1867
DISRAELI, GLADSTONE
AND REVOLUTION

Cambridge Studies in the History and Theory of Politics

1867

DISRAELI, GLADSTONE AND REVOLUTION

The Passing of the second Reform Bill

BY

MAURICE COWLING

Fellow and Tutor of Peterhouse, Cambridge
University Lecturer in History

CAMBRIDGE
AT THE UNIVERSITY PRESS
1967

Published by the Syndics of the Cambridge University Press
Bentley House, 200 Euston Road, London, N.W. 1
American Branch: 32 East 57th Street, New York, N.Y. 10022

© Cambridge University Press 1967

Library of Congress Catalogue Card Number: 67–13801

Printed in Great Britain
at the University Printing House, Cambridge
(Brooke Crutchley, University Printer)

THIS WORK
IS DEDICATED
TO THE
PRIME MINISTER

CONTENTS

PREFACE

The author is indebted to Mrs I. M. Martin, Miss Ann Parr, Mrs E. D. Beebe and others for typing various parts of the drafts of this book, to Mrs N. A. Blenkin for making the Index and to Mrs Steinberg for helping to read the proofs.

He is indebted to the owners, custodians and archivists of manuscripts whose names are listed in the Bibliography, to Lord Cairns and Lord Wemyss for lending parts of their own collections and to Mr Robert Blake for allowing free access to papers belonging to Lord Derby while these were in his possession in Oxford.

He is grateful to Mr Paul Smith for allowing him to see his *Disraelian Conservatism and Social Reform* before it was published.

He is grateful to Mr A. B. Cooke of Peterhouse and Edinburgh for checking references and reading proofs, to Dr J. R. Vincent of Peterhouse, Professor H. J. Hanham of Edinburgh and Dr. D. R. Shackleton Bailey for commenting on the manuscript and to the Master of Peterhouse, Professor Butterfield, for criticism at an early stage.

His thanks are due to the editor of the *Historical Journal* for permission to reproduce material in Chapter II which has been published previously in article form.

He is grateful to the staff of the University Library for recurring help and to the staff of the University Press for their attention.

Finally, he owes debts to Professor C. H. Wilson, and to the Master and Fellows of Peterhouse collectively for providing conditions in which work—particularly historical work—can be done.

'The influence of the country gentlemen of England rest[s] on a more solid basis than that of any electoral franchises. . . A country gentleman, one of large territorial possessions, living with his people, and, as Queen Elizabeth used to say, for his people, wield[s] an influence superior to any other class in this or in any other nation in the world. This bill [is] a great and comprehensive measure—and the most liberal ever offered to Parliament.'

> Sir Thomas Lloyd, Liberal MP. for Cardiganshire in *Hansard*, May 27 1867 (1157).

'The Reform bill may be considered "through". . . What an unknown world we are to enter, but I believe more, or at least as safely, and more permanently than a £5 franchise would enable us to do. If the gentry will take their part, they will be adopted as leaders. If we are left to the demagogues, God help us!'

> Gathorne Hardy, Home Secretary and Conservative MP. for the University of Oxford. *Diary*, August 9 1867, Cranbrook MSS East Suffolk County Record Office.

'If we wish to commit political suicide, it is not difficult to do so and, as far as I am personally concerned, I have no particular objection; but politically I have a very strong one. I accepted office very unwillingly, but having accepted it, I mean to keep it as long as I can. . .'

> Derby to Sir John Pakington, December 4 1866. Derby MSS Box 193/1.

INTRODUCTION

The understanding of mid-Victorian politics which the pre-war generation of historians transmitted to its successors has, over the last twenty years, been subjected to extensive emendation. A period of psephological and sociological analysis has established the received fact that nineteenth-century political society was more aristocratic than earlier historians had been willing to admit, and its politics socially more conservative than they had tended to suppose. In a society of great fortunes, many of them new and some politically unrewarded, the ethos of political deference, the strength of executive government and the concern felt by owners of even new wealth for their continued possession of it have been given their place in the still-life picture which historians present. The farther away 1860 recedes in time, the less volatile and radical the structure seems to become.

Yet, though these truths are understood by every student of the period, they have left virtually no mark on the accounts which have been given of the process by which political decisions were made. Most full-scale published accounts of the major political decisions taken in England between 1846 and 1880 were written in the late nineteenth century or early twentieth, or, if written later, take at its face value the structure of interpretation in which, for example, Molesworth, Trevelyan, Justin McCarthy and Herbert Paul put them. They assume that Radicalism was more powerful, the gentry weaker and middle-class politics uniformly more progressive than sociological analysis might suggest, and they fail, where they try, to understand the conservative character of the politics they were attempting to describe. They see mid-Victorian parliamentary politics as Liberal politics. They see Liberalism as a doctrine rather than a political party, and Radicalism as truth rather than ideology. They see industrial change on the one hand and political change on the other, and assume a simple, one-way relationship between them. They by-pass, ignore or explain away both the hostility to change and the power to resist it which analysis of society at large suggests might be found, not just on one side of the House of Commons but in most parts of both.

They assume, moreover, a straight progression from the reforms of the 1830s to the reforms of the 1870s, neglecting the recession in progressive feeling which Palmerston reflected as much as he wished to create. The death of Chartism, the mid-Victorian boom and the hints given, alongside a militant trade unionism, of a contented, loyal and royalist working class in some of the larger cities, produced a sense of political stability and distrust of Radical motion which impregnated the social attitude of a great part of the House of Commons. If the Reform bill of 1867 symbolized the beginning of a period of rapid political change, it did so in a parliament which not only thought of itself as the ruling assembly of a highly stable society but was also in strong reaction against any suggestion that it should be otherwise.

In an earlier work[1] John Stuart Mill was seen not as the central moralist he has become but as a radical critic of the society in which he lived. This book examines the political system Mill attacked, displays the process of decision-making with which it worked and shows how one central decision was made, not by Bright, Mill, Fawcett, Thomas Hughes and other leaders of the Radical assault, but by a House of Commons in which the parliamentary Radicals were a small, extreme group reflecting neither the general body of opinion inside Parliament nor the only centre of political equilibrium beyond. This has been done by seeing the Reform bill of 1867 as an incident in the history of party; by showing that the movement of the action is unintelligible outside this context; and by emphasizing what Lowe, Bagehot and Bernal Osborne[2] noted at the time—that its substantive merits as it was eventually passed were given prior discussion, at a moment at which choice was possible, neither in Parliament, as Osborne suggested, nor in Cabinet, as it is now possible to know. The deployments of principle with which nostalgic publicists credit the parliaments of the 1860s will be seen not as examples of 'the classical parliamentary system' where 'the debates were public, the issues were known and the personal struggle for power could take place on the floor of the House or on the hustings'[3] but as assertions of individual and party opinion and personal and party power in a battle—as private as it was public—not just to establish the best constitution but to decide who should establish it. They will be seen in this way, not because this is how some of the actors saw them at the time, though some of them did, but because there was so solid a measure of agreement among four-fifths of the members who sat in the Parliament of 1865 about the importance of electoral arrangements in maintaining the social and economic structure, and about the overriding need to maintain it, that the action is unintelligible if its significance is supposed to lie in differences of fundamental opinion or disputes about fundamental principle.

The Reform Act of 1867 was not the consequence of relevant decisions relevantly taken about the substantive merits of questions: but neither was it the outcome of simple consonance between public agitation on the one hand and agitated assent from government on the other. There was a development of party commitment, established opinion and governmental policy which, however much the leaders of public agitation claimed it had been determined by them, was not so determined in fact. Because the Reform League was politically active at moments of crisis, it is easy to attribute outstanding importance to its role. This is doubly easy when the historian has an interest in the working-class movement or the historical sociologist a belief that political manœuvre is incidental to the progress of popular social movements. There is, however, a sociology of power as well as a sociology of protest. In the period under discussion new social forces did not make their impact directly, were effective through existing concentrations of power, and, in the process of decision, were transformed in order to be made tolerable to ruling opinion. The passage of the Reform Act of 1867 was effected in a context of public agitation: it cannot be explained as a simple consequence. Parliament in the sixties was not *afraid* of public agitation: nor was its action *determined* by it. Its members did not believe that public agitation necessarily represented public opinion. Public opinion included a variety of acquiescences and protests, which interacted continuously with Parliament. The interaction took the form of dialogue: the dialogue was a real one. The interaction reached its most fruitful peak in Parliament. It is in Parliament, and in the light of Parliament's view of public feeling, that the centre of explanation will be found.

This book, therefore, may be treated as an essay in political sociology—an attempt to uncover the logic of conservative resistance, to show how class consciousness permeated consideration of an electoral system and to display the impact of political respectability on political agitation; and to do this by drawing together two factors to which historians pay their respects—parliamentary manipulation and consciousness of popular pressure—at a point at which it might be expected that clear decisions would have issued from the consensus if decisions had not been blurred and blunted by the mechanism of the political system through which they were taken.

In Parliament predominant opinion was affected by, affected and concentrated itself around a fluctuating combination of the personal standing of political leaders, the permanent interests of political parties and a vague sense of the preferences of not one, but a number of public opinions outside. Public opinion did not mean just the Reform League, or even the Reform Union. Nor did it mean merely *The Morning Star, The Daily Telegraph* or the authors of *On Liberty, Sartor Resartus* and *Culture and Anarchy*. It did not mean just the existing electorate or the new electorate which Parliament might create. It meant Conservative working men as well as Liberal ones. It meant the deferential workman in the small borough as well as the radical urban artisan. It meant the assumed Conservatism of rural England as well as the Radicalism of the metropolis. It meant Conservative merchants, bankers and industrialists as well as Liberal ones, and, more important, Liberal ones who might become Conservative. It meant different things at different times, from day to day and month to month, and it meant them connected and tied together, for practical political purposes, in parliamentary parties led by particular leaders. However loose party ties were in Parliament, in the Liberal party at least, however independent of central control the emergence of MP.s in constituencies, however fissiparous the tensions between leaders within parties, however great the ignorance shown by politicians in Parliament of the real movement of public opinion outside, party was the mould in which parliamentary ambition had to set. The context in which politicians were operating made it impossible to think of achieving any permanent political objective without attempting to control, or modify, the course adopted by one party or another. Any particular measure in these circumstances may be explained as an incident in the career of a politician or the life of a party: the Reform Act of 1867 no less than any other. The context of public agitation explains some aspects of the Conservative government's policy, chiefly by reaction against it. By itself it explains

4

nothing of the change which occurred in Conservative thinking about Reform, and Liberal thinking about party, between October 1865 and August 1867.

The second object of this book is, therefore, to suggest that sense of continuing tension *between* and *within* and *across* party, which is important, not merely because it had special significance in the twenty years following the fall of Peel, but because it was a central part of the process of decision-making in the political system we are discussing. Particular leaders were never so certain of their political following that they could govern without fear either of competition from within or of opposition from without. Conservative governments were not the governments of the Conservative party, but the governments of Peel or Derby or Salisbury: Liberal governments, the governments of Russell or Palmerston or Gladstone. For each of those who succeeded, others failed, or hoped to succeed in future: knives were never so far below the surface that a victor could ignore them.

Nor, under British parliamentary arrangements after 1832, were politicians so confident of the climate of opinion that they could ignore it. What made the political classes tolerable and, by acquiescence, acceptable to public opinion were the slogans and images presented by ministers and parties, and their ability to deal with real or new problems, when these pressed, in terms which could be made to appear consistent with previous declarations or honourable to those who shared their assumptions. This combination of pressures and contexts in changing situations gave *any* political statement an ambiguity which is characteristic, no doubt, of all political rhetoric, particularly where large electorates vote, but which was peculiarly intense when an important factor in any political decision or any political career was a capacity for polarizing differences, while working within a framework of common assumptions; and when as much attention was given, as was given in mid-nineteenth-century England, to the sort of politico-metaphysical refinement of principle of which Gladstone, however untypical, was the master. Government by synthetic conflict is not obviously the most rational form of polity: when surrounded with deliberate reticence and calculated ambiguity, it will not yield its reasons without a struggle.

In the political system we are considering, tension—whether institutionally inherited or deliberately enhanced—was an integral part of the process of decision-making: statements made, or actions taken, by any participant must be scrutinized, not as expressions of *belief*, but in their logical place in the chronological sequence. A major defect of much recent narrative writing about nineteenth-century British politics is that, concerned as it is with one man or party, it neither sees each group in relation to all the rest nor searches for the movement of events which is the outcome of tension between the wills of all. A defect of the contributions made by Seymour, Park, Trevelyan, Professor Briggs and Dr F. B. Smith to an understanding of the function and passage of the Act of 1867 is that, aware as these authors are of the existence of tension in the Parliament of 1865, they neither follow the tension in detail as it impinged on the actors at the time, nor show that it was tension itself—within parties as well as between them—which prevented the House of Commons passing the sort of bill a majority of MP.s would have been happy to accept from any government, if any government had been able to free its action, and their votes, from all consideration of party interest, duty, situation and advantage. An attempt, inadequate and incomplete as this one is, to shed light in a specific instance on the politics of continuous tension is the core of such special message as this book contains.

Finally, since the amount of material is large, the subject provides an opportunity to discuss a question central to all historical thinking—how far does the material available to an historian provide conclusive indication of the motives we assume to have been imbedded in the minds and wills of the actors whose activities we are attempting to explain? The politics of mid-nineteenth-century Britain provide an opportunity to discuss this question, not because they were more typical or important than any other, but because the combination of a loose party system, a vigilant public opinion, a high level of literacy among politicians, the permanence of families and survival of letters, an absence of typewriters and telephones and the length of the parliamentary recess have produced a body of material as rich as, perhaps richer than, is available for any comparable historical problem.

This book sets Disraeli, Derby, Russell, Gladstone, Elcho, Cranborne, Lowe, Beales and Bright in the historical situations in which they were operating. From what one finds them writing and from what others wrote about them, and from the context in which they wrote, one intuits their intentions. Even with material so extensive, and apparently as categorical, however, intentions can seldom be established certainly. Yet the historian has to judge, and to work with the judgement he has made. He must do this assuming that much of the material was *meant* to be opaque and that political convention left little room for private conviction as opposed to public. He is dealing with men whose function was histrionic, whose words and actions were meant to be ambiguous and who are most likely to be understood, not by asking whether they believed what they wrote but by showing what role each cast himself for in the political world. With politicians of high intellect, wide experience and continual involvement over many years in party conflict, these roles developed an autonomy of their own, arousing loyalties which fact had somehow to be prevented dissolving, raising expectations which decision did not always sustain. Yet what seems at first to be dishonesty, trickery or disingenuousness appears, once the context is understood, as sensitivity to the limits of political possibility or attempts by politicians to edge themselves, and everyone else, into reconciling the roles they felt obliged to play with what they took to be the necessities of situations. This process occurred, no doubt, halfconsciously, manifests itself fragmentarily and is difficult to discern. Nevertheless we assume that it occurred, and is central to the problems with which we are dealing.

' I always hold', wrote Gladstone in 1873, 'that politicians are the men whom, as a rule, it is most difficult to... understand completely and for my own part I never have thus understood, or thought I understood, above one or two.'[1] Historians have smaller contact, though sometimes more evidence, than Gladstone: their claims need be no more categorical. Their evidence is slender: justification of use is essential to historical activity. For all these reasons, beyond the intrinsic interest of the subject, this book takes the form in the first place of categorical narrative, and then finally of justification of the decisions on which the narrative has been made to rest.

I

PRELUDE

'There is no country in the world where every class can speak its own mind and exercise its influence so openly and earnestly as in England: no country where there is so little practical separation between the several classes...; none where the freedom of the individual is so absolutely secured; and none where social rank and personal influence enjoy a stronger sway over every class. There is no country therefore more free or less democratic.'

> Thornton Hunt (of the *Daily Telegraph*) to Layard, May 1 1866. Add. MSS 38993

'If the nation is to be split into two parts and there is to be a wide gulf between them, there is nothing for the future but subjection for you are powerless to obtain your end: but working with a large portion of the middle class and with the most intelligent and just of the highest social class, we may find these great measures accomplished without any violation of public peace and without any disruption of that general harmony which ought to prevail throughout all classes of the people.'

> Bright to Leeds Manhood Suffrage meeting, October 8 1866
> (*Morning Star*, October 9 1866)

'Come, then, Fellow-workmen, and let your orderly conduct, your respectable demeanour and law-abiding qualities, be so many thousand mouths, whose united voice shall make your enemies stammer forth the sacred truth that the vast Aerarian classes of this country are worthy of the Franchise.'

> Hugh McGregor, Hon. Sec. Working-Men's Rights Association, on proclaiming break-away from Reform League and determination to meet in Hyde Park on Good Friday 1867. H.O. OS 7854

(i) THE EVENTS

The government which Earl Russell formed on Palmerston's death on October 18 1865 met Parliament first on February 6 1866. On March 12 it introduced a franchise bill, the chief objects of which were to lower the 1832 borough franchise qualification in England and Wales from £10 to £7 and the county franchise from £50 to £14, and to give votes to £50 savings bank depositors, £10 lodgers and certain others, enfranchising altogether about 400,000 new voters. On May 7 it introduced a seats bill which provided for grouping of thirty-eight boroughs with populations smaller than 8,000

8

and removal of second seats from eight small boroughs with two members; and which proposed to distribute the seats thus freed so that Liverpool, Birmingham, Manchester, Leeds and Salford would have one extra seat each, London four, Scotland seven (to be detailed in a separate bill), London University and seven new boroughs one each and the English counties twenty-six in all. These measures were recommended by Gladstone, as leader of the House of Commons, in the hope, which the Queen shared, that they would put an end to the Reform question for a generation. Their authors, Russell and Gladstone, intended them to wind up the line of abortive measures which had been presented to Parliament in the previous seventeen years. They expected, innocently as it turned out, that a degree of enfranchisement which the Cabinet had accepted, however reluctantly, which had been tailored in order to pass through Parliament and 'which we had so much cut down...from the standard of the Palmerston measure of 1860',[1] would be accepted by the Liberal majority in the House of Commons.

In this they were disappointed. The nucleus of the Adullamite 'Cave' had been created in March 1865 in opposition to precipitate lowering of the franchise, and had operated in the debate and division on Baines's Reform motion in May of that year. It operated now more intensively around Lowe, around Clanricarde's Irish connection (of whom W. H. Gregory was the most prominent), around alienated Whigs (Earl Grosvenor, Anson and Horsman in the one House, Earl Grey, Lord Lichfield and the Marquess of Lansdowne in the other) and under guidance from an ex-peelite MP. (Lord Elcho) in whose home the Cave at first normally met, who was a close relative of Lichfield and Anson (themselves brothers) and who persuaded Grosvenor (a colleague from the Volunteers and desirable as 'a whig swell')[2] to provide titular leadership in the House of Commons. Before the session began, Horsman thought there would be seventy or eighty rebels.[3] In each of five of the six major reform divisions between March and June more than twenty-five Liberal MP.s voted against the government (in the final division— Dunkellin's—on June 18, on which the government was beaten, more than forty), and there were others who disliked either the government or the bills but did not vote against them because they disliked the Cave and the opposition leaders equally. MP.s who voted with the Cave on April 28 or June 18 were not all Whigs or

9

apprehensive Irish landowners. There was a London industrialist—Doulton of Lambeth—and a Yorkshire industrialist—Crosland of Huddersfield. There was an advanced Liberal mapmaker—Wyld of Bodmin—who thought the bill did not go far enough. There was a Dublin Quaker (Pim), a Scottish railway administrator (Laing), a number of Scottish MP.s who wanted a better deal for Scotland and a handful of Liberal country gentlemen who either disliked the abandonment of the rating qualification or were repelled by Gladstone's handling of the House of Commons. There were, in addition to those who voted with the Cave, a great many more who nearly did so, and at least twenty Whigs in the House of Lords who seemed likely to do so if the bill ever reached them.[1] Nevertheless, the Cave never numbered, properly speaking, more than about a dozen MP.s not all of whom (Gregory and Grosvenor, for example) were unwavering in support, and none of whom, except Lowe, carried the biggest political guns.

In organizing resistance in the Commons, in helping Lansdowne to prepare for resistance in the Lords and in keeping Grosvenor up to the mark, the drive was provided by Elcho, with Lowe as chief speaker. Neither thought of himself as head of the movement (a role reserved for Lansdowne as representative of a great political family) but in combination they did most of the work. Lowe—*Times* leader-writer, ex-don, ex-barrister, ex-official and MP. in Australia and Lansdowne's MP. for Calne—was a cynical, strident, fifty-five year old half-blind albino outsider in whig politics with a wife whom Whigs thought 'unfortunate' (though she reminded Bright 'with thankfulness, of the quiet ladylike reserve of my own wife when she is in company');[2] a systematic utilitarian and ideologist of respectability who even Gladstone thought lacked both the smoother arts and the common touch, but who was one of the most powerful debaters the House of Commons was to see in his generation. The role cast by Lowe for himself involved a pungent, highly intellectualized advocacy and defence, tailored as much to the political aristocracy as to the commercial and propertied classes, of enlightened government, a free economy and the absolute rights of property against the inroads which democratic protectionism, democratic socialism and a concern for Irish improvement might make on the enjoyment by existing owners of the wealth they now possessed.[3]

Elcho, like Lowe, though seven years younger, had been a junior minister under Aberdeen, was chairman of an insurance company in London and was heir to 60,000 acres in Scotland. He thought of himself as 'moderate Liberal', which he thought the country was also, believed in a balanced constitution and the representation of interests, and was opposed to the rule of 'mere numbers in the State'. He feared the political power of trades unions, but claimed credit for contributing, by his contact with trades union leaders, by the part he had played in enabling working-men to join the Volunteers and by his interest in Master and Servant legislation, to fruitful co-operation between the gentry and the working classes. In constitutional questions he was opposed, not to all change, but to changes made without deliberation. Once the franchise qualification of 1832 was lowered, he agreed with Lowe that there would be no stopping short of household suffrage, in counties as well as in the boroughs: he wanted the merits of change discussed in the light of the fullest information, thinking that, once discussion began, the merits of the existing constitution could not be ignored. He had energy rather than charm, more character than intelligence, and was endlessly persistent, 'amiable', 'high-spirited' and 'vain'. He was the enemy of Gladstone and the power behind Grosvenor whose name made the Cave look more formidable and become more successful than it could otherwise have been. In spite of uncertainty among their supporters on the one hand and blackguarding from the government on the other, Elcho and Lowe succeeded in June 1866 because they were saying in private, and in debate in the House of Commons, in a way which Gladstone could not counter, things which many Whigs and some Liberal MP.s came to feel about the bills themselves, about Gladstone's management of the House of Commons and, in Elcho's case, in his class-conscious way, about Gladstone's adequacy as leader of a party of gentlemen; and because the Conservative party voted solidly against.

The alliance between the Cave and the Conservative party forced the government to promise a Seats bill in March, though it had not wanted to: it created situations at the end of April and in mid-June in which the government had to think of resigning. Though the Cave wanted to replace Russell's government by a Whig-dominated Whig/Conservative coalition, it was replaced by a purely Conservative one which Derby, with 290 supporters in a House of

Commons of 658, formed on July 2 to the accompaniment of a series of public demonstrations in London organized by the London Working Men's Association and the Reform League in rivalry with one another and culminating in the massive meeting outside Hyde Park in July when, although forbidden by public notice to enter the Park, the crowd broke down the railings, invaded the Park and marched in varying degrees of order and conflict to a political rally in Trafalgar Square.

Parliament was prorogued in August and did not return until February 5. In its absence an extensive public agitation was mounted in most of the major cities of England and Scotland. There were marches and meetings in London, and meetings, banquets and monster demonstrations in Birmingham, Manchester, Leeds, Newcastle, the other Northern cities and Scotland—all dedicated to denunciation of Adullamite treachery, Conservative trickery and Parliament's failure, all demanding replacement of Derby's usurping Toryism by a government which could give the people what it wanted. Though no one was killed, the language was high, the demands extensive, the warnings of violence, particularly from Bright, prominent. Though there was no repetition of the public alliance between civic dignitaries, advanced reformers and aristocratic Whigs which had characterized the agitation of 1831/2, the demonstrations in Brookfield, Birmingham, on Woodhouse Moor, Leeds, on Town Moor, Newcastle, on Glasgow Green or in Queen's Park, Edinburgh, were reminders of the power exercised over popular feeling in the large cities by leaders of industrial society more respectable than the professional agitators by whom the Reform League seemed to be led in London. Though not many demonstrators were arrested, Elcho and Lord Chelmsford, Derby's Lord Chancellor, had their windows broken in London: Horsman was jostled by a crowd: at the opening of Parliament the Queen was booed, partly, it was thought, because of her connection with John Brown.[1]

When parliament reassembled, the Queen's speech announced that the government intended to deal with the Reform question without showing how. On February 11 Disraeli, as leader of the House of Commons, announced that it would do so by asking the House to discuss thirteen very general resolutions, which members of Parliament saw first in the newspapers next morning. On February 15 he announced that the resolutions, if approved by the House, would be converted into a bill, and its terms sketched, but not introduced, before the resolutions were debated on February 25. On February 23 the Cabinet decided to announce at the beginning of the debate that approval of the resolutions would be followed by a bill to establish rated residential (i.e. household) suffrage in parliamentary boroughs, but, under threat of resignation from Cranborne, Carnarvon and General Peel, compromised at lunch-time on Monday the 25th by deciding to promise a less extensive enfranchisement instead. That afternoon, without abandoning the original resolutions, therefore, Derby explained to a party meeting and Disraeli to the House of Commons that approval of the resolutions would commit the government to propose a bill to reduce the borough franchise qualification in England and Wales from £10 p.a. to £6 p.a. rating, and the county franchise from £50 p.a. to £20 p.a. rating. While totally disfranchising only four constituencies with seven seats which had to be disfranchised because they were corrupt, they proposed to remove one seat from each of the twenty-three English and Welsh double-member boroughs with populations of less than 7,000 in order to give fifteen seats to county constituencies, twelve to newly created parliamentary boroughs, two to the existing Tower Hamlets constituency (after division), one to the University of London, and none at all to the largest cities from which the major agitation had come[1].

Next day Disraeli announced in the Commons that the resolutions would be abandoned and the bill introduced sometime in the following week. On Monday March 4 he and Derby announced in the two Houses separately that three Cabinet ministers had resigned, that the bill would not after all be a £6 Rating bill, but the rated residential Suffrage bill the Cabinet had abandoned on February 25, and that it would not be introduced before March 18. It was not until then that Disraeli introduced a bill—to give effect to the redistribution of seats mentioned on February 25; to give the vote to every male householder in a parliamentary borough who had occupied his house for two years, been rated to the relief of the poor and had paid his own rates; to give the vote in county constituencies to anyone who had resided for a year and owned or occupied property of £15 p.a. rateable value, provided the rates had actually been paid; to enfranchise in both counties and boroughs all residents who had

13

£50 in government stock, paid a certain amount in direct taxation, or held a wide range of professional qualification (i.e. 'the fancy franchises'); and to give a second vote (i.e. 'duality') to any borough householder who paid 20/- p.a. in direct taxation.

Although this bill would have produced hardly any working-class enfranchisement in London, and a very small one in Birmingham, and although no proposal was made to increase the number of seats in Scotland, Gladstone failed to persuade the Liberal party to oppose the second reading which passed without a division on March 26. His attempt to make up for this by devising a central modification—Coleridge's Instruction—before the committee stage began, was ended by the Tea-Room revolt of about fifty Liberal MP.s on April 8. The bill went unopposed into committee on April 10. On April 12, the day before the start of the Easter recess, Gladstone's first amendment in committee was defeated by 310 votes to 289: on April 17 he withdrew temporarily from leading the Liberal party in the House of Commons. Parliament reassembled on April 29: by the time the bill had left the committee and had been given a third reading on July 15, it had been transformed by a series of amendments moved from both sides of the House. Duality was virtually abandoned before the committee stage began. The committee itself increased the scope of the redistribution by a half and trebled the size of the proposed addition to the electorate. It did this by adding to the borough electorate not only £10 lodgers, who had never had the vote before (Torrens' amendment), but also compound householders who had not previously been responsible for paying their own rates (Hodgkinson's amendment). It further increased the size of the electoral roll by reducing the period of qualifying residence in boroughs from two years to one (Ayrton's amendment), by lowering the county franchise qualification from £15 p.a. to £12 p.a. (Locke King's amendment), and by adding £5 leaseholders and copyholders to the county register. It was still the case that no householder in a parliamentary borough could vote unless he was assessed for the rates and had actually paid them. But, whereas in the 1832 Act and in all subsequent bills a minimum rateable or rental value (i.e. a 'fixed-line franchise') had excluded large numbers of householders, this bill excluded only those who had not actually paid their rates or resided in the same borough for a year.

After its third reading had passed the bill went to the House of

Lords, where four major amendments were carried, all but one of which (for cumulative voting) were rejected by the House of Commons. The Commons' decisions were accepted by the Lords in August. The bill received the royal assent on August 19, as did Reform bills for Scotland and Ireland in 1868 and a Boundary bill, providing for extensions to the boundaries of seventy English and Welsh boroughs, on July 25 1868.

(ii) THE PROBLEM

As soon as the main Act had passed, the main protagonists began to climb on to the bandwaggon. The Reform League's objective throughout had been manhood suffrage and the ballot. No member of Parliament wanted manhood suffrage: the government had conceded neither. The League's leaders congratulated themselves, nevertheless, on the part they had played in making the government capitulate.[1] In March Bright had urged Disraeli to establish household suffrage. He had supported Gladstone's £5 rating proposal once he saw that Disraeli's bill proposed not a household, but rated residential, suffrage. In July, in writing to Russell, who did not like the form of household suffrage the bill eventually established, he admitted that 'a £5 Rental Franchise with the rate-paying clauses abolished would probably give you a better electoral body than will spring from this bill', but, wanting to remove 'the impression that the followers of Lord Derby are less afraid of the people than those who have been and are associated with you...ask[ed] for [him]self not to be introduced into the [Lords] debate [on the reform bill] as tho' [he] wished the House of Commons had adopted a more restricted franchise.'[2] To Gladstone, who until mid-May had attacked the bill because it would go too far, the Act seemed a 'great progress in the career of British liberty'; he was 'thankful...to say that we [had] had that which, perhaps, may be called the highest triumph of a party...to see [our] opponents themselves compelled to be the organs of giving effect to [our] principles and fulfilling [our] wishes (cheers)'.[3] Disraeli, aware of the accusation that his policy had been to 'yield anything but his place'[4] insisted that 'we had a policy of our own from which we would never deviate', that he had 'always considered the Tory party...the national party of England' and that 'when change [is] carried out in deference to the manners, the customs, the laws and the traditions of the people...and when the people are led by their natural leaders...then the Tory party is triumphant, and...under Providence, will secure the prosperity and happiness of the country'.[1]

Though some Conservatives—particularly in the Cecil family—regarded Disraeli as 'trickery enthroned', his wife as 'a dirty old woman' and 'found it more than political human nature can bear... to be dragged helplessly through the mud—bound hand and foot behind the Jew's triumphal car',[2] the Conservative party after twenty years of impotence had a great measure to its credit. Elcho remembered Gladstone at dinner 'at Lady Egerton's...saying to you and me...a heavy responsibility will rest with you if you...do anything to induce...the government...to propose household suffrage'.[3] Lowe found in the congratulations Gladstone offered the country on achieving household suffrage 'the very naming of which by a minister of the Crown he told *me* would be a gloomy day for England' evidence that Gladstone was the 'poor creature' he had come to suppose he was.[4] J. B. Smith, Radical MP. for Stockport and a Tea-Room rebel himself, found it 'curious' to 'observe that...Mr Gladstone congratulated [a] meeting [he was addressing at Oldham] on the passing of the household suffrage, Mr Platt, one of the "*Tea-Room*" party being in the Chair'.[5] Duncan McLaren, Bright's brother-in-law and Radical MP. for Edinburgh, 'with all [his] admiration for [Gladstone's] talents and character...[could] not admit' to his constituents 'that the main improvements in the Reform bill were carried by Mr Gladstone, or by his influence, far less by the influence of the assailants of the "Tea-Room" party, who have so strangely magnified their own importance'.[6] Yet the Liberal party as a whole pocketed its pride, patched up its wounds and nailed its flag to the Act as evidence that its principles had triumphed.

It has long been understood that historians should not too readily accept the claim that the Act of 1867 radically transformed the constitution. The great increase in the size of the electorate and a moderately extensive redistribution of seats, even when combined with eminently quotable prognostications of doom uttered by critics on the one hand and expressions of victory uttered by professional reformers on the other, could not sustain the impression, once Seymour[7] had made statistical comparisons, of change as radical, and fundamental, as from their different standpoints Lowe and Beales

claimed to have seen effected. Though Seymour confined his attention to published statistics, public debates and the incomplete
quotations which existing biographers had made from the vast
volume of private letters, his work supplied warnings against assuming that the Act was as far-reaching as it had come to be to the
interest of all politicians to suggest. It was clear, for example, that,
though nearly a million electors were qualified to vote after the bill
had been passed who had not been qualified before, a good many
would never vote because they would either fail to register or fail to
pay their rates. It was clear that the redistribution of seats in the
1867 Act not only left sixteen very small boroughs with separate
representation but transferred twenty-five English and Welsh small-
borough seats to county constituencies as against twenty to the
English boroughs. It was clear, also, that, whereas a borough like
Calne with a population of 5,000 and about 600 electors still had a
member of its own, many great towns, like St Helens, with populations ten or fifteen times as large, were not represented directly at
all. Once this was seen, it should have been asked whether Disraeli's
actions could be described as 'a capitulation to Radical pressure'
and whether 'half a dozen great outdoor demonstrations at the principal centres of population and a dozen speeches in great halls by
Bright' really had, in Trevelyan's words, 'sufficed to awe the
Conservative party into submission'.[1]

Nevertheless, a belief in the radical significance of the Act re-
mains, and seems likely to revive. One recent writer[2] treats the enfranchisement both of the £10 lodger and of the compound householder as, quoting Trevelyan, a demonstration of 'that wise old
English fear of their fellow-countrymen which has done as much to
save England as many more heroic virtues'.[3] To Dr Harrison the
passage of the 1867 Act, and especially of these two provisions, rep-
resents a capitulation by government to the Reform League: a problem is supposed to face the historian who wishes to understand why
a Conservative government should have been party to a capitulation
of this sort, and why the Conservative party as a whole, whose members had no desire to assist in establishing a democratic constitution,
should have helped its leaders to do so.

Some attempts at explanation have emphasized the parliamentary
situation: some the climate of public opinion: some the importance
of public agitation. Dr Harrison, rejecting each as a total explana-

tion, underlines the decisiveness of one particular demonstration—the Reform League demonstration in Hyde Park on May 6 1867—in converting a moderate into a radical bill, and in impressing on Disraeli and Derby the revolutionary character of the situation and the revolutionary dangers which would follow failure to go along with some at least of the Reform League's demands. Reform, which Dr Harrison recognizes to be 'a gamble taken in the interests of party expediency', did not, he believes, remain, as in the 1850s and 1860s, 'a harmless flutter'. In 1867 it became a

relentless game of brag which began in February and ended in August... It was surely the presence of the Reform League which stopped the players crying off as they had done so often in the past. If the pressure exerted by the League is held to be negligible, then innumerable public and private admissions about the influence of its agitation have to be discounted: the wide-spread preoccupation with preventing the formation of revolutionary forces has to be ignored,...the proximity to revolutionary situations in 1866 and 1867...neglected,[1]

and Disraeli's decision to treble the increase he had already proposed in the electorate by accepting the principle of Hodgkinson's amendment on May 17 rendered inexplicable.

Dr Harrison does justice to the complexity of motive by which Reform League leaders, like Beales, were moved in confronting the government on May 6, but catches no hint of the meagreness of their expectation. The mass meeting was an assertion of the League's right to use Hyde Park, which it had been forbidden to do in July 1866. In 1867 it was allowed to meet there because the government wished to avoid the showdown involved in exercising its right to close the Park to everyone, and had no power to discriminate in advance between a meeting held by the League and a meeting held by anyone else. May 6 was a demonstration of the League's effectiveness, in the context of the co-operation which Beales's concern for legality created between the League on the one hand and the police and the government on the other. It was, as Dr Harrison suggests, other things besides. But the Reform League leaders had no reason at the beginning of May to alter their long-term assumption that public agitation would affect neither the immediate judgement of the House of Commons nor the policy of the Conservative government. There had been a moment of expectation between March 4 and March 18 when Disraeli had announced publicly, and had re-

assured Bright privately about, the household suffrage bill he proposed to produce, and when it was not certain whether it would be
surrounded with counterpoises and compensations to which the
League would object.[1] Hope, however, had disappeared with the
form given to household suffrage in the bill itself, with the checks
put on Disraeli by the Cabinet and with the defeat of Gladstone in
the first reform division on April 12, when the House of Commons
supported the government's insistence on confining the suffrage to
borough householders who had personally paid their rates. There is
some reason to suppose that the climate of concession which Disraeli had persuaded some Radical MP.s to believe he was trying to
create had been discussed by the League on April 12.[2] The League
at this stage, for a time, lowered its sights from manhood suffrage
and the ballot to specific alteration of his bill. It may have done this
because it had come to think that Disraeli would concede if he could:
it may have done it in order to make Gladstone insist less ambiguously than he had so far on the concessions that it wanted. The defeat
of April 12 forced it to invite co-operation from the Reform Union[3]
which, until then, many of its members had wanted to avoid, and
which the Union's desire to begin activity in London made it desirable to keep close watch on. But in organizing the demonstration on
May 6 the League had no reason to expect the government to
capitulate. On the contrary, there was a mixture of objectives—an
attempt, on the one hand, by Beales to rescue his reputation from the
damage it had been done by the support he had given Gladstone, by
Gladstone's refusal unambiguously to propose household suffrage
pure and simple (let alone manhood suffrage and the ballot) and by
his failure, even so, to defeat the government on April 12; an
attempt, on the other hand, to counter the Reform Union's arrival
on the London scene and to keep up the pressure in order to help
Reform League candidates make a respectable showing at an election, whenever that might come in the future.

The commonplace to anyone who reads the letters of advanced
advocates of electoral reform is not the certainty of victory but consciousness of weakness in face of working-class deference, middle-
class complacency, aristocratic monopoly[4] and a Parliament and
ruling-class which clung to the 'grovelling superstition... that
human society exists for the sake of property in land'.[5] It is the
manifest feeling of powerlessness which reformers outside Parlia-

ment felt at the strength and obstinacy of a House of Commons 'which was richer and more aristocratic than any which had preceded it for many years past',[1] whose 'spirit' was less 'just and . . . liberal' than in 'Sir Robert Peel's time',[2] which was 'too corrupt for [Bright] to hope anything good from it',[3] and which confirmed its 'shabb[iness]' and 'utter absence of political thought and principle'[4] by supporting the restrictive personal payment principle in opposition to Gladstone on April 12 and May 9. Bright expected 'a real and probably not a small revolution' when Palmerston died. He thought it would take courage on the part of Russell and Gladstone to effect it: he saw no sign of courage once their government got under way. He knew himself to be 'a pariah among politicians [who could] not be thought of' for office, though it is probable that he would have liked to be offered it.[5] As Disraeli began slowly and deviously in 1867 to move the ground of discussion far beyond anything the Liberal party had proposed, Bright was buttered up by such of the great Whig leaders as did not join the Cave.[6] Nevertheless, there is no reason to suppose Bright ignorant, even after the agitation of 1866/7, of the strength, depth and pervasiveness of the resistance to his politics which had been established by Palmerston's unscrupulous use of 'the ignorance and credulity and passions of the people'.[7] Even Beesly, Congreve and Frederic Harrison—armchair politicians who thought of themselves as revolutionary leaders—expected revolution, not in 1867, in spite of the fact that 'thousands [were] starving'[8] but as a result of the strengthening and realignment of radical forces which would follow a combination at some time in the future of chronic economic breakdown and the persistent refusal of the existing House of Commons as representative of the political order they were attacking to yield power to those who claimed it. Whatever Disraeli's calculation in accepting Torrens' and Hodgkinson's amendments in the following fortnight, there is no reason to suppose that any of the organizers of the demonstration on May 6 expected him to do so or thought that a revolutionary situation was imminent.

The belief that there was a revolutionary situation in 1866/7, or that Disraeli's remedy was a revolutionary one, was shared by some public figures at the time. The Queen, Lowe, Beresford-Hope, Cranborne, Carnarvon and Earl Grey are some of those who agreed with Carlyle[9] and Dr Harrison. The distinguishing characteristic of these, however, is that, apart from the Queen, they were not in office when the crucial decisions were made, or, when active in Parliament, inhabited an intellectual world far different from that of most ministers and members of parliament. The Queen wanted a bill passed as soon as possible, because she feared the effect if one were not. But so far was she from making the running in persuading Derby to act that it is difficult to believe that Derby was influenced by her opinion at all. His chief anxiety about her involved her general withdrawal from public life, the danger of scandal from John Brown's appearances in public and the fears her doctors expressed, and the Cabinet discussed, at the effect on her health of the nervous vomiting to which she was subject as a continuing consequence of Prince Albert's death in 1861[1]. The Queen's willingness to help, by opening Parliament in person and creating a climate of goodwill among Whigs, and the co-operation offered by General Grey in that direction, may have helped Derby to see his way through the House of Commons. The Queen had both an instinctive feeling that the régime would be in danger if something were not done soon and a desire to ensure that Russell and Gladstone did not do it. But Derby's correspondence with Disraeli and General Grey makes it impossible to see the Queen as a major policy-maker, and difficult to find in his attitude to her anything more than skilful use by an experienced politician who had too few pawns of his own of one more pawn in a complicated game.

Cranborne, Carnarvon, Beresford-Hope, Lowe and Earl Grey were highly articulate political intellectuals with a doctrine to peddle, a review to produce, reputations to make or disappointments to make up for. Though the first three belonged to the Conservative party and Grey and Lowe to the Liberal party, they leave the impression of having in common a desire to be something between prigs on the one hand and doctrinaires on the other. Grey was the son of the author of the 1832 Reform bill and brother of the Queen's private secretary. His *Reform of Parliament*, published in 1858, was a defence of parliamentary government against the threats presented by American practice and democratic theory. He had been colonial secretary under Russell and chairman of the parliamentary commission whose statistics of working-class voters put an end to the Reform bill of 1860: he spent 1866 and 1867 at work on the letters which passed between his father and William IV in 1832, intending his edition to be a warning. He had not been in office since 1852: the intensity of his correspondence reflects this. In Lowe's case there were intellectual affinities which enabled him, in an ironical Comtean fantasy, to place himself above Beales and Mill who stood, in his view, in the metaphysical stage of human development—a fantasy which made Frederic Harrison 'wish [he] had not attacked him so' because he was 'the only one of them with the true key' and had 'produced the only thing on Reform worth reading'.[1] Mill was a Comtean Radical who had alarmed Cobden by suggesting that half the members of parliament should be elected by the working classes,[2] Cranborne a conservative Anglican who had no wish to establish a working-class preponderance. Yet Cranborne 'rebuked...[MP.s who had] laughed very much and [been] very inattentive' during Mill's introduction of a modified version of Hare's scheme as an amendment to the bill in 1867, saying that 'any plan proposed and entertained by such a great thinker as Mr Mill deserved respect'. Mill believed the scheme 'was taking hold of one after another of the thinking men'. In pressing the House to take Mill's motion seriously, Cranborne pointed out that Hare's plan was a commonplace of the literature of the subject, though Lady Amberley, who thought she knew the literature and was watching the debate, found 'the speeches against... very foolish because they showed ignorance of [Hare's] book'.[3] Carnarvon nearly followed his brother[4] into the Liberal party in 1869: it was neither accident nor political calculation but a common cord of sympathy which made Gladstone use the occasion of an advanced speech to the Reform Union in London in May 1867 to praise the 'liberality' of the Cranborne Cave. Their earnestness, their literacy and their willingness to read what was written by the journalists of opposition cut them off from a great many of their colleagues. They stood as far apart as Gladstone did from Liberal lawyer-parliamentarians like Serjeant Gaselee, to whom Mill's interjection of the 'philosophical eccentricities' of 'Gooseberry Hill' seemed likely to turn the House of Commons into 'a debating society'.[5] They stood as far apart from Conservative back-benchers like Lord Galway who, at the moment of political breakdown in March 1867, thought 'this infernal Reform question must be giving [Disraeli] no end of trouble' because 'none of your opponents have the manliness to say what they... want'.[6]

Cranborne, Carnarvon and Beresford-Hope were party Conservatives, but they did not think like the body of Conservative
MP.s. In a low, partly evangelical and strongly protestant party,
none was evangelical, two were Puseyite and ritualistic, and Cranborne was dogmatic, intense and too clever by half.[1] Nor did they
believe, like some Conservatives, in the political value of deferential
deception. They believed in political education as a prerequisite of
political enfranchisement, assumed that political knowledge was
necessary to electoral duty and feared that 'large masses of people
who had had no political education were being endowed with political power'.[2] Like Laing, Lowe and Elcho among Adullamites and
like Gladstone among Liberals, they wanted to ensure co-operation
between the intelligence, industry, property and respectability of
the whole country, and they wanted co-operation to be open and
articulate. While many Conservative back-benchers, and a good
number of Liberals, thought of the small boroughs as 'conservative
institutions because. . . the peasant householders would vote as their
landlords wished. . . [Beresford-Hope] thought it would be a most
fallacious and unfortunate position for the Conservative party to
base itself upon the ignorance and subserviency of the country
population'.While Disraeli and some of his followers were prepared
to encourage this, 'he flattered himself that Conservative politics
stood the test of reason and examination; so he should be sorry to
find that their supporters depended upon mere passion and the influence of landlords'.[3] Though Cranborne and Carnarvon wanted a
Whig/Conservative alliance in order to stop Gladstone and Disraeli,
there was nothing about them which smelt of the restrictiveness of a
reactionary country party. Cranborne in some respects was a crude
utilitarian. So far from being a gentry party, the Cranborne Cave
included a director of the Bank of England, who was a militant
opponent of Gladstone's taxation policy: it was as much committed
as Laing or Lowe to the interest and weight and importance of the
world which the free market had created. Whether or not they
agreed with Beresford-Hope's attack on the freeman franchise, they
would have accepted his argument that

its operation in these days, when the labour market ought to be free and
class interests ought not to be encouraged, was to hold out a direct pre-
mium to young men to drag on, living in poverty in the town in which
they were born, waiting for election time, in the hope of getting some of

the good things of this world in the shape of five pound notes rather than go out in the world to prosper where the labour market was at the highest.[1]

Grey, Lowe, Laing and these systematic Conservatives were asserting a long-term connection between extensive enfranchisement, American institutions, democratic domination and the extension to England of the continental socialism which had so far been resisted: the prospect they presented was one which ninety-nine MP.s out of a hundred wished to avoid. They wished to avoid it, and would have supported Disraeli's critics if they had believed that Disraeli's bill would have brought it closer. The tension between their politics and the politics of Potter, Beesly, Bradlaugh and Odger was a tension between different political objectives. The existence of tension of this sort, and the presentation of alternatives it implied, served as a backcloth on which the parliamentary conflict was played.

It served also as a backcloth against which the parliamentary conflict must be contrasted. Whatever impression one gathers from studying Cranborne's or Lowe's writings and speeches, it is not the impression one gathers from those who were important in office or effective in Parliament. Russell's view of Bright's first warning of the danger of physical force if a Reform bill were not passed was that, though it 'will produce sham terrors among the Tories...it is in fact quite ridiculous. If Derby has not the support of the House of Commons, he will resign: if he has, the English people love the law... too well to use physical force against him'.[2] This is not an isolated opinion: it can be matched with innumerable parallels. For every warning of the possibility of violence offered by Bright, a parallel expression may be found of the belief that the 'reform demonstrations...have set forth in plain colours the differences between revolution and reform, and ought to have prepared men's minds to accept a fair settlement of the question',[3] that 'Bright's progress and speeches ...have produced the same feeling among the professional and mercantile classes in Scotland as...in England...[i.e. agreement] in deprecating any reduction of the borough franchise',[4] or that 'it is everyone's duty to keep Mr Bright and his friends out...[by introducing] "a wise and moderate measure"'.[5] For every assertion of the effectiveness of Reform League demonstrations there are parallel claims that 'the reform demonstration of February 11 made no trouble', that 'all passed off quietly in the Park so far as I have heard' or that 'the "great" meeting today seems to have been a fiasco'.[1] For every expression of cosmic anxiety, expressions of pity may be found for the condition 'the poor devils' on the Trades' march through London would be in 'by the time they g[o]t to Beaufort Gardens' through 'mud' and pouring 'rain',[2] or the view that, despite the Home Secretary's desire to mention it, 'allusion had better not be made' in the Queen's speech to the demonstrations of July 1866 because they 'would be made too important'.[3]

'It has not been the mob' wrote a Cabinet Minister after watching the Home Secretary at close quarters in July 1866 'that has frightened me so much [during a most] anxious week. . .as the indecision of some who have to maintain the peace and order of the metropolis.'[4] 'There was', this middle-aged Young Englander wrote of the Trades' march he watched from the roof of St James's palace in December, 'no disorder, no hooting, hardly any cheering; many of the banners and inscriptions had nothing to do with Reform', and the 'Processionists' amounted to about '25,000. . . inclusive of county deputations, bands and Reform Leaguers, the latter a very scrubby, disreputable lot'.[5] For every expression of the belief finally that the demonstrators represented deep-rooted or irresistible working-class feeling, counter-assertions may be found from Bright on the one hand, for example, that 'the Aristocratic Institutions of England [had] acted much like the Slavery Institutions of America. . .[in] demoralis[ing] large classes outside their own special boundaries. . .[in producing] a long habit of submission. . .[and in] enfeebl[ing] by corrupting those who should assail them',[6] and from Shaftesbury, on the other, that Bright's party was a minority among the working-classes and that 'the gentlemen who go in deputations to Lord John Manners are ingrained Democrats and Infidels [by appeasing whom (he meant Hartwell)] you will alienate the sound and thoughtful men. . .the best portions of the working classes of Great Britain. . .[whom] it is within your reach to secure'.[7] These assertions may be combined with claims that, despite the 'false and ridiculous statements [given by the newspapers] of the numbers that attend the demonstrations', 'the very best testimony can be adduced to show that. . .instead of 150,000 [at one meeting in Manchester in October] at no time was there

25

more than 1/10–15,000'.[1] They were supported by the tactically orientated evidence offered by one of the few catholic Liberals whom Disraeli succeeded in capturing—that the Reform League demonstration in Trafalgar Square on February 11, which he watched from a club-house nearby, amounted to 'great numbers of zealous democrats, some of them on horseback, profusely decorated with stars and ribbons, evidently in imitation of the aristocracy...and...all ...out...for a day's holiday' and that the London Working-Men's Association meeting there on Saturday March 16, which 'some of the papers...represented...as a great political event', consisted when he passed it 'of a hundred and fifty people assembled together in the middle of the Square [with] Mr [George] Potter mounted between two of the British lions...making a speech', with 'the greater part of the people...laughing at him...and a good many...saying, as they looked up at him, "what a damned fool"'.[2]

Examination of the letters of politicians nearest to events shows that those who came closest to *fearing* the mob were not Conservatives, but Gladstone and the Whig/Liberal leaders on the one hand and Reform League and Reform Union leaders on the other. Conservative backbenchers disliked mass demonstrations, objected to the government's failure to restrain them and demanded strong measures to preserve the peace and order of the capital. But the intensity of distaste which Conservatives felt for public displays of mob power prevented them being 'awed into submission'. The Conservative attitude throughout the session of 1867 was that, though *something* must be done, because 'wherever [one] went, whether in town or country...no man was satisfied with the present House of Commons on the question of Reform', no countenance should be given to 'the mere riots of a mob'.[3] The one factor which is perfectly consistent, from July 1866 right through to August 1867, is that, whatever was done must be done, as Disraeli recognized in accepting Hodgkinson's amendment, with at least the pretence that it was done in deference, not to 'the terrors' which Gladstone had 'depicted...and the agitation with which [Parliament] ha[d] been threatened',[4] but to respectable opinion, to the House of Commons as a whole or to the wishes of the Conservative party inside it.

Nor was this an unintelligible position to adopt. Not only was the

Conservative party a party of order: its members had nothing to expect from capitulation of this sort. Resistance to public agitation was likely both to conform to Conservative instinct and to be politically advantageous for the party—either in its role as defender of order against the Whig/Liberal alliance with violence, or, as the party of wealth, property and respectability to which existing wealth, property and respectability would turn in face of a newly enfranchised, economically menacing working-class electorate in the future. It is in the Liberal party and among Reform League and Reform Union leaders themselves that we find something resembling *fear*. What Whigs and Liberals feared were the smears the volatility of public agitation would attach to the Liberal party by association. They thought that a socially respectable, economically contented electorate would react against Bright, positivism and republicanism. They thought that this would make the existing electorate more conservative and enhance the attractiveness of the Conservative party to the contented classes in the future. They knew that the satisfied classes did not wish to be disturbed in the security of their possessions, but would accept a measure of enfranchisement if it was presented tactfully. They believed that Palmerston had known this and were much less certain that Gladstone had shown signs of knowing it in the course of attempting to enfranchise a sizeable part of the working-classes in 1866.[1]

They knew moreover that whig leadership had been followed in the past because the working-class movement had not been organized as a separate political power. They knew that the trades unions had never been effective in conventional political terms: they were afraid that they might be now. One cause of the shift in whig feeling in 1866 was the evidence the agitation left that the 'working-classes ...[were] doing...what they never thought of doing *really* before and what those who accused them of doing did not believe at the time...using their trades combinations all thro' the country for the purpose...of a political organization to be brought to bear against the party in power and indeed against Parliament itself'.[2] A movement of this kind would not only destroy the whig hold over working-class feeling but would produce a reactionary flight from the Liberal party on the part of 'employers of labour...[who] kn[e]w what monstrous tyranny [was] exercised by the trades unions and how wholly powerless the workman would be to resist the leaders of

27

these combinations if they chose to make use of their power...for political purposes'.[1]

The Palmerstonian alliance had been based on the belief that a Whig/Radical combination would carry active working-class feeling with it without abandoning anything essential in the process. Fear of the unknown when Palmerston died operated in different ways on different people. It pushed Earl Grey, Shaftesbury and Elcho for a time towards Derby: it made Russell, Halifax, Gladstone and Granville redeploy in order to keep the alliance in existence. This was why whig promotion was neglected in 1866: why Forster, Stansfeld and Goschen were so prominent in 1866/7: why pains were taken to promote Radicals who were not creatures of Bright. But though Halifax, for example, thought that no Reform bill that was in sight would alter the social composition of the House of Commons, none wanted to be branded as allies of rampant proletarianism. They knew, what Gladstone knew also, that, whatever extra-parliamentary forces might follow it, the Whig/Liberal party was, first and foremost, a parliamentary coalition. One aspect of Gladstone's public personality in the middle sixties, was the appeal he made to advanced opinion outside the House of Commons. His identification with a wide range of popular causes from Italian freedom onwards made progressive reformers think of him as the one ministerial leader to whom they could look for sympathy and support. Yet the fact that Gladstone, in the course of the narrative which this book unfolds, succeeded on two or three occasions in putting himself in tune with a progressive wave of public feeling, should not mislead us into seeing him, at this time, as the 'People's William'.

Gladstone was exercised by public selfishness and self-interest and anxious to raise the public to a high level by infusions of concern for the public interest. He was moving, slowly and circuitously, to a position of hostility to the exclusiveness of the Anglican establishment and renewing on a new basis the whig alliance between Catholic, Irish and English dissent, of which his attack on the Irish Church in 1865 and his vote in 1866 in favour of the annual motion against Church Rates were symbols. In this process, party necessities coincided with intellectual commitments. In the gap left by Newman's destruction of the national regeneration which Oxford Anglicanism had promised in his youth, in the political isolation in which he was left by the deaths of the most elevated of his Peelite contemporaries and in the felt need to lead the Whig/Radical/dissenting alliance at large, Gladstone had come to see the parliamentary process itself as the agent of moral unity. Whereas the prospect of a revivified State–Church in the thirties had inspired the best men of his generation with a sense of the moral unity of the nation, this was a something he had ceased to think it possible that the Church of England should do. Newman's secession had broken its nerve: in a society whose prevailing tendency was for 'the establishment of the principle of popular self-government as the basis of political constitutions . . . and the disintegration of Christendom from one into many communions', Anglicanism by itself could no longer provide moral cohesion. Nevertheless 'consciousness of moral duty [had] been not less notably quickened and enhanced'.[1] The consonance between parliament and people was already considerable: it was desirable to increase it in the future. It was desirable to increase it by extending the franchise because the Act of 1832 had shown 'the great *positive* strength which is added to the government and institutions by any addition to the constituency subject to the single limitation that it shall not be such as to do damage by violence'.[2] Though there were numerous examples, of which no one could be ignorant, of 'outrages' committed by the 'labouring classes', they would be removed most effectively by attaching working-class political activity to the existing parliamentary régime. The process of attachment would extend economic knowledge and forestall incipient socialism. Though the benefits the working classes had gained from the operation of the market were considerable, an imaginative effort would have to be made if they were to understand that this was so. It was desirable from time to time to 'tot it all up before them'.[3] They would be led to 'adopt more universally the laws of freedom in their dealings among themselves in the labour market' only if 'they [were] placed in as close connection as possible with the representative system [Oh!]'.[4]

On the other hand, Gladstone was by upbringing, context and training first and foremost a parliamentary statesman, with all the caution about extra-parliamentary politics which scepticism among parliamentary politicians induced about alternative sources of power. If Gladstone moved in these years to a position which seemed likely to alter the relationship between Parliament and the public platform outside, the move was made hesitantly, with no clearly articulated understanding of the process for which he was responsible. Gladstone's relations with the Reform League and with the London Working-Men's Association were formal and official. Like Derby, Stanley and Disraeli in April 1867, he received delegations: though he wrote to the *Morning Star* and to Beales personally, he at no time addressed their meetings. George Potter caught his imagination in 1867; but as a symbol of the intelligent working-men to whom Parliament had a duty to perform, not as the leader of a movement with a right to dictate policy. Gladstone gave the League no support at the moment in May 1867 at which its defiance of government was strongest, 'fac[ed] both ways'[1] on the Royal Parks bill and took pains to remove the impression that he supported illegality. His relations with the Reform Union were closer, but even these until May 1867 displayed more warmth than contact.

Gladstone's difficulty was considerable. It was not only not expected that ministers and potential ministers would 'run about the country delivering speeches': it was also expected that 'as a general rule' they would not.[2] One objection to Gladstone was that he did so more often than a minister should, but, when he did, he did it in conformity with parliamentary convention and recognizing that the party he was attempting to lead consisted of respectable merchants, manufacturers and country gentlemen who had no desire to be led by Radical demagogues and of suspicious Whigs who would not be 'reconciled to *adventurers* in high places' unless they had made themselves indispensable 'like Disraeli or Lowe'.[3] Gladstone wanted to make the parliamentary process attractive to the 'millions of hard hands' who had to be governed by 'force, fraud, or good-will'.[4] He wanted to do this, not by force, not by fraud, but with the sort of goodwill which had already begun to be effective. If, however, we are to understand the struggle he fought in the Whig/Liberal party after 1865, we must recognize that he had neither popular organization nor hereditary power behind him; that he was neither a civic Radical nor 'born in [the Whig] kennel';[5] and that, though Argyll 'toadie[d]'[6] him and Granville handled him, he had neither instinctive 'sympathy nor connection with any considerable party in the House of Commons'.[7] We must take account of his uncertainty and comparative isolation. We must give weight to his consciousness of the dignity of Parliament, and must begin at the point at which in 1864 when, writing 'with great freedom', to George Wilson, the president of the Reform Union, he attempted 'thoroughly [to] dissuade those who are interested in the extension of the franchise from taking any step to connect my name with it, outside the walls of Parliament; I mean in any manner requiring presentation of an address'.

Already [he went on] people seek to damage the cause itself, which it is rightly considered is a good cause, by alleging that my declaration last session [i.e. the speech of May 11 1864 on Baines's Reform motion, *Hansard* (312ff.)] was an attempt to create a faction in support of myself —considering that I did no more than speak in my place as a member of Parliament, in favour of a proposition in which I had long before cordially concurred as a member of the Cabinet. I do not feel that there is any force in the reproaches as against myself, or what I endeavoured to recommend and support; but were I to become a party to proceedings out of Parliament individually, on a matter of this interest, and not belonging to my department, I think it would be a violation of duty to my colleagues, and would also tend, without any compensating advantage, to break up that political connection to which we must look to aid in the future advancement of the question.[1]

This consciousness of the forces determining political possibility affected not only parliamentary politicians, but even the Reform League leaders themselves. The point of the Reform League, the centre of its rhetorical concern, was to attack aristocratic monopoly. Yet brazenness of language was not always matched by brazenness of mind. Like Mill, Lord John Manners saw Beales and others at close quarters in July after they had lost control of the demonstration of July 23: he thought they were 'more frightened than those whom they have frightened'.[2] Though they took pains to respect the limits of legality, this was not true of all advocates of extra-parliamentary action. Bradlaugh was an atheist journalist whose *National Reformer* had a primarily religious objective. He was also a minor demagogue with a name to make: he made it by attacking the League's leadership. Ernest Jones was an old chartist without real sympathy for Beales's alliance with Gladstone and the Reform Union.[3] Beesly, Harrison and Congreve were positivist proselytizers with plans for a fundamental revolution to supersede a 'Venetian' by a Comtean polity. To them 'old Beales' was useless, the 'Liberal MP.s . . . a pack of curs' who did not understand that 'strong measures, processions and physical force' were necessary if Gladstone was to be 'dragged out' of his shell. Their object was to capture Bright: the longer a settlement was delayed, the more certain they felt of achieving manhood suffrage.[1] But Ernest Jones lived in Manchester and had little effect on League policy. Bradlaugh resigned from the League Executive in 1867 because his atheism was embarrassing the movement. Harrison was a barrister who lived by his pen, took little part in the day-to-day politics of Reform except as a journalist, and, though nominated alongside Thomas Hughes as the trades union nominee on the royal commission on Trades Unions, did not join the League because he had neither the time nor the money to do so.[2] Beesly was not an MP., but a professor at University College, London. He spoke at Reform League meetings, but, so far from being one of its leaders, failed when he stood for election to the League Executive. Beesly provided a comprehensive rhetoric with which to approach the future but his ejaculations were premature and his day-to-day judgements defective. In 1861 he had seen in the builders' strike of 1859 an event which 'seem[ed] to have a chance of standing in the same relation to the coming industrial régime, as the meeting of the States-General in "eighty-nine"... to the subsequent history of Europe'.[3] Like other reformers, he objected to the House of Commons which was the real enemy: the day Palmerston died he declined membership of the League because the old cries would make no impact on it. Bright commanded positivist attention as a possible leader of a revolutionary movement in the future. When Bright gave the word in favour of Gladstone's bill in 1866 despite the inadequacy of its contents, Beesly offered his services[4] but expected so little, and was so little in touch, that he, alone with Corry (Disraeli's secretary), General Grey and the Queen, thought the Derby government's abortive £6 rating bill of February 25 1867, which was universally criticized in the House of Commons because it did not go far enough, 'as good a bill as was expected... if not better'.[5]

The Reform League, however, was led, neither by Bradlaugh nor by Beesly but by Beales. Beales was a promoter of good causes: a middle-aged barrister who was chairman of the Reform League in much the same way as his 'imperative sense of duty and justice to the Circassian race' had made him chairman of the Circassian committee and a member of the Polish, Jamaica and Garibaldi

committees.[1] Beales was conscious of being a middle-class edu-
cator with interests different from those of his followers.[2] His support for Gladstone was not helped by the obscurity of Gladstone's
position: he too had to face the problems of political leadership.

He received criticism from George Potter and from Hartwell (who
had been passed over for the Reform League secretaryship). He was
attacked by Bradlaugh for timidity and unnecessary deference to
Shaftesbury's and Gladstone's religious susceptibilities, and by
Ernest Jones for excessive legality. The government's inability to
establish that the League meetings in the Park in 1866 were illegal
and its failure to prevent the meeting of May 6 1867 were interpreted as victories which he presented to his followers as
such. Beales was suspended from his post as revising barrister for
Middlesex in 1866: he lost two members of his family in early 1867
and was in evident financial difficulty.[3] He spent a great part of the
winter spreading the message in provincial halls and lecture-rooms.
Just as Gladstone shifted and shuffled in order to keep together a
diverse motley of Radicals, Whigs and respectable parliamentary
Liberals, so, even from the limited material we have to hand, Beales
can be seen shuffling and shifting to keep together in a responsible
political movement, a miscellaneous body of middle-class improvers,
old chartist agitators, young revolutionaries and a good many un-
influential, unimportant and in one case persistently drunken,
respectable-working-men. The members of Parliament closest to
the Reform League—Bright, Mill, P. A. Taylor, T. B. Potter,
and Thomas Hughes—were party Liberals because they pursued
objectives more extensive than reform of the electoral system,
and regarded the Liberal party, under Gladstone's leadership,
as the only instrument for effecting inroads, however slow, on
aristocratic or Anglican monopoly. Although they wished to limit
aristocratic power, however, they did not underestimate its strength.
The restraint they put on the League was put, not just out of dislike
of violence but from fear of the reaction of respectable opinion at
large and of the Liberal party in the House of Commons.

Bright's rhetoric was militant and forceful. He talked the language of power, threatened to use it and predicted downfall for an
aristocracy which failed to concede to the demands of the class of
which he was the self-appointed mouthpiece. Yet the attacks on
aristocracy in the autumn and winter of 1866, the demand—

CDG

cautiously hedged in and explained away as soon as made—for an extensive transfer to tenants of the estates of absentee Irish land-owners[1] and the warnings of violence if a Reform bill were not passed[2] do not exhaust the story of Bright's relations with public agitation. Whereas, when the Liberal party was in office, he had attacked aristocracy in his own party, he could now assault the aristocratic prejudices of the Conservative party. Whereas the Reform League wanted manhood suffrage, Bright at no time advocated anything more extensive than a household suffrage in which 'all persons who are rated to some tax—the relief of the poor being the most general now—should be admitted to the franchise'.[3] Bright had no desire to enfranchise any but the most prosperous lodgers. He did not want to enfranchise a million paupers, the unemployed or those who could not pay their rates. He did not doubt that the 'residuum'—a 'small class...of almost hopeless poverty and dependence...in all or nearly all our boroughs'— should be denied the chance to vote, if only because they had 'no independence whatsoever' and had interests and attitudes opposed to those of our 'intelligent and honest working men'.[4] He objected to Sir Rainald Knightley's attempt to forbid corrupt payment of rates on the ground that in Birmingham 'any active politician [would] go...to the overseer's office and look over the list' when the time for registration came in July, would 'pay the rates and clear the account' of anyone who was entitled to register but had failed to pay his rates, and, in doing so, had so little of a 'corrupt purpose' that 'in the majority of cases the money [was] repaid by the voter (ironical cheers from the ministerial side).'

Though those by whom he was attacked thought he wanted to destroy aristocratic power, his words suggest no such intention. There is every reason to think that he wanted what he said he wanted—neither an assault on property nor the destruction of aristocracy, but a sharing of its power; and that he wanted this because, in the society in which he lived, he could not conceive of success for revolution fundamental enough to sweep away aristocratic institutions altogether. It was, he told Congreve in September 1866 on being offered leadership of the vague, non-existent independent revolutionary working-class movement which Congreve wished to establish for the future, 'simply impracticable...to undertake leadership and guidance and even a government which many are

34

unwilling and none have the power to place in my hands'. He adequately reflected the limits of his political world when he added that the organized power of the existing aristocracy 'forms a citadel which can hardly be invested, and can only be taken, it may be, by the labour of generations'.

However extensive his demagoguery, Bright saw himself as a practical politician, 'not much believ[ing] in far-reaching schemes ...content with doing a day's work as it presents itself', aware of the importance for practical purposes of party connection, and conscious of the need, if anything was to be achieved, of pulling at the levers that were within reach—the suffocating of reactionary Whiggism inside the Liberal party, the election of a more popular Parliament, and a public exertion of moral pressure which, combined with 'a free press and platform and with what is passing in Europe and America before our eyes', would produce movement which 'must be forward'.[1]

Bright was ill and depressed in 1866 and 1867. He addressed one outdoor meeting in London, joined no marches, was involved in no disorder. He gave as his reason for criticizing Derby's suspicion of the Reform League meeting in the Park in May 1867, not a justification of violence, but the fact that 'contrary to the feelings of some ...the character of the English people [was] guarantee for a peaceful issue on a day like that'.[2] He attacked the government for threatening to close Hyde Park in July 1866, but did not join the demonstration. He sent George Howell, the Reform League secretary, a letter of denunciation, but tried, and failed, to stop him publishing it because 'it so strongly condemn[ed] the *Tory government* for that which [he remembered after sending the letter] Sir George Grey [the Whig Home Secretary] had already ordered to be done' before the Russell government left office.[3] Bright was unusual among parliamentary politicians in his consciousness of the possibilities of public agitation, but he wanted to accommodate the extra-parliamentary movement to the standards of respectability inside it. Like other parliamentary Radicals, Bright knew what image he wanted a working-class movement to present. He knew, also, what image it ought not to present. Like the Radical author of *Tom Brown's Schooldays*, he wanted it to be manly and honest on the one hand and dignified and restrained on the other. Other examples may be found of the embarrassment caused to Radicals in Parliament by their followers outside—Fawcett's refusal in January 1866 to appear on League platforms; the refusal of Alderman Lusk, MP. for Finsbury, to demonstrate on Primrose Hill in May; Mill's meeting with the League Executive during the Hyde Park conflict in July; Hughes's attack on the Sheffield trades unionists at the Sheffield meeting of the Social Science Association in 1865, his unwillingness to appear on a public platform in Islington, despite the help given him by the League in Lambeth at the election of 1865, his mediation between the government and the League and his attempts to prevent the Hyde Park meeting in May 1867; Bright's insistence that the League abandon the policy of presenting individual petitions to Parliament because of the 'annoyance' it would cause the League's 'friends' in the House of Commons; the warning given by Culling Hanbury, the brewer MP. for Middlesex, who was not a Radical, that 'an agitation at the present time on [the] basis...of Manhood Suffrage [would be] likely to prejudice the cause of Reform in the minds of many whose support is both desirable and necessary.'[1] None reflects this better than Bright's criticism of the public image the League left of itself in inadequately prepared newspaper reports —reports in which, for example, Mr Mantle, a London working-man and a League vice-president, made the League Executive laugh, but in Bright's view made it ridiculous, by mentioning the interest taken by Colonel Dickson—a leading League member—in 'Dr Mary Walker (laughter)',[2] and which showed Beales in the course of the same meeting declaring that, since it was

impossible to get...gentlemen [like Bright, Stansfeld or Taylor as speakers at a League meeting on New Year's Eve] they should have a certain number of good singers, a good quadrille band and...should ask Lady Amberley and others to be patronesses so that the affair might be carried on in a fashionable way (Hear, hear).[3]

Under Beales's guidance the Executive reminded itself of the legality of its actions, took pains to organize orderly demonstrations, blamed the government for the breakdown in July 1866 and co-operated with and asked for co-operation from the police in order to keep its followers under control. There were, it is true, marches, demonstrations and public meetings. There was a prolonged struggle with the government, which the League won, about the right to assemble, first, while Sir George Grey was Home Secretary, on Primrose Hill and in Trafalgar Square, then, under Walpole, in Hyde Park itself. But there was no defiance except when the law confirmed its positions, and there were elaborate para-military plans to ensure that the meetings were not ruined by roughs and rowdies who could not be excluded altogether. There were Reform League songs,[1] Reform League pamphlets, Reform League ribbons and a Reform League poet.[2] There were lecture courses, not only about the suffrage and the ballot but also about Russell's, de Lolme's and Creasey's views of the British Constitution. There were soirées and fêtes as well as public demonstrations; there is no evidence, despite Bright's warnings and talk in Bright's circle,[3] of any intention to arm its members. This atmosphere of controlled legality embraced even the most vigorous. Bradlaugh sounded like a revolutionary firebrand. Yet Bradlaugh prided himself on his knowledge of the law, insisted on holding the demonstration on May 6 1867 because of the legal right to do so, and spent his afternoon during the Re-form League rally in Trafalgar Square on February 11 not on the rostrum, certainly not battling with the police, but on horseback alongside Baxter Langley as deputy marshal to keep order in which role, 'wearing tricolour scar[f] and armlets', he rode his horse up the steps of the National Gallery in pursuit of 'a young fellow who had thrown a stone...on the crowd below'.[4]

A breakdown of public order would have helped no one. It would not have helped the government, though violence might do it good with electors, because Conservative backbenchers would not stand for it. It would not have helped the Liberal party because its repu-tation as a party of government would have suffered. It would not have helped the Reform League leaders themselves (Marx thought them foolish for thinking so)[5], because even those who looked forward to revolution in the future, saw that the time had not yet come at which it could occur. Although, therefore, it would be wrong to speak of agreement between responsible leaders inside Parliament and outside, the absence of actual violence was, in part, a result of the embarrassment any violence would have brought to everybody.

Nor, on the other hand, did the government want a violent con-frontation. Although Conservative backbenchers criticized the gov-ernment's failure to prevent the League demonstrating in London in 1867, there was reluctance in Cabinet under Disraeli's guidance to have a show-down. Though Cranborne, like Marx, wanted a show-down and thought there could have been one if the government had exercised its right to close Hyde Park on May 6, the Park was not closed: though troops patrolled the streets before the meeting, there seems to have been an understanding[1] that they would not appear in the Park. On the morning of May 6 the League Executive decided not to provoke the government during speeches at the meeting. The detective detailed to serve warnings in case its members caused a 'nuisance' called at the League's office while the Executive was making final preparations: these were completed in time for him to serve notices peacefully and civilly in Howell's office.

Although Walpole was blamed, there is reason to suppose that the government's decision was Disraeli's. Disraeli had good reason to avoid a confrontation, not least because he wanted to carry Radical votes in the House of Commons. From the moment at which the demonstration came to his notice, he played it down as much as possible. Walpole was blamed by party and Cabinet for issuing a notice which he could not honour, but the notice was issued, after consultation and Cabinet discussion, on the assumption that the government would close the Park on May 6: if the Cabinet had intended to do so it would have been a reasonable thing to publish. It seems certain that Walpole was nervously exhausted. It was Disraeli's pressure which made the Cabinet decline to act. When Walpole was blamed, in Parliament and outside, he did not criticize Disraeli in public, though it was Disraeli's insistence that the Park should not be closed which made his notice look ridiculous. But in private Walpole thought he had been let down.[2] The fact that, once the demonstration was over, Disraeli took a more militant line in order to appease the Conservative party in the House of Commons, should not prevent us seeing that he was involved at least as much as Walpole in the Cabinet's failure to anticipate the demonstration by closing the Park as it had in July 1866, or, once that alternative was rejected, by acting boldly on the assumption that the League must be appeased.

At various moments between 1865 and 1867 Derby and Disraeli wrote of the possibility of an anti-revolutionary coalition, but they did not think they were living in a revolutionary situation. They thought Bright's mention of revolution offered a chance to accumulate anti-revolutionary support, but they thought this as politicians calculating within a settled system, not as men of action confronting a revolutionary upheaval. They did not spend the winter of 1866 preparing some comfortable Chislehurst in Spain, Portugal or the Azores: apart from six weeks in London for Cabinet meetings and the Guildhall dinner, they spent the winter as they had for many years past, at Hughenden and Knowsley. Though the winter was hard, cholera rampant (in London at least) and food prices high, they seem not to have been conscious of the political implications of under-nourishment.[1] Since many of Beales's and Potter's followers spent half a guinea to take part in demonstrations,[2] their political judgement was probably accurate.

It is true, as *Hansard* and the letters of politicians reveal, that there was, in Parliament in these years, acute and continuing consciousness of public opinion and working-class feeling. The London builders' strikes of 1859/62 and the Staffordshire iron-workers' strike of 1865, for example, presented a threat to political economy and the control of industrialists over their labourers. The breaking of the Park railings in July 1866, the dynamiting of a non-trades unionist saw-grinder's house in Sheffield in October and the Fenian outrages in Ireland and England in March 1867 induced, in a public which had been habituated to threats of violence from below, a re-action of some force. A confused analysis made a connection between Bright's threats, vast meetings, Fenian violence and an Irish alliance, which Bright's visit to Dublin and The O'Donoghue's prominence at Reform League meetings did nothing to remove. Yet, though this unco-ordinated conjunction of events left an impression of danger, it would be wrong to attribute to the House of Commons fear or uncertainty in response. Though the government had been slow to act, 'it was', wrote Hardy of the suspension of Habeas Corpus in Ireland in February 1866 'a grand thing to see a great assembly, where need was, act with the decision and vigour of our execution'.[3] Sir George Grey had been Home Secretary when the Chartist demonstration of April 10 1848 had been put down by Wellington and Sir Richard Mayne. Though he was proposing to limit the freedom of some of their supporters, no one in the parliamentary Liberal party could discredit his attitude to the Reform League's attempts to meet in public in London in 1865/6, or doubted the desirability of keeping a close check on

Reform League meetings in 1867. No passages in English oratory are more barely expressive of the class struggle than Lowe's attacks on the lower orders. No British politician in mid-twentieth century would imply as clearly as a Liberal leader like Gladstone the need to ensure that any renovated franchise excluded the 'residuum', by-passed 'the mere peasantry' or took pains, in enfranchising the working-classes, not to admit 'the poorest, the least instructed and the most dependent members of the community... [at the expense of] the most skilled and most instructed of our working men'.[1]

In these circumstances much must be said for Dr Harrison's view that 'unless a synthesis is made between the "party conflict" and "class struggle" interpretations, the history of 1866/7 is unintelligible'.[2] However, to do this involves understanding ministers in the situations in which they were acting. It involves understanding that, while official Whigs and many Liberals wanted a Reform bill in 1866 in order to prevent class conflict in the future, others anticipated class conflict in Parliament if a large working-class electorate were admitted to the franchise. Earl Grey and Carnarvon differed from Halifax and Granville in the fear they felt for the independence and integrity of Parliament in an electoral system in which the working classes had a majority of votes. While Halifax foresaw no difficulty in keeping hold of working-class feeling so long as Liberals honoured their promises, Earl Grey and Carnarvon believed that the existing Parliament, which was not, they thought, a class Parliament, might easily become one. Earl Grey's fears may be explained, no doubt, as a function of political under-employment, Halifax's confidence as a facet of the fact that he was fully employed. But, though differences about immediate policy must not be disregarded, it is still the case that they, Carnarvon, Derby and Gladstone (if not Disraeli for reasons which will emerge later) were guided by the assumption, which all held with varying degrees of sincerity but held nevertheless, that the object of policy should be to maintain conditions in which class conflict was kept out of the House of Commons.

In this, perhaps, they were deceiving themselves. Once they began to think in class terms, they were, almost necessarily, rationalizing their positions. Once one asks why they wanted to maintain existing arrangements, one sees material reasons more extensive than avoidance of class conflict. Nevertheless, the historian must take account of the language in which they talked, the fears they felt and the ideas they expressed, and must not too readily explain away the fact that, even if the existing situation worked to their advantage, neither they nor Bright nor anyone else had conceived of the working of any other.

Moreover, to connect the 'class struggle' with the 'party conflict' interpretation involves distinguishing between the making of decisions and the manner in which decisions were discussed. Dr Harrison claims that Derby and Disraeli 'frequently talked with a flippancy which is only possible for men who have surrendered to events': he supports his claim with four examples, none of which justifies his conclusion that 'the Tory statesmen were bowing to a process which it was beyond their power to control'.[1] Derby did write, it is true, that 'household suffrage would be a wonderful hare to start',[2] but he wrote this in December 1866 three months after household suffrage was first discussed in Cabinet, mentioning it as one subject among many which the Cabinet might refer to an all-party commission of enquiry.[3] Derby was thinking of appointing a commission to examine the next step in dealing with the question because he thought that a viable way, given the prior decision not to drop the Reform question altogether, *of avoiding commitment to introduce a bill as soon as Parliament met.* So far from showing him 'bowing to a process which it was beyond [his] power to control', it suggests that at this time he felt free to contrive a tactical delay before Parliament began to legislate.

Again, as Dr Harrison says, Disraeli 'request[ed] Stanley to come and speak on the lodger clause, explaining that it made no difference whether he spoke for or against it, so long as he spoke'.[4] There is about this letter a Disraelian cynicism which Stanley did not reciprocate.[5] Nevertheless, it was written, not in the middle of a debate, in which situation it might have been highly significant, but at Windsor during the Easter recess. Disraeli had committed the Cabinet three weeks earlier to consider any lodger franchise to which the House of Commons might agree. He may not have known what rental qualification Stanley thought desirable, and was probably fishing to find out. At the same time as Disraeli was sounding out Stanley, Cairns was sounding out Hardy about conceding over Hibbert's amendment. It is likely that Disraeli wanted to know how far the Cabinet would go, and would want Stanley to speak, just as Derby wanted him to speak in the confidence debate on May 9,[1] because he and Hardy were the two ministers whose presence in Cabinet was treated by dissident or unwilling Conservatives, like General Peel, as a guarantee of integrity. Nor, in the third case cited by Dr Harrison, is it reasonable to say that 'poor Walpole', the Home Secretary, after his handling of the demonstration of May 6, was 'offered up as a sacrifice to the outraged dignity of the upper and middle classes'.[2] Walpole left the Home Office on May 9 because he had damaged the government's reputation and lost the confidence of his friends, and because he thought that Disraeli had let him down. But, despite Walpole's inadequacy, which was manifest both to the House of Commons and to the Cabinet,[3] Derby at first refused to allow him to leave the Home Office *because it would look as though he was being made a scapegoat*, and agreed (on condition that Walpole stayed in the Cabinet) only when Walpole's wife wrote urgently to say that Walpole's mental state was such that he was in no condition to continue.[4]

Finally, although there are questions to be asked about the connection between the demonstration in Hyde Park on May 6 and Disraeli's acceptance of Hodgkinson's amendment eleven days later, it would be wrong in this connection to speak of the government's 'surrender'.[5] Dr Harrison's justification for this word is Disraeli's assertion, made to Hardy after the event, that acceptance of the amendment would 'destroy the present agitation [i.e. the Reform League agitation] and extinguish Gladstone and company'.[6] Yet this narrative will show that Disraeli would have preferred to accept Hibbert's amendment in the form in which Hibbert proposed it long before the Park demonstration was thought of, and almost certainly accepted Hodgkinson's instead because the Cabinet had discussed and rejected Hibbert's, and had not discussed Hodgkinson's at all. Hodgkinson's amendment, so far from settling anything, created great confusion in all boroughs in England and Wales where compounding for rates was the norm, but it speeded up the passage of the bill. Disraeli accepted it for this reason, it will be argued, and for this reason only—that it facilitated passage in the current session by removing pretexts for Radical filibustering *in the House of Commons*. The Hyde Park demonstration of May 6 did nothing to Disraeli which the general movement of public feeling in the winter had not done already. So far as it had an impact on him, it was in a reactionary direction, making Conservative backbenchers so hostile to the government's failure to resist the League's use of the Park that he could not concede as much as he wanted to in Hibbert's direction, and had to couple an inadequate concession to Hibbert on May 6 with what Gladstone called a 'reactionary' motion of confidence on May 9 and a bill to prevent similar demonstrations in the Royal Parks in future. In winning the vote of May 9, Disraeli demonstrated his command of the House of Commons: when he accepted the principle of Hodgkinson's amendment on May 17, he was in a position, not of weakness, but of the greatest personal strength. The bill had been passed as far as it had been less by Conservative and Radical votes than by Conservative and Adullamite ones. The Conservative vote in the divisions of April 12 and May 9 had been reinforced not by Radical votes alone, but by a mixture of Radical, advanced, constitutional and reactionary Liberals voting against Gladstone, or with Disraeli, for reasons at least as various as their labels. In each case Disraeli wanted to concede more than he did, but was prevented by the Cabinet from doing so. In each case the desire to concede sprang, not from the feeling that Radicals as a body would support him, but from the uncertainties forced on him by the ambiguity of Gladstone's attack and the unreliability of the Cave.

Throughout the session Gladstone had combined an attack on the restrictive aspects of the bill of March 18 with the warning that, if the restrictions were removed, the suffrage it would establish would be more extensive than it should be. Though Gladstone failed to receive the wide measure of Conservative and constitutional Liberal support he was undoubtedly hoping to attract, Disraeli could not have predicted the outcome of either division. Since Adullamite and Conservative votes could not be relied on, therefore, Radical support had to be bid for too. Radicals had not responded in large numbers on April 12, but the rallying of constitutional forces in both parties behind Disraeli on May 9, when combined with a greatly increased Radical vote and Gladstone's adoption for the first time two days later of an unambiguously progressive position, established Disraeli in a position of overwhelming strength. The fact that a sizeable number of Radicals and advanced Liberals had voted with him displayed possibilities: the fact that they would filibuster if not conceded to made concession desirable. The doubt that persisted about support from Conservative and constitutional Liberals for any vote which was not a reactionary one made it desirable to avoid a vote at any point at which concessions were to be made. Though the Park demonstration may have made filibustering more likely on the part of Radicals who had no wish to let Disraeli make the running without pressure from them, it is certain that, so far from being a 'capitulation', Disraeli's acceptance of Hodgkinson's amendment should be seen as a signal, 'exulting'[1] demonstration of his ability, on his own terms and in his own time, to provide what Whigs believed that they alone, as guardians of executive government, could provide—an instalment of progress which was both real and safe.

Moreover, it is necessary to understand the significance of the clauses to which so much importance is attached by Dr Harrison in common with all other historians who have written about the question. The Hodgkinson amendment and the lodger clause were only parts of the bill. They affected voters in the English and Welsh boroughs, did not apply to the counties and in no way altered the distribution of seats. The lodger clause was not expected to have 'any large practical effect' since lodgers, alone among new electors, had themselves to take active steps each year to claim to be put on the electoral register.[2] With a £15 p.a. qualifying bar, they 'would [have] swamp[ed] only constituencies which are already as radical as they...can be':[3] with the £10 qualifying bar that was eventually accepted in the modified form proposed at the last minute by Gabriel Goldney, the Conservative MP. for Chippenham, the effect would have been not very much different. The step which made it possible, at one spectacular blow, to enfranchise well over 400,000 new borough electors with Disraeli's acceptance, on his own responsibility and without Cabinet discussion, of Hodgkinson's amendment on May 17, trebled the enfranchisement permitted by the bill of March 18. By itself, or as an earnest of what was to come, it looked startling, novel and thoroughly democratic. However, it had been anticipated, three days earlier, by the introduction of a Reform bill for Scotland. There was no compounding for rates in Scotland, though occupiers of the poorest houses were excused from paying them. The Scottish bill proposed a rated residential suffrage almost as extensive as would obtain under the bill of March 18 in the twenty-nine English boroughs where compounding had not been adopted and where no occupier was automatically excused from paying his own rates. Hodgkinson's amendment had little or no application to these twenty-nine boroughs or to the thirty or so others in England and Wales where compounding for rates had been adopted in only a minority of parishes and where, therefore, the bill of March 18 had established rated household suffrage without restriction in the rest.[1] Every householder who was affected by Hodgkinson's amendment already had the right to vote if he paid his rates on opting out of composition. Registration would now be easier for those who wanted to vote, but, since the abolition of compounding would increase opportunities for avoiding rates on the part of the poorest ratepayers, there was one sense in which the conjunction of Hodgkinson's amendment with the personal payment principle would be more likely than the original bill to reduce the number of the very poor who were likely to vote. In addition to the 390,000 working-men, acceptance of the Hodgkinson principle brought onto the electoral register between 80,000 and 90,000 occupiers of houses rated at more than £10 p.a., the rateable value of which would have given their occupiers votes under the 1832 Act but for the fact that the 1832 Act excluded from the franchise any occupier who did not pay his own rates unless he claimed annually to pay them, and that they were situated in twenty-one boroughs where the borough rating authority had made compounding compulsory for all rented houses up to a comparatively high rateable value.[2]

Sir William Clay's Act of 1851 had entitled these occupiers to opt out of composition once and for all and to vote on paying their share of the reduced rate. But registration depended on occupiers taking the initiative which, since 1851, only a quarter of those who were entitled to do had in fact done—chiefly in Manchester, Birmingham and Brighton.[3] Since, although rateable values were high in some of these twenty-one constituencies they were not high in all, some of these 80,000 or 90,000 occupiers were reasonably prosperous citizens who did not belong to the lowest stratum of the working-classes: the full force of the abolition of compounding in relation to it was felt in something between 135 and 150 boroughs. This is not to say that the Hodgkinson amendment, in conjunction with the original bill, did not effect a major change or that Disraeli, in accepting it, did not accept far more than the House of Commons or the Cabinet would have accepted if either had been asked beforehand.

But, when viewed in the context of the whole, it is a good deal less significant than the assertion that it trebled the proposed addition to the electorate implies.[1]

The post-1867 electorate in England and Wales was nearly twice as large as the electorate in 1865: the proportion of male citizens qualified to vote after 1867 was about twice the proportion qualified in 1833. Whatever meaning is attached to the phrase 'working-class', the potential working-class electorate in English and Welsh boroughs in the period immediately after 1867 was probably about *five times* the size of the working-class electorate in these boroughs before, and over a half their total electorate. Also, the Act of 1867 made possible the enfranchisement of over three times as many electors as the bill of 1866 would have done if passed, and was followed by an election in which the Liberal party increased its majority in the House of Commons. These are facts which it is no part of this book to question. Nor would it be sensible to deny the genuineness of the alarm felt not only by Conservative critics like Cranborne and thwarted Whigs like Clarendon but also by representatives of the intellectually respectable Whig–Liberal upper-middle class alliance, like Bagehot, Lowe and Earl Grey, whom Professor Herrick has rightly cited as believers in the merits of the 1832 constitution.[2]

All these things are true. Yet they should not be emphasized without emphasizing also that almost everyone who discussed the question assumed that the lower the franchise qualification was set the smaller the ratio of registered to possible voters would become, that the redistribution of seats, though smaller than in 1832, positively favoured the Conservative party, that the number of borough seats did not increase as much as the size of the borough electorate and that a permanent settlement of the question was an object for which most non-Radical MP.s and some Radicals were willing to pay a considerable price. Elcho, more than anyone apart from Disraeli, was responsible for the fact that the Act of 1867 was more extensive than any previous bill: self-respect no doubt made him support the consequences of the personal and political hostility to Gladstone by which his actions had been governed. But Elcho did not think of household suffrage in parliamentary boroughs as a 'democratic' measure. In 1865 he thought it the only permanent alternative to the existing £10 franchise. He objected to Gladstone's £7 rental bill in 1866 because it would settle nothing. He would have supported a rated residential suffrage if Disraeli had proposed that on February 25 1867 provided that counterpoises and compensations were retained: he reiterated his support for Disraeli even after Hodgkinson's amendment had been accepted.[1] The only criticism another Adullamite—Grosvenor—made of clause 3 of the bill *before* Hodgkinson's amendment was accepted was that, with the greatly increased electorate established by the bill, existing compounding regulations would give local authorities a disproportionate political power, which Hodgkinson's amendment went a long way towards removing.[2] The one objective aimed at by the Cave, and one which the Reform League specifically rejected, was to reach a settlement which would stand for a generation, without going so far as the League's manhood suffrage on the one hand or equality of electoral districts on the other. Elcho thought Disraeli had settled the question for a long time without conceding anything vital. Indeed, with every desire to avoid paradox and an even stronger unwillingness to be deceived by Disraeli's rhetoric, it is idle to ask: why did the Parliament of 1867 not resist democratic reform? The fact is that many of its members thought it had resisted it, had taken the wind out of the democratic movement, had made plausible the claim that Parliament had moved with the opinion 'not of the mob (for that would matter little) but of the bulk of the class now actually voting and holding political power',[3] and had delayed, for at least a generation on a matter in which delay was of first consequence, the democratizing of the British political system.

The purpose of this book, therefore, is to show that these measures, though radical in certain directions and promising 'democratic' measures in the future, were not as 'democratic' as they might have been; to take seriously the fact that, compared with the apparently less extensive bill of 1866, the Act of 1867 offered positive advantages to an extended conception of the 'conservative cause' as well as to the Conservative party; and to emphasize that, although there are questions to be asked about the connections between Disraeli's and Gladstone's parliamentary tactics and the climate of public opinion, these questions become less difficult to answer, and their parliamentary actions less paradoxical to explain, once it is seen that the bill of March 18, and in some respects the final Act itself, represented the point at which an initially radical movement could safely be taken up by *any* conventional party, and was proposed by the Conservative leaders, and supported by the Conservative party, because they had convinced themselves that it would not only not significantly alter the existing political structure, but would also give the Conservative party specific electoral advantages and a settlement of the question for the future.

(iii) PARLIAMENT, CLASS AND THE POLITICAL STRUCTURE

By 'existing political structure' must be understood—what the bill's defenders were persuaded by Disraeli to mean—not the Act of 1832 or any particular modification of its franchise clauses, but the situation in which gentry, aristocracy and the respectable classes continued to be responsible for the conduct of English political life. Neither the Liberal nor the Conservative leaders expected the Act of 1867 to establish a democratic constitution: nor would they have supported it if they had thought it would. The existing House of Commons was '*defective*', in Russell's view, 'in not having a sufficient representation of the working-classes', but Russell did not mean to imply that working men should represent themselves— at any rate in large numbers. '[He] entirely dissent[ed] from Bright's dictum that the present House of Commons does not represent the people, but only the interests and prejudices of a class.' Members of the House of Commons were extremely wealthy or took their colour from those who were. Nevertheless, they succeeded in *representing* 'the people' and were 'entitled to speak for it': they would do so more effectively if other classes were given the opportunity to vote for them in the future. Russell may not, when talking of the Reform bill in 1866, have 'suddenly exclaim[ed to] the Cabinet...that... the middle classes were those to whom the political power of the country ought to be entrusted, and that the working classes were not fit': but since it is certainly the case that 'not a few of the Liberal party and perhaps some of the Cabinet, thoroughly agreed with Lord Russell in their hearts',[1] there is no reason why he should not have done.

Nor, though there was a difference of emphasis, was Gladstone's position very much different. Gladstone's language had been democratic in 1866: he did not think his bill had been. What Gladstone wanted was enfranchisement of a literate, independent, non-conforming element—'the skilled labour of the country'[2] which would warm to guidance from forward-looking, educated Whig-

Liberals under his own leadership, and carry the more advanced and literate working-men along with them into a future replete with free trade, commercial prosperity, removal of religious disabilities and increasing regard for the public interest in relation to the personal and class selfishness which Mill had taught him called for transformation if the age was to fulfil its duties. He sensed the political possibilities of an extended franchise, and the desirability of encouraging a larger share of the population to feel that the centre of its political attention should lie in Parliament. But Gladstone was not undiscriminating: his concern was for the political classes, for those 'whose will, whose thought, whose intelligence, whose education is directly to be interested in the political action of the State'.[1] Whereas reactionary Whigs, like Pleydell-Bouverie, were willing to support household suffrage if they had to support anything because 'constituencies will be more corrupt and less liberal, but...won't be more democratic',[2] Gladstone's, and Russell's, objection to Disraeli's Act was that it would enfranchise too large a part of what was variously called the 'residuum', 'the mere peasantry of the country', the 'very lowest and most ignorant class' or the 'cellar-holders' (to use the expressions of a Gladstonian duke).[3] In the boroughs, especially the small and agricultural ones, this might enhance the importance of bribery and 'increas[e]...the power of the landed aristocracy'.[4] It might make the 'money-making classes... return to a sort of Tory dread of the lower orders'. It might produce a working-class movement against free trade.[5] Gladstone sensed the advantage—to the party and to the régime of which that party was a part—from embracing the independent working-class, but he wanted it to support the existing type of Liberal party. There is no reason to believe that he wanted to see working-men or shop-keepers in the House of Commons, or supposed that the bill of 1867 would enable them to get there in large numbers. Gladstone differed from Russell in many important respects, but by independent electorate both understood an electorate which would defer to *them*. Gladstone did not express his objection in the same way; he almost certainly objected to the 1867 Act because a 'suffrage...more extensive than that of the United States...by introduc[ing] many of the most unfit class; men dependent on their landlords and employers or open to the temptation of bribes or beer'[6] would make that deference more difficult to achieve.

Similarly Derby and Disraeli, in passing a bill to make possible the enfranchisement of over four times as many electors as Gladstone had proposed to enfranchise in 1866, did not claim that *they* were establishing a democratic constitution. On the contrary. 'The county franchise [was] not very low':[1] there was a strong vein of feeling that it could, from the viewpoint of the territorial interest, usefully have been lower. Richard Bagge was a Norfolk landowner and Stanley's agent in King's Lynn: his twin brother was a Conservative MP. In 1866 one had favoured reducing the county occupation franchise from £50 p.a. to £10 (rather than £20) in order to swamp dissent in the rural towns. The other was an advocate of household suffrage in the boroughs for the same reason.[2] Malmesbury had been Foreign Secretary and was a landowner in Hampshire. He used his experience of landed society as justification for equalizing the borough and county franchises.[3] R. J. B. Harvey, banker MP. for Thetford and shortly to be a bankrupt suicide, was the only Conservative to vote with Gladstone in 1866: he had 'always felt that the peasantry of the country ought to be represented [because they were] hard-working, conscientious and religious'.[4] T. E. Headlam compounded the need, felt by any Liberal MP. for Newcastle upon Tyne, to appear thoroughly advanced with an instinctive desire not to by claiming that equalization of the borough and county franchise qualifications would be 'conservative...in the highest and truest sense...[and] that any dangerous or impulsive tendency in any one town or district would be checked...by the average good sense of the whole community'.[5] Nor was this feeling confined to Conservatives or constitutional Liberals. 'In [a] country', wrote Holyoake in 1858, 'where reverence for law...rank and wealth is the religion of the streets and lanes...so many of the people are uninformed, prejudiced and indifferent upon politics that ignorance, animus and bigotry may be relied upon to vote for things as they are'. It was not Malmesbury, Bagge or Newdegate, but a Christian Socialist—J. M. Ludlow—who objected to joining the Reform League because its demand for manhood suffrage in the counties would enfranchise ignorant, deferential and illiterate electors, 'give an immense power to the Tory party and throw back the cause of social and political reform for years'.[6]

What was hoped for by those who convinced themselves that they

did not fear extensive franchise reduction—at any rate in the
countryside and agricultural boroughs—was an electorate socially
more deferential than Gladstone was trying to create. They may, in
this, have been deceiving themselves or making the best of a bad
job, but, once they decided that the franchise level should be
lowered, they convinced themselves that they believed it. 'The
large towns', as Stanley said, had been 'democratic before.'[1] There
the 'working-classes [were] powerful trades formed into unions and
the employers [were] dependent on them':[2] the electorate established by the bill would not be deferential. Since it would not, with
some exceptions, be Conservative either, that might simply make
the Liberal party more radical. In the small boroughs, since 'the
working-classes...are those who are under the patronage of the
Upper Classes and depend on them for employment and existence',[3] and since, even 'in the...middle-sized boroughs, the class
feeling of the artisans does not predominate',[4] conditions would be
different. In these boroughs the 'beer-barrel influence', which Disraeli no less than Russell expected the Act to increase, was regarded
as a barrier *against* democracy. 'Democracy' did not mean a system
in which representation of the working classes would be undertaken by their betters as hitherto. 'Democratic' was not to be used
of a franchise which 'g[a]ve the land a great number of voters in the
rural boroughs', where landed power was so strong and deference so
marked that even household suffrage, if given to the same sort of
voter in the surrounding counties, could, in Malmesbury's probably erroneous view, have established on the support of 'country
mason[s], smith[s] or [rural] labourer[s at whom] Radicals...
always sneered...a broad popular franchise with a powerful aristocracy'.[5] Democracy meant, on the contrary, as Elcho put it,
'hand[ing] the country over to the Trade Unions' and the 'rule of
numbers', enabling 'the poor' to tax 'the rich'[6] and destroying the
monopoly exercised by the existing parliamentary régime. Neither
the critics nor the defenders of the 1866 bill wanted this, though the
critics persuaded a large part of the House of Commons that this
was what Gladstone's 1866 bill would eventually produce. Lowe's
defence of existing arrangements, however, cut little ice in the session of 1867. Disraeli then, in a different party situation, succeeded
in establishing a belief that, although the suffrage that was eventually
accepted 'would give the working-classes a majority of nearly 2–1

[when] even Gladstone [in 1866] repudiated the idea of giving them *any* majority',[1] it would operate within the political structure Lowe was attempting to defend because by 'going lower [it would] bring other elements into play'[2] and because, as one Conservative backbencher explained when the major decision was taken in 1867, 'household suffrage would bring in a large number of men, honest, simple-minded (using the word in the best sense) who, in disposing of their votes, would look to men of respectability and character and would vote for them in preference to excitable men'.[3]

Disraeli created this climate of opinion by referring to a number of principles. Throughout these years Disraeli was addressing himself, not to the *Edinburgh Review* but to a House of Commons over half of whose members were unalienated aristocrats, gentry or adventurers who had adopted aristocratic ways of thinking, and most of whom thought, not in terms of equality or the rights of man, but in the language of representation of interests. Representation of interests meant that no one was afraid to advocate sociological polarization between town and country in order to create, or maintain, community of interest between the inhabitants of a constituency. One objection to the 1866 bill in its original form had been that, since it took no account of demographic change since 1832 and was not concerned with the redistribution of seats, it would destroy the existing basis of representation by introducing into county constituencies 'strangers whose thoughts, feelings...interests, capital and labour are employed and occupied in another place'.[4] One does not have to ask whether Disraeli *believed* this: everyone asserted it and understood criticisms which made this assumption. Disraeli made them as a party leader, but the objection did not arise from party considerations alone. Given the assumptions about the nature of a constituency which probably three-quarters of the members of that Parliament shared equally, it was dangerous to flood counties around the large towns (where rent and rateable values were likely to be higher than elsewhere) if the franchise qualification was reduced without boundaries being redrawn. As a party leader Disraeli had much to gain from dealing with the county franchise, from appointing a boundary commission and from keeping the redistribution of seats in his own hands: no doubt he was talking a great deal of the time as a party leader. Nevertheless, territorialism was not just a party doctrine. Conservatives were not the only politicians who assumed that the landed interest was legitimate and defensible, and wealth and property a ground for representation. Disraeli was not just reflecting a party interest in declaring that 'there is a principle in the county franchise when you deal with it, and it is this—the franchise must be a county franchise. It must be a suffrage exercised by those who have a natural relation to the chief property and the chief industry of the county. Those who are to exercise it ought to be members of the same community, and not strangers.'[1]

Nor was it assumed that a reduction in the county franchise level would necessarily damage the Conservative party. Over thirty boroughs[2] already existed which had the area and character of county constituencies, but which were parliamentary boroughs with a borough qualification. In all the 1832 boroughs, the borough franchise qualification applied: in these boroughs there was virtually a rural £10 occupation franchise. Yet the party representation of these was not notably different from that of other rural constituencies. If Tavistock returned a Chartist in 1852, less than a dozen of the others had normally been represented by Liberals in the nine Parliaments which had been elected since 1832. At Christchurch, Wenlock, Droitwich, Eye and Woodstock no Liberal had been returned. In Shoreham, there had been no Liberal since 1837. In Wallingford there had been none until Dilke was returned in 1865. Only one of these constituencies—Tiverton—had been uninterruptedly Liberal, and Tiverton was by no means wholly agricultural. In the majority of cases there had been an even party division, which sometimes reflected a patron's wishes. The 1867 Act established rural household suffrage in these constituencies: their significance in the context of discussion in 1867 was the evidence they provided that a £10 occupation franchise did not necessarily make a county more radical than before. There can be no doubt that Disraeli both knew what he was doing and struck responsive notes among members of both parties in claiming that his bill was designed to recognize 'a rural community...and an urban community', that even if one ought 'not [to] be *encouraged* to draw hard lines between counties and towns', 'because *very* hard lines... do not and can never exist', it was still the case that, in recognizing 'the propriety of the representative of a borough resisting any invasion of his rights', one must allow 'the natural feelings of those who represent the rights of counties...[to] be respected...also'.[3]

In short, one has to understand that, even when Disraeli and Gladstone were attempting deviously to push members of parliament into doing what they had no *desire* to do and would not have done without prompting, they did so in a language which was designed to appeal to the existing political classes. They were talking to the existing House of Commons which wished to be reminded, and was by both, that there was a level below which enfranchisement was dangerous, which attached special meaning to class and territorial representation and which, so far from wishing *democratically* to extend the franchise, was intensely suspicious of any proposal to do so. This applies to the great body of Liberals as well as to the Conservative party. It applies to Michael Bass, the Liberal brewer from Burton and supporter of Disraeli's bill whom Adderley found at the beginning of 1866 advocating a reduction of the 1832 franchise because 'a lower franchise would reach a class of workmen more under their Master's influence [than] the present £10 workmen [who were] intolerable'.[1] It applies to the youngest Liberal MP., Charles Tilston Bright, the marine engineer employer from Greenwich who, while fighting the 1865 election against a Reform League candidate, rejected the view that 'every man of sound intelligence and years of discretion had an inherent right to the suffrage', doing so on the ground that, in a Parliament elected on this principle, 'it would...be to the interest of indirect tax payers [who would be in a majority] that whatever increased expenditure they might carry by their votes...should not be paid for by any increased taxation upon the tea or sugar, or other duty-paying articles consumed by themselves'[2]—in other words, that manhood suffrage would present a direct threat to existing wealth. It applies to Labouchere, the Liberal MP. for Windsor, who supported the introduction of voting papers because 'it would act to a certain extent as an educational test [and] if a man could not write the name of the candidate he wished to vote for distinctly or legibly, he was not a fit person to be entrusted with the suffrage'.[3] It applies to John Duke Coleridge who, whether tactically or not, in the course of supporting Gladstone on April 11 viewed household suffrage 'without the slightest fear or apprehension, because, on the whole, he thought that intelligence, wealth, education, station and other social distinctions of that character would exercise their due influence in the country and would keep us pretty well where we were at present'.[4]

It applies to Charles Neate, senior fellow of Oriel, professor of Political Economy at Oxford and MP. for Oxford city, who combined Liberal opinions and trades union sympathies with extreme hostility to Reform agitation in London, 'objected to a house of two rooms being authoritatively stated by the House of Commons as a fit residence for a citizen of England' and, in defining 'house' for electoral purposes, wanted to 'protect the public against the influx of the lower classes of voters who he was afraid would obtain admission in large numbers'.[1] It applies to Ayrton, the Radical MP. for the Tower Hamlets, who 'never entertain[ing] for a moment the idea that it was expedient to admit every person to the enjoyment of the franchise because he happened to be a man...thought that [the franchise] line...could be best drawn by separating those who had a fixed position in the country from those who might be regarded as a mere fleeting and unsettled population'.[2] It applies, even, to Edward Baines, nonconformist proprietor of the *Leeds Mercury*, Liberal MP. for Leeds and proposer of an annual Reform motion in the House of Commons, who was afraid that the 'rating franchise' to which the Reform Union committed itself at its first meeting in 1865 meant something 'considerably more extensive than household suffrage' because it 'included lodgers...and the occupiers of tenements which are not houses' and who, in company with other West Riding Liberals, boycotted Bright's Leeds meeting on October 8 because of its connection with manhood suffrage.[3] It applies in the first half of the session of 1867 to Gladstone even more than to Disraeli. With hind-sight which sees a straight progression between the Reform speech of May 11 1864 and the victorious propaganda of late 1867, it sounds liberal when Gladstone criticizes the bill of March 18 because it ignored the principle that 'we ought not to establish artificial distinctions among men belonging to the same class'. It sounds less than democratic when we notice that he was thinking in terms of representation of classes, and wanted throughout to confine the working-class suffrage to skilled, literate or educated artisans.

Once the plunge into household suffrage had been taken, Radicals and Liberals could see the danger that it could easily become a 'hovel suffrage'.[4] They could see that ignorant, illiterate lodgers might be at the mercy of registration associations. They could see that a deferential electorate might be at the mercy of landlords in the agricultural boroughs. They knew that a landowner who owned land in a borough could build a shoddy building and create a tenant in order to get a vote. Under any arrangement of borough boundaries there would be landowners who could do this: under arrangements in which a good many boroughs contained large tracts of agricultural land, there really was a danger, as Duncan McLaren put it, of a 'cow-house suffrage.'[1]

The three weeks following the House's confirmation of the personal payment principle on May 9 saw the adoption of a lodger franchise and of Hodgkinson's amendment, both of which were enfranchising measures. It saw, on the other hand, a renewed attempt by Poulett Scrope, who was not a Conservative but a Liberal economist, to limit the effect of Hodgkinson's amendment by excusing the lowest class of householder from liability to rating, thereby depriving them of the chance to vote. MP.s found it difficult to know what sort of person would be enfranchised by one lodger qualifying line rather than another: there was extensive discussion of the difference between a £10 and a £15 line, as well as between a £10 qualifying line which excluded the cost of furniture and a £15 qualifying line which included it. After the lodger franchise was settled there was discussion about joint occupation in which two Liberal barristers, Sir Francis Goldsmid and T. E. Headlam, and a northern Radical, Candlish, joined hands to exclude joint occupiers from the franchise. There was discussion about the definition of 'a house' in which Duncan McLaren and E. W. Watkin, the Liberal railway-magnate from Stockport, tried to limit enfranchisement by establishing that

no tenement should be considered a dwelling-house for the purposes of the Act which contained less than two rooms, many of the tenements in the large towns being [as Bright's brother-in-law pointed out] often dark, ill-ventilated, damp...If votes were given to the occupiers of all such houses...[which] were erected for the poor and the greater number of [which] were paying poor rate,...the door would be open to bribery and corruption by political agents paying for poor persons the trifling amount of poor rates laid upon them in order to secure their votes; and this might be done to an extent which no man could foresee.[2]

The restrictive rhetoric of Horsman and Lowe was, indeed, distinctive rather by reason of its stridency, and the manifest personal inadequacy of the speakers, than because of the eccentricity of the opinions they were expressing. They were eccentric in the certainty with which they attributed political disaster to the bills of 1866 and 1867; they came to be eccentric in their view of the revolutionary character of the situation. But their assumptions about the British constitution were not eccentric. There was nothing eccentric in the House of Commons of 1865 about the belief that the lower orders should not be allowed to exercise predominant power or that representation should be concerned with interests. Many Conservatives who would have agreed in 1866 did not agree with Carnarvon in 1867 that a balanced constitution (i.e. 'the complicated system of English constituencies they knew') made it essential to avoid electoral arrangements which 'would admit...the working classes... in such proportions, and under such conditions, as would place them in absolute pre-eminence and control over all other constituents'.[1] They believed, nevertheless, in the balanced constitution and the complicated system of English constituencies, and accepted a suffrage in which the working classes outnumbered all other constituents because they convinced themselves that those parts of the working classes which would exercise the right to vote would be neither politically united nor socially irresponsible, and would, in the sorts of constituency Conservatives were interested in, be suitably deferential. Though Earl Grey, Clarendon and Halifax feared the impact the starkness of Lowe's oratory would have on Whig ability to keep hold of working-class support in the future,[2] there was nothing novel about the opinions he expressed except, perhaps, that he expressed them as often as he did. His comments on the venality and drunkenness of the lowest classes supplied a convenient slogan for Reform League banners and a suitable text for Reform League speakers. But they were an echo of what Bright had said in 1859 and repeated in 1867. They were matched by Roebuck, the ex-Radical from Sheffield, who supported the first draft of Disraeli's bill on March 25 1867 because, although there was 'a very large class [of working-class citizens that] he desired to keep in... there [was] a very large class [he] desire[d] to keep out...who are not educated, who are vicious [and] who are unfit to have in their hands the government of mankind'.[3] Roebuck and Bright were matched by J. B. Smith who, from his knowledge of Stockport where there were no compound householders, offered as justification of the personal payment principle the fact that, where every man paid the full rate, 'the lowest class of householders' took pains to be 'acquainted with those who were idle and profligate in the town', regarded men who received parish poor relief 'somewhat in the light of plunderers' and 'constituted the best police against the spread of pauperism that could well be imagined'.[1] Nor was it Lowe, Gladstone, Disraeli or Derby, but Hodgkinson himself who in the course of debate defended his own amendment on the ground that it 'would get rid of "the residuum" because that would be composed of a class which would never pay the rates in any case'.[2]

However, their desire to exclude a substantial working-class element involved MP.s in no hostility towards the working classes as a whole. There was nothing but solicitude on the one hand and the desire to extend the range of responsibility and respectability on the other. There was hostility to trades unions: there was a distaste for political agitation. A line was drawn between allowing the working classes to be represented, and encouraging them to usurp political and industrial power. But in all parts of the House of Commons there was a belief in the good sense of the English people, and especially in the sense of responsibility of the better-off artisan on the one hand and the agricultural labourer on the other— so long as both were allowed to follow their natural leaders. One may see this belief as complacent ignorance, or as tactical rhetoric designed to prevent the emergence of effective revolutionary politics in the future. But, whichever way it is seen, the conception of natural leadership, and a belief that it would survive any altera- tion of electoral arrangements that was in sight, was a factor which helped a great part of the House of Commons to accept Disraeli's bill. Though some MP.s gave their support even when they did not want to, because opinion among their constituents was favourable and could not be resisted once a Conservative government had proposed it, there is no reason to doubt that, as soon as Conserva- tives recovered from the shock of supporting an extensive lowering of the borough franchise, their judgement of the people among whom they lived gave them ground for optimism of a sort.

These opinions in public were common to nearly all MP.s. They were the language they knew and understood. Anyone who wanted to be listened to used it, or made public genuflection to it. Mill, Hughes, Fawcett, P. A. Taylor and Bright (among the handful of

MP.s closest to the Reform League) were attempting to assault the existing class structure, but even Bright, the most blatant enemy of aristocracy, was attacking, not the *existence* of an aristocracy or the power of Parliament (of which he was, both tactically and genuinely, the defender), but the predominance of a class—the aristocracy—to the exclusion of all others.

The persistent Adullamites were, first and foremost, enemies of Gladstone, who saw in his policies a foretaste of the relegation they would suffer in the Liberal party and the revolution that would ensue at large: Cranborne, Peel and to some extent Carnarvon had the same feeling about Disraeli's power in the Conservative party. What both groups wanted was a policy based on manifest principle —the principle that real power should be kept out of the hands of the working classes. What almost everyone else—including the most advanced parliamentary Radicals—wanted was to keep real power out of the hands of the working classes without insisting as rigorously as these did on the need to assert the principle. Being practical men, MP.s who did not follow him were repelled by the dogmatic rigidity with which Cranborne's positions were put, and by his refusal in 1867 to believe that a bill could be produced which *looked* as democratic as he said it was without, so far as they could see, being democratic in fact. At no stage in his 'revolution' did Disraeli question, or reject, this principle. He made a point of stressing that the 1832 Act removed some of the political rights enjoyed beforehand by working-class electors. He did his best to leave the impression that Russell's Whiggism was hostile to working-class interests. But at no stage did he assert that his bill was founded on any principle which conflicted with the principles of Cranborne or Peel. All he did, in a House of Commons which accepted their principles, was to suggest, or pretend, that the bill he was proposing was a development which would resolve the difficult practical problem raised by the manifest need to pass *something* through a House of Commons whose party alignment was not such as to assist its passage.

Wherever one looks in the parliamentary debates on the Reform bill of 1867, one finds no general advocacy of a democratic franchise, electoral districts or equality between the worth of one vote and another. One finds, on the contrary, in both parties and all sections, an overwhelming anxiety to establish that nothing should be done to destroy the alliance between responsibility, respectability, wealth and status on one hand and the possible new electorate on the other. Where differences appear about the extent of the enfranchisement proposed, they arose either because of the desire of Conservative leaders to show that the Liberal party was more restrictive than they were, or because Conservative county members, who did not fear the lesser occupiers, wanted to claim for their own constituents the right to vote as extensively as the inhabitants of boroughs. Given this language, given these facts and given the care Disraeli took to talk a language which took account of them, the question that has to be asked is; did he do more than these assumptions permitted? Did he bamboozle the Conservative party and the House of Commons into accepting a bill which their assumptions did not allow them to accept?

In the first place the Conservative party accepted a great deal more in May, June and July than it intended to accept in February. Hardly anybody in February thought of accepting household suffrage without counterpoises or compensations. Nobody wanted to accept a twelve-month residential qualification. The bill that was finally passed, though possessing finality in some respects, was not a final settlement in most. To that extent Disraeli, assisted by Gladstone's manner, edged Conservatives into adopting policies they had at the beginning no desire to adopt. Yet, once they had been pushed over the edge and had looked at the other side, what they saw was by no means as bad as they had expected. What they were under persuasion to see was not the future erosion of gentry power and aristocratic politics, but a new opportunity in which gentry and respectable wealth would be allied with whatever part of the working classes would follow. If they disliked the large increase in the borough electorate, they could see that any future agitation would greatly increase the size of the rural vote and the number of agricultural seats, and might induce in the minds of the paper democrats from whom the Liberal party took its cue a recognition that social stability mattered a great deal more than indiscriminate progress.

It is desirable, secondly, to be clear about the relevance of two further factors—the public movement for electoral reform which had been operative since the 1840s and the public demonstrations which were organized by the Reform League in 1866 and 1867. It

was certainly the existence in the 1850s of a public Reform movement—however insignificant its popular following—and the presence of reforming MP.s—however small their numbers—which
produced a situation in which a decision to propose alteration of the
1832 settlement became a practical problem for parliamentary politicians. Nor should anyone seek to deny that public agitation *was* a
factor which affected the decisions of the Conservative government
from July 1866 onwards. The point in both cases is that between the
journalism and agitation of Potter, Howell and Beales and governmental or parliamentary decision a filtering process was interposed
which converted demands for manhood suffrage and equal constituencies into proposals more likely to be acceptable to the
Parliaments by which they had to be accepted.

It is certain, for example, that the Conservative government's
decision in autumn 1866 to deal with the Reform question in some
way or other was stimulated, not by *fear* of Reform League agitation, but in part at least by a feeling that the extravagance of the
Reformers' language had provided an opportunity both to gain the
credit, which the Conservative party needed, of dealing with a major
matter, and to do so by introducing a bill which would be so much
more moderate than the bill of 1866 that it would cause dissension
in the Liberal party if it did not succeed in passing the House of
Commons. Again, it was not the Reform movement which made a
Conservative Reform bill a possibility in 1858, but Lord John
Russell's acceptance in 1851 of the idea that the 1832 Act was not a
point of finality. The climate of parliamentary opinion in the fifties
and sixties was *affected* by extra-parliamentary forces, but not
created by them. Within Parliament some politicians took pains to
give an impression of sensitivity to what they took to be public
opinion, maintaining positions in Parliament which would appeal
to advanced opinions outside it. Russell was a leading exemplar of
this policy—which was the basis of the Whig attempt to buttress
Whig power by alliance with popular Radicalism. But Russell,
though conscious of one extra-parliamentary atmosphere as
Palmerston was conscious of another, had no intention of capitulating to it. Russell wanted to be admired by advanced thinkers outside
the House of Commons, but he wanted this because he equated
Whiggery with Liberty and thought it would perpetuate Whig
power inside it. Russell no more intended to capitulate to the Reform

League programme in 1866 than he had in 1854: if, as a responsible parliamentary statesman, he left the impression on the minds of some reformers that he did, that is evidence only of his success in bamboozling *them* and, also, in a way, himself into supposing that he was on the same side as they were.

Russell—however impossible as a person—was a responsible, central figure in an aristocratic régime, who had no desire to destroy that régime, whose closest associates were aristocratic and who assumed that, if Radicalism was to be rampant, it must be controlled, and its sting removed, by aristocratic leadership. The Reform League's programme was manhood suffrage and the ballot: Russell's programme, at its widest, involved a £5 rating franchise and a redistribution of sixty seats. The Reform League welcomed household, as a step on the road to manhood, suffrage: to Russell, household suffrage meant extensive bribery and the further degradation of the electoral process. There is not much doubt what the Earl Russell branch of the Reform League would have thought when it was founded in 1866 if its members had known that Russell would threaten to move the rejection of household suffrage if it was proposed to the House of Lords, would support cumulative voting there in August 1867 and was not sure in October 1866 'that we can or ought to resist the strengthening of the landed interest... by taking towns out of the counties to a moderate extent'.[1]

Russell was not a critic or enemy of the 1832 settlement. He had been one of its architects; but once he had breached the unanimity with which it was defended in Parliament, other parliamentary leaders had to ask whether they could take their stand on finality either. It is possible that a dominant Conservative party, united under Peel's leadership, or led by whatever successor Peel had designated, might have taken a stand on its known achievement as a progressive party in refusing to alter the settlement of 1832. It is possible that it might have done this (though extremely unlikely), but for the Conservative party of the fifties this was a difficult thing to do. It was not just that Disraeli wanted to kill the accusation that it was the party of 'bigotry and intolerance' but that the one chance it had of success in Parliament was by alliance, however temporary, with the Irish, the Catholic, the Radical and the Peelite groups in the House of Commons. Even if there were occasions on which Conservatives could expect to fight an election in defence of the constitution, Disraeli's hope to detach one, or more, of these groups from the Whig/Liberal party, however chimerical, made his policy preferences as flexible as possible.

Therefore, once Russell had committed himself to tamper with the settlement, the Conservative leaders felt compelled to do so also. As soon as they had done so, competition became inevitable between Whigs on the one hand and Conservatives on the other to see which side could claim credit for, and control the details of, any Act that might eventually be passed. Derby's government introduced a Reform bill in 1859 without proposing a reduction of the borough franchise, in order both to establish that it was in the van of progress and to ensure that any measures that were adopted would not do it electoral damage. The bill was defeated by Whigs, Liberals and Radicals before the second reading, because they wished to bring down the government, and in order to prevent the Conservative party gaining credit for passing it. One factor which produced the 1866 bill was a feeling among Whigs that, if Russell's government did not introduce a bill, the Conservative party would do so eventually: one element in Derby's attitude, once he had taken office in 1866, was a desire to pay back the Whig/Liberal alliance for its part in stopping the Conservative bill in 1859.

The Liberal party's reaction to the bill of 1867 was affected by a feeling that it had behaved factiously in 1859: Gladstone's belief that the parliamentary process was in danger of discredit seems to have sprung from recollection of this episode.[1] Apart from Lowe, no leading statesman was willing to say publicly in the sixties that a reduction of the borough franchise would be intolerable. There was a marked recession in public demand which induced pessimism in the minds of parliamentary reformers like Bright about Parliament's willingness to consider any alteration in the electoral system, and in the minds of extra-parliamentary reformers like Beesly a disposition to await 'political changes...of a far more fundamental description' than were contained in even the most radical demand for electoral change.[2] But the policy in all parliamentary quarters was to accept the fact that, if there was to be a bill, it must not go too far, while never denying that a bill might be necessary. It was this half-conscious edging into a situation in which no one asked what assumptions these half-considered commitments involved that made Elcho speak, as he did, of disingenuousness: it was this same situation which made Gladstone speak, as he did, of the discredit which in this matter alone attached to the reformed Parliament of 1832.

There was, therefore, nothing in its record about electoral reform which made it impossible in 1866 for the Conservative party to co-operate with Russell in passing an agreed bill of modest dimensions. It did not do this because Russell did not ask it to, attempting in-stead, without success, to detach Stanley from the opposition front-bench, and because Disraeli hoped that Palmerston's death would make it possible to destroy the Palmerstonian coalition, not, as in the past, by detaching the Irish, the Peelites or the Radicals, but by detaching dissident Whigs. How far Disraeli in the first half of 1866 believed in the possibility of permanently extending this policy is an open question: whether or not he believed in it as a desirable objective, he used it as a tactical device, abandoning it only when it began to be used in July by others as a way of getting rid of him. It is far from clear when a Reform bill would have been introduced, or what it would have contained if a Conservative/Whig coalition had been formed, but at no stage in the debates on the 1866 bill did Disraeli, or anybody else, commit the Conservative party to abandon electoral reform altogether.

Although there was no reason why the Conservative party should not have proposed a Reform bill at some time, any proposal which it or a Liberal government might make would affect the interest of the politician or party by whom it was made. In this connection motives must not be imputed too precisely. Disraeli made the running in the Conservative government after the beginning of January 1867, even if he did not, or did not choose to, make it before that. Within the parliamentary climate created by the decision to introduce a bill in the circumstances in which a bill was promised on March 4 Disraeli was trying to destroy Gladstone's control over the Whig/Liberal coalition by detaching both Whigs and Radicals: for a time he succeeded. Nor is it certain that Disraeli, left to himself, would have chosen 1867 as the year in which to bring forward a Reform bill. Nevertheless, in considering the strategic possibilities open to Dis-raeli, one must be aware of a number of factors, however nebulous their operation and however difficult to establish that they operated. First, that, since 1852, though the Conservatives had never had fewer than 275 seats, they had not done particularly well out of the existing constituency and in 1865 had been less successful even than in 1859: there was no part of the United Kingdom, apart from Ireland, in which they had more seats in 1865 than in 1852. Secondly, that while some Conservatives sometimes believed that the lowering of the borough franchise would not necessarily damage Conservative control of Conservative cities, it was clear both that a lowering of the franchise level in the small boroughs would damage Whig control, and that the reduction of the franchise level in the Liberal cities, Wales and Scotland would increase the difficulty Whigs were finding in driving off Radical infiltration there. This induced a belief that one effect of franchise reduction would be to push the Liberal party a good deal further to the Left than it had gone hitherto—with the result that the Conservative party would establish total control of the respectable middle-classes as the working classes became more radical.[1] Although there was no simple sociological polarization between parties, it seems probable that Disraeli hoped at one level to create one, not exactly by turning class against class and not just by increasing county representation as much as representation in the cities, but by ensuring that, however effectively the Act restricted working-class enfranchisement, the Conservative party might become the party of deference, respectability, order and property, even if it succeeded at the same time in becoming both the party of reform and the agency for restoring to the working classes as a whole what Whiggery was alleged to have taken from them by disfranchisement in 1832. Disraeli's politics were conducted in the rhetoric of the age. They took account of the forces of the age. He was the most militant opponent of Whiggery in his generation. His hostility pervades his writing and speaking. The question we have to ask is: behind the rhetoric, was there any difference of substance between Whig doctrine and Disraeli's conception of political duty, except that Disraeli wanted to replace the Whigs at the centre of the political scene? The Whig/Radical alliance emerged from a party, not a popular, context: Disraeli's Radical alliance in 1867 was a parliamentary convenience. Tory Radicalism, of which we cannot speak with confidence at this time, though Laing, Bagehot and Beresford-Hope did, was a transposition into electoral terms but without Radical allies apart from Roebuck, of the desire Disraeli had caught from Peel, Palmerston and the Whigs to accommodate a fundamentally conservative party to every shade of centrally-held, securely-based opinion. This was not, as is sometimes supposed, the beginning of a demoralizing, unprincipled professionalism in poli-tics.[1] Nor was it the translation into policy of the visions of the young Disraeli. It was the attempt of a parliamentary politician who was anathema in its circle to imitate the Whig claim to be the only credible government. It was an attempt by one who, as Bright said in 1852, was 'ambitious, most able and without prejudices'[2] to usurp the position of the party by which he had been excluded. It was an attempt, in the conditions created by Gladstone's arrival at the head of the Whig/Liberal party, to provide an alternative manner which some Liberals preferred[3] and which, whatever the 'best men'[4] may have thought, was much more in keeping than Gladstone's 'high-minded'[5] Puseyism with what most MP.s expected in a parliamentary leader. It was made in a situation in which the prop—Derby—on which his power depended was no longer young, and was never well; in which it was not certain who would succeed him, and in which failure to succeed, if Derby re-tired, might well destroy even the power Disraeli had at present. One need not attach too much importance to passing declarations— his declaration to Bright in March 1867 that he would want to retire once the Reform question was settled: his declaration to his wife in July 1866 that he might *have* to retire soon.[6] Nevertheless, in understanding the path chosen by Disraeli between 1865 and 1867, it is necessary to remember that he had not had much more than a year in office at a time in nearly thirty years of political life and that, even if he did not *want* to retire, there was a danger that he would have to if the protection which Derby had given him was suddenly removed.

In 1865 Disraeli did not control the Conservative party. He was Derby's manager in the House of Commons and by far its ablest leader. He was in continuous contact with Derby and had enormous influence on his thinking. But the government was Derby's govern-ment, not Disraeli's. When Disraeli's influence mattered, it mattered because Derby was ill or because he let it. Disraeli had a few, but not many, political friends: there was no general approval of him. He had a number of enemies, many of them bitter and some in the Cabinet. The Cabinet was Derby's, not his: it included Cranborne, Chelmsford, Malmesbury and General Peel, who all felt the strong-est aversion for him. Some of its members were friends—like Lord John Manners—or nominees—like Naas and Northcote, who had been snatched from Gladstone's arms. He had others waiting in the wings, like Cairns, who seems to have been promised the Lord Chancellorship whenever he might want it.[1] But the Cabinet was held together by regard for Derby, not for him. It was neither his creation nor likely to be responsive to his wishes.

(iv) THE MECHANICS OF DEFERENCE

Finally, in setting the scene in which the 1867 session began, one must spell out the advantages which might accrue from the fact that a minority Conservative government, by the very fact that it was in office, would have some measure of control over the details of any Act that was passed—though, in doing this, one must make two qualifications. Since the Conservative party was the minority party in the House of Commons, the government could never be certain in advance that any particular provision would pass. Secondly, since the final shape of the Act was a result of innumerable amendments suggested from both sides of the House, Disraeli and Derby could not, in any exact sense, have planned its final details. Nor need one pay attention to the redistribution parts of the bill of March 18, which proposed no advantage for the Conservative party, which seem to have been designed to establish the government's unwillingness to play a party game and which were superseded at Disraeli's instigation in the House of Commons at the end of May. What is important is the final bill, including, in particular, the details of the redistribution clauses. The operative motions as to the scale of redistribution did not come from the government, but from a Conservative and from a Liberal MP. The extent of the redistribution was a decision reached by vote of the House in opposition to the government's advice. Nevertheless, the government accepted the decision, and the Conservative party supported it in doing so. In asking why the party accepted the bill, one must examine the assumptions about the boundary and redistribution questions which a majority of MP.s shared equally, and must remember that Disraeli and a Cabinet committee arranged for the allocation of most of the seats these motions decided should be redistributed, took advice by letter and by meeting in London from Conservative party agents and local deputations and produced a scheme which was much more favourable to the party than Gladstone's bill had been in 1866.[2]

5-2

There was a belief, in the first place, that counties were entitled equally with cities to an increased share in representation. There was the belief, among all but a small number of Radicals, that equal electoral districts must be avoided. There was the belief that representation must be given to communities not to numbers, that the claims of conflicting communities should be judged by their importance to the nation considered as an embodiment of agricultural, mineral, industrial and commercial wealth, and that the representative system should be based on the need for members of Parliament 'when they rise in their places to advise the House on questions of public interest...[to] be able to describe to the House what view is taken upon these questions by the communities they represent'. There was a recognition, in both parties, that the landed interest must not be swamped and that, if it lost some part of its hold on the small boroughs, it should be compensated by an increase in the counties. So strong was the feeling about county representation and the landed interest that those who came closest to supporting the Reform League's demand for equality of representation between men were not parliamentary Radicals, who despite lip-service saw the danger to themselves, but Conservatives who did not cease to emphasize the disparity between the '11,500,000 people in England and Wales residing in the counties [who] were directly represented by only 162 members [and the]...334 representatives of 9,500,000 people residing in the English and Welsh Boroughs'.[1]

Although it was recognized that representation of large towns must be increased, it was understood that the effect of franchise reduction there would be to increase the revolutionary potentiality of urban politics. This produced a desire for a *cordon sanitaire*—an attempt to create Radical ghettoes by confining the largest franchise reduction to the boroughs and large cities, by refusing to make any reduction except in the large cities or by creating varying sorts of franchise for the varying sorts of constituency.[2] County representation was treated in terms quite different from the terms applied to the cities: it was assumed that county MP.s had a particular claim to speak about the distribution of the new seats which would be given to the counties,[3] and that a problem arose from the fact that a large number of borough freeholders[4] who were qualified to vote for county seats made significant inroads, which the Whig managers did not mind, on the cohesiveness of the county electorate.

Even within the framework of the assumption that the rural interest was a separate one, however, the 1866 bill was likely in every way to have been disastrous to the Conservative party. The party was, to start with, in a minority in the House of Commons—with not more than 290 seats out of 658. The party leaders believed that a moderate lowering of the borough franchise would damage them in some borough seats, and that the insertion of borough leaseholders on to the county register from which they had been excluded in 1832 would introduce into the county constituencies what Gladstone called an 'independent' and what they thought of as a Liberal and nonconformist element. Although the redistribution bill was drafted by Brand with a view to appeasing Liberal MP.s for small boroughs rather than to damage the Conservative party, it offered no hope in a Conservative direction. One cannot estimate the effect at a general election of the provision (Schedule A) for grouping fifty-seven seats from thirty-eight small boroughs into twenty new seats, but, since thirty-one of these fifty-seven seats were Conservative in 1865, it is likely that the Liberal majority would have increased marginally. It is likely that the provision (Schedule B) for removing one member from each of eight two-member boroughs would have made no difference to party strengths, though it should be noticed that, whereas two of these boroughs (Huntingdon and Marlow) had two Conservative MP.s, no borough was included in this schedule which had returned two Liberals in 1865. The division of south Lancashire (a three-member seat in 1865—2 C, 1 L) into two divisions, each with three members, combined with the creation of a separate (Liberal) borough for Burnley, might conceivably have added two Conservative seats at an election fought in the circumstances of 1868. The creation of a parliamentary borough for Chelsea–Kensington, the division of the Tower Hamlets with two sitting Liberal members into two divisions with four seats altogether and the establishment of a seat for the University of London could be expected to add not less than four to the Liberal majority: four of the new single-seat boroughs (Burnley, Gravesend, Middlesborough and Dewsbury) were likely to be Liberal seats as against two possible Conservative seats at Stalybridge and Hartlepool.

The bills of 1866 did not include a redistribution for Scotland, though a bill would have followed if the English bills had passed, and there was to be no redistribution of seats in Ireland. The redis-

tribution bill for England and Wales provided, however, for the creation of seven extra Scottish seats—to be detailed in a separate Act
—of which it is impossible to think that more than one, if that,
would have been Conservative. The addition of one seat each to
Liverpool, Manchester, Birmingham, Leeds and Salford, though
it might not have increased the Liberal majority, offered no promise
of compensation for the Conservative losses that were expected
from the operation of a lower franchise qualification and the addition of borough leaseholders to the county registers elsewhere. Nor,
more significantly, was there hope of compensation from an increase
in the number of county seats. It was a commonplace of electoral
discussion in the 1860s that, by comparison with the small boroughs,
not only the large towns but also the counties had been under-
represented after 1832. One reason why Conservatives were willing
to contemplate electoral reform was that, even when they did not
particularly want a redistribution, they could see that both the
landed interest and the Conservative party might gain enough from
an increase in county representation to offset the inevitable loss in
borough seats involved in any reduction of the franchise qualification and the creation of new seats for Scotland, the new boroughs
and the large cities. They hoped that this would happen on *any* redistribution plan, but it would not have happened if the 1866 bill
had become an Act. The addition (Schedule D) of one member to
each of seventeen two-member county constituencies, so far from
assisting the Conservative party, would have given the Liberal party
a reasonable hope of adding two or three to its existing majority.
Since no election was fought on the franchise or redistribution
clauses of the 1866 bill, these calculations must be rough, but there
can be little doubt that the Liberal party—quite apart from the extensive gains it might have been expected to make from a moderate
lowering of the borough franchise—stood to increase its majority by
something between eight and fifteen as a result of its redistribution
bill, and that it was this, combined with the insertion of borough
leaseholders on to the county register and the failure to provide the
Conservative party with a counterpoise in the counties to offset the
Liberal gains anticipated in the boroughs, which made Derby
describe the bill as 'the extinction of the Conservative party and . . .
of the real Whigs'.[1]

It is against this background that one must examine the Act of

1867: in examining it, one must not assume that the Liberal party 'swept the country' in 1868, or that its victory at the election was the result of the gratitude expressed by new electors for Gladstone's part in passing a Reform bill. At the election of 1868 almost two-thirds of the strictly comparable seats[1] were held by the same party as in 1865, despite the lowering of the franchise. The Liberal majority in 1868/9 is difficult to estimate since it varied with the subject on which votes were taken. On Irish Church disestablishment, it was about 120. It is not certain what the Liberal majority was in 1865. Derby found 283-7 regular Conservatives in August that year. Ten months later the Conservative Chief Whip found 287. In March, Knatchbull-Hugessen thought there were 295.[2] Analysis of known allegiances and division lists leaves the impression that there could not have been more than 290 Conservative MP.s in 1865—giving a Liberal majority of about 77, and an increase at the election of 1868 of, say, thirty-five to forty.

If this increase is broken down, the importance of the redistribution clauses becomes apparent. Of the seats where the franchise level was lowered but whose boundaries and numbers of MP.s were unaffected by the 1867 Act, ninety changed hands in 1868—of which the Liberal party gained fifty-seven (twenty-four of them in largish boroughs and twelve in Ireland) but lost thirty-two—an increase in the Liberal majority of fifty (see Appendix I).[3] The conversion of eight Scottish seats into thirteen added nine to the Liberal majority, which was further reinforced by the creation of three university seats (two of them in Scotland). The extra parliamentary seat in Salford which was Conservative in 1868 balanced the seat for Merthyr Tydvil which was an obviously Liberal gain, as were the new London seats and two or three of the five new seats that were given, as in 1866, to the largest English boroughs. One cannot assume, because a seat changed hands in the circumstances of the election of 1868 *after* franchise reduction, that it therefore occurred *because* of it. Even allowing for a political (rather than psephological) explanation of the increase of sixteen in the Liberal majority in Ireland, it seems safe to assume that if these provisions had not been compensated for elsewhere, the Act of 1867 would have been as disastrous for the Conservative party as Derby thought the 1866 bill would have been if it had been put into operation.

In fact, the directions in which new boroughs were created and

extra seats distributed in the fourteen counties where major alterations were effected by the 1867 Act and the 1868 Scottish Reform
Act combined possibly with the tendency in some cases for the enlarged county occupation franchise to reduce the importance of the
urban freeholders' county votes[1] to offer the sort of counterpoise
which Conservatives needed, though some of them thought it should
have been larger than it was. In 1865 these counties had within their
boundaries fifty-two county MP.s whose constituencies were altered
geographically by 1868 and fourteen MP.s sitting for boroughs
which were disfranchised by 1868.[2] Of these seats the Conservative
party in 1865 held thirty-four, the Liberal party thirty-two. In
1868 these sixty-six seats had become eighty-seven, of which fifty-
seven were Conservative—representing a *reduction* of twenty-five
in the Liberal majority (Appendix II). Since there is no sign of a
regular swing to the Conservative party in any of these counties,
except in London, Middlesex, Lancashire and, just possibly,
Staffordshire, since even the Conservative gains in Lancashire and
Middlesex may be attributed as much to the Act as to changes in
political opinion, and since, in general, the new electorate elsewhere
was uniformly more Liberal than the old, significance must be attached to the choice of principles on which to select counties in
which to increase representation, and from the deliberate decision,
adopted in principle in March, to create new county divisions instead of adding extra seats to existing ones.[3] Whereas, for example,
in Surrey the 1866 bill proposed to add a new member to the Eastern
division, which was held by two Liberals in 1865, the 1867 Act
created two divisions out of the existing East Surrey division and
gave each two MP.s, two of whom, in mid-Surrey, were Conservative in 1868. The conversion of Chelsea–Kensington into a parliamentary borough, the expansion of the borough boundaries of
Finsbury under the Boundary Act of 1868 and the consequent removal of a Liberal element from the Middlesex county constituency undoubtedly helped Lord George Hamilton to the top of
the poll in 1868 in the process of winning the first Conservative
victory in the county since 1847. The 1866 bill proposed to give a
new seat to the existing North Derbyshire constituency, held by a
Whig and a Liberal. The 1867 Act created a new Derbyshire constituency (East Derbyshire, with two members). At the election of
1868 three out of the six MP.s returned for the county were Con-

servative, though there had been none in 1865. The division of West Kent in order to create a new mid-Kent division, returning two members in 1868, combined with the establishment of Gravesend as a (Liberal) borough to give the Conservative party two seats, which the absence of additional county representation would not have done on the 1866 plan. The division of Essex and of Lincolnshire, to which three of the Lincolnshire members gave attention,[1] added four Conservative seats. The division of Devonshire and the absorption of four small boroughs, where Liberals could sometimes buy their way, into surrounding county divisions, where they could not, helped to turn Devon into a Conservative county.

Even in the cases of the four large-borough enfranchisements made necessary by acceptance, with Disraeli's approval, of Horsfall's motion on June 28 and the seven disfranchisements forced on the government in order to provide eight new seats for Scotland during the passage of the Scottish Reform Act in 1868, the Conservative loss was more apparent than real. Horsfall was not a Liberal, but a Liverpool Conservative. His motion was discussed by the Cabinet before being discussed in the House.[2] Disraeli's amendment of July 2 converted Horsfall's principle[3] into specific proposals to add a third member each to Manchester, Birmingham, Liverpool and Leeds. The first two had been Liberal, with one brief exception in Birmingham, since 1832. Leeds had had a Conservative as well as a Liberal MP. at each election, except in 1852; Liverpool had had one Conservative and often two at every election apart from the election of 1847. These four seats were provided for, despite Bright's objection, not at the expense of the small boroughs, but by removing the constituencies the government had proposed to create for Luton, Keighley, Barnsley and St Helens in the redistribution made necessary by acceptance of Laing's amendment on May 31.[4] All four might well have been Liberal in 1868; Disraeli was able to abandon them in return for agreeing to an increase in representation for large cities,[5] which Bright pressed as well as Horsfall, because, although continued opposition support had been made conditional on something being done for the large cities,[6] it was certain that 'if there be one subject on which both sides of the House are unanimous, it is that the moderate addition to the county representation which the government [had] propose[d] should be supported'.[7]

At first sight it might seem that the creation in the 1868 Scottish Act of eight new seats in the more populous districts of Scotland must greatly increase the Liberal majority. All these seats were Liberal at the election of November 1868: in addition, the only Scottish seat (Peebles and Selkirk) which had one of its members removed in order to effect this redistribution had two Conservative MP.s in 1865. Yet, if one looks at the other seven disfranchisements involved, the Liberal gain is not as great as it might have been. Three of these seats were taken from small double-member English boroughs—Honiton, Thetford and Wells—which had already lost one seat under the 1867 Act. In each of these seats there was a Liberal as well as a Conservative in 1865. It is by no means certain that any would have been Conservative in 1868: it is almost certain that Honiton would have been Liberal.[1] In two constituencies— Arundel[2] and Ashburton—whose only member was removed by the 1868 Act, there were sitting Liberals in 1865 who would almost certainly have been sitting after the next election. Only two of the disfranchised constituencies were Conservative in 1865: if they had kept their separate borough representation with the greatly increased borough electorate established by the 1867 Act, there is at least a chance that they would have gone Liberal in 1868. Complete disfranchisement of a borough, as distinct from grouping, meant not only that the borough had no separate representation: it meant also that its electoral roll would be based in future on the county franchise qualification. The *county* franchise qualification under the 1867 Act was not much higher than the *borough* qualification under the Act of 1832, but the merging of these seven boroughs into their surrounding counties meant that the increase in the size of their electorates which would have occurred under the 1867 Act if they had remained boroughs did not occur, and that they were swamped in the counties in which disfranchisement placed them. It would be foolish to attach too much significance to comparisons of this sort, or to impute predictive accuracy to Disraeli and his party managers; nevertheless, it is probable that the Conservative party gained something, and that the Liberal party lost, by the removal of these seats in what Russell thought of as 'Disraeli's corrupt bargain with the Scottish members'.[3]

Disraeli's handling of the Scottish Reform bill suggests that he used it both as a bait to Radicals on the one hand and as an inducement to Conservatives and conservatively-minded rural Liberals on the other. The promise of new seats to a country which was solidly Liberal was of some importance. In a country where no compounding for rates existed (though all occupiers of houses below £4 p.a. were excused rates), the proposal to give the burgh vote to every occupier who had paid his rates was more extensive than any previous one: at the point at which Disraeli announced it (i.e. before Hodgkinson's motion had been moved), it went further than the proposals he had made for the borough franchise in England and Wales. In these circumstances it was reasonable for Disraeli to expect Scottish support for the English bill: in view of his announcement that he would do nothing to carry the Scottish bill until the English one was passed, it is reasonable to imply a bargain. On the other hand, though the Scottish burgh franchise was extensive, the Scottish bill offered compensating advantages to conservative and territorial interests. The division of the Glasgow constituency into two constituencies, when one might as easily have been added to the existing constituency, promised something if the Conservative party was to become the party of respectability in the future. If Disraeli's Scottish bill had passed, eleven medium-sized burghs would have been removed from the six county constituencies in which they were situated: they would have been grouped (as the burgh districts of Falkirk, Kilmarnock and Hamilton) along with eleven other burghs which before the bill shared two burgh seats between them. Though this would have added one to the number of Scottish burgh MP.s, it would have consolidated the rural character of the counties from which the eleven burghs were removed.[1] The reunited Liberal majority in 1868 cancelled both the Falkirk/Kilmarnock/Hamilton grouping and the division of Glasgow. Since it also joined together Selkirk and Peebles, which had previously had two Conservative county seats, and created a burgh district out of Hawick, Galashiels and the burgh of Selkirk, this reinforces the conclusion, already reached in connection with the English bill—that, while Disraeli was getting what he could in the parliamentary vacuum created by the destruction of Liberal unity in 1867, the restoration of Liberal unity over Irish Church disestablishment in 1868 confirmed the fears which he and Derby had always felt about the effect on the Conservative party of any united Liberal attempt to deal with the redistribution of seats.

Throughout the session of 1867, Conservatives had pressed, no less than Liberals, for a more extensive redistribution than the bill of March 18 had proposed.[1] Gaselee's motion of June 3 to disfranchise boroughs with populations smaller than 5,000 implied a more extensive disfranchisement than Laing's: unlike Laing's, it was not designed to compensate the counties with seats taken from the boroughs. Gaselee accused Laing of trickery in getting priority for his own motion, and dishonesty in stealing parts of it from him:[2] if debated before the House had decided on the enfranchisement proposed by Laing, it is possible that Gaselee's motion would have been accepted for want of any other.[3] Once its unity had been restored in 1868, the Liberal majority voted in favour of the substance of Gaselee's amendment in the process of finding English seats to transfer to Scotland during the passage of the Reform bill for Scotland. It also reduced the number of cases in which Disraeli's boundary commission had proposed extensions of borough boundaries in order to free county constituencies in England and Wales from urban-style populations which were spreading from adjacent cities and towns. Nevertheless, if one ignores the events of 1868, it will be seen that the Act of 1867 in its final form both established a boundary commission with wide powers to remove the urban overspill from county seats and left sixteen of the smallest boroughs with independent representation.[4]

Acceptance by the House of Laing's motion of May 31 regulated the *extent* of redistribution by removing one MP. from every two-member borough with less than 10,000 inhabitants, but this was neither a victory for Radicals and large-borough members, nor prevented the government allocating to the counties twenty-five of the thirty-nine small-borough seats scheduled for disfranchisement. Though acceptance of Gaselee's amendment in addition to Laing's would have reduced the size of the agricultural and territorial interest in the House of Commons by about fourteen seats (assuming that the same number—twenty-five—of the disfranchised seats would have been transferred to county constituencies), the defeat of Gaselee, the limited allocation to large cities and the allocation eventually made to counties ensured that the Act reduced the number of MP.s for agricultural and territorial constituencies by two or three, if it reduced it at all.[5] Laing was not a Whig but an Adullamite: he thought the bill, if amended, would enable 'moderate men in future Parliaments to rally round it' and resist 'the slope along that incline which would lead us to democratic institutions almost parallel with those of America'.[1] His object was to increase representation in the counties as much as in the large cities, though his plan for an even larger redistribution was defeated on June 13.[2] Laing's motion of May 31 was supported, not only by the body of the Liberal party, but also by sixty-five Conservatives, of whom thirty-two were members for English or Welsh counties, and of whom eight more were either defenders of the agricultural interest or closely identified with a very conservative attitude to electoral reform. In this division 179 MP.s voted with Disraeli, but of these only about 150 were Conservative, since he had with him the Liberal Chief Whip and about twenty-five Liberals—fourteen at least of whom were recording their votes against the partial disfranchisement their own constituencies would suffer if Laing's amendment were passed (in the hope, no doubt, in the event of the bill not eventually becoming an Act, to be able to repel the attacks they would suffer for disloyalty to their constituents). Only five members of the Cave voted with Disraeli. No fewer than twenty-three of the Liberals who had voted against Gladstone's bill in June 1866 voted with Laing, as did five more who had voted, or flirted, with the Cave, including Laing himself and Lowe, who did so on the ground that, under the new franchise established by clause 3 of the bill, small boroughs 'are indefensible and must become dens of corruption of the lowest order'.[3] There is one hint that the Government wanted Laing's amendment to be accepted, and evidence that one 'county member, who came down prepared to vote with the Government . . . eventually voted with Laing at the earnest solicitation of . . . Spofforth', the Conservative chief agent, who 'was diligently whipping in favour of it, and, with considerable audacity . . . and a list in his hand, which professed to give the statistics why Laing's amendment ought to be carried . . . asserting that the Government wished to be beaten on this point'.[4]

Spofforth's list does not survive, but there is independent confirmation of the view that in boroughs with populations between 7,000 and 10,000 there was thought to be a small Whig majority.[5] Perhaps because he wanted to avoid presenting Gladstone with something to knock down, perhaps because he wanted to avoid seeming anxious to make too large a change, Disraeli, though he almost certainly wanted this and at least one other vote to go against him, thought it better neither to take the initiative nor to say so. It is difficult to resist the conclusion that one reason why Disraeli thought it safe to 'take the sense of the House' on the seats question once the Liberal party had fallen apart was that, whatever might happen once the Liberal party was reunited, some of its members, if left to their individual preferences, could be relied on to provide compensation for an increase in the large-borough representation by 'backing us up in a good distribution for counties',[1] and that Conservatives really did 'hope', as one of their opponents thought, 'by a large accession of county members to raise a barrier against democracy, and many of our people are of the same mind'.[2]

Although, therefore, it must not be imagined that Derby and Disraeli could have predicted in detail the course of the redistribution clauses at an early date in January or March, or were anything but surprised to have got away with the bill they passed in 1867, they had every reason to suppose that, even if they were going as a party to lose from a lowering of the borough franchise, which was not in any case certain,[3] there was no reason to fear the instinct of a very conservative House on redistribution questions. The redistribution clauses of Disraeli's bill of March 18, as Disraeli was at pains to point out, would probably have been marginally favourable to the Liberal party. But Disraeli can hardly have been blind to the fact that the more extensive redistribution accepted on June 2—so long as its details were regulated by the government—would so effectively consolidate county representation that Bright expected the redistribution clauses which were eventually adopted to induce among Radicals in the future 'a growing disposition to accept something more like electoral districts to get rid, to some extent, of the close phalanx of country gentlemen who seem unable to see clearly either the true interest of the country or their own'.[4]

Once the question is asked, there can be little doubt that Disraeli, like Bright, thought the 'question of redistribution...the very soul of the question of reform',[5] and saw that there were advantages to be gained from a Conservative-controlled settlement, whatever the cost in concession over the borough franchise. When one finds Disraeli assuring Bright that, in dealing with Reform in 1867, he 'did not care much for the counties', one feels, like Russell, that he 'always thought [Disraeli] meant [to introduce household suffrage without duality] when he proposed an abstract resolution against it'.[1] In March 1867, Bright half-promised Disraeli support for a household suffrage bill. But Bright attacked the bill Disraeli intro-duced on March 18 as 'being so unpleasant, so unjust, so insulting to those whom it excludes that it will establish...a raw on the public conscience'.[2] Bright admired neither the final bill 'in [which] I feel now to have lost all interest' nor its author whose dishonesty was equalled only by the 'rotten[ness]...of not a few...on our own side'.[3] It is important to notice Bright's objection. It is important to recognize that Liberal disunity was unlikely to be permanent, and that a Liberal party united under Gladstone's, or anyone else's, leadership would be much more concerned with party advantage, and much more conscious of the party context of all electoral reform, than in the passing phase in 1867 when the Liberal party had ceased to exist as a parliamentary unit. The moment at which Disraeli was in command was a transitory moment—long enough to pass the major part of a measure which his party feared—but too insecure to be expected to persist. At the moment of power in May, June and July, Disraeli did as much as he could to get what he wanted, but he did not succeed, even then, in nominating the whole of the boun-dary commission, which produced a remarkable Liberal unity in face of the threat it presented to Liberal electoral prospects in the future. These are important contextual aids in the attempt to provide intel-ligible explanation of Disraeli's and Derby's apparent willingness to accept almost anything the House of Commons might approve of. It is in this framework that we must ask: why did they decide to deal with the Reform question by introducing a bill? how did it get into committee? why did most Conservatives, some Radicals, a good part of the Cave and even Gladstonian Liberals at various stages assist its progress? why, above all, did a House of Commons which was 'opposed to any violent reform and to any reform of any kind which is immediate'[4] assist Disraeli in passing a bill which was both immediate and apparently more extensive than anything it would allow Gladstone to pass in the session of 1866?

II

PRELIMINARY: THE UPROOTING
OF THE WHIGS

'I never saw thro' a glass so darkly as now in regard to politics. A numerous and hungry Conservative party, a Whig one to which office has become a second nature, and two very clever and very ambitious middle-class men, namely Disraeli and Gladstone, who never can act in the same play and who...never will assist any fusion into which they would respectively be joined.'

Malmesbury to Derby, November 8 1865. Derby MSS Box 146

(i)

The election of 1865 left the Conservative leaders in a condition of total depression. Once more the Conservative party was the minority party in the House of Commons. In Scotland there had been 'utter rout'.[1] Spofforth, the chief Conservative agent, could not 'help expressing my regret that the result is so disastrous'.[2] To Gathorne Hardy, shooting with Colonel Taylor, the chief whip, who found 'the elections...unaccountable', it seemed that they 'have...I fear...almost demolished the party'.[3] Disraeli, offering his own resignation but hinting at Derby's, reflected that 'the leadership of hopeless opposition is a gloomy affair and there is little distinction when *your* course [the adjective was perhaps ambiguous][4] is not associated with the possibility of future power'.[5] To Derby it seemed 'at the age of sixty-six and after forty-four years of public life, a man may well be content, as I shall be, to take no greater share in public affairs than that which may attach to any personal influence which I may exercise'.[6] As Derby and Disraeli looked out there was only a faint glimmer of hope. Palmerston was eighty: 'his bladder complaint, tho' in itself not fatal, deprives him of his usual exercise, and of sleep which was his *forte* and carried him through everything.'[7] He might live for a long time yet—long enough to outlast Derby himself: it was certain that 'Palmerston will never retire'. But, as they viewed the wreckage, it seemed just possible that, if anything happened to Palmerston, the Conservative party might turn the corner. In these circumstances the only possible policy was to 'endeavour to keep [the party] together, so as to be ready to avail ourselves of any contingency which may arise, or any serious breach in our opponents' ranks in the event of Palmerston's death, however little we may expect it even then'.[1]

Palmerston's death eight weeks later, before the new Parliament met, opened up all the possibilities on which they had reckoned. The Liberal party at once seemed to become, in the words of Clarendon who succeeded Russell as Foreign Secretary, 'a great bundle of sticks [which]...are now unloosed [with]...nobody to tie them up'.[2] It seemed possible, to say the least, that the alliance of Radicals, squires, lawyers, Whigs and businessmen, bereft of its anchor and captain, might disintegrate more easily, even, than Peel's party in 1846. Nor was there merely a vague feeling that the 'bundle of sticks' might break up. It was obvious what would break it up, and in which directions the sticks would fly. The Liberal party in Parliament consisted of a small number of Whigs, many of them peers, who were bound together by family ties on the one hand and governmental experience on the other, of a small but militant group of Radicals, and of a large body of predominantly Anglican landowners, lawyers and businessmen (some of them Whig by opinion or connection) who had no expectation of office or open influence and who were willing to follow their parliamentary leaders so long as their conduct seemed reasonable; but whose opinions in bulk were decisive in relation to the party as a whole. Though the party as a whole was not radical, the parliamentary Radicals had, since the beginning of the 1860s, both committed themselves to regular support of the Liberal party and expected consideration in virtue of their willingness to do so. At the same time as they made themselves party Liberals, however, the climate of opinion—both public and parliamentary—had begun to move against them. The reaction of the 1860s had many sources; its effects on party alignment was blurred. The eclectic ambiguity of Palmerston's appeal, 'an idiotic belief in his longevity'[3] and the virtual alliance between Derby and Palmerston tended both to limit the expectations entertained by parliamentary Radicals and to perpetuate the situation in which, although 'the Liberals [had] so mismanaged matters that the country is conservative...the Tories had so mismanaged matters that the country, although conservative, would rather be governed by Whigs than by Tories'.[4]

In Palmerston's Cabinet the opponents of electoral reform had been successful. Opposition to reform did not mean opposing it outright: it meant surrounding it with the provision that nothing should be done hastily. Nothing of consequence had been done at all except the redistribution of four corrupt borough seats from St Albans and Sudbury: it was widely supposed that this was because Palmerston thought it unnecessary that it should be. At the same time, however, as the public mood was supposed to have hardened against, Gladstone's mood seemed to have hardened in favour. Extension of the franchise was not the major plank in Gladstone's platform, but since 1864 at least it had become a plank. Gladstone had not been asked to form a government: nor were his commitments about the franchise explicit as to scope or timing. Gladstone, nevertheless, as Chancellor of the Exchequer, 'principal member of the administration' and leader of the House of Commons, would insist, it was thought, on immediate action.

Behind Gladstone Bright was supposed to loom. Dislike of Bright was as strong inside the Liberal party as anywhere else: the name of Bright, more than that of any other Radical MP., aroused class and chauvinistic antagonism in the House of Commons: by ostentatiously announcing support for Gladstone, Bright increased suspicions which Gladstone's language did little to remove. Bright in private thought public feeling put a major Reform bill out of the question: this did not make him less menacing in public. 'Mr Gladstone' had not, as the *Morning Star* (Bright's organ) claimed 'been converted by Mr Bright as Sir Robert Peel was converted by Mr Cobden';[1] but it was not implausible to suggest that he had been. In these circumstances there was real fear in the Liberal party, and expectation in the Conservative party, that Bright would bring pressure to bear on Gladstone which Gladstone might not resist. Gladstone, in this company, might go too far and 'alarm the middle classes';[2] he might go too far in the House of Commons, and the prospect emerged of full-scale conflict there. The prospect raised three questions—whether 'there will be a number of men on the government side sufficiently plucky to go with Lowe, Horsman, Gregory, Elcho...thirty men would do it...but that is a large proportion of mutineers for a new parliament';[3] whether there was anything the Conservative party could do to bring this about, and whether, if a parliamentary rebellion brought down the Cabinet, a coalition would follow.

The precariousness of the Liberal majority became overnight an article of Conservative belief. 'There is', wrote Spofforth, 'a general impression pervading all classes on both sides that the government will not last long.'[1] 'The necessity of reconstruction', Earle, his private secretary, told Disraeli, 'is on every Conservative mouth'.[2] 'Reconstruction', from a Conservative point of view, meant accommodating Whigs who, Tory in all but name, would be willing to resist excessive lowering of the franchise and any assault on property. It meant, so far as Derby was concerned, 'avail[ing] yourself of those confidential connections which you have among the Whigs, and let[ting] them clearly understand...that you are free and prepared to form an anti-revolutionary party on a broad basis'.[3] It meant that Whigs, if that could be done without compromising church positions, might bring with them Liberal politicians like Lowe who were not themselves Whig. While preserving the Anglican commitments of the party, it meant above all an attempt to rally middle-class Palmerstonians by emphasizing the trade union and working-class threat to expropriate wealth, and to turn the Conservative party from being the party of the landed interest to being the party of all existing property. The end of *The Times*'s alliance with Palmerston and Delane's hostility to Russell, the hope that Borthwick might bring over *The Morning Post*[4] and a feeling that 'the current of public opinion [in relation to reform] had been turned'[5] combined with the continuing restlessness of Irish Whigs and rumours of Whig attempts in August 1865 to rig the succession against Russell[6] to arouse the belief that the Conservative party might become a major instrument in preventing 'considerable changes...both in Church and State which neither the necessities of the country require, nor its feelings really sanction'.[7]

The Liberal ministers, also, knew that they were in danger. The Liberal party, which was already weak in the House of Commons, was made weaker by the fact that Palmerston was dead and that the new Prime Minister and Foreign Secretary, and two major spending ministers—Somerset at the Admiralty and de Grey at the War Office—were all in the Lords. The objects at first, therefore, were to strengthen the front-bench in the Commons and embrace, so far as possible, all the dissident elements of which the Liberal party consisted. Each of the Cabinet lobbyists had an axe to grind—Russell for a reform ministry, Gladstone for an economy one, Wood and Brand for comprehensiveness. Each had his own Radicals for promotion, and urged the need for parity between factions, but all identified the same basic problem. It was Granville, no enemy of reform, who wanted Lowe in the Cabinet and thought, six months later, that if offered office on condition of supporting a moderate Reform bill, Lowe would have accepted:[1] it was another Whig, Sir George Grey, who pressed on Brand the view that Russell would need to remove the impression his Cabinets too often left that he moved in a narrow aristocratic circle.[2]

Decisions about appointments were made by Russell himself, after discussion, not always very full, with Gladstone, with Wood[3] when he chose to intervene, and with Brand, who thought the Russell–Gladstone combination would be difficult to manage, and announced, soon after the session began, that he would resign as soon as the Reform question had been settled. Consultation was a struggle for influence between these three, none of whom was uniformly successful. Gladstone did not get control of the spending ministries: Somerset was not turned out and Milner Gibson, Gladstone's nominee, did not become First Lord of the Admiralty in the February reshuffle.[4] Although de Grey was persuaded (by Brand) to offer his resignation in October so that the War Secretary might be in the Commons, Wood prevented Russell accepting it.[5] When de Grey succeeded Wood at the India Office in February, he was himself succeeded at the War Office by Hartington, whom Gladstone did not want there, and who was as little committed to reducing military expenditure as de Grey. Gladstone succeeded in preventing Russell offering office to Horsman, which Brand thought would have removed some of the sting from the Cave,[6] but failed, if he was trying, in October, to get in Lowe (also an economizer) before the government's reform commitments had been agreed on.[7] Wood, too, lost over Lowe, whom Russell would not have at any price, and over Bouverie, if, as Bouverie thought, he wanted him:[8] but he won over de Grey's resignation in October, and over the appointment of Stansfeld to the India under-secretaryship in February 1866. He won again when Russell made de Grey his successor at the India Office, which Gladstone wanted for the Duke of Argyll who felt 'shunted' as a consequence.[9] Goschen was brought into the Cabinet by Russell without taking advice from anyone, and, possibly, without asking Goschen himself.[1] Gladstone was blamed for the appointment of Goschen (by Bouverie and Knatchbull-Hugessen, for example), though he objected to it because he thought it would upset junior ministers, and quarrelled with Sir George Grey when Grey failed to see that men like Knatchbull-Hugessen, who had been a junior whip for seven years, had a right to expect promotion, at least to an under-secretaryship.[2] Goschen was a highly literate, highly talented undoctrinaire banker with Radical attitudes on church, administrative and financial questions. His combination of impressive intellect, practical experience and progressive inclinations, when combined with openly expressed hostility to Bright's class-consciousness and a desire (if his father's ambitions were a guide) to 'raise his rank' in the world, promised a convenient extension into the next generation of the safe Radicalism which Russell admired. But his appointment to the vice-presidency of the Board of Trade in November 1865 was made at the expense of Sir William Hutt, who had been there for six years, who expected to be in the Cabinet and whose removal from office once the reform commitment was accepted was attributed by Cranborne to the fact that he had been too outspoken. Goschen's admission to the Cabinet not only annoyed Whigs and Liberals who had been passed over in the first batch of appointments in favour of W. E. Forster, who had 'since his election in 1859 [1861 in fact] voted no less than sixteen times against the government': it also annoyed fellow Radicals like Layard, and further depressed morale at a time when the inherent difficulty of the situation had depressed it already.[3]

In all these matters Gladstone's function was to soothe tempers even when disagreeable decisions had to be made. When Chichester Fortescue replaced Sir Robert Peel (son of the Prime Minister) at the Irish Office as part of a concerted appeasement of Irish Liberals, it was Gladstone's idea that the Queen should be asked to give Peel a viscountcy.[4] Lowe was left out in October because of Russell's aversion: he could not be included thereafter because of his unequivocal position about Reform. The Cabinet, nevertheless, at a meeting at which Gladstone presided,[5] asked Granville to tell Lowe, whom Russell would not see, how much it appreciated his services under Palmerston, regretting that 'the strong opinions declared by him in opposition to that of the government, that there ought not to be any lowering of the suffrage in the boroughs, inter-posed for the moment an insuperable obstacle' in the way of office.[1] The proposal, made by Russell on Gladstone's suggestion, to bring Stanley, Derby's son, into the Cabinet, together with any other Con-servative he might bring with him,[2] so far from providing evidence of a Radical tendency, is evidence rather of a desire to 'redress...in the best manner practicable the balance of the government',[3] to strengthen the hand of aristocratic progress, to damage the Con-servative party, and to bring the Reform question to an agreed, moderate and reasonable conclusion.[4] Even in Bright's direction it was at Gladstone's insistence that caution was observed. Though Russell thought seriously in December of having him in the Cabinet if he would come now that a Reform bill was to be introduced, Glad-stone pointed out that, although Bright had 'for many years held language of a studious moderation about Reform, in the present critical state of feeling on your own side with respect to the franchise, his name would sink the government and their bill together'.[5]

Though Bright was not asked, the other major Radical appoint-ment made the government's balancing-trick more difficult to main-tain. In late October, when W. E. Forster was offered the colonial under-secretaryship in order to confirm Radical support without incurring the odium of offering office to Bright, a price had had to be paid, though Russell had no objection to paying it. Forster would not accept office until it was understood that the Reform question would be dealt with by introducing a bill, instead of by appointing a commission of enquiry. The commission had become a practical issue when Elcho suggested it after the debate on Baines's motion as a preliminary to the discussion of principle to which he was com-mitted, but the idea of a commission had been attacked on Radical platforms at the election of 1865. Russell had not wanted a commis-sion, but pressure from Whig ministers, from Brand, reflecting party feeling in the House, and from Elcho, whose recital of its desirability in a letter written, by request, to Lord Stanley of Alderley, had been read out at a Cabinet meeting at the beginning of November,[6] had made him 'suppose we may be forced into having one'.[7] The decision to proceed by bill, which Forster's insistence precipitated, seems not to have been thought decisive at the time: so far from in-volving commitment as to content, it was almost certainly tactical. Russell thought Forster was looking for an excuse to destroy the

Liberal/Whig alliance, 'his object being, as [Lord Russell] has been told, to get rid of the present government, and, after a short interval of Tory rule, to come in himself in high office'.[1] The decision in favour of a bill, which the Cabinet had to confirm before Forster joined in mid-November, seemed a harmless way of neutralizing him, just as the decision to collect statistics—which, to Bright, was evidence of 'a huckstering spirit. . . as if a few thousands of electors more or less were of the smallest consequence'[2]—seemed a harmless way of meeting Elcho's demand for a commission. The difficulty was that, given the balance of forces within the party, the decision to proceed by bill, and the decision to collect statistics, though meant to paper over cracks, were crucial and conflicting, since the statistics turned out to be so startling in their novelty that the decision in favour of an immediate bill could be represented, as and was, a capitulation to Radical pressure.

Once the commission had been abandoned, Russell and Gladstone had first to persuade the Cabinet to agree on a bill, and then to edge it through the House of Commons. The Cabinet problem was, in a way, the smaller—first, because, with the replacement of Palmerston and Halifax by Goschen and Hartington, the Cabinet was less conservative than before: secondly, because no one in the Cabinet was willing openly to oppose a lowering of the franchise. The Whig members showed a marked reluctance to leave office themselves so long as a Liberal government remained a possibility: knowing the strength of Liberal opposition in the House of Commons, they could expect a bill to be defeated even if the Cabinet approved of it.[3] Though the older Whigs disliked the bill which emerged from Cabinets and Cabinet committees in January, no member of the Cabinet resigned. Somerset had offered his resignation shortly after Palmerston's death, partly because of the threat Gladstone presented to the level of naval expenditure, partly because of the threat Russell might present to the small boroughs;[4] he did not offer to resign thereafter. Clarendon made a show of reluctance at the same time, but not in relation to Reform. Wood resigned at the end of January because he had injured his head in a hunting accident, choosing to do so then in case resignation in the middle of a Reform crisis later on, though resulting from the accident, should leave the impression that 'I retired because I differed from [the government]'.[5]

The proposal, in February, to substitute rental for rating as the franchise qualification produced from the Whigs the fabian reaction that the whole question must be reconsidered: it produced no resignation. On March 6, less than a week before the Franchise bill was to be introduced, when Gladstone proposed reducing to £7 the £7.10s. rental the Cabinet had accepted (as the equivalent of the £6 rating qualification it had decided on in the first place), there were again complaints (directed largely at Russell's attempt to make the change by circulating memoranda instead of calling the Cabinet),[1] one veiled threat of resignation,[2] a difficult meeting, but no sustained attack on the substance of the change. Sir George Grey certainly, Clarendon and Somerset probably, treating the vote as an excuse for dropping Reform altogether, wanted the government to resign at the end of April when the division on Grosvenor's motion confirmed their predictions about the strength of opposition in the Commons:[3] when Gladstone and Russell ('it is a small majority but five times as many as I had for the second reading of the great reform bill')[4] insisted on carrying on with the bill and the government whatever the Whigs might do, they agreed to carry on also.

Whig criticism in the Cabinet, moreover, was not directed very decisively at the content of the Russell/Gladstone proposals, and this requires explanation. 'Safe progress' in relation to Reform meant, in theory, stopping short of the point at which a preponderant influence would be given 'to one class and that the lowest'.[5] One thing a commission would have done would be to discover what proportion of working-class electors already had the vote: when the statistics for which Elcho was asking had been collected through the Poor Law machinery and consolidated by Lambert, the Poor Law board secretary, they showed that the proportion of working-class voters already on the urban electoral rolls was more than double what it previously had been supposed to be—'more than one-fifth of the whole number are of this class [actually 26·3 per cent], and the persons making the returns generally understood what class of person was meant by your description'.[6] So little was this conclusion anticipated when returns were called for that Russell's claim—'our returns come in rapidly and will be full of information more than Lord Elcho would ever collect'[7]—could hardly have been more typical of Russell's conduct in these months if he had known in advance what the statistics would prove; while the weapon they gave to enemies of almost any bill compelled Russell and Gladstone to spend time attempting, unsuccessfully, to prove, from their own sources,[1] that the returns had exaggerated the size of the working-class electorate.[2] The critics in the Cabinet, however, did not use them in this way. It was not until they were published in March that the Cave and the Opposition drove home the point that the Russell/Gladstone bill would give working-class voters a 'preponderance' in at least a hundred constituencies.

The position of the Cabinet Whigs was delicate. They were distinguished from the most militant of the Adullamites, to whom in general they did not explain their plans, by the fact that they were in office and the Adullamites were not. While Earl Grey, Bouverie, Horsman, Laing and to some extent Lowe were disappointed politicians who had no particular commitment to existing arrangements, the Cabinet Whigs wished above all to keep the boat running smoothly. Their object was to maintain the Liberal party as the party of 'real and safe progress', and they knew that a price had to be paid if this was to be convincing. A price had to be paid in relation to policy: a leader had to emerge who could carry Radicals along without capitulating to them. It was not that the Liberal party in the House was Radical, which it was not, but that its most powerful leaders outside the Whig circle (especially Gladstone) could easily become so. Whig resignations would throw the Liberal leadership sharply leftward, leaving the Whigs either as floating bodies with no party of their own or as allies, not necessarily dominant, of Derby, whose politics they disliked, and of Disraeli, whose personality the older ones detested. The Whig object, therefore, was not to carry a *particular* measure of reform, but to slow the pace of reform to the speed of the slowest man—to keep the Liberal party in existence by squaring the circle of disagreement. It was 'not' because he was 'in the least afraid of the working-classes' that Halifax (Wood) was alarmed by Gladstone's bill but because a 'more moderate measure' would have stood a better chance both with existing Liberal voters in the country and with the Liberal party in the House of Commons. Once the bill had been adopted, however, and Gladstone committed to it, it had to be handled carefully. Gladstone's talents qualified him to carry along a united party in the future, but Gladstone, if defeated in the House, 'emancipated from all control of Whig colleagues' and 'thrown . . . into the hands of the radicals' could lead a popular working-class movement which, if not likely to be dangerous 'as long as matters are smooth in the country' might become so 'if bad times come'.[1] Whatever backbench Whigs were trying to do, the Cabinet Whigs were trying to keep the party together, and they were led on, at first, by the belief that Gladstone was also.

In the months before the bill was introduced, Gladstone displayed no urgency about Reform.[2] It was Gladstone who pressed Russell, against Russell's better judgement, to invite Stanley to join the Cabinet, Gladstone who discouraged Russell from offering office to Bright, Gladstone who would not have minded having Lowe in the Cabinet. It was Russell's son, not Gladstone's, who was an advanced Radical: it was in Pembroke Lodge and 37 Chesham Square, not at Hawarden or Carlton House Terrace, that the 'sham' Liberals were being separated from the 'real' ones.[3] In the decisions which were taken between November and January, Russell, despite his own uncertainty, was the dominant partner. It was Russell's, not Gladstone's, treatment of the Cabinet which provoked mass resistance in March: Russell's resignation, not Gladstone's, which was thought of as a sensible solution.[4] Russell criticized Gladstone in February 1866 for wanting to make *all* appointments from 'the left wing of the party', but in an economical context, not a reforming one. In October Gladstone had been slow to accept the lead in the House of Commons: in January he tried to get rid of responsibility for Reform questions in order to find time to reorganize the Treasury.[5] There is every indication that Gladstone was 'all for putting off Reform at first, tho' that was the question on which he was supposed to go further and to be more eager about than any of the others'.[6]

It may be that Gladstone was allowing Russell to make the running, just as he wished Sir George Grey to take the lead in the House of Commons because Grey was a safe and sensible parliamentary Whig. He may have thought it easier to foist a Reform bill on an unwilling party under shadow of the threat of dissolution, which could not be offered immediately after a general election. It is likely that he wished to build up a reliable ministerial following of his own before undertaking a major task,[7] and thought the first task to be reduction of government spending and an assault on income tax. It has even to be asked whether he may not have thought, from the start, like everyone else, that the Russell Cabinet would neither survive nor carry a Reform bill, wished to be untainted by the stain of defeat, and was swept along by his own combativeness when Russell committed both of them in a way which made withdrawal impossible if Radical expectations were not to be disappointed.

Whatever his reasons, Gladstone's situation was complicated. 'Unmuzzling' was well advanced: the direction of his commitments was unequivocal. Unmuzzling, however, did not mean handing himself over bag and baggage to Bright, and it meant meeting the accusation that he had done so. It meant demonstrating, in face of Bright's impatience,[1] that Gladstone could edge whatever com-bination Gladstone led in some of the directions which Bright would have chosen and which progressive opinion in general wanted, but it meant taking the precaution of having a combination to lead. It meant asserting control over a governing party, and discovering in these months how far it was possible to go with the Liberal party in the House of Commons. Gladstone's repertoire of slogans was catholic: his judgements of suitability varied with the situation. The Reform slogans of 1864 lacked specific content and avoided specific commitment: nevertheless, they seemed to be democratic. The slogans of 1865 and early 1866 were not. Economic policy was in the front of his mind in late 1865: there was a danger that a Reform crisis would get in the way of that. So long as it was uncertain what atti-tude the Liberal party would take, provocative demonstrations were avoided in the hope of edging the Reform bill through the House as successfully as it had been edged through the Cabinet.

This cautious policy was also the policy of the Conservative leaders—but with a difference. While Russell and Gladstone were attempting a balancing trick in order to maintain party unity, Derby and Disraeli were playing a waiting game in order to destroy it. They sensed a hardening of middle-class feeling, the electoral possibilities if the government swung sharply leftward. They saw that there were strains inside the Cabinet, and that the climate of public opinion was reflected in the Liberal party in the House. They feared, also, the damage the Conservative party would suffer if Russell constructed a central coalition. There was a delicate moment in November when Russell tried to detach Stanley: perhaps because he thought the government would not last, perhaps because his opinions were more conservative than Gladstone supposed, perhaps because he could not openly oppose his father,[2] Stanley did not join.

Care was taken to ensure that the Conservative party avoided positions which would hamper manœuvrability when the government published its bill. Sir John Hay, fighting a by-election in Palmerston's seat in January, on asking for guidance about the party's Reform policy, was told to 'say nothing to give the government a notion of the course likely to be followed—but to hold for Conservative progress and refute Mr Bright'.[1] Sir John Pakington, an ex-Cabinet minister, preparing to speak at a Conservative rally at Droitwich, was told by Derby to 'do full justice to the tact and adroitness with which in domestic matters Palmerston...kept... hostile opinions [in the Liberal party] in check', to suggest that 'now...the...guiding...hand is withdrawn...[it is] impossible not to feel that security...is impaired', and, while vindicating the Conservative party against the charge of being obstructive ('and you may instance our introduction of a Reform bill in 1858') '...to avoid holding out anything which can be construed into a pledge that...we would bring in another'.[2] As late as March 8, four days before the first reading of the Reform bill, Hardy refused to talk, when approached about the party's Reform tactics by Lowe, who had been his tutor at Oxford, because, as he put it in the privacy of his diary, 'Lord Derby impressed caution and silence upon us'.[3]

Conservative policy, right up to the publication of the bill on March 12, was to make the most of other issues—the Governor Eyre controversy so long as public opinion was thought to support him, the cattle plague question because that made it possible to claim that only one member of the Cabinet (Gladstone) had extensive practical experience as a working landowner—but to remain absolutely uncommitted; to let 'our policy...be regulated by that of the government' so that, 'if they [the government] quarrel with the Radicals, we [may] do our best to support them and thus widen and perpetuate the breach; [or] if they throw themselves into the extreme party, we [may] offer them a strenuous opposition, relying on the aid of their moderate men to prevent mischief'.[4] It is possible that Derby would have liked to 'agree a measure', though he thought this almost impossible. Disraeli seems to have wanted an agreed bill at the time of Palmerston's death, but backed down when Russell's offer to Stanley made accommodation dangerous to the party.[5] For Disraeli also, as we shall see later, the position was complicated: it was made more complicated by the fact that he was not sure that he could rely on Derby, and that Gladstone was spoken of in some Conservative quarters, before the bill was introduced, as the possible leader of a broad-based coalition.

Gladstone's parliamentary appeal was in its way potentially as broad as Palmerston's. Gladstone lacked many elements in Palmerston's armoury but made up in others. He made up in Radical directions: he made up as a conceivable agent of Conservative progress; he made up, finally, in church matters—among the younger, most devout generation of churchmen like Acland, Bath, Lyttleton and Northcote who all combined cross-bench opinions with an elevated opposition to Whig, cynical or Palmerstonian Erastianism. In these respects Gladstone seemed to present a threat to the existing Conservative party. Northcote's admiration for Gladstone had suffered when in March 1865 'Gladstone...denounced the Irish Church in a way which shows how, by and by, he will deal not only with it but with the Church of England too'.[1] Northcote had always been close to Gladstone and was one of his executors: the prospect of a Conservative/Adullamite coalition reduced Northcote's expectation in the Conservative party. Northcote, nevertheless, represented something when he told Disraeli in February 1866 that 'some of the High Churchmen [in the Conservative party] are so alarmed at the danger of Erastianism that they are for a free church and look to Gladstone as their leader to that result', and, if faced with a Conservative Cabinet including 'men who have so little of their confidence[2] as Stanley, Lowe and Horsman, the breach may be precipitated and men like myself...forced to join the Free Church party as the lesser evil'.[3]

In conversation with Malmesbury, before the bill was introduced in March, the Marquess of Bath, whom the Chief Whip thought a 'blockhead',[4] expressed a preference for 'a coalition under a Whig premier, but although Gladstone is not a Whig, I believe he was the man meant'.[5] Gathorne Hardy reported to Cairns in December that 'Gladstone talks Conservatism and sneers at Lord Russell—at least so I am told by Lady M. Hope who met him at the Archbishop's'.[6] Sir Robert Phillimore 'thought Gladstone was not likely to become very Radical: that he was anxious to found a family and would like to see his son a Peer'.[7] Lady Colchester, at a moment when rumours reported by *The Times* of Russell's retirement, though known to be false, set off speculation about the succession, 'expressed great alarm at the reports that Gladstone was making advances to the Conservatives'.[1] In the same situation Lady Salisbury predicted, more reasonably, that if the government broke up and Derby failed, or refused, to form a government, 'the Queen would send for Gladstone of whom she is very fond and he would...take General Peel and Stanley and yourself [i.e. Northcote]...Cardwell and Lowe...Argyll, de Grey and Hartington'.[2] Derby, even, was reported by Disraeli to believe that if (for reasons which we shall examine later) Disraeli gave up the leadership of the Conservative party in the Commons, 'there was nobody for it but Gladstone "who is quite prepared to take the high Conservative line"'.[3] Derby himself, assuming that the government would propose 'so mild...[a Reform bill] that it may thoroughly disgust the real Radicals', was thinking in November of 'fresh combinations' of a 'Liberal–Conservative' sort: while recognizing that 'the Liberals would not...act under [Disraeli] nor the Conservatives under [Gladstone]', he attributed this to no deep difference of policy but to 'personal difficulties...the rivalry of Disraeli and Gladstone—the strong aversion felt by each for the other and for each by the great body of their respective opponents, and not a few of their respective supporters'.[4]

The significance of these rumours is not that they were true,[5] but that they illustrate the climate in which the parliamentary battle began. If Gladstone had succeeded Russell in March 1866, as some Whigs wanted him to, he would probably have offered office to Stanley and Northcote: if they had accepted—they probably would not have done—his language about the franchise might have been more conservative, and his success in the House of Commons greater. It is possible that Derby and Disraeli used these rumours in order to reconcile dissident Conservatives to Disraeli, whom many disliked personally, by reminding them that the alternative was Gladstone, whose opinions they disliked even more. But the strength of the rumours came from the fact that they were not inherently implausible, and from the danger Gladstone, or any other coalition leader, was thought to present to the cohesion of the Conservative party. They pinpointed the need, therefore, to destroy the image of a moderate Gladstone whom some sorts of Conservative might in some circumstances support. Just as Bright's support eased the government away from the conservative Whigs outside it,[6] so the assaults made on Gladstone by Disraeli, Cranborne and Cairns were designed to edge the Whigs and the body of the Liberal party away from him: to accentuate the difference between Gladstone on the one hand and Liberals and Conservatives on the other—to make Gladstone seem, what Cranborne in the *Quarterly Review* had said he was, what Elcho and Horsman thought he was, but what he certainly was not at the beginning of the session—the prisoner of Bright, Mill and Odger, the ally of positivism and the conniver at the policy, which a reformed electorate was said to favour, of 'securing [for working-men] freeholds out of the landowner's estate or larger wages out of the capitalist's wealth'.[1] The necessities of the situation were pressing: its destructive possibilities considerable. Disraeli's keynote speech at the party meeting held at Lord Salisbury's house on March 16 was a bitter attack 'throwing all the blame for the present agitation upon Gladstone'.[2] When told by Northcote a fortnight before of Jolliffe's belief that 'it might not be a bad plan to let the government pass a moderate Reform bill and so get rid of the question...[he] received...this view...with the deepest contempt, considering that such a course would seat the Whigs for a lifetime'.[3]

The meeting of March 16 was treated by the government as a Conservative 'bid for office'. It was, however, preceded by—it did not follow—the decision, taken by Disraeli, Northcote, Cranborne, Sir William Heathcote and Spencer Walpole on March 8—before the details of the bill were known—to co-operate with the Adullamites in opposing whatever the government proposed.[4] It is certain that there was dissatisfaction in the higher reaches of the party with Derby's failure to give decisive leadership, possible that Disraeli was concerned for his own position if a lead were not given, and clear, in any case, that the decision of March 8 was stimulated in part by a feeling that the policy of non-commitment could not survive the introduction of a bill. Although, therefore, the decision to co-operate with the Cave, and not the government, was taken on tactical grounds, the government's proposals, once they were published, convinced everyone that the bill must be opposed on grounds of substance also.

In the three weeks following, the parliamentary battle was joined. The electoral returns were presented on March 9. They showed 116 boroughs in England and Wales where more than a quarter of the electorate was working-class: they established that 26·3 per cent of the whole electorate was working-class. Elcho, Cranborne and Lowe drove home the point about the danger of working-class preponderance. Grosvenor tabled a motion to postpone the second reading of the Franchise bill until a Seats bill was introduced also. Gladstone announced the Cabinet's willingness to introduce a Seats bill, but not in the terms of Grosvenor's motion. On Brand's advice, under Cabinet authority[1] and in order to rally the parliamentary party, he staked the government's existence on its Reform policy by firmness in the House and categorical assurance ('we have passed the Rubicon') in his two speeches (both at Liverpool) in the country. Grosvenor's motion was made, at Elcho's insistence, without consulting anyone outside the Cave. This made it necessary that the government should assert its authority, and gave Gladstone the opportunity to claim that he was the offended party, because party leaders had a right to be consulted when motions of this sort were made. Of all the Liberal leaders Gladstone could least afford to let it appear that the popular element in the party was being put down by the aristocracy: Grosvenor's intervention (both the way in which it was conducted and the support it received) made it likely that Gladstone would sharpen his public manner. There is no reason to suppose that Gladstone wanted to move leftward at the time, every reason to think that, 'though too much disposed to the [Radical] line before', it was Grosvenor's motion which drove 'the government to depend more on the Radicals than ever'. This is what Halifax thought:[2] it is almost certainly what happened.

In their tactics, the Conservative leaders were encouraged by a belief, right from the start, that Gladstone's bill could not pass, or the government stand; by the change which Lambert's statistics made to the climate of opinion; and by Gladstone's willingness, once Elcho had made their significance clear,[3] to justify the working-class preponderance the bill would establish in some constituencies by offering a highly sharpened, 'absolutely democratic'[4] apologetic which, though consistent with what he had said and including the same reservations as he had offered in 1864, was more Radical than anything he had said since Palmerston died.[5] They were encouraged by the information about Cabinet feeling which Stanley received from Wood (Halifax), both before and after his resignation,[6] and which Disraeli and Derby received—perhaps through Derby's daughter, who had married Clarendon's son,[1] perhaps through Lady Salisbury, whose family was Whig and to whom Clarendon wrote at length. They were sustained by the belief that the existing electorate did not want a Reform bill. They were assisted, finally, by rumours about the Liberal party itself—rumours, for example, of Layard's resignation in protest against the appointment of Goschen, though that had been withdrawn almost as soon as offered, and of the 'very general offence' the appointment had given:[2] rumours, which 'may be depended on' that, in the middle of Russell's resignation audience with the Queen in February (an audience which never took place), a telegram announcing the death of Sir Charles Phipps, a member of the Queen's staff, had arrived and the Queen had said 'This must be postponed: I can attend to no public business now';[3] rumours, finally, of the Duke of Somerset, Clarendon and de Grey walking out of a Cabinet meeting in February 'in disgust',[4] of the majority of the Cabinet wanting to drop the bill and 'Lord Russell and Gladstone [being] determined to go on with it immediately'; and of Gladstone saying that 'he did not want to run the risk of bringing in a budget for other men to pass'.[5]

Before the session began, there was little direct co-operation between the Adullamites and the Conservative party. When it did begin, though Horsman and Lowe did not trust Disraeli, co-operation about parliamentary tactics was close. Co-operation was kept secret so far as it could be. Liberal backbenchers did not respond to Gladstone, but they were sensitive to signs of disloyalty to the party.[6] Clay's motion for an educational franchise was used at the start of the session as a way of provoking division among Liberal reformers. In April Grosvenor took pains to deny that his motions had been drafted by 'a Tory hand' (a great deal of Grosvenor's work was done in fact by Elcho),[7] but, contact between the Cave and the Codservative party was very close. Disraeli had correspondence and conversation with Earl Grey, direct contact and conversation with Elcho and Horsman and seems actually to have attended or been present at the same time as a Cave meeting in Elcho's house.[8] Stanley, Heathcote and Carnarvon were in touch with Elcho, the first two with Lowe. Earle negotiated daily with Clive, Lowe, Elcho, Dunkellin, Bouverie and the younger Hayter, drafting Hayter's and modifying Bouverie's motions, and arranging the course of debates with the Adullamites. In March Carnarvon, with Disraeli's know-

7   **97**   CDG

ledge, opened negotiations of his own with Lichfield and Earl Spencer, but allowed them to lapse when Grosvenor's motion made it clear that some Whigs would be active against the bill.[1] Sir Edward Kerrison, the Conservative MP. for East Suffolk, was in constant touch with Elcho and Grosvenor.[2] Derby had contact with Clanricarde and Sir Robert Peel, whose support he canvassed before the vote on Dunkellin's motion. In the weeks before Goschen's appointment, Bouverie convinced himself that *he* had a chance of the Duchy of Lancaster.[3] Convincing himself in the weeks afterwards that the government could not survive, he carved out in imagination a Cave consisting of 'a considerable section of the most respectable Liberals in the House...of which I [i.e. rather than Lowe who was not respectable] might easily become the exponent and leader':[4] immediately the Franchise bill was published, Baillie-Cochrane, Conservative MP. for Honiton and 'an old Cambridge friend', began 'butter[ing] me up to the eyes...say[ing] I had the fate of the bill and country in my hands', and that 'Dizzy and all the Tories were looking to what I meant to do'.[5] On the initiative of Knatch-bull-Hugessen, who sat for Sandwich, in the month after Forster had been promoted over his head, Spofforth was negotiating for help in returning a Conservative in the event of a by-election in the other seat there, with the prospect of Knatchbull-Hugessen himself join-ing the Conservative party if other anti-reforming Liberals would do so also. Though it is difficult, in the absence of Taylor's papers, to find evidence that this was done, the Conservative chief whip in-tended in preparing election petitions to show 'hesitation to ques-tion the return of moderate men returned to support Lord Palmer-ston and who may now not unreasonably be expected to shake them-selves free from an allegiance to Lord Russell if...he brings in a comprehensive Reform bill'.[6]

(ii)

The government was throughout in a position of considerable diffi-culty from which closest attention to the mood of the party alone might have rescued it. The difficulty arose not so much from the extravagance of its proposals, as from the speed with which the bill was prepared, the procedural problems connected with passing it, the hostility which Gladstone aroused and the use made by the opposition of it.

In the early Cabinets and Cabinet committees, for example, rating had been accepted as the qualifying principle.[1] It is not certain that Whigs, like Somerset and Lord Stanley of Alderley, supported the rating franchise *because* its operation would vary from place to place, and would, in some places, whatever the qualifying figure, produce a very small enfranchisement; but they certainly did support it. The objection to a rental franchise was that, unless accompanied by stipulations about the payment of rates, it opened the way to establishing manhood suffrage, by reducing the rental qualifying level to nothing. In February, on the initiative of Lambert (who, in addition to being secretary to the Poor Law board, was an advanced Liberal journalist), rating was replaced by rental:[2] the absence of a rating stipulation formed the subject of the decisive vote, on Dunkellin's motion, on which the government was beaten in the House of Commons on June 18. Again, neither Russell nor Gladstone objected in principle to introducing a bill for redistributing seats alongside the bill for lowering the franchise. They decided not to do this for the tactical reason that if the franchise were lowered and constituencies left unchanged, it would be unnecessary[3] to have an immediate dissolution, and that this would remove opposition from MP.s who had spent extensively at the election in July. At the same time, as Sir George Grey pointed out, glaring inequalities between constituencies made it impossible to defend the existing distribution once discussion of the question began seriously, while to lower the franchise without redistributing seats would mean that a new Parliament elected on a new franchise might make a more dangerous redistribution.[4] This was established as Bright's public position by the beginning of the year. Even Russell saw objection to adopting it because 'Bright has shown his cards, and if we follow suit, we shall be considered his partners':[5] when this policy was adopted notwithstanding, Bright's approval probably inclined some Liberals who were willing to support a government bill so long as it looked reasonable to resist the bill they were offered.

At the same time, if franchise reform were coupled with redistribution of seats, involving disfranchisement or regrouping of small boroughs, it seemed certain at the beginning of the year that MP.s whose seats would disappear would oppose the bill. It was on Brand's advice, not Bright's, and in view of feeling in the House of

Commons, that redistribution was dropped from the original proposals in January.[1] At about the same time, though the government's proposals were not yet public, Earl Grey had guessed from
reading one of Russell's few public statements that a Seats bill would
not form part of them. He persuaded Bouverie (on the rebound from
the Goschen appointment) and Edward Ellice to ally themselves
with Elcho, Horsman and Lowe. Bouverie and Ellice voted with the
government against Grosvenor's motion, but lobbied actively in
favour of the view that a Seats bill was a necessary part of the scheme.
Though the government won the division on Grosvenor's motion
(by 5 votes out of 631) the Grey/Ellice/Bouverie/Adullamite combination was an extensive segment of backbench opinion. It was
decided, therefore, in March to promise a Seats bill in spite of the
dangers involved,[2] and at the end of April actually to introduce one
before the committee stage of the Franchise bill:[3] its provisions,[4]
though helpful to the Liberal party, made some members for small
boroughs vote against the grouping their seats would suffer if the
bill were passed.

Given Conservative tactics—of avoiding confrontation on the
principle of Reform, and, until late in the session, leaving the major
assault to the Cave—it is impossible to say that the course the
Cabinet adopted was a wrong one. Whatever course had been
adopted would have been open to obstruction: if redistribution had
been coupled with franchise reform at an earlier stage, MP.s whose
seats were vulnerable would have rebelled earlier. Grouping was
extremely unpopular with members for small boroughs. It was, in
some cases, not just a question of policy. On seeing one draft (by
Russell) of a possible Seats bill, the Liberal chief whip 'could not
honourably be party to the introduction of a bill which thus muti-
lated a borough [Lewes] at my own door which I have represented
for fourteen years'.[5] Lord Ernest Bruce had 'represented Marlborough during the whole of [his] parliamentary life' with only two
contested elections 'on both of which occasions I have been returned
at the head of the poll and Henry Baring...with me. No election has
cost me or him one shilling more than the legal expenses. We should
be ashamed to show ourselves in the streets of London if we deserted
our old friends and voted for a measure which could lead to their
disfranchisement.' Others undoubtedly felt, as Clarendon's agent
did, 'who is a Liberal and knows everybody in the county, [that the

bill] will lower the tone of the House of Commons, which is already too low; that no one wants reform and that people ask why they can't be let alone, instead of being forced to oppose a government that they would like to support'.[1]

In the major tactical task—of edging Gladstone away from the Whigs and dividing the Liberal party in the House—Conservatives succeeded abundantly, though they would not have succeeded so readily if Bright had not been so helpful, Lowe and Cranborne so powerful, Grosvenor and Elcho so incautious or Gladstone so unconciliatory. Whigs knew perfectly well that they should welcome Radical support for a Whig–Liberal bill: that was the pattern on which the party had come to be drawn. There was nevertheless, they thought, a danger that, where they wanted Gladstone to keep hold of Bright, Bright might merely capture Gladstone. It was not because he did not think Gladstone a 'dangerous man', but because responsibility might tame him, that Earl Grey had wanted Gladstone to succeed Palmerston as Prime Minister. In these circumstances Bright was the last person Sir George Grey, Somerset, Clarendon and their followers in the House of Commons wanted to hear warning Grosvenor that 'if he should succeed in dissevering the most intelligent of the Whig nobility from the great popular party...you may rely upon it that the popular party will win, and the nobles will go down'.[2]

To all these difficulties must be added the fact that Gladstone fought the parliamentary battle without adequate support; that, despite their lack of contact with the Cave, the Cabinet Whigs (especially Clarendon) made their dissent known widely; that, not for the first time, it was alleged that Russell was locked up in Pembroke Lodge where he listened to his family[3] and to no one else:[4] that he seemed, to one fair-minded Conservative, to be 'very much aged and...remarkably feeble...and twaddling'[5] and displayed, even on paper, a curious combination of petulance, optimism and self-congratulation. To his Whig enemies Gladstone, though 'full of genius', seemed to have 'not a particle of tact, temper, knowledge of the world [or] commonsense':[6] to be 'neither honest, moderate or gentleman enough...to be the whig minister':[7] to have an 'incorrigible...temper and impatience of contradiction': to be a 'wild man',[8] and, after the 'shuffling, bad taste and impertinence' of his attack on Grosvenor 'unfit...to lead an assembly of gentlemen'.[9]

He had 'the impulsiveness of woman without her instinct', showed signs of being 'in a chronic state of conversion'[1] and was thought of as 'that d—d Gladstone—Tory as he was, High Churchman as he is and revolutionist as he will be...more dangerous and not half so good a fellow as Bright'.[2] He struck a Conservative enemy (Cranborne) by the 'extravagant affectation of humbleness' he displayed 'during the intervals of the [parliamentary] conflict' and by the 'consideration [and] almost awe' with which he 'treated the radicals'.[3] He struck a Conservative admirer (Sir William Heathcote) 'by the apparent loss of power of his mind...[and inability] to grasp, or to decide, anything'.[4] He struck Clarendon as being a 'driver' rather than a 'leader',[5] and appeared, even to old friends and members of the government, to be unapproachable and uncompromising, and to be attempting to bully the House and appeal from the body of the Liberal party to the Radicals on their left.[6]

Gladstone and Russell, under pressure, developed an obstinacy which neutralized the effect even when they intended to conciliate. No doubt Gladstone was intuiting what he took to be the state of public feeling: he seems nevertheless to have been hurt personally by the effect his manner had in the House of Commons. Russell thought it '"a proud position" to be...at 75...no longer [the] leader of the...whig lords...but the head of the most advanced Liberals of the country':[7] none of the Cabinet Whigs shared his belief that 'I have done my duty' and 'after all...shall not mind [if the government is defeated] for it is fine weather to go out in'.[8] The decision to produce a Seats bill and the decision to introduce it before the Franchise bill went into committee were meant to meet reasonable doubts: when they were made—particularly when Russell and Gladstone explained the position to a meeting of the parliamentary party—they did so.[9] But, though all but the firmest Adullamites wavered in consequence, they gave Elcho the chance to press home the point that what was virtually a complete Reform bill could not be passed between May 7 and the end of the session in July or August.

In Gladstone's frame of mind, the danger was that, having avoided disaster on the first assault, he might press too hard on this one. 'If', Sir George Grey is reported to have said on accepting the Cabinet's decision to go on with the bills after the division of April 28, 'if he is cordial and accommodating', and accepts the fact that the bill cannot be passed 'by repeating or declaring...obstinate adherence to declarations that [it] shall be carried this session', then 'the position will be stronger than before', but 'if there is anything ...like a spoilt child in his tone...it will be much better that the government should resign at once'.[1] The immediate dissolution, which Russell and Gladstone began to threaten in face of resistance from the party, increased Whig fears that an election on the Reform issue would 'break...up the old Whig party for the benefit of a new Radical party headed by Bright'.[2] If the government went to the country, it would 'have to go...pledged to *this* bill': it 'would identify itself [in the public mind] with the party [i.e. Bright's] which certainly is earnest about advocating an extensive reform, but whose supposed influence on the government has been one great cause of our weakness'. This would 'break up the Liberal party, opposing by men of extreme views Whigs and Liberals, who on this question have deserted us, driving them permanently into the ranks of the opposition'.[3] When the Whigs first feared that they would be 'dished', it was not by Disraeli in 1867, but by Gladstone in these months in 1866 when Brand, Halifax, Granville, Clarendon and Sir George Grey exerted themselves to pull on the brake, Halifax and Sir George Grey in correspondence with Russell, Granville with Gladstone, all three with General Grey at Windsor. Halifax made it his business to persuade backbench Liberals and Delane, the editor of *The Times*, that, so long as the government was allowed to take the bills into committee, they would 'somehow not be proceeded with'.[4] Clarendon claimed in face of Russell's desire for dissolution in June that this was a matter for decision not just by the Cabinet, which he thought in any case would oppose it, but for 'my own conscience'.[5] Brand, as soon as it seemed possible that Russell would support dissolution, threatened to resign if he did so in fact.[6] The Queen had a consistent non-party desire to see the Reform question settled and thought that a general election would help Parliament to approach a settlement: one draft of one of the Queen's letters to Russell, discussing dissolution, was shown to Granville by General Grey, who on Granville's advice persuaded the Queen to tone it down.[7] When Russell and Gladstone proposed dissolution, Halifax, Granville and Sir George Grey all wrote to General Grey to let him know, so that the Queen might know also, that a majority of the Cabinet did not want dissolution; that steps

were being taken to enable the government to carry on, and implying that Russell's resignation ought not to be accepted.[1]

In these negotiations the Cabinet Whigs were alarmed beyond
measure, and with good reason. Russell's knowledge of backbench
feeling was small: after the second reading was passed, he had 'great
hopes of...being able to settle the Reform question by pressing,
pressing, pressing hard'.[2] The appeals made to Russell by the
Queen, who wanted the government to stay and a bill to pass but
who thought this could not happen unless the House was handled
carefully, were met by self-exculpation. 'The course of obstruction
so openly followed by the opposition', the Queen was told, 'makes
it...very difficult to yield to them on any point without incurring
just reproach on the part of the public at having abandoned...
principles on light and insufficient grounds': 'if by any premature
concession [Lord Russell] were to expose his own character and that
of Mr Gladstone to the loss of public confidence...those who
would most...reproach them with such a concession would be
their implacable and insidious enemies'.[3] Self-justification was
given a new lease of life by the desire which some Conservative
county members expressed to pass a bill by agreement with the
government and by the failure of Stanley's attempt, apparently on
Adullamite advice but without Adullamite votes, to win a snap
division without notice on June 7[4]—a procedural trick which both
strained relations between the Cave and the Conservative party and
so greatly irritated backbench Liberals that Derby thought it
'would enable [the government] to carry the bill'.[5]

As the strain grew and the possibility of victory increased, Gladstone seems to have become less conciliatory even than before,
generating the conviction, not only in public, that the passage of the
bills was a debt he owed the public—an attempt to redeem Parliament from the deviousness and dishonour with which the Reform
question, alone of the issues with which Parliament had dealt since
1832, had been treated. Though the Cabinet did not think he had
been conciliatory, he thought he had been conciliatory enough.
Though he had tried to argue the *principle* of Reform, the opposition
had tripped him up by arguing on the detail. 'All other battles [since
1832] ha[d] been honourably fought'; if Parliament was 'to keep
faith with the people' the Reform issue must be fought honourably
too.[6] The warning had been given, at the beginning of April, that

'a critical point in the history of the nation' had been reached and that 'it rests with the public to determine what shall be the issue'.[1] He could rely, he thought, on '300 men or thereabouts who support the Government and the bill conjointly', but the Liberal party in its present form was not an instrument of 'great public purposes'.[2] Hence his positive rigidity, after the adverse vote in June, when Halifax attempted to mediate between the Cabinet and the Liberal party in the House. Hence his advocacy of dissolution, despite Brand's warning that dissolution would be damaging, in the hope that 'a general election which should somewhat reduce the party would be of great use if it should also have the effect of purging it'.[3] Hence, finally, at Gladstone's insistence, the Government's resignation in an orgy of recrimination, Clarendon telling Russell that 'the construction of a party for Derby & Co....will be the inevitable consequence of what we are doing', that he could not bear that 'the last act of your official life should be to break up the party by which you have so long and so faithfully been supported', and that 'when the truth comes to be known, it will be fatal to Gladstone whose services and abilities would fit him to guide the destinies of his country if his arrogant ill-temper did not repel the sympathies upon which a leader must rest for support'.[4] Gladstone's first period as leader of the House of Commons ended as, strengthened by Bright, Forster and T. B. Potter, by backbench supporters and by demands, transmitted from Reform League meetings in the country, that the party should fight an immediate election 'for a great principle and a great cause',[5] he raised his flag to catch, control and intensify the wind, offering himself to reforming opinion and the public everywhere as *the* advocate of Reform, urging the London Working Men's Association 'to wait in patience the course of great events', warning it 'to be...on...guard against any illusory or reactionary measure simulating the...character of reform', and announcing 'in the hour of defeat...the presentiment of victory'.[6]

(iii)

With the resignation of the Cabinet, the Conservative party had achieved a major victory. The Liberal leaders had been edged on to a radical foot. The government had been defeated. Fusion seemed possible. Yet Derby's Cabinet, when it was completed in July, contained no important renegades. No broadbased coalition of

Conservatives, Adullamites and Whigs emerged to withstand 'Gladstone and democracy'.[1] Majority opinion in the House of Commons was suspicious of extensive measures of Reform, but the majority did not organize itself as a governing party. Parliament did not come, suddenly, to be dominated by a self-confident, reactionary majority-government, committed only to minor modification of the franchise of 1832: it was led for the next two years by a minority-government which, committed at the beginning to nothing, was not certain of a majority on any important question. When Russell resigned, there had, for nine months, been a general expectation that a link would be established. So extensive were these expectations that not only were Derby, Granville, Lansdowne, General Peel, Cranborne, Clarendon, the Dukes of Devonshire, Somerset and Cleveland and Lord Stanley canvassed as possible leaders but Carnarvon, walking with Hardy in the Park at the beginning of the crisis in June, even 'ha[d] a strange theory of putting the Duke of Cambridge at the head of a mixed government' which, as Hardy commented, was 'impossible in all senses'.[2] Fusion or coalition was in the air. Yet fusion did not occur.

The Queen at first would not allow Russell to resign: she refused to leave Balmoral on hearing that he wanted to. Though the government had been defeated on Dunkellin's motion, the bills, with Dunkellin's amendment included, had passed into committee without a division. The delay the Queen imposed—partly because she wanted to finish her holiday, partly in order to avoid a change at the foreign office during a European crisis—gave Halifax, Sir George Grey, Brand and Clarendon the opportunity to draft, and canvass, a form of parliamentary resolution to enable the government to stay in office, despite hostility to the government's bills. It is not certain what Halifax was trying to do: his intentions at this point are surrounded in impenetrable ambiguity. It is certain that he wanted to prevent a dissolution. He appeared to want to keep the government in office. There is a hint that he wanted a Liberal–Conservative coalition under his own leadership and a suspicion that he was urging on Gladstone and Russell a form of pacificatory resolution which he must have known they could not accept.[3] Attempts to keep the government in office failed—because Gladstone wanted them to, because Russell, at the last moment, decided that they should not succeed, and because neither would accept any alteration in the government's Reform programme. It was not until Russell made it plain that accommodation was impossible that the Queen, now at Windsor, invited Derby to form a government, and gave him an indefinite time in which to decide to do so. On June 28 twenty-two leading Conservatives met Derby at his house in St James's Square.[1] The meeting decided that Derby should try to form a coalition government (first with members of the outgoing government, afterwards with independent Liberals) but should form a Conservative one if the attempt failed. Derby then approached Clarendon, the Duke of Somerset, the Marquess of Clanricarde, Sir Robert Peel and Shaftesbury separately, and Grosvenor and Lansdowne in succession—as representatives of the Cave—with a view to offering posts to all of them and, in Clanricarde's case, his dependants, in the new government.

Clarendon, who may just possibly have hoped to be Prime Minister,[2] refused the Foreign Office: Somerset refused to call on Derby and declined office 'in much curter language'.[3] Shaftesbury, who was asked because he 'would be a representative of Palmerstonian sympathies and influences; powerful with the religious middle-class etc. etc.' and because his presence would refute the charge that the Conservative party was 'hostile to the working classes',[4] while admitting that he 'regarded [Russell's] ministry (except three or four of its members) with great distrust', refused when it became clear that no other major figure would be joining, adding that, if Derby failed, he should tell the Queen to send for Clarendon.[5] W. H. Gregory, one of Clanricarde's followers, refused the secretaryship to the Admiralty which he had refused from Russell in 1865. Clanricarde refused office himself, having already explained that Dunkellin, his son, would refuse too,[6] though Michael Morris, MP. for Galway City, 'a very moderate Liberal and Roman Catholic', became Irish Solicitor-General—the only Liberal accession Derby gained.[7] The name of Peel '[was] still a great [one] in the country, besides [which] in society there is an impression that the present representative of it always joins the winning side'.[8] Sir Robert Peel was offered the chancellorship of the Duchy of Lancaster without a seat in the Cabinet. He refused (it was what he had refused from Russell on being removed from the Irish secretaryship six months earlier) and was then offered the Board of Works in the Cabinet, which he refused also. Lansdowne and Grosvenor called in succession at Derby's house on June 29. When offered three posts, including one in the Cabinet, though 'most cordial', they asked for time to consult the rest of the Cave.

At the Cave meeting at 10 o'clock that night both Lowe and Horsman whom Derby, as he told Grosvenor a couple of hours before, 'was not at all anxious...should join his government,'[1] argued against doing so. Elcho was clear that, since his influence rested on the fact that he had renounced ambition for office, he could not in any circumstances consider taking it. Gregory, who had left and rejoined the Cave at least three times, had always been opposed to a Liberal–Conservative alliance. The Cave decided not to join. Grosvenor returned at midnight to tell Derby that the Cave agreed to give him 'independent support':[2] it seems more likely that 'the gentlemen present did not come to any resolution to give "an independent support" to your future government, although no feeling whatever of hostility was expressed'.[3]

During preliminary soundings four or five days earlier (before it was certain that the Cabinet would resign), Grosvenor had told Derby (through Grosvenor's uncle, Lord Wilton, who was a relative of Derby) that he 'could not guarantee...the support (in the strict sense) of the Cave', that 'a government under a Whig in the House of Lords, such as Lord Clarendon, would be most desirable on all accounts, with Stanley leader of the House of Commons', and that a meeting attended by himself and Lansdowne, and by Lowe, Elcho, Horsman, Gregory, Gilbert Heathcote and Anson—in other words by all the major Adullamites in the House of Commons—saw 'every reason for believing that a very strong government could be formed under these auspices'.[4] Disraeli had a letter from Elcho on June 21[5] suggesting that Derby should discuss with Grosvenor and Lansdowne the possibility of serving under a Whig Prime Minister (Clarendon). It is not certain that Derby saw this letter, but it is certain that Elcho called on him without invitation on the 25th and told him the same thing, adding that Granville also was a possible Prime Minister.[6] Derby, however, seems not to have raised this possibility when Grosvenor and Lansdowne visited him on the 29th: on seeing Grosvenor's letter to Lord Wilton, Disraeli's comment was that 'the terms intimated by Lord Grosvenor, in his letter to Lord Wilton, are not consistent with the honour of the Conservative

party, and are framed in ignorance and misconception of its elements and character',[1] thus leaving the impression, as Buckle
following Disraeli claimed, that the sole reason why a coalition was
not constructed was that the Adullamites were demanding so 'pre-
posterous' a 'subordination' of the Conservative party that 'ready
as Disraeli might be to efface himself, neither he nor Derby could
possibly accept it'.[2]

The Adullamites were playing for high stakes. Like the Peelites
before them, but with much less reason, they seem to have supposed
that they could provide the leaven in every lump and the navigation
for every voyage. To Elcho the Cave was a body of 'determined men
acting...unselfishly and patriotically in each House...and independently of party' which would 'keep things straight' by 'look-
[ing] with comparative indifference on ministerial crises and
changes', which would ensure that 'whoever is in power, whether
Cons: or Libs: must follow pretty much the same line', and which
was obliged, in the situation *it* had created by 'shunting' Gladstone
when he 'tried to leave the line', to retain its freedom so as to 'hold
...the balance between Whigs: Rads: and Tories so long at least as
great constitutional questions remain unsettled'.[3] Its members had
expected to exercise decisive influence in the crisis, and had been
worried by the fact that Derby had done nothing to consult them
between June 18 and 28.[4] It is clear (as Russell suggested before
the crisis occurred)[5] that they hoped to produce a situation in
which, if Derby failed to form a government, one of them, or
Clarendon or Granville, would be asked to do so instead: there may,
in addition, have been a more than ordinary element of misunderstanding.

Disraeli's version of the misunderstanding was that Elcho had
been the innocent instrument of a 'long-matured intrigue' in which
Halifax's had been the guiding hand.[6] Since he resigned in January, Halifax had been trying to stop Gladstone and the Cave destroying the Liberal party between them. It is possible that he wanted at
this time to replace Russell by a central Whig (himself?): it is more
likely that he wanted what he said he wanted—to keep the Russell
government in office. So far from being the instigator of a 'long-
matured intrigue', Halifax was almost certainly conducting a rescue
operation which the Liberal conflict had made necessary. If there
was a 'long-matured intrigue', it is at least as likely that it was a

Conservative one—that the prospect of fusion under Whig auspices had been held out in the preceding months by Earle or by other intermediaries as a means of inducing co-operation between the Cave and the Conservative party. At the start of the session Elcho was assuming that 'if the government are beaten, which is believed to be a certainty, Lord Derby is to be sent for and he is to hand over the government to Stanley who will form it on a moderate basis—Lowe and yourself etc'.[1] In mid-May, after talking to Disraeli, he claimed that 'all minor considerations [are] merged in resisting the one great tyrannical democratic majority which...would flow from the passing of this bill', that 'all idea of office [on the part of Derby and Disraeli] is abandoned' and that 'they are ready to aid in any way...in forming and supporting a moderate Liberal government'.[2] Rightly or wrongly (and, so far as the first half of his sentence is concerned, consistently with Derby's language at the time), Elcho had received the impression, as he told Earle in June, 'that Lord Derby from the beginning of the session [had] intended to decline office for himself and to advise his friends to serve under some Whig statesman'.[3] It cannot be said certainly that fusion on these terms was held out as an inducement to the Cave. The initiative in opposition came from Elcho, Horsman and Lowe, not from the Conservative party: at the beginning they needed no inducement. At the same time, the Conservative leaders were not sure how persistent Adullamite opposition would be: whether it was necessary or not, Disraeli may have thought inducement desirable. Though Earle denied this[4] (and there is no certain evidence either way) it is by no means impossible that some hint, or inducement, was held out in the course of the session.

In addition there is reason to suppose that Lowe and Horsman expected office in whatever government was formed, and were looking forward with high ambitions to the future. Lowe's object from the start of the session had been to bring down the Russell/Gladstone government, partly because of its commitments on Reform, partly because he reciprocated Russell's hostility;[5] perhaps, also, in the earlier months of 1866, while Gladstone was moving cautiously, from the expectation that, if Russell fell, Gladstone himself would form a government in which 'talent and eloquence as apart from connection...would predominate'.[6] Horsman was thought of as a man who wanted office as much as he was unsuited to it:[7] he was also a genuinely moderate Whig who wished to preserve Whig power inside the Liberal party. This meant rescuing the party from Gladstone and Bright and destroying Gladstone as Liberal leader. A coalition led by Clarendon with a strong Adullamite infusion might have been acceptable to Horsman, but a Conservative-dominated coalition was not. Alone of the Adullamites, Horsman felt that Derby had tricked them by refusing to make way for a Whig: he, more clearly than anyone else, had seen from the start that Gladstone had to be stopped, and that if he was not stopped, his leadership of the Liberal party might be the making of Disraeli, whose policy had for long been 'the extinction of the moderates', who had an 'understanding with Bright' about getting rid of them from both parties, and who believed that 'a democratic programme [in the Liberal party] will drive all the moderates into the Tory ranks... ensur[ing] the Tories the same reign as the unpopularity of Fox and Sheridan gave them after the French revolution'.[1]

A Clarendon, Granville or Stanley coalition would have suited Lowe because that would alter the character of the Conservative party, but his rational Radicalism gave him little expectation in a Derbyite party otherwise. His identification as the pedlar of that 'essentially selfish breeches-pocket morality which in every country more or less accompanies *exclusive* middle-class legislation'[2] struck few notes: the impression he left of 'looking to a Ministry of the Future which should stand on a middle-class basis, on principles of pure reason and in an attitude very unfriendly to the church',[3] would disqualify him. Despite his command of the House, Lowe's language compromised his own position as much as Bright's had compromised the government's. His onslaught on the working class provoked in the Queen the reaction that 'they are the best people in the country':[4] it stimulated similar reactions amongst Conservatives. Northcote and Carnarvon (both friends of Lowe) agreed in thinking that, in negotiating with the Adullamites, 'the great point to gain would be to get some of the great Whig families', that 'it is better to approach the third party through them than them through the third party', and that 'if they like to propose Lowe for our colleague, [we might] take him as their [i.e. the Whigs'] nominee'.[5] It is just possible that Lowe hoped to succeed Gladstone as Russell's heir-apparent;[6] it is likely that he saw himself as a 'blot' in Conservative 'arrangements'.[7] A Granville or Clarendon government, or a government in which Granville was a prominent figure, despite Granville's irritation at Lowe's conduct between March and June, would, in any case, have suited him better.[1]

If high stakes were being played for by the Adullamites, high stakes were being played for on the Conservative side as well. In particular, one of the stakes involved was Disraeli's future. Derby and Disraeli both knew that if a coalition were formed it would be at their expense. Derby was told this by Jolliffe, the Conservative ex-chief whip, in August 1865:[2] Derby and Disraeli assumed it when they discussed the political future later that month. Derby made it clear to Malmesbury in April 1866: Disraeli accepted it as a fact in discussion with Northcote on a number of occasions in March. Nor was this feeling private to the two leaders. In June General Grey thought one of the advantages in 'Lord Clarendon continuing at the Foreign Office [if a coalition were formed] would [be] getting rid of Mr Disraeli who could not remain after his personal attack upon him—and this would be popular with the bulk of the Conservative party'.[3] Cranborne and Carnarvon thought that Derby himself might be replaced. Sir Hugh Cairns, at the beginning of March, thought 'a *party* might be formed under the Duke of Somerset with General Peel to lead the Commons, [with] Lord Derby stand[ing] aloof, as he would probably not serve under anyone... [with] Disraeli either stand[ing] aloof or...tak[ing] some office like the Duchy of Lancaster, *not* the Foreign Office',[4] and probably including Cardwell and Roundell Palmer.[5] Sir Rainald Knightley, whom the Marquess of Bath claimed as a supporter of fusion,[6] gave as his reason for refusing the Foreign Under-Secretaryship in July the fact that 'with every feeling of respect towards yourself and Lord Stanley...I have not sufficient confidence in Mr Disraeli to justify my accepting office in any administration of which he is the leader in the House of Commons'.[7]

Both leaders knew that, apart from General Peel, the only Conservative acceptable as coalition Prime Minister would be Derby's son, Lord Stanley. Stanley's relations with Clarendon, Halifax and perhaps Lowe were close, his attitude on Church questions undogmatic. His view of the Reform question was flexible, but capable of being as conservative as the Whigs': it embraced the belief that a settlement could, if necessary, be put off for ten years. He was not, in any sense, however, a Derbyite. Unlike Derby he had neither a

cynical nor a reactionary past. His image was of an admirer of Mill
and advocate of progress; but of safe progress under aristocratic
guidance towards the higher objects of the intellectual reformer—
religious equality, competitive examinations, the establishment of
public libraries and mechanics' institutes, and the abolition of the
purchase of Army commissions.[1] Earle was not the only person to
whom it seemed, on Palmerston's death, that, if the Conservative
party was searching for 'a new platform which we can only receive
from a new leader', Stanley should 'declare that, although there are
many things to be done in many departments of administration, a
minister in earnest to do them would find all the support he requires
from a parliament elected by the present constituencies'. 'Stanley's
name', he wrote, 'is the only one that can inspire faith in such
language...he alone can manage the finality which the country
desires in the way of the franchise with the progress and movement it expects in other directions'.[2]

His liberal opinions on Church matters weakened Stanley in the
Conservative party, but General Peel (the Prime Minister's brother)
who was in some respects a keeper of the Tory conscience, was willing at the meeting in Derby's house on June 28[3] to serve under 'my
young friend here' [i.e. Stanley] if 'our old Commander...under
whom I hope we shall fight...gives up'.[4] Roundell Palmer
records the view that Lowe would have served under Stanley:[5]
Shaftesbury, riding in the Park before breakfast one morning after
he had refused to join, 'seemed to regret that Lord Derby had not
suggested his son, Lord Stanley, as one whom the Liberals might
have served under', though 'I told him he was mistaken and that his
motion the other day (which he admitted was a mistake) would alone
prevent it'.[6] Derby was advised by Malmesbury, who had been
given the hint by Mrs Lowe, 'to tell the Queen what was said about
Lord Stanley being supported by a section of the Moderates [and
that] forty Adullamites would join him, whilst only ten would join
Derby'.[7] The Whig members of a Stanley coalition would have
been hostile to Disraeli, but Disraeli would probably have had to
join it, if Stanley had been allowed to have him in a reasonable office.
It may well have been the case, as Stanley and Disraeli seem to have
thought, that Stanley would have been an inadequate leader of the
House of Commons and an even more inadequate Prime Minister,
though the evidence about Stanley's opinion of his own abilities

113

comes through Disraeli: nevertheless, he commanded a wider measure of support outside the Conservative party at this time than did either of its actual leaders. There is, despite 'all his heresies'[1] and perhaps because of them, no doubt of the breadth of Stanley's appeal.

Derby, however, gave Stanley no more opportunity than he had given Clarendon and Granville—perhaps because he thought the Conservative party would not follow him,[2] perhaps because he was by now so greatly alarmed both by the Reform bill he had just escaped 'which would simply be the extinction of the Conservative party'[3] and by Stanley's attitude to the Irish Church that he would not trust Stanley to lead a government of resistance; perhaps because, although Derby, whose relations with Stanley were cool, might have been 'disposed to sacrifice himself for the advantage of his country, he was much more likely to do [so] for [that] than for the sake of his son'.[4] He allowed the Queen to press Clarendon to join the Cabinet, but '"*could* not throw Mr Disraeli over in order to get [him]"'.[5] He did not mention coalition except under his own leadership when he talked to Grosvenor and Lansdowne: he discouraged the Queen from pressing them to change their minds when they refused to join on the terms he was offering.[6] Although, in other words, he may, as both of them thought, quite genuinely have wanted to form an expanded government, Horsman was probably right in thinking that 'he knew beforehand that his proposal to Liberal members of the two Houses to serve under Mr D'Israeli could not for a moment be entertained'.[7]

Once the question is put in this way, Disraeli's conduct presents problems. If Disraeli knew that fusion could not take place, then his assertion that fusion was possible takes on a peculiar colour. At the meeting in Derby's house on June 28, the Marquess of Bath was the only person who urged Derby to face the fact that he could not form a coalition himself. 'A pure Derbyite government', he said, 'could not stand;...the Whigs would reorganize themselves in opposition, turn us out and come back under Gladstone and Bright. He urged Lord Derby to hand over the task...to Stanley who would, he thought, unite the Whigs with us.'[8] Disraeli, who had been warned by the chief whip to expect this intervention,[9] emphasized that he, like the rest of the party, was willing to accept sacrifices, adding that 'he thought the chances of an alliance more promising than did Lord Bath'.[10] Three days earlier, when Grosvenor's letter to Wilton had shown him the scope of the Adullamite demands, he had claimed, in writing to Derby, that 'what is counted on and intended...is that you should refuse [to be Prime Minister]: that a member of the late government should then be sent for [like Granville or Clarendon],' and that 'there is only one course with this question, to kiss hands: and...in four and twenty hours or so, Lansdowne, Granville (if you want him), Clanricarde...will be at your feet'.[1]

On at least two occasions, in other words, at tactical moments Disraeli gave the impression of believing in the possibility of fusion. Yet Northcote, calling on him on June 29, before Derby had seen Lansdowne or knew Clarendon's answer, 'discuss[ed] the question of fusion in which [Disraeli] does not himself believe'. He was told that Disraeli 'did not see how Lord Clarendon could in honour accept'; that 'we should gain little by addressing ourselves to the Adullamites [for this reason, among others, that] Lowe's appointment would be rather too much of a challenge to the Reform party and would look like the decided adoption of an anti-reform policy, while after all we perhaps may be the men to settle the question;' and that, in any case, 'we were relieved of our difficulty by the forwardness of this party to announce that they should not take office under us'.[2] Disraeli had good reason for talking in this way to Northcote, who was reserving his position in case of coalition,[3] but it seems certain that, although, as Disraeli claimed, 'all these interviews and offers do good',[4] neither Derby nor Disraeli expected very much from them.[5] Derby seems to have gone through the motions reluctantly, as a duty he owed the party he led and the dangers that loomed: once Disraeli's actions in this week are understood, it becomes clear that, if he wanted coalition at all, he wanted it with such isolated figures as Clanricarde, Gregory, Peel and Shaftesbury but wished nevertheless to seem to want more. There were party reasons why, if the Conservative party were to take part in government, the government should have a more decisive image than a coalition might produce. This was a possible view to take: some members of the party took it. Disraeli at large, however, adopted the opposite view, which raises the questions: why, throughout the session, had he been the advocate of fusion? why, at the point of decision, did he not want it? why, if he did not want it, did he say that he did?

In the first place, the success of Conservative policy had produced a situation which was dangerous both to Disraeli personally and to the Conservative party as a political instrument. 'Fusion' had served a destructive purpose in the Liberal party: it must not be allowed to destroy the Conservative party. The danger was that, if Derby failed, or refused, to form a government 'a member of the late government should then be sent for, and...an application...made to a section of [the Conservative party] to join...; which application', though it might not include Disraeli, 'will be successful, for all will be broken up'.[1] The danger to Disraeli was that, if a major Whig/Liberal invasion of a new government occurred, the coalition it produced would have little room for him. Such a government might have a profusion of political talent: it might become what the Conservative party had never been since the fall of Peel—the party of 'the official corps'.[1] But Whig and Adullamite hostility might put an end to Disraeli's influence, and to his political career. Disraeli, in other words, through his own parliamentary success, had produced a situation in which he had to fight for parliamentary survival.

But, it may be said, some Conservatives did not want coalition: why did Disraeli not put himself at their head? First, if this sort of opinion existed in the Conservative party as a whole, opinion among its leaders (certainly at the meeting on June 28) was almost unanimously the other way. Secondly, if Disraeli thought fusion impossible, there was no need to protest against it: it would be better to be applauded, as he was at the meeting, for showing willingness to sacrifice himself.[2] One of the arguments in favour of fusion was that it would put control of the Reform question into the right hands: this was an argument that had to be handled respectfully. Thirdly, although some of the fusionists (e.g. Cranborne) at this time were supporters of Disraeli, others (e.g. Bath and Knightley) hated him even more than the Whigs did. Finally, although Derby was reconciled to forming a minority-government if he had to, and had probably become more willing as Gladstone had become more 'democratic', he had no positive desire to return to office without a majority, had frequently said he would not do so after his experience in 1858, and would probably have to be kept up to the mark if he was to persevere at the point of decision. He would probably try to form a Conservative government if fusion failed, but it was not certain that he would be able to do even that.[1] Whether or not Disraeli thought fusion possible, it may well have seemed necessary to arouse Derby's enthusiasm for the task of government in general by encouraging him to think an enlarged government possible in particular. Disraeli had found it difficult in the months before to convince Derby that it was worth taking office but, if Derby declined office altogether, Clarendon, Granville or some other central figure would attempt a more dangerous fusion than any Derby could achieve. Earle's warning to Disraeli that 'all our fellows have got hold of this absurd Granville notion, so you must not let Lord Derby out of your sight'[2] reveals the danger. Hardy's judgement that 'I do not see my way to a pure Derby government however one might desire it' shows that the negative aspect of Earle's view, in relation to one potential Conservative minister, was not extravagant: Cairns' assertion that 'nothing but a new lead [by Lansdowne] to a moderate party can answer' reflects the same feeling in another.[3]

Fusion might have been dangerous to Disraeli even under Derby's leadership,[4] but the situation in which Derby failed to form a government might, given the desire for fusion which some Conservatives felt, 'make it much easier for Lord Granville or whoever[5] Your Majesty might entrust with the task'.[6] If the Conservative party split over the question, the danger would be acute. Disraeli's position in the Conservative party depended on his manifest superiority in the House of Commons, but his position in English politics depended on the fact that he was manager, and leader, of the Conservative party there. Whether or not Disraeli was necessary to Derby, Derby and the existing Conservative party were essential to Disraeli. Despite Cranborne's desire to get rid of Derby while keeping Disraeli,[7] it was far from certain that Disraeli would have succeeded if Derby had died at this time. Therefore, we are suggesting, Disraeli went through the motions of seeming to want fusion, of offering to stand down in order to make fusion possible, and of desiring to make the Conservative party an enlarged instrument of government in which, however, his role would be a minor one.

Disraeli's conduct did not follow a fixed pattern. Nor, though he saw the advantage to be gained if a Conservative government could settle the Reform question, is it likely that his desire to prevent reconstruction arose from a coherent decision to prevent the Conservative party becoming a reactionary party. There is every reason to suppose that his preoccupations at *this* time were personal, no reason to suppose that he would have objected to forming an anti-revolutionary or, indeed, any other coalition if that had been convenient. Disraeli's desires were not the only factors which determined events: reconstruction might still not have occurred if Disraeli had wanted it, and been willing to stand down in order to achieve it. Derby was not enthusiastic: Whig Erastianism would have received no welcome. The Whigs were unwilling to destroy their own party unless they could dominate something more congenial. Conservatives were unwilling to be dominated. Leading Conservatives had been in opposition for eight years: the older ones had been in opposition for most of their political lives. In spite of the brave face which was put upon the need for sacrifice if fusion was to be achieved, the Conservative party was indeed 'numerous [and hungry'.[1] Nevertheless, pressure from Derby or Disraeli at crucial moments to persuade the party to offer coalition in conjunction with a change of leadership might well have brought a favourable response, and we must conclude that, although Disraeli and perhaps Derby may, speaking comprehensively, be said, in Disraeli's words, to have 'wanted the appearance of a great and organised adhesion',[2] it is much more reasonable to suggest that what they wanted, speaking precisely, was the 'appearance' rather than the 'adhesion'.

III

THE CORNERING OF THE
CONSERVATIVE PARTY

'The late government thought they had a sufficient majority, and they
found their mistake. We know we have not...'
> Derby to Pakington, December 4 1866. Derby MSS Box 193/1

'...a measure of Reform is indispensable. But you can, I am sure, construct
one, extensive, safe and satisfactory.'
> Shaftesbury to Derby, October 19 1866. Derby MSS Box 114

'We may have to meet a tortuous bill by a tortuous motion.'
> Gladstone to Brand, October 30 1866. Brand MSS

Out of the political crisis which lasted from June 19 when Russell
offered his resignation until July 3 when Derby finally accepted
office, neither a reconstructed Whig nor an enlarged Conservative
party had emerged. Nevertheless, the four central contenders for
political power—Disraeli and Derby, Gladstone, the Cabinet
Whigs and the Cave—had all learnt much from the events through
which they had passed in the nine months since Palmerston
died.

Gladstone had learnt that he could not ride roughshod over all
feeling in the Liberal party in the House of Commons. He had come
to understand that, if the Liberal party was to be led, it had to some
extent to be followed, and that in its present condition it could be
neither followed nor led on the Reform question. At the same time,
Gladstone had no desire to capitulate to either of its opposing factions. He knew, or thought, he could rely on 300 or so of the Liberals
behind him who were neither Whig nor Radical, and that they would
follow him so long as he seemed neither Radical nor Whig. He knew
that some of the non-Cabinet Whigs and the Cave wished to stop
him succeeding Russell, and that the sense of the party was not
Whig. He knew also that it was not Radical in the sense in which
Bright was, and that, although he had committed himself to some
Radical positions, he had to take pains to avoid *identification* with
Bright.

Gladstone's position in the Liberal party, like Disraeli's in the Conservative party, depended on his outstanding merits in the House of Commons—on the impression he left of energy, eloquence intelligence and power. Nor did the fact that he was disliked by many Whigs (particularly by disappointed ones) diminish the strength of his support elsewhere. Although Grosvenor and Earl Grey thought they had seen too many passes sold already, others were more cautious. Halifax, Granville and their colleagues clung to the belief that the Liberal party was a coalition in which it was idle to 'threaten and openly combine against the Radicals'. 'Without applauding their violent doctrines', they wanted to continue the Whig policy of 'coaxing them and, if possible, working with them'. As Elcho was told by Earl Spencer, a young man of thirty-one with a great name, no ministerial experience and much under Granville's influence, on being offered and, on Granville's advice, refusing the leadership of the Cave in early 1867: '[although]...myself a Constitutional Liberal opposed to the violent doctrines which Bright and his organs...propound...when agitating for Reform...I do not believe that [these doctrines] imperil the Constitution' or are likely to 'embarrass the head and body of the Liberal party'. The Liberal leaders, he added, 'including Gladstone, are Constitutional Liberals'. To detach 'a separate party' from them, as Elcho was proposing, would 'weaken the Governing Power of the Liberals'. Although

every Liberal since Charles, Lord Grey's time...had relied for carrying its great measures to some extent on the Radical section of the party, [he could] call to mind no measure dangerous to the Constitution [which had been carried] by a Liberal Government...Until [the present leaders] distinctly show by their acts that they are not [Constitutional Liberals], I am prepared to support them.[1]

In these conditions the ambiguity of Gladstone's position ensured that, while Radicals looked to him because he seemed to be speaking their language and to be appealing to popular opinion outside the House, non-Radical Liberals, and many Whigs, had not lost the habit of looking to him because they knew, from close personal acquaintance, that, while his language in many respects appeared Radical, he was 'not...at heart an advanced Liberal' and could be relied on both to carry, and to curb, the Radicalism which many Whigs feared, and some detested.

Gladstone, however, was not leader of the Liberal party, and it was not certain that he was going to be. Russell was blamed as much as Gladstone for the destruction of Palmerston's majority, but Russell had no wish to be removed. In mid-1866 Russell was not less militant, and not less anxious than before to be in touch with the more Radical members of his Cabinet.[1] He expected more certainly than anyone else in the Liberal party that Disraeli would force an election in early 1867. He decided to anticipate it both by improving party organization[2] and by devising a formula which, while accommodating Adullamites who would, would exclude those who would not, support the Russell/Gladstone axis.[3] In defining his own position in relation both to Bright and to the prospect of a Conservative bill, he was clear that he was opposed to household suffrage and wanted nothing more extensive than a £5 rating suffrage which he took to be equivalent to the 1866 bill's £7 rental.[4] He declined invitations to Reform dinners. Before he left England for the winter, he settled down to the expectation that the government would find it impossible successfully to carry through any of the courses that were open to it.[5] There is no evidence of an extension of Russell's range of acquaintance in these months. From November until the beginning of the session he was not in England at all. His unpredictability on his return underlined his inadequacy as leader.[6] His health seemed to exclude him for the future.[7] Nevertheless, he was in formal control of the party, and clearly intended to remain so.[8]

Even if Russell were removed, Gladstone's position was by no means impregnable. Gladstone was not a Whig: his claim depended on success in keeping the coalition together while solving difficult problems. In the previous session, he had destroyed the coalition and solved nothing.[9] In October 1866 when Derby's government seemed likely to break up under the strain of producing a bill, Brand expected that 'Granville will be the next Prime Minister';[10] Granville himself, while staying with Knatchbull-Hugessen and fishing, perhaps, for compliments, explained that 'he liked [Sir George Grey] so much and thought so highly of him that there was hardly any office he would not accept under him if [Grey] were forming a government, and...that his doing so would be of service'.[11] Gladstone—at least by those who wanted to think it—was thought to be in an 'excited state of mind'[12] and in danger of complete mental breakdown.[13] His holiday in Italy from October to January, though it demoralized some of his supporters, was a way of relieving himself of the difficulty of preferring one faction to another. The fact, of which he was conscious, both before Palmerston's death and after, that some Liberals wanted him to succeed instead of Russell, the clarity with which he saw that any attempt to put himself forward for leadership in a party to which he came 'an outcast [with] none of the claims [Earl Russell] possesses'[1] would 'seal [his] doom in taking it'[2] and the speed with which he offered himself to Russell on Palmerston's death[3] suggest acute uncertainty about his position. The erratic firmness with which he had led the Commons in 1866, the seriousness of the Liberal split he found on his return in 1867 and the difficulties Derby was having with the Cabinet all provided need, or opportunity, for reconciliation.

Nor were the lessons of 1866 lost on the other Liberal leaders. To Brand, Russell, Halifax, Clarendon and Sir George Grey who supplied the central management, it seemed that the Liberal party had almost been destroyed, could not for the present act as a governing party, and, in spite of having 'a majority of near seventy upon every question *but* reform and a majority of some twenty or thirty upon *that*, except upon one or two points of detail',[4] would be foolish to turn out the government so long as there was a chance 'in spite of what you say', that the Reform question 'will break up the Tory party'.[5] The situation was dangerous, but, as the Liberal leaders viewed the scene in late 1866, there were compensations for the damage for which Gladstone and Russell had been responsible. If Gladstone and Russell had made the Liberal party look foolish in the previous session, their conduct had generated a movement of public expectation which nobody could ignore. This did not mean that a Conservative Reform bill would be a radical one or that public agitation would do the Liberal party undiluted good.[6] But any government would find a decision difficult to make. No government which refused to introduce a bill could survive in the House of Commons: if the Cabinet decided that no bill was necessary, then, since hardly any politician outside the Conservative party except Lowe would support it, the government would be turned out. Derby knew this as well as anybody else: all the Liberal party had to do was to wait until a definite Conservative commitment produced a definite Conservative split. Though Clarendon, Russell, Brand, Sir George Grey and even Gladstone would have been willing at various times to give 'a reasonable bill' a chance if it was Derby who proposed it, they believed that it was Disraeli not Derby who was 'master of the situation'.[1] They did not believe that the government could carry a 'good bill without offending all those of their party who ha[d] any principles'. A firm proposal—if firm proposal there was to be— would be 'narrow', 'tortuous' and 'probably tricky after the fashion of Disraeli'. They expected a 'dodge' in the distribution of seats, an attempt to remove 'all towns...out of the counties [and] an increase in the representation of purely agricultural counties at the expense of towns'. Seeing the Cabinet situation for what it was, they expected Disraeli to avoid specific commitment until the latest moment possible.[2]

In late 1866, in short, though they thought they were losing control of the working classes and were in process of being alienated from respectable opinion as well, the Liberal leaders were relieved that they no longer had to govern. They hoped that, so long as Gladstone was restrained, and given normal good luck, they would be able in the next session to pay back Derby and Disraeli for their success in the previous one: if they offered a limited, mean, dishonest bill—the only sort of bill they thought acceptable to Conservatives —by moulding it into reasonable shape; or, if the government declined all action, by forcing it to resign in order themselves to return to office in a situation of strength.[3] They more or less declined all political activity in the winter of 1866, therefore, adopting a 'policy' of 'reticence' and 'forbearance towards the government, waiting to see what they will do',[4] in the expectation that the movement of public feeling would make it difficult for the Conservative party to operate within the limits suggested by its public commitments.

Brand, Halifax and Clarendon were conscious of the danger Bright presented to the Liberal party. They had lost one by-election because a wavering Whig had withdrawn support.[5] They suspected that the Liberal party was 'more conservative...than a year ago'. They knew that some of their supporters believed Bright to be doing 'much harm to the cause of practicable reform' by making the working classes so determined for 'revenge' on Lowe and the Cave that 'the middle and upper classes [were] for leaving things alone'.[6] They knew that 'Bright's speeches, particularly about Irish land, were frightening all Whiggish Liberals into absolute Tories',[7]

and that 'in Scotland...Whig country gentlemen...[were]...
sadly afraid of Bright and democracy, and bitter against Gladstone
and becoming very Conservative'.[1] They agreed with Sir George
Grey that it 'would be the greatest folly for us to connect ourselves
with the cry for manhood suffrage and the ballot'.[2] But, while Sir
George Grey and Argyll, for example, saw only that Bright 'had
destroyed the prospect of union among the Liberal party', making
it clear that 'we should have difficulty in dealing with the Bright
party if we were in again', and 'greatly increas[ing] the difficulty of
substituting any other government than the present one, which
I have no doubt feels greatly obliged to him',[3] the others at first
saw also that although 'Bright's language [had] been indiscreet...
he [had] done good service' in keeping up the pressure on the
government by 'showing that the working classes are not indifferent to the subject of reform'.[4] Gladstone 'd[id] not like what
[he saw] of Bright's speeches'; he thought the public agitation was
separating Bright from the Liberal party. Nevertheless, it was clear-
ing the way. Gladstone wanted to avoid the appearance of wilful
obstructiveness. He was not sure how he would deal with a plausible
trick: he needed a climate which no Conservative government could
satisfy. He drew the conclusion that, though the Liberal party need
not commit itself to any particular measure of reform, Disraeli's
difficulties could usefully be increased by encouraging Liberal
journalists to warn the public against the possibility of a 'bad bill',
and to assure it that 'a bill from [the government] to be accepted by
the people must be larger and not smaller, than would have been, or
even would be, accepted from us'.[5]

The continental holidays of Gladstone, Russell, Argyll, Cardwell
and Sir George Grey, though normal necessities to ministers who
had been in office for seven years at a stretch, saved Gladstone the
embarrassment of publicly criticizing, or failing to criticize, Bright
for the violence of his public language.[6] Uncertainty about Gladstone's ability to deal with Bright made Brand glad to see him go at
the same time as he tried to keep back Sir George Grey 'to [whom] a
large section of the House of Commons will be looking for sensible,
crucial and sound advice' and 'from [whom] a few words about the
meetings and the Parks [had] put the party right with the House of
Commons and with the Queen and with the country'.[7] Although
Brand and Russell, no less than Gladstone, wanted to avoid com-

mitting themselves about Bright in public, commitment could not be delayed indefinitely. Brand himself refused to attend a Reform Union banquet in Manchester,[1] but had to give advice to Liberal MP.s who asked for it when they in turn received invitations to similar meetings also. The advice (given in a letter to *The Times*[2]) at first reflected the belief established by Russell, Gladstone and Brand at a meeting at Woburn in September[3] that, though the public agitation would cause inconvenience to the Liberal party, it would cause greater inconvenience to Derby. In the early autumn, Brand and Halifax thought they could manage Bright. They thought they could do this, not by dealing with him direct, but by encouraging judicious Radicals like Stansfeld, MP. for Halifax, Halifax's protegé and from late 1866 Brand's assistant on electoral questions, to speak at Reform banquets where 'he will endeavour to take the rough edge off anything that Bright may have said in the direction of...physical force'.[4]

On the other hand, Liberal reactions to the size and energy of the agitation and the determined and articulate warnings of violence which Bright offered in the course of his speeches went far beyond anything Brand had anticipated. Instead of embarrassing Derby, they had the opposite effect. Instead of driving Derby into action he could not sustain, they made 'the country' so 'Conservative' that Brand thought a general election would destroy the Liberal majority if Derby were given an excuse for having one. It was not just that the electorate felt this way, or that middle-class Liberals were as tired as the Whigs of Bright, but that hostility between the two chief Liberal groups had become so intense that it was impossible to have an eve-of-session dinner to include such diverse personalities as 'Grosvenor, Bright and Lowe'.[5] This did not mean that the government could ignore the Reform question and survive. But if the Cabinet was turned out or broke up, the moral advantage a Liberal government would gain from Conservative failure would not necessarily outweigh the difficulty it would have in governing or fighting an election[6] before the party was reunited. The party would not be reunited by the sort of government that had left office in June.[7] If the government took steps of its own, any counter-step from the Liberal leaders which left the impression of 'doing anything which would impede a settlement of the question of reform or be represented as betraying an impatience for office'[8] would give

Derby the chance to have, and win, an election on the cry 'let us have a moderate measure from Lord Derby rather than a wild one from Bright'.[1] It was in this situation that Brand asked Gladstone to make a point of being in London for the beginning of the new session.[2] It was to a situation in which 'Gladstone [did] not possess the confidence of the Whig party', in which 'the moderate section [of the Liberal party] *preferr[ed] Lord Derby and a reasonable Conservative policy* to one whose policy [was] guided by Gladstone and Bright', in which Whigs and Liberals alike had been depressed by the absence of guidance from Russell[3] and which, therefore, from a personal as well as a party point of view called for careful handling that Gladstone arrived 'well and exceedingly keen'[4] on January 30.

The uncertainty of the situation was not much altered by the Queen's speech, which showed that the government intended to proceed with Reform, though this was the first time the opposition knew for certain; by Disraeli's introduction of the resolutions on February 11; or by his intention, announced on February 14, to sketch on February 25 the form of bill the resolutions would commit the government to propose if they were accepted. It was not much altered because the Liberal leaders had a 'very strong impression that [the Cabinet] [were] not agreed'[5] or were even 'quarrelling among themselves' and had adopted resolutions for this reason',[6] and because, although they could see why, from his own standpoint, 'the Jew is on the whole right not to make premature disclosures, particularly as, [since] they...have settled nothing... he has nothing to disclose',[7] there was a reasonable chance that Disraeli would fail to carry a united Cabinet to the point of commitment to a bill.[8] Disraeli's announcement of February 14 took the wind out of their sails by establishing that the resolutions were a prelude to legislation. It made Gladstone, Russell and Brand suppose that the time had come to commit the Liberal party to a franchise level. The difficulty they found in getting agreement to any particular level was considerable.[9] This sharpened the relevance of the policy which had been devised by Russell, Gladstone, Halifax and Brand at the beginning of the winter and reiterated at Halifax's insistence when Russell seemed likely to want to introduce resolutions of his own[10] and Gladstone to mount a premature assault[11]—of avoiding specific commitment on their own part, of insisting that

they had renounced the search for party advantage and of emphasizing their willingness to do almost anything 'to clear the way as
speedily as possible for [the government] being in a condition to
propose a bill'.[1]

The advantage, finally, of this policy was not only that the attempt
to produce a government bill would break up the Cabinet so long as
outside pressure did not prevent it breaking up, but that production
of a bill, or manifest failure by the government to produce one,
would push the Adullamites off the fence. Since no situation had
arisen since 1859 in which Derby and Disraeli had had to commit
themselves to a specific measure of reform, Conservative policy had
so far been negative.[2] Since Disraeli had taken pains to imply that
the Cave's views would be listened to by the Cabinet, the Cave
believed that the Cabinet would respond to advice: so long as these
conditions remained, Liberal action in relation to the Cave was unlikely to be effective. Gladstone had had desultory and chilly correspondence with Grosvenor in the summer.[3] But, though Brand,
Granville and to some extent Halifax spent time then and later in
1866 trying to decide what to do about the Cave, they had 'come to
the conclusion that [although]...here and there a stray sheep may
be gathered into the fold...we can do little with any of them until
the government shall have shown their hand'[4].

The Adullamites, like everyone else, had learned a lesson in 1866
—that, although they could succeed in breaking governments, they
could not succeed in making them. They had organized a large, if
miscellaneous, body of Liberal opposition to the Reform bill, and
been offered, and refused, office under Derby's leadership as a
result. But they had failed to resurrect a Palmerston-style Whig/
Conservative coalition under Stanley, Granville or Clarendon because Derby and Disraeli did not want them to succeed: it was by no
means certain that the opportunity would recur. The Adullamite
position in mid and late 1866 was that, while its leaders had no desire
to leave the Liberal party unless they could dominate the Conservative party, the one thing on which they insisted was that the
Liberal party, so long as they belonged to it, should not be allowed
to follow Russell and Gladstone into the arms of Bright. In this
respect, the Cave was the creature of a very few men. Just as the
opposition consisted of Gladstone, Grey, Russell, Halifax, Clarendon and Brand, and the Cabinet, where initiative in policy was con-

cerned, of Derby and Disraeli playing before an audience of fifteen, so the Cave was an attempt by half a dozen disappointed Palmerstonians to determine the character of Liberal policy and the direction to be taken by the Liberal leadership. They were making a bare bid for political power by creating, through their knowledge of opinion in the House of Commons, a third party to rival the party leaders already in possession of the scene. They were perfectly articulate about their purpose—to make Russell, Gladstone and 'their republican allies' see that 'whoever governs in this country can only do so with the help and confidence of the constitutional Liberals',[1] and they had some of the means available to pursue it. They found the money to start a newspaper: when they started it, they did not know that the leader-writer they appointed was in Disraeli's pocket.[2] About electoral reform they represented a wide range of parliamentary opinion whose practical effectiveness was limited by the fact that MP.s who agreed about that question were divided into conflicting parties on others. Though there was nothing to keep their followers together except electoral reform and, in some cases, the Liberal leadership, they presented a threat to the leaders of both parties. They presented this threat because they were free to take the initiative in proposing motions and making amendments, and used this freedom to the utmost. They presented it, again, by reason of the range of their contact among secondary frontbench figures in both parties, which gave them tolerably accurate knowledge of the progress of Cabinet decisions. In addition, and most important of all, in the session of 1866 they had been highly successful. Though Lansdowne's death on July 7 1866, unexpectedly at the age of fifty, weakened the Cave as a political instrument, reduced its potential power in the event of a Reform bill being opposed in the House of Lords and may well have increased its difficulties at moments of crisis in February and May 1867, it made little difference to immediate manœuvring in the House of Commons. In 1865 Elcho had failed to persuade the Russell/Gladstone Cabinet to deal with the Reform question by appointing a Royal Commission, but the tabling of Grosvenor's amendment in March 1866 had demonstrated the possibilities of the parliamentary initiative, even when the Cabinet had a theoretical majority in the House of Commons. Now that a Cabinet was in office without a majority, the possibility increased that, by maintaining contact and forcing motions, the Reform question could be dealt with as it should be, and the Liberal party directed as it ought to have been.

Nor did Disraeli and Derby fail to make an impression on the Cave. Though the Cave had been denied a central coalition in July 1866, Derby's reputation had emerged unharmed.[1] Though the government mishandled the Park demonstration in July that year, the damage its reputation suffered was offset by the damage Gladstone suffered by his failure to make any sort of critical intervention.[2] Though it is probable that Disraeli tricked Elcho in the session of 1866, Elcho maintained contact with the government in the winter—advocating a royal commission on the trades unions (of which he became a member), amendment of Master and Servant legislation and the need to deal with electoral reform, as in 1865, by appointing a commission.[3] Pakington, Northcote, Carnarvon and Cranborne received Adullamite confidences direct: Derby received Earl Grey's through General Grey at Windsor. Through his contact with Cranborne, Carnarvon, Northcote, Chelmsford and Lady Salisbury, Lowe exerted himself to prevent the government introducing a bill to lower the franchise, and thought he was succeeding.[4]

For Derby and Disraeli, finally, the lesson of the Russell/Gladstone government was that, whatever form Liberal feeling might take outside the House of Commons, Palmerstonian Liberals inside it were suspicious of Gladstone's supposed alliance with Bright. They knew that their victory had been the result of Bright's and their own accentuation of Whig/Radical divergence. They thought that the Liberal party might be divided more seriously if settlement of the Reform question were delayed, or if proposals were made to settle it on terms which Radicals could not accept. But, although the tactical objective—of prising the Liberal right, the Cave and some Whigs away from Gladstone and Bright—continued in the months following to be an objective of Conservative policy, the lesson of the Cabinet crisis was that nothing would be gained by relying too heavily on dissident Liberals, and that it was idle, if not positively dangerous, to expect the reconstruction of parties which had been canvassed since Palmerston's death actually to be carried out unless the Conservative leadership was changed also. The persistence of the Liberal wound, which Brand and Halifax were attempting to close, opened possibilities for a Conservative future, but there is no reason to suppose that Derby and Disraeli were attempting to construct a reactionary coalition in the months following the formation of the Cabinet, or thought coalition possible except at their expense.

Derby's government, moreover, when it came into office, was a minority government in the House of Commons. It was in office because the Liberal party had fallen apart. It had fallen apart over Reform (with an Irish background), and because of personal conflict between the growing power of Radicals and the apparently diminishing prospects of Whigs and moderate Liberals. There was no reason to expect extensive dissension on any subjects except Reform and Ireland. About Ireland the Conservative party could do little beyond on the one hand drawing a line between legislation to establish an 'English' degree of tenant-right and the actual expropriation of Irish property,[1] and jumping in, on the other, at a point at which Russell's government had failed to satisfy the Catholic bishops, by providing a charter for the Catholic university. About electoral reform the Conservative leaders were in two minds and totally uncommitted. There was the opportunity to govern: when they took office in July 1866, there was a belief that the longer a settlement could be delayed, the greater the damage the Liberal party would suffer on the way. They wanted to avoid dissolving Parliament because they did not feel certain that a dissolution would improve their position in the House of Commons. Having been edged unwillingly to the point of accepting office, Derby did not intend to throw away the opportunities office might offer of letting Bright drive a wedge down the side of the Liberal party, of bringing the Reform question to a satisfactory conclusion or of establishing the Conservative party as a major instrument of government for the future.

In these circumstances the Conservative leaders had a number of courses from which to choose. They could produce the rest of their programme and do nothing about Reform in the hope that the Liberal party would be broken up by pressure from Bright. They could ensure co-operation from the Liberal party or the moderate Whigs in the hope of passing an agreed measure at some time in some subsequent session, or they could go ahead under their own steam with a bill or with parliamentary action which would lead to production of a bill later. Each course had disadvantages. If the first were adopted, there was danger of a hostile motion as soon as Parliament reassembled followed by parliamentary defeat and the alternatives of resignation or a general election, which neither Derby nor Disraeli thought they could win—in this, as it happens, differing from Russell and Brand who thought the Liberal party would not win it either. This policy might well have been adopted, have kept the government in office through the next session of Parliament and produced marked conflict between Radicals inside and outside the House and the body of the parliamentary Liberal party. It was rejected by Derby at the end of September because, although public agitation had not bullied him into accepting its require-ments, he thought the country expected the government to rise to the level of the events which the Reform Union and the Reform League were creating.

Derby's attitude to the Reform question, and to public feeling, underwent a change between July and mid-September. He was responsible for the closing of the Park in July, was the target of pub-lic attack in August and September and saw the leaders of public agitation claiming to be repeating the successes of 1832 and 1845. At the same time, he sensed not only that the public agitation was gaining strength but that a reaction was growing up against it. The size of the meetings may have been as large as those of thirty years before, but they lacked a significant ingredient. They were chaired, in some towns, by the Mayor; their platforms accommodated rows of respectable manufacturers. But they did not now, as then, include the Whig or Liberal gentry.[1] Although, therefore, the agitation was a formidable one, it was not a united expression of Whig/Liberal feeling; its demands were so extensive, and its language so powerful, that it could be relied on in the right circumstances to produce a cleavage in the Liberal party, not just in the House of Commons but also in the country. Derby could see that, even if the movement ran away with itself, its chief effect would be on Gladstone who would not be able to run very far with it. From a parliamentary standpoint Derby had a built-in desire to reject total inactivity so far as he could: having accepted office, he had no desire to leave it. But, even if this affected his decision, the decision was designed at least as much to step on the wave of reaction *against* Bright as to capitulate to him. It was an attempt to use Bright's threats in order to renew the Conservative role as the anti-revolutionary party, not by rejecting *all* action about electoral Reform which it would be difficult to persuade Conservatives was possible, but by proposing a bill which would rally conservative forces in both parties against the threat of a revolutionary change in the political system. It was based on the assumption that, although Bright's language and the public demonstrations had made it possible to create an anti-revolutionary front, the climate they had created 'in our favour [was] not in favour of resisting all Reform for which I believe there is a genuine demand *now*, however it may have been excited, but in favour of the acceptance of a moderate and conservative measure'.[1]

The second course was adopted for a time as a way of carrying Adullamites and some Whigs, but there was a difference between the policy, advocated by Cranborne, for example, of close and permanent fusion between the Conservative party and the 'constitutional Liberals' and Derby's virtual insistence that co-operation should take place under his leadership, or not at all. There was a difference again, between playing along Whigs like Earl Grey, and the policy of using Earl Grey and General Grey as intermediaries with Halifax, Sir George Grey and the Cabinet Whigs in order to get agreement to a measure which would not only be, but would also be known to be, the result of compromise between the parties. There is no reason to doubt that Derby's eyes were open as much as Disraeli's to the possibility of dissension in the Liberal party. It is unlikely that Russell or Gladstone would have risked their reputations on the left by co-operating openly with Derby. It is clear that Derby intended, if the question could be settled, to settle it himself. It would not be true to say that he thought he was pursuing the third course; for he took pains to consult, and to let it be known that a bill could be carried only if compromises were accepted by both sides. But by compromise it is far from clear that he meant an agreed compromise. If he did mean it, he seems to have meant it because agreement between the leaders of the two parties would cause disagreement in the Liberal party.

No doubt at the point at which discussion was going on in Cabinet and with Disraeli, Derby was searching for questions to refer to the all-party commission it was proposed to appoint under the chairmanship of Earl Grey. No reader of his letters to Disraeli between November and January[2] can doubt that he was assuming that there really would be a commission if the resolutions were passed, and was taking seriously the implications which would follow from the decision to appoint it. The Cabinet thought it was committed to proceed by resolutions in order 'by gradually feeling the pulse of the House of Commons and ascertaining how far a community of opinion might be relied on between the moderate sections of both sides...[to arrive at] an ultimate, and so far as anything can be, a final settlement of the question'. It is almost certain that Derby at one level thought so too. Derby knew that a policy of this sort would depend on establishing that common sentiment between the Conservative party and the Constitutional Liberals which it was one part of his policy to achieve. He knew also that this would destroy Liberal unity by effecting 'the exclusion [from the Reform discussions] of the extreme Democratic party'.[1] The decision to proceed by 'affirm[ing] principles and postpon[ing] details as far as possible' so as to 'establish...that all differences between us are differences of *degree* only' was, therefore, not just a decision to do the right thing to settle the Reform question, though it was that. It was also a decision to take advantage of the fact that, though the Liberals 'can defeat us if they combine...they cannot agree as to *what* they want', and a decision which, while not necessarily stimulating Liberal acquiescence in whatever the government might propose, would produce a situation in which 'if they try to precipitate matters, we [may] beat them, or if we do not, shall have a good ground on which to go to the country'.[2]

There was, in addition, a deliberate refusal to allow the Adullamites to effect their manifest desire to give public demonstration of the fact that *they* were determining the government's policy. On accepting office in July, at least three ministers offered to stand down if Derby should construct a Whig/Conservative coalition later in the year.[3] On various occasions in the winter Cranborne, Carnarvon and Pakington all pressed him to closer co-operation with the Cave.[4] But it was his policy, and the policy of Disraeli, both to prevent the Cave taking the initiative and to play down its importance. It was useful to keep it in existence as a disruptive force inside the Liberal party. It was desirable to offer office to a minor member under Derby's leadership in preparation for the parliamentary session.[5] Since the votes of its members mattered even if their quality was not high, it was necessary to know what the Cave would vote for. But it was essential to play a balancing game; to avoid inflating its leaders' importance by going so far in the direction of 'recogniz[ing] the Adullamites as a party [as] to send them' for example, '[an advance copy of] the [Queen's] Speech'.[1] Derby and Disraeli were in office because the Cave had rebelled against Gladstone, so they had no desire to alienate its sympathy. At the same time, since they were in office because they had beaten off the Whig/Adullamite plot to replace themselves by Stanley, Granville or Clarendon, they did not want to encourage Adullamites to play a decisive part in the politics of the future. These were undoubtedly the reasons why, at all crucial moments in the first year of office, though the views of the Cave mattered, they never mattered to the point, aimed at by Elcho, of publicly *determining* the Cabinet's policy.

The decision to do *something* about Reform was taken by Derby in September. By then he had rejected the course, proposed by Salisbury from one standpoint and by Disraeli from another,[2] of taking up the Gladstone/Russell Franchise bill where Dunkellin's amendment had left it (i.e. with rating substituted for rental). In September he did not know what a Reform bill would contain, when it would be introduced, or whether, and when, it would become an Act. But he rejected the Salisbury/Disraeli proposal because, however little the Liberal party might be in a position to pass a bill of its own, its leaders intended to make it as difficult as possible for him to pass one either. He had seen an outline bill drafted in late July by Dudley Baxter which reflected Baxter's desire to keep in step with Adullamites and Constitutional Liberals[3] by proposing a £6 rating franchise for boroughs and a £14 occupation franchise for counties, the removal of some borough freehold votes from the counties, the grouping of small boroughs, the extension of the boundaries of large boroughs and the establishment of a number of educational franchises. Though it was designed, like the bill the Cabinet eventually accepted on February 23, to 'strengthen the moderate party and the landed interest...in the counties and small boroughs' while enfranchising 'nearly as many of the working classes as Mr Gladstone's bill', Derby was not committed to it. There were at this time only decisions to proceed, to take pains to avoid a situation in which a bill had to be introduced as soon as Parliament met, and to persuade first the Cabinet and then the House of Commons to discuss a set of very general resolutions in preparation for a commission. It was understood that the resolutions could be altered to suit the taste of the Cabinet, that the Cabinet would not be committed to any resolution in particular, and that they would not commit the government to a specific measure. Introduction of resolutions, so long as a commission was not already in existence, would not commit the government to any particular course of action. Disraeli's desire to appoint a commission immediately (without calling the Cabinet) was rejected because it would 'virtually pledge us to act at the first possible moment upon its recommendations'.[1] Procedure by commission was attractive because the Cabinet would not have to decide in the earliest stages about the contents of a bill, could throw on to Parliament as a whole the burden of discussing the specific decision and would make it extremely difficult for the Liberal leaders to mount an attack on a governmental policy. It was attractive, also, because Elcho suggested it in August 1866 as a step the Cave would support. Nevertheless, although it was a possible policy, to adopt it involved rejecting the policy of inaction about Reform, and this decision, once made, exerted a power of its own on all subsequent decisions.

As soon as inactivity had been rejected, it was necessary to show that the government intended to introduce a bill at some time. This involved delicate decisions about the commission. A commission, headed by Earl Grey and including Radicals as well as Conservatives, would not only provide a '*buffer*',[2] but would also be supported by the Cave. On the other hand, while one object of the exercise was to gain credit by passing a bill—which could not be done so readily if too much of it was the work of privy councillors headed by a Whig—a Commission of Enquiry (as distinct from Recommendation) would give the opposition a chance to accuse the government of using the Commission as a 'dodge' to cover up its own internal difficulties. Sir Stafford Northcote was not, at this time, in Derby's confidence (though he was to some extent in Disraeli's). He would have preferred to leave the question alone, but there is no reason to think him untypical of Cabinet opinion in his insistence that it was 'even more important than the settlement of the Reform question that the government should take no step which would look like a procrastinating policy for the sake of keeping themselves in office, and that they had better either propose a plan of their own by which in its main features they could stand or decline to deal with the subject'.[1]

The idea of having a commission was Derby's. At the same time it was conceived by Earl Grey as the outcome of Adullamite discussion. In order to make it acceptable General Grey persuaded the Queen to offer mediation between Derby and such leading Whigs as Grey thought might be responsive. The Queen was strongly anti-Radical, was hostile to Russell and Gladstone, and had an intense desire to pass a moderate bill as soon as possible by agreement between the parties. The two Greys were alarmed by the danger Bright presented to the existing establishment: they hoped, by manipulating the Queen, to achieve the safe and lasting settlement which the collapse of the Liberal party had made impossible in 1866.[2] Though General Grey's contact with Halifax, Somerset, Clarendon and Sir George Grey seems at this time not to have been close, the object was to arrange agreement through them 'and perhaps Lord Granville', even if that meant cutting below Gladstone's and Russell's leadership in the process.[3] Although they were probably right to think that neither Gladstone nor Russell would have facilitated agreement between the parties, it is almost certain that Derby and Disraeli would not have been willing to do so either. They could see advantages in having the Queen's support in case of emergency, but they had no intention of renouncing the opportunities of government, of saving the Whigs from the consequence of their Radical alliance or of being led on by the manifest initiatives of others.[4] The attempt made by General Grey and the Queen during Northcote's period in attendance at Balmoral to interest him in a royal initiative[5] in preparation for an all-party commission was considered and rejected by the Cabinet on October 31 as an immediate project, though Derby, in writing to the Queen, kept the proposal in store against the need.[6] In late December he decided that a commission must do more than enquire, but should not make decisions of principle. He rejected Disraeli's proposal to include Mill and Ayrton on the ground that, though Mill favoured plurality and Ayrton 'hate[d] the mob', 'their private and philosophical opinions would be...subservient to their...interests...[as] members for Radical constituencies'. Earl Grey's approach of October 30 seems to have received no direct answer, despite extensive discussion about it between Derby and General Grey.[1] At every turn in his contact with the Queen and General Grey, Derby was not only reticent about his intentions and insistent on the need for reticence on their part,[2] but took such opportunities as offered to rivet the Queen's support to himself by drawing a contrast between his own co-operativeness and the acerbity, querulousness and manifest search for party advantage which he imputed to Russell and Gladstone.[3]

The first Reform Cabinets were held between October 31[4] and December 2: by December 2 provisional approval had been given to a number of resolutions,[5] which Derby and Disraeli are said to 'have forced through the Cabinet'. With one exception these were the resolutions Disraeli presented to Parliament on February 11 1867. They were the result of previous preparation by Disraeli and Derby, and of the fact that, when Cabinet ministers were asked to send written suggestions, only Lord John Manners did so, though his formed a substantial part of the finished product. They did not commit the government to immediate legislation. On the contrary, they were felt, not only by those who disliked them but also by Derby, to commit the Cabinet to do no more than introduce resolutions with a view to obtaining parliamentary sanction for a commission to prepare information on which a bill would be drafted. They were kept vague in order to be acceptable to everyone in the Cabinet: the possibility that their vagueness might produce an unfavourable reaction when they reached the House of Commons, though it occurred to Derby and Disraeli, did not deter them. They were dealing with each problem as it arose. The first problem, since Cabinets *had* to meet, was to carry the Cabinet to the point of presenting a united front in the House of Commons.

The November/December Cabinets did not come to a decision about the content of policy, though there was discussion, both in Cabinet and outside, about the principles on which a bill would eventually be drawn if a bill were ever presented. It was not until January 10 that it was finally decided to introduce resolutions with the promise of an all-party commission of enquiry if they were accepted by the House, in the hope that, since the resolutions would have established the principles on which a bill would be based before the commission reported, Parliament would then be able to 'consider [its] recommendations without the party prejudice [attaching] to a specific proposition brought forward by any government'.[1] The decision was conveyed to the Queen, but not published. The Queen, who had seen none of the draft resolutions up to this time and saw only one then,[2] was warned that her mediation should not begin, and that nothing should leak out, until they had been introduced by Disraeli on February 11. The reference in the Queen's speech to electoral Reform was agreed by the Cabinet on January 30:[3] it was left vague so as to keep the opposition guessing 'whether the intention of the government [was] to proceed by way of bill or resolution'. The final form of the resolutions was approved in Cabinet on February 9, sketched out by Disraeli to the House of Commons two days later (with a promise of extended discussion on February 25), and made available to MP.s next morning.[4] On February 14, in answer to a question from Lord Robert Montagu, Disraeli announced that the government would outline the details of its policy before the resolutions were discussed. This announcement confronted the Cabinet with the need to decide what its policy was.

There is no evidence that Disraeli consulted the Cabinet before announcing that the government intended to commit itself to specific proposals in advance of the House's discussion of the resolutions. This raises two questions about his relations with the Cabinet in the three weeks between the opening of Parliament on February 5 and the speech on February 25, in which he announced the government's terms; was he trying to edge the Cabinet to commit itself to a bill instead of to resolutions leading to a commission? was he trying to press the Cabinet to accept a policy—of rated residential suffrage—to which its members did not really want to be committed?

The first question may be dealt with by asking another: why was the proposal to proceed by commission leading to a bill after approval of the resolutions replaced by decisions first to abandon the commission[5] and then to announce, before the resolutions were discussed, the terms of the bill the government would introduce if they were passed? To this, a number of answers may be given. In the first place it was clear, when the House met on February 5, that a wide range of MP.s, from varying standpoints and for various reasons, wanted conclusive treatment of the question. It was clear, therefore, that the government would need to work hard to create a climate of opinion in which it seemed credible that it should deal with it.[6] The commission of recommendation under Earl Grey, in the only form in which it was acceptable to the Cabinet, was abandoned because it would leave an impression of insincerity.[1] When the commission had first been thought of in October, it was intended (by Earl Grey) to play an important part in deciding what should be done. The decision to give it powers of enquiry rather than recommendation[2] was consistent with the desire to avoid the impression that the government was being driven by the Whigs. Disraeli and Derby spent time during the winter searching for enquiries it could reasonably be expected to make. By mid-January they seem to have come to the conclusion that, though they might be accused of establishing a commission in order to avoid the Cabinet split which would follow an attempt to reach an agreed Cabinet policy, it would still be safe to establish one. Given the temper of the House of Commons when it met, however, it seemed certain that announcement as government policy of a commission of enquiry, when so much was known about the electoral system already, would destroy whatever confidence there was in the government's intentions. Though Derby left open the possibility of appointing a commission if the House decided that it wanted one during discussion of the resolutions, there can be no doubt that he abandoned the intention to propose this, not because Disraeli was hustling him, but because he had come to think the House of Commons hostile to it.

Secondly, it is almost certain that the one thing Disraeli wanted was to introduce the resolutions and have a debate on them. He wanted this, not because he was pressing the Conservative party to accept proposals of which it did not approve, but because a debate would almost certainly upset the Liberal party. When Disraeli and Derby first thought of introducing resolutions with a view to appointing a commission, they assumed that this would produce extensive parliamentary discussion which would enable them to find out what the House would accept and in the course of which the 'Liberal party' would 'probably be broken up'.[3] Whig/Radical conflict, intensified as it would be by any restraining pressure the Queen and General Grey might bring to bear on the Liberal leaders, would either ensure a Conservative victory in the House and 'establish' the government, or enable the government to have a dissolution 'on an issue between Bright's policy and our programme'.[4] The difference between the situation in November and the situation at the end of the second week in February was that the resolutions, which had been emasculated in order to appease General Peel, had been introduced by Disraeli evasively, ineptly and inadequately and caused little pleasure in any part of the House of Commons,[1] and that, although the Queen had been set to work on the opposition as soon as it had been decided to introduce the resolutions, the Liberal leaders had done their best to avoid the Conservative 'trap'[2] by announcing that they would both press the government to introduce a bill and encourage it to do so by allowing the resolutions to pass without scrutiny. This meant, contrary to Derby's and Disraeli's expectation, that, unless they raised their stakes or declared their intentions, there would be discussion, not of the *substance* of the resolutions, but about the desirability of converting the resolution into a bill—which would cause much less conflict in the Liberal party than they had intended.

On the other hand, they knew, both from the debate on the resolutions and from their knowledge of Liberal opinion, that 'the Liberal counsels' were 'hopelessly divided'. They knew that Gladstone was being agreeable to the Cave and moderate Whigs even if Russell was not, and that discussion of the substance of the resolutions, especially of resolution 3, for which Derby 'ha[d] little doubt that there [would] be a large majority',[3] would produce a situation in which 'Mr Gladstone would have to declare himself in favour of it in opposition to the Democratic party'.[4] Even at this stage (on February 14) Disraeli was not committed to each of the resolutions as it stood, or to introduce a bill after the passage of the resolutions. He was trying to establish that 'parliamentary Reform should no longer be a question [to] determine the fate of ministries': he was 'ask[ing] the opinion of the House and see[ing] whether they will sanction the course [he] recommend[ed]'.[5] There can be little doubt that it was his own and probably Derby's desire to provoke the dissension they wanted, and were in danger of being denied, which persuaded him to open himself to the point of promising, not a bill, for that was not promised for February 25, but a sketch of the contents of the bill they would introduce if the resolutions were passed.

It is in this context, rather than by implying a desire to hustle the Cabinet, that one may best understand Disraeli's commitment on February 14 to announce the terms the government supposed the resolutions to amount to before the resolutions were debated. There had been discussion between Disraeli, Derby and members of the

Cabinet individually about the terms the government should propose. Despite Cranborne's and Carnarvon's belief (expressed after
their resignation on March 2) that Disraeli was trying to hustle
them, no objection was raised at the Cabinet meetings on February
15 and 16 to the fact that Disraeli had already committed the
Cabinet to declare its hand at the same time as the resolutions
were debated. General Peel objected to the *content* of the plan which
Derby and Disraeli proposed, and was led on in discussion to object
to the introduction of any Reform bill. But no one else objected to
the proposal Disraeli then made—for a £5 Rating bill combined
with second votes, not for occupiers of houses rated at above £10, to
which there was said to be strong objection in Parliament, but for
holders of professional qualifications, Savings Bank investors, and
direct taxpayers. This was accepted by 'all...as a very conservative
measure', which would have formed the basis of the policy Disraeli would have announced to Parliament on February 25 if
General Peel had not at that point announced his 'unconquerable
aversion to all reform, for it amounted to this, and his virtual determination to leave us'.[1] What requires explanation, therefore, is
neither the decision to indicate, before the resolutions were discussed, the terms of the bill the government would propose if the
resolutions were accepted, nor the decision, of which the whole
Cabinet apart from Peel approved, to accept a £5 rating and duality
bill, but the proposal, made and accepted apparently without conflict at the next Cabinet meeting on February 19, to replace the £5
rating proposal with a rated residential suffrage one.

In the general Cabinet discussion which had gone on inside and
outside Cabinet meetings between July and January, a number of
schemes had been canvassed. Adderley had a plan for introducing a
special franchise qualification for the large towns.[2] Pakington had
one for remodelling the franchise on a German basis, which Derby
summarily rejected. Cranborne wanted a bold, new and well-
prepared measure, if any was to be introduced at all.[3] It was clear to
everyone that, if anything was proposed, it must be different enough
from the 1866 bill to justify the destruction of Russell's government. Gladstone had been attacked in the previous session for failing to provide a secure resting-place for the borough franchise.
His £7 rental franchise established no principle with which to
counter further agitation, abandoned the connection between rate-

paying and the franchise on which the 1832 Act had rested, and had done this, both by refusing to make liability to pay rates a condition of enfranchisement, and by setting the rental qualifying level low enough to ensure that a good many new electors would not pay rates in fact. The Small Tenements and local rating Acts passed during the previous forty years had empowered the local rating authorities to compel landlords to pay on their tenants' behalf all rates due on houses rated at less than £6 p.a. The rate paid by landlords in these circumstances was lower than the rate the tenant would have paid if compounding had not been in operation. Since 'almost every £7 *rented* house would be *rated* under £6', the Gladstone bill would have brought on to the register 'a vast number of persons...who pay no rates and on whose houses (being compounded for) rates are really only in practice paid upon one half of the rateable value'.[1] This meant that the only restriction imposed on borough enfranchisement if Gladstone's bill had passed, would have been a value limit (£7), which, given the wrong combination of political circumstances in the future, could slowly be reduced until all connection between property, tax-liability and the franchise disappeared as *every* man who lived anywhere came to have the right to vote.

Conservatives who defended the connection between enfranchisement and liability to rating did not know empirically, as it were, that this would produce a better type of elector. But, whether they knew this or not, it was a principle to which the Conservative party as a whole, and conservative opinion in Parliament, had come to be committed in 1866, and to which the Cabinet returned in 1867 in the course of seeking a proposal which would be both impressive and, in these terms, safe. In late 1866 and early 1867 Cabinet ministers, so far from trying to enfranchise on a large scale, were not certain that they should enfranchise at all. They were determined, if they did so, to do so in conformity with Conservative commitments and to prevent the predominance of any one class in the electoral system. They had too little psephological knowledge to know what effect each combination of proposals would have, but they knew enough to see that, once the £10 occupation level was abandoned, a proposal to restore the connection between rating and the franchise might provide an effective long-term barrier against such indiscriminate enfranchisement as Gladstone's £7 rental bill seemed likely to promise for the future.

There were two further considerations in the minds of Cabinet ministers in mid and late 1866. They knew, in the first place, that, if the Conservative party was to legislate about the electoral system, it must do so in a way which seemed credible from the start: they knew that if it could not do this, it would be better not to try. The government was in a minority in the House of Commons. Credibility meant a proposal which would seem to go so far beyond the expectations Liberals had created about the Conservative party in the past that they would not be able to mount a destructive attack as soon as a proposal was made. This did not mean that the proposal would have to go far in fact: there was no desire to establish a working-class preponderance. But it meant that a proposal which went a long way in one direction might enable the government to provide a counterpoise or compensation in the other.

It was in these circumstances that Cabinet ministers first came to think of proposing household suffrage, provided it could be coupled with stringent requirements about rating and with the granting of second or third votes (plurality) to richer and better-educated electors in much the same way as they had already been given them in Poor Law elections. Since plurality would counteract the effect of any increase in working-class power which household suffrage would produce, this was generally attractive. It was not Disraeli alone who was responsible for it. At the Cabinet of November 8 Carnarvon proposed 'household suffrage accompanied by Conservative restrictions and safeguards [though he] was...overruled'.[1] In December Derby had suggested, as one question for a commission to examine, the connection between household suffrage and the size of enfranchisement. In the course of January, Dudley Baxter produced figures which showed that 'a household suffrage would give a smaller number of electors than generally was supposed—a little more...than 800,000, and that payment of rates and a residential qualification of three years would reduce this by one-third'.[2] In fishing to find out what the Cabinet would accept, Disraeli had tried rated residential suffrage with various sorts of plurality by way of safeguard. Walpole seems positively to have supported it and to have discouraged retention of plurality.[3] Derby was clear that 'without plurality we could not propose household suffrage', but seems equally to have been clear that this was a combination that might be proposed. On February 1 Carnarvon told

Disraeli 'that the mere payment of rates and a three-year residence would not be a sufficient safeguard': he agreed, nevertheless, in writing to him next day that, provided more than one safeguard *was* proposed, household suffrage, coupled with 'a residential qualification of three years [and] payment of rates and taxes [would be] excellent'.[1] Northcote, while believing in the viability of 'absolute inaction' and preferring, 'if [he] could, to take [his] stand upon the present limit of the Borough franchise', was clear that, if inaction was rejected and resolutions were proposed 'which do not show upon their face that we contemplate a reduction of the borough franchise, we shall be met by a motion to the effect that the House will not consider a plan which does not embrace such a reduction'. Since the policy of proceeding by resolution had been adopted and a motion of this sort would be successful, he 'believe[d] that we shall find no standpoint short of Household Suffrage...and, if we go boldly down to this point...shall have a fair chance of coupling [it] ...with conditions which would make it safe'.[2]

The difficulty in assessing the significance of these references to 'household suffrage' is that 'household suffrage' could mean a number of different things according to the way in which it was applied. The point in thinking of it in conjunction with restrictions, counterpoises and compensations, was to meet the desire, which not all Conservatives yet felt, to 'go far enough to *stop*, instead of stopping short, as the last bill did, to invite further agitation on the subject'.[3] In the search for the smallest enfranchisement consistent with a permanent resting-place and a credible party platform, it was thought to have many advantages. It had, however, two disadvantages. First, that a household suffrage 'measure [once] passed, agitation against the restrictive portion of it [would] commence' and would be likely to be successful 'if restrictions upon the freedom of the franchise are narrowed to one single, tangible, very definite point of opposition'.[4] Secondly, that General Peel would not be party to it. Peel had presented his resignation on February 7,[5] because household suffrage had been mentioned by Disraeli in one draft of the resolutions, but had been persuaded to remain in office on condition that the phrase was withdrawn. The phrase was withdrawn at the next Cabinet in favour of the resolution that the 'principle of plural voting, if adopted by Parliament, might lead to the adjustment of the borough franchise on a safe and satisfactory footing'.[1] It is unlikely that Derby or Disraeli at this time had anything resembling an intention to try carrying a household suffrage bill without counterpoises, or wanted to do more than make the resolutions attractive. Both, however, sensed the tactical advantage in making household suffrage in some form or other part of their proposal to the House of Commons, and dropped it under pressure from Peel, not because they thought it ought to be dropped, but because 'the House and the country (more important) would understand' that, even though household suffrage was not mentioned, it was, nevertheless, what the substitute resolution meant. 'If the resolution be adopted [by the House]' they thought, the government's position would be so strong that 'we could do without Peel', while, 'if [it was] rejected, we should have to fall back on a moderate reduction of the franchise... with fancy safety valves;... [in which case] Peel could honourably remain until we attempted to carry it into action according to our interpretation of it; and if the House did not sanction our doing so, then, of course, he need not resign'.[2] It was in these circumstances, and because Cranborne independently objected,[3] that Disraeli proposed the £5 rating with fancy franchises to the Cabinet on February 16, though even that made Peel once more offer his resignation.

Between February 16 and 19, four things had happened. Disraeli had fulfilled an engagement, made before Peel's resignation, to go to Windsor to see the Queen, who seems already to have been greatly impressed by him.[4] Carnarvon had called on Peel, probably at Derby's or Disraeli's request, to ask him to give way.[5] Derby had had a talk with Grosvenor. The Cave had held a meeting, the upshot of which Grosvenor had conveyed to Derby. Disraeli's visit convinced the Queen, who seems previously to have thought that the government could lose Peel safely, that she should press Peel to stay. She wrote to him at once:[6] in doing so, she pressed him not about the details of any bill that might be proposed, but about the desirability of doing something to settle the question. The fact that the Queen's letter to Peel was general and successful gave Derby and Disraeli a wider measure of flexibility than they had had before. It gave them in particular the opportunity to revert to their original plan.

Finally, though no account exists of the Derby/Grosvenor meeting, it is almost certain that the views expressed by Grosvenor then as representative of the Cave, made it doubly desirable, in one way or another, to revert to some sort of household suffrage. In the previous three weeks the Cave had come to believe that it could use Gladstone, and that the Liberal party offered opportunities for the exercise of its power. Its members would have preferred to preserve the £10 qualification established in 1832 in relation to the borough franchise, extending the franchise laterally but not lowering it. Since the government's third resolution made it impossible that the government should do this, and since Gladstone had no intention of doing so either, it had fallen back on its second objective—a permanent resting-place for the borough franchise by establishing household suffrage combined with attempts to compensate for the increase this would produce in the working-class vote by giving second or third votes to richer and better-educated electors, and by providing opportunities for the richer classes to give all their votes to one candidate (cumulative voting). They believed, rightly, that this sort of proposal would attract widespread support in both Houses: they expected support to issue, under guidance from them during discussion of the resolutions, into a clear preference for a sensible, acceptable and conservative bill. Lowe's hostility to *any* lowering of the borough franchise was not shared by other members of the Cave. After the Cave meeting of nine people on February 17, Derby was given a note explaining the conclusion to which they had come. This was that 'there is no standing point between the present qualification and household suffrage, the householders paying their own rates and a certain time of residence', that 'if guarded in the way proposed by plural and cumulative voting...[household suffrage] might be safely established', and that the Cave was willing, if the government accepted their principles, to propose amendments to the resolutions so that '*after*' the House had given its approval of 'the principle of plurality [and]...the cumulative vote', they would then 'support what the government might propose as to a reduction of the borough franchise on a rating qualification'.[1]

On February 20 the Cabinet decided against cumulative voting because it would endanger Conservative control of county seats. On February 23, after hearing Baxter's statistical analysis, it committed itself to rated residential suffrage, duality and fancy franchises. There is no evidence about the attitude Derby and Disraeli took to the Cave's proposal except that they attached importance to the

Cave's opinions in general. Nevertheless, it seems probable that, although the Cabinet, with the exception of General Peel, had been willing on February 16 to accept a £5 rating franchise with counterpoises, they took the chance, which the Queen's success with Peel gave them, to revert to their original plan, which Peel had disliked even more strongly. It is possible that they did this in order to prevent the Cave taking the initiative; it is certain that in doing it they were trying to ensure that the Cave was carried along with them. In other words, it is likely that a united Cabinet first came to be committed to rated residential (i.e. household) suffrage as a result of the intervention of the most militant of those who had defeated Gladstone's bill because it went too far in 1866, and that a measure (a £5 rating suffrage) which the Cave, Cranborne, Carnarvon and Gladstone all took up in the next month as *their* solution of the Reform problem, was abandoned as a joint result of Peel's threatened resignation and the Cave's commitment.

Disraeli's object was not to commit the Cabinet to a proposal of which it did not approve, but to give the government a chance of producing extensive discussion of the resolutions in the House of Commons. Neither Derby nor Disraeli wanted to introduce a bill before the resolutions were passed. As late as the lunchtime Cabinet on Monday the 25th, they hoped that the sketching of a government bill without formal commitment would help command a majority for the policy of *considering* resolutions, and that, in the dislocation caused by a Radical/Whig divergence, they would accumulate a large measure of Liberal support for whatever measure they might propose. They hoped that discussion of the resolutions would intensify the dissension in the Liberal party which they had stimulated at the beginning of 1866. It was only the situation created by the compromise they had to reach at the emergency Cabinet called on the 25th at Cranborne's request after he had looked at Baxter's statistics which made it necessary to think about introducing a bill instead.

It is not certain what Cranborne was trying to do in demanding the emergency Cabinet. His own account is recorded both in a memorandum, of which Lady Gwendoline Cecil gives a critical account, and in a letter to Elcho dated February 25.[1] On February 16 Cranborne had acquiesced in the decision to sketch the government's proposals before the resolutions were discussed on February

25, and had agreed to abandon the commission so that Disraeli could announce the government's commitment before the resolutions were introduced. The essence of his complaint was that at this point he had begun to feel that the Cabinet was being hustled. On February 25 he had accepted Disraeli's rated residential suffrage because Baxter's statistics, which Disraeli had read out without circulating,[1] seemed to imply that the enfranchisement involved would be comparatively small, but noticed 'accidentally' on working through them in their circulated form on Saturday the 23rd and Sunday the 24th that, although the overall enfranchisement would not be large, it would be uneven and in 'boroughs of less than 25,000 inhabitants in which the Conservatives had an interest', of which his own was one, would give an absolute and 'alarm[ing]' majority to the working classes even when 'allowance ha[d] been made for all deductions and all *counterpoises*'.[2] This, he said, was why on Sunday afternoon he had consulted first Carnarvon and General Peel, and then Hardy, and had written Derby a letter, which was stuck in Derby's letter-box the whole of Sunday night, demanding a Cabinet before the meetings of party and Parliament already planned for Monday afternoon. There is no suggestion in Cranborne's memorandum, in the letter Carnarvon wrote to Derby on the morning of the 25th[3] or in Cranborne's letter to Elcho, that his action was premeditated: it is unlikely that the form it took was premeditated. Also, it is certain at one level that he and Carnarvon were attempting to find out whether the statistics, which they suspected Disraeli of cooking, meant what Cranborne thought they meant, and, then, to do what they could to ensure that no proposal was made unless it was a safe one.

Nevertheless, there are four things to notice. First, Cranborne was chronically suspicious of Disraeli, even though his intense suspicion of Disraeli's attempts to liberalize the Conservative party in the early sixties had been followed by a period in which he seems actively to have approved of him.[4] Cranborne's account amounts to the allegation that Disraeli deliberately concealed from the Cabinet, until the latest moment possible, both the details of the bill he would sketch on the 25th and the statistics on which they rested. Yet, although it is likely that Disraeli wanted as little discussion in Cabinet as possible, he had had the statistics only the day before he presented them: until then, they were being prepared by Dudley

Baxter.[1] Baxter's position about electoral reform was, if anything, more conservative than Cranborne's. If he had interpreted his statistics then as Cranborne interpreted them and as he interpreted them himself after Cranborne had made his point, it is unlikely that he would have offered them as the basis for a safe extension of the franchise. It is equally unlikely, if Baxter did not anticipate Cranborne's objection, that Disraeli would have done so either. Unless we make the assumption—a highly implausible one—that Baxter was part of a Disraeli plot, it is likely that Baxter meant what he said in the memorandum of February 23 which was read out to the Cabinet— that, although the number of voters *qualified* to register in boroughs under the bill the government would propose if the resolutions were adopted would be 810,000,[2] the number *likely* to register would be not more than 625,000. Since only 375,000 of these would be working-class votes, the bill, while being a household suffrage bill, would increase the working-class majority on balance by only 125,000. There can be little doubt that, in contrasting this with Gladstone's bill of 1866, 'the result of [which] was to give 204,000 additional votes to the working classes', Baxter intended to act as draftsman of a very conservative bill. Disraeli may have intended to concede a great deal in the course of discussion if the Liberal party did not break up. He almost certainly wanted to commit the Cabinet to something as soon as possible. But there is no need to assume that he knew at this moment what he would do with the Cabinet's commitment once it was made, or that he was trying to trick the Cabinet into supporting a bill which went further than Cranborne and Peel wanted.

Secondly, Cranborne's uneasiness was known not only to Disraeli, but also to the Queen, to General Grey and to Halifax. Cranborne was in close touch with Elcho, met him on the evening of February 23 to explain what had happened in Cabinet that afternoon and wrote urgently on Monday to say that the policy had been reversed.[3] There is no evidence of direct contact between Halifax and Cranborne on the one hand or between Cranborne and General Grey on the other. At other times Carnarvon seems to have talked freely to Earl Grey. There is nothing to establish that he did so at this time and no reason, if he did, to suppose that he was using Earl Grey's contact with Halifax and General Grey as an instrument of concerted action. Nevertheless, General Grey was emphatic in writing to Derby on February 26 that, when he, General Grey, had had the day before to contradict the assertion made to him by Halifax ('who seemed perfectly acquainted with the nature of the proposals including the double vote') that 'the Cabinet was not agreed', Halifax replied that 'at all events it was not 48 hours ago', and 'mentioned Lord Cranborne's name particularly as object-ing'.[1] Thirdly, Cranborne was the most articulate advocate of fusion in July 1866. Since he advocated it even at the risk of breaking up 'personal and traditional ties' which had so far '[kept] apart those [Tories and constitutional Whigs] who are of one mind upon the most vital question of our generation',[2] one must ask whether his resignation was designed to produce a situation in which it again became a possibility. Indeed, since the supporters of fusion in mid-1866 included Carnarvon, Elcho, Hardy and General Peel, who all played a prominent, and conservative, part in the Reform crisis of 1867, and since Cranborne seems to have wanted an informal elec-toral pact with the anti-Radical Whigs,[3] one must ask whether his resistance was part of a larger plan to establish a Whig/Conservative coalition and get rid of Disraeli.

One must ask the question only in order to dismiss the idea that there was a planned conspiracy. First, because there is no evidence of it. Second, because there seems to have been no collusion be-tween Carnarvon, Peel and Cranborne until Sunday, February 24. Third, though this scarcely amounts to evidence, because, if there had been a conspiracy, it would have been more sensible to press it at the moments at which Peel himself had threatened to resign on February 5 or 16. It is true that Cranborne's first instinct on Febru-ary 24 was to resign instead, as Carnarvon insisted, of asking for a Cabinet to investigate the statistics.[4] It is not certain who would have succeeded Derby if the government had fallen as a result of Cranborne's resignation, had that been offered on February 24. It might have been Russell or Gladstone, but it is equally likely that it would have been Granville, Halifax or Clarendon at the head of a central coalition. Even though Cranborne must have known that his resignation might set off others and bring down the government, it is probable that what he wanted at this time was not coalition but Con-servative persistence in a conservative reform policy, so that 'if. . . changes are to be made [in the constitution], the Conservatives should be in opposition when they are made'.[5] The party situation was in the forefront of his mind in February when he objected 'not to household suffrage' which Disraeli had 'named', but to mentioning any franchise level at all because that would give the Liberal party something specific to attack.[1] It was in his mind on February 22, when he emphasized the importance of fixing a direct taxation counterpoise at the right level for the small boroughs 'on [which] we depend', where 'household suffrage [would] bring in the largest number of voters' and where 'the wealthiest voters [would] be fewest'.[2] It was in his mind when he wrote to Elcho on February 25. There is little doubt that he was looking to a long-term future in which, when Gladstone's position had consolidated in the Liberal party, Whigs and constitutional Liberals would be driven into the arms of a Conservative-dominated coalition as in fact happened under his own leadership in different circumstances twenty years later. Whatever Cranborne intended to achieve, his intervention resulted initially in the decision (reached at the end of a tense and angry Cabinet meeting at lunchtime on February 25)[3] to abandon rated residential suffrage in favour of a £6 rating proposal. This decision, which was suggested by Stanley as an interim compromise, was announced by Derby to a party meeting that afternoon and by Disraeli to the House of Commons that evening, but satisfied hardly anybody.

It failed to satisfy the Cave because it was not what Grosvenor had told Derby they wanted on February 17, and because its members could not see why, having helped to turn out Gladstone in protest against the £7 rental bill in 1866, they should support a Conservative bill of almost exactly the same sort which would *settle* nothing. It offered nothing which Radicals could not expect to get by waiting for another Liberal government. It was unwelcome to the Conservative party because it seemed neither to stand much chance of being passed through the House of Commons nor to provide a reasonable platform on which to go to the country. It showed that the Conservative party could not propose a bill that would stand the slightest chance of being successful. It put the party in the gravest danger. Above all, it exposed Disraeli to a specific commitment which he had little hope of persuading either the House of Commons to accept or the country to approve of.

IV

THE REASSERTION
OF CONSERVATIVE POLICY

'If we cannot retain power, I do not see how a Conservative policy is ever
again to prevail in England.'
Lord John Manners, *Journal* n.d. [but July 1866]

With Disraeli committed to a £6 rating franchise, it seemed to Gladstone and the Liberal leaders that they had paid back the Conservative party for the defeat of June 1866. Right up to the introduction
of the resolutions, their object had been to make the government
introduce a bill. The government had not yet done this, but the bill
to which it was committed if the resolutions were passed, was unlikely to be acceptable to the House of Commons. It was, the Liberal
leaders knew, not the bill Derby had taken to Windsor on Saturday.[1]
It had been accepted by the Cabinet with great reluctance, but the
difficulty the Cabinet had had in agreeing would be nothing beside
the difficulty Disraeli would have in piloting a bill of this sort
through the two Houses. It was not only that Radicals and Gladstonian Liberals would reject the limited enfranchisement involved,
but that Whigs and Adullamites would not accept a situation in
which, having turned out Gladstone in 1866 for a £7 rental bill, they
were expected to accept a £6 rating bill which, as Gladstone pointed
out,[2] was very much the same thing. It was necessary to tread cautiously, to avoid pressing the government too hard, to betray no impatience for office and to leave an impression of willingness to give
the government every inducement to proceed, while keeping the
confidence of advanced opinion in the country at large.[3] Neither Sir
George Grey on February 25 nor Gladstone on February 26 pressed
the government to abandon the resolutions.[4] Nevertheless, Liberal
caution seemed to have produced its reward—the opportunity to
unite the Liberal party on a destructive policy which would be
acceptable to everyone in it.

Gladstone's reply to the government's proposal, and to the willingness Disraeli showed to abandon such of the resolutions as might

not be acceptable to the House,[1] was therefore to press him to convert the resolutions into a bill, give them more detailed shape or explain which of them should be taken to embody principles on which the government would stand or fall. On February 25 and 26 he did not make an alternative proposal. Despite Disraeli's belief, or need to induce in Derby, the House of Commons and the country, the belief, that he had done so,[2] Gladstone gave no hint in his speeches that he intended to commit himself to the £5 rating proposal Disraeli attempted to saddle him with. He confined himself, in the House of Commons on February 25 and 26 and at the party meeting of February 26, to reminding the government of its obligation, as a government, to make a definite proposal for the House's consideration. On hearing Disraeli's announcement on February 26[3] that the government intended at last to introduce a bill, he made a point of leaving the impression that the opposition would support it if it could, and

express[ed] a confident hope, and further, a very earnest and sincere desire, that we may find [the] bill to be such that we can not only assent to it, but even promote and expedite its passage through its earlier stages [which was taken to mean the second reading] so that, if it be conducive to the public interest, we may join issue with Her Majesty's Government [in committee] on those subjects...upon which we may, unfortunately, be compelled to differ from the conclusions to which Her Majesty's Government may have come.[4]

In doing this, he thought he could carry the whole of the Liberal party with him, including Elcho, Grosvenor and their followers, who spoke in support of Gladstone at the party meeting in Gladstone's house on February 26. He thought, also, no doubt that it would lead to the defeat or break-up of the government. Nor was this an unreasonable thing to think. Gladstonian Liberals would follow him. Radicals could not be expected to vote for a Conservative bill unless they found it particularly attractive, which they did not. The Cave had no desire to vote for it either. Gladstone could not have been blamed if he thought he had the ball at his feet.[5]

In fact, though the ball was at his feet, it was kicked away at once. The announcement of the £6 rating proposal was as devastating to the Conservative party as it was to the Cave. Conservatives were not *wanting* to be Radical, but they wanted to be led. They wanted office and success: they had the one, and did not want to be denied the other. Not all knew that the £6 proposal was an interim compromise which had been reached in order to keep the Cabinet united, but they could see that it would not meet the situation in which it was proposed. They knew that the Conservative party was in danger. They knew that Gladstone was waiting for them. They needed to be told how to take up a position which Gladstone could not occupy.

What Disraeli had done on February 25 was to announce the government's intention, not to introduce a bill. Nor, before the debate began, was it proposed to introduce a bill before the resolutions were discussed. The point in discussing resolutions was to divide the Liberal party while sounding opinion in the House of Commons: until the Cabinet was forced, on February 25, to agree to a £6 rating bill instead of to rated residential suffrage, it had seemed possible that this might happen. The course of the debate on February 25, the disappointment felt by Conservatives and Adullamites at the proposal itself and the unity which Gladstone had succeeded in establishing in the Liberal party, however, removed all expectation of profiting from Liberal dissension. It made it impossible to think of appealing against him to the country. It made it seem likely that Gladstone would 'play with us till we are contemptible'.[1] The attempt to divide the Liberal party had failed. The resolutions no longer had any point. Gladstone, as leader of the majority party, had the initiative. It was necessary, if the initiative was to be regained, to remove Gladstone's power of manœuvre.

Gladstone's power of manœuvre stemmed not from any real unity in the Liberal party on the Reform question but from the incidental fact that the dissension on which the government had relied had been destroyed by the timidity of the government's proposal and the target its inadequacy presented to anyone who wanted to attack it. If Disraeli had been able to hold out hope of a serious settlement of the question on February 25, the inadequacy of the resolutions would not have mattered. But their inadequacy, when combined with a specific proposal which satisfied nobody and would settle nothing, seemed likely to remove any goodwill there might have been before. Whether Disraeli had, or (as we suggest) had not, been trying in the previous six months to commit the Cabinet to legislation more quickly than it wanted to, ministers seem now to have had no doubt that unforced commitment to immediate legislation was unavoidable if they were to prevent themselves being driven by Gladstone's pressure into commitment that was not spontaneous. At the same time as Gladstone was deciding to table a notice to the same effect, the Cabinet decided on the morning of February 26 to replace the resolutions by a bill—which Disraeli announced he would introduce to the House of Commons in a week's time.[1]

The Cabinet which took this decision was the Cabinet which had come into office in July 1866, including Cranborne, Carnarvon and General Peel. Though Cranborne had wanted to resign on the previous Sunday, he had not done so. Nor did he resign now. It was Peel's refusal to support household suffrage in any form which had produced the first crisis in February: on this occasion, the initiative was Cranborne's. The last decision the Cabinet had made on February 25 had been made in deference to him: there was no reason why he should take the initiative in resigning. It is unlikely that he minded very much what bill was adopted, so long as it would not damage the party's reputation. Assuming, like everyone else, that Gladstone would propose a £5 amendment to the government's £6 rating bill if that was persisted in, he was happy 'to take our stand on 6 against 5'.[2] Carnarvon was an earnest, doctrinaire, illiberal young man who wanted, if possible, to follow any lead which Derby might give. He had 'no objection. . . to the general principle of the scheme which we abandoned on Monday', but had withdrawn his support because Disraeli had produced no answer to Cranborne's demolition of Baxter's statistics.[3] Peel, while clear about what he would not accept, had a strong desire to keep the party together. There was no reason why any of these should take the initiative in pressing the Cabinet to abandon the policy their intervention had forced it to adopt, even though that policy would be disastrous in the House of Commons.

However, although they did not want a change of front, Derby and Disraeli did. Cranborne's letter and the Cabinet meeting of February 25 had been particularly irritating to Derby. He seems to have thought (and thought rightly) that he could handle Peel, so long as Peel was acting alone. Carnarvon was a follower. It was objectionable to have a carefully managed assault on the Liberal party thwarted by an arrogant, highly intelligent and manifestly contemptuous junior minister. Whether Disraeli thought Cranborne was acting in collusion with the Whigs or whether 'treachery' meant nothing in particular[4], Derby knew that Cranborne was the enemy, and decided to defeat him. In this he was both pressed and supported by Disraeli for whom the decision of February 25 was a defeat of a signal and significant sort. Having succeeded, by deft and devious diplomacy, in bringing a united Cabinet to the point of decision on February 20 and 23, Disraeli, like Derby, had been routed at the last ditch. He had been routed personally: the consequences would be disastrous politically. He knew that the £6 rating proposal stood no chance in the House of Commons. Cranborne did not mind (because he wanted to maintain a conservative position more than he wanted to pass a bill), but Disraeli minded very much. At a moment at which it seemed that he and Derby had squared the circle by persuading a united Cabinet to agree to proposals which would stand a chance in the House of Commons, both he and the party had been put at Gladstone's mercy. The question now was whether Disraeli and Derby were going to be driven by Gladstone and Cranborne, or whether Disraeli and Derby were going to drive them instead.

From February 26 onwards, therefore, Disraeli reverted to the policy he had proposed in early February and withdrawn in deference to General Peel, which he had revived on February 19 and withdrawn again on February 25, and which he now pressed Derby to accept, even if doing so divided the Cabinet and forced dissident ministers to resign. The rated residential suffrage policy returned to the forefront of Disraeli's mind, not as a kite to be flown in order to give discussion of the resolutions a chance to destroy the Liberal party, but as a firm commitment which would give the government a chance to regain some part of the initiative it had lost. Since it was unlikely that a united Cabinet would accept it, Derby's support was critical: since at least three ministers would resign, replacements were essential. Since it was by no means certain that the Conservative party as a whole would accept household suffrage from a truncated Cabinet, acceptance had to be prepared carefully.

The object was not just to produce a piece of useful legislation; it was to prevent the 'utter ruin' of the Conservative party.[1] It was not a detached decision taken without reference to party and personal considerations, but a deliberate attempt to repair the 'ignominious disruption' of the party by which it was taken. In other circumstances or under other leadership, it might have been possible to co-operate with Gladstone or the Whigs. Derby's first reaction was to ask the Queen for mediation: Walpole's to think of coalition with the Adullamites, and then of resignation. Under guidance from General Grey, the Queen offered mediation between Gladstone and the government on the basis of the £6 rating proposal of February 25.[1] Her, or perhaps Grey's, anxiety to keep the government in office made her suppose that 'the first impulse of some of the staunchest Liberal members was to be satisfied with it'. Even if it could not be persisted in, she was willing to support Derby in any action he might take.

In a situation in which the Conservative party was 'in a broken and disorganized condition', it is unlikely that Gladstone would have co-operated except on his own terms: it is certain that Disraeli did not want co-operation. He did not want it because he could gain nothing from it and would probably lose, and because a bill passed by agreement with the Liberal party would confirm the impression that the Conservative party could not govern, deprive it of the chance of damaging Liberal unity, and greatly inflate the power of Cranborne and Peel. Whether he wanted to avoid it because he knew that Gladstone could not persuade a united Liberal party to accept a £6 rating suffrage, or because the safest way through the crisis from his own point of view was to generate tension in Parliament, and a distinction in the country, between Gladstone and the Conservative party, there can be no doubt of the vigour with which on February 26, 27 and 28 he exerted himself to dissuade Derby from considering any sort of crossbench arrangement.[2]

This was, in Disraeli's mind, a moment of crisis, in which, as in July 1866, it was necessary to keep close to Derby in order to ensure that he kept control of the party. Coalition with the Cave had been averted in 1866; Disraeli did not want it now. Whereas the initiative in Reform decisions in late 1866 came almost invariably from Derby, at this moment the initiative was Disraeli's. It was Disraeli who suggested replacing Cranborne, Carnarvon and Peel by Richmond and Lowry-Corry, though Derby's first reaction made it seem unlikely that he would do so.[3] Though he knew that Baxter now agreed with Cranborne that 'the larger scheme of rating household suffrage and duality...would...hand over all these small boroughs to the working classes',[4] he nevertheless pressed it, and pressed others to press it, on Derby.

Baxter was in touch with the Adullamites. On February 28 he was trying to interest them in the £6 rating bill by making personal payment of rates a precondition of the right to vote and by removing houses rated at and above £6 p.a. from the operation of the Small Tenements Act, in this way providing 'a better chance of finality... and a barrier to further change'.[1] It is unlikely, however, that Disraeli at this point had any intention of taking special pains to trim his sails to anybody. There is no evidence to show what part he played in determining the form of rated residential suffrage that was chosen by the Cabinet on March 2, but it is certain that the bill which was eventually accepted was different both from what Gladstone seemed likely to support and from what the Cave was supposed to want. Since we do not have Dudley Baxter's papers, and since Disraeli kept no letter-books, it is difficult to be certain of the reasons for the rejection of Baxter's policy. But the policy Baxter proposed in drafting the bill the Cabinet had adopted on February 25 was not adopted: the pains he was taking to keep in touch with Adullamite opinion were disregarded.

Right from the point on February 26 at which the Cabinet decided to introduce a bill, it seems to have been Disraeli's idea to replace the bill the Cabinet had accepted by the widest measure possible: it is difficult to believe that he was not, even on February 26 and 27, aiming not only at the Cave which, though it wanted rated residential suffrage, wanted counterpoises too, but also at the left of the Liberal party on the one hand and an open-handed electoral appeal to 'the country' on the other.[2] Though there is no sign of any attempt to suborn Radicals before this, the weakness which Cranborne's action had produced made co-operation with Radicals desirable. If the government had been stronger and more united, Disraeli might have been willing to propose, and keep to, a restrictive bill. If there had been no sign of public weakness, he might have persisted in the hope that a Cave/Conservative combination would be able either to pass it or to produce conflict in the Liberal party extensive enough to justify a general election. If the rated residential suffrage with counterpoises and compensations which the Cabinet had adopted on February 23 had been proposed to the House of Commons on February 25 as a basis for discussion of the resolutions, it is possible, on the other hand, that Disraeli would have tried to persuade the Cabinet to dismantle the counterpoises and compensations if parliamentary opinion had crystallized against them. Whether he would have adopted the one course or the other would have depended on the strength shown by Cranborne, Hardy, Carnarvon and Peel in resisting persistent expressions of parliamentary opinions contrary to their own. What is certain is that Cabinet dissension, Liberal unity, Cranborne's resistance and the reception given to the £6 rating suffrage proposed on February 25 had made controlled sounding of parliamentary opinion impossible, and that, if the Cabinet was to be persuaded to abandon counterpoises and compensations, it would have to dismantle them of its own accord.

At some point between February 25, when the Cabinet adopted Stanley's £6 rating compromise, and March 18 when Disraeli introduced the first reading of the rated residential suffrage bill, his chief object was, therefore, to persuade the Cabinet to *anticipate* parliamentary opinion which he had previously wanted only to *sound* by removing most of the counterpoises and compensations before they were removed for it. There is nothing to show what he intended when the Cabinet gave unanimous approval to rated residential suffrage on February 23. However much he may have wanted, as one possible course of action, to remove the limitations established by that proposal on rated residential suffrage, it was the critical weakness produced by the Cranborne rebellion which both made him and enabled him to press the policy of removing restrictions with the decisiveness he gave it in the weeks following.[1] A Cabinet in which Cranborne, Carnarvon and Peel had been replaced by Lowry-Corry, Marlborough and Richmond was not likely to be vigilant: the threat from an opposition which smelt victory, and a Cave which had been disillusioned, made decisive action essential. Just as Peel's resistance to household suffrage in early February had produced conditions in which the Cabinet could be committed to it, so, if Cranborne had not resisted on February 25, Disraeli might well have conceded much less in the months following if he had been able to concede anything at all. Although Cranborne was wrong in thinking that the Conservative party as a whole would support him, he reflected the realities of the situation when he answered Derby's announcement of the change of policy on March 1 by saying that 'with the opinions you entertain...you are taking the most expedient course, [and that] the removal of dissension from your Cabinet will undoubtedly tend to strengthen it'.[2]

A conversation between Disraeli and Bright in the Lobby of the House of Commons on March 1 which left Bright the impression that 'Derby and Disraeli will try to go on. . . and we shall help them to carry. . . a better bill',[1] Disraeli's willingness, after a moment of suitable reticence, to encourage Graves, Goldney, Jervis and Laird —four Conservative MP.s—to set on foot a movement in the Carlton Club against Cranborne, Carnarvon and Peel, his pressure on Derby to reconstruct the Cabinet by replacing these three with his own nominees, all testify to the critical nature of the situation by which he was faced. The success of the Carlton Club movement, Derby's agreement to reconstruct the Cabinet and the Cabinet's adoption of the more extended plan mark a signal and significant triumph over the group which had tried most persistently to remove him. Whether this possibility was in Disraeli's mind in proposing household suffrage to the Cabinet before February 16, the demand he stimulated now for a bold, independent initiative was both a *party* and a *personal* necessity. It was the need to differentiate his own and the party's position from Gladstone's, and not any particular hostility to a £5 or to any other rating franchise, which made him persuade first Derby, then the Cabinet, and finally the party as a whole, to revert to his original and 'larger' policy of rated residential suffrage.

Derby claimed to have noticed, in talking to the party meeting after the lunch-time Cabinet on the 25th, that some backbenchers would have preferred the rated residential suffrage which had been rejected by the Cabinet that morning.[2] Derby was not, either then or in the week following, as certain as Disraeli that the party as a whole would accept it.[3] But, even if he did not deliberately invite a demand by letting the party hear of it as a rejected alternative when it would have been enough to announce the government's £6 rating policy as an agreed decision, he was prepared, even before Disraeli's pressure began, to prefer it. Disraeli, nevertheless, brought pressure to bear. The small boroughs had been the centre of Cranborne's attention; the chief Whip was told to prepare reports showing the effect of the original bill on them and to collect opinions from 'every [small borough] member on our side of his individual feelings and wishes'.[4]

In the seven months which had passed since Gladstone's defeat in June 1866, there had been a marked change in Conservative feeling.

This was partly a reaction to Derby's decision that the government must deal with the Reform question itself: it was much more a feeling, of which that decision was an aspect, that the climate of public opinion made action essential. If Derby had not decided that something must be done, Conservatives would not have reached the position many had by now reached. If they had been able to remain negatively resistant to Gladstone, the opinions they convinced themselves that they had always held would never have been expressed. Nevertheless, once Derby's decision had been made, they took stock of the situation: once they did so, they saw advantages, and much less danger than they had expected, from a measure which would be bold, decisive and final. They saw that, whereas for a long time the Conservative party had been the 'stupid' party[1] for which intelligent opinion had great contempt, there was now a chance that this phase was passing. Palmerston's mantle was descending on Derby: the arrival of Gladstone, and the contact between public agitation and the Liberal party, was making the Conservative party more respectable than it had been for many years past. It was, therefore, not fear of public agitation which made Conservatives willing to grasp the Reform question, but a vague sense that a settlement might be reached which would put an end to the question for good without damaging existing constitutional arrangements or their own prospects for the future. When to this was added the fact that the advantage the Conservative party had gained from dissension in the Liberal party was being destroyed by 'a vacillating and subservient policy' in their own, it became clear that 'the *only* course that [could] serve our credit before the country [was] for [Derby's] master-mind to determine what [was] the best bill',[2] for 'all of us...[to] stand by [him] to the utmost of our power'[3] and for 'the government [to] make up their minds what is the ultimatum which they intend to propose or to accept, announce that to the party and the House, and then stand or fall by that decision'.[4] It was at the point at which this climate of feeling was induced that the largest steps forward were taken as Conservatives convinced themselves that not only was franchise reduction feasible but that household suffrage might positively help them.

The Cabinet had adopted rated residential suffrage in the first place because, while sounding a serious contribution to the question (i.e. household suffrage), it could, because it was a serious contribution, be surrounded by suitable safeguards and presented as a conservative measure. The Cave had for long thought it adequate because it provided a final resting-place which could be combined with plurality, cumulative voting and three years residence. In early and mid-February, when Cabinet unity was the first consideration, any resignation (particularly General Peel's) could have been disastrous. Rated residential suffrage had been abandoned then in order to keep the Cabinet united. The position now in Disraeli's view was that it was essential to get as much support as possible in the House of Commons and to establish maximum credibility in the country. Even if that involved dividing the Cabinet in order to do so, the critical character of the situation made it much more reasonable than before to suggest that persons (even persons as popular as General Peel) should be abandoned in order to save the party.

Rated residential suffrage with safeguards was regarded as a socially conservative measure, which had operated conservatively in some places under the municipal franchise and had the additional merit of enabling the party to take a step which would not be a capitulation to Gladstone. Whether with a view to carrying it into law or as a means of constructing a party platform, this combination of feelings was wide-spread and deep-rooted in the days following the fiasco of February 25. Disraeli did his best to stimulate it, but Disraeli by himself could not have produced the expression of opinion which between a third and a half of the party gave at a meeting of 150 MP.s on Thursday the 28th at the Carlton Club—that rated residential suffrage would not just solve the Reform question, but would also save the party. This was not a movement of county MP.s ditching the boroughs in order to get a reasonable redistribution of seats, or of borough members calculating that electors below the £7 rental or £5 rating level would be more Conservative than those above. Although Graves, Goldney, Jervis and Laird—the initiators of the movement—were members for English boroughs, the movement was more extensive and deep-rooted than that. It spread across the whole party and did so because the party was thinking of immediate survival as much as of ultimate electoral possibility. There was a feeling that 'we should fix upon the franchise we thought best and then stick to it, declining to carry our opponent's measures'.[1] There was a feeling that, since we 'could not..go to the country' if beaten in the House on the £6 proposal, 'we should stand by...whatever we proposed [instead]...and not accept amendments dictated by Gladstone'.[1] Opinions differed about the merits of £5 rating as opposed to household suffrage, but household suffrage was acceptable to the meeting because, at the moment at which it was proposed, it was not intended that the restrictions and counterpoises should be abandoned. Though there are occasional hints[2] at the possibility of passing a rated residential suffrage bill *without* restrictions or counterpoises, there is no sign in the correspondence of ministers of any *intention* to abandon them, and there were many ingenious attempts to make sure that the right ones would be adopted.[3] In moving towards 'household suffrage, two or three years residence [and] rates paid by occupiers and not compounded for by landlords',[4] the Conservative party was supporting a franchise which, if not necessarily intended to be more limited in *scale* than any fixed-line franchise without personal payment, was expected, as Laird told Derby, to 'be a more Conservative and satisfactory measure' and more 'likely to promote the interest of the Conservative cause than any mere lowering to £5 or to £4', and was, in any case, designed to fall short of household suffrage pure and simple by the omission of the very large number of occupiers who would have neither resided for two or three years nor paid their own rates.[5]

Though there was no unanimity about the desirability of rated residential suffrage, there was enough support to justify Derby and Disraeli proposing it: their reaction to the hostile reception given to the £6 Rating bill was to do so. The decisions taken between February 26 and March 2 were not just decisions about the merits of the bill: they were decisions about the future of the Conservative party. They were decisions to reject the policy, pursued half-heartedly hitherto, of taking particular pains to play along Adullamites and dissident Whigs,[6] in favour of a policy of marking out a distinctive Conservative line in the hope that these others, and the left of the Liberal party, would follow. They were decisions to present the counterpoises and compensations, which Cranborne had already disposed of,[7] as material guarantees which backbenchers would not for the moment see through. They were decisions to create in Cabinet, though not yet in public, a climate which would make detailed calculation irrelevant and statistics unhelpful, and which implied a deep-seated 'trust' in 'the people'.[8] They were decisions that Disraeli and Derby were going to run the Conservative party, not Cranborne and Peel, and that those elements in the party which wanted to get rid of Disraeli would have to destroy the party in the process. They were designed to demonstrate that Disraeli and Derby knew better than 'General Peel and Lord Cranborne [who] have acted in a complete ignorance and misapprehension of the real feeling of the Conservative party'.[1] The decision the Cabinet had made on February 23 but rejected two days later, was taken again now, not with the risk of 'being booted out' by the party (as Peel had predicted when it was taken),[2] but in the certainty that something like two-thirds of the party supported it. Cranborne's analysis of Baxter's statistics had demolished the justification which ministers offered themselves in accepting it on February 23: they supported it now even though the justification had disappeared. They supported it because 'our present plan excites no interest on our own side, will be mercilessly pulled to pieces by Mr Gladstone and we shall fall ignominiously',[3] because resignation would be humiliating in the extreme, and because a Gladstone government in these circumstances would be able 'to dictate [its] own terms,...introduce a more Radical bill than last year' and inflict immense damage on the Conservative party in the process.[4] This was a decision to appeal to the body of the Conservative party in the House against dissidence in the Cabinet and the menace of Gladstone. It involved a widening of the range of policy the Conservative party as a whole was willing to consider, and a widening of the sort of franchise the party was willing to propose. It involved doing what Lowe predicted would be done if the government dealt with the Reform question—approaching the House of Commons as a minority with no power absolutely to determine what was done or decided about the contents of the bill. Since the feasibility of the policy depended on the Conservative party remaining united, it necessitated a heightening of party tension.

The Carlton Club meeting took place on Thursday, February 28. The decision to ask the Cabinet to revert to the original plan was taken by Derby and Disraeli on February 28 or 29. Peel, Carnarvon and Cranborne (with a warmth which diminished in that order) were warned by Derby that the policy would have to be reversed. Northcote was sent to persuade Carnarvon to stay.[5] Derby had an unsuccessful interview with Peel who, though he thought new proposals would be accepted by the party, was 'immovable' about his own position.[1] Each member of the Cabinet was asked in Cabinet on March 2 to say whether he agreed. When only these three said they could not, and announced their intention to resign (Peel with the greatest reluctance, Carnarvon because he no longer thought an answer could be given to Cranborne's statistics), the Cabinet as a whole accepted the proposal. The policy to which the Cabinet agreed was to revert to rated residential suffrage combined with fancy franchises, the counterpoise of duality for direct tax-payers and £10 householders, and the restrictions of two or three years residence and the personal payment of rates. At first the Cabinet committed itself to abandon none of these. At the Cabinet meeting of March 2, and at the drafting meeting Hardy had with Derby and Disraeli on March 6, the commitment was unambiguous. It remained unambiguous just so long as the crisis persisted.

V

THE DESTRUCTION OF
LIBERAL UNITY

'If the government stand or fall by dual voting, they and their bill are
doomed; but I fear, when it comes to the point, they will conform to the
Jew's opinion in all things. . . and yield to [his] arguments for the sake of
keeping the party together.'

Sir Rainald Knightley to Cranborne, n.d. [but March 1867].
Salisbury MSS

(i) THE ESTABLISHING OF THE CONSERVATIVE BILL

The policy of March 2 was adopted because no other policy was
available, because dependence on the Whigs and the Cave was to be
rejected, and because the 'unenviable and humiliating position'[1] in
which the Conservative party found itself made it seem so 'contemptible'[2] that it had to make the bravest show possible. Nevertheless it transformed the situation. The outcome of the events it set in
motion was victory over Gladstone, not so much on the second reading of the bill, though that passed without a division on March 26,
but in the Tea-Room revolt of April 8, in the withdrawal without a
division of the second half of Coleridge's Instruction on going into
committee on April 10, and in the defeat of Gladstone's first amendment to clause 3 of the bill on April 12, when the split which had
been threatened, and averted, in the Conservative party was carried
to the point of actuality in the Liberal party and the Cave. The question we have to ask is: how did this happen?

The point in changing policies was not, just yet, to pass an Act of
Parliament. Disraeli and Derby had been edged to the point at
which they had had to stake their future on a bill, but they did not
necessarily frame it in order to pass the House of Commons.[3] In the
first week of March, on the contrary, they were moving boldly in the
dark, searching less for an Act of Parliament than for an alibi or
slogan on which to unite their own party, attack Gladstone and, if
necessary, face the country. The immediate question was not the
passage of a bill, but whether the bill which the Cabinet had agreed

166

in principle on March 2 should be proposed on March 18 would be accepted by the Cabinet in final form: whether it would get through its second reading and into committee; or, if it did not, whether the party might fight and win an election in defence of it.

For all these purposes a rated residential suffrage bill was particularly suitable. It was suitable because it faced both ways. To the Cave and to many Conservatives, household suffrage combined with personal payment of rates, plurality and a two or three year residential qualification involved an intelligible principle on which the borough franchise could be settled for a generation. So long as restrictions and counterpoises were retained (and no one outside the Derby/Disraeli circle was thinking of abandoning them on March 1), there was a chance that this would be a very conservative measure which would not be much more extensive than the bill of 1859, except in respect of the borough franchise level.[1] Liberals might hesitate to oppose a household suffrage bill, which some of their constituents were supposed to want, however limited the form it was given. Radicals might note the affirmation of a rated residential suffrage principle and expect the restrictive clauses to be removed in committee and the personal payment principle modified to remove the anomalies it would produce. Bright seems at first to have been the only Radical with whom Disraeli had contact: whether because he thought the Conservative party would accept it, or because he thought it would not, he offered support for a £5 rating franchise or household suffrage. After their meeting on March 1, he expected Disraeli to propose a bill which he would be able to support.[2] Stanley left the impression, in speaking in the House of Commons on March 5, that, if household suffrage were proposed, it would be heavily restricted. Four days later Bright nevertheless (perhaps therefore) encouraged Disraeli to think he would deal sympathetically with a Conservative bill provided household suffrage was not 'accompanied by any novel propositions, in themselves evil or undesirable, and proposed only as restrictions on, or compensations for, household suffrage'.[3] When Disraeli's bill was eventually produced, Bright, like every other leader of the public agitation, thought it dishonest.[4] Since, in the course of preparation, he invited Disraeli to bid for support, it is reasonable to assume that Disraeli on March 1 had encouraged him to think it worth his while to do so.

When the broad outline of the bill was first adopted in Cabinet and canvassed inside the party between February 26 and March 18, most ministers undoubtedly intended, as Stanley explained when criticized by Lowe in the House of Commons for attempting to 'outbid the late Government,...that their proposal would be found to contain safeguards and compensations and that they would stand or fall by it'.[1] The 'safeguards' which were to be offered were two or three years residence and personal payment of rates (i.e. exclusion of householders whose rates were paid on their behalf by composition). 'Compensations' at no time meant more than two sorts of duality,[2] duality being part of the original package-deal because it assured Conservative doubters of the conservative character of the bill. The whole was treated by Cabinet ministers like Stanley, Manners,[3] Malmesbury[4] and Hardy[5] as a firm commitment which the Cabinet would defend against opposition inside or outside the House and which they were prepared, if necessary, to take to the country on a Reforming and anti-revolutionary ticket.[6]

Whatever other ministers thought, it is certain that Disraeli thought differently. Once the Cabinet was publicly committed on March 5 to revert to the wider measure which Cranborne's, Derby's, Carnarvon's and his own speeches had hinted at without explaining the content of, he began to step up the pressure for conciliation. Whereas in the winter of 1866/67 he had been flexible and accommodating in Cabinet, he began now to press for rapid concession. Having got rid of his critics, he could do so: the decision to do so surprised some of those who were closest to events. Hardy, Buckingham, Manners, Walpole and Henley (who had been offered the Home Office in 1866 and refused it because of his age[7]) at various moments in the fortnight following were all shocked by Disraeli's willingness to concede. When Disraeli first tried to persuade the Cabinet to drop duality, Hardy recorded his 'amazement as Disraeli left the ground [about duality] which I imagined was at least permanently agreed on since last Thursday'. He found it 'sad to have dissentients behind us' on the second reading,[8] and 'generally left [Cabinets]', as he recorded the day duality was abandoned, 'without much satisfaction and in this instance not more than usual'. On April 11 he wanted 'a good steady resistance to Gladstone and no more surrender'. On April 13 (in circumstances which we shall look at again) he doubted whether he 'could again serve under so unscrupulous a man as Disraeli'.[9] Earle had been Dis-

raeli's contact man with the Cave in the session of 1866 and an advocate of co-operation with the constitutional Whigs; he had been a
follower of Disraeli for a good many years before that. Earle was an
adventurer, and was regarded as such by respectable members of the
party. He was much put out by the preference Disraeli showed in
office, as confidant and private secretary, for Corry who was not an
adventurer. Earle was also member for a geographically extensive
small borough in Essex whose political character would be transformed by Disraeli's bill. Whatever the reason for doing so, he
resigned the minor office he held under Hardy at the Poor Law
board on March 18 on the ground that 'the Reform bill which has
today been introduced . . . is one which it is impossible for me to support'.[1] Dudley Baxter—the sole draughtsman of Reform proposals
until March 14—was a persistent advocate of a conservative bill by
prior agreement with the Cave. He showed little understanding of
the change of tempo. The transfer of responsibility for drafting the
bill to Thring, the regular Treasury draughtsman, who was 'a very
safe man, a good draughtsman and a fair politician'[2] and whom
Baxter found 'determined to remodel the bill and animated by no
conciliatory spirit towards myself' was, no doubt, in part a recognition of administrative practice.[3] It was in addition very probably a
decision by Disraeli to free himself from the rigidity of an upholder
of the principles on which the Conservative party had conducted itself over the last twenty-five years, a man who was 'a puritanical
prig' for 'presum[ing] "to tell" a prime minister' that in the small
boroughs rated residential suffrage with duality would produce
'beer-barrels and douceurs',[4] and who, on hearing of the Cabinet
decision that Thring should replace him, could 'only hope that the
government may not find their bill completed on principles at
variance with those on which it has been drawn and not in harmony
with the wants and wishes of the Conservative party'.[5]

Rated residential suffrage was accepted in principle by the
Cabinet on March 2. The bill was drafted thereafter by Disraeli,
Derby and Baxter, discussed in Cabinet on March 9 and 12,
approved in principle on March 14 and explained in principle to a
party meeting next day. It was redrafted by Thring on Derby's
instructions on March 15, printed that night in preparation for
Cabinet discussion, approved on the 18th and published the morning after Disraeli had introduced it in the House of Commons.[6] As

early as March 9 Disraeli tried to persuade the Cabinet to drop duality. He succeeded then in confining it to payers of direct taxation, because that was the only qualification to affect substantial numbers, but failed to persuade them to abandon that.[1] He failed again on March 11, 20 and 23 in face of resistance from Hardy, Buckingham and Walpole. Gladstone made duality the major target for attack on March 18. It was abandoned by the Cabinet before the second reading on March 25 in circumstances in which *The Times* was against it, in which some Conservatives objected to it because 'it took away with one hand' the working-class enfranchisement that 'it gave with the other'[2] and in which others—including enemies of the bill—believed that 'it would be...wholly inadequate to secure the object for which it was introduced...to maintain a fair balance of power between the various classes of the community'.[3] It was abandoned because Derby, who had been clear in the different party situation of early February that 'without plurality of voting we cannot propose household suffrage which would give the working classes a majority of nearly 2:1', asserted his authority on Disraeli's behalf, directly in Cabinet and through correspondence with Naas, the Irish Chief Secretary who was in Ireland, and indirectly through the correspondence of his private secretary with Malmesbury whose wife's illness kept him away from London throughout March.[4]

When duality was abandoned, although abandonment was serious, it was less serious than it might have been because its supporters, while regarding it as a symbol of intention, attached 'little or no weight' to its practical effect.[5] It was less serious, also, because, when abandonment was accepted, the main restrictions appeared to remain. Although Disraeli on March 18, and again on March 25, promised to consider any opinion the House of Commons might express about the lodger franchise and the detailed application of the personal payment principle, the bill the Cabinet accepted included a two-year residential qualification, excluded the compound householder and was intended to do so. Although there were boroughs in which compounding occurred in respect of houses rated at more than £6 p.a., the great body of compounders occupied houses rated at less than £6 p.a. In discussing the possibility of household suffrage on February 11[6], Baxter had drawn attention to the fact that 'the measure of enfranchisement granted below £6 depends entirely upon...the decision whether vicarious ratepaying is made sufficient or not'. It is probable that most, if not all, Cabinet ministers, and a large part of the party, regarded the personal payment principle as a restriction, and accepted it, not just because it supplied a principle which Gladstone had not thought of, but because, while giving the Conservative party the tactical advantage of having a principle to propose, it would confine the enfranchisement to a comparatively small number of electors.[1]

In supporting the proposals of March 2 in the form in which they were presented on March 18 and 25, they were committing themselves to a comparatively small enfranchisement and to a principle, in relation to the borough franchise—the personal payment of rates —which was regarded as a guarantee that those who had enough property, however little, to pay rates would be careful not to give power to those who, having none, would wish to attack those who had a great deal. If a Cabinet minister or MP. had been asked in the second or third week of March to defend the adoption of rated residential suffrage, he might well have replied, in the words of an elderly, literary Conservative backbencher, that the difference between the £5 rating line, which Gladstone was expected to suggest, and rated residential suffrage on these terms was thought to be 'very small', that it was not 'at all certain that in many boroughs the lower-class voters would not be quite as Conservative as those just above them', and that its adoption would give the Conservative party a position from which 'it could not be assailed from the Liberal side of the House', 'some chance of confronting the Hustings with success' and 'strength better to fight the conservative parts of the bill—the limited amount of disfranchisement and redistribution, the withdrawal of the borough voters from the counties, the increase of the county representation, the...fancy franchises and the voting papers'.[2] He would have emphasized, in addition, not only the fact that the government was proposing a *principle*, but also the limitation the principle would impose on the enfranchisement of 'numbers'. This is reflected in one aspect of Disraeli's speeches of March 18 and March 25, in which he commanded assent among Conservatives and in some parts of the opposition both by touching on the smallness of the certain enfranchisement involved and by emphasizing the government's insistence on the personal payment principle.

These speeches are notable, not just for what they say, but also for what they say in parentheses or omit to say at all. While emphasizing the smallness of the *certain* enfranchisement involved in bringing on to the register all householders who personally paid their rates already, Disraeli was vague about his intentions with regard to those who did not. He not only did not commit the government to exclude them (as he might have done if his policy had been to restrict the *size* of enfranchisement): he attacked Gladstone for limiting enfranchisement in exactly this way. To calculate that, by adopting one figure (a £7 rental) 'a certain portion of [the working classes] would be admitted, but that, if another figure were adopted...the number admitted would be excessive', and to propose a franchise qualification on that basis, he told the House, had produced in 1866 a bill founded 'not...on a principle...but on expediency'.[1] The principle the House had accepted, in accepting Dunkellin's amendment in June 1866, was that the electoral qualification should be a rating qualification, and this was right. It was right 'because [to be liable to pay rates] is the best evidence of the trustworthiness of the individual':[2] because, by adopting that principle, 'you know where you are; you know that the power of electing members of parliament must be exercised by men who, by their position in life, have shown that they are qualified for its exercise';[3] and because, where Gladstone's reduction of the borough franchise qualification to £7 rental would have invited persistent agitation until the value limit was reduced to nothing and *manhood* suffrage established, removal of the value limit altogether, combined with insistence on a personal rating qualification, would produce a permanent arrangement against which agitation could not easily be mounted.

In asserting this 'principle', Disraeli was giving Conservative MP.s what they wanted—an answer to the claim to a *monopoly* of principle to which Gladstone's and Bright's mode of utterance lent itself,[4] an opportunity to show that the Conservative party had principles which were relevant to the major question of the age, assistance in reconciling themselves to disagreeable necessities by differentiating Conservative principles from the principles of Bright,[5] and a lead in doing so by asserting that rated residential suffrage and the personal rating principle, so far from being democratic or radical in tendency, were both 'popular' and 'conservative in the highest sense'.

However, although the principle had a rhetorical function to which Conservatives and some Whigs responded, the prominence Disraeli gave it involved a subtle, but discernable, shift of emphasis within the framework of Cabinet and party policy. Instead of making the central feature a desire to prevent the enfranchisement of 'numbers' (over which Cranborne and Carnarvon had resigned, in relation to which Liberals were pressing for papers,[1] and about which Gladstone was probing),[2] he emphasized that 'it is [not] our business to act the part of electioneering agents and to make estimates, always of a most speculative character, of the number of persons who will vote under the plan we propose'.[3] Instead of stressing the desirability of excluding the compound householder, he emphasized the offer of a 'popular and rational principle'[4]—the 'constitutional principle of the old borough franchise in use for centuries, extending back to the Normans and even to the Saxons'[5] which, by pointing out in parenthesis that compounders were not to be excluded 'as such', left open the possibility (as the bill proposed) that existing ones who chose to pay their rates in person would be enfranchised. The shift away from consideration of numbers was marked in the speech of March 18. It became stronger in the 'brilliant'[6] and 'not uncandid'[7] winding-up speech in the debate on the second reading a week later in which, while leaving the impression that 'he [had], with binding effect, conceded *nothing* but the dual vote',[8] he not only offered to yield to the House's wishes on the lodger and county franchises, but left the impression, if not on Gladstone then on others, that even personal payment was 'doubtful'.[9] From a tactical point of view, as Disraeli well knew, the bill could be attacked as a 'revolutionary' or a 'restrictive' measure[10] according to whether one took into consideration the numbers *automatically* enfranchised by the bill or the numbers who could *claim* to be enfranchised by settling and paying their rates (if migratory paupers) or by opting out of composition if their landlords paid their rates on their behalf. While sounding, in Disraeli's hand, as conservative as before, it issued in the principle, as the core of the government's proposal, that 'the foundation of the franchise should be rating and a payment of rates... *not as a check, as some would say*, [as, indeed, Hardy said a week later][11] but on the contrary, as a qualification': that 'because [this] is the best evidence of the trustworthiness of the individual, we have no hesitation in saying ourselves that we do not think that the compound householder, as a *compound householder* [my italics], ought to have a vote'[1] but that the 'principle...on which the measure [was] founded...that a householder who is rated to the poor...personally pays his rates and...has occupied his house for two years, shall possess the franchise...[was] of general application, without any restriction whatever; and [that] any person who fulfils the conditions which are...as I believe, entirely approved by the majority of the people, may possess and enjoy the suffrage in this country'.[2]

In enunciating this principle Disraeli did not commit himself to anything the Cabinet had not accepted. On March 18 he did not abandon duality, having tried, and failed, to get the Cabinet to do so. On March 25 under Cabinet authority he removed duality from the list of essential principles and left other unspecified questions to the decision of the House. But he suggested no resolution of the difficulty Liberals felt about arrangements for enfranchising the compound householder who opted out of composition. Conservatives and Adullamites who wanted to restrict numbers while asserting a principle could see that the financial discouragement to opting out would be considerable. Liberals and Radicals who wanted inconsistencies to attack could contrast the treatment accorded to the 1832 Act compounding occupier of a house rated at *more* than £10 p.a., who could pay the *reduced* rate in order to be enfranchised on opting out of composition (under the provisions of Clay's Act of 1851) with the government's insistence that compounding occupiers of houses rated at *less* than £10 p.a. should pay the full rate on doing so. Nevertheless, the shift involved a skilful, distinct and deliberate replacement of the idea that a Conservative bill should recognize Parliament's fear of 'numbers' by the idea that it was not 'numbers' that were to be feared but those who did not personally pay their rates. This, though conforming formally with the Cabinet and party decisions which had been made between March 2 and 24 and with clauses 3 and 34 of the bill, shifted the basis of discussion, increased the flexibility of Conservative policy and enlarged the number of electors which might be enfranchised by a bill founded on this principle, if one set of detailed arrangements about compounding was adopted rather than another.

Nor is it likely that Disraeli, in asserting this principle, did not know what he was doing. He could see, as well as Baxter, that the *size* of enfranchisement depended on the treatment accorded to existing compound householders. He could see also that a bill which was recommended on the ground that it would enfranchise one number of electors rather than another, would run into great difficulty. Though a majority of MP.s would have agreed about the appropriateness of one (smaller) number rather than another (bigger) one had agreement between parties been politically possible, the possibility of agreement had been rejected both by Gladstone and by Derby and Disraeli in the course of realignment between February 26 and March 18. Realignment involved an assault on Gladstone and was in process of becoming an assault on his left. Most Liberals did not want household suffrage pure and simple; but neither did they want to be left out of account in the process of legislating about a matter on which they claimed authority. Since, therefore, they had to pick on *something* to attack in the government's proposals, they chose the manifest injustice of giving 1867 Act electors treatment different from that given to electors under the Acts of 1832 and 1851, in respect both of the franchise qualification and of the 'fine' suffered by the compounder on opting out of composition.

Since a large part of the Liberal party seemed likely to follow Gladstone in attacking restrictions, and since on paper Gladstone had a majority of sixty, inducements were necessary to attract enough of these to support the bill if the government was to have a majority. If the Adullamite Cave had been bigger, or more reliable, and if it had been certain that no Conservatives would vote with Gladstone, the Adullamites could have supplied enough cross-votes to do this. Since it was certain in March neither that the Conservative vote for Gladstone would be as small as it was on April 12 nor that the Cave would be as large as it was in 1866, it was necessary to have some hope of picking up at least a handful of Liberal votes proper. The Cave had decided to keep the government in office after February 26 because it did not want to replace Derby by Gladstone. It had been confirmed in the decision after March 2 by the belief, induced by both leaders, that both parties might wish to retain counterpoises and compensations if household suffrage were adopted in principle. Disraeli could not rely on their votes at any time before about April 8. Though he did his best to accommodate them, however, he did not restrict his freedom of manoeuvre, as

Grosvenor had suggested,[1] by proposing the duality clause for discussion before the lowering of the borough franchise was agreed to. Nor, despite the ease with which this could have been done, did he follow Baxter's advice, once duality was seen to be impossible, by proposing to make compounding universally compulsory for all houses rated at less than £5 or £6 p.a. in order to exclude their occupants from the franchise.[2] Having invented a line of his own, he obviously intended to stick to it. It is difficult to avoid the conclusion that his object in shifting the emphasis from numbers to the personal payment principle was to provide an instrument which by its ambiguity could be bent in either direction—and particularly, if necessary, in the direction of the Liberal left.

Because Liberals of the left and centre felt obliged to seem to want to enfranchise a larger *number* of electors than anyone else, commitment to enfranchise a specific number, given a prior decision in both parties to divide on party lines, could not be certain of success. The personal payment principle, however, was a much more open-ended commitment. Though the *bill* was unambiguous, the principle was not. The principle, indeed, if applied generously, could conflict with the intention which most Conservatives imputed to the bill: this may well have been what Disraeli intended. It would be too much (in the light of the evidence available) to suggest that Disraeli thought in March or early April of *abolishing* compounding altogether in parliamentary boroughs (as he claimed in accepting Hodgkinson's amendment on May 17). But a close reading of the two speeches of March 18 and March 25 leaves no doubt that the principle was used as a means of edging the Conservative party out of the position in which Clause 34 put it, where its views would be reciprocated in the body of the Liberal party but not on its left, into another in which he pointed a gun at the Liberal left.

Disraeli, then, as Conservative spokesman in the House of Commons, so effectively changed the emphasis of Conservative policy that the Liberal left was attracted to it. He could do this because his rear in Cabinet was guarded, and because the body of the Conservative party believed Northcote's, Stanley's and Hardy's assurances about the conservative character of the bill.[3] Although Thomas Baring, Lord Eustace Cecil, Henry Baillie, Sir Brook Bridges, Lord Hotham, Baron Dimsdale, Sir Rainald Knightley, James Lowther,

George Bentinck, Lord Henry Scott[1] and his brother, the Earl of Dalkeith (who had refused office in 1866)[2] at various moments between March 18 and April 12 all thought of voting against the bill, none of them did so.[3] Lord Robert Montagu was bought out of the Cranborne Cave by being offered junior office. Though Baring and Bentinck refused office because they objected to household suffrage, the offer to Bentinck seems to have appeased both him and Lowther because of the compliment it implied to Lord Lonsdale.[4] There were rumblings from Lord Percy, who had not been given office, and from his eighty-eight year old father who had not been given the Garter[5] and who allowed the two Caves to meet in Northumberland House. But there was no effective resistance from the Conservative party in the House of Commons. Although there was a strong feeling of distaste, distress or apprehension at what was being done, only Sandford, Earle, Cranborne, Heathcote, Beresford-Hope, Alexander Baring and J. G. Hubbard voted with Gladstone on April 12. On May 9, while Sandford alone of these voted with Disraeli, none voted with Gladstone.

After the three resignations of March 2, the Cabinet position was delicate, and became more so in the next fortnight. If the Cabinet, in changing its front on March 2, had remained united, the difficulties would have been smaller. But the resignations themselves, a wrangle between Derby and Carnarvon in the House of Lords immediately afterwards and the sharpness of Cranborne's attack in the Commons demoralized the party even more completely than Sir John Pakington's revelation, in a by-election speech at Droitwich, that the Cabinet had changed its mind on February 25 because it could not decide which franchise to propose. Replacements had been found for Cranborne, Carnarvon and Peel. The Dukes of Marlborough and Richmond supplied great names to guarantee the conservative character of a liberal measure: Lowry-Corry was Shaftesbury's brother-in-law. But the general result was not impressive. Hardy did not know what the party would think about abandoning duality.[6] Like Lord John Manners, the Earl of Devon and the Duke of Richmond, Marlborough had refused the Lord-Lieutenancy of Ireland in 1866: having accepted the Lord Stewardship instead, he found he did not like it. He had been wanting to resign for some time and would not necessarily be deterred by being appointed President of the Council.[7] Ward Hunt, the Financial Secretary to the Treasury, was feeling that he could no longer remain in office after an incident in debate in the House of Commons on March 11 in which Disraeli had suddenly thrown him over on a matter not directly connected with Reform.[1]

Although three ministers had resigned, resignation did not mean that they ceased to have contact with members of the Cabinet. Resignation, indeed, brought into the open resentments which each had previously kept to himself or confined within a circle of two or three. Doubts about Disraeli's honesty, which seem previously not to have been given extensive expression, were given expression now. A subtle blackmail was tried on ministers who might want to be thought well of by the party. The objection to what had been done, as Richmond was told ten days after joining the Cabinet, was not just that household suffrage would 'produce...in many boroughs [a] result' which, whether 'good or bad...[would be] a revolution'. Nor was it that 'the compensations and securities which [were] proposed were...illusory', or that there was 'imminent danger...[of] the Conservative party...going to pieces...if it [did] not disappear in the deluge that the government [was] bringing on'. It was, in Carnarvon's carefully chosen words, that 'in this most delicate question...no one's facts, figures, or judgements [were to be] trust[ed] but [one's] own', as to the 'disastrous effects...of [the Cabinet's] contemptible tergiversation' on the 'honour' of the party, and the 'incurable distrust which henceforth must prevail in the country of the principles and professions of public men'.[2] Carnarvon was a young, virtuous, intellectual high churchman who had been brought up, after his father's death, by Sir William Heathcote. He had been educated at Christ Church by Mansel: his conservatism involved, as much as Gladstone's liberalism, a supraclass conception of national moral solidarity. This national moral solidarity already existed in England, he thought. In attempting to preserve it, the electoral machinery must be manipulated, not in order to establish a working-class preponderance in individual constituencies, but to maintain the existing mixed, representative Parliament, which had avoided both 'the dead uniformity of any one class or interest or opinion' and had prevented conflict, which the bill would produce, 'between two clearly defined and perhaps ultimately hostile classes—a rich upper class on the one hand, and a poor artisan class on the other'.[3] Peel's reputation as an honest and sensible figure was high. He was thought of in some quarters as a possible leader of the party[1]. While keeping the party united, he wanted to discredit Disraeli and strengthen ministerial resistance to him. Hardy had nearly resigned with him: Peel mentioned his continuance in Cabinet as evidence of integrity.

Hardy came from the second generation of a Bradford iron family. He had been taught by Lowe at Oxford and had practised successfully for fifteen years at the London and Northern bars. On being refused silk in 1856, he had abandoned the bar and set up as a country gentleman first in Hampshire, then in Kent. Like his father, he was a Conservative free-trader who embodied in straightforward intensity most of the qualities which reactionary Tories admired— a protestant defence of the Anglican establishment and deep distrust of the liberal climate in one direction, a public patriotism which made him think Cobden 'too much cosmopolitan' in another.[2] He had replaced Gladstone as member for Oxford in 1865: though he had hardly any ministerial experience, his Tory reputation made him a prize worth keeping. He had thought of resigning in sympathy with Cranborne and stayed in office, not because he was pleased with what was being done, but because the 'personal honour' of the Cabinet had been involved by 'allowing our chiefs to state that we were prepared with a bill'.[3] He was given intensive indoctrination and praise by Derby and Disraeli,[4] associated with the drafting of the bill in March and the redistribution of seats in June, and, in face of Gladstone's part-radical, part-conservative assault, given prominence in the debate on the second reading on March 25 when he spoke effectively and in a way more certainly calculated to appeal to Conservative backbenchers than Disraeli the day after.[5] Hardy was a barometer of backbench opinion and seems to have disliked differing from it. Cairns was an impeccable Protestant who had resigned from the government in October in order to become Lord Justice of Appeals. When Hardy had doubts about abandoning duality in March, about conceding over the compound householder in April and about reducing the residential qualification in May, Cairns was recruited to persuade him to stay. He seems to have done so so skilfully that Hardy did not realise what was happening.[6]

Sir Stafford Northcote was a forty-nine year old devout Anglican baronet from Devonshire, who had been an Irvingite at Oxford. As a young man he had been Gladstone's secretary at the Board of

Trade, had developed a personal and financial admiration for him and had written both a Gladstonian financial tract[1] and a defence of Gladstone's personal character[2]. During discussion of Gladstone's bill in 1866, he had committed himself as unambiguously as he could against any reduction of the borough franchise. Disraeli had insisted on his inclusion in the Cabinet in 1866, and had allowed Northcote to know that he had done so: Northcote developed a strong political affection for Disraeli in the months following.[3] Nevertheless, though there seems to have been no question of resignation on his part, he was extremely unhappy. Few things were more ludicrous in the session of 1867 than his attempt to claim that the borough franchise, so far from being *lowered* by the bill, was still a £10 occupation and freeman franchise to which a fancy franchise—a rating franchise—was being added.[4] The Duke of Buckingham had moved to the Colonial Office at Derby's request on March 2 in order to 'support the Conservative ministry and party' and help Derby 'to prevent, if possible, the ascendancy of the democratic feeling now spreading'.[5] Finding himself faced at the next Cabinet a week later with the proposal to abandon duality, he threatened to resign if the proposal was accepted, was reminded by Derby of his duty to the party and was set on by Hardy and Walpole to remind him also.[6] Resignation by any of these at any time up to May 9 would probably have destroyed the government, but they did not resign. Nor did the Conservative party follow the lead given by Cranborne and Peel. Disraeli's pressure succeeded over duality, not because the Cabinet as a whole wanted to concede, but because, however much they were misled by the decision of March 2, they, like Peel and Carnarvon,[7] were reminded by Derby or Disraeli of the damage the party would suffer from any step they might take to break up the Cabinet, and of the dangers they would face from a Liberal Reform bill 'the effect of which would ...be the entire annihilation of the Conservative Party in the House and in the country'.[8]

Though Derby was ill in the winter, was drugged for the session and was out of action on a number of occasions between March and July, his influence was paramount. Whatever other uncertainties were felt, Walpole intended 'to stand by Lord Derby through thick and thin'.[9] Buckingham withdrew his resignation out of a 'strong desire to support [his] chief and [his] strong feelings of regard to

[Derby] personally'.[1] Since Lord John Manners left Cambridge nearly thirty years before, Derby had been his 'exemplar and model of what an English Statesman ought to be'.[2] His control over the Conservative party was complete. He paralysed the House of Lords and stifled debate within it.[3] His wealth and station, his experience and intellect, his want alike of cant and pomposity and his unconcealed hostility to Catholicism ensured for him in a party of inexperienced but Anglican country gentlemen an authority which persuaded even the most reactionary that the bill had its advantages. At the party meeting of March 15 no one questioned his policy apart from Heathcote and Beresford-Hope.[4] Wilson Patten was 'much annoyed at the proposals of the government', but did not speak against them. Cavendish Bentinck and others 'disapproved, but might have to support [them]'.[5] The new Lord Exeter had been MP. for Northamptonshire and Treasurer of the Household until his father's death in January: he was now Cranborne's patron at Stamford. On March 9, before he had taken the air in London, he approved of Cranborne's resignation. On March 25, after visiting London and corresponding with Derby, he found 'the bill [not]...nearly as objectionable as [he] had anticipated while judging from hearsay'. On March 9 he did not want 'household suffrage pure and simple', expected the proposals, as Cranborne had explained them, to enfranchise a 'low class of voters' in the small boroughs who might elect 'a low class of politician', thought Disraeli 'was playing ...the usual Dizzy game with the House of Commons' and denounced the educational counterpoise as

not altogether a safe one without some provision as to property,...the most dangerous classes in any State...throughout the history of the world [being] those who, though possessed of cleverness and general knowledge [and] able to take any degree...are without a rap of money, and look to Revolutions and popular commotions as the means for replenishing their pockets, or giving them what they never had.

By March 25 he knew that 'the bill' did not propose household suffrage pure and simple and might be 'hammered into a very useful measure with a few alterations in committee'.[6]

Disraeli succeeded secondly, because, although willing to press for as much concession in radical directions as he could get, he accompanied concession with an affirmation of conservative principle and the strengthening of conservative clauses, even though in one respect at least he did so by mistake. Having persuaded the Cabinet between March 5 and 25 to accept a lodger franchise if necessary and virtually to abandon duality (which he definitely renounced in the House of Commons on April 1[1]), he had coupled concession with unambiguous assertion first, of the personal payment principle, and then, of an 'adequate' residential qualification.[2] Since early February the personal payment principle had been the central feature of the borough franchise as Disraeli presented it. Assertion, and reassertion, of it were designed to facilitate concession at points at which concession was necessary. Gladstone's failure to persuade a united Liberal party to attack it made concession easier. The residential qualification, on the other hand, was not one to which Disraeli attached particular importance. It became an 'essential principle' when Gladstone seemed likely to make it the first target for attack in committee, but only in order to establish that an early defeat in committee would be treated by the Cabinet as a defeat for the bill as a whole and presented to the country as proof of the Liberal party's insincerity about Reform. For tactical reasons which are far from clear, Gladstone changed his target.[3] But Conservatives who voted with the government on April 12 were voting, as they thought, for a bill which not only embodied the personal rate-paying principle (including the fine on the compound householder), but was restrictive in the further sense that it involved a two-year residential qualification. The Conservative party as a whole might or might not, at this stage, have stomached advance commitment to concede further. There is no doubt that the commitment to maintain the two-year residential qualification (which was made with one order of opposition amendments in view but not abandoned when Gladstone changed the order) reinforced Conservative belief in the conservative nature of the government's intentions, while at the same time neither discouraging Liberals from believing that it would be abandoned if the House at a later stage voted against it, nor, when the House did so, preventing the government in different circumstances accepting its decision.

Disraeli's pressure succeeded, thirdly, not because Peel, Cranborne, Heathcote, Carnarvon, Earle, Sandford, Hubbard and Beresford-Hope did not have a case to put, but because they were neither united nor effective in Parliament. They were ineffective because Sir William Heathcote was not an accomplished parliamentary figure, because Cranborne had a tendency to olympian exaggeration and failed to mix socially,[1] because neither Earle nor Sandford was a respectable figure,[2] and because, although at least one disappointed under-secretary—Adderley—used his friendship with Gladstone to let the opposition know through Acland how precarious Disraeli's position in Cabinet was, the opposition to him was too little organized to succeed.[3] They were ineffective because they were driven by Cranborne's hatred of Disraeli and Heathcote's admiration for Gladstone to support Gladstone, whose militancy against restriction and desire to destroy the government made it easier for Disraeli to handle the Conservative party and the Cave, and because Cranborne's manifest wish to get rid of the government was something which Conservatives, at the low point from which they had started on February 26, feared more than anything else.[4] Though Cranborne collaborated with Elcho, and Heathcote with Gladstone, they failed to establish a three-cornered alliance—Elcho, Grosvenor, Anson and Gilbert Heathcote being driven, despite Cranborne's warnings, to prefer Disraeli in face of the violence of Gladstone's attacks on the counterpoise—duality—to which they were particularly committed. They failed because, at the same time as he was promising to concede to Radicals on the compound householders' fine, Disraeli was leaving Conservatives the impression that he would accept a fixed line as well as personal payment.[5] They were hampered by the fact that, while some Conservatives were willing to give way on the borough franchise in the expectation that they would gain on the redistribution of seats, all of the Cranborne/Heathcote Cave—apart from Knightley—either sat for small boroughs or, like Hubbard and Beresford-Hope, were Conservatives because they identified 'Toryism' not with the land but with the cause of 'intellect' which 'did not inseparably go with acres' and with 'wealth' which 'was represented by commerce... as much as by land'.[6] They were hampered by the fact that the only one of the resigning ministers who had the smallest personal following in the Conservative party—General Peel—took Stanley's assurances seriously,[7] refused to vote against the party in the dangerous situation in which it was placed despite his threat to do so if duality was abandoned,[8] moved the Army estimates after he had

183

resigned[1] and, after transferring himself below the gangway and speaking against the Government's policy, voted with Disraeli in the divisions of April 12 and May 9. Above all, Disraeli's pressure was assisted by Gladstone's inability to divide the Conservative party and his failure to control the Liberal party.

(ii) THE DEFEAT OF GLADSTONE

'I suppose you don't for one moment imagine that to the Reform bill alone —to the opinion of its merits or demerits, is to be ascribed the check Gladstone has now met with.'

Edward Ellice to Halifax, April 17 1867. Garrowby MSS

In the three weeks following his return from Italy, Gladstone continued the policy he had set himself before he left—of regaining the support of the Cave, and of Whigs and constitutional Liberals. He allowed himself to be guided by Halifax and Brand, let it be thought in the right places that Bright was an 'impracticable demagogue', decided not to hold the usual eve-of-session dinner (because 'he dares not ask Bright') and, while not actually criticizing Bright in public ('he funks omitting him from the dinner...a bad symptom'), left the impression, as Sir George Grey had suggested, that he wished to be rescued from him.[2] Sensing, like Brand and Halifax, the importance of not 'betraying an impatience for office' or seeming to do 'anything which would impede a settlement of the question of Reform',[3] persuaded as he was that the House could no more be *bullied* into turning out the government than it had been into passing his bill in 1866, and conscious, as his advisers had made him, of the importance of keeping the Liberal party united if only in order to mould a government bill, he found himself faced by a chance to confront a challenge to ambiguous moderation which his critics began to believe he had accepted. Whereas in 1866, under the strain and stress of his first months as leader of the House in a delicate situation after seven continuous years of office, he had been uncompromising and unconciliatory, attempting, on Cabinet advice, to teach Grosvenor and the Cave a lesson but in fact being taught a lesson himself, the challenge to show that he was capable of leading the Liberal party, and the benefits to be gained from leading it successfully, stimulated a judicious geniality which went a long way to create the impression '*consensu omnium*', in the words of a sharp critic, '[that he was] fitting in to the place he ought to occupy'.[1]

Nor did he leave it to his Whig advisers to give assurances on his behalf. Though Brand expected nothing from it, he, Halifax and Granville had taken pains with such individual members of the Cave as they met in the winter recess. Gladstone himself took such opportunities as he had to prepare Lowe's mind for the need to resist the government if it proposed household suffrage. He was being represented by Francis Lawley, his ex-private secretary, a close friend of his family and brother-in-law of Grosvenor, as 'a man...tenderly, devotedly loyal to the Crown, and (whether you believe it or not) to Land and to old families'.[2] It is impossible to know how far Gladstone authorized Lawley's approaches to the Cave, but there is no incompatibility between the impression left on interlocutors by his own conversation and the impression left by reports of Lawley's attempts to dissociate Gladstone from his radical and republican followers. Just as Earle had been Disraeli's contact man with the Cave in the previous session, so Lawley was Gladstone's at the start of this, reminding Anson (who had won the Victoria Cross at Lucknow) of the dangers involved in 'leav[ing] Gladstone to be manipulated by the Radicals', assuring him that 'no one can do more good not only to the Liberal party but also, I verily believe, to England than yourself if you can bring Gladstone and Grosvenor into communication at this critical moment' and asserting that although

his impressionable and susceptible heart overflows with admiration for Mill—his general character and conduct as a Member of Parliament and some of his more recent works and especially his address to St Andrew's— surely it would be worth while for Grosvenor and all that large school of Liberals who...believe that, while progress is the law for England, it is critically important to moderate and guide new progress—to hold out a hand to Gladstone and make him their friend.[3]

In all this, as February 25 approached, Gladstone's success was considerable—not only by contrast with Bright and with Russell's unpredictable militancy but also in face of the difficulty Derby was having in bringing the Cabinet to a point of decision.[4] Though Ellice and Bouverie—two jealous Whigs—went off to Cannes at the end of January in order 'to be out of the way of any opposition there may be to the Government',[5] one of them believed that

'Gladstone's wish now is to come out as a moderate Liberal': the other was so greatly impressed by what he saw on his return that he thought 'Gladstone has behaved so well that he ought to be encouraged in a moderate line'.[1] Gregory and Dunkellin, partly perhaps because of Derby's failure to offer office to Clanricarde,[2] partly, perhaps, because of his refusal to take up Gregory's Irish land bill,[3] had left the Cave once more at the beginning of February. Lowe, who in October 'would never serve under Gladstone'[4] began to see in Gladstone a barrier against household suffrage. Horsman, whose dislike of Gladstone was equalled only by his dislike of Disraeli and Bright but who had found Derby insufficiently responsive to advice, was induced to visit Gladstone in mid-February 'for one and three-quarter hours urging the adoption of a system of plural voting'. He left Moncreiff the impression that the Cave was 'disgusted' with Derby, and wanted Gladstone's leadership 'of the Liberal party including themselves to continue' so long as 'a sharp line [was] drawn between Mr Gladstone and the Bright party'.[5] Anson could 'not stomach either Lord Russell or Bright'. For Gladstone he had 'nothing but respect and affection'. He saw 'but one prevailing feeling in every Adullamite heart—we are all Liberals and we all yearn for Mr Gladstone as our leader'.[6] To Elcho, who in August 1866 had attributed his 'broken windows and all broken heads not to Bright or the Reform League but to the conduct and flesh-and-blood arguments and appeals of the late leader of the House' and had found Gladstone's 'silence during these disgraceful riots...disgraceful to him[self]',[7] it seemed that Gladstone 'on [whose] part...the anti-Bright feeling is...very strong...is, I know, in a frame of mind well adapted to' the attempt, general on both sides of the House, to frame not 'a Radical measure', but a 'comparatively moderate' one.[8]

Gladstone may at this time have wanted to turn out the government: the Cave, apart from Horsman and Lowe, did not. Gladstone may have been hoping to return to office soon, or he may have been searching for a position from which to determine the shape of any bill the government might propose. It is more likely that he did not know what he intended, beyond preparing for the varying possibilities which would be thrown up by a genuine bill, a Disraelian trick or a Conservative split. Whatever he wanted, he was so successful with Elcho and Grosvenor that they came to think it possible that it might be what *they* wanted. Though they treated his change of mind as a victory for them rather than evidence that Gladstone should lead the party, they co-operated closely. Elcho called on Gladstone on the evening of February 25.[1] Through Lawley's, Anson's, Granville's, Spencer's, Mrs Gladstone's, the Duchess of Sutherland's[2] and Elcho's mediation, Grosvenor was invited to call on Gladstone. He not only did so on February 27 but, in addressing the crowded Liberal party meeting the day before in Gladstone's house, 'mentioned with great praise the judicious way in which Mr Gladstone had led the opposition this session' and 'declared in general terms his attachment to Liberal principles and the Liberal party'.[3]

The announcement, as government policy, of a £6 rating bill had put Gladstone in a position of overwhelming strength. It united the Liberal party behind him. Faced with a £6 rating, he could afford to wait. A bill of this sort, if allowed to go into committee, could almost certainly be amended. A tolerable amendment—for a £5 rating, for example—would be accepted by a majority of the House of Commons.[4] If it was, it might have to be accepted by the government, might settle the question for a long time without enfranchising the residuum and would demonstrate Gladstone's ability—even in opposition—to deliver a further instalment of progress which was both 'real' and 'safe'. It was in these circumstances that he committed himself to allow the government to get to the point of presenting a bill, and held out the hope that he would not expect the Liberal party to oppose the second reading.

His line of advance at this point was halted by Disraeli's decision, first to convert the resolutions into a bill, then to undercut any credible Liberal position by reverting to the household suffrage he had had to abandon on February 25. Though it was not certain on March 5 that the Cabinet would propose a household suffrage bill, the speeches of Stanley, Carnarvon, Cranborne, Disraeli and Derby in Parliament, Pakington's by-election speech at Droitwich on March 13 and the reports Gladstone received of Conservative feeling in the House of Commons made it likely that it would be. This presented Gladstone with a difficulty. He had no intention of advocating household suffrage pure and simple because that went far beyond anything the body of the Liberal party had thought of wanting. In the previous six weeks he had presented himself in a conservative light to Whigs and dissident Liberals. He had leant over backwards in doing so because it seemed safe, in view of Conservative commitments, to do this. He was now confronted by a bill from Disraeli which, though thoroughly ambiguous, could be made to appear to lean in the opposite direction. Where previously he had agitated against the restrictiveness of Conservative policy in the certainty that the Conservative party would work out the restrictive role which Liberals regarded as its 'legitimate function',[1] the boot was now on the other foot. There would now be no Conservative longstop. 'The mention of household suffrage by the Conservative government would make it impossible to recede'.[2] It seemed now to be the Liberal party's turn to 'limit...*somehow* to the more respectable classes of householders...[the] operation [of]...household suffrage'.[3]

Liberals had not previously listed the limitations they assumed would be imposed on the movement to extend the franchise, because the Conservative party had done this for them. Now that they were in danger of getting from the Conservative party a good deal more than they expected, some of them began to see that it might well be a great deal more than they wanted. One conclusion to which this led was that Disraeli's bill should be supported as it stood, so as to prevent it going further. The other was to reject it outright because, while being more progressive than anything offered by Liberal governments in the past, the momentum of progressive feeling would demand concessions to make it more progressive still.[4] Though a cohesive party might have presented a token opposition so as to keep up party tension while allowing the bill to pass more or less as Disraeli proposed it, the importance attached to a progressive image by all the Liberal leaders combined with Gladstone's insistence on playing a major part in legislation to put this out of the question.

Gladstone did not want to enfranchise 'the residuum'. Since the Reform question was his speciality, he did not want an agreed measure except on his own terms, though he tried to leave his party the impression that he did. Nor did he want to be led by the Cave. He objected to the independence of the initiative which Disraeli had taken. He objected to its manifest crookedness. Study of the statistical effects of the bill, as it would become in committee, reduced him to a 'state of anxiety, approaching to despair'.[5] He was, moreover, a party leader in a party whose progressive momentum could not suddenly be checked. Though some of its members had begun to realize that it would have to be checked, the process of checking it would be painful. If the party was to come smoothly to a halt, a point had to be found of ambiguous equilibrium at which all sections could meet.

In searching for it Russell was of little help. No one reflects the Liberal perplexity better than Russell: no one dealt with it less effectively. Russell disliked household suffrage pure and simple and threatened to move its rejection if it was proposed to the House of Lords. He objected to plurality because it was 'new [and] unbearable' and to personal payment because it would increase bribery. He felt it necessary to strike at duality and to make the government's 'fraudulent' bill a 'reality'. Removal of duality would produce household suffrage pure and simple, but what he really wanted was a £5 rating bill. It is not surprising that his advice to 'adopt the strongest...course...which Bright on the one side and Grosvenor on the other will support' irritated Gladstone as much as Russell had irritated Halifax earlier in the session.[1]

Gladstone, in fact, needed not a policy statement, but a slogan on which both to fight Disraeli and to unite his party. Just as Disraeli intended to propose household suffrage because Gladstone had not, so the fact that Disraeli's was a rated residential suffrage bill meant that Gladstone's could not be. The difference in actual enfranchisement between a £5 rating bill and rated residential suffrage less some of the counterpoises and compensations was small.[2] But it served a purpose. Rated residential suffrage with counterpoises and compensations, as hinted at on March 5/6, explained to a Conservative party meeting on March 15 and introduced as a bill on March 18, was objectionable, in Gladstone's view, because the counterpoises and compensations would have to be struck out in committee[3] by the Liberal majority which, by thus establishing household suffrage pure and simple, would enfranchise more extensively than most Liberals had ever conceived of as a practical (or desirable) possibility.

Moreover, a household suffrage bill could not easily be modified in committee. To reduce to £5 the £6 franchise proposed on February 25 would have been comparatively simple. No principle would have been involved, merely a detailed application.[4] But to modify a household suffrage bill would be perilous in the extreme. Gladstone did not conceive it his business to advocate household suffrage pure and simple, but any modification of Disraeli's principle which a *Liberal* leader could move in committee would have to be directed against the counterpoises and compensations. Removal of these would produce a bill even more at variance both with Gladstone's preferences and with the views he had expressed since his return from Italy in the course of the attempt to appease the Liberal right.

Nor did the actual announcement of household suffrage at first make him change his position. He had not seen the text of Disraeli's bill when he spoke on March 18. His comments were made in criticism of the outline given by Disraeli on asking leave to introduce the bill (which would be printed next morning), and on what Gladstone had gleaned of the speech Derby had made to a private meeting of the Conservative party three days earlier. Nevertheless, his object was clear—to emphasize at the start that, if the restrictive clauses were removed, the bill would establish household suffrage pure and simple. The point in doing this was to remind Adullamites and the Cranborne Cave that his 'conviction of the mischief and injustice'[1] of counterpoises and compensations whose sole purpose was restrictive, would compel him to lead the Liberal party to attack them in committee—with the hint that they ought therefore to kill the bill before it got into committee; and to assure his non-Whig, non-Radical supporters, about whose reaction he was uncertain,[2] that he would not connive in committee at objectionable restrictions which their conception of the party's function made them unable to support.

If Gladstone had not needed to establish that the Liberal party was still *the* authority about Reform, he would not have needed to reject the bill. If he had been willing to advocate household suffrage pure and simple, he could have attacked the counterpoises and compensations without suggesting alternative restrictions in return. But the party he led, and the House of Commons to which he belonged, had not convinced itself that household suffrage pure and simple was a practical possibility. It would not, if left to itself, have gone as far as the form of household suffrage Disraeli had presented; it would have deserted Gladstone if he had pressed this at this time. Though the words were Whig words, and evidence is wanting, there may well have been a desire to warn the Conservative party that the initiative they were being led by Disraeli to steal from a reformer as striking as Gladstone would involve them in 'eating' a great deal more 'dirt'[1] than they had eaten so far. Hence the attempt—both before March 18 and increasingly thereafter—to square the circle; to ensure that his own supporters followed him in attacking fraudulent restriction, while leaving open the possibility that those who feared household suffrage pure and simple as a prospect in committee would support him if he moved the rejection of the bill on the second reading a week later.

Although this was an attempt—both personally and on the Liberal party's behalf—to dispute Disraeli's right to determine policy, it gave little pleasure to any of Gladstone's followers. So far from pleasing both wings, it pleased neither. So far from ensuring support from the Adullamites and the Cranborne Cave, it divided one from the other. Despite an attempt to prove 'the antiquity of the principle of equality among voters',[2] his criticisms of duality and inequality of enfranchisement between electors, and his attacks on the restrictions the bill imposed on the enfranchisement of compounders, shook Elcho's confidence. The impression he left of wishing to lead the Liberal party to reject a household suffrage bill struck blows at his following among ordinary Liberals.[3] His ferocity and 'indignation' drove away Conservatives who might otherwise have responded.[4] Though Cranborne and Sir William Heathcote understood his objective—to leave open the possibility of moving the rejection of the bill before it went into committee— and pressed him to press the Liberal party to support him in doing so, the plain hint he had given of a desire to demand this produced a reaction of great force inside it.

The contents of Disraeli's bill began to be known from March 16 onwards: the effect was striking. On the one hand Liberal MP.s saw the affirmation of principles—the duality and personal payment of rates—which, as the party of progress, they knew it to be their obligation to oppose. On the other hand, they saw the shadow, not just of household suffrage, but, if these principles were abandoned, of household suffrage pure and simple.[5] They objected to duality, not because they did not want to protect property and intelligence against democratic pressure, but because it was an Adullamite trick which some of their constituents would not like. They objected to the personal payment principle because it put great power into the hands of Poor Law overseers and election agents. They objected to it, also, no doubt, because they had not proposed it; but they did not carry their objection to its logical conclusion. They were party Liberals who had no wish to support a Conservative bill, but they were responsible landowners or manufacturers who, in the words of a wealthy banker, could not 'question...the object of the Conservatives in adhering to the rate-paying clauses below the £10 franchise...[which is] to limit the number of voters'. Conservatives supported the personal payment principle because Disraeli persuaded them that it provided a permanent resting-place. 'One of the strong objections felt [to the bill] on [the Liberal] side [was] that the final democratic move thereafter [would be] to do away with such personal rate-paying clauses (already felt to be objectionable)', which would 'land us in household suffrage pure and simple'.[1]

If the bill had been proposed by a Liberal government, the Radical assault might have been resisted. Having no confidence in the ability of the Liberal party to resist erosion of a Conservative bill, Liberals needed either to turn out the government at once or to devise a restrictive alternative. In choosing a £5 fixed-line franchise with rating and composition meeting at a fixed point, they were hoping, no less than Disraeli, both to exclude the residuum and to provide a permanent resting-place for the future. This was taken, by Disraeli at least, to be implicit in Gladstone's speech to the party meeting on February 26.[2] As early as February 28 Halifax thought that a £5 rating franchise would 'settle the question'.[3] In the three weeks following the first reading, probably all but fifty Liberals came to support it.[4]

Unfortunately, although this feeling was widespread in the Liberal party, it was confronted, sometimes in the same person, by another feeling, equally strong and fundamentally conflicting, that, once the Conservative party had committed itself to household suffrage, the Liberal party could not afford to appear more restrictive in return.[5] Though one Radical[6] wanted the second reading rejected because Disraeli would concede anything that was asked in committee and then sweep the country with the product, this feeling was held, not just by Radicals like Hadfield who had no objection to household suffrage pure and simple, but by many of those, like Enfield and Beaumont, who wanted most of all to produce a situation in which it could be avoided. They saw that outright opposition

would be politically suicidal. They thought that, if outright opposition was given on a party basis, Disraeli would not be in a position
to concede. They drew the conclusion that, if a sensible settlement
was to be reached, Disraeli must be induced to reach it. By March
26, when Enfield opened negotiations with Hardy, he claimed to
have 100 followers.[1] It was, therefore, not just attention to Radical
and advanced Liberal feeling which made Gladstone decide not
to oppose the second reading after all, but the fact that central and
constitutional Liberals wanted the opinion of the House taken without hindrance from party tension or commitment.

Before the bill was introduced, Brand and Glyn (Brand's successor as chief whip) had decided that the Liberal party would not agree
to move the rejection of a household suffrage bill. They had been
willing to think of *supporting* a motion against the second reading if
it were proposed by the Cranborne Cave; Gladstone had tried to
persuade Heathcote to propose one.[2] The Cranborne Cave was
weak in Conservative support, knew it was weak, and wished to
conceal its weakness. It wished to avoid destroying in advance the
morale of the new Cave it hoped to create if the bill got to the House
of Lords and would do nothing to damage its chances there.[3]
Heathcote's refusal to take the initiative and the weakness of his
following, which was obvious despite attempts to conceal it, convinced Brand that opposition to the second reading would be idle.[4]
Gladstone's speech of March 18 implied, without saying so, that the
second reading might be opposed.[5] Since this was the opposite of
what he had said on February 25, 'it produced a most unpleasant
effect on the party'.[6] It drove Lord Enfield, in whom as an ex-
minister 'this was very improper', to prepare a requisition against
it.[7] In Halifax's company Brand called on Gladstone the morning
afterwards to persuade him to withdraw opposition to the second
reading unless it was certain that the Liberal party would follow
him. Soundings taken that day by Halifax among peers, and by Sir
George Grey, Beaumont, Brand and Gladstone himself among
MP.s, established that the party would not. At a meeting of party
leaders on the 20th, Gladstone agreed not to try to make it, and
conceded the point gracefully to a united, and relaxed, party meeting two days later.[8]

However, although he agreed to do this, he still wanted to push
Disraeli as far as he could. Having been denied the desire to reject

the bill as a whole, he decided to strike at its central principle. Having been assured of party support, he thought it safe to do so. In doing so, he was continuing the attempt to move with a diverse body of Liberals, Adullamites and Conservatives who, since they were opposing the bill for diverse reasons, would not be able to work together in moving detailed amendments in committee. This made it essential to have a confrontation before the committee stage began. In attempting to have one, Gladstone was hoping to force Disraeli either to abandon the bill or to risk rejection by the Conservative party if he accepted modification of its principle. He knew that a large body of Liberals wanted to avoid household suffrage pure and simple, and that a feeling was growing that rating and composition should meet at a fixed point. He saw an amendment tabled by Grosvenor to this effect before the start of the debate on the second reading on March 26. At the same time, therefore, as he attacked the restrictive clauses of Disraeli's bill on March 25 and 26, he drafted a restrictive proposal of his own. Recognizing that, if Disraeli's restrictions were removed, the bill would not be restrictive enough, he tried to replace Disraeli's principle—the personal payment principle *without* a fixed-line franchise—by a fixed-line franchise above which all occupiers would have the vote (whether compounders or not), but below which *nobody* would have it. This formula (Coleridge's Instruction) was devised by Gladstone in collaboration with Heathcote and Cranborne, vetted by Brand and Halifax,[1] given to Coleridge to propose as an Instruction from the House on going into committee, and accepted by an under-attended Liberal party meeting in Gladstone's home on April 5 in spite of objections raised by Clay and Locke.

In drafting the Instruction Gladstone was doing his best to unite Disraeli's enemies, but from the standpoint of the Cranborne Cave, it was a second-best. Like Bright and Lowe,[2] Cranborne and Heathcote had wanted to oppose the second reading outright. Since the diversity of opposition to the bill made it impossible that 'any [detailed] amendment [in committee] could be so framed as to make it easy for Mr Gladstone's party and the Conservative Cave to unite', the Liberal party's refusal to do this was a major blow for them. Since Liberal amendments in committee would be 'in a radical sense' and might 'reunite the...[Conservative] party', they were willing to take anything they could get before the committee stage began.[1] Since Conservatives would not vote for a motion to remove restrictions, it was necessary to make a motion as general as possible.[2] Since Gladstone was committed to attack restriction while having a restrictive objective, the motion had to be ambiguous. Disraeli was committed to exclude householders who did not personally pay their rates; so Gladstone had not to be. Disraeli claimed that it was possible to enforce personal payment of rates: Gladstone believed that it would be impossible to shift to the occupier a liability to the direct payment of rates, and that the personal payment principle would act as a deliberate disfranchisement.[3] Disraeli had established the differentiation; so Gladstone had to avoid the odium of differentiating between householders who paid their own rates and those whose landlords paid their rates on their behalf. He had to do this while still excluding the majority of householders whose rates were paid by composition,[4] without excluding them explicitly for that reason. Coleridge's Instruction, if accepted by the House, would have given the committee power to 'relieve... occupiers of tenements below a given rateable value from liability to personal rating' and to make this level the level at which the franchise qualification began. It displayed the difficulty of finding a proposal which would perform the same function as Disraeli's while being different from it. It reflected the ambiguity of the role Gladstone conceived himself obliged to play as leader of a parliamentary alliance which needed to embrace Radical and advanced Liberal preferences as well as Whig and Conservative ones, and which was being constantly pressed to greater exertion by the public agitation outside.

In fulfilling the purpose for which it was intended, it was unsuccessful. Though the party meeting accepted the Instruction on April 5, Liberals were not reconciled to it. The meeting was held despite widespread opposition and was boycotted by at least seventy members.[5] The Instruction was sprung on the meeting without notice in order to prevent opposition to it.[6] Bright supported it.[7] It was pressed by Gladstone so dictatorially that some of those who were present felt unable to question, or contradict, him. Gladstone seems to have had no sense of danger.[8] But the Instruction convinced the Cave that he wanted, not just to modify the bill, but to bring down the government. His conduct of the meeting aroused intense anger in Locke and Clay, who decided to sabotage it.

Locke was a barrister, the son of a merchant, member for a heavily populated Radical London constituency, and unequivocally committed by earlier declarations to household suffrage. He thought that the constituencies would never 'understand or appreciate Mr Gladstone's distinctions' and that an election would destroy the Liberal party.[1] James Clay, Radical MP. for Hull, was an old, and at one time intimate, friend of Disraeli. He had co-operated with him in the previous session, had been asked to Hughenden in January 1866 (though he could not go), and had been in touch before the second reading. Like a great many other people,[2] he interpreted Disraeli's speech on the second reading as a promise of reasonable concession. After a meeting with Harvey Lewis and others in the Reform Club on April 6 or 7, he wrote to ask Disraeli whether the government would accept Coleridge's Instruction if it were amended to leave out all reference to the personal payment and fixed-line principles.[3] At the same time McCullagh Torrens, the Radical MP. for Finsbury, had given the Conservative chief whip a list of forty-six Liberals who would vote, if necessary, against Gladstone's resolution.[4] Though the Tea-Room meeting of April 8 is usually seen as a spontaneous demonstration by MP.s who felt that the decision of April 5 was mistaken, it may also be seen as a party revolution organized by Locke, Torrens, Akroyd and Clay with Disraeli's connivance. Clay's approach to Disraeli and Disraeli's answer, which we do not have, were followed by a meeting of fifty-two Liberal MP.s in the Tea-Room of the House of Commons on the afternoon of April 8. Candlish, Edmund Potter of Carlisle and Dent spoke against altering Gladstone's decision: Morrison of Plymouth declined to commit himself. Having decided at first to instruct Locke to move an amendment to Coleridge's Instruction, the meeting was persuaded by J. B. Smith to send a delegation to Gladstone instead. Forty-eight of the fifty-two then called on Gladstone 'to tell him that they could not support the Instruction' which was to be moved almost at once, for 'fear [of] being...made to appear in the eyes of their constituents as having been opposed to going into committee upon, and fairly considering, a bill which gave, ostensibly, that household suffrage which they had always advocated'.[5] This demonstration was so decisive, was produced at such short notice and showed such willingness to support Gladstone if he moved the substance of the Instruction as an amendment to Clause 3 in committee, that Gladstone had to accept it. Coleridge's Instruction to the committee, when moved on April 8, was in two parts. The first altered the law of rating: it was accepted by the government by prior agreement. The second instructed the committee 'to provide ...that occupiers of tenements below a given rateable value be relieved from liability to personal rating, with a view to fix a line for the Borough Franchise at and above which *all* occupiers [i.e. including compounders, whether out of composition or not]...shall have equal facilities for the enjoyment of such Franchises as a Residential Occupation Franchise'. It was withdrawn by Coleridge on Gladstone's orders in order to avoid a Liberal amendment and an adverse vote.

The position by April 10, therefore, was that the Liberal party had forced Gladstone to abandon opposition to the second reading. His attempt to commit the party to replace Disraeli's principle had been thwarted. He had listed ten major respects in which the restrictive aspects of the government's bill would have to be altered, and knew that a good many Liberals would follow him in attempting to alter it. But the attack on the restrictiveness of the details of the bill was not an attack on its principle. Disraeli had offered to accommodate himself to the House's wishes. The only matters to which his offer did not apply were the residential qualification and the personal payment of rates. Before the withdrawal of Coleridge's Instruction, Gladstone had intended to mount his first attack on the residential qualification, if the bill got into committee. He chose now to attack the personal payment principle instead. In doing so, he was making a major challenge, to which, as we shall see later, he must have known that the Adullamites would not respond.

What Disraeli had done, in the course of his two speeches on March 18 and 25, was to make clear what parts of the bill the government would stand by or fall. He had not committed himself to personal payment of the *full* rate, though he tried unsuccessfully on April 11 to persuade the Cabinet to accept the reduced rate if the House insisted. But he had made it clear that personal payment (i.e. excluding compounders so long as they were compounding) was an essential pre-condition of the right to vote. Gladstone's attack on it, in his first amendment to clause 3 of the bill on April 12, was, therefore, no less than a motion to reject the second reading, an assault on a principle to which, in the absence of other restrictions, many Conservatives attached great importance. Even those who did not like the government's bill could see that abandonment of the principle, if the bill survived, would establish household suffrage pure and simple. Gladstone did not want to advocate household suffrage pure and simple: he wanted a £5 Rating bill without insistence on personal payment of rates. But he wanted to exert energy and assert authority. Because it was difficult to be certain that his followers would 'vote for a restriction in amount unless they first received the assurance of destroying the personal rating', he made a point, in drafting his motion of April 12, of avoiding mention of the specific amount to which the franchise should be reduced. In order to persuade Conservative supporters of Cranborne and Heathcote to vote 'for the abolition of personal rating without first securing the £5 limit',[1] he was compelled to make clear the fact that his amendment involved a £5 line. He had not wanted to make this clear, because of the warning the Tea-Room meeting had given against any sort of restrictive action on his part. He had resisted as long as he could, and agreed now only because the Cranborne Cave would not have followed him if he had not done so. Having left the clutches of a 'rogue', Cranborne did not propose to hand himself over to a 'lunatic'.[2] It was under pressure from Heathcote, edged on by Cranborne, that Gladstone made up for his reluctance to fix the line at any particular point by providing the piece of 'very plain speaking' they both wanted in order to give dissident Conservatives a chance to explain 'out of doors (what can be made clear in the House) that the amendment is part of a whole and implies £5'.[3] Even so, the amendment itself did not mention a fixed-line franchise. Though Heathcote did mention it and Gladstone had tabled a £5 amendment for later discussion, the ambiguity of Gladstone's position produced a negative response among Conservatives. It gave government speakers the chance to suggest that the amendment had been 'calculated to catch votes on both sides',[4] and made it easier for Disraeli, in the long run, if not on April 12, to prise off Radicals and Liberals who had no wish to attack a bill which, in the form in which it was presented, had already established household suffrage pure and simple in over twenty constituencies.

The secession of forty-seven Liberals from Gladstone's leadership in the division on his amendment to clause 3 on April 12 must not be confused with the Tea-Room meeting of fifty-two on April 8.

There were, in fact, not forty-five to fifty Liberal rebels, but well over a hundred. Although there was a small overlap (only about half a dozen of the Tea-Room rebels abandoned Gladstone on April 12), they were markedly dissimilar in character. Though a Whig (W. O. Stanley) presided, the Tea-Room meeting was a genuine expression on the part of 'a formidable body of members whose Liberal sympathies were beyond suspicion'[1] of the dilemma with which Disraeli had confronted them. Though a number of Radicals were there because they wanted household suffrage pure and simple and thought Gladstone would stop them getting it, the great majority neither had any particular desire to establish it nor doubted the desirability of the objective Gladstone was pursuing. On the other hand, they did not want to abandon the progressive posture to which they had become accustomed in the past. They objected to the Instruction which could be attacked 'by those who are opposed to us' on the ground that 'we are lessening the number of persons to be placed on the register'. They objected to it because the Instruction could be represented as an attempt to replace Disraeli's positive, enfranchising proposition 'that a man who is a householder and pays his own rates is to have a vote' by the negative, disfranchising one 'that if a person is a householder but is rated below a particular line, he is to have no vote'.[2] They saw that the Instruction, if successful, might involve the resignation of the government or the dissolution of Parliament. While preferring a fixed-line franchise, '[they] wish[ed] all the same to say to [their] constituents that [they] did so as it was not possible to get household suffrage'.[3] For most of those who attended the meeting (as distinct from the Cave, which, on the whole, did not), refusal to support the Instruction involved, therefore, a demand to preserve the party's progressive image. Its decision brought it into conflict with Gladstone's announcement on April 5 that 'it is impossible for me, under any circumstances and conditions whatever, to accept the suggestions which Mr Clay has made'[4] (i.e. to abandon the second half of Coleridge's Instruction). Nevertheless the delegation, which forty-eight of the fifty-two Tea-Room members sent to Gladstone, not only was not primarily directed against his leadership, but was supported by MP.s like Fawcett who were among his strong supporters. A few discontented Whigs like Hastings Russell, W. O. Stanley and Lord Enfield attended the meeting, though most deliberately stayed away. There was contact between Locke and Clay on the one hand and Elcho on the other. There was an unwillingness to defer to Gladstone's arrogance. But the Whigs did not make the running.[1]

The forty-seven Liberals who voted with Disraeli and the fifteen or so others who abstained on April 12 were a varied, but in general very different, sort of Liberal from the Tea-Room delegation. The secession of April 12, so far from consisting of advanced Liberals and Radicals who supported Disraeli because of the supposedly or potentially Radical character of his bill, consisted primarily of Whigs and constitutional Liberals who were alarmed by the consequence of failing to accept Disraeli's bill while they could, and who wanted no part in replacing Derby and Disraeli by Gladstone and Bright. It included great employers like the two Basses of Burton, Akroyd of Halifax, Platt of Oldham, and Doulton of Lambeth who wanted the question settled as soon as possible. It included Roebuck who hated Gladstone and sat for a city whose trades unionists were among the most notorious in England. It included Irish landowners or their dependants like Lord John Browne, the two Grosvenors and C. W. W. Fitzwilliam. It included advanced Scottish Liberals like Crum-Ewing, Dalglish, and M'Lagan, who had been persuaded by Disraeli to expect a tolerable redistribution for Scotland. Though more Radicals and advanced Liberals sitting for English seats would have voted with Disraeli if the Cabinet had agreed to make greater concessions, there was only a handful who can be said to have wanted household suffrage and thought Disraeli the person most likely to give it.[2] There was a number of Catholic MP.s for Irish seats, who, so far from being primarily interested in electoral Reform, were responding to hints of an Irish University bill or thought Disraeli had promised to set up a sympathetic Select Committee on McEvoy's bill to repeal Russell's Ecclesiastical Titles Act.[3] Some, while not necessarily wanting household suffrage, did not want it to be 'supposed' that they were voting against it.[4] Others, while willing to accept a £5 rating franchise if that had been proposed by a Liberal government before Disraeli had proposed household suffrage, thought it impossible for the Liberal party as a party 'to insist upon the retention (with a change from £10 rental to [the] £5 rating [which Gladstone's amendment was taken to imply]) of the harsh barrier between the rich and the poor which was set up by the Act of 1832.'[5]

In addition there was an influential group which feared that the bill would produce household suffrage pure and simple in committee, realized that they would have to accept it unless Disraeli was willing to avoid it, and had no desire to increase tension between the government on the one hand and the House on the other. They saw that Disraeli, if he wanted to avoid household suffrage, could not do so by abandoning the principle to which he was committed. They had no desire to replace a cautiously reforming Conservative government, which might settle the question for good, by a divided Liberal government which might not. They could see that the government, if beaten, might win an election by fighting on household suffrage against £5 rating. They saw no evidence that Gladstone, if he won the election, would 'be placed in a better position for [passing a Reform bill]...than he was twelve months ago'.[1] They feared, far more than the Conservative leaders did, the effect on opinion outside Parliament if the question was not settled soon. They wanted to prevent the Reform bill becoming 'the football of contending parties'.[2] They may even have believed that Disraeli, if confrontation were avoided, would accept a fixed-line franchise in addition to the personal payment principle.[3] A number of Liberal MP.s were unwilling to see the Liberal party returned to office until all hope of another Grey/Halifax/Clarendon/Russell hegemony had been avoided and boycotted the meeting at Gladstone's house on April 5 because 'they suspect[ed] the members of the late Cabinet to be eager for office'.[4] A handful of Liberals, in the view of the whips, voted against Gladstone or abstained on April 12 from 'fear of dissolution' or from 'worse motives',[5] including the two Mackinnon brothers, members for Rye and Lymington, 'who thus revenged the non-elevation to the peerage of their father by Lord Palmerston or Lord Russell, for which he had been long striving...but to which he has really no claim unless for his money'.[6] The great body of Radical MP.s and of Liberal MP.s for county constituencies seem in general to have supported Gladstone in the first fortnight of April.[7] But more than twenty of the Liberal cross-voters were Adullamite followers of Grosvenor, who, though leading a body which was much reduced from the Cave of June 1866, represented a deliberate rejection of Gladstone's leadership on grounds more general and fundamental than were involved in the question under discussion.

(iii) THE SHUNTING OF THE CAVE

'Mr Gladstone's interviews with G[eorge] Potter and Co. have led him to the conclusion that all right, justice, generosity and good feeling are on the side of the Trades Unionists. Alas! alas! that this should be the man on whom the hope of the country rests.'

Elcho to Grosvenor, March 30 1867. Wemyss MSS

The Cave's effectiveness as an independent party depended on the Conservative party having some measure of attractiveness to constitutional Liberals and dissident Whigs. In this respect the government's proposals of February 25 had been as menacing to Grosvenor and Elcho as they had been to Disraeli. The government's position at this point no longer had the merit of uncertainty. Its position was plain and inadequate; it would fail to attract any dissidents at all. The Cave leaders had attended Gladstone's party meeting of February 26 in the hope of keeping Gladstone straight in a difficult situation, and had held a well-attended meeting of their own on February 28. But the government's manifest uselessness presented a threat. It meant that the government would fall as soon as Gladstone wanted it to, that Gladstone's position would be unassailable, and that the Cave's ability to keep him on the central line would be destroyed. It meant that the conditions on which the Cave had depended for effectiveness in the past year would disappear: 'for I know that some of our sensible men in it would be likely to be satisfied with Gladstone's suggestion of a trench dug below a £5 line of rating.' In policy terms this would be a victory for the Cave, but a policy victory was not the only victory that Grosvenor wanted to win. Gladstone, it was true, did not 'himself wish to go to [the] lengths [to] which the Radical party' would go in general, 'and was against any sudden enfranchisement'. But Gladstone, though he had been edged off it by the Cave in the previous months, nevertheless 'leans much on the Radical party', and, if *free* to do so, would do so in future.[1] Grosvenor and Elcho would not have supported the government if it had persisted in its £6 rating proposal. They trusted Derby more than they trusted Gladstone. Though they would have preferred to have the prolonged discussion on the resolutions which the government had promised,[2] it seemed essential both that the government should be kept in office in order to prevent a worse one—including Bright—succeeding and that the Cave should attempt to restore *its* influence by taking steps, *before* the government fell, to submit 'resolutions...if the procedure of the House permits', which might 'obtain the support of the Conservatives *en masse* and of a large proportion of Liberals', and enable the government to carry a rated residential suffrage bill with plurality and cumulative voting.[1]

Disraeli, however, got in first with the announcement, on March 5, that the government would introduce a rated residential suffrage bill: the possibility of an *independent* initiative of a fundamental sort disappeared. Nevertheless, the need to prevent the government's proposal for rated residential suffrage with counterpoises being converted by governmental concession into household suffrage pure and simple gave an opportunity for the Cave to give a lead. What the Cave had decided it wanted on February 17 was rated residential suffrage combined with a residential qualification, plurality, personal rating and cumulative voting. It was reasonably certain on March 5 that Disraeli's bill would offer a rated residential suffrage. The question was whether it would offer personal payment of rates, cumulative voting, duality and two years residence as well. Disraeli had made plain his willingness to do anything on which the House might insist. It was necessary for the Cave to ensure that the House insisted.

Duality was an easy target for anyone who wished to attack it. It was blatant 'Toryism'.[2] It 'could not be carried, and if carried would not last beyond the first general election'.[3] It differentiated between electors enfranchised by the 1832 Act and those who would be enfranchised by the new one. It seemed likely, if Gladstone attacked it, that it would be removed. It seemed likely, on the other hand, if Gladstone defended it, that it would be retained, and this both increased Gladstone's importance and involved him in a difficulty. He seems to have been genuinely shocked by the possibility of household suffrage without safeguards, and by the ruthless cynicism involved in the fact that it was the Conservative party that was taking the first step to propose it. From a very early date, he regarded a £5 rating franchise as the lowest point to which a government could safely go, and attacked the restrictive aspects of Disraeli's bill in order to establish that *his* proposal was the *only* alternative to the household suffrage Disraeli's bill would become if its restrictive features were removed. A £5 rating franchise was less attractive to the

Cave, because it was not so obvious a resting-place. As soon as they knew that household suffrage was to be proposed, the point about which they were clear was that, whatever the franchise level, counterpoises and compensations must be established 'with Gladstone's help if possible, [but] without it if needs be'.[1]

The Cave was by now an unhappy place. Not only had Gregory and Dunkellin left it: Samuel Laing had joined it. Laing was an able and versatile man who had been a fellow of St John's College, Cambridge in his youth, a railway administrator and magnate for most of his working life and Financial Secretary to the Treasury and Finance Minister in India. Like other leading Adullamites he was a disappointed politician who might have supported the 1866 bill if he had been given office after his return from India in 1865. In the earlier stages of the session of 1866, he had been prominent in opposition to Gladstone because of Gladstone's refusal to redistribute seats. He voted against Gladstone on April 27 1866, but was appeased by the promise to introduce a Seats bill before the Franchise bill went into committee. His return to the Cave in 1867 was in some respects a source of strength, but it gave Horsman the impression that *he* was being put out.[2] Though Laing did not vote with Disraeli on April 12, he embodied many of the fears which gave the Cave its power to reflect central opinion in the House of Commons. He wanted a more extensive redistribution than Disraeli had proposed, not as a step on the road to democracy, but because the large centres of wealth were more important than the small boroughs in his conception of a modern state. He objected to the borough franchise clause, not because he approved of household suffrage pure and simple, but because to give something like household suffrage with one hand so as to restrict it with the other would satisfy no one and settle nothing. He objected, finally, to the personal payment principle, not because he objected to confining the franchise to ratepayers, but because, in a rating system in which Poor Law overseers decided whether composition was permitted in a borough or not, it was 'impossible [i.e. undesirable] to suppose that [the] question [whether the scale of enfranchisement permitted in each borough would be large or small] could be left to be decided by local bodies, actuated by local party feelings and local jobbing'.[3] From the beginning of 1867 Laing took a prominent part in the Cave, occupying the place Lowe had occupied in debate in 1866 and reflecting more adequately than Lowe, in the climate created by Disraeli's bill, the doubts which Liberals who wanted to do *something* about the franchise felt about the leaders of both major parties.

Whatever they thought when it was first mentioned in public at the beginning of March, a great many Liberals had seen very clearly by the end of March that they were opposed to household suffrage. They were opposed to it, not because they objected to the scale of enfranchisement embodied in Disraeli's proposal, but because they felt obliged to reject the vestiges of restrictive Toryism which he had attached to it. What they wanted instead was the enfranchisement embodied in the proposal Gladstone wanted to make—a £5 rating suffrage without insistence on personal payment. They wanted this because, if rating liability and voting rights began at a £5 rental line, the settlement would be permanent enough to last; because '...[while] doubl[ing] the present constituency', it would 'eliminate...the least independent portion of house-holders';[1] and because they thought it the right or duty of the Liberal party to be in office when decisions of this sort were made. It is not clear whether Gladstone let it be known that he was committed to this before the government made its proposals under the impression that he was going farther than the government had gone on February 25 and found only later that he had edged himself into the more restrictive position, or whether he adopted it as a response to the government's proposal of March 5. Whatever the sequence, adoption by Gladstone of a position which in some respects seemed more conservative than Disraeli's was no bad thing so far as the unity of the Liberal party was concerned. There was at least a chance that criticism by Gladstone of the *scale* of enfranchisement permitted by the bill would both rally the Cave and attract a larger body of dissident Conservatives than he succeeded in the end in attracting.

His difficulty was that, once Disraeli had taken a major initiative, he had to take a major initiative too. Once Disraeli had begun to woo the left of the Liberal party, it became essential that Gladstone should woo it also. Bright did not abandon Gladstone in any of the Reform divisions. The fact that Bright would support him in proposing a £5, £4 or £3 fixed-line franchise in opposition to the personal payment principle was in some respects a source of strength. Nevertheless, Disraeli prefaced the adoption of the new policy by talking publicly to Bright in the lobby on March 1.[1] One Radical, White of Brighton, while deploring the 'un-English air of mystery' maintained by 'the "little Isaac" class of politicians' in the period of uncertainty between March 5 and March 18, 'believe[d]' that 'the party to which [he] had the honour to belong would be benefited by a twelve-months' absence from office', and implied that he might support the government if its bill came near to meeting his requirements.[2] The fact that Disraeli was succeeding to some extent in chipping away at Gladstone's Radical wing meant that Gladstone, at the same time as he was beginning to convince the Cave that he wished to be rescued from Bright, had to run after Radicals in order to keep up with Disraeli. This undoubtedly is one explanation of the 'want of tact and temper, not to say taste' and 'violent' denunciations of duality on the first reading on March 18, which, though it attached Bright even more firmly than in the past, made Elcho unable to see 'what we can do with him' and persuaded Grosvenor that, although duality *had* to be carried, it would probably have to be carried in spite of Gladstone.[3]

The other difficulty, almost certainly, was that Gladstone did not wish to be *managed* by the Cave. Disraeli distrusted the Cave because of the threat it presented to him. Gladstone, though he needed to carry the Cave along, could not afford too obviously to be led by it. Its members wanted an open breach with Radicals and advanced Liberals: they did not mind the consequences. Though they mirrored many of the instincts most prominent among Liberal MP.s about undue extension of the franchise, they faced none of the problems which arose from the need to keep hold of a miscellaneous coalition. Gladstone was not exactly the manager of an aristocratic party, but his function was to perpetuate the Whig alliance with popular Radicalism. Whig managers shared the Cave's fears about Reform, but they knew that 'a breach with the advanced Liberals was neither politic nor possible, and that we needed all'.[4] To precipitate a breach of this sort would destroy Gladstone's reputation as a popular statesman. It would limit his usefulness as a party leader. The point of decision with which he was confronted—whether to abandon Radicals in favour of Whigs or Whigs in favour of Radicals—was not one that could easily be resolved. At first he tried to avoid it, and seems even to have supposed that the Liberal party would remain united.

But once Disraeli's willingness to appease every section of the House forced choice upon him, he chose the line most likely to rally the party at a point somewhere left of centre.

The decisiveness of the Conservative commitment on March 4 had put the Cave in a difficult situation. The government's attractiveness to the Cave had depended on the expectation that it would be a willing recipient of Adullamite advice. Now that an unsatisfactory commitment had been made, there was much less point than hitherto in supporting the government against Gladstone with whom, for some members of the Cave as distinct from its leaders, there would be no serious conflict once the Reform question was out of the way. Though Elcho ran the Cave as an anti-Gladstonian rump, not all his followers were so simple. They had been affronted by Gladstone's manner in 1866, but they were 'moderate Liberals'. They had been able to resist a wrongly conceived Reform bill in 1866, because the existence of an uncommitted opposition strengthened their importance in the Liberal party. But the breaking of the Conservative dam against Gladstone's pressure demolished some of the ground on which a group of this sort must stand. The Conservative party was trying to remove the Reform question from party politics—which might help it to pass a bill—but, if this policy succeeded, those who had acted against Gladstone on Reform grounds alone would find that much less separated them from him in the future. Lowe's objection to a lowering of the borough franchise was seen to emerge from a well-understood view of public policy. But part of his hostility to the Liberal party was a personal hostility to Whig exclusiveness—to its tendency to reserve 'the Cabinet...for men of one particular connection or family' unless they were Radicals.[1] Lowe had wanted the government to stand firm. He had wanted this not just because he objected to a reduction of the franchise qualification nor because he wanted to keep Disraeli and Derby in office and join them himself, but because, if they fell (as they would once they refused to lower the borough franchise), a Liberal–Conservative coalition of the sort Lowe had tried to construct in July would be possible under Stanley 'if he would only use [his]...opportunity'.[2] Throughout the winter Lowe had tried to persuade Conservative ministers to prevent the government dealing with the Reform question at all. He turned against it as soon as the resolutions showed that its members had 'no opinions of their own' and had 'only been fishing for a policy'.[1] Stanley was included in this condemnation. The events of the winter had shown that he would not detach himself from Disraeli. His manifest indecisiveness when coupled with Gladstone's rightward shift edged Lowe once more towards Gladstone. Lowe thought duality impossible[2] and disliked what he thought of as the logic of Disraeli's situation (which was that, once a decision was taken to lower the franchise, there was no reason to stop short of household suffrage). Household suffrage to Lowe meant 'ruin' and would be a capitulation to Bright. He decided that the government must be turned out. Though he cannot have expected a Liberal government to stand firm on the £10 franchise of 1832, household suffrage was more likely to be resisted by Whigs than by Tories in the frame of mind in which Tories allowed themselves to be led by 'a reckless, foolish adventurer who neither respects himself nor anyone else'.[3]

The decision to proceed by resolution, and the *prospect* of a Conservative bill, caused no difficulty to Elcho, Grosvenor, Anson, Gilbert Heathcote or at first Horsman, who were satisfied by the belief that 'd'Israeli is *the* man to draw a good bill that will admit the right part of the working classes'.[4] The Cabinet decision of February 19 in favour of rated residential suffrage with duality was not far from what the Cave wanted. Yet of the forty-two Adullamites who had voted with the Conservative party in June 1866, thirteen voted consistently with Gladstone in the Reform divisions of 1867. Only twenty voted with the government in the first division on April 12, while of these twenty, only five[5] voted consistently with the government in major divisions throughout the session.

It would be absurd to suggest that the decisions of March 2 were adopted *in order to* destroy the Cave. Detachment of as many Liberals as possible from Gladstone's leadership was an item in Disraeli's policy. Nevertheless, Derby and Disraeli wished to avoid being led by the Cave. They were probably influenced by the Cave in adopting both the policy of proceeding by commission in October and the rated residential suffrage in February and May. But, despite Pakington's, Cranborne's, Carnarvon's and the Cave's manifest desire that they should not, they kept the Cave guessing about their own policy, Derby adopting an attitude of enquiring reticence which enabled him to get information without necessarily giving it. None of the Adullamites was offered serious office at any time in the first four months of 1867. Anson, who was offered the Treasurership to the Household in January, refused it with the assessment, which was accurate from an Adullamite point of view, that 'when the proper time arrives for that rapprochement between the moderate Liberals and moderate Conservatives, so earnestly to be desired, it must, to be of any use, begin with the leaders rather than with the rank and file'.[1]

The policy of February 25 had driven not only Lowe and Horsman, but also Elcho, Grosvenor and Laing, into Gladstone's arms. It would have done so permanently, even after the government's reversion to rated residential suffrage on March 5, if Gladstone had not coupled virtual commitment to a fixed-line suffrage with strong attacks on duality and the personal payment of rates during the debate on the introduction and first reading of the bill on March 18. The policy objective of Elcho, Grosvenor and Laing was a clear resting-place to put an end to the Reform question for a generation. Unlike Lowe, they had supported the policy of proceeding by resolution, though at first they had no particular desire to pass a bill in the present session. What they wanted was a prolonged sounding of parliamentary opinion, leading to a coagulation of moderate opinion around themselves. In spite of doubts about Conservative reliability even before February 25, they would have welcomed Disraeli's announcement then if it had promised a clear resting-place (i.e. the rated residential suffrage with counterpoises and compensations which Disraeli had originally proposed to the Cabinet). Disraeli knew this.[2] If the Cabinet had allowed Disraeli to make a proposal of this sort on February 25, as it had two days earlier at what was to have been its last meeting before he did so, Grosvenor and Elcho would have done their best to mediate between Gladstone and Disraeli in an attempt to give greater precision than the resolutions permitted to the nature and the essential character of the counterpoises. What Disraeli had to propose on February 25 in order to prevent Cranborne, Carnarvon and Peel resigning was a £6 rating, which did not satisfy the Cave. In the days which followed, Elcho had canvassed a rated residential suffrage bill (with counterpoises) among Conservatives, and had discussed with Gladstone the possibility of an initiative from the Cave to propose it in Parliament.[3] There can be little doubt that he did this in all seriousness, expecting that enough Liberals would support the Cave and the government to enable the House to accept it, so long as Gladstone did not attack it.

Nor did the government's change of policy on March 4 very much alter the situation. If the government could change its mind once, it could, so the Cave thought, change it again—particularly when it had been weakened by the resignations of three ministers, two of them close to the Cave. Elcho could see the danger, if a rated residential bill got into committee, that Disraeli would want to abandon the counterpoises altogether. Also, he was under pressure from Cranborne not to believe anything Disraeli said. This, however, though it made Elcho cautious, did not deter him. A situation in which neither of the major parties was acting decisively was exactly the situation for which, in his view, the Cave was designed, providing, indeed, a confirmation of the view he had taken for at least two years that, though no *party* could settle the Reform question, it *could* be settled by the Cave.

In the spirit of the Liberal meeting in Gladstone's house on February 26, therefore, Elcho set about rallying support for a Cave initiative to produce a bill of sufficient scope to be differentiated from Gladstone's bill of 1866, but which would contain enough safeguards to justify going as far as household suffrage. In the fortnight following announcement of the more extended measure of March 4, he and Grosvenor concentrated on Gladstone, and thought they were succeeding. It was only the ferocity of Gladstone's assault on duality in the speech of March 18 which convinced them that rated residential suffrage would have to be abandoned if the Cave was to stand any chance of piloting an agreed and moderate bill through the House of Commons.

What Gladstone was trying to do on March 18, in attacking duality and the other restrictive aspects of the bill, was to confront the House of Commons with a choice between the household suffrage pure and simple which Disraeli's bill would become if it went into committee, and the moderate fixed-line enfranchisement which Gladstone wished to propose instead. He did not commit himself on March 18 to making composition and the franchise meet at a fixed point. But his message was understood as a warning that, though *he* did not want household suffrage, he would be compelled, if Disraeli talked the language of inter-party co-operation without being willing to co-operate seriously, to press the Liberal majority to convert the bill into a household suffrage bill pure and simple. Elcho and Grosvenor would have preferred to support a rated residential suffrage combined with personal payment of rates, duality and cumulative voting. But this was not possible. The fact that Gladstone intended to prevent duality being adopted made it necessary, if co-operation was to be effective, to manufacture a position which would appeal not only to the Cave but also to Disraeli and Gladstone as well. It was in these circumstances (i.e. because Gladstone had driven them) that they abandoned rated residential suffrage in favour of a £5 rating franchise. In doing this, there was almost certainly a desire to take advantage of Gladstone's willingness to conciliate them, and to do this by getting him committed conclusively to a measure to which he seemed to be more or less committed already.[1]

Gladstone did not want to advocate household suffrage pure and simple; in this respect nothing divided Elcho and Grosvenor from him. It was clear that he would not follow Disraeli's lead. It seemed likely, also, once rated residential suffrage had been proposed by a minority Conservative government without agreement between the parties, that the restrictive clauses would be struck away in committee. Since, in these circumstances, it was dangerous to continue support for Disraeli's bill, Elcho, Grosvenor and part of the Cave ceased to support it. In trying to avoid the dangers it involved, they needed, however, to consider not only their own wishes but also Gladstone's. On considering them, they decided that what all three might agree in wanting was a franchise in which compounding would be compulsory for houses rated at less than £5 p.a., in which only occupiers of houses rated at more than £5 p.a. would have the borough vote and in which no one else would have the vote at all.

In the week following the introduction of the government's bill on March 18 and Gladstone's assault on it, this was the object to which Cranborne, Grosvenor, Elcho and Laing were moving, to which they thought Gladstone seemed likely to be committed and for which Disraeli, once he saw Cave support receding, convinced Elcho that he had some sympathy.[2] To Grosvenor it seemed likely to appeal to Gladstone because it would exclude the lowest portion of the working classes. He got the impression from Gladstone that Gladstone wanted the question settled through the present government and that it 'would be likely to be adopted by the Liberal party' as being 'one which...might combine the various opinions on our side of the House with a view to carrying a measure of reform this session'.[1]

Because he was away from London, Grosvenor had an amendment embodying this proposal drafted by Elcho who tabled it before the debate on the second reading on March 25. The object in doing this was threefold—to give a lead to the large body of Liberal opinion which feared the effect of sending Disraeli's bill into committee without preliminary alterations; to anticipate the move Gladstone had led them to suppose he would make in the same direction; and to ensure that the attempt to modify Disraeli's bill would not be weakened by Conservative reluctance to follow a lead if the lead came from the leader of the Liberal party. They seem to have been right in thinking that the great body of MP.s would have voted for a £5 rating bill if that could have been proposed without party feeling interposing.[2] There was much less reason to suppose that it would be supported by Conservatives after Gladstone's assault on duality on March 18, and every reason why the Cave should avoid a situation in which a Gladstone amendment to a government bill would be likely to produce, as a consequence, a Gladstone government.

Though anxious to avoid proposing anything to which in principle Gladstone would object, having, indeed, tried too late to get Elcho to drop the phrase 'personal payment of rates' from the amendment in order to avoid excluding compounders rated at more than £5 a year,[3] Grosvenor intended, as much as Elcho, to keep the initiative out of Gladstone's hands. They tabled their amendment *'before the debate'* on March 25/6 'in order to occupy the ground and anticipate Gladstone'.[4] Despite Gladstone's desire to call one,[5] they refused support for a party meeting to draft a party amendment because they 'had no wish to see Bright in the new government'.[6] Finally, having drafted a second motion on April 3 to be moved on going into committee, Grosvenor sent it to Gladstone for approval.[7]

On receiving notice of Grosvenor's motion on March 25, Gladstone had asked whether, if a £5 rating line were fixed, the compounder above the £5 line would have to *claim* in order to be rated. His only response to this second approach was to 'regret deeply that in this critical state of circumstances [Grosvenor thought] it necessary to proceed without consultation with the general body of the

Liberal party'[1] and to ask him to delay tabling the amendment until the party meeting two days later. Having decided at first to do so, Grosvenor refused to do this, apparently on Elcho's advice.[2] He advised the Cave to boycott the party meeting on April 5, prepared to move a motion against the second half of Coleridge's Instruction,[3] and urged the Cave to vote against it on April 8. He did so on the ground that the Instruction struck at 'the main principle of the bill, viz. the personal payment of rates'. A week earlier, when he thought he had a hold on Gladstone, he had been willing to leave open the possibility of enfranchising compounders above the £5 rating line provided voting rights began at that point and compounding was made compulsory below it. Personal payment of rates now became a 'principle' he was 'individually prepared to support' and had framed his amendments to conform to. He took this view because 'for Liberals as a party to win a division on Coleridge's Instruction, so far from advancing the settlement of the question, would make it impossible to settle it without a change of government and a general election'.[4] Gladstone's and Grosvenor's policy objectives had to some extent become identical—a franchise in which rating and composition met at £5. Both agreed that no householder of houses rated at less than £5 p.a. should have the vote. Grosvenor's refusal to attack the personal payment principle, so far as it excluded compounders rated at more than £5 p.a., affected a comparatively small number of electors. Nevertheless, an amendment like Grosvenor's, which did *not* attack the personal payment of rates, might be accepted by Disraeli without renouncing the principle on which his bill was founded. Rejection of it made it impossible that he should accept Gladstone's or Coleridge's. Since he could not accept it, he allowed Taylor to tell Grosvenor and Elcho that he would dissolve if beaten.[5] In a situation in which Bright would make the running, Grosvenor and Elcho had no wish to see the Liberal party fight an election. In these circumstances, Grosvenor prepared to vote with Disraeli on April 8, and voted with him on April 12. There is no sign of contact between Gladstone and Grosvenor between April 4 and the end of 1868.

To Knatchbull-Hugessen Grosvenor seemed a 'fool' for supporting Disraeli on April 12. Once Gladstone had established that 'the occupier [need not] be personally rated', he thought, 'all the Conservatives and most of the moderate Liberals would have supported [Grosvenor] and...carried [his] £5 rating...as the only alternative to simple household suffrage'.[1] Nevertheless, the division between them was Gladstone's work even more than it was Grosvenor's. Just as Disraeli wanted to keep hold of the Cave in order to move enough Whigs away from Gladstone, so Gladstone in February and March 1867 knew that he must play the Cave along with him if he was to lead a majority in the House. Hence his approaches to Elcho and Grosvenor, and some measure of rapprochement with Lowe. Hence the meetings between Elcho and Gladstone on the one hand and Grosvenor and Gladstone on the other. But for Gladstone, as for Disraeli, there was a difference between playing the Cave along, and following its leadership. Derby and Disraeli had done nothing to suggest that they would do that: Gladstone did nothing to suggest that he would do that either. In suggesting that no *party* move should be made to amend the bill, Elcho and Grosvenor undoubtedly reflected genuine feeling among Gladstone's opponents, but they were distinguished from Gladstone by the fact that they had no party to lead, and that their influence depended on the fact that party discipline was breaking. Gladstone was leader in the Commons of an opposition in which his leadership had suffered damage both in 1866 and in the course of the attempt to persuade it to oppose the second reading. Reform was one of Gladstone's, and the Liberal party's, specialities: he wanted the party to present a united policy. He had been manœuvred into resisting what looked like a potentially liberal bill and was being accused of capitulating to the Whigs. He had no desire to fall in line behind the leaders of the Cave, who had refused to attend a party meeting, and who were not only deliberately occupying the ground in order that Gladstone should not do so, but had actually told Gladstone that they had 'been rather accused in one quarter of having "appropriated" [his] scheme'.[2] Gladstone was conscious of the need felt by Heathcote and Cranborne to ensure that any amendment was moved by 'someone of prudence and moderation ...not...Grosvenor'.[3] He was conscious, not just of the Cave but of Bright, of central and advanced Liberal followers of his own in Parliament and of persistent calls from outside to rescue himself from 'the...treachery and insincerity of a large portion of what is called the Liberal party in Parliament'.[4] Although his objective at this time, so far as the content of policy was concerned, was not far distant from Grosvenor's, he allowed the moment of agreement to pass,[1] forced the party meeting of April 5 to accept a formula which struck at the personal payment principle and, when this had to be abandoned as a result of the Tea-Room revolt, tabled a motion on April 10[2] to make the personal payment principle the first target for attack in committee on April 11 and 12.

Whether this was a mistake depends on the view taken of Gladstone's conception of his role in the Liberal party at that moment. So far as uniting the party was concerned, it was disastrous. So far as it was designed to carry a large reactionary Cave/Conservative group into a division against the bill, it was useless. At the same time as he was failing to satisfy the Cave, Disraeli was succeeding in doing so. At the same time as Gladstone failed to answer its letters, Disraeli was leaving the impression that the government would accept Grosvenor's amendment once a favourable vote had established the bill. Disraeli's assurances became valueless as soon as the victory had been won on April 12:[3] that victory destroyed Grosvenor's position altogether.[4] Nevertheless, although they had none of the written promises on which Cranborne had told them to insist,[5] Disraeli's assurances helped Elcho, Grosvenor and twenty-one of the Cave to decide that nothing must be done on April 12 which would lead to a 'ministerial crisis',[6] the break-up of the government or the replacement of Derby and Disraeli by Russell, Gladstone and Bright.

Coleridge's Instruction demanded a franchise in which compounding and the voting qualification met (at a figure which the Instruction did not specify) and insisted that *all* occupiers above that level, whether compounders or not, should be entitled to vote. Gladstone's motion of April 12 called for the rejection of the personal payment principle. The Instruction was objectionable to the Cave because they had decided that Gladstone was trying to bring down the government. Grosvenor's amendment, for a fixed-line franchise (without striking at the personal payment principle), might well have been accepted by the House, if it had been accepted by Gladstone, in which case the personal payment principle would have been modified in committee thereafter. But Gladstone would not abdicate political leadership to the Cave. The Cave would do nothing to help Gladstone turn out Derby. Grosvenor did not want a Gladstone/Bright Cabinet. Elcho did not want to be 'the means of making...[Lord Halifax]...Prime Minister'.[1] Nor did they want a recurrence of the unprincipled evasions for which Halifax and Sir George Grey had been responsible in 1866. Determined, therefore, that the government must neither be defeated nor allowed to go out of office, they refused to attend Gladstone's meeting on April 5. They kept Grosvenor's amendment on the order paper after the tabling of Coleridge's Instruction and tried to persuade Roebuck or Enfield to take it up. They maintained contact, through Akroyd, with the dissident Conservatives and the Tea-Room rebels, proposed a motion to delay consideration of Clause 3 until after Easter, and, when this was knocked down by Gladstone, Disraeli and the general feeling of the House on April 11, voted with Disraeli on April 12.[2]

VI

THE VICTORY OF DISRAELI

'D'Israeli...*is* the government.'
Knatchbull-Hugessen: *Diary*, May 29 1867

The dissension in the Liberal party, culminating in the Tea-Room revolt and withdrawal of Coleridge's Instruction, had three consequences. It destroyed any chance there might have been of a large Conservative Cave. It established the government's bill as a going concern. It persuaded Gladstone that he must make a stand if he was to create the Liberal party in his own image. Though there was little chance at any time of a large Conservative vote for Gladstone on April 12, the Tea-Room revolt put it out of the question. At a moment at which the Liberal party was afraid to follow Gladstone in adopting any part of the Conservative party's restrictive role, it was unthinkable that he should attract a restrictive following elsewhere. There was no guarantee that a Gladstone government, if that followed a successful vote, would be more successful than Derby's. There was no guarantee that Gladstone would be able, if he wanted, to call a halt to progress. Although Gladstone had been 'all that is frank and straightforward, as well as kind', even so certain an enemy of the government's bill as Sir William Heathcote, who voted with Gladstone on April 12, found it 'alarming' to be involved in 'joint action with a party which neither knows its own mind nor its obligation to its leader for twenty-four hours'.[1] In drafting Coleridge's Instruction before the Tea-Room meeting took place, Heathcote and Cranborne had tried to stop Gladstone committing himself to a specific franchise level, because the £5 level he would want to mention would be too low for the sort of Conservative they hoped would support them. After the Tea-Room revolt, their chief object was to get Gladstone committed to that for fear of seeming committed to no restriction at all.[2] But the uncertainty of Gladstone's following and the necessary ambiguity of his position made Conservative support difficult to produce.[3] If the government dissolved on being defeated on April 12, Heathcote explained, 'our men [would] go to the country as having opposed their own party for the sake of destroying personal rating which, although *we* may think it worthless, is much thought of by their constituents and by most of the members themselves'.[1] Though at least twenty-nine of the Tea-Room rebels voted with him on April 12, the humiliating demonstration of their unwillingness to follow Gladstone's lead was devastating.

Moreover, the joint facts that there was hardly any Conservative cross-voting on April 12 and that Gladstone had been deserted by the dissident Whigs, seemed to Russell and Gladstone to suggest the uselessness of attempting any longer to conciliate them. If they would not follow, then they should not be led. They had been given every opportunity to follow, though Grosvenor's lead had not been taken by Gladstone: it was necessary, for the future of the party, to fry other fish than were to be found in the Cave. Though Gladstone moved more slowly, the defeat of April 12, involving rejection by the House of the policy of the fixed line, meant to Russell that 'the £5 rating franchise must be laid aside'.[2] Household suffrage in itself was greatly to be deplored, introducing, as it would, all the worst evils of demagoguery in the cities, excessive deference in counties and small boroughs and bribery everywhere. But when the Conservative party was showing a progressive front, the Liberal party could not afford to lag behind. Since household suffrage pure and simple in the larger boroughs might well 'give the representation to men like Orator Hunt in place of moderate Liberals', safe, if advanced, Liberals, like Forster and Stansfeld, must be helped to beat the demagogues at their own game.[3] It had been right to try to convert a household suffrage into a fixed-line franchise on the assumption that this could be done. It would still be right to do so if there was the slightest chance of succeeding. But the fixed-line principle had been decisively rejected by the House of Commons. The Liberal party should no longer sacrifice the long-term interests of its own large-borough members in the hope of remedying deficiencies which were inherent in the characters of existing members of Parliament. Nothing could prevent a household suffrage bill becoming law. The object must be to make it an 'honest household suffrage...with rating of the occupier, with 12 months residence ...[and] without [personal] payment of rates'.[4] Russell had to be persuaded by Gladstone to accept a one-year residential qualification instead of the two proposed in the bill. He objected to house-

hold suffrage even more strongly after Hodgkinson's amendment
was accepted than he had before April 12. But there is no doubt
that, from this point on, he reverted for tactical purposes to a
position of Liberal militancy, wanting 'Bright, Forster, Baines and
Stansfeld...admitted to all our counsels'[1] and leaving it to dissident Whigs to make up their own minds what they wanted to do
without help or persuasion from him.

Nor can there be much doubt that Gladstone's conduct, both
before the division of April 12 and afterwards, was determined by
an equally strong desire, not so much to affect events in the immediate future, as to raise a flag and gain the future for himself and his
personal following in the party. His first reaction to the defeat of
April 12 was to 'speak of retiring to the back benches'.[2] His re-
nunciation of day-to-day leadership in the House on April 17 was
not made simply in anger or irritation, though anger at Grosvenor
and irritation at Russell's indecisive incontinence were probably
present.[3] It was a response to appeals addressed by central and advanced Liberals, who looked to him as the guardian of their interests,
thought of him as the one hope of freeing the Liberal party from
the domination of the 'sneaks'[4] and believed that the division of
April 12, though 'deplorable in itself...was the first step towards
the construction of a sound and reliable Liberal party', from which,
if Gladstone conducted himself sensibly, 'he should...[by the
time] he takes the position which must inevitably be his...have
driven all the rotten and effete elements...now associated with it'.[5]
These calls had begun to be made before the division of April 12.
While Halifax and others were stretching themselves in order to
keep the party united,[6] Neate, Acland, Denman, The O'Donoghue,
the *Morning Star* and, from a different point of view, Sir William
Heathcote[7] were urging Gladstone to draw his line clearly, to stake
out a Gladstonian position and, if necessary, since the party was
divided already, to make his own contribution to the division.[8] They
were calling on him to abandon the attempt to patch up the
Palmerstonian coalition, which he had pursued consistently and
unsuccessfully since he left office in 1866. They were urging him
to remove himself from leadership where compromise was both
necessary and impossible. They were demanding that he 'run [the]
risk of being beaten and, if your followers desert you,...sit below
the gangway and wait for another Parliament',[9] confident in the

certainty that 'there is but one name of power in the country'[1] and that 'the recalcitrants...when [they] become aware how impotent they are for any good when standing aloof [from the party]',[2] would recognize that 'you are more important to the Whig party than they are to you'.[3] It was a call to 'assume an attitude of command, or rather of *free service on your own terms*',[4] to lift the Liberal party out of itself and bring Gladstone in line with the 'free flow of Liberal thought and feeling'. It involved a demand to demonstrate to 'selfish ...or timid men [who], having regard to their pockets, veil their motives by carping at you, or vote against you' that, unless you retire from politics, you cannot help being the recognized leader';[5] and to do this by establishing egalitarian discipline between one set of members and another, rejecting the policy of treating with dissident Whigs 'as a party', declining to deal with them 'through Lord this or Lord that', but 'requir[ing] their *personal* assurances through Mr Brand'.[6]

These were clear and articulate attempts to rescue Gladstone from what his followers thought the compromises[7] forced on him by leadership. They were initiated as a result of Disraeli's success on March 26, stimulated by the personal humiliation of the Tea-Room revolt and strengthened by the vote of April 12. They were calls, not so much for a new programme as for a personal assertion of the way in which Gladstone would exercise party power in future. In relation to the body of the Liberal party, they involved no policy commitment. In relation to the dissident Whigs, they were demands for action against 'a narrow clique who want to prevent your being prime minister'.[8] These calls were made, if not in weakness, at any rate in alarm. There is little doubt that Gladstone responded—by refusing to follow Grosvenor's lead at the beginning of April, by pressing his opposition to the personal payment principle and by withdrawing from day-to-day leadership in the House. He refused to move the motions he had tabled before April 12[9] and for a time abandoned contact with some of his Whig advisers.[10] He offered, nevertheless, to 'accompany others in voting against any attempt, from whatever quarter, to limit yet further the scanty modicum of enfranchisement proposed by the government',[11] assured the *Morning Star* of his gratitude for letters he had received from readers since April 12[12] and urged Disraeli to make concessions more extensive than he had made so far, in the hope both that the Cabinet might collapse[1] and that by resolute and independent action he would confront the Liberal party with its choice.

Once the bill had got into committee the need for, and possibility of, concession from the government, increased. The vote of April 12 had been a major Conservative victory: 'the government...now [had] every chance of passing their bill and remaining in power'.[2] The fact that they had, however, did not mean that they would be able to pass it in the current session. Gladstone had listed respects in which the bill was defective, and emphasized his personal intention to fight the committee stage clause by clause. It is not certain that Disraeli had reached a point at which passage in the present session had become a practical objective, or that he was, even now, pressing the bill as very much more than an instrument of party existence. Nor is it certain whether Gladstone was trying to destroy the government, or merely to make it capitulate to his pressure. Whatever the several objectives in their minds, each was attempting to make a viable majority from the same sort of mixed parliamentary material, and had, therefore, to persist in an attitude of deep ambiguousness— Gladstone coupling his ten necessary improvements with refusal to take responsibility for the household suffrage pure and simple which these improvements, if adopted, would establish; Disraeli coupling willingness to adopt some of them with assertion, and reassertion, of the personal payment principle which, in the form in which other ministers presented it, was more restrictive than the form of household suffrage which Gladstone's amendments would establish.

In one sense, the government's position in the House, in the Conservative party and, prospectively, in the country, was immensely strengthened by the vote of April 12. It had been challenged by Gladstone and had beaten him, even on the left of his own party. So far as victory had been Disraeli's work, it had been achieved by conceding a good deal and implying a desire to concede more; by coupling concession with assertion of a principle which, in the form in which it was asserted, not only conceded nothing but attracted criticism from Gladstone; and by threatening resignation in the event of defeat, which would lead either to an expensive, and perhaps disastrous, dissolution or to installation of a Gladstone-led, Bright-dominated Cabinet. Though the bill was now a credible instrument, it was very far from being an Act. Though Conservative morale was enormously improved, it was far from certain that Conservatives would stomach further concession. A bill which had been supported by forty Liberals looked a more viable electoral proposition than a bill which had been opposed by the Liberal leaders without public dissension inside the Liberal party, but there were many clauses and amendments on which it would not be possible to go to the country. Whereas a Conservative defeat on the second reading, on going into committee or on an amendment as central as the amendment moved by Gladstone to clause 3 on April 12 would have provided an impressive electoral platform, it would be much more difficult to take a similar stand if defeated on other amendments individually. It was possible to treat some divisions as votes of confidence by announcing in advance that the government would resign if beaten, but it was impossible to do this to all. Yet amendments which would be acceptable individually, in bulk would transform the bill. So long as the opposition chose them carefully, concentrating on anomalies, and avoiding assertion of a general principle which struck at the bill's roots, there was much to fear from the Liberal majority. If Gladstone had not left the impression that his first amendment to clause 3 was an attack on the bill as a whole, the threat he presented to each clause would have been greater, though, since his intention in attacking each clause was to convince the House that it would not want to pass this sort of bill once the restrictive provisions had been removed, the generality of the assault was central to his strategy.

It would be wrong to assert that there was for the government now no resting-place until the bill as a whole had passed. But, unless the risk were taken of actually having a dissolution as distinct from threatening MP.s with the possibility, it was clear both that the parliamentary timetable would necessitate extensive concession and that, if concessions were to be made acceptable to the Conservative party, care must be taken neither to make them too obviously at the command of Gladstone, nor to be willing too obviously to make them at all. Gladstone's withdrawal from day-to-day leadership on April 17 might, at first sight, have made it easier for Disraeli to extend his arrangement with the Radical left. On the other hand, the hostility which Gladstone aroused in the Cave and Conservative party after March 18 had helped to keep the two together. If Gladstone had coupled temporary withdrawal with silence thereafter, the Conservative party might have become more restless as Disraeli's Radical alliance grew stronger. Gladstone's object, however, almost certainly was not just to tip Disraeli off his balance but to keep a hold on the vast reservoir of Liberal feeling by establishing himself as the sole proponent of a safe enfranchisement. In these circumstances, despite a warning from Brand,[1] he could not now remain silent, and he did not. Disraeli's 'insolent tone'[2] made intervention more necessary: intervention made it easier for Disraeli to rally Conservatives against him. The baiting of Gladstone helped Conservatives to accept the concessions they were being persuaded to make. There can be no doubt that Derby and Disraeli, after announcing their refusal to consider amendments from Gladstone, knew what they were doing when they decided to announce their willingness to consider amendments proposed by anyone else.[3]

The bill, if it had been passed in the form in which it went into committee on April 10, would have given the borough vote only to those among the 486,000 compound householders in parliamentary boroughs who took the trouble, and suffered the expense, of opting out of composition. The bill in its final form abolished compounding altogether in parliamentary boroughs and entitled every householder who had paid his rates to have his name put on the electoral register. The bill as it went into committee included no lodger franchise, though Disraeli had committed the government to accept one if it had to. The Act enfranchised all £10 lodgers in parliamentary boroughs. The county occupation franchise in the bill began at £15 p.a. In the Act it was lowered to £12 and supplemented by a £5 franchise for copyholders. The period of qualifying residence was two years in the bill, one in the Act. The provision to allow voters to vote by voting papers, which was included in the bill, was removed by the time it was passed.

The initiative in making these changes came either from Gladstone or from Radical or Liberal members of Parliament. Nevertheless, the amendments that were proposed were not invariably Radical in character or Liberal in origin. Nor were all Radical or Liberal amendments successful. Some successful amendments were moved by the government or its supporters. Some amendments were resisted by the House as a whole. Some were in no way damaging to the Conservative party. Others were obviously advantageous, given the shape the bill was taking. In one case, Laing's first amendment, it seems likely that the government *wished* to be defeated, in order to accept an amendment which uncertainty about its following in the Conservative party made it impossible that it should take the initiative in moving. In another[1] Gladstone accused it of ensuring the defeat of the motion which Disraeli's acceptance in principle of Denman's amendment in May[2] had committed the government to propose. On two occasions[3] at least, Disraeli tried to make private arrangements with movers of opposition amendments in order to move amendments quickly through the House. It is possible on at least one other that he agreed to accept one *form* of amendment, whose *content* had been agreed already instead of another, because Gladstone had supported the other.[4] On a number of major occasions he took the initiative in proposing motions which, so far from being radical in character, were both extremely conservative and successful. On a number of others—particularly after Hodgkinson's amendment was passed and in the case of Hodgkinson's itself —he committed the government to accept amendments without formally consulting either the party or the Cabinet.[5] In two cases he seems to have settled the final wording of clauses by confidential 'mutterings' across the table of the House 'not a syllable of which reached hon. members below the gangway'. Despite the difficulty back benchers must have had in keeping check on the large number of alterations which had been made in committee, Disraeli refused to reprint the bill until the committee stage was over.[6]

Disraeli's language at first sight seems to justify the belief that he had not only surrendered but was being carried out to sea by an irresistible wave of Radical feeling. Once he had broken resistance in the Conservative party, he made a point of presenting it as the party of enfranchisement. Having carried a generous borough franchise clause through the House of Commons, there was every reason to claim to be as forward-looking and responsive to the country's wishes as Gladstone. The tables had turned so far in this respect that it is not surprising to find him claiming on more than one occasion that 'motions from the hon. gentlemen opposite had a common character...that they were all aimed at the limitation of the suffrage'.[7]

The point behind the rhetoric on both sides, however, was not generosity or niggardliness of enfranchisement as a principle, but the sort of the elector to be enfranchised on the one hand and the

redistribution of seats on the other. The government on the whole
wanted to enfranchise county voters in such a way and in such numbers as to strengthen the influence of landlords. Conservatives
wanted to keep the counties as free as possible from urban influences
while keeping the landed interest as strong as possible in the smaller
boroughs. In this some Liberal backbenchers undoubtedly agreed.
What most Radicals wanted was to strengthen the existing urban
element in county constituencies (as Gladstone had proposed in
1866), to prevent a proliferation of dependent votes and to keep
the landed interest as weak as possible in the smallest boroughs.
Since this made the government willing to enfranchise freely in the
counties and since most Radicals were unwilling to seem restrictive in return, it meant that for different reasons Conservatives
and Radicals sometimes spoke with the same voice.

Though the lowering of the county occupation franchise from £50
p.a. to £12 p.a. was a major step, it is far from certain that it would
damage the Conservative party. County constituencies were extremely varied in composition: they included not only villages and
small towns but also towns of considerable size. The villages and districts were assumed to be Conservative at most financial levels. In
villages and small towns rents on the whole were low: a £12 occupier there would be equivalent 'in social position and Conservative
feeling' to those who paid a higher rent in the larger towns. In 1866
Disraeli had been advised not to oppose the £14 county occupation
franchise. Although occupiers up to £20 in the larger rural towns
were assumed to be predominantly Liberal, it was believed that
the Conservative party would have a majority among occupiers
between £20 and £50, and that the Liberal majority to be expected
among occupiers of cheaper houses in the larger towns would be offset by gains in these other directions.[1] Baxter gave this advice after
careful investigation. There is no reason to think that the situation
was different in 1867.

Indeed, the more closely one follows the committee stage of the
bill, the more difficult it is to see it as just a 'Radical triumph'.
Though many Radical objectives were achieved, they were matched
by conservative clauses, motions and amendments, the success of
which guaranteed Conservative acquiescence in the bill as a whole.
Though the lodger franchise was low, it had a twelve-month
residential qualification and stipulations about furniture added to it,

which seemed likely to neutralize its effect. The clause (clause 46) to extend from seven miles to twenty-five the residential catchment-area for voters in the City of London was proposed by R. W. Crawford, the City Liberal. It was supported as 'a very conservative measure' which Conservative agents had urged for general application to all the largest boroughs 'as the men of property were those who generally lived farther from their place of business'.[1] The Savings Bank and professional and academic franchises, when proposed in March, were offered as counterpoises to the working-class enfranchisement. However, they were unpopular with Conservatives and were removed in committee because most of the voters they would have enfranchised had already been enfranchised by the lodger clause (which did not form part of the original bill). The attack on them was led not by Radicals but by official Liberals like Roundell Palmer and Conservatives like Beresford-Hope, who had visions of a 'noble savage' paying 'neither rates nor rent' nor residing anywhere at all, but with 'a little judicious...cramming... three months training and three days answering questions', being entitled to 'a vote for life'.[2] The educational qualification was defended by advanced Liberals like Wyld and Radicals like Fawcett as a way of enfranchising 'many young men of intelligence who could not easily gain a vote in any other way'.[3] Since they were not necessary, Disraeli almost certainly intended to abandon these clauses if he had to. When he did so he took the opportunity to claim that he was doing so 'in deference to the influence in this House of the reactionary party'.[4]

Fawcett's motion to transfer part of candidates' election expenses to the rates was designed to help working men to stand for Parliament. It was heavily defeated, as was Berkeley's amendment in favour of the ballot.[5] Mill's motion to give the vote to women was voted down. He withdrew his proposal to give special representation to minorities. The minority question had exercised a wide range of conservative opinion in early March. Like plurality, cumulative voting had been pressed both by the Cave and by Conservatives as a counterpoise against the dominance of numbers.[6] It was rejected by Disraeli because, although it would help the Conservative party by ensuring adequate representation for property and intelligence in the large cities and urban counties, it might have the opposite effect in rural constituencies, where the most obvious coherent minority consisted of Liberal owners of borough freeholds.[1] Nevertheless, it was revived by Cairns during the Lords' debate in July, passed there in its most general form, attacked by Bright in the Commons but added to the bill in early August.

The motion to deny the borough vote to borough landowners unless their land had a £5 house erected on it was an attempt to reduce the landed interest in the boroughs. It was opposed by the government and defeated by eight votes in a small division.[2] Liberal amendments, on the pattern of the 1866 bill, to repeal clauses in the 1832 Act which removed from the owner of a borough leasehold or copyhold the right to a county vote if the occupying tenant had a vote in the borough, were defeated by substantial margins.[3] These amendments, proposed by Colvile and Vivian, were not designed to insert a new urban element into the counties. Their object was to prevent the extensive disfranchisement—Vivian said one-sixth of the whole county vote—which existing owners of borough copy- and leaseholds would suffer if the Act were passed without them. Though *owners* of borough freeholds were not excluded from the county vote in 1832 in cases where their *tenants* voted in the boroughs, rejection of these two amendments in 1867 meant that, as the number of copyhold and leasehold *tenants* on the *borough* register increased with the establishment of household suffrage, the number of copyhold and leasehold *owners* entitled to vote in *counties* fell in equal proportions. The justification offered for these unsuccessful amendments was that there would be actual disfranchisement if Disraeli's bill were passed without them, and that the new borough franchise would otherwise create a marked inequality between owners of borough freeholds and owners of copyholds and leaseholds, even though the copyhold and leasehold proprietors were sometimes the wealthier men. It was met by a Lincolnshire Conservative with the question whether it 'was...or...was...not desirable that the county representation should reflect the agricultural interest'.[4] It was met by Adderley's advice that 'if it was desired that there should be symmetry in their legislation as respected freeholds and copyholds...freeholds [should] be put on the same footing as copyholds in that matter', i.e. owners of borough freeholds should be *excluded* from the county vote and 'the principle' carried out 'that every locality should return its own representatives to [that] House'. The clause to

15-2

increase the number of polling places in each constituency was a help to county members. Cranborne, Trollope and Sir Matthew Ridley supported it. It was attacked by a Liberal Irish member on the ground that 'a proliferation of polling-places' in thinly populated places, where there was no public opinion to control the 'proceedings', would enable 'landlords [to] have their tenants more under their control'.[1]

Sir Edward Colebrooke's motion to confine the occupation franchise in the counties to dwelling-houses was opposed by some Radicals and nearly all Conservatives. Radicals were trying to defeat a motion which restricted enfranchisement, Conservative county members to keep open the possibility that retention of the words Colebrooke wanted removed would leave maximum flexibility to landlords in exerting influence in constituencies in the future. Colebrooke was a Scottish landowner and MP. for Lanarkshire. The clause to which his amendment referred was clause 4 section 2 which provided that 'every man [should] be entitled to be registered as a voter...for a county...who...is on the last day of July in any year and has during the twelve months immediately preceding been the Occupier, as Owner or Tenant, of Premises of any tenure within the county of the rateable value of £15 or upwards'. His amendment proposed to replace the phrase 'premises of any tenure' by 'a dwellinghouse or other building'.[2] It was designed to prevent the 'practice of splitting votes' and the 'creation of faggot votes', and to avoid a situation in which 'the natural and resident constituency of a county [was] overborne by strangers' who might buy land in quantities sufficient to entitle them to vote. Edward Ellice, the Scottish Whig, moved an amendment, which Colebrooke accepted, to remove the phrase 'or other building'. He did so on the ground that, if buildings other than dwelling-houses were allowed to count, cowhouses and cowsheds might be offered as franchise qualifications when Colebrooke's object, and his own, was to make 'residence necessary'.[3] The object, therefore, was to increase the probability that county constituencies would be constituencies of residents and to remove opportunities for corruption. The substance of the amendment had been proposed in 1853, 1860 and (by Gladstone) in 1866, but had been abandoned then in deference to Conservative criticism. Colebrooke's amendment was attacked by Lord John Manners, presumably on behalf of the government.

After a short discussion, two votes were taken.[1] The first, by a majority of three, approved the removal of the words 'premises of any tenure', thus assisting Colebrooke towards his object. The second, also by a majority of three, refused to approve the replacement of these words by the words 'a dwelling-house', thus denying the object of his intervention. Hardy, for the government, then proposed the insertion of the phrase 'land or tenements', in this way restoring to the clause the meaning Colebrooke was attempting to remove. Ayrton, the Radical MP., thereupon proposed inserting instead the phrase 'with a tenement erected thereon' so that the 'clause would give a county vote to the occupier as owner or tenant of lands with a tenement erected thereon of a certain rateable value'.[2] After a short discussion, in which Conservatives accused Colebrooke, Gladstone and Sir George Grey of wishing to exclude citizens from access to the franchise, the discussion was adjourned until May 27.

On May 27 Hardy made his proposal again. Ayrton withdrew his for technical reasons in order to substitute another which meant much the same thing. This was discussed briefly and was attacked by Sir John Trollope, a conservative Lincolnshire landowner. He did so on the ground that it would not only disfranchise a good many county inhabitants, but would also disfranchise 'a much larger class of very respectable dwellers in towns who occupied lands beyond the boundary of those towns', though it is difficult to believe that Trollope wanted to see town dwellers voting in the counties.[3] He supported his view with the claim that he did not want to create faggot votes and was seconded in this by Russell Gurney who explained that, though there were ways of creating faggot votes (i.e. he had encountered life rent charges and forty shilling freeholds), this was not one he had ever encountered. Ayrton then withdrew his amendment. Hardy's was accepted, and another from Colebrooke—to insert 'with a house'—rejected by ten votes. Although there is no reason to suppose that Disraeli would have insisted on rejecting the amendment if the House had accepted it, there is no doubt that the government wanted it defeated.

Over Colebrooke's motion Disraeli got his way: over voting papers he did not. The government proposal to allow electors to vote by voting paper was defended by county Conservatives, by Cranborne, by Karslake and by Labouchere on the various grounds that voting papers would induce a habit of voting in 'a good many quiet people [who at present] were afraid of going to the poll,'[1] that they would reduce the expense incurred by county members in bringing electors to the poll[2] and that, even if they enabled a single man to vote in seventeen different counties, they would at least have the advantage that they were men of education.[3] Labouchere, a Liberal himself, accused Liberals of opposing the clause because they believed 'that many of these quiet persons who...did not now vote at elections but were likely to do so under the proposed system were Conservatives (No, No!)'.[4] Liberal criticism of voting papers was justified by Bright, Ayrton, and Sergeant Gaselee on the ground that it was a major innovation,[5] that cheaper elections would mean more contested elections[6] and that in the counties especially voting papers, attested as they would have to be by a magistrate, would 'increase the gangrene of intimidation [as] the peasant...taken to the drawing-room of a magistrate...would be subjected to...the influence of wealth and power...which it would be impossible to free himself from'.[7] It is not certain whether Disraeli wanted the clause to pass because it would increase Conservative control of county constituencies, or whether it was put into the bill of March 18 in order to quieten Conservative consciences. Sir John Walsh mentioned it then as a 'conservative' aspect of the bill which concession on the borough franchise would enable the Conservative party to carry. It is reasonably certain that it would, if carried, have had a conservative effect in many constituencies.[8] Whether Disraeli intended to drop it or not, it is likely he was willing to drop it if necessary. He did not make it an issue of confidence. It was defeated by 38 votes on June 20, despite sizeable Adullamite support, dropped then and not revived when the House of Lords reinstated it during its discussion of the bill.

The abandonment of voting papers and the fulfilment of Derby's prediction, with the rejection of Dyott's and of Darby Griffith's amendments, that it was useless 'even to try to remove owners of borough *freeholds* from the county register'[9] were setbacks from a territorial point of view. However, it was likely in practice that the county votes actually used by borough freeholders occupying houses worth less than £10 p.a. would fall sharply as these freeholders acquired borough votes under the new borough franchise.[10] The enlargement of borough boundaries around a number of boroughs was a serious step in consolidating the rural and territorial character of the county seats. A Boundary commission with wide-ranging and indefinite powers was proposed in the bill of March 18. On June 25 it was given the task of examining all boroughs in England and Wales with a view to recommending cases in which it was desirable to enlarge them. It was not given the chance to reduce them. Reduction was excluded from its purview in terms which made it clear that Disraeli was intending to press this exclusion,[1] though Forster, Locke King and Sir George Grey had pressed, and lost, the point about the desirability of making the municipal boundary 'which was often a restricted one, the basis of the Parliamentary constituency'.[2] Since it had also to examine and propose for Parliament's approval any alteration it might think necessary in the boundaries of the new county and borough seats, its potential power was considerable. Disraeli tried at first[3] to propose a heavily-weighted commission, whose interest would be a county rather than an urban one and whose temper, so far as it was not Conservative, would be, if anything, Palmerstonian. The danger to the Liberal party from a body of this sort was considerable: it produced an unusual closing of the ranks. Under pressure from Sir George Grey, Gladstone and Bright, Disraeli dropped Pleydell-Bouverie, who was a Palmerstonian Whig, Bramston, a Conservative MP., and Lord Penrhyn, the recipient of one of Derby's few peerages in 1866, who as the Hon. Douglas Pennant had been a prominent county backbencher in a number of Parliaments. He kept the Chairman, Lord Eversley, the ex-Speaker of the Commons, whom Derby had expected to vote against Gladstone in 1866.[4] He kept John Walter of *The Times*, who, in Bright's view, had an unhealthy regard for territorial rank. He kept Russell Gurney, the Conservative Recorder of London, and Sir John Duckworth, an ex-MP. who had been first elected to Parliament in 1845 as a Protectionist. He added Sir Francis Crossley. Crossley, industrialist, Liberal MP., and object of suspicion to Yorkshire Conservatives and county Tories alike had supported Derby in 1859 up to the point at which the Reform bill was introduced.[5] He was offered as one who 'though his own opinions were known to be what were called Liberal and...from his social position...showed that he had a constitutional sympathy with the Whig party, nevertheless from his territorial possessions... might be supposed to have some interest common to the country party'.[1] Even this more carefully balanced commission proposed enlargements, in some cases extensive, to ninety parliamentary boroughs, which would have significantly increased the rural character of the county seats affected. These proposals might well have been carried in the following year if the reunited Liberal party had not referred the report to a more Liberally-constituted Select Committee, which removed fifteen of the largest boroughs from the Commissioner's list. Nevertheless, the Boundary bill which passed the Lords without amendment and received the royal assent in July 1868, removed an element of overspill from more than thirty county constituencies by enlarging the boundaries of fifty-eight English boroughs and ten Welsh groups of boroughs, and succeeded, as Serjeant Gaselee complained in 'tak[ing] away from the county and plac[ing] in the towns [a good many] town voters who were really... Liberal'.[2]

As we have seen, the government accepted Laing's first modification of the redistribution clauses. But it carried the rejection of Laing's second motion, of Gaselee's motion and of the motions made by Roebuck, Berkeley and others, to give third seats, not just to Liverpool, Birmingham, Manchester and Leeds, but to Sheffield and Bristol as well. In accepting Horsfall's motion, it rejected the connection Horsfall implied between the claim for increased representation on behalf of these four cities and what Adderley called 'the American principle' that 'each [had] a population (according to the last census of 1861) of upwards of 250,000'.[3] It coupled it with the condition that Disraeli would 'reserv[e] to [him]self, on the part of the government, the necessary right of remodelling the [redistribution schedule] so far as the intended necessary borough representation is concerned'. It was followed by a remodelling which, in order to meet Horsfall's requirements in relation to the four great cities, removed the borough status which had previously been proposed for four industrial towns. Though the distrust felt for Disraeli by Bright and Gladstone is manifest throughout discussion of the redistribution clauses, Disraeli was in a position to resist them because the House of Commons did not wish to transfer seats to industrial England on a purely numerical basis. He was able to resist them, also, because at each point at which he did not want to concede, he threatened them with loss, or postponement, of the whole bill, or with a redistribution which would take greater account than his 'compromise' proposals did of the fact that 'a majority of the people of the country do not live in parliamentary boroughs...and are represented by a very small number of members'.[1] This might not have been effective before he had a bill to show to the country, but at a stage at which household suffrage had already been established for the boroughs, it presented a threat. Disraeli made rejection of Laing's second redistribution motion, involving complete disfranchisement of certain boroughs, a question of confidence. He resisted Bright's and Gladstone's attempts to turn the debates on Horsfall's motion into the occasion for a general reopening of the Seats question.[2]

In other words, it is wrong to think of the great body of successful amendments as being Radical in content. Though abandonment of the Royal Parks bill in August as a result of Radical filibustering was a Radical success, it is doubtful whether Disraeli had ever treated it as anything more than a reassurance to angry Conservatives when he introduced it in May, or minded very much whether it was accepted or not. Though rejection of voting-papers, acceptance of the lodger franchise, the abolition of compounding, and the establishment of the £12 occupation and £5 copyhold franchise in the counties must be counted major Radical successes, the allocation of seats, the ratepaying principle, the boundary commission and a number of other clauses were so obviously concessions in the opposite direction that one may almost think of Disraeli as honouring an unwritten, though sometimes express,[3] 'contract' to let Radicals have their way in the boroughs so long as he had his to some extent in the counties.

The decisive vote at the beginning of the committee stage of Clause 3 (the borough franchise) was taken on April 12. The Easter recess began immediately and lasted until April 29. The first discussion of Clause 3 thereafter began on May 2. Discussion of Clause 3 continued until May 20, ending only when Disraeli had accepted Hodgkinson's amendment. Discussion of Clause 4 (the County Franchise) occupied the rest of May 20, May 23 and May 27. It was not until Clause 34 was brought forward out of numerical order on May 27 (in order to receive the government amendment which acceptance of Hodgkinson's amendment to Clause 3 necessitated to Clause 3) that discussion of the borough franchise was finally concluded with acceptance of amended versions of both clauses. On July 15 the bill received its third reading which passed without opposition being carried to the point of division. Only one government motion in these months—Disraeli's motion of May 9 to insert 'as an ordinary occupier' into the first section of Clause 3— was made into a vote of confidence[1] on which the government threatened its followers with dissolution, and Radicals with loss of the bill, if they were defeated. Although the votes of April 12 and May 9 gave the government a chance of carrying the bill in some form or other, there was no *guarantee*, even after the decisive majority of sixty-six on May 9, that the bill would pass in that session: it was only in the ten days following that this possibility became an immediate practical objective. It is in this context that one must examine Disraeli's acceptance of Hodgkinson's amendment in principle on May 17 1867, Hodgkinson's withdrawal of the amendment three days later on the understanding that the government would make alterations to clause 34 in order to meet his point, and the proposal, amendment, and final acceptance by the House, in amended form, of the amendments Disraeli proposed on May 27.

The problem with which Hodgkinson's amendment dealt was the problem of the compound householder. It dealt with it by proposing to abolish the practice of compounding in parliamentary boroughs in England and Wales. The amendment was called on May 17 as part of the discussion on the committee stage of Clause 3 (the borough franchise). Neither Hodgkinson nor Gladstone expected the amendment to be accepted. Gladstone seems to have preferred Childers' amendment to Hodgkinson's, and to have been prepared to commit himself to the one without committing himself to the other. When he arrived at the House of Commons on the 17th, he was surprised to be told by one of his own whips that the Conservative whips had promised that Hodgkinson's would be accepted in the course of the debate. During the debate, therefore, instead of denouncing the government's refusal to concede, he spoke judiciously. After Hodgkinson had proposed the amendment and Gladstone and Bass had supported it, Disraeli announced acceptance of the principle and promised either to bring in a government amendment to give effect to it or to introduce, as a separate bill, a major measure for consolidating the rating laws as they would be left after the abolition of compounding. He did this, he said, not because of public agitation outside, but in deference to the wishes of the Conservative party. He did it without consulting the Cabinet, without informing Hardy, the minister most closely involved, and without warning Conservative speakers in the House that he would do it. He did it, nevertheless, despite the pretence adopted in writing to Hardy that evening, premeditatedly and deliberately, ensuring, if Gladstone's memory was accurate thirty years later, that Gladstone knew in advance even though Disraeli's followers did not, and despite the fact that the amendment, if taken to a division, would almost certainly have been defeated.[1] It was, whether Gladstone's memory was accurate or not, almost certainly a calculated act of policy. The question is: what had Disraeli done? why did he do it?

Under an Act of 1563,[2] every occupier of a house in England and Wales was obliged to be rated for the relief of the poor. Freeholders were responsible for paying their own rates. In cases where the occupier was not a freeholder but a tenant, the obligation was still placed, not on the landlord but on him. The Small Tenements Act of 1819,[3] and a number of Rating Acts passed subsequently, provided, however, that landlords might, on decision of the inhabitants in vestry, be called on to make bulk payment of the rates due on the houses they owned (i.e. payment by composition) in place of the provision for payment by the tenants themselves which was embodied in the original Acts. The advantage of compounding was that it facilitated collection of rates and encouraged a better standard of housing for the working classes. In return for the saving made by local authorities in collecting small rates, the rate was reduced when a landlord paid the rates due in bulk by composition. The compound-householder was the tenant whose landlord paid his rates in bulk on his behalf, and whose rate therefore was smaller than that levied on householders who paid their rates direct.

The bill of March 18 had proposed to permit the enfranchisement of all householders who had 'been rated...to all rates (if any) made for the relief of the poor and had before July 20 in [any] year paid all poor rates that had become payable by [them]...up to the preceding January 5' (Clause 3). On these terms no compounder would have been enfranchised by the bill. A compounder could obtain a vote only by opting out of composition and paying the *higher* rate he would have paid (i.e. 'rates calculated on the Full Rateable Value', Clause 34), if his rates had not been paid on his behalf by composition. In the hands of critics, insistence on *personal* payment of rates could be made, therefore, to look like a 'fine' on the compounder who opted out of composition. It could be, and was, attacked on the one hand and defended on the other as the most serious restriction the bill offered to household suffrage pure and simple. Compounding had been adopted in some parishes, or in all, in something between 130 and 150 boroughs. If the provision for opting out of composition was financially discouraging, as it was under the terms of the bill of March 18, the personal payment principle would be a major check on the enfranchisement of numbers.

The 1832 Act had established the principle, as the basis of the borough franchise, that in addition to freemen, any occupant of a house worth £10 a year or more should have the vote, provided he had resided for a year, been rated for poor relief and the rates had been paid. There was no difference between the parties in 1867 about the need to lower the franchise qualification or about the importance, in doing so, of framing legislation so as, nevertheless, to 'exclude the residuum'. The difference between them by mid-April was that, whereas Gladstone, without committing himself, had made clear his desire to do this by lowering the qualifying line from £10 to £5 p.a. and enfranchising all occupants of houses rated at more than £5 (whether it was the occupier who paid the rates or the landlord), Disraeli intended to do so by enfranchising occupants of all houses whatever their rateable value, so long as the occupier had been rated for poor relief and himself had paid the rate. The difference in potential enfranchisement was small. When Disraeli's rated residential suffrage was combined with insistence on a two-year period of residence, the difference was a difference of party independence and personal assertion by two leading contenders in Parliament. For a variety of reasons, which have already been described, Disraeli won the first battle in the decisive vote of April 12.

The victory of April 12 and the assertion of the personal payment principle did not, however, in Radical eyes dispose of the problem of the 'fine' suffered by the compounder who opted out of composition. In this connection there were two objections to the bill—it really did impose a fine; it differentiated between the richer compounders enfranchised under the 1832 Act (as modified by the Clay

Act of 1851) and the compounder whose right to vote would be established by the bill. The solution proposed by Hibbert allowed the new compounder, like the old, to pay the reduced rate on opting out of composition. This would not *facilitate* opting out, which involved a deliberate choice and formal registration, but would remove the positive discouragement to doing so. It would also be a signal demonstration both of the power of Radicals themselves and of the willingness of Disraeli to concede to them. If adopted by the government, Hibbert's amendment would demonstrate Disraeli's willingness and ability to go farther than Russell and Gladstone had ever proposed to go. Even if he did not accept it, the attempt to make him do so would remind the Whig party that Radical support was never unconditional.

It is not clear whether Radicals took the initiative in approaching Disraeli, or whether he took the initiative in approaching them. But from the last week in March it seemed likely that something would be gained from appeasing Hibbert—at least among those who were not 'tooth and nail' against the government, just as something would be gained by abandoning the two-year residential qualification at a moment at which the Cave's erratic progress made it necessary to attract as much support as possible from elsewhere. Acceptance of Hibbert's amendment could be justified because the inequality between the old compounder and the new one was glaring, and would give little pleasure even in the Conservative party.[1] As, under pressure from the Cranborne Cave in the week before the division of April 12, Gladstone made plain his intention to destroy the government's bill because it went too far, the possibility of a Disraeli/Radical alliance increased. As Disraeli's anxiety to concede broke in upon everyone concerned, it seemed more likely than before that support might come from 'independent Radicals' who would 'not be dragged through the dirt, simply for the pleasure of seeing Mr Gladstone sit on the right-hand of the Speaker'.[2] Radicals and advanced Liberals who had always left the impression that they wanted household suffrage, did not want to destroy a bill which, however closely surrounded with conservative safeguards, *looked* like a household suffrage bill, and under pressure might become one. Since it was not certain, before April 10, that Gladstone would concentrate his first assault on the personal payment principle, it had not seemed necessary to make a point of conceding in Hibbert's direction. As soon as it became necessary, Disraeli tried to persuade the Cabinet to meet him.

The Cabinet at which he tried to do this was held secretly on April 11 in the house of Derby's private secretary, Lord Barrington. It was held secretly in order to avoid the impression that a change of policy was being considered, and was held under Disraeli's chairmanship because Derby was ill.[1] It was asked to decide whether to accept 'overtures' which Disraeli had been summoned to the House of Commons the day before to hear from 'Hibbert and his friends' who were willing 'if we would concede the point as to the compounder's fine...to support us on Gladstone's amendment'.[2] It issued, under guidance from Hardy, Stanley and Northcote, in the decision not to do so.[3] Nevertheless, that afternoon[4] Taylor told Dillwyn, the Liberal MP. for Swansea, that Disraeli[5] was in favour of meeting Hibbert's wishes and would urge them on the Cabinet, and seems to have given some sort of verbal approval of a memorandum recording the conversation. Dillwyn in his turn in the lobby on April 11 and 12 showed this to a number of Liberal MP.s, urging them to vote on this basis with the government the following day. Among these was Bernal Osborne,[6] MP. for Nottingham, who drew attention to the conversation and memorandum in the debate on the adjournment for the Easter recess before the second day of the main debate on April 12, accusing Taylor of committing the government in private to measures which it was not clear that it would commit itself to in public, and asking where the government in fact stood. There is no evidence that Taylor knew that Osborne's question would be raised:[7] whether by design or by genuine accident, he was not present in the House during Osborne's statement. Disraeli, in replying to Osborne, denied knowledge of the memorandum, pointed out that, since Derby was ill, he had not seen him for some time and explained away any assurances he might have given Hibbert, who had not seen the Dillwyn/Taylor memorandum,[8] by referring to the 'happy characteristic of this House that...notwithstanding the excited feelings sometimes to which none of us are superior,[9] there has always been among us on both sides of the House that trust and confidence which can only exist where there is the thorough breeding and feeling of gentlemen' and adding that 'the moment I leave the House and get into the lobby, I readily converse with any gentleman whatever his opinions may be, with the same freedom that I should in society and...should feel extremely embarrassed...if every statement which is so made by us is to be afterwards the subject of conversation in Parliament'.[1] Though there had in fact been a Cabinet not only the day before but also that morning, at which his attempt to accommodate Hibbert had once more been rejected, he neither committed the government against Hibbert's proposal nor suggested that it had already been rejected. It was only Stanley's intervention a couple of moments later to say that he 'knew absolutely nothing of the communication to which reference ha[d] been made until [he] entered the House [that] evening' which established that,

whatever may be the nature of the communications that have passed between [the Chief Whip] and certain [MP.s] on the other side of the House in whom he seems to have confided...[he wished] distinctly to say, and ...[was] authorised by [his] colleagues to state, that we go into this debate perfectly free and unpledged and upon no understanding direct or implied between Her Majesty's government and any individual member of this House as to any concessions that will be made in the bill.[2]

Like Stanley, Hardy was conscious that concession at this stage would be unpopular with Conservative backbenchers: in the course of the debate, he said the same thing. Although over twenty non-Whig Liberals voted with Disraeli, less than half a dozen of the Liberal cross-voters were Radicals, including neither Hibbert nor Clay who were almost certainly deterred by the brake which Hardy, who thought Disraeli 'unscrupulous' and Stanley, who evidently believed Disraeli's explanation to be 'untrue',[3] had so obviously put upon him.

Nevertheless, for reasons which we have explained already, the division was won: the bill was established as a going concern. Nobody in Radical quarters minded Disraeli appearing to be crooked.[4] MP.s went away for Easter. At this time it was not certain that the bill would pass, or that the Cave and the Conservative party would provide permanent support in numbers sufficient to enable Disraeli to disregard the Liberal left. Disraeli's contacts (through Taylor) with Clay, McCullagh Torrens, Hibbert and Dillwyn were close. He knew now that something could be done with them if assurances were given. He did his best to produce a situation in which they could be.

The first amendment to be taken after the Easter recess was Grosvenor's—to establish a £5 rating line. Grosvenor withdrew this, in view of the vote of April 12, while keeping open the possibility of moving another amendment, which was already on the order paper, to make voting and composition meet by reducing the Small Tenements Act from £6 to £5.[1] The second amendment was Ayrton's— to reduce the period of qualifying residence in parliamentary boroughs from two years to one. One objection to the two-year residential qualification was that it differentiated between existing electors (who had to reside for one year only under the terms of the 1832 Act) and electors who would be enfranchised by the bill. Another was that it would not restrict enfranchisement of the poor alone since the delays connected with the process of registration meant that, in order to satisfy a two-year residential requirement, many other electors had sometimes to reside for three or four.[2] The government had intended to propose a twelve-month residential qualification in the bill of February 23 which was dropped on February 25.[3] If Gladstone had stayed on this ground for his first attack in committee, he would have stood a chance of defeating the government decisively. So likely did this seem that Disraeli on April 9, despite the fact that he was in a position of some strength because of the Tea-Room humiliation, felt it necessary to write Conservative MP.s a letter (which was published in *The Times* on April 10) to say that the two-year residential qualification was an issue of confidence, the defeat of which would involve withdrawal of the bill. Gladstone had then shifted his ground, altering the order of his amendments in order to put the personal rating principle to the test. He had done this in order to demonstrate his independence of Grosvenor, who did not want the personal payment principle attacked, and in order to keep support from Heathcote and Cranborne, who could not vote against a restriction like duality. Under Taylor's guidance Disraeli reacted, first, as we have seen, by reaffirming the personal payment principle and hinting to Elcho that he was in favour of a fixed line as well; secondly by trying to give way to Hibbert in the matter of the 'fine'. The fact that he was overruled by the Cabinet, though it reduced the size of the Liberal vote and discouraged Hibbert, did not discourage all Liberals from voting with him.

Gladstone's defeat on April 12 had boosted Conservative morale.

The fact that, despite Taylor's and Disraeli's manifest duplicity, they had defeated him without conceding more than was conceded in principle on March 25 and had still been supported by a handful of Radicals and advanced Liberals, was a matter for congratulation. There were difficult questions to face and difficult decisions to be made, but at the beginning of the Easter recess the Conservative party, so far as day-to-day parliamentary management was concerned, had emerged from the critical gloom into which Cranborne had cast it on February 25. Some passes had been sold, but the personal payment principle had been affirmed and might well result in an Act as restrictive and conservative in practice as most Conservative MP.s wanted it to be. Though Taylor was not sure that he could carry the two-year residential qualification and seems to have wanted prior concession in order to avoid defeat, the fact that there had been a major Conservative victory made this easier to contemplate.

Nevertheless, the end of the Easter recess brought with it a change which radically altered the feeling of the Conservative party. It produced a renewal of public agitation which shook Conservative confidence in the government's ability to control it and spilled over to become a major source of discontent about Reform. Since the events of May 6/20 were profoundly affected by this change of mood, since the impact of popular disturbance on governmental policy in these months is not as simple as is sometimes supposed, and since the connection between public disturbance and the climate of opinion is one of the themes of this book, it is necessary if the passage of Hodgkinson's amendment is to be understood, to follow the objects of the various agents of public agitation from their foundation in 1864/5 up to the point at which the Reform League organized a defiant meeting in Hyde Park on May 6 1867.

VII

THE PUBLIC AGITATION

'The [Reform] question is the sole property of Liberals, because they alone are conscious of and sympathize with the claims which Reform is needed to satisfy.'

Morning Star, October 8 1866

In attempting to disentangle the objectives towards which the creators of the public agitation were directing events between 1865 and 1867, it is necessary to distinguish between the substantive objectives of their policies and the tactical purposes by which the objectives were surrounded. This is obviously necessary in dealing with parliamentary politicians; it is no less necessary in evaluating the activities of those whose centre of power lay outside Parliament. It is necessary in the case of Bright, whose mind and manner were conditioned by an acute sense of parliamentary possibility. It is necessary in the case of the Reform League, the Reform Union, the London Working Men's Association and the London Trades Council. It is necessary in all these cases because, although all wanted a Reform bill at some time in the future, there were significant differences about scope and timing which made the Reform agitation a more miscellaneous alliance than is suggested by the manifest unity it was able to maintain between July 1866 and April 1867.

In the first place, there is a distinction between the Reform Union style of organization on the one hand and the Reform League style of organization on the other. The Reform League and the London Working Men's Association had a working-class membership which was led, for its purposes and theirs, by an intelligensia of middle-class and ex-working-class journalists, litterateurs and professional organizers, many of whom were short of money and some of whom wanted, more than was thought suitable, to keep their own hands on subscriptions raised from benefactors.[1] The Reform Union was the creation of Radical politicians and Lancashire merchants and manufacturers who were attempting under the leadership of George Wilson, Bright's lieutenant in the anti-Corn Law agitation, to repeat the successes of the 1840s. The Reform Union was founded in April 1864 as an offshoot of the Leeds Manhood Suffrage Association, but, unlike the Leeds association, was a strongly civic body with heavy representation of merchants and manufacturers, nonconformist clergy and a sprinkling of the progressive intelligentzia from elsewhere.[1] The Union did not embrace all Lancashire merchants and manufacturers. But it was an attempt by a self-conscious bourgeoisie to provide leadership and exert power in the determination of public policy, and to display its strength by carrying the higher artisans along with it. It had civic pride and corporate purpose. Success in relation to a predominantly 'territorial' Parliament was an essential prerequisite to success in keeping the support of the lower classes within the area of its influence. Like Cowen's reform movement in the North East (which, however, had a manhood suffrage platform),[2] and like Bright's movement in Birmingham, the Reform Union in Manchester and its environs was an attempt to keep control of any working-class movement that was in sight by proving its own power in relation to an aristocratic Parliament, and by providing politico-industrial leadership which was so effective that leadership would not be given by working-class politicians themselves. The movement assured its working-class audiences that there was no hostility between wealth and the working-classes, that 'in nearly all the great towns of the kingdom there [was] a powerful middle class in favour of the enfranchisement of the working classes'[3] and that the outcome of successful agitation on its terms would be a consolidation of national unity, a series of fundamental reforms in church, financial, and Irish policy and a general elevation of the power of the industrial bourgeoisie and the intelligent artisan to produce a polity which was both conservative and secure. Its leaders saw the social and political advantages of working-class complaisance. They saw the dangers to be feared from working-class hostility. They knew—none better than Bright—how far it was safe to go.

The Union's original programme included the ballot, a redistribution according to population and property, triennial Parliaments and a franchise in counties as well as in the boroughs for 'every male person householder or lodger, rated or liable to be rated for the relief of the poor'. It is not clear what was intended by the franchise proposal, but pains were taken to avoid the phrase manhood suffrage. Though this platform was more advanced than any *party* had advocated by 1864, the Union's leaders understood the limits of political possibility with the existing electorate. They were conscious of the uneasiness felt by the upper classes in Lancashire, Yorkshire and elsewhere. They remembered that 'the chartist agitations of 1837 and 1848 [had]...failed because of the indiscretion of the leaders and the antipathy of the middle classes'. They had no intention of repeating its mistakes.[1] They knew that manhood suffrage was not an objective to which the prosperous classes would respond. It was not an objective to which they wished to be committed: they took care that they were not committed to it. Though Beales, Howell, George Potter and other Reform League leaders appeared on Reform Union platforms in Manchester, and though the Union sent delegates to Reform League meetings in London and elsewhere, an understanding was established by mid-1865 that the Union would not propose manhood suffrage, and it became clear, as the agitation developed in 1866 and 1867, that in certain circumstances it would oppose it.

Its leaders opposed it because they did not think it safe and because they knew that the climate of Liberal opinion was against it. Liberal opinion mattered because they were party Liberals with a desire, to which the parliamentary party did not yet respond, to replace Whig domination by their own conjunction of Liberal, progressive and nonconformist positions. The Reform Union in Manchester, Cowen's movement in Newcastle and Bright's movement in Birmingham were demonstrations of the power of industrial radicalism—attempts to prove to an aristocratic Parliament and the Whig element in the Liberal party that it too had followers more effective, more impressive and more readily articulate than the mute agrarian legions on which territorial power depended. In Bright and Gladstone they had idols whose working-class sympathies were undisputed, and who could blame the Conservative party or dissident Whigs for any want of enthusiasm they felt themselves at the prospect of enfranchisement as extensive as the one Disraeli eventually gave them. They succeeded in carrying along a large body of working-class opinion with comparatively little disaffection right up to the point at which the Reform bill was passed in August 1867, while imposing restraints on the policy platform of the movement itself.

The journalism of agitation spoke of rights and the people's will: so

did the Reform League. The Union looked to Mill, Bright and Gladstone: so in 1866/7 did the League and the London Working Men's
Association. Bright and McLaren declared their independence of
the Whig party;[1] so did Potter and Beales. The rights of dissenters
and the wrongs of the Irish had their place in the minds of both.
Bright, Cowen and Wilson spoke of the need to suffocate the Cave,
and to destroy Derby's government. The League and Potter left an
impression of unanimous coherence with Gladstone and Bright.
The League and the London Working Men's Association, as much
as the Reform Union, directed their attention at Parliament, and
timed meetings to coincide with the major turning-points in Parliament's discussion of the question. Though there was suspicion of
Parliament, the object throughout was to set up a dialogue between
Parliament and people.

Yet between the League and the Union there were significant
differences. Whereas the movements in Manchester, Birmingham,
Newcastle and elsewhere were led by such wealth and respectability
as was available, the Reform League was almost entirely devoid of
both. Colonel Dickson was a retired soldier—a bankrupt pensioner
not a leader of industrial society. He had served in the army in
India, had been a Carlist in Spain and had stood, alongside Wellington's son, as Conservative candidate for Norwich. He had held
minor administrative office in South Africa, had developed a personal grudge against Earl Grey and had been a member of the
Executive committee of the Conservative Land Society. He had
been dismissed from the Tower Hamlets Militia for misappro-
priation of mess funds but had won a lawsuit which partly cleared
his name. He had stood as a Radical in Marylebone in 1859. Beales
was a barrister—an Etonian without wealth or great social standing.
Beesly was something between a journalist and a prophet. The rest
of the League's leaders, apart from Dresser Rogers, Baxter Langley
and a handful of others, had been compositors, bricklayers, tailors,
soldiers and so on. Some were still working their craft; others were
pursuing a life of intellectual respectability in the lower regions of
the self-taught journalistic and political intelligentsia. Lord Teynham provided a title, but not very much more. A small number of
dissenting manufacturers like Thomasson and Samuel Morley provided money for the League (as well as for the Union) though in the
case of the League so much less, and so much less regularly, than

it needed it that at one stage the Executive was not sure it had enough money to let Howell 'call in a man to examine the gas pipe...and have it...repaired'.[1] Despite the Lord Mayor's presence at meetings organized by Beales in August 1866 and by Potter and the London Working Men's Association in the Guildhall later in the winter, the commercial leaders of London were unfriendly: they tended to avoid the League. The support supplied by the London Trades Council as a body was negligible until the beginning of 1867. The intelligentsia dragged its feet. Even Baxter Langley wanted to know what sort of company he was being asked to keep.[2] Not more than eight or nine Liberal MP.s were in close touch and of these Fawcett, Mill and Torrens were philosophic radicals, Hughes was a Christian Socialist, The O'Donoghue was O'Connell's nephew and T. B. Potter was Cobden's successor in Rochdale. Only Bright, if such categories are appropriate to him, and P. A. Taylor, the Courtauld magnate and Cowen's candidate in Newcastle in 1859, can be said to have combined wealth and industrial respectability, though it is doubtful whether these were the salient political characteristics of either. These facts did not prevent Howell, Rogers, Dickson, Odger, Leno, Cunnington, Merriman, Mantle, Langley, Bradlaugh, Osborne, Weston, Taylor, Connolly and Marx's friend, Lucraft[3] stimulating a powerful expression of working-class feeling in the capital and elsewhere. It did not stop them asserting a claim to represent men who, though not holders of property, were 'equal in position and intelligence to the [existing] possessors of the franchise'.[4] Nor did it prevent them tapping, by association and connection, the innumerable trades, temperance and welfare societies and the pockets of antinomian working-class feeling which working-class newspapers and clubs reflected and stimulated throughout the country. But it helps to account for the contempt with which its activity in the capital was treated by those who watched its progress there.

The League was founded in London in 1864 in the wake of a meeting which the police had dispersed from Primrose Hill during Garibaldi's visit. It was founded with the object of establishing manhood suffrage and the ballot, and of opposing all other proposals (including any redistribution of seats proposed by the existing House of Commons). It was founded with the support, personally and individually though not corporately, of the main leaders of the London

Trades Unions, and was infiltrated from the start by working-men nominees of the International, whose function, if Marx is to be believed,[1] was to prevent Beales and his followers imposing capitalist respectability on it. As a result of a quarrel with Applegarth and the Junta in early 1865, George Potter left the London Trades Council in order to found a parallel organization of his own—the London Working Men's Association—to campaign for a lodger franchise. Potter's anxiety to make his Association work brought him into conflict with the Trades Council he had left. Since its leaders were closely involved with Beales and Howell, the tension between the League and the London Working Men's Association at times was acute. Since Potter was also a member of the Reform League, the tension was carried into the League itself. The tension arose less from any policy conflict than from Potter's journalism which was vigorous and idiosyncratic, from his personality which was exuberant, perhaps from his religion which seems to have been Christian, and from the feeling others had about him (as they had about Howell) that he enjoyed hobnobbing with the great. Potter's objectives were as extensive as anyone else's : they were expressed more powerfully. But Potter caught Gladstone's imagination much more than Odger, Applegarth or Allen. It was to Potter, not to the League, that Lord Ranelagh—ex-Carlist and Tory peer—offered Beaufort Gardens for the Trades rally when the government had refused Hyde Park in December 1866. Though it is difficult to see a fundamental difference between his objectives and theirs, there can be little doubt that Potter, despite the extravagance of his language and the militancy of his trade unionism, was less unacceptable in high places than other trades unionists in the League.

From the early months of 1866 and increasingly after July, the two bodies worked on parallel lines with some common membership and a measure of common direction, taking pains to emphasize that the Tory government could not produce a tolerable Reform bill and that the Whig/Cave element in the Liberal party had no popular following. In the agitation of mid- and late 1866, Beales, Howell and Potter played a significant part in providing journalistic and rhetorical comment, in organizing meetings, lectures and branches and in establishing contact between their own organizations in London and similar organizations elsewhere. The innumerable meetings, lectures and branches which were organized not only in the large but also in the medium-sized towns throughout the country, and the impression they leave of being a highly organized, successfully managed national institution, even when run on a shoe-string, was in large part their achievement.

There were, then, three elements in the public agitation, not one. Each had a different ulterior purpose, though all co-operated to leave an impression of common direction. The Union was a Liberal body with a desire to help its chosen leaders destroy the reactionary element in the Liberal party. The League in Liberal terms was a fringe group with many members whose political objective was to create an independent working-class movement out of a vastly extended electorate in conditions of economic depression in the future. Potter's Association was based on the belief, about which some parts of the Junta at first had reservations, that industrial success was impossible without direct political action. The London Trades Council's decision in January 1867 to give corporate support to the Reform League was probably an attempt to reduce Potter's powers,[1] as well as a recognition that the hostility shown towards trade unionism by public opinion at large and in the Hornby *v.* Close case made direct political action essential, at any rate so far as franchise extension was concerned. There was backbiting between Potter and the League, and suspicion between the Union and the League. Nevertheless, right up to the point at which Disraeli began to dismantle the restrictive aspects of the bill of March 18, there was something resembling a common direction.

In Bright the movement had a leader who transmuted defiance of aristocracy into an assertion of moral solidarity between the middle and working-classes, who was conscious of the danger Cobden had foreseen that in any struggle with the aristocracy the middle classes would desert the working classes[2] and who reflected more exactly than anyone else that broad blurring of distinctions, that powerful accommodation of all reforming positions which was designed to keep together those who might otherwise have stood apart on all important questions. Bright gave the movement its common direction. While Gladstone's name was as powerful, and Mill's as widely respected, Bright alone had the record, the freedom from formal party leadership and the necessary accessibility. Though he was depressed by Cobden's death and though his public pessimism about the possibilities of extensive franchise reform in the existing

Parliament did him no good with the League,[1] the memory of the campaign he had waged against Disraeli's bill in 1858/9, his standing as the hammer of aristocracy and the vigour with which he put himself in touch with the movement in 1866 placed him in a position to damp down the differences that existed between the constituent elements. Though the differences of substance which divided Bradlaugh and Potter on the one hand from Cowen and Wilson on the other were deep, Bright, despite doubt, hesitation and some suspicion, was the only man whose unconcealed ambiguity enabled him to maintain relations with all.

Bright was a parliamentary politician who wanted to make the Liberal party in his own image. He had a specific purpose—to reduce the power of reactionary Whiggism. Beales agreed. Other League members did not. Marx's contingent wanted a show-down; they were probably the 'working-men' Mill found so much more anxious than Beales to challenge the government in Hyde Park after July 23 1866.[2] The trades union wing of the movement was concerned less with the Liberal party than with an extension of the franchise, improved contractual or working conditions or rates of pay for its members and an opportunity to demonstrate the importance of the organizations to which they belonged. Yet Bright succeeded for a time in imposing his tactical calculations and rhetorical objectives on all of them. Bright at no time attacked Gladstone. Before the Gladstone bill was defeated in June 1866, he attacked the Cave and the Conservative party for trying to destroy it. When the bill had been defeated and Russell had resigned, he attacked the Conservative party for bringing down a government which had 'acted upon the principle of trust and confidence in the people'. He greeted 'the accession to office of Lord Derby [as] a declaration of war against the working classes'. He presented Derby as 'the fomenter of discord' and his party as 'a turbulent element in English political society', and welcomed the fact that trades unions had been forced by the House of Commons to take direct political action. Bright emphasized his detachment from party.[3] He stressed the need to show Parliament that the 'people' was 'the only...power in the country that can do anything'.[4] He applauded the gatherings he addressed as 'demonstrations of opinion and if you like...exhibition[s] of force [which] if they be despised and disregarded, may become exhibitions of another kind of force'.[5] He claimed that, though patience was necessary and dignity essential, the united demonstration of the people's will made action inevitable.

In late 1866 Bright did not conduct himself as the straightforward exponent of a programme. He did what Disraeli had done to Russell and Gladstone at the beginning of the year, destructively uniting all the government's enemies in the hope that its attempt to meet all the requirements of its situation would bring about its downfall. The League programme included manhood suffrage: Bright 'was not afraid of it'.[1] On the other hand he did not want it, and justified his reluctance on the ground that anyone who knew the House of Commons could see that it would not give it. Though there were obvious differences between the League, the Union and the Liberal party, he papered over cracks by showing that all roads led the same way. Bright expected Disraeli to produce a bill, but seems to have been intent on raising his terms so high that the Liberal party would not be able to support it. Not only did Bright try in advance to destroy any liberal mask the government might put on: he predicted the government's destruction. It may well have been the government's success in 1867 in avoiding the disaster which Bright had predicted which made him keep up the pressure to the latest moment possible in the hope that it would be unable to do what Disraeli by May 1867 had clearly decided it was going to do.

These groups, then, did not begin as one. In 1865 they had a common body of recognizable causes—Italian freedom, the Irish church, the modification of Anglican monopoly, but their assumptions and purposes were by no means identical. They were held apart by the fragmentary character of the opportunity public feeling gave for united action on major topics, by Palmerston's success in taking the sting out of the Radical movement and by the League's reluctance to connect itself with any platform but its own.[2] This feeling did not prevent the development of a rhetoric and journalism at all levels of social life which was designed to hold the literate working classes for the varying reforming causes. But it left its leaders the impression that there was an uphill struggle to be fought, that little would be achieved in the immediate future and that there need be no thought in 1865 of a movement of united public agitation. Though Palmerston's death, and its prospect beforehand, and a deep-rooted belief in Gladstone's effectiveness, had opened up rays of hope, the beginning of the session of 1866, with its promise of a bill so limited as to be valueless, saw these various groups at the nadir of their expectation.

Nor was this feeling altered by the introduction of the Russell/ Gladstone bill which was welcomed as an instalment because Bright supported it, but which was unimpressive in itself[1] and aroused little interest outside Parliament. Meetings were held and petitions presented. But the most respectable Liberal papers at first ignored them.[2] Even the most ardent reformers agreed with Lowe and Horsman that there was no steam in the agitation. Though there was little interest in Reform, however, there was considerable interest in parliamentary proceedings and a capacity, which every newspaper induced, for dramatizing the parliamentary conflict. The interest aroused by the conflict between Gladstone and Grosvenor, the vigour of what seemed to be Lowe's denunciation of the whole of the working classes, and the proof given by July 1866 that even Liberals disliked, distrusted and abused the people made it possible to stimulate extensive public interest in nearly all the major cities. One must not exaggerate the political concern of the working-class audiences which provided support at public meetings. Millions did not turn out to cheer Bright. Many of those who did so turned out, no doubt, because they had been given a holiday for the purpose. But from the point at which Lowe's remarks became public knowledge, interest was aroused. The tabling of Grosvenor's amendment in March and the government's narrow victory in April gave agitation events to which to gear itself. With the government's defeat in June and the refusal to hold a general election, the agitation became serious. With the arrival of Derby's government, an opportunity arrived to mount a major assault, not just in favour of a lowering of the franchise but in order to purify the Liberal party, attack the Whig party and demonstrate that the Tory party was incapable of meeting working-class demands.[3]

Right from the point at which Russell and Gladstone were defeated on June 18 there was a desire in all parts of the public movement to work together to create a climate of opinion in which Adullamites and Tories should be seen to be defying the people's will. At first this was a demand for a dissolution. When the dissolution did not take place, it became a call to recognize that, if enough pressure was brought to bear, the new government would have to produce a bill.[4] Derby knew, it was claimed, that the age would not tolerate real

Toryism. He had given Stanley the Foreign Office instead of Malmesbury who had had it in 1858. This 'concession to the spirit of the age' would be matched by others if agitation was persistent: 'the Tories [would] sacrifice anything which require[d] to be sacrificed.'[1] It was only after the closing of Hyde Park on July 22 that 'the whole bent of the Tory mind' was seen to be 'towards... Austrian maxims...[and] a continental despotism'.[2] Thereafter, Derby, who had previously been 'personally a kind and good landlord'[3] became the reactionary who had resisted Grey's enquiry into the Irish Church in 1834 and helped to destroy Peel in 1846.[4] The outbreak of window-breaking and the incidents in the Park on July 23 and 24 were blamed on Mayne and Derby, and on a crowd of roughs who marched through the Park on the 24th, abusing the fashionable in Rotten Row until they were chased off by the police. The meetings which were actually held in the Park on July 24 and 30 were represented as triumphs for the League. The power the League's leaders had to bring Derby into violent conflict with the people was taken to show that he was at their mercy.[5] The meetings and demonstrations now became 'demonstrations against Toryism' and were 'meant to prove...that the Tories in office are not the Ministers of the English people', that 'Lord Derby [held] office as a usurper' and that 'there [was] no way to satisfy the public but for Her Majesty to dismiss the present ministry and recall Earl Russell and Mr Gladstone'.[6] Throughout the rest of 1866 and the first four months of 1867 there is the same line of policy—to blame the government for the breakdown that occurred in public order in July and for any that might occur in the future, to establish the peacefulness of the agitation's intention and to insist, after a movement so 'majestic', that even 'Lord Russell and Mr Gladstone [must] mark that the time for £7 franchise bills and the grouping of rotten boroughs ha[d] gone never to return'.[7]

As the movement gathered strength, its claims in relation to the Liberal party became more powerful, its attacks on its enemies more emphatic. Liberal constituency associations were encouraged to persecute Adullamites.[8] It was claimed that 'the next Liberal government must be so constituted as to include a much greater proportion of the popular element than has been usual in Whig ministries'.[9] The next Liberal ministry would not be long coming since 'the moment ha[d] gone [so] far beyond the possibility of a Derby measure [that] anything which could satisfy the people would place the Tory government in more violent opposition to their own party than the repeal of the Corn laws'.[1] Though there were moments of uncertainty when Bright's warnings of violence were used by Tory newspapers in order to discredit him, the resistance Bright provoked among the upper classes was used as an obstacle against which to mount a frontal assault on those who might 'meditate crimes against liberty and the commonwealth'.[2]

Derby's decision to deal with the Reform question was as much an attempt to keep in step with the reaction against Bright as a capitulation to him. The possibility that he might stay in office to do so did not please the leaders of the agitation. When the possibility of Conservative action about Reform was first mentioned, warnings were issued against a Disraelian trick. Since Disraeli had already presented Derby as the author of the 1832 Act,[3] these warnings were thought to have substance. Brand's warning that the Liberal party might have to improve a bill if the government proposed one, produced denunciation 'beforehand [of] all Tory attempts to settle the Reform question as sinister in meaning, unwholesome in method, detrimental to political morals [and] certain either to do nothing or to do harm'.[4] When W. E. Forster discussed the possibility of Disraeli doing a Peel, he was reminded that Peel had had a majority in 1845 and that the Cave would abandon Disraeli if he proposed any lowering of the franchise. Disraeli, Walpole and Stanley were singled out as 'pliable men' who would like to propose a bill.[5] But 'if [Disraeli] tried to induce the Cabinet to pass a good Reform bill, a majority of his colleagues would refuse', while 'if, as the organ of the government, he were to propose a small or tricky Reform bill, he and the ministry would be summarily expelled from Downing Street'.[6]

The desire to strengthen the climate of resistance was acute. Rumours, securely based and extensively reported, of proposals to couple 'the name of household suffrage...with some extravagantly long period of residence and other qualifications' were 'a Tory dodge' which must be met by a firm refusal from 'all that is manly, intelligent and progressive in the British nation'.[7] The recollection that Disraeli 'began political life as a follower of O'Connell' produced the assurance that 'no Reform bill worth having can come from the Cranbornes and Malmesburys and Hardys'.[8] Lord John Manners' praise of the British working-man[9] was met with the accusation that he had not contradicted Lowe's slurs on the working classes in the previous session.[1]

As the possibility of a Conservative initiative grew more plausible, two threats emerged to the unity of the movement. There was the League's fear that the Reform Union, 'in an anxiety to complete the enfranchisement of the middle classes', might follow the Liberal party in 'disregard[ing] the enfranchisement...of the working classes'.[2] There was a danger that the conduct of the League and the London Working Men's Association might discredit the movement as a whole. Both fears are obvious from September onwards.[3] They were met to some extent by the Reform League banquet in Manchester on November 20 when twenty Liberal MP.s sat down with Lords Houghton and Teynham alongside Baines, Bright, George Potter, George Wilson and 'the cream of the middle class politicians of Yorkshire and Lancashire—...the self-made men of industry,...who can subscribe £1,000 for a purpose ...to benefit the country without expecting anybody to quote it as a reason why they should be permitted to do political wrong for the rest of their lives'.[4] They were met by the orderliness shown by 'many thousands of the élite of the working classes'[5] on George Potter's Trades march through London on December 3, though anxiety had been felt beforehand that rowdies or drunks would ruin the effect.[6]

With the return of parliament and more specific rumours about the government's intentions, anxiety grew to ensure that the agitation should not stop merely because the session had started. It was necessary to keep up the pressure, because a meeting of Parliament would restore a reactionary House of Commons to the centre of the scene. It would expose the fact that not only on the Tory side but also among the Whigs there were 'many who,...too cunning to become avowed Adullamites,...would be only too glad to see even a Tory government succeed in postponing the hated reform for a year'.[7] In 1867, it is true, there could be no question of Disraeli attempting, as in 1859, 'to conciliate the Radicals and widen the breach between them and the Whigs'.[8] In the climate of expectation created by the popular movement, he would not be able to 'unite the most advanced section of the Liberals with the most bigoted of the bucolic members'.[9] For Disraeli to do anything and survive, he would have to keep hold of the Adullamites who might support him in return for 'an illusory bill' if that would prevent 'Mr

Gladstone's [coming] back, with the country up and clamouring for manhood suffrage'.[1] Disraeli's *Reform Speeches*, published under Corry's editorship in January, contained 'hardly...a single sentence which would not...be an argument against any sort of step of parliamentary reform which the people of England could possibly care to have'.[2] They underlined, what real reformers knew already, that 'the Tories fear the working man, not because they think he is a revolutionist or a socialist or...a dullard...[but] because they know that...he is not a Tory'.[3] In these circumstances '[since] there must be a Reform bill...it follows inevitably...that the Tories should resign'.[4]

Uncertainty about the government's policies in one sense assisted the task of public agitation. If the government had declared its intentions, the Liberal party might have had to declare its own. The government's silence meant that the whole of the opposition—parliamentary and extra-parliamentary, Liberal, Radical and Democratic—could continue to be united. So long as no bill had been proposed, it was possible to keep together the whole range of opinion. When the government had reached the point, first of proposing resolutions and then of announcing the content of its policy on February 25 and March 5, Disraeli's tactical ambiguity still made it possible for the opposition to present a united front. The League had held a public meeting the night Parliament was prorogued. The day after it reassembled final arrangements were made for two meetings to be held the day Disraeli introduced the resolutions. On February 11 there was an afternoon rally in Trafalgar Square. That evening a mounted messenger brought the outlines of Disraeli's policy to a vast rally at the Agricultural Hall. As T. B. Potter read out the 'proposal of a rating...which would be included in the resolutions...and...[pointed out that] the counties...[would be] handed over bound hand and foot to the Tories..., shouts and groans in intensity went up from the crowd ..."out with the Tories"'.[5] When the resolutions were read in the newspapers next morning, they seemed 'a clumsily devised scheme based almost altogether upon that which met with so scornful a rejection...in 1859—...the revision of boundaries, the elimination of the urban population from the counties, the fancy franchises and the voting papers all over again'.[6] The bill promised on February 25 merely made the government look ridiculous.[7]

The first doubts about the viability of Gladstone's tactics arose from the Liberal decision to let the resolutions pass without scrutiny. They were reinforced by the truth which dawned between February 11 and February 25 that 'an unscrupulous and audacious strategist...[was] choos[ing] his own battle ground' more effectively than had seemed possible in the winter.[1] Gladstone continued to attract respect but the 'exaggerated courtesy' and 'wholly misplaced generosity' with which the opposition was treating the government was dangerous.[2] Doubts were increased by Gladstone's failure on February 25 to understand that 'warfare cannot be carried on without blows'[3] and by the realization that, if Disraeli could get rid of the dissident ministers and bring in a bill, he might stand a chance if 'the measure...he submits to the House...[was] a better bill than Mr Gladstone's'.[4]

Despite anxiety in some quarters,[5] the unity presented by Gladstone and Grosvenor at the Liberal meeting in Gladstone's house on February 26 restored a certain measure of optimism. Russell, Bright, Gladstone and Grosvenor had all condemned the government. Given a continuation of pressure, the Liberal party might avoid a Whig compromise. The resignations of Cranborne, Carnarvon and Peel—'the obstinate party'—made it seem 'within Mr Disraeli's power to carry a Reform bill'.[6] It made it doubly desirable to mount an 'agitation more extensive, more fierce and more resolute than any' previous one, in order to remind the Liberal leaders that 'the unenfranchised millions' mattered more than 'the great aristocratic houses of Westminster, Sutherland, Bedford, Lansdowne and Derby'.[7] In the bill when it eventually appeared, there was little that was not 'positively objectionable except the bare name of household suffrage'.[8] Duality would produce class warfare: personal payment was 'shabby, stingy and stupid'.[9] Expectations varied from the belief that 'it [was] impossible that [the bill] should ever be passed into law'[10] to a belief that it might be, if the Liberal party could insist on the enfranchisement of the compound householder and a more extensive redistribution of seats, together with the abandonment of duality, personal payment, the long term of residence, the fancy franchises and the high county qualification.[11] The Liberal decision not to oppose the second reading gave no pleasure to the leaders of public agitation.[12] Though this second reading was obviously an exception to the rule that 'the second reading affirms the principle of [a] bill', it was alarming that Disraeli had got past it while 'conced[ing] nothing of the slightest importance'.[1]

Despite the passage of the second reading, however, it was still possible to hope that the bill would be defeated very shortly and the government turned out. It was possible to hope this because it was assumed that Liberal MP.s would see through Disraeli who, having abandoned nothing conclusively except duality, was saying in effect ' "shut the gates of committee behind you and then, when you are helplessly locked in...we will tell you what we mean to do for you" '.[2] But, though it was possible to hope that Disraeli would be turned out, it was far from certain that he would be. Since a good many Liberal MP.s were not to be trusted, it was necessary to remind them of their obligations. Just as the public movement had wanted the government turned out on the second reading on March 26, so on April 8 it wanted Disraeli turned out before the committee stage began. Just as the Liberal party itself had prevented Gladstone opposing the second reading, so now the Tea-Room delegation refused to follow Gladstone's lead. Though doubts were felt about Coleridge's Instruction because it made household suffrage impossible,[3] it was recognized outside Parliament as an attempt to impose conditions to which Disraeli could not agree, and was supported, whatever the reservations, because it would put an end to a fraudulent government. The 'sudden burst into factitious independence'[4] on the part of the Tea-Room meeting on April 8 and the forced withdrawal of the second half of Coleridge's Instruction meant that the bill had got into committee. It meant that Disraeli had won a major victory without committing himself to meet the central demands for which the public movement was campaigning. When this was followed by the defeat of Gladstone's attempt to destroy the bill by destroying its central principle on April 12, all the fears which suspicion of the House of Commons had aroused among earnest reformers at their moments of gloomiest expectation had been confirmed. It was clear now that the Tory government would not fall as easily as had been expected. It was clear that a measure of success had been achieved for a 'gigantic attempt to keep the Tories in office in an age when they have long been left behind by the intelligence of the country'. It was certain that something drastic would be needed if expectations were not to be disappointed.

The difficulty was not just that the movement was not being given what it wanted, but that it would not easily hang together once Gladstone had demonstrated his inability to deliver the goods. From July 1866 until the production of Disraeli's bill on March 18 1867, it had not been difficult to maintain unity among the various Reforming bodies. The harrying of the Adullamites, the claim that the people would make the Liberal party in its own image if Gladstone would let it and the want of commitment on the government's part had made it easy to construct a platform of destructive intensity in which the main objects of hostility were reactionary Whiggism and the obstinacy of the 'stupid party's' resistance to the people. So long as Conservatives were committed to nothing, and so long as it was believed that nothing to which they could be committed would go far enough to satisfy even a majority of the House of Commons, so long was it supposed that effective agitation would make it possible to capture the Liberal party in the future. Though they had been deprived of a chance to fight a general election in 1866, the movement's leaders looked forward to the government's inevitable failure to produce a bill which its followers could accept, anticipating, no less than Halifax among Whigs, a situation in which they would be able to claim some share of the credit for producing the conditions which produced its failure.

The objects of policy right up to the end of March, therefore, were to mobilize opinion against Whig power in the Liberal party and to demand the expulsion of the Tory government. The second objective, so far from being weakened, was strengthened by the terms of the bill Disraeli introduced on March 18. The personal payment principle, the inadequacy of the redistribution clauses and the fact that, in the absence of a lodger franchise, virtually no enfranchisement was proposed for London[1] all showed Disraeli to be the trickster he had been said to be: they showed that the Tory party could not be an instrument of the people's will. It was only Gladstone's failure to bring down the government at once, his conciliation of Halifax, Brand and the parliamentary Liberal party and delayed evidence of his earlier flirtation with the Cave which produced the first signs of dissatisfaction with his leadership.

Unfortunately for the public movement, at the same time as it was pressing Gladstone to get rid of Disraeli, Disraeli was raising his terms in the House of Commons. Though there is no sign on Bright's part of willingness to concede publicly to Disraeli, whom he had denounced throughout the winter, the climate of concession which Disraeli created on the bill's second reading made Liberals and parliamentary Radicals wonder whether he would not go as far as it was safe to go. The dislocation of the Liberal party, produced as it was by the collapse of Gladstone's relations with the Cave, created a vacuum in which the power of the popular movement seemed likely to be so menacing in the future that it would be better to settle with Disraeli while there was time. In the last week of March Liberals and Radicals in the House of Commons began to see that the popular movement might get out of hand at the same time as it became clear to the movement itself that not only the Cave but also parliamentary Radicals and these anxious Liberals were ready to be deceived by Disraeli.

From the defeat of Gladstone's amendment on April 12, therefore, a number of conclusions were drawn in the rhetoric of agitation. It was recognized, without pleasure, that some Liberal MP.s had opposed Gladstone because they believed that 'household suffrage pure and simple [would be] more easily obtainable from the government's scheme...than if Mr Gladstone's instruction were to be incorporated into it'.[1] It was emphasized that the fixed-line franchise was at least as objectionable as personal rating and that Bright and Gladstone should not have proposed it.[2] It was pointed out that 'the Liberal party was utterly demoralized' and that, although 'no doubt [could] be entertained [about] Mr Gladstone's individual fidelity to the cause of working-class enfranchisement', there was a difference between Gladstone as a person and Gladstone the party leader, who was affected by his 'aristocratic surroundings and the anti-Liberal influences to which he was constantly exposed'.[3] There was little sympathy for Disraeli, and no lightening of abuse for 'truculent Tories, treacherous Liberals and spurious Radicals'[4] who had got him so far, but there was a decision that, if anything was to be achieved, something must be done to induce Gladstone to 'rely more on himself and [to] care less about threatened defections'.[5] There was a tendency, on the part of the most militant reformers, to criticize not only Gladstone and the Liberal party but also Bright whose support for Gladstone's bill in 1866 showed him to have 'the sentiment of a Tory, or, what is worse, of a lukewarm Liberal'.[6] So near, indeed, were parliamentary Radicals to losing control of the movement that Bradlaugh explained that it was not just Whigs or Tories who were on trial but the whole House of Commons which, if it would not abandon 'the contemptible' personal payment principle, must be met by widespread refusal to pay taxes.[1]

All reformers agreed that renewed agitation was necessary, but they did not agree about the way in which to conduct it. On April 18 the League changed its target from manhood suffrage and the ballot to the removal of personal payment and the residential qualification from the bill. It authorized Beales to approach the Union for a common platform on that basis.[2] The leaders of the Reform Union, on the other hand, had close connections with Liberal and Radical MP.s. They saw that the Reform League, if left unchecked, would do the Liberal party great damage. They knew that, in London especially, respectable reformers had not made themselves felt so far because of the working-class character of the League's agitation.[3]

From the beginning of the Easter recess, therefore, the League, the Union and the London Working Men's Association organized a new wave of meetings, though with rather less cohesion than before.[4] The Union, committed to household suffrage but committed to nothing beyond, decided to invade London where the League had so far had a monopoly. It is not certain at what point the League began to fear the Union's arrival in London. Beales asked Wilson for an interview immediately after the vote of April 12. At the meeting between a League and a Union deputation on May 10 1867 under the chairmanship of Samuel Morley,[5] the Union representatives—Morley, P. A. Taylor, Ayrton and Stansfeld—did their best to pacify the League without meeting its objections. A Reform Union meeting at Westminster Palace Hotel and a deputation to Gladstone followed on May 11. These were intended as signals for middle-class political activity in London. Beales was not present, though George Potter was. There were twenty Liberal MP.s including Bright, Stansfeld, Cowen and Sir John Gray (the enemy of the Irish Church), a large number of aldermanic northern reformers, George Wilson himself (who had travelled south for the occasion) and a small contingent of London doctors, clergy and respectabilities, including Sir Henry Hoare. The deputation presented an address to Gladstone and received in reply a firm commitment to abandon personal payment whenever he returned to office.

The League itself looked for a more spectacular confrontation. In the previous two years it had had twin objects. It had wanted to establish its right to meet publicly in the Royal Parks in the capital. It had wanted to show that the London working classes were both powerful, and willing to use their power sensibly. Throughout the agitation its leaders had been concerned to avoid violence. On two occasions, in 1866 and 1867, they had accepted the government's refusal to co-operate in arranging meetings in the Park,[1] though the absence of meeting-places elsewhere in central London meant that marches had to be held or rallies arranged at greater distance and considerably greater expense to individual members. In the period up to April 12, Beales prevailed, despite Bradlaugh's opposition, because everyone expected Gladstone to get rid of the government. It was Gladstone's failure to do this which made the League more militant and made it more difficult for Beales to resist the desire to test what had persistently been said to be a legal right. Though the danger continued to exist that 'roughs' and 'rowdies' would discredit the meeting and though there was no more evidence than before that the police would co-operate, the decision was taken once again to meet in the Park.

The decision was taken at first on April 18 to meet on Good Friday.[2] The date was then altered, at Gladstone's and Shaftesbury's request, because of the religious offence it would cause. The decision to meet on May 6 was taken in the belief that precedents had been established by the meetings which had taken place there on July 24 and 30 1866 and by the meeting held by a break-away Reform League group on Good Friday in protest against the League's decision to defer to Gladstone's and Shaftesbury's wishes.[3] Whereas earlier decisions to use the Royal Parks for public purposes had been coupled with requests for permission and co-operation from the government, on this occasion the decision was taken to publicise the intention without consulting the government. Once the League had made its decision on April 18, plans were made and committees set up to arrange an orderly, and inexpensive, demonstration. There were to be no bands, marches or much organization, and sympathizers were to go spontaneously to the Park on their way home from work.[4] As soon as the decision had been made, it was announced in the newspapers.

The government's attitude to the announcement of the meeting was determined by its reaction to the events of mid-1866 and by its refusal to allow meetings to be held in the Royal Parks in the ten months since. It had never doubted its right to close the Parks completely. The meetings which had been held after the railings had been broken down had made the right seem academic, but this was the right it had asserted in July 1866.[1] The justification it offered was the need to protect non-political people from interference to life and liberty. Its reason for refusing permission was, no doubt, the feeling that the Park was a public place in which the people as a whole, and the upper classes in particular, displayed fashion, aired their children, rode their horses and made public manifestation of their status. It was moved by a sense of the duty all governments felt to curtail public demonstrations, and by the obligation Conservatives felt to maintain every semblance of public order.

The decision was taken to close the Park altogether on July 23 1866, to station troops nearby for use in case of emergency and to empower Sir Richard Mayne, the Police Commissioner, to meet the leaders of the delegation at the Park gate, warn them of the illegality of the meeting and ask them to go away. This was done. As soon as Beales and Bradlaugh arrived at the Park gates in a horse-drawn carriage, they were met by Mayne who refused them admission.[2] The pressure the crowd then brought to bear on the Park railings was almost certainly accidental. The destruction of the railings, the clashes between demonstrators and the police and the window-breaking which took place on the 23rd were not planned by Beales and his followers. The meetings which assembled in and out of the Park on July 23 and 24 probably assembled without Beales's foreknowledge. Once they had met, the difficulty the police had had in dispersing them made Walpole and Disraeli think Beales's cooperation desirable. Mill mediated on Beales's behalf in order to pacify League members who were more militant than their leaders. The conflicting impressions received by Beales and Walpole of the meeting they had at the Home Office in company with Holyoake produced the belief that Walpole had agreed either to authorize a meeting in the Park or to take his claim to forbid meetings to the courts. Walpole seems not to have done so; whether he did so or not, he denied it. Meetings were held in fact on July 26 and 31.[3] Walpole's fumbling, the use made by Beales of it, the difficulty the government knew it would have in establishing its right to prevent the League meeting in Hyde Park if the Park was left open and the impossibility, on the League's side, of meeting there if it was closed, produced a situation of the greatest uncertainty.

The uncertainty of the situation did not, however, produce action to remedy it. Though Derby, Walpole and the Lord Chancellor knew that there were loopholes in the government's powers, nothing was done to test them in the courts or to propose legislation to increase them. It is difficult to explain this. Walpole's inadequacy may have been one reason: unwillingness to inflate the League's reputation another. It may even have been felt that, since the breakdown of order had damaged the League as much as it had damaged the government, it would be better to do nothing.

The uneasiness felt by all the leaders of the public movement was considerable. They blamed the clashes on the police and made of Sir Richard Mayne a working-class bogey. But they sensed the damage they had suffered. They invited police co-operation, and when this was not forthcoming, appointed 'police protectors' to ensure that rowdies did not get out of hand.[1] They took pains to establish that the agitation consisted of 'well-dressed, independent manly citizens',[2] declared their loyalty to the 'noble and illustrious' lady who from the throne had seven times 'urged upon Parliament the extension of the franchise',[3] and emphasized that the question of forcible resistance had been settled once and for all in 1832 by the ruling classes' recognition that the people's will could not be resisted. Bright warned the government of the danger of violence but gave no incitement to disorder. In November Potter made a point of asking permission to start his Trades' meeting and march in Trafalgar Square.[4] The Cabinet, knowing that the meeting and march were not illegal and could not be stopped, gave the permission it had no power to refuse because of 'the advantage which [might] result from the *implied* recognition of the *right* of refusal'.[5]

The renewed agitation, however, deprived of some of its allies and thwarted in respect of its major demands, was released from the inhibitions it had suffered so far. Though there was still no desire to provoke violence, the decision had been made to assert a right, whatever the consequences. Though there may have been a belief that a demonstration of independence on May 6 would affect the House's treatment of the bill, it is much more likely that no expectations were maintained except the perennial one that the House was too corrupt for anything to affect its judgement.

If it was believed that Disraeli wanted to avoid a confrontation, this belief was correct. Though the government had been unyielding in the nine months since it came to office, there is no sign that it proposed to be unyielding now. Though the conservative posture it had adopted between July 1866 and February 1867 had been reinforced by the sternness of its public image, the atmosphere of broad accommodation which Disraeli was trying to create made this anachronistic. Disraeli was not trying to give way to public agitation. Nor could he gain anything from manifest weakness. But there can be no doubt about the anxiety he showed at this time to prevent a recurrence of the tension which had been generated in 1866.

In July 1866 Walpole had been opposed to closing the Park, had been overruled by Derby and the Cabinet and had stood up badly to the tension which followed. He had impressed Beales by his fairness and his Cabinet colleagues by his weakness. He had been given backbone by Lord John Manners and Derby, but had not been reconciled to the danger that a flat refusal to League requests to meet in the Park would produce violence. In April 1867, when the League announced its intention to meet in the Park on May 6 whatever the government might wish, all the dangers he had expected in 1866 seemed likely to recur.

Walpole's first reaction was to get Mayne to confirm that the League's announcement of its intention to meet would be followed by a meeting in fact. When Mayne confirmed that it would be and that it would be 'largely attended',[1] Walpole asked Derby's approval of a letter he proposed that Mayne should send to Beales. He also sent the government law officers a copy of Beales's announcement, together with the opinion given by the law officers when a similar attempt had been made to hold public meetings in the Park in protest against Lord Robert Grosvenor's Sunday Trading Bill in 1855.

At the two Cabinets on April 26 and 27, Walpole emphasized the inadequacy of his powers and left the impression of having nothing to suggest. The Cabinet decided not to close the Park because it wanted to avoid the 'peril and certainty of a collision'.[2] Instead it authorized the issue of a royal proclamation against creating a riotous assembly and sanctioned the collection of 'enough military force to support the police' in case of necessity.[3] Even this half-measure had to run the gauntlet of the law officers who thought a formal warning against a riotous assembly was 'not a purpose for which a royal proclamation ought to be issued'.[1] Walpole wanted the warning issued as a police notice if the Cabinet could decide in advance 'what course of action [was] to be taken upon or in consequence of it'. Disraeli seems to have been opposed both to the proclamation and to the notice.[2] Nevertheless, a notice was delivered to the League on the evening of May 1 and published subsequently. It drew attention to the fact that 'the use of the Park' for the purpose of a political meeting was 'not permitted' and 'warn[ed] ...all persons...to abstain from attending...or taking part in any such meeting or from entering the Park with a view to attend, aid or take part in it'.[3]

The object in issuing this notice was, presumably, to show Conservatives that the government did not approve of the meeting, to discourage the public from attending it and to leave the impression, without saying so, that anyone who attended it would be in danger of military coercion. Since the government had no right to prevent a meeting while the Park remained open, it can hardly have been supposed that the League would be discouraged. If this was supposed, the League's reaction disposed of the idea. The morning after the notice was issued, the *Morning Star* published a letter from Beales (sent, probably, before the notice was issued) which attacked the notion that the government had a right or intended to suppress the meeting by force, recalled that the League had met in the Park in July 1866 and asserted that the maintenance of order would not be assisted by repression. Beales followed this with further letters to the *Morning Star* on May 3 and 4, and the *Times* on May 6, in which he questioned Walpole's power to prevent the meeting, rejected the claim that the League had ever accepted its legality and denied that he, or the League, had advocated violent assertion of what they held to be a legal right.

At the same time Thomas Hughes was attempting to persuade the League to negotiate with the government about what was to be done in the event of an attempt being made to arrest the League's leaders in the Park.[4] Beales's letter, however, established that he was so certain of his position that he would call the government's bluff. In the course of mediation, Hughes and Auberon Herbert[5] received from a source close to the Cabinet an assurance that the 'government wished to avoid...a collision' and that the meeting would not be suppressed by force, whatever warnings the government might give in public.[1] The uneasiness felt by some League members at the danger of violence and the discredit which violence would bring, made it necessary to reiterate the peacefulness of the League's intentions. The knowledge that conflict need not be feared made it possible to combine firm assertion with peaceful rhetoric. At the meeting on May 6 attacks on the government's Parks policy were avoided. Despite the presence of troops in the vicinity, the meeting passed off quietly, with no attempt to arrest the leaders and no disorder at all.

The League, in other words, having decided to ignore the government's refusal to let it meet in the Parks, had succeeded in its objective. The public agitation, having been awed into submission by the danger of violence in the winter, had done as a right what it had previously asked for permission to do. The government, having threatened without power to execute its threats, had been made to look foolish at the moment at which MP.s were returning from the Easter recess.

In these circumstances there was every reason for Conservative MP.s to lose confidence. Confidence was lost because the government had implied that it intended to prevent the meeting and had not done so, and because the League had humiliated the government. It was lost, also, because at the same time as the government was faced by a violent conspiracy in Ireland, it was failing to deal firmly with the Fenian movement's allies in England. It is not surprising that Walpole felt the sharp edge of a good many tongues and offered his resignation as a consequence, or that, when the Easter recess ended, the confidence felt by the Conservative backbenchers in Derby's management of government slumped to the lowest point since early March. There is no evidence to show that this loss of confidence stimulated withdrawal of Conservative support in the division on Ayrton's motion on May 2, though a handful of Conservatives voted with Ayrton. There is abundant evidence that this was why on May 5 and 6 both Derby and Disraeli thought the government might be defeated in the next major Reform division. It is in this context that one must approach the events of May 6 to May 17.

VIII

THE ACCEPTANCE OF HODGKINSON'S AMENDMENT

'I cannot but think that the opportunity [the 3rd reading of the Reform bill] would be a good one for making an appeal to the instinct and good sense of Englishmen, and, tho' it may be a repetition, to dispel the apprehension that the measure is a democratic one...The Ministry and the House of Commons have shown (Mr Gladstone and Mr Bright notwithstanding) that they trust the people of England.'

G. A. Hamilton, memorandum to Derby dated July 14 1867.
Hughenden MSS

By May 2 Ayrton's motion had been passed with some Conservative support and a sizeable Conservative abstention[1] in opposition to the government, which, though it had Adullamites voting with it, had no Radical support at all. It had been passed in circumstances in which, although the two-year residential qualification had been made an issue of confidence in the first week of April, it could not sensibly be made the occasion for a general election. As Taylor knew, and the division lists made clear, it was not even a restriction which all Conservatives felt happy to maintain. It was impossible in his view to resign on it, and it is clear that resignation did not appeal to Disraeli. On the other hand, though the immediate problem was solved by the Cabinet's decision to accept the amendment despite Hardy's objections, it seemed likely that there would be similar problems in the future. Disraeli's willingness to concede was inexhaustible, but, if the situation recurred in which he had to concede after resisting and being defeated in the House, confidence in the government's control of the situation would vanish. This would have been true at any time. At a time when the government's inability to keep order in the capital had been made manifest, it would suffer greater damage than usual. Though Pakington had made clear in advance that the residential qualification would not be an issue of confidence,[2] Ayrton's motion (to reduce the period of residence from the two years to one) was the only major occasion on which the Cabinet, having been genuinely defeated,[3] accepted an amendment

267

which it had not been intended beforehand that it should accept. Thereafter Taylor's advice[1] was taken. So far as possible concessions which the House was thought to favour were made without a division.

However, although it was better to accept amendments without a division than to wait for defeat before accepting them, it was by no means certain that the Conservative party would agree. The Conservative party had swallowed a good deal since Derby's government had come to power. It had swallowed the introduction of Irish Land bills.[2] It had swallowed Disraeli's equivocation about Church Rates and Catholic Oaths.[3] It had watched the Reform League asserting its right to meet on Primrose Hill, in Trafalgar Square and in Hyde Park, and had seen General Peel resign from the government because he disliked its policy. It had swallowed household suffrage in general. It had now to swallow it in detail, and it was far from certain that it would. In particular, acceptance of Ayrton's amendment, combined with the need to do something about Hibbert's before that too was accepted by the House, might well be too much for the Conservative party, whatever the damage the party would suffer if it did not accept it. Disraeli needed to persuade the party to support the Cabinet's acceptance of Ayrton's amendment: he was committed to a lodger franchise. Disraeli had wanted from the start to accept Hibbert's amendment. Taylor thought that, if pressed to a division on it, the government would be defeated. The Cabinet's refusal to accept it on April 11 and 12 neither disposed of the problem, nor made it unnecessary to find alternative proposals which it would accept. Hardy was the leading resister in April and the minister most likely to resign. Cairns had been used to keep him in office in March. He was used again to keep him in office in April. It is not certain which of them chose the formula, or whether the formula came from Disraeli. But the solution embodied in the Cabinet decision of May 5—that the compounder, while paying the full rate on opting out of composition, might deduct it all from the rent he paid his landlord—was pressed on Hardy by Cairns, as Disraeli's intermediary, in the Easter recess before it was pressed on Hibbert by Disraeli.[4]

The uncertainty of the situation on May 3, 4 and 5 was increased by Walpole's failure in the Park. It was not that Conservatives were afraid of the demonstration, for which many had great contempt, but the unpleasantness of the evidence it provided of the government's inability to deal with it. It was not that Disraeli, Derby, the Cabinet and the Conservative party *wanted* to meet the demands which the Reform League leaders were making, but that Conservatives wanted the government to remove itself from the position of discreditable debility into which it had been put. If the government had not been beaten on Ayrton's amendment, this might not have affected the Reform bill itself. But when weakness had been shown in face of Radicals in the country, it was impossible to connive at unadorned concession to Radicals in the House. In other words, though there is little evidence, there can be little doubt that Disraeli needed a Conservative formula which, while comforting his own followers, would attract Radical votes because of Radical reluctance to lose the bill altogether.

At question-time on May 2 before the debate on Ayrton's motion Disraeli explained that the compounder would in no circumstances be allowed to pay the reduced rate on opting out of composition.[1] On May 3, he not only announced the government's acceptance of Ayrton's amendment but also assured McLaren that the burgh franchise in Scotland would be the same as in England and Wales. At the end of proceedings on May 3, Walpole asked leave to introduce a bill to give the government the right to prevent demonstrations in the Royal Parks in future without actually closing them.[2] On May 6, while reiterating his commitment to a lodger franchise, Disraeli refused to commit himself to a figure (no doubt in case the £10 he wanted to accept would be too low for his party). At the same time as he moved a motion to insert the substance of Ayrton's amendment into the bill, he announced that Hibbert's proposal would be met not, as Hibbert wanted, by allowing compounders who were enfranchised by the bill to pay the reduced rate on opting out of composition, but by permitting them, once they had paid the *full* rate, to deduct the whole of it from the rent they paid their landlords. He also moved a government amendment to clause 3 to ensure that, on opting out of composition, all compounders—whether exercising rights established by the Clay Act or by the new bill—would be rated as, and pay the rate of, 'an ordinary occupier' (i.e. the full rate), announcing that this would be a vote of confidence on which the government intended, if beaten on May 9, to dissolve.[3]

In doing this he was attempting once more to rescue the party from disaster. On May 5 Derby expected to be defeated if Hibbert's amendment was put to the vote the day after. On May 8 he so little expected to win the division of May 9 that Hardy's appointment to succeed Walpole at the Home Office was delayed because no vote could be spared. On both occasions he expected to lose because the unwillingness of Conservatives to concede on the bill had been strengthened by a feeling that Walpole had conceded too much in the Park. Derby intended, if he lost, either to resign or to dissolve. The two-headed policy which Disraeli had produced, and which Derby explained to a party meeting on May 6, was devised to meet that eventuality by reiterating the principle for which the party was standing, and by providing ambiguously various attractions to both Radicals and Conservatives.[1] Having seen in the debate on April 12 that the personal payment principle would bind the Cave to the Conservative party, he played it again. Having insisted on the principle in order to quieten Conservative consciences, he was able to quieten Radical ones by agreeing to allow the compounder to pass his 'fine' on to the landlord. It is not certain that the Cabinet, having refused once more on May 5 to abolish the 'fine',[2] was asked to agree to this, but the Cabinet supported it when Disraeli suggested it to the party meeting on May 6.[3] Though this seems to have satisfied Hibbert,[4] it was represented as an independent initiative which Disraeli had taken without consulting him, and was, in any case, both an assertion of conservative principle and not what Gladstone and Hibbert had said in public that they wanted. Disraeli was forced, in other words, by the discontent which Walpole's failure to deal with the Reform League had produced in the Conservative party and the danger the government would be in if it were beaten again on an opposition motion, to reject Hibbert's amendment (because the Cabinet would not let him accept it), to reassert instead a principle which was at least as conservative as the principle he had asserted on March 18 and 25 and to threaten dissolution in case of defeat. On May 9, when the House of Commons gave Disraeli the largest majority it gave him on a major question in the course of the whole Reform discussion (i.e. 66 by contrast with his majority of 21 on April 12), it was, therefore, supporting a government amendment which was reactionary, not radical, in content. It was given the opportunity to do this in order to satisfy Conservatives who were reacting *against* Beales's agitation, and in order to anticipate the accusation that the government was conceding all along the line. This majority consisted, nevertheless, of a mixed bag of Adullamites, central Liberals, Conservatives (voting solidly, apart from the Cranborne Cave) and a larger body of Radicals than voted with the government on April 12.

Gladstone's reaction to Disraeli's amendment was to nail it as a reactionary measure, and to assert that the principle it embodied, despite the concession it offered to Hibbert, would not satisfy the public at large. While hinting once more at a preference for a fixed-line franchise with 'many more not personally rated than at present', he struck a clear line in his speech on May 9 in defence of popular feeling outside the House. He reminded a House, which had no wish to be reminded of popular power, of the danger presented by unsatisfied agitation, and attempted once more to press it to reject the bill by rejecting its fundamental principle. It seems likely that Hibbert wanted to withdraw his motion on receiving Disraeli's assurance about the fine, and was pressed by Gladstone to persist. Whether he thought he would win or not (and he had some reason to think he would), Gladstone failed completely.[1]

In the division of May 9, no Conservative voted with Gladstone.[2] On April 12 only nine Tea-Room rebels had voted with Disraeli. On May 9 seven other Tea-Roomers voted with him as well as fourteen of the Liberals who had voted with Gladstone in the earlier division. On May 9 four of the Tea-Room rebels who voted with Disraeli in April voted with Gladstone, as did seven other of the Liberal cross-voters then. But fifty-eight Liberals voted with Disraeli, including all the Adullamites and Radicals who had voted with him on April 12. In addition he had with him Dunkellin, Edward Ellice, W. O. Foster, Richard Fort and Laing who had all at various times been part of the Cave. He had T. E. Headlam who had 'always believed' that 'every man [should have the vote] who ha[d] a true and substantial interest in the welfare of the town in which he lives'.[3] He had Sir Robert Peel. He had Bright's friend, J. B. Smith, who was voting against the destruction of the bill. He had Bright's brother-in-law, Duncan McLaren, who was moved by the promise of extra seats and household suffrage for Scotland, and who almost certainly saw in a bill of this sort the best hope of breaking the stranglehold exercised over the Scottish Liberal party by Whig and constitutional Liberals.[4] He had Walter Morrison, the Plymouth

Radical, who thought household suffrage in Disraeli's version 'the best settlement [to] fall back on' in circumstances in which, if the government went out of office, 'the Liberal party...disorganized as it [was] by the events of the session, might...fail to pass a Reform bill and...we might see a Conservative government bringing in a Reform bill again...in 1869'.[1] He had, finally, advanced Liberals like Sergeant Gaselee, A. W. Kinglake and Bernard Samuelson, who thought that Disraeli had gone as far as it was safe to go and could see no reputable ground for opposing him. Until this demonstration of support, there was considerable uncertainty about the future of the bill. The range and volume of support put its success beyond doubt.

Whatever the reasons—whether it was 'dislike of Gladstone', unwillingness to follow him in making Reform a party question, 'unwillingness to see the old Whigs back [in office], fear of dissolution [or] *fear of offending the new constituencies*',[2] the victory of May 9 decisively altered the situation. It confirmed the necessary character of the personal rating principle, established that Gladstone had lost control of the Liberal party and, for the first time, made it certain that a bill could be passed in the current session. It relieved Conservative leaders of the need to adopt positions which would be useful not only for the passage of a bill, but also (what was sometimes in contradiction) for an anti-revolutionary platform in case of dissolution. It reinforced Disraeli's predominance as leader of the House of Commons. It drove Gladstone into a position in which for the first time he felt obliged openly to attack his enemies in the Liberal party.

Gladstone's reaction to this second defeat was to abandon the £5 rating line altogether which until then was a practical alternative, and to deliver a sarcastic address to the Reform Union on May 11[3] in which he attacked the Adullamite Whigs for the first time in public, praised the Conservative Cave and went as near as a responsible politician could to committing himself as soon as he returned to office to reject the personal payment principle 'which in our view is...intolerable'. He did this with an eye to the feelings of his own supporters and by way of reply to the Whig/Adullamite element in the Liberal party, demonstrating that, if they would not have him as leader, they should not have a Whig–Liberal party at all. He did it by way of encouragement to the thousands of demonstrators who had met in the Park on May 6, many of whom were probably Liberal and some of whom had votes already.[1] He did it, in a situation in which he had lost the support not only of Radicals like J. B. Smith, Dalglish and Duncan McLaren, but also of respectable manufacturers like Akroyd and the two Basses. He did it to the Reform Union, most of whose members were respectable Northern MP.s and industrialists. In doing it he transformed the situation.

Right up to the point at which he spoke to the meeting on May 11, there was a danger, from the government's point of view, that any proposal to dismantle the restrictive aspects of the compounding regulations could be attacked by Gladstone as a final dishonest abandonment of the policy of *avoiding* household suffrage pure and simple from which the great body of MP.s did not dissent, and which the government from the start and by repeated declarations, had pledged itself to pursue. At each stage up to this point Gladstone's position had been as ambiguous as Disraeli's. Just as Disraeli had attached to each concession he made to Radical or Liberal critics a reassertion of the one fundamental principle—the personal payment of rates—which most members accepted because it would limit the numbers to be enfranchised, so Gladstone had attached to each of his attacks on the fraudulent restrictiveness of the government's bill the claim that he objected to the bill, not just because it was restrictive, but because, if the objectionable restrictions were removed, it would not be restrictive enough. He had attacked personal payment on April 12 because, although Liberal feeling had prevented him opposing the bill outright on the second reading, Disraeli had so fully committed himself to the principle that a successful motion against it would involve rejecting the bill altogether. Gladstone had failed then because of a general crisis of confidence in his leadership and because advanced Liberals would not vote against a household suffrage bill. But he had not abandoned the attempt to produce a situation in which, while removing the restriction to which Disraeli was committed, either a bill was passed which fell short of household suffrage, or a bill was not passed that session at all.

The situation now, as Derby and Disraeli saw it, was that Gladstone had finally, publicly and unmistakably kicked dissident Whigs and Adullamites in the teeth. He had demonstrated beyond possibility of misunderstanding that he proposed to run the Liberal party, and that they had very little to hope from him in the future. He and his supporters had made it clear that they would not treat the present bill as a settlement of the question.[1] With the abandonment of his £5 rating commitment, Gladstone seemed to have removed all hope that *he* would be party to an attempt to restrict the operation of the government's bill, and to have freed the Conservative leaders from the need to guard against a conservative manœuvre on Gladstone's part, for which he might until then have commanded support. In this they misunderstood or misrepresented Gladstone, who was responsible the following Friday for the decision (to which Russell, Sir George Grey, Halifax, Brand and Clarendon agreed) to ask Wilson Patten to open negotiations with the government for establishing a £4 line below which in future nobody would be rated.[2] It convinced Derby and Disraeli, nevertheless, that the chance had come to brand Gladstone and his allies as 'obsolete incendiaries' and 'spouters of stale sedition'[3] and to start rallying Whig/Adullamites under their own leadership and on their own terms against the 'unmitigated democracy advocated by Bright and partially also supported by Mr Gladstone'.[4] In the reshuffle made necessary by Walpole's resignation, they decided to offer office to Grosvenor. They decided also to make an offer either to Sir Robert Peel or to the Peelite, Earl Stanhope, who had been driven back into the Conservative party only two years earlier by the leftward shift in the Liberal party. The Queen vetoed the offer to Peel. Stanhope disliked the Reform bill[5] and had not recovered from Derby's failure to offer him office before: he refused. The fact that Grosvenor still hoped for the restoration of Liberal unity at some time in the future and that Derby did not expect any of them to accept, did not affect his estimate of the situation.[6]

Gladstone's speech on May 11 transformed the situation, secondly, because it was made, not to the Reform League, but to a Reform Union deputation sent by a meeting of nearly twenty Liberal MP.s and over a hundred northern worthies. It represented, not the working classes of the capital but a threat to arouse the middle classes everywhere. It was the beginning of a campaign to arouse the middle classes who had so far dragged their feet, and to do so in the belief that Gladstone would lead it. It represented an extension to London and a national basis of the provincial demonstrations which had been effective in the winter. Though the split it implied in the Liberal party encouraged Disraeli to continue the policy he had pursued throughout the session, it promised a formidable threat in electoral terms if a Reform bill were passed, or if a general election were held in the event of the bill being defeated. If Gladstone had addressed a meeting of the Reform League in Hyde Park on May 6, he would have guaranteed Disraeli's position for a decade. The fact that the speech was made to a 'very earnest'[1] Reform Union deputation supported by such respectable Parliamentary Radicals as Stansfeld, Forster, J. B. Smith and Watkin made the threat more formidable.

The speech transformed the situation, thirdly, because it strengthened the possibility of passing the bill in the current session. It did this because there was now no danger of Whig/Adullamite support for Gladstone, and because the firmness of the Conservative party in face of an 'agitating'[2] Gladstone, made it possible to think that, once the borough franchise question was out of the way, the redistribution of seats and the county franchise could be dealt with by effective alliance between Whigs, moderate Liberals and Conservatives. Now that Gladstone seemed to have adopted an absolutely Radical position without regaining his Radical following, there was both opportunity, and need, for moderate Liberals and Conservatives to keep the passage of the bill in the government's hands.

Indeed, if Gladstone's following in the Liberal party was now committed to marking itself off from Whigs and Adullamites by rejecting both the compounding restrictions *and* a fixed line, then Disraeli's freedom of manœuvre had widened markedly. Whereas previously, Gladstone had left an impression of insincerity in attacking the restrictive aspect of the compounding regulations because he was committed to a restrictive position himself, he was now free to lead a frontal assault on the bill as a whole. Whereas at any time before May 11, a further extension of the borough franchise (by abolishing compounding) could have been met by a conservative reaction from Gladstone on the ground that he had attacked the government bill, among other reasons, because it went too far, Gladstone had now renounced this position altogether. His new position might not be effective in the House of Commons, but if the question were not settled soon, it was likely that his following would grow outside. It was likely that he would in the process 'drive moderate men out of [the Liberal party],'[1] making it impossible for a reasonable Whig to belong to it. The Conservative leaders, therefore, had nothing to fear from a Whig movement against them. So long as the Conservative party followed, they could do almost anything they liked and still be certain that the Whig/Adullamite/Conservative body would be so greatly alarmed by the prospect of a Gladstonian future that it would do nothing to prevent the government passing the bill.

The chief difficulty in the way of passing a bill in the current session was that its Liberal supporters did not intend to allow this to happen unless the bill became the sort of bill they wanted. Though Radical support was larger on May 9 than on April 12, Radical acquiescence was still conditional. J. B. Smith and E. W. Watkin, for example, had voted with Disraeli (and Ayrton had abstained). Despite the reactionary content of the amendment, they had done so because they believed that Disraeli wanted to meet Radical wishes and would continue to try to do so. Their vote on May 9, however, did not prevent them joining the Reform Union meeting on May 11. Though Bright's control of the Radical party had manifestly crumbled, it had done so because his followers supposed that they would get what they wanted by strengthening Disraeli's hand. This did not mean leaving Disraeli free to pass the bill in its present form. It meant, on the contrary, persisting with attempts to make the bill the honest household suffrage it ought to be. From this viewpoint reiteration of Disraeli's principle on May 9 had been a major blow, but discussion in committee imposed no restriction on their time. Discussion of Clause 3 had lasted a month already. It seemed likely to go on for at least as long again.

The major amendments[2] next for debate after the division of May 9 were Denman's (providing for notice to be given for arrears of rates by the overseers), Torrens's (for a lodger franchise), Hodgkinson's (for the abolition of compounding in parliamentary boroughs) and Childers's (to make compounding optional everywhere). The principle of Torrens's amendment had been accepted by Disraeli on May 6 without specifying the amount of the lodger franchise. Disraeli's secretary visited Torrens on May 12 to say that the Attorney-General had no objection to the form of Torrens's proposal and that 'time would be saved if Torrens was disposed to make a compromise as to the amount of the qualification'. Torrens 'inti-

mated his intention of sticking to £10 if supported by the House'.[1]
£10 was accepted the following day after Torrens had met opposition objections by excluding everything (i.e. furniture) from the
qualifying amount, and after the government had won a division in
support of Goldney's insistence on a twelve-month residential
qualification, despite McLaren's claim, which Goschen, Torrens and
Thomas Hughes supported, that this would disqualify four lodgers
out of five. Denman's motion was accepted in principle by Disraeli
and the Attorney-General[2] and a government amendment promised
later. When this was eventually proposed in June, Denman and
Gladstone, seeing Cabinet ministers voting against it, decided that
they had been double-crossed. The same attitude of speed and
despatch was taken to Hodgkinson's.

The exclusion of the compound householder, whatever Disraeli
might say, was in fact a restriction. To anyone who believed that the
bill of March 18 was fundamentally conservative, it was a matter of
great consequence. One of the counterpoises—duality—had been
abandoned. The two years residence had been reduced by parliamentary vote to one, and the reduction accepted by both government and party because it was not a question on which an election
could be fought. It is not certain that Disraeli *wanted* to abandon the
safeguard against numbers provided by the exclusion of compound
householders. But his repeated insistence on the personal payment
principle throughout the first month of discussion of Clause 3 was
designed not only to provide an alternative to Gladstone's £5 rating,
but also to keep hold of such Conservatives and Whigs as did not feel
happy in support of a household suffrage bill, and might still be
tempted by a practical commitment in favour of restriction from
Gladstone.

Nevertheless, alongside a belief in the personal payment principle as a means of excluding compounders, objections were felt to
compounding itself and to the effect the modified form of Hibbert's
amendment would have on landlords' attitudes to it. Hibbert's
amendment, in the form accepted by Disraeli, allowed the compounder to deduct the full rate from his landlord's rent on passing
voluntarily out of composition. This raised the expectation that
landlords would try to break the composition.[3] It reinforced a dislike
of compounding which was common to all parts of the House. The
practice of compounding, though universally legitimate in England

and Wales, was not everywhere adopted. Whether it was adopted in a particular borough depended on the decision of the overseers. With the greatly enlarged electorate proposed by the bill, they would have in their hands the power they already had in boroughs where rateable values were high radically to transform the electoral situation. This in itself was objectionable since, so far from removing the Reform question from political discussion, it would transfer the Reform agitation to 'three-fourths of the parishes in the boroughs of the country'. Overseers would be free at any time to change their minds: MP.s and candidates would never know how large their constituencies would be. Rating would be connected with politics in a way which, distasteful in itself, would be made more distasteful by the fact that the Small Tenements Acts were, as an elderly Tory pointed out, 'a device...to oppress the poor' by making them pay rates through the rent 'even when they received outdoor relief'. The prospect was objectionable to intellectual Radicals who saw that in towns[1] where 'nearly the whole of the property was owned by one proprietor...it would be in [his] power to refuse to have any tenant who would not remain a compounder'.[2] It was objectionable to intellectual Radicals and Conservatives alike, because it would increase the amount of bribery and add to the expense to be expected in the political process.[3]

Concern about bribery was not the preserve of Radicals or high-minded Liberals alone. It was felt also by those who would have to foot the bill. Although it was understood in all parts of the House of Commons that manifestly established corruption must always be met by disfranchisement, a great deal of bribery existed which no election committee could establish the existence or illegality of. Elections were expensive. With the larger electorate established by the bill, they would be more expensive still. If, at the same time as the size of the electorate increased, a new source of electoral expense was created, the situation would be intolerable. So long as the number of compounders entitled to vote on opting out of composition was small, a candidate would not have to spend heavily on paying rates. So long, moreover, as a two-year residential qualification made it difficult to plan ahead, corrupt payment of rates could not really be effective.[4] But with the reduction of the residential qualification, it seemed likely that candidates in parliamentary boroughs would find large calls on their pockets in the future.

To the question of expense there were two attitudes. On the one hand, it was an investment against revolutionary proletarianism in the future:[1] on the other, an instrument of advancement for the new rich who would pay anything to get what the old rich had already. To those who, without being rich themselves, still wanted to exercise the power which territorial connection gave, the cost of politics was crucial.[2] Throughout the session of 1867, expense was a recurring preoccupation. The voting papers question, the prohibition of payment for carrying voters to the polls,[3] the increase in the number of polling places and the attempt to keep committee rooms out of hotels, public houses and other licensed premises[4] were all attempts to reduce it. A Bribery bill was proposed in 1866 and an Act passed in 1867. Both were the work of Conservatives. Cranborne wanted voting-papers.[5] It was not just Bright, McLaren, Fawcett or Mill who attacked bribery with an intensity which increased as the Radicalism became more philosophical, but a Conservative MP. for a rural borough—Yorke[6]—a Lowther[7] and a number of other Conservative borough MP.s who objected to household suffrage in March because it would cost MP.s a great deal more to fight elections than it cost at present.[8]

It is not to be supposed that Hodgkinson's amendment was adopted by Disraeli *because* it would reduce bribery in parliamentary boroughs or because the practice of compounding was extensively disliked. There is no reason to think that Disraeli objected to bribery as a political practice or to compounding in general, or wanted at this stage to do more than get past Clause 3 in order to pass the whole bill without an autumn session. What he wanted was to get on, but he could not do so certainly because he had no power to stop debate. Debate could be stopped, if at all, only by removing the grounds on which criticism would be based. Criticism would be silenced by removing the restrictions on enfranchisement which Radicals, whether genuinely or not, had made it their business to attack.

Whatever else it did, the personal payment principle, when combined with the practice of compounding, acted as a major restriction on the size of enfranchisement. The government, though committed to maintain personal payment, was not committed about compounding at all. Since the Cabinet had refused to touch personal payment, Disraeli had to leave that alone. Since he wanted to make a large concession, he had to take steps the Cabinet had not discussed. The decision to abolish compounding was, therefore, a trick on Disraeli's part to maintain the principle to which the government was committed by removing the conditions in which its restrictive aspect would operate. Although it was a trick, however, it was not a trick which could have been played if conditions had not been ripe. Nor would Disraeli have succeeded in playing it if the climate had not been favourable.

The climate, in fact, was favourable. The Cabinet the day after 'passed off quietly'. Hardy, who distrusted Disraeli and had no desire to extend the process of accommodation, did not object to the 'disappearance' of the Compounding Acts, which he 'dislike[d] in themselves', though he probably shared the Cabinet's 'dissatisfaction' with the 'mode of doing...it'.[1] Sir William Heathcote, who disliked Disraeli intensely, remembering that 'we [had] made a great point of the mischief which the combination of these acts with the requirement of personal rating would produce...[did] not see [now that the House had insisted on personal rating]...that we can very well oppose the acceptance by the government of doing away with the Small Tenements Acts'.[2] It is difficult to be sure of the significance of these facts. But it is certain that Grosvenor, in writing to Derby on May 13, listed as his chief objection to the existing bill the fact that it put so much power in the hands of local authorities,[3] and that Lowe began his assault on the bill on May 9 by complaining that 'the franchise which we are asked to confer is one which it will depend on the caprice of the parochial officer either to give or take away: upon the disposition of individual owners of large masses of small kinds of property: upon the organization of local bodies; upon anything, in fact, except the permanent and stable conditions of our society'.[4]

There are, then, three questions to be asked: why did Disraeli accept Hodgkinson's amendment when, if he had not done so, it would almost certainly have been defeated? how did it come about that he got away with acceptance in the Conservative party? to what extent was he guided in his actions by fear of public reaction? In answering these questions, one must establish in the first place that he was not concerned about the substantive merits of the question. This is not difficult: it would be difficult to establish that he was. No particular electoral calculation seems to have been involved: Conservative agents were surprised when compounding was abolished.[1] Having accepted Hodgkinson's amendment in principle on May 17, Disraeli at once tried to back down from it. Not only did he do this: he did it in a remarkably blatant way.

The amendment next for discussion after Hodgkinson's was the motion from Childers to make compounding optional in all boroughs. Childers's and Hodgkinson's amendments had been tabled before the House had reaffirmed the personal payment principle on May 9. Since they did not believe it possible that Hodgkinson's could be accepted, Childers's had been intended, both by its author and by Gladstone, as an alternative. Now that the personal payment principle had been accepted, Gladstone had committed himself to repeal it when next returned to office. This was a long-term commitment. It anticipated a situation in which Disraeli had refused further concession. Though a long-term commitment, it was accompanied by a decision to try once more to press the government to accept concessions which would both meet Gladstone's wishes and avoid household suffrage pure and simple. For this purpose Childers's and Hodgkinson's amendments, *when combined with a renewed attempt to establish a fixed line below which no one would be rated*, would meet all the requirements of the situation.

The fixed-line proposal in one form or another had been in the minds of most MP.s of all parties for most of the session. It already operated in Scotland. There seemed to be every reason to apply it to England also. In attempting to open negotiations to establish it at this stage, Gladstone reflected a widespread feeling. In doing so, he was trying both to avoid the indiscriminate enfranchisement which he feared more than anything else and to continue the policy of urging the government to concede to him under manifest pressure.

There is no doubt that, by May 17, Gladstone hoped that both amendments would be accepted, intending to couple the abolition of formal compounding with permissive arrangements to enable householders to persuade landlords to pay rates on their behalf. There is no doubt either that he hoped in this way to exclude householders who made these arrangements at least until he returned to office and intended thereafter permanently to exclude all occupiers of houses rated at less than £4 p.a. whose relief from liability to rating and voting would persist even when a Liberal government had repealed the personal payment clauses.

281

What Disraeli did on May 17 was to accept Hodgkinson's amendment in principle without undertaking to exclude householders rated below £4 a year from liability to rating. Having done this, he then claimed, when the question was next discussed on May 23, that he had accepted Childers's amendment as well. Childers's, if proposed as an amendment to the original bill, involved a considerable increase in the size of the likely enfranchisement. When taken as an amendment to the bill in the form in which it would be left by acceptance of Hodgkinson's principle, it would have made the bill more restrictive than in Hodgkinson's version because, instead of *abolishing* compounding, as Hodgkinson proposed, it provided an opportunity for some compounding to occur.

In pretending that the House wanted both amendments accepted, it is possible that Disraeli was either drunk or confused. Dr F. B. Smith shows that he was confused about some aspects of the bill. Holyoake and the Duke of Argyll refer to Disraeli's partiality for drink during debate. Since, however, Lord John Manners makes it clear that the question had been discussed in Cabinet in advance, this explanation has been rejected (though it is right to mention it). On the other hand, it is right to consider the claim, made in debate by Mill and Gladstone, that Disraeli accepted Hodgkinson's principle in order to remove opposition to the Reform bill as a whole in the hope that application of the principle would be delayed until the following session or, if he won an election, postponed indefinitely. The decision to abolish compounding had far-reaching implications for rating policy in general. There is no inherent implausibility in the idea that Disraeli accepted Hodgkinson's amendment in principle on May 17, with the promise of a government amendment to the clause later, presented an emasculated version for insertion on May 23, with the promise of a rating bill once the Reform bill had passed, and was compelled to accept a stronger version on May 27 only because the Opposition was on its toes and made clear its intention to delay progress unless he did so. This seems not only plausible but also probable. It is even possible that some Conservatives thought Disraeli wanted to abolish compounding at the beginning of May.[1]

In answering the second question, it is necessary to return once more to the period February 26/March 25. Although Disraeli tried to convince the Conservative party in May that the Cabinet had acted consistently throughout, he could not in March have persuaded his followers to support enfranchisement on the scale allowed by Hodgkinson's amendment. What he could not do in March, however, for one reason, he could now do in May for another. In March Conservative demoralization gave him the opportunity to take a forward step, though there was a limit to the 'progress' the party would stomach. Nevertheless, in March Disraeli within limits could do more or less what he liked, because the party was in danger. He went as far as he could under a mask of ambiguity; because of the party's weakness, he was followed. He was followed in March and April, and led his followers to victory—on April 12 and May 9. With Gladstone's second defeat, he had restored the morale of the Conservative party, and established his own ascendency in it. This did not dispose of all complaints against him, but it gave him greater freedom of movement than at any time in the previous ten years. Just as, within limits, he could do whatever he liked in March because of the party's weakness, so now, again within limits, he could do more or less whatever he liked, because of its strength. Conservatives who had swallowed household suffrage in March because they did not want the party to be destroyed, were unlikely to reject the possibility of *permanent* victory now that, for the first time since 1846, the Opposition was beginning to wonder 'what will become of us...if the Conservatives carry this bill'.[1] That the victory had been won by diplomacy verging on duplicity did not alter the scale of the achievement.

Finally, in answering the third question, it is necessary to distinguish between Radical feeling in the House of Commons and democratic feeling in the country. There is no reason to suppose that Disraeli needed, at this stage, more than at any other, to capitulate to the latter. He had been hoping in the long run to put the Conservative party in tune with every shade of respectable thinking, had been thwarted by Gladstone's equivocal opposition and was now freed from restraint by Gladstone's commitment on May 11. Though he was now in a position to do more or less as he liked, a desire to avoid obstinate resistance did not make it *necessary* to accept Hodgkinson's amendment. Neither Gladstone nor Bright[2] expected him to accept it. It would probably have been resisted by the House of Commons if he had insisted on its rejection. Refusal to accept it, after acceptance of household suffrage in general, would not have been seen as obstinate resistance in the House with which he was dealing. If he was trying to appease Radical opinion in the House, it was because, in the context of the parliamentary time-table, parliamentary Radicals were able to delay the passage of the bill long enough to prevent it passing that session, and because the threatened extension of Reform Union activity under Gladstone's leadership left little doubt that they would do so. Though it is possible that Disraeli had in mind the danger presented by an extension of Reform Union activity under respectable parliamentary leadership in the future, it is much more likely that the immediate parliamentary prospect was more pressing.

However, although he had parliamentary Radicals in mind, it is unlikely that co-operation was close. Hodgkinson was not a regular Radical. He was a little known Newark solicitor, who had been an MP. since 1859 and had made of parliamentary Reform a question of which he had expert knowledge. His constituency, like Hibbert's and J. B. Smith's, was one of those in which, because compounding had not been adopted, the terms of the bill of March 18 would have established household suffrage pure and simple.[1] The amendment seems not to have been devised by Bright, though Bright supported and pressed it.[2] Bright had promised Disraeli co-operation in March on condition that the right sort of household suffrage was introduced, but his promise did not survive the introduction of the bill which, though it provided an extensive enfranchisement in Oldham and Sheffield, provided a very small one in Birmingham. Relations between Bright and Disraeli deteriorated in the course of the session: despite a long-standing regard, they never recovered. Bright undoubtedly intuited a desire on Disraeli's part to make all concessions possible within the framework of the personal payment principle so long as it was not Gladstone who proposed them, but Bright had no desire to detach himself from Gladstone's leadership. The fact that other Radicals had done so and the coolness this induced in his relations with them was a blow as much at Bright's leadership of the Radical party as at Gladstone's leadership of the Liberal party. Hodgkinson's amendment was designed to conform to Disraeli's 'plan and principle'[3] while vastly extending its application, but Bright had no reason to expect Disraeli to accept it. In helping Hodgkinson to press it, it is probable that he wished merely to show that Disraeli was not as radical as the public might suppose, to indict the Conservative party as the party of fraudulent reform and to press Disraeli into demonstrating by his own resistance that Conservative reform was as much a sham as Birmingham knew already.

In view of the want of direct evidence about Disraeli's state of mind, it is difficult to be certain. It seems very likely, however, that it was a combination of the facts that criticism of compounding arrangements was widespread, that Hodgkinson's resolution of the problem was different from the one that Gladstone favoured[1] and that Disraeli saw the chance to move on to the redistribution clauses at a point at which Gladstone had renounced his conservative position rather than any capitulation to public agitation, which explains the decisions of May 13 (in relation to Torrens) and of May 17 and 28 (in relation to Hodgkinson). The anxiety to move quickly is marked—on May 13,[2] after his acceptance of Hodgkinson's principle on May 17[3] and in the Attorney-General's reply to Ayrton's, Forster's and Childers's attempts to make the passage of the Reform bill dependent on production of a satisfactory bill to reform the rating law.[4] Whatever the intention, acceptance of Torrens's and Hodgkinson's amendments establishing Clause 3 in its final form, was the 'turning point of [the] measure', and made it likely that 'no further opposition to the Reform bill' would 'take place'.[5] It was followed by a promise of support from the *Daily Telegraph* which had supported Mill in Westminster at the election of 1865,[6] by agreement between Disraeli and the House to begin morning sessions on May 28,[7] by the announcement that there would be no Irish Reform bill in the current session[8] and by a clear warning, given to a Scottish member's enquiry about the probable progress of the Reform bill for Scotland which had been introduced on May 13, that the government would 'proceed with no business whatever until the English bill was passed through committee'.[9] It made it impossible to expect any substantial support in either party for Poulett Scrope's motion[10] excusing from rating and voting all occupiers of houses rated at less than £4 p.a., though there is overwhelming evidence that this sort of proposal, whether in his name, in Wilson Patten's, in Coleridge's or in Grosvenor's, had commanded the instinctive assent of a very large number of MP.s in both parties throughout the session.[11]

There is no doubt that the existence of the Reform League, and its public agitation, put this possibility in the air, and that the special hostility the League showed to compounding restrictions played their part in creating the climate in which Disraeli's decision was taken. Nor can a reader of his speeches at this time doubt that Gladstone was conscious of the need to keep hold of advanced Liberal and Radical feeling, and was moved by the prospect of public agitation in the future. Whether Beales's followers were £10 occupiers or £10 lodgers, whether they were actual or prospective voters, no doubt their wishes, and the opinions they were symptomatic of, played a part in helping Gladstone to make up his mind. Also, as we have seen, there was a strong strain of Conservative feeling which genuinely thought that a lowering of the franchise would be more helpful to the Conservative party than *any* restrictive move. It is doubtful, however, whether mere agitation at a moment when Gladstone had lost control over the Liberal party in the House of Commons would have made Disraeli accept the principle of Hodgkinson's amendment on May 17, when all previous policy and calculation had been designed to make the Conservative party the centre of resistance to agitation, and when this policy had been successful to the point of pushing Gladstone so far off balance that Derby and Disraeli for the moment had nothing to fear from him as a parliamentary leader.

IX

CONCLUSION:
PALMERSTON'S MANTLE

'I have no personal predilection for any party. My interest in party politics ceased when my father left office in 1834. I still believe in Whig doctrines and principles as I was taught them forty years ago and if I was to choose the side of the House on which I find them best represented, it might very probably be yours.'

General Grey to Derby, October 28 1866: Derby MSS Box 159

'There is really no difference between the two, except some small rages of bigotry and intolerance that stick unwillingly to them. Let them get rid of these—let the Tories throw overboard the talk about the Church rates, the talk about the Universities—and they will do it—and even the Liberal, the moderate Liberal party, will join them, and form such a strong Ministerial party in England as will enable us to maintain the power of England throughout the world; as will make her feared by her enemies and loved by her friends, and be the protecting power of the people. I am sure that this will take place. I am sure that Lord Derby will disappear. I hope that Lord Russell will disappear, and that other men will rise up in their places representing the united feeling of the people of England; and that then we shall be enabled to preserve the people of England from the control of ignorance and vice with which we are now threatened; and, in spite of all the demagogues in the world, the people of England will ride triumphant.'

J. A. Roebuck (1866), in Leader: *Life of Rt Hon. J. A. Roebuck*,
1897, p. 312

It is neither possible nor necessary to give to the rest of the passage of the bill the detailed attention which has been given to its progress thus far. There was no guarantee of unconditional Liberal acquiescence until the allocation of extra seats to the large cities at the beginning of July, but the passage of the borough franchise clauses in the form in which they were passed by May 28 made it impossible for Liberals to think seriously of challenging any reasonable advantage Disraeli might take for himself elsewhere. Instead, therefore, of following what the material does not allow us to follow adequately and what many MP.s were apparently too bored to follow at all, we shall try in this chapter to see the Reform bill in its largest party context and to show that, though we are interested in it as a special case with a beginning and an end in time, the politicians with whom we are dealing regarded it as part of an endless process by which leaders emerged and parties were transformed.

It must by now have become sufficiently apparent that the connection between public agitation and parliamentary decision was more complicated than is sometimes supposed. The action we have described was a battle within the political classes to sustain support and achieve power. 'Political classes' includes parliamentary politicians: it includes the leaders of the Reform agitation. The Reform agitation, in London at least, did not grow up without mediation or stimulation from professional politicians. It was stimulated and mediated by professional politicians who felt themselves part of a political system, cast themselves for roles in it and sought for support with which to make these roles effective. Beales, Bradlaugh and Potter were as much parts of the political system as Disraeli or Gladstone. They did not accept it as Gladstone and Disraeli did, but they knew how far they could go. They wanted to extend the range of political practicability, but they knew that, if they went too far, the assumptions on which existing politics were conducted would be turned against them. They had no desire to unloose the passions of the people.

Much of the parliamentary belief in Disraeli's credibility arose from a feeling that Gladstone might unloose the people's passions by accident. This feeling affected Liberals as much as it affected Tories. Indeed, it affected Liberals far more than Tories, who seem not to have feared the effect of resisting the League, who were willing to adopt an anti-revolutionary position and a restrictive bill in relation to it, and who were led by Disraeli to go farther than they intended because his success in dividing the Liberal party promised a more Tory future than they had expected. So far as they thought in terms of 'revolution', they welcomed the revolution which Bright and Disraeli seemed likely to have effected. To see Gladstone pushed into a position of sympathy with public agitation not only confirmed their worst suspicions: it promised closer sympathy between the Tory party on the one hand and territorial Whigs, a worried intelligentsia and strike-breaking urban magnates (of whom they had had too few in the past) on the other. If it would not be true to say that the problem of social order had become the central problem of the age, the events we have described reflect a major shift in ruling opinion.

In explaining the fact that an Act was passed in 1867 which went farther than any bill could have done at the end of 1865, we must examine the varying impacts made by the movement of events on the major political leaders. It is important to examine the leaders one by one. Although we speak of a movement of events which it is the historians' business to uncover, that movement was the outcome of conflict between the wills and minds and actions of the actors who were responsible for creating it. No one actor was responsible completely. No one actor could know the inwardness of the whole movement. The historian cannot know completely, but he alone has the chance to see what went on over the heads, beneath the feet or despite the intentions of all the actors in the movement. He alone can begin to distinguish the parts they controlled or knew from the parts about which they had no knowledge or understanding at all. If he is to show to what extent they were carried along by forces they did not control and forced by circumstances into reactions they did not intend, he must not only recognize that some of them knew exactly what they wanted and got it, like W. E. Forster who saw an opening for competent parliamentary Radicals in 1866 and took it;[1] he must also deal with them in the first place individually.

Defects of knowledge and prevision are obvious in all the major actors in the story. They are most obvious in the leaders of the Cave. Whatever strength of feeling the Cave reflected in Parliament and among Palmerstonians in the country beyond, it was the Cave which was routed most completely. The Cave did not succeed in keeping the borough franchise at the 1832 level. It did not succeed in surrounding household suffrage with counterpoises and compensations. It did not impose a fixed-line franchise with compulsory compounding for houses rated below £5 or £6 a year. In pursuing these objectives, it was expressing feelings to which many MP.s responded —in the third case to which the vast majority were only too anxious to respond at the time at which it was proposed. Yet not only did the Cave fail to carry these measures: it both failed to establish that dominance over Liberal feeling which would make permanent resistance to Gladstone possible and produced a situation in which Gladstone had to shift sharply leftward if he was to have any hope of controlling the Liberal party in the future.

For this there was a number of reasons, the first of which was the inadequacy of its members and the character of Elcho. Elcho in these matters was central. Grosvenor was a limited, straightforward, dilettante politician—'one of the nicest fellows that ever stepped'[1]: he went shooting in Cheshire during the crucial days at the beginning of March 1867 when the reconstruction of Disraeli's policy was effected.[2] The drive came from Elcho who emerges as a man of booming, crude, unsubtle energy. Elcho was right to think that his own hostility to Gladstone was shared by a great many parliamentary Liberals. He was wrong to attach to their feelings of unease, distress and uncertainty a matching certainty that the obvious reply to Gladstone was some sort of alliance with Disraeli. He miscalculated because he did not realize how little concession Disraeli was willing to make in his direction, and underestimated the unwillingness of party Liberals to break up the party on which they thought that stability and progress depended.

Unlike the other members of the Cave, Elcho was neither a Whig nor a Liberal, but a Peelite. He represented in a blustering way that same combination of attitudes on which Peel's Conservatism had depended. Like other ambitious politicians, he had his own working-class connections—with Macdonald, the Scottish miners' leader, with George Jacob Holyoake and with the London Trades Council whose parliamentary advocate in Master and Servant questions he was for most of 1866 and 1867. Along with his relative, Lord Lichfield, who had had close experience of trades union questions during the Staffordshire ironworkers' strike, he was the only official member of the royal commission whom trades union leaders thought had given them a hearing. His appointment to it reflected a desire, of which the government's support for his Master and Servant bill was another example, to find harmless ways of 'putting us right with the working classes' for the future.[3] Elcho had never left the Carlton Club. For him to return to the Conservative party, so far from involving a breach with his past, would be no more than a recognition that the Conservative party had restored itself to the position of broad-based accommodation from which Peel's fall had removed it.

In the session of 1866 Elcho was effective. He was effective because the absence of a decisive demonstration of popular interest in Reform left Liberals free to give expression to their instinctive feelings, and because the absence of a Conservative desire to outdo the Whigs in Reforming directions made it sensible to translate these desires into parliamentary votes. But even in 1866, in favourable conditions, Elcho could not bring all Liberals who shared his objection into the division lobbies with him. Their objection was not just to the content of the bill, but to the impression the Russell government gave of 'identifying itself with men whose claim and merit [was] merely a wish to upset all the present and revolutionize the country'.[1] Since it was this (as much as an objection to the Reform bill itself), the extent to which Liberal disaffection was translated into parliamentary voting was affected by the conduct of the opposition. Of all the opposition leaders, Stanley was the one who appealed most to Whigs. When he began to play a party game, there was a marked, if temporary, Liberal consolidation in reply. Nevertheless, when Gladstone's mishandling of the situation drove a large proportion of the dissidents together in June 1866, Elcho had good reason to think that, whoever governed in the existing House of Commons, had to take account of the feelings the Cave reflected.

What Elcho did not understand in 1866 was that Derby and Disraeli had no more intention than Russell and Gladstone of being run by him. He seems not to have foreseen that, once the government had reacted to the public agitation by adopting the cautious line the Cave wanted between September 1866 and February 1867, the Cabinet would back down under pressure from those of its members who stood closest to him.[2] He did not anticipate the Cabinet's change of policy on February 25 and the three resignations a week later. He did not predict the need Disraeli then felt to guard against his own unreliability by shifting sharply towards such Radicals as were available. Though Elcho supported Disraeli from March 30 onwards, Disraeli's Radical shift after Cranborne's resignation made it difficult to carry the original Cave into division lobbies with him. Whereas on June 18 1866 over forty Adullamites had followed Elcho and Grosvenor, only twenty-one did so on April 12 1867. Though over fifty Liberals voted with Disraeli on May 9, the Cave ceased to function after the beginning of the Easter recess.

For this a number of explanations may be given. First, that the initiative had passed so decisively to Disraeli that there was no opportunity for a central group to make the running. Secondly, since Disraeli had left the impression of removing the Reform question from party politics, there was little to be gained from wrecking the Liberal party, with which on many other questions much of the

Cave had no real disagreement and which might, in some constituencies, be greatly strengthened by the enlargement of the franchise. It would be wrong to anticipate Gladstone's restoration of Liberal unity in 1868: in mid-1867 the Liberal party was not united. But the removal of the dam provided by the Conservative party against all Reforming positions transformed the situation. The fact that Disraeli was in control of Conservative policy and not Stanley, who had given assurances whch had not been honoured,[1] reduced the attractiveness of anything resembling a Conservative alliance. The fact that Gladstone was asserting his own position, that Forster, Stansfeld and Coleridge were occupying the vacuum left by the collapse of Whig control and that many Liberal constituencies were intensely hostile to Whig backsliding made it more difficult than before to think of an effective third party in the House of Commons. There is a hint that Grosvenor was tired of Elcho. It is clear that Lowe and Horsman had seen that they had made fools of themselves. There is not much doubt that they had.

The Cave was an attempt to control the Liberal leadership. So was Bright's public agitation. But whereas Elcho used parliamentary knowledge, exact calculation, Whig resentment and Gladstone's manner, Bright's weapons were broad, simple, imprecise statements of the direction in which all right-thinking men must necessarily want to move. Bright's speeches in 1866/7 were powerful statements of intention, masterly evocations of mind and manner which brought together in common harmony, a large, uncoordinated, unsystematic body of sympathetic public opinion. In creating a climate in the lower reaches of the Liberal party, in forcing Whigs to show their hands and in enabling Radicals to chop them off once they had done so, Bright's assault was successful. In providing Gladstone with a hole to run into and a movement to fall back on when he had been outmanœuvred by Disraeli,[2] Bright was a major creator of events.

Bright knew that an election in July 1866 would have driven a good many Whigs away from the Liberal party: he cannot have doubted that the agitation of the winter would do this also. The care taken by Liberal leaders in March/April 1867 to listen to his opinions, the Whig defection of April 12 and Gladstone's leftward shift in May were changes in the balance of power which brought Bright a step nearer both to creating the Liberal party in his own

image, and to capturing a good deal more of Gladstone than Gladstone had thought it safe to allow it to be supposed had happened
beforehand. Yet it is doubtful whether Bright was doing very much
more than follow his nose, with no certainty that it would lead anywhere in particular: it is unlikely that he anticipated the outcome.
It is unlikely that he expected the Conservative party to propose a
bill which was anything like the bill he wanted. Nor did he expect
the government to survive or a bill to be passed if Disraeli persuaded
a Conservative Cabinet to propose anything that came within sight
of acceptability. In that sense Bright's calculations were mistaken.
On the other hand, Bright respected Disraeli's sensitivity to the cur-
rents of the age and understood his skill in the mechanics of deception. There was no question of Bright abandoning the Liberal party
in favour of Disraeli so long as Gladstone remained a possible
Liberal leader, but it is by no means certain what he expected from
his public speeches in 1866/7. He wanted to drive a wedge down the
side of the Liberal party so as to get rid of reactionary Whigs. He
wanted to capture Gladstone more completely than he had so far.
But it is unlikely that he thought from the start that Disraeli could
persuade the Tory party to pass a reasonable Reform bill. Though
he may not have anticipated the effect his actions would have in
consolidating conservative opinion in both parties and in all sections of the Liberal party in support of Disraeli, Bright believed in
principle that the House of Commons was extremely reactionary.
Though he willed the confrontation whatever the consequences, it
is even less likely that he anticipated conditions in which, so far
from compelling Disraeli to go farther than he intended, the agitation made Disraeli the safest and most credible reforming figure in
Parliament who would not have had to go as far as he did in late
March if the Cave had not deserted him; and who was able to go as
far as he did in May, not because he had been forced by Bright to
do so, but because the doubts felt by many Liberals about Gladstone's ability to keep hold of the Liberal party, gave him a very
wide range of flexibility indeed.

Bright, as we have seen, was willing to settle for a £5 franchise if
Gladstone proposed it, or a £3 or £4 one if that could be guaranteed
to keep the Liberal party together. But he made a point of pressing
Disraeli to remove from the bill of March 18 the checks and counterpoises, abandonment of which would establish not a £5 rating

suffrage but household suffrage pure and simple. About the evasiveness of his position there can be little doubt. So long as the Gladstone bill was under consideration, no conflict had arisen since Bright and the League were supporting the £7 franchise as a payment on account. Nor was conflict possible between July 1866 and March 1867 when there was no guarantee, and little likelihood, that the Conservative government would go even as far as household suffrage. Bright's language in late 1866 was based on the assumption that Disraeli's proposal, if he made one, would be unsatisfactory. In these circumstances he did not need to specify. It was only the gun pointed by Disraeli at all Radicals in April and May which made it necessary that, if a Disraeli bill were to be passed, it should obviously be passed under pressure from Bright. Though Disraeli's bill, when interpreted in his speeches between March 18 and March 26, was not far from what the Reform Union wanted, neither Bright nor anyone else who had promised the downfall of the Derby government could afford to let Disraeli get away with it. In these circumstances Bright was willing to support the £5 rating proposal because he wanted Gladstone to keep control of the Liberal party and knew that acceptance of a £5 rating by the House, in the form in which Gladstone proposed it, might destroy the government without committing the Liberal party to any particular measure for the future. He attacked Disraeli on this basis because he did not think Disraeli could accept it and survive (though he had told him that he would) and because acceptance by Disraeli after further agitation would demonstrate the power of the popular movement, demoralize the Conservative party and dish the Cave. Above all, Bright needed to keep up the pressure not just in order to make it difficult for Adullamites in the Liberal party but in order to keep hold of those parts of the public agitation which did not want to stop short at household suffrage pure and simple.

Bright's preferences and objectives were vague and flexible. He had the incentive that Birmingham would not gain much from the bill of March 18. But it is difficult to avoid feeling that the constant pressure for which Bright, the Union and finally Gladstone were responsible after April 12 sprang from the feeling that, since Disraeli intended to get his hands on the central body of existing electors, their own political fortunes depended on their ability to keep hold of the politically conscious Radical working classes in the future. It is in this sense—that they had been trumped by Disraeli and feared further trumping in the future—that the public movement, while not determining the government's policy, took hold of Bright, whose name and rhetoric had made it what it was.

Bright, then, probably did not anticipate the outcome of the action—at any rate in detail. He foresaw neither the defection of Radicals from him, nor the consolidation behind Disraeli in May. Nevertheless, Bright—of all the actors in the story—was the one who succeeded most abundantly in exposing the raw nerves of the Liberal party, in imposing his opinions on its leader and in ensuring that, if there was to be a Liberal party in the future, he would be somewhere near its centre.

What Bright won the official Whigs lost, and saw from the first that they were losing. With them there were no defects of prevision. They saw it all before it started. They saw that the party was 'a bundle of sticks'.[1] They saw that Lowe was a danger.[2] They saw that Gladstone was not the instrument they had hoped he would become, and they did not know what to do. They did their best. They bided their time. They gave Disraeli rope to hang himself with. They thought, at one stage, that they had won. If Elcho had played the game, they might have won. But the Cave did not trust the party leader the Whigs had chosen; so they lost, and lost resoundingly. They lost not only among Radicals, but among Whigs and regular Liberals as well. They did not turn out the Derby government. They did not keep control of their Radical allies. They did not restrict the enfranchisement proposed. The names of Sir George Grey, Halifax and Clarendon became symbols of an unhappy period that was past. They were more appalled than anyone else by the breakdown in Hyde Park in 1866. Above all they did not pass a Reform bill, and there was little sign that they would regain control of the Liberal party in the future.

Not only had they lost control: Disraeli had shown them to be 'humbugs'. Whereas previously they could profess concern for progress without needing to be more progressive than was safe because the Tory party would be less progressive still, they were now exposed to ruthless thrusts from an operator as cynical as they were. Disraeli had not only stolen their radical clothes: he had left the impression that he was more conservative as well. What Disraeli had in common with Radicals was a desire to give the Whigs a shock.

The Whigs were frightened that, if he pushed the Conservative party too far, they would 'lose a defence on which they [had] relied against the others'.[1] As a consequence of this, and through defects of mind, manner, decision and application, Russell had lost control of the party. In face of Disraeli Russell floundered absolutely. On the one hand he sketched out a bill of his own consisting of the borough franchise he had proposed in 1854, together with compounder and lodger franchises and the redistribution of fifty seats. On the other, he rejected the counterpoises and compensations—especially duality which was 'new, strange and unbearable'.[2] When duality had been abandoned and personal payment circumvented in May, he attacked the bill in the House of Lords and disgusted Bright by helping Cairns to force Derby to accept cumulative voting which no advanced Liberal approved of.[3] His unpredictability reduced any influence he might have had with Gladstone. His raw hostility to extensive enfranchisement did him no good in the body of the Liberal party. His want of prudence destroyed his reputation as a popular statesman.

If Halifax, Clarendon or Sir George Grey had plans to succeed him, they had not done so: they were unlikely to do so now. Gladstone had lost control. If he regained it, he would do so on his own terms and in his own way, and would not allow his preferences to be hampered, and his style cramped, by Whigs of his own and earlier generations. In a party whose popular following would become more advanced as the franchise was lowered and in which only Gladstone's name, and Bright's, struck roots in the country, the prospect was plain. Forster was a Bradford manufacturer, Stansfeld a Halifax brewer and solicitor, Coleridge and Roundell Palmer successful barristers, Goschen and Charles Glyn, the new chief whip, partners in banking firms. All six came forward in the vacuum left by the Whig collapse. Along with Granville, Kimberley, Cardwell, Childers and Argyll, they were the men of the future. They were men of the future not because they were or were not Whigs, nor because they liked or disliked the Reform bill, but because they were neither involved in the follies of the past nor equals in age and experience to Gladstone. Whatever *positions* they might hold in future, the management of Halifax, Clarendon, Brand, Russell and Sir George Grey was ended.

The cases we have considered are comparatively simple. With

Gladstone simplicity is absent. There is abundant evidence that in 1866 Gladstone thought an opportunity would arise in 1867 to pay back Disraeli for the disruption he had caused in the Liberal party in the previous session. He expected the movement of public opinion to compel Disraeli to propose a bill and felt that no bill he proposed could be accepted by the Conservative party. Since he had a nominal majority in the House of Commons already, it is unlikely that he was looking forward to attracting dissident Conservatives. All he had to do was to prove that the Conservative party was not a credible instrument of government. In this, up to a point, Gladstone succeeded. The government was split by the attempt to produce a bill: Cranborne, Carnarvon and Peel resigned. Instead of resigning as a consequence, however, the Cabinet stayed put, reorganized on a basis of hostility to Gladstone and survived. It survived because Gladstone, no less than Disraeli, had to keep together a mixed bag of opinions, interests and personalities and failed to do so. He failed partly because of his parliamentary manner, partly because of defects of doctrine, rhetoric and record, and partly because of his churchmanship, which was too clerical for an Erastian party, too enthusiastic for men of the world, too catholic for Anglicans and too closely identified with that broad range of Irish, dissenting, positivist and atheist opinion which constituted one part of the religious aspect of the democratic movement to which he was supposed to have capitulated.

In one sense, his enemies were right. Gladstone had cast himself off from Oxford deliberately. In mind and manner he was neither a man of the world nor an Erastian. Throughout these years he spent a number of evenings a week rescuing prostitutes: if Acton, who was an admirer, misunderstood this aspect of his life, others probably did so too.[1] If Gladstone was not in practice a democrat, he had adopted language which sometimes left the impression that he was. His comments on the Irish Church and his support of the Church Rates motion in 1866 were attempts to continue the Whig policy of pacifying Catholics and dissenters, but they could be mistaken for something a great deal worse. His attacks on manufacturers' pursuit of private profit instead of the public interest during the Lancashire cotton famine,[2] his silence while others denounced trades union activity and the impression he left at moments of stress, not only of wishing to carry the democratic movement along with him but also of believing intensely in its claims, promised a significant difference in the balance of power and state of mind of the Whig party under his leadership. What was thought to be a needlessly high tone about patronage, an intense involution of mind bordering on 'mystification'[1] and a climate in which coolness towards the Irish Church could be mistaken for hostility to the property of Irish land-owners, further helped to create conditions between 1865 and 1867 in which rebellion could occur among those whose personal prospects under Gladstone were slender.

Nevertheless, in entering into Gladstone's mind, there is the difficulty that Gladstone at no point committed himself in public to go as far as his enemies thought he would go if left unchecked. Even when coloured, as in 1866, with rhetoric which seems most democratic, his speeches and letters suggest a tortuous, powerful and casuistical attempt to keep all options open. The most categorically advanced of his Reform speeches—the speech of May 11 1864—was surrounded with qualifications which could be interpreted to satisfy the most cautious of Whigs. The most offensively democratic of his parliamentary speeches in the session of 1866—the speech of April 27—was made in defence of a bill which was not as extensive as Palmerston's bill of 1860, and which the Reform League had supported only because it deceived itself into treating it as an instalment on the road to manhood suffrage. In 1867, right up to the speech to the Reform Union on May 11, and in one sense even then, there was a tactical ambiguity which succeeded in carrying along a good many central Whigs, and the great body of Liberal country members, despite Adullamite and Radical rebellions.

Gladstone's failure to control the Liberal party arose, then, we may say, less from what he wanted to do than from loss of confidence in his ability to keep in judicious juxtaposition the forces he was expected to carry with him. Everyone agreed that the Whig/Liberal role was to carry the public movement along: there was disagreement about Gladstone's ability to do this. If one lists the party Liberals who were repelled by Gladstone in the two sessions which followed the death of Palmerston, the range of dissidence is remarkable. It included doctrinaire Whigs like Earl Grey. It included regular, impeccable, undoctrinaire ones like Somerset, Clarendon, Hastings Russell, Enfield, Brand, Edward Ellice, C. W. W. Fitzwilliam, Bouverie, Grosvenor, Eversley and Lord Ernest Bruce. It included

Clanricarde, Dunkellin, W. H. Gregory and Horsman, and it included Russell himself whose support for cumulative voting was not
part of Gladstone's programme. It included Radicals like Platt,
Hibbert, Dillwyn, Clay, Locke, Torrens, Oliphant, Steel, Ewing,
Hodgkinson and White of Brighton. It included rural Liberal backbenchers of no particular opinion like Hanbury-Tracy, Sir Thomas
Lloyd, Tomline, Dering and Knatchbull-Hugessen, respectable
industrial Liberals like Bass, Doulton and Akroyd and idiosyncratic
Palmerstonians of the first and second rank like Lowe, Laing,
Shaftesbury and Sir Robert Peel. It included a sizeable Irish defection and a small Scottish one. It was not a doctrinal rebellion but the
disintegration of a coalition, which occurred despite the fact that
Gladstone was trying at one level to square the circle by encouraging all sections of opinion. It occurred, not because Gladstone was
ignorant, not because he was not trying to act as a Whig leader
should, not even because he had uncomplicated working-class
sympathies which his followers did not share; but because he was
less capable than Disraeli or Palmerston of the highest sorts of
ambiguity.

If we ask why Gladstone inspired doubt, the answer cannot be
simple. In 1866 Gladstone did not set out to offend Whig/Liberal
susceptibilities. On the contrary. Just as he opened the session of
1867 with a consistent attempt to conciliate them and was driven by
the Whig attempt to control him into rejecting the Cave altogether,
so in 1866 it was the stand taken by Grosvenor and Elcho which had
pushed Gladstone off the hook. The events of 1866 are inexplicable
except on the supposition that Gladstone, the Cabinet and at first
Russell, conscious of the tension within the Liberal party now that
Palmerston was dead, were playing the Reform question as cautiously
as they could and had to assert their authority once the Cave had
questioned their decisions. Gladstone was almost certainly put up
by the Cabinet in the House of Commons and at Liverpool to knock
down the Cave.[1] His speeches at Liverpool in April were assertions
of a ruling Cabinet against a dissident group, not of democrats
against constitutional Liberals. What the Cabinet did not expect was
that Gladstone would lose control of himself to the point of bullying
the House of Commons and giving his enemies the chance to present
him as the prisoner of the democratic movement. It is difficult to
establish the point in time at which the interaction between the Cave

and the democratic movement began. Gladstone's speech in May 1864 was a major stimulus to public feeling. It induced a reckless euphoria among some advocates of electoral Reform, and produced an answering reaction elsewhere. Grosvenor, who voted for Baines's motion in 1864, seems to have withdrawn support for any lowering of the franchise:[1] the creation by Elcho of the climate in which the Cave grew was a consequence. The existence of the Cave in 1866 was more important than anything else in turning Gladstone from being the judicious accommodater of February into being the democratic orator of April. The fact that he uncovered himself in this way without being democratic himself was a victory for Elcho who wanted others to see that Gladstone was as democratic as he believed him to be.

Nor was Gladstone the prime mover in instigating his own shift to the left in mid-1867. Once the Reform question had driven Income Tax from the centre of his mind, Gladstone wanted to carry a united Liberal party at the point at which some sort of Reform bill was passed. So long as the Conservative party was not committed to propose one, or was likely, if it did, to propose a restrictive one, Gladstone did not need to go far in order to convince the public that he had done as much as he could. If Derby had fallen on February 25 1867, Gladstone could have carried a £5 rating bill, kept hold of Whigs and Adullamites in the process and lost nothing of his reputation as a popular statesman. He would have pushed Disraeli off the central ground, which both were trying to occupy from October 1865 onwards. If a united Conservative Cabinet had proposed a heavily restricted household suffrage bill on February 25, Gladstone's position would have been impossible. It was only the fact that the household suffrage bill, when it was finally presented on March 18/19, was presented by a Cabinet which had lost its most restrictive members that compelled Gladstone to shift his ground. Whatever the position before Cranborne, Carnarvon and Peel resigned, their removal from the Cabinet, when coupled with the Cabinet's survival, meant that Disraeli had a chance to pass a bill which would take the wind out of the public movement and show that he, as well as Gladstone, could deal with the central governmental problems from a position which accommodated Radicals as well as everyone else. The government, at this point, had the advantage of uncertainty: it was uncertainty about Disraeli's intentions which compelled Gladstone to adopt the two-way insurance he took out between March 18 and March 25. Despite the effective identity between their substantive proposals, it was Gladstone's failure to match Disraeli's ambiguity which produced the fiasco of April 12, the withdrawal of Adullamite support and the compulsion he felt to shift once more to the left as the central ground deserted him. Many non-Whig county backbenchers stuck to him throughout the session. His reputation outside parliament tied official Whigs more closely to him than before.[1] But it was the fact that Gladstone was shifting to the left, in conjunction with a renewed instalment of public agitation and the certainty that he no longer led the Liberal party in the House of Commons, which gave Disraeli the freedom he used to such advantage in May, June and July.

Disraeli outmanœuvred Gladstone and Elcho, and trumped Bright. He was the victor of the session: his reputation was made by it. Yet even in his case, it is far from certain that he knew what he intended from the start. In 1865 he was sixty-one, seven years younger than Derby. He had led the Conservative party in the House of Commons for nearly twenty years and had had remarkably little success. He had led it as a party leader: he had led it with skill, with style and with self-control. He had kept it together in depression and expectation, but he had never had real power. Throughout the 'fifties and 'sixties, though it was often the largest single group in Parliament, Whig flexibility, Radical hostility to a wide range of Tory positions and Derby's reluctance at crucial moments had deprived it of the chance to govern. Its strength had made it formidable: the fragmentary character of opposing coalitions had given it opportunities. These opportunities had been taken, so far as Disraeli could ensure party support in taking them. His objective throughout these years was to create a credible government on a Tory base to replace the coalitions on Whig bases which had followed the fall of Peel. Though he cannot be said to have succeeded, he was attempting both to broaden and to deepen the Anglican and agrarian foundation onto which the party had forced itself in 1846.

The first thing to understand about Disraeli's policy between 1865 and 1867, therefore, is that its flexibility in relation to Catholic, Whig, Irish, Adullamite, Liberal and Radical MP.s was a continuation of one aspect of the policy he had adopted since he first had to combat the Russell/Aberdeen/Palmerston coalitions in the 'fifties. The second thing to understand is that there is no reason to suppose that Disraeli knew in advance in 1865 which group he would be able most successfully to detach. In 1852 he had tried to detach Bright. Throughout the 'fifties he had tried sporadically to detach various Irish contingents.[1] In 1859 he had tried at various times to detach both Palmerston and Gladstone.[2] He had detached twenty Irish and Catholic MP.s in the Danish debate of July 8 1864, which was a vote of confidence in Palmerston.[3] The death of Palmerston made it possible to expect greater success than in the past for the attempt to reconstruct the broad-based conservatism which Disraeli had played a part in destroying in 1846. His first reaction in 1865 was to prise off dissident Whigs. The object in the first half of 1866 was to draw Adullamite support away from Gladstone. The fact that two or three Adullamites were not Whigs but urban Liberals was a matter of consequence, but the overriding objective was a destruction of the unity of the Whig party in whichever way this could be accomplished. Nor, despite contact with James Clay and a desire to include Mill and Ayrton on Earl Grey's electoral commission,[4] was this altered in the first eight months of office. The object, right up to the point at which Cranborne resigned, was to carry a Cave/Conservative combination which, for Reform purposes at least, would disrupt the Liberal party and might, in some circumstances, enable Conservatives to fight a general election as defenders of the constitution. In this Disraeli had the same objective as Cranborne—to create an anti-revolutionary party on a constitutional basis. It was Cranborne's refusal to follow at the end of February and the Cave's return to Gladstone which compelled him to shift from one line of policy to the other. It was Cranborne's failure to organize resistance which enabled him to do so successfully. It is difficult to be certain at what point he decided that Radicals might be detached as well as the Cave. The decision to appease Radicals, which the Cave's and Cranborne's defection forced him to consider, became a practical possibility when loss of confidence in Gladstone's leadership and fear of a runaway public agitation drove Adullamites and constitutional Liberals back into his arms at the same time as Radicals began to respond to him also. He could hardly have predicted this in making tactical dispositions in 1866. Though he had bid for Radical support in 1852 and 1858 and had actually used it over the India Act, there was no reason to expect success at a moment at which Russell and Gladstone had succeeded Palmerston in the leadership of the Liberal party. There was even less reason to suppose that he could persuade the Conservative party to go far enough in a Reforming direction to make Radical support possible. Though he was certainly aiming to destroy Gladstone's control of the Liberal party, he probably had little idea in which way the split would come and thought, like Derby, if he thought specifically at all, that Gladstone would have to detach himself more completely from the 'democratic party' than in the end he did.[1]

Disraeli's was a policy of consistent opportunism—an attempt to be prepared for any chance that might arise to occupy as much of the central ground as he could, to hold out expectations to such Liberal or Irish groups as might be detached and to smooth down the rough edges of reactionary Toryism. Reactionary Toryism was patriotic, Anglican and agrarian. Its topics were the malt tax, national defence and the Church of England. The malt tax was a symbol of agricultural subservience in an industrial society. The campaign for its repeal was an organized movement to which territorial Tories responded. As Chancellor of the Exchequer Disraeli was as economy-minded as Gladstone, but his eye was on the income tax. He had no intention of being driven off it by prior demands to abolish the malt tax.[2] Naval defence and Somerset's conduct at the Admiralty were targets for Tory attack. Tory policy in opposition was to strengthen naval installations: the attack on Somerset continued after Derby's Cabinet had come to power. The logic of the attack involved large increases in naval expenditure but this was not possible in an economical House of Commons. At the same time as Pakington attacked Somerset, Disraeli used Pakington's junior minister, Lord Henry Lennox, to impose a major economy on him.[3] The Conscience Clause was an earnest of religious accommodation, dividing Cranborne and Carnarvon on the one hand from Adderley and Pakington on the other. In 1867 it was played down. English Catholics were 'naturally Tory . . . [had] behaved admirably to us . . . influenced . . . elections in our favour' and supported the attack on Palmerston in 1864 on Austrian and ultramontane grounds: Irish Catholics were in some respects up for auction. There was a recurring attempt to break down the Anglican party's unwillingness to contemplate concessions about Catholic oaths and education in England, and about the Catholic university in Ireland.[1] Above all, there was the desire to prove that the Conservative party was not the party of agriculture alone, but the party of the 'landed interest' which 'includes all those interests that spring from the land such as the mineral treasures developed from the land' (i.e. in coal-fields where strikes happened).[2] One should not attach too much importance to the letter Disraeli wrote to Stanley on November 6 1865 when it seemed possible that Stanley would join the Russell/ Gladstone government. Many of its words were not Disraeli's, but Earle's, who suggested them for use in another context.[3] They were designed to prevent a major loss to the Conservative party, to avert a major threat to its future, and to deny to Russell and Gladstone the central ground they wanted Stanley to help them occupy. Nevertheless, a great deal of Disraeli's outlook is embodied in the claim that a public declaration by Stanley against electoral Reform and in favour of progress in other areas of governmental activity would produce a situation in which 'the mass of the Whigs,...the great towns...[and] the great employers of labour [like] the Bass' and the Petos [would] rally round you, and [in which] the bulk of the Tories, our own people, humbled by their defeat on the hustings and frightened by the threatened Reform bill, [would] accept you as their leader with all your heresies'.[4]

The variety of those whom Disraeli thought it possible to detach from Gladstone, or to attach to himself, was as wide as the variety of those whom Gladstone offended. The Queen was given more detailed and vivid accounts of parliamentary proceedings than she had ever had before: she seems to have responded. Though Disraeli did not want to be swamped by a large, well-organized Whig accession which would destroy his position in the Conservative party, his ideas for appeasing figures of the second rank were extensive. The Boundary Commission nominations and his negotiations with the Cave, Shaftesbury and Sir Robert Peel have been examined already. He wanted to please Irish Catholics by preventing Whiteside becoming Irish Lord Chancellor and by sending Lord Arundell of Wardour, an English Catholic, as private secretary to the Lord Lieutenant.[5] The new Duke of Newcastle, unlike the old one, was not a Gladstonian Peelite. His estates were being administered by Gladstone: he would 'formally and completely join' the Conserva-

tive party if offered the Garter.[1] Somerset Beaumont, brother of
Wentworth the Liberal MP. for Northumberland North, had been a
constitutional Liberal MP. for Newcastle from 1860 until defeated
by Cowen's Radical machine in 1865. The Beaumonts were Yorkshire and Northumberland gentry: Wentworth Beaumont was Clanricarde's son-in-law. Somerset Beaumont was offered the private
secretaryship to Disraeli. When he refused it, it was accepted by
Montagu Corry, who was part of the post-Palmerstonian *Owl* circle
which Borthwick and Evelyn Ashley had established at the *Morning
Post*.[2] W. H. Smith, the newsagent, was a Palmerstonian who had
been black-balled by the Reform Club in 1862. On standing as a
Liberal/Conservative Palmerstonian for Westminster in 1865, he
was given Conservative support, even though he did not ask for it.
On being beaten by Mill and a Grosvenor, he was complimented by
Disraeli. He attached himself to the Conservative party in the two
years following. Sir Hugh Rose, on retiring from being Commander-
in-Chief in India, was said to have been offered a peerage by Russell
provided he would support the Liberal government. Since he was
a Conservative, Disraeli asked Derby to offer him a Conservative
peerage instead. The Marquess of Bath, a Conservative admirer of
Gladstone, had wanted coalition under Gladstone's leadership in
1866: in 1867 he was offered, and accepted, the embassy to Vienna.[3]
Lichfield's brother, Anson, was offered household office in 1867.
Lichfield himself was made a member, along with Elcho, of the
Royal Commission on Trades Unions. Elcho's Master and Servant
bill was given governmental support.[4] Roebuck also was put on the
Royal Commission. Torrens, who collaborated with Taylor, the
Conservative Chief Whip, during part of the session, was given
help with his Artisans' and Labourers' Dwellings bill which he had
failed to pass in 1866.[5] A Commission on London water supply
was established under pressure from Shaftesbury.[6]

Not everything went as Disraeli wanted it to go. Derby did not
offer Newcastle the Garter. Newcastle's brother was not offered
office in 1866.[7] Shaftesbury's opinion of Disraeli remained as unfavourable as his opinion of Gladstone: he did not much like Derby's
ecclesiastical appointments.[8] Neither Anson nor Somerset Beaumont accepted offers when they were made. Roebuck and Elcho were
captives. Torrens gave support when it mattered. Akroyd was impressed by the government's attitude to Factory Acts Extension.[9]

305

Stanley was set to persuade Whiteside to renounce his claim to the Irish Lord Chancellorship: in this he was successful. Sir George Bowyer, McEvoy and others responded. Of the ninety-five Irish MP.s who voted on April 12, fifty-four voted with the government. But appeasement of Irish Catholics did not go far in 1867.[1] The Charter question was not resolved. Disraeli received little support from Irish Liberals in 1868. Morris was a Catholic, W. H. Gregory and Dunkellin racing rakes. Together with Lord John Browne, they made up something resembling a Clanricarde contingent. Clanricarde was a Whig who had been excluded from office after matrimonial scandal in the 'fifties.[2] He offered support to the highest bidder in return for a policy of Catholic concession and tenant-right recognition. In July 1866 Derby saw Ireland as a ground for fusion[3] and thought an Irish Land bill a necessity. Mayo was made Chief Secretary as an earnest of liberal intentions. Clanricarde was given serious attention. An Irish Land bill was introduced, though not in the extreme form proposed by Gregory. Browne voted with the government in a number of divisions from early 1866 onwards. Morris joined the government in July as Irish Solicitor-General. Though Dunkellin died in 1867, he moved the motion on which the Russell government fell in 1866. Gregory did not join Derby in 1866 and reverted to Gladstone in 1867, but he gave support for a time.[4] In 1868 Gladstone forced Disraeli back upon a Protestant Irish base: for the first time in fifteen years his attempt at a Catholic Irish alliance floundered completely. Nevertheless in 1867 the situation in which English and Irish Whigs, Irish Catholics and English Radicals might all be picked up was one to which Disraeli gave attention.

In the attempt to recover for the Conservative party a central position on the political stage Stanley was of great significance. He was a man without crotchets, without party passion and with a want of the Anglican edge on which Conservative doctrine depended. He spoke the language of enlightenment. He combined the practical political and reflective skills in a way which was attractive both to the official and to the literary intelligentsia. His inherited rank, his inherited Whiggism, his reputation as a friend of the working classes, and his responsiveness to the higher tendencies of the age combined with a sceptical distrust of popular claims to make him a credible point of equilibrium for a party which wished to attract the

towns as well as the countryside, the centres of intellectual respectability as well as the territorial power on which its strength depended.
Russell's attempt to woo him in 1865, Lowe's desire to follow him
in 1866, Disraeli's anxiety to keep him, all reflect the significance
of his position. If he had been more assertive personally or decisive
politically, and had taken the trouble to concert action with Clarendon, Granville or Halifax, he could have emerged as the unques-
tioned leader of whatever combination he had chosen to create.[1]

In explaining the fact that Disraeli carried the Conservative party
so much farther in May 1867 than he had shown signs of wanting to
carry it before, it is necessary to understand that he was pursuing a
personal as well as a party line, and that the two at certain points conflicted. From a party point of view the obvious objective was to
attach a major Whig/Liberal contingent to it. From his own, this
would be as dangerous while he was not established as Derby's successor as it would be impossible once he had been. He was not yet in
a position to lead the party, and needed urgently to be so. This was
why, despite tactical willingness to destroy the Liberal party, he
resisted fusion in July 1866, kept the Cave at arm's length while
playing it along in 1866/7, retained the initiative in his own and
Derby's hands in 1867 and in May was prepared to do almost anything he could get away with in order to remove the opportunities
others would take to construct an alternative government if Derby's
fell. So far from being a Tory Radical, Disraeli was doing what
Stanley, Halifax, Lowe, Northcote, Russell and Gladstone were all
trying at some time or other to do—pursue a central line in order to
make the Cabinet which pursued it a credible instrument of sane,
sensible and safe government. The Reform League helped this process by defining the extent to which a respectable government could
go. Gladstone's failure to maintain a broad-based Liberal position
enabled Disraeli to go farther than he might otherwise have done.
But it was Derby who gave him the party support on which
flexibility depended.

In asking what Derby intended, one must beware of supposing
that he predicted the course taken by the session of 1867. It is unlikely that Derby anticipated the resolution Gladstone would offer
of the dilemma with which he was confronted. So far from supposing
that Gladstone would straddle between a moderate and a radical
position and then slip down on to the more radical one, Derby seems

to have assumed that, in the event of the split in the Liberal party, Gladstone would denounce Bright and rally such moderate Liberals as would support a modest bill. At first his expectation was realized: from the end of January until mid-March, Gladstone ran along a very conservative line. What Derby seems not to have foreseen was Disraeli's appeasement of the Radicals whom Gladstone had lost and Gladstone's lurch to the left in April and May. Despite Disraeli's attempt to co-operate with them in 1859, it is improbable that Derby expected him on Clause 3 to concede almost everything that Radicals had ever demanded. This is not to say that Derby would not have approved if he had predicted it, or that he could not see the advantages to be gained on the redistribution clauses by compromising over the borough franchise. But it is to suggest that, even if Disraeli foresaw the outcome, Derby almost certainly did not, had no intention of conceding to popular agitation or the parliamentary Radicals, and was led on, like everyone else in the Conservative party, because he convinced himself that no measure that was in sight would make much difference to the social structure and wanted to win more than he wanted anything else.

The point, therefore, that has to be grasped is that it is wrong to think of the division between Gladstone and Disraeli as a division of basic and fundamental principle. There were differences of manner, temper and direction. But, so far as aiming at different audiences, Gladstone and Disraeli for large parts of 1865, 1866 and 1867 were aiming at very much the same one. Both had at various times been followers of Sir Robert Peel. Both had a large body of conservative supporters—territorial or industrial—who wanted to avoid excessive enfranchisement. Both rejected mere numbers as the basis for a bill, though Disraeli, starting from the more conservative position, had to avoid the imputation of restrictiveness over the borough franchise and stressed the numbers question in order to establish that the counties would claim a larger number of seats in the future. Neither found it possible to prevail by relying on conservative forces alone. Though neither in any simple sense was a Radical, Disraeli had begun life as one and Gladstone had become the ally of Bright. Both needed at some point to lean on an advanced section of the House, though both at first made a point of appearing not to do so. The first battle between February 25 and April 12 was fought over the conservative Whigs and constitutional Liberals, and

Disraeli won it. But the Cave's defection in March made him seek support from Radicals in the process. It was the Cave's defection from Gladstone which enabled Disraeli to satisfy them. It was the Cave's refusal to play Gladstone's game which made Gladstone move leftward. It was this leftward shift which made it possible to maintain Conservative unity. Even in these circumstances the Conservative reaction between May 1 and May 8 made Disraeli's Radical alliance difficult to maintain, while the difficulty in which Disraeli was placed prevented Gladstone toppling himself off the point of calculated balance on which he remained until May 11. It was not until the defeat of May 9 had pushed Gladstone off balance that Disraeli was able more deliberately to follow him on May 17. It was only because Gladstone had lost, or rejected, the support of the Cave in April that Disraeli was in a position to do this at all.

It is idle to ask, and impossible to say, who took the lead. What matters is that both were pursuing the same combination of forces— a Conservative/Liberal/Radical spectrum of the sort which Gladstone and Russell had inherited from Palmerston, and which Disraeli wanted them to lose. Disraeli's flirtation with the Radicals did not begin until mid-March: it produced no permanent accession apart from Roebuck. His flirtation with the Cave produced nothing beyond Elcho. Distrust of Disraeli, Gladstone's success in reuniting the Liberal party in the following session, the Conservative party's Anglican platform at the general election of 1868 and the even stronger Liberal majority it produced, leave an impression of linear aggrandisement on the part of the party which Palmerston had left in the two years after he died. But the aggrandisement was erratic. That Disraeli failed, until the 'seventies, to capitalize the advantages he gained in 1867, it is no part of this volume to record. What is its business is the success he achieved in the exercise he had pursued from the day Palmerston died in attempting to unite in the sort of viable governing party which Palmerston had left that same combination of Whig, Radical, Irish and conservative forces on which Palmerston had relied. Between October 1865 and July 1866 Disraeli, Elcho, Lowe and Grosvenor between them destroyed the Palmerstonian coalition. Having failed by February 1867 to reconstruct it on a purely reactionary basis, the movement of Disraeli's policy must be seen thereafter, not by looking for a Disraelian doctrine or a political theory, but as an attempt in a moment of crisis for the Conservative party to persuade it to be as broad-based as Palmerston's had been, in the hope, as Lord Henry Lennox had put it when urging Disraeli to attend Palmerston's funeral, 'now [that] the lion is dead...to persuade the public that we are the right parties to roll ourselves upon the lion's skin'.[1]

What conclusion do we draw? There was no 'capitulation' to popular pressure. The Conservative party was not overborne by Beales and Bright. Disraeli did not revert to being a Radical. Derby did not suddenly discover Marx. Since there was to be a predominantly working-class electorate in the boroughs, they had to put themselves right with it, just as Lord John Manners expected Master and Servant legislation to 'put' them 'right with the working classes' among the old electorate. The result was a Tory social policy in the 'seventies. But what Derby and Disraeli were imitating in 1867 was Palmerston or Peel, and until March 1867 more Palmerston in his most conservative phase than anything else. There was nothing inevitable about the course they followed. If a restrictive Act could have been passed on a conservative basis, they would have passed it. If party conditions had been suitable, they would have persisted in March 1867 with a restrictive proposal, and would have appealed to the existing electorate if defeated on it. But the Cave's reluctance, Whig refusals and Disraeli's preferences had destroyed the chance of comprehensive resistance in July 1866. The consequence was a minority government and disjointed resistance in February 1867. Once he had been ousted on the more conservative line, Disraeli staked out his own. Just as Russell and Gladstone had to agree to immediate legislation in 1865/6 since they could get Forster to join the government and not Stanley, and adopted a more radical line because they were compelled to by the Cave's resistance, so the Cave/Cranborne resistance in 1867 drove Derby and Disraeli to greater concession than they may otherwise have intended. It was not the weakness of conservative feeling in the House of Commons which drove Disraeli this way, but the fact that Radical demands were not too extensive to be met and the obstacle he, among others, presented to any attempt to give viable party shape to a policy of resistance. If a united Conservative Cabinet had led the way on February 25 1867, it could have formed the nucleus of an unbeatable party. In the divided condition of February 26, it opened itself to any wind that blew.

EPILOGUE: THE LIMITATIONS OF
HISTORICAL KNOWLEDGE

'I will explain to you. . .all the arts by which [I passed the Reform bill]. . .
All the black devices I applied were simply these—upon every question I
took my own party into my confidence and when I had to appeal to an independent opposition, I remembered at all times that they were men of sense
and gentlemen.'

> Disraeli to working-men's meeting in Edinburgh, October 30
> 1867 (*The Times*, October 31)

The reader who has read thus far will want to know what right one
has to impute motive, intention and disingenuousness to the actors
whose personalities we have created out of the letters and speeches
which survive from the past. He will want to know by what process
we speak of Gladstone desiring, Disraeli wishing or Derby declining
to make this decision or that. He will ask how certain we are of the
existence of the tensions we have posited, and how far they can be
said to have determined the actions of the actors we have presented.
He will want to know how we justify the estimate we have made of
the extent to which they were affected by the context in which they
worked and the movement of events of which they were a part. This
chapter will explain that we cannot *justify* very much.

History in one sense discovers the past: in another sense it creates
it. To what extent historical writing is reconstruction is a question
which we are not concerned with here. But it is certainly construction—the rendering into continuous prose of as much as the material
justifies of the account we have decided to give. In construction of
this sort the preliminary assumptions are crucial. No 'past' can be
'created' without them. No material can be enlivened except by their
instrumentality. Any justification that may be offered of the use to
which the material has been put must begin by elucidating their
nature.

What this work has assumed is that politicians in positions as
responsible, as powerful and as difficult to manage as the politicians
we have watched leading, or failing to lead, the parties over which
they presided, cannot usefully be said themselves to have wanted,
desired, or believed anything except what was wanted by all other

participants in the system. It assumes, on the contrary, that, by the time they emerge as commanding figures, they have adopted a way of thinking and acting whose function is the playing of a role which their positions as repositories of the hopes and ambitions of their followers, forces them to respect. In a sense, therefore, it is idle to ask whether they self-consciously believed, personally desired or independently wanted anything in particular. Since others followed where they led, innumerable opportunities arose for the exercise of creative power, but they were limited by the situations in which they found themselves, and reflected as much as they created the climate in which they worked.

The assumptions this view involves about our understanding of political activity were laid out in the introduction to this work and in various parts of the author's two earlier works. They would not necessarily apply to all sorts of political activity. They might be inadequate guides to the politics of autocracy. But if it be asked why these assumptions were adopted, the answer must be that no antecedent reason exists why they should be more useful than others in understanding the politics of mid-nineteenth-century Britain. The belief that substantive judgements of policy cannot be understood in isolation from the personal and parliamentary context in which they were taken is an instrument of enquiry whose usefulness, if it is demonstrable at all, can be demonstrated only by detailed application. This book is such an application. The question it raises is—given these assumptions, about which argument is unnecessary—what justification does the material provide for the construction it produces?

In constructing a particular past, three sorts of knowledge play a part—knowledge derived from the first-hand material, knowledge derived from other historians' accounts of the period that is under consideration, and knowledge derived from explanation of the way in which earlier historians have come to their conclusions (i.e. the historiography of the subject). None can be irrelevant: in the continuous consciousness of the historian all play a part, whether they ought to or not. In approaching the first two, no historian can detach himself from that knowledge of the third which is embodied in the historiography of a subject.

Nevertheless, the third sort of knowledge is knowledge with a bar sinister, knowledge at second-hand, knowledge deflected and distorted by the preoccupations of people other than ourselves. Knowledge is comprehension without distortion of this sort. The essence of historical writing is the confrontation between the raw material from which it is made and the mind of the historian by whom it is given. The historiography of a subject is an historical exercise in its own right, but unless it embodies material we no longer have is irrelevant to the task of making sense for ourselves in the idiom we understand of the material the past has left us to deceive ourselves with. Each generation has its own task. Liberal history from Morley to Trevelyan established the belief that the Liberal party in Parliament was on the side of progress, not just in social, church and administrative questions which, given its assumptions about progress, on the whole was true, but also on matters affecting political rights and the distribution of political power, where its record was not so certain. The annexation of the political rights questions to these others produced an account of the events of 1867 which this book has not accepted. It is for this reason that, though raw material has been extracted from them, no reliance has been placed on the interpretations offered by G. M. Trevelyan, Herbert Paul, John Morley and Justin McCarthy.

Where earlier histories of the Reform bill are concerned the difficulties are no less great. Homersham Cox's *The Reform bills of 1866 and 1867*, published in 1868, was a Liberal contribution to the election of that year: it is not history, though it pinpoints the paradoxes history has to explain. Seymour's work[1] is a compendious summary of printed material about the electoral system in London and Wales. It says little about the political context of which the Reform question was a part, but suggests the need to explain why the franchise was not extended more quickly and equally than it was. J. H. Park's *The English Reform Bill of 1867* uses a great deal of magazine material as well as providing a political narrative: though it records the movement of events without attempting to explain it, its incoherence about governmental policy indicates the problems which need to be solved. Professor Herrick's[2] two articles are concerned with the enemies of Reform: they imply the need to explain, without actually explaining, why politicians of such impeccable integrity were defeated. Professor Briggs's chapters in *Victorian People* and *The Age of Improvement* assert connections between public and parliamentary politics: they have not been adopted in this work, but they indicate the points at which the central problems arise. Professor Gillespie's chapter on the Reform bill in her *Labor and Politics in England 1850–1867*, though not concerned with governmental policy in depth, makes clear the meagreness of expectation with which the Reform League approached the task of agitation. Dr Royden Harrison's chapter,[1] despite the criticisms offered in the prelude to the present work, gave specific twists to Professor Briggs's explanation which forced the present writer to ask his own questions more specifically. Professor Winter's article on the Cave[2] was not read until late in the process of composition. Though Professor Winter is wrong to think the division of April 12 decisive in parliamentary terms, it confirms much of the interpretation suggested here. Mr Paul Smith's *Disraelian Conservatism and Social Reform*, which was read in typescript after the body of this book had been completed, strengthens its view about Disraeli's party objectives in 1867. Ireland is not mentioned, but it suggests that Disraeli used a wider range of topic for accommodation than was originally supposed. Dr F. B. Smith's *The Making of the Second Reform Bill*, which was also consulted in typescript,[3] suggested at a number of turning points a number of questions to which answers have been given with which Dr Smith might not agree. If none of these works explains the passage of the bill itself, this is because none takes as specifically as it might the socially conservative character of the House of Commons or examines in detail the impact on the leading protagonists of the need they felt to react to one another.

In one sense a book of this sort depends absolutely on what has been established already. One would not know what to look for in the material relevant to mid-nineteenth-century parliamentary politics without the accounts given by Gash, Hanham, Kitson Clark, Burn, Thompson, Owen, Moore and Vincent[4] of the socially conservative attitudes which prevailed among the classes from which the two Houses of Parliament drew their members. Nor could one grasp the nature of the public agitation without the apparatus of scholarly investigation produced by exponents of what may be called the 'Labour School of History'. In understanding the part played by the trades unions, the welfare societies, the Reform League, the London Working Men's Association and other connected Reform organizations in the social history of the mid-nineteenth century, one can but be grateful to the Webbs, to the *Bulletin of the Society for Labour History*, and to Gillespie, Saville, Harrison, Cole, and so on.[1]

Yet, considering the work involved and the results produced, it is remarkable how little has been done to explain the connection between these two sorts of material. In the case of the first body of writing, the omission reflects the valid judgement that preliminary investigation is needed if the governing ethos is to be understood. In the case of the second, the difficulties are more fundamental. It is not just that its exponents provide no explanation, but that politico-sociological assumptions free them of the need to face the problem. Believing that class government is likely to be stupid as well as bad, they underestimate its attitude to working-class politics. Assuming, what they would not do for working-class action itself, a caricature instead of conducting an investigation, they produce a parody of the process of decision-making in which government and Parliament were involved. This affects the questions to which attention is given as much as it affects judgement itself. Even Dr Harrison and Professor Briggs, who are sensitive to the tactical complications of governmental thinking, show little grasp of the material available for providing an account of official, governmental or parliamentary action.

In relation to some phases of working-class politics in some societies this might not be surprising. But when applied to mid-nineteenth-century Britain it is extremely surprising. It is surprising in the first place, because the effective reaction of the rich and the ruling classes to the stirrings of which they were conscious beneath them was conditioned, so far as legislation was concerned, by the situation with which practical statesmen were confronted in Parliament. It is surprising, secondly, because close study of the mid-nineteenth-century Parliament strengthens the assumptions made by this school about the restrictive attitude of its members. It shows that parliamentary Liberals, as much as anyone else, wanted to keep power out of the hands of the working classes. It establishes as certainly as a systematic sociology could desire that, despite the existence of a reforming strand in the Liberal party on a wide range of social, church, economic and administrative questions which distinguished it from the body of Conservative backbenchers, the mid-nineteenth-century Parliament as a whole was united in consciousness of an obligation not to abdicate power to an organized urban proletariat.

It is surprising, finally, because, whatever desire the motivators of working-class political action may have felt to supersede Parliament, they wanted to be listened to in Parliament. Whether the leaders of agitation expected Parliament to give them what they wanted or whether they thought they would have eventually to take it for themselves, it was possible for Bright, Mill and Gladstone to establish popular reputations in the 1860s because they provided a link between the excluded classes and the inner sanctum of political power to which the leaders of agitation looked. However slow the London Trades Council may have been to connect itself with political demands for political rights, however extensive its suspicions of the guile of the Whig party, however strong its primary concern to exert industrial power, the centre of the agitation for the extension of the franchise was a desire to be in conflict with the existing House of Commons. Conflict may in some cases have been used in order to organize working-class feeling rather than to pass a Reform bill. Among those who had no parliamentary axe to grind, there was a desire to prevent the movement being used for the purposes of political groups within the Liberal party. But at every point in the story, the public movement was affected by what was done in Parliament and Parliament by what was done outside, even if the chief impact made by public agitation was made, not on Parliament as such, but on the Liberal party inside it. The author is conscious of his ignorance of large tracts of working-class history. Nevertheless, its concept of interaction is so limited and its understanding of governmental thinking so small that less attention has been given, at the point where parliamentary and popular radicalism met, to the judgements made by this school than to the knowledge by which its judgements are supported.

Our question, however, concerns neither the assumptions nor the historiographical tradition, but the material. The question is; does it sustain the interpretation argued in this book? And, first of all, what is the material?

Of the material which survives from 1865, 1866 and 1867, three main types have been used—the letters written by politicians to one another; their speeches in Parliament and outside, and their public acts as recorded in bills, statutes, parliamentary papers, newspaper reports and so on; and the comments of outside observers upon them. The last type of source has been used sparingly, where at all, unless, in the case of *The Times* under Delane and Lowe or the *Morning Star*, with Justin McCarthy writing leaders, it represented a well-informed body of first-hand knowledge or political participation close to the centre of events. The *Morning Star* reflects the attitude of those who, like Bright, were active at the point at which parliamentary and popular radicalism met. It has been used in chapter v as evidence of this in the absence of anything better. *The Times* provides evidence of a shift of one body of respectable opinion away from Russell after Palmerston's death. Both parties paid attention to *The Times* and took care, where they could, to carry Delane along with them. But *The Times* provides little evidence about the motives and calculations of politicians. Beyond suggesting the existence of a political atmosphere whose impact on politicians has to be established elsewhere, there is no reason to suppose that other newspapers provide this sort of material either.

With the speeches of politicians and their public acts the difficulties have been considerable. It has been assumed that a body of assumptions could be discerned if enough parliamentary speeches tended in the same direction, and that the socio-political assumptions laid out in the prelude to this work emerge with sufficient clarity from the speeches of 1867 to justify the belief that they constituted an effective opinion. Nevertheless, parliamentary speeches are neither self-explanatory nor to be taken at their face value. In using them one knows neither what moved a speaker to speak nor what objective he had in mind. This is so in three senses.

It is so in the first place because the mid-nineteenth-century Parliament was at least as much a place where business was conducted as a place where oratory was displayed. The point of oratorical display was to command assent, and to make reputations or keep them. Assent and reputation depended on the ability to say what was interesting to the House of Commons or would command a following in it. What ministers or members offered as reasons for actions they wished to recommend, however, need not be the 'reasons' by which we explain them. Throughout the session of 1867 Disraeli claimed to be applying Conservative principles. There is no doubt that some MP.s thought he was, and supported him because they thought this. Yet the historian has still to ask whether

Disraeli can be said to have treated speeches as anything more than convenient instruments for the conduct of business.

Caution is necessary, secondly, because parliamentary speeches do not show whether backbenchers were put up by frontbenchers to make them, whether they made them as instruments of self-advancement or whether they made them on their own initiative as heartfelt expressions of opinion. Sometimes one knows who was put up and why, though in these years there are not many cases in which one does. More often one has to guess from the context that this was done without knowing certainly that it was done. It is possible, for example, that Gabriel Goldney's modification of the lodger franchise was concerted with Disraeli or Taylor, but there is no evidence of this.[1] Before deciding to stand as a Conservative in 1865, R. J. B. Harvey was willing to support whichever party would be more likely to give him a baronetcy. Though they are significant if he thought them acceptable to the House of Commons, the words quoted on page 50 from his speech of March 25 1867 may well have been designed to assist him in getting one. But one diary reference from Kimberley, who had refused to support him as a Liberal candidate on that basis, is not enough to establish the connection.[2] Some of the Conservatives who defended household suffrage in the debates of March 18 and March 25 spoke as supporters of the government. The Cabinet's reversion to household suffrage in March 1867 was recommended in discussion in Cabinet on the ground that 'we' should 'trust the people'. This phrase was used in the second reading debate by H. G. Liddell, the son of Lord Ravensworth. Ravensworth had been a Conservative MP. in the 'thirties, 'forties and 'fifties and was a close friend of Derby with a common interest in the translation of classical verse: in addition he was uncle to Viscount Barrington, Derby's private secretary. From an early stage in March, Barrington encouraged ministers to drop the duality clauses from the bill, and may well have passed on word to Liddell before Liddell spoke.[3] It is impossible to establish this. The absence of evidence does not mean that he did not do so. Liddell in any case had independent interests of his own in paternalistic legislation.[4] One may be attributing power to Derby or Disraeli which they did not have. Nevertheless, in evaluating speeches of this sort one must consider the possibility that ministers were able to persuade MP.s to express opinions which they would hardly have held if they had not been induced to turn their rhetoric in one direction rather than another.

The third respect in which parliamentary speeches present problems is no less important. A great deal of information is available in newspapers, in Dod's *Parliamentary Companion* and McCalmont's *Parliamentary Poll-book*, and in parliamentary debates about the character of the constituencies MP.s represented, and about the nature of the issues about which personally they felt most strongly. It is possible to draw a picture of the grass-roots psephology of a great many MP.s and a chart of their personal orientations. This has not been done systematically in the present work, but an attempt to do it might show that a very large number of MP.s—much larger than the number suggested here—voted in Reform divisions on grounds which had little to do with the merits of the Reform bill itself. The difficulty in each case is to establish that this was so. Few MP.s went as far as the new Lord Beauchamp who thought the Conscience Clause 'a matter of far higher importance'[1] than the Reform bill, but it is impossible to avoid believing that many more had their attitudes determined by local, personal or extraneous factors which do not always appear on the surface.

Sometimes they do appear on the surface. Bright wanted to make the municipal and parliamentary boundaries coincide. Hibbert wanted to keep them separate. He wanted this because much of his own support lay outside Oldham: he came as near to saying so as an MP. decently could.[2] The amendment moved by Colonel Gilpin to restore to Luton, Keighley, St Helens and Barnsley the separate representation removed by Disraeli in order to provide for the seats to be given to the cities as a result of the Cabinet's acceptance of Horsfall's motion, was blatant. Gilpin was Conservative MP. for Bedfordshire. Since the House had already decided that no existing parliamentary borough should be disfranchised completely,[3] he did not suggest, as a Radical might, that the four seats he needed should be taken from the small boroughs. He proposed instead that the principle of Laing's first motion—the removal of one member from every two-member borough with a population of less than 10,000—should be extended to cover the four boroughs next above 10,000 in population, intending in this way both to remove from his own constituency a large urban element in Luton and Dunstable and to convince electors there (in case they remained constituents) that he had done his best to give them the borough status and extended enfranchisement they were supposed to want and which they would be particularly annoyed at being deprived of if, once promised, it was withdrawn.

To do this, however, involved removing one member each from four other boroughs—Tiverton, Tamworth, Warwick and Barnstaple—which stimulated among members for these boroughs a similar attitude in reply. It united the Conservative Walrond of Tiverton with Denman, who on almost every other Reform question was an advanced Liberal and who expected household suffrage to shake the Liberal party in Tiverton. It united Jonathan Peel and Sir Robert Peel (not relatives) of Tamworth, Arthur Peel, Sir Robert's uncle (Liberal), and George Repton (Conservative) of Warwick against the motion. It united Colonel Stuart of Bedford, Algernon Egerton of South Lancashire and Henry Beaumont of south-west Yorkshire, the last two of whom had Burnley or St Helens connections, in favour. It made Denman contrast Tiverton with Luton and Dunstable, whose sole 'interest [was] the plaiting of straw for the manufacture of straw bonnets...carried on in agricultural cottages by large numbers of women and children'. It made Gilpin describe as 'very silly' Repton's assertion that it was bad taste on his part to have placed Luton at the head of the list. It produced exchanges between him and Sir Robert Peel 'who did not know where Keighley [was]', who thought that the houses built in Luton in the last twenty years had 'all been built of straw' and who, without wishing 'for a moment to cast a slur on the morality of Luton' claimed that 'when we have a population in Luton in which the women exceed the men in numbers, there cannot be any doubt ...and I should move Returns as regards legitimacy and illegitimacy if the clause passed...that if the town [had] increased [in size]', the reasons could not have been creditable. It brought out Newdegate, the spokesman of territorialism, in favour of disfranchising completely the four smallest boroughs with populations below 5,000. When Disraeli, who wanted the motion dropped in order to get on with the bill, succeeded in defeating it, Gilpin 'was not at all surprised that...after [his] vaccilating and inconsistent conduct on the bill...[Disraeli] should now ridicule a proposal of his own of a few night's ago'.[1]

In these cases connections do not need to be made. In other cases, they are more difficult to establish. It is, for example, a fact that the bill of March 18 proposed a large enfranchisement in Oldham and a very small one in Bradford and Birmingham. What is not a fact is the connection between this and Bright's, Forster's and Hibbert's attitudes to it. Gladstone got in for South Lancashire in 1865 when his Liberal partners did not because he attracted Conservative voters as well as Liberal ones, but it is not clear what, if any, connection this had with Gladstone's conduct in the House of Commons in 1866 and 1867. J. G. Hubbard, like Cranborne, was a bitter enemy of the Conscience Clause, Pakington, its most effective exponent, a member of the Cabinet. Was this why, though he seldom appears in Cranborne's and Heathcote's discussions, Hubbard voted consistently against the government in 1867? Lowe and Horsman were notorious anti-tractarians: did this increase their hostility to Gladstone? Pim, the Dublin Quaker MP., was a broad-based Radical who collected a wide variety of Dublin votes in 1865 including Cardinal Cullen's: was he an Adullamite on electoral grounds or on Irish ones? Was he twisting Gladstone's arm or hoping, like Clanricarde, McEvoy and Bowyer, to be able to twist Disraeli's?

Edward James QC. had been elected as a Palmerstonian Liberal in Manchester at the general election of 1865. In June 1867 he voted with Disraeli against Laing's proposal to give third seats to large cities (including Manchester), giving as his reasons the fact that the bill without Laing's amendment would be so far from settling the question that there would have to be a better bill later. What motive can one impute here? Was Roebuck's reaction a reflection of respectable opinion in Sheffield: or was it a facet of Roebuck's hatred of Gladstone? In Roebuck there seems to have been a bleeding heart: 'kind words' he told Disraeli 'to me are so rare that when they come they make a great impression.'[1] Did he support Disraeli because both were enemies of Whiggery? Did he hate Gladstone because of Gladstone's religion, his manner, his doctrine, or his success in a party in which Roebuck had been a failure? Isaac Holden, the Liberal MP. for Knaresborough, proposed an amendment to prevent owners of land within borough boundaries creating faggot votes for borough members: why, as Sir Henry Edwards, who knew Knaresborough, asked, except that Holden's Conservative colleague—B. T. Wood—and his Conservative predecessors both 'had a good deal of land within the borough which gave votes as there were several buildings upon it of stone or brick having doors and, he dared to say, windows also that were occupied by cows and horses'.[1] Was Torrens's co-operation in 1867 affected by the government's support for his Artisans' and Labourers' Dwellings bill, or was the support coincidental?[2] How many Catholic Irish MP.s were regular Liberals? Can W. H. Gregory's fluctuating membership of the Cave be explained by reference to anything except the party leaders' attitudes to his Irish Land bill? Was The O'Donoghue's support for the Reform League (when he had supported Disraeli in the early sixties) connected with his bankruptcy, and the success he had in borrowing money from Liberal members?[3] Above all, did Fenian violence in Ireland and its threatened extension to England help to make English MP.s so reactionary that they accepted from Disraeli a more extensive bill than they would have accepted from Gladstone? Individually, most of these questions are marginal to the problem we are considering: together they transform the interpretation. If this factor has been under-emphasized, it is because the author knows less than he should and is willing to guess less often than he might.

These sources have all provided material on which to work. Nevertheless, the centre of this book is rooted in the raw material—the collections of letters written by ministers and politicians to one another in the course of the years under discussion. This source is voluminous and on its face rich. It might seem to present no problems. Yet problems exist.

We have been asking what influences played upon, what intentions were maintained, what prevision was possible and what success was achieved by the leading actors on the political stage. Since all were literate and highly articulate, it might seem that one has only to underline and quote the various sentences which indicate influence or intention at a particular time. Whether one does this as summarily, however, depends on the view taken of the character of the writer and his relation with his correspondent, and on the guess one hazards at the purpose correspondence served. In a polity and Parliament whose rhetoric assumed a public level of motivation, guesses are difficult to sustain: where they rest on judgement of personal ambition and calculation, they are more difficult still. This must almost necessarily be so. Even if the original version of Knatchbull-Hugessen's diary[4] described his attempt to join the

Conservative party in 1865/6 at the same time as he was trying to get promotion from Russell in the Liberal government of which he was a member, the version he left for posterity in later life did not. We know about it because letters passed between Spofforth, the Conservative chief agent, and Disraeli in which Spofforth's negotiations with Knatchbull-Hugessen are described from their starting-point at a meal in the Grand Hotel, Brighton.[1] Whether Lowe believed that he could lead the Whig party or a Whig/Liberal coalition, he said the opposite in terms which suggest that he never expected to do so.[2] We guess, and perhaps guess wrongly, that he believed he could by tying together his manifest jealousy of Gladstone, the pains he took with Lady Salisbury and Stanley and the judgement that a man who combined intellectual clarity, political energy and personal insensitivity in Lowe's proportions might well have thought this possible. Halifax's intentions are hidden: the discovery of further material is unlikely to show what they were. He resigned from the Russell government in February 1866, tried to keep the government in office in June, imposed himself on Russell and Gladstone in the winter and waited for the Derby government to fall. He nowhere wrote that he wanted to be Prime Minister: he was never mentioned as a possible leader except by Elcho in anger,[3] and by Disraeli by implication[4]. The leadership was much on his mind, but, despite great experience he seems not to have been a serious contender. The fact that he was not so in fact, however, need not have stopped him thinking he might be. There is no doubt that he injured his head in a riding accident in January 1866: there is no *reason* to doubt the genuineness of the reasons he gave for resigning. Yet he had hinted at resignation when Palmerston died, was in no sense an ardent reformer. He may have decided to strengthen his position by detaching himself from the errors for which he expected Russell's Cabinet to be responsible. There is some evidence of an attempt to create a Liberal/Conservative government under his leadership in June 1866, but the evidence is uncertain, does not implicate him directly and is almost illegible.[5]

This range of consideration is of great importance. Lowe, Laing, Elcho, Horsman and Earl Grey had all been ministers at one time or another. All probably wanted to be ministers again. If the best of the Cave's leaders differentiated themselves from other frontbench Liberals because of personal disappointment, and if policy disagreement might have disappeared if personal disappointment had been removed, then while not denying that the views they expressed struck notes with Liberal backbenchers, one may wonder what view should be taken of the policy itself. In maintaining party connection men were as important as measures. Good names guaranteed more certainly than good opinions that policies whose direction was agreed would be administered sensibly. Shaftesbury distrusted the Russell government as much because of what it was as for what it did. Much of the disaffection felt by the Hutts, Hugessens, Bouveries, Peels and Lowes[1] in the 1860s arose less from doubts about policy than from the evidence they saw that the best way to get on in the Liberal party (if one were not a Whig of the highest connection) was to vote against the government. That there were differences of direction and manner is not in doubt. That others would have played the parts they played if they had not played them themselves is by no means impossible. But policy clashes, parliamentary dissension and oratorical conflict of the sort which Lowe created in 1866 do not necessarily provide evidence of cleavage as fundamental as Lowe's presentation suggested.

This applies not only to the Liberal party, but to the Conservative party as well. It is difficult at first sight to see why Conservatives followed Disraeli in April, May and June 1867. The possible explanations are numerous—Derby's authority, hatred of Gladstone's manner and Disraeli's ability to play on both; the feeling that, if the Conservative party could not solve the Reform question it would never solve anything; the belief that the Church of England would be in greater danger from a Gladstone government and Reform bill than from any immediate extension of the franchise; the fear that any redistribution of seats which a Liberal bill might pass would be worse than Disraeli's; the instinctive belief, crucial to party existence, that the Liberal party was run for the benefit not just of Whigs, who were sometimes less honest than they should be, but by 'snobs' like Bright—public deceivers who maintained the odious pretence, in appealing for the suffrage of the poor, that they too were enemies of the rich when, in the words of a duke's brother, who could not afford to take the Lord Lieutenancy of Ireland in 1866, 'the people in these days who add house to house and field to field' were not the heirs of territorial wealth, but 'Bright's own class, the Mathesons and Morrisons [and] Marshalls and Strutts'.[2]

These feelings, whether held as social prejudices by Manners or Sir Henry Bulwer or as literary adornments by the younger Lytton,[1] come to light with comparative ease: when held by obscure backbenchers, they do not. But even when uncovered, they do not explain all that calls for explanation. They explain why Disraeli had a chance in March 1867 once party feeling was aroused. They do not explain why Cranborne, who shared these feelings,[2] lost, why Disraeli won, why General Peel's misgivings were not translated into action; or why Hardy supported the bill through all its changes.

Hardy shared all the doubts backbenchers felt about Disraeli and his objectives. Had he resigned between March and May, the government would probably have fallen. He did not resign. He made up for the good resignation would have done him with Conservative backbenchers by achieving success as a ministerial speaker. While Disraeli spoke with one voice, he spoke with another. The fact that he spoke as well as Disraeli reassured those who disliked Disraeli. The fact that two voices spoke made it difficult to object.[3] Since Hardy did not resign, he was given prominence. Since he was given prominence, he had to attack Gladstone. Having done so successfully he was more than a little committed. We shall never know, for his diary does not tell, what combination of personal flattery, ministerial inexperience, genuine uncertainty and unexpected success combined to make him a supporter of proposals he instinctively distrusted. We can but wonder. We can do very little more.

In some cases more can be done: if there were no landmarks nothing could be done at all. One can, for example, almost certainly take at its face value a great deal of Derby's correspondence with Disraeli in late 1866. Derby—ill, tired, detached, anxious to avoid a repetition of 1858/9 and old and perhaps inconsiderate enough of the feelings of others not to worry about the effect his actions might have on the prospects of a successor—almost certainly said what he thought in a series of letters about the parliamentary situation in the months following the session of 1866.[4] This is an historical judgement: it may be wrong. It stands at the basis of the interpretation given here of his policy in late 1866 and a good part of 1867.

If it is reasonable to make this judgement about Derby's letters to Disraeli, the same cannot be said of Disraeli's letters to Derby.[5] Disraeli faced the same problem—that the Liberal party, while unable to pass a Reform bill of its own, did not want the Conservative party to pass one either, and expected a Conservative failure or botched-up attempt to establish it in office for another generation. But Disraeli's situation was different from Derby's. His career, unlike Derby's, was not at an end: he did not spend parts of the session in bed, too ill to turn over without help.[1] Where, at a certain point, Derby could afford to throw off the party politician in a certain statesmanlike grandeur, Disraeli could not. In correspondence with Derby in late 1866, Disraeli was cautious about Reform commitments for the coming session: he showed no *enthusiasm* for any. Yet if Derby could see that something would have to be done if the government was to survive, Disraeli cannot have failed to see this also. It may be that he was unwilling to take the initiative on a dangerous question. It may be that he was sheltering behind Derby so that Derby would take the blame if anything went wrong. It may be that he was expecting to be able to fight an election on an anti-Radical platform, though neither he nor Derby seems to have thought this possible without some Reform proposal or other. It may be, as he said, that he thought the best thing from every point of view was a prolonged Reform crisis which would damage Whig control of the Liberal party. His letters are long and detailed, but they provide no certain explanation. They contain no statement of his attitude to the leadership question: the only ground for thinking that he wanted to shift the blame to Derby is a letter to Cranborne in late December in which he made it clear that though 'Lord Derby, about the time you were here, thought it inevitable [and had] now modified...his views...I have, throughout, been against legislation'.[2]

Yet the suspicion persists that this factor must have affected his judgement throughout the period we have been discussing. The Conservative party had spent the previous session resisting Reform: there was no reason to think it wanted to change its position now. Cranborne was the minister most vigorously opposed to legislating in the immediate future. He reflected, if he did not represent, a wide range of party opinion: earlier in the year, though a long-term enemy of Disraeli, he had wanted to keep him while getting rid of Derby. In 1866 Disraeli had thought much about the leadership. It was certainly in his mind in March and April:[3] it is unlikely that it was not in his mind in November and December and throughout the period we have been discussing. But there is no evidence that it was.

Disraeli, it may be said, is a difficult case, involving particular difficulties. But Disraeli is not alone in presenting problems. Personal prospects at the highest level are difficult to uncover. Where unsuccessful politicians emerge from the darkness in which history has left them, their *personal* intentions are blatant. Earl Percy, Sir Robert Peel, Baillie-Cochrane, Lord Arthur Clinton, Sir William Hutt and Bouverie[1] are one-dimensional figures who leave little room for conjecture. But where an operator like Halifax, a calculator like Lowe, or great exerters of creative energy like Gladstone and Disraeli are under consideration, the difficulties are insuperable. Gladstone was a dialectical artist using as the subject for virtuosity a finely drawn casuistry of exact commitments. Disraeli was a destructive showman manipulating the necessities of opposition in order to ridicule the inconsistencies of government, but unwilling to be committed in advance to anything which would put government out of his reach or make it, once undertaken, more difficult to conduct. Even when innumerable hints emerge that this or that was intended by either of them, and they can be found confirming that it was, we can no more be certain of penetrating the complicated intelligence, suppressed agitation, eloquent self-justification and strength of mind and will which make up Gladstone than we can combine in coherent proportions the uncapturable combination of contrived ordinariness, controlled geniality, brazen insincerity and utter verbal unscrupulousness which constitute Disraeli. It is with these considerations in mind that we may look more closely at the material which sustains the impression we have left of the central lines of movement in the years under discussion.

The first thing to notice is that, with three or four notable exceptions, the evidence is fuller for the periods of the parliamentary recesses than for periods of the parliamentary session. The reasons are mechanical—that letters were less necessary when politicians met daily. The consequence is that we can justify a good deal more certainly our view of Derby's and Disraeli's intentions between October 1865 and February 1866 and in those parts of the period between August 1866 and February 1867 when neither was in London than we can for the period when both were. Similarly, the Whig/Liberal managers reveal themselves more fully for the same periods and less fully for the periods of actual parliamentary activity. This means that one can be more certain of the considerations which guided the leaders on both sides of the House of Commons in preparing for the two sessions than one can in assessing their reactions to events once the session had begun. One's ignorance must not be exaggerated: the number of letters written during the sessions and still existing is enormous. In constructing atmosphere volume is invaluable. But if in attempting to describe the leadership of the two parties, one had to rely on the letters ministers and opposition frontbenchers wrote to one another *during* the sessions, though a narrative could be constructed, its defects would be extensive.

Fortunately, other sources touch on the sessions themselves and provide material for explanation of governmental and opposition activity within it—the letters written by Derby and others to Malmesbury, whose wife was ill, and Derby's one letter to Naas, who was in Ireland at the moment of crisis in February–March 1867: Brand's correspondence with Gladstone and Halifax: Elcho's letters to Grosvenor: Derby's letters to General Grey and the Queen: and the diaries of prominent figures on both sides of the House which are as full for the periods when Parliament was sitting as for the periods when it was not.[1]

The letters to Naas and Malmesbury, though they are few in number and cease as soon as the recipients returned to London, are of value as accounts of Cabinet decisions at the beginning of March. Brand's correspondence exposes the tactical considerations in his mind, though they do not establish that these considerations were Gladstone's. Derby's letters to the Queen and General Grey, though suspect as simple statements of intention, are invaluable in establishing the dates and content of Cabinet decisions. Elcho's letters reveal, as certainly as letters can, the objectives aimed at by the Cave in the central period between the middle of February and the first week of April. All these have been used freely.

Excluding Gladstone's, which is not available for study, and Shaftesbury's, which was not consulted, eight diaries were used— Carnarvon's, Malmesbury's, Halifax's, Northcote's, Lord John Manners's, Knatchbull-Hugessen's, Bright's and Gathorne Hardy's. All present problems. They present problems firstly because only Hardy's and Lord John Manners's have been available in their original form. Both provide sufficient material about Cabinet

328

opinion: Hardy's reveals both the doubts felt by Conservatives and the methods Disraeli used to counter them. Though Hardy's is fuller than Manners's, both are useful, and both appear to be authentic. Northcote's diary covers the period from January to June 1866: it exists in the British Museum in a typescript form of which the original seems not to have survived. It has been used as an accurate account of the gossip Northcote picked up in these months from Disraeli and from others he met at the house of his brother-in-law, T. H. Farrer, the permanent official at the Board of Trade, and as evidence, sometimes unwitting, both of Northcote's personal fears and of the possibility of fusion in 1866. Carnarvon's *Journal* almost certainly no longer exists: it has been used in the truncated form in which Sir Arthur Hardinge quoted from it in his *Life of Carnarvon*. It has been assumed that he quoted it accurately: it has been used as evidence of Cabinet feeling in late 1866 and early 1867. Malmesbury's *Diary*, again in a printed version of which the original has not been found, has been used sparingly except where it underlines material which receives confirmation from elsewhere. Extracts from it were published by Malmesbury himself in his *Memoirs of an Ex-Minister* in 1884: it is useful chiefly to suggest the atmosphere in which Reform questions were considered. In the case of Bright's diary the original is not available: the version published by Walling in 1930 has been taken to be accurate so far as it goes, with the provision that one would expect to find more about the organization of the public agitation and that some parts of it may have been omitted for 1866 and 1867. In all these cases the diaries have been used to suggest the atmosphere in which Reform politics were being considered. Though all contribute to the general picture, no part of it depends so much on any one that a want of authenticity in the version used would damage the structure of the narrative.

Of the two remaining diaries—Knatchbull-Hugessen's has been used in the manuscript form in which it is available in the Kent County Record Office. The original has not been seen. The Maidstone copy is a version which Knatchbull-Hugessen seems to have prepared for publication (but never published) at some time after he became a Tory in the 1880s. It is a rich store of political gossip which there is no reason in most cases to think was not an accurate representation of the original. There are hints that, writing in retrospect for publication after the Reform Act of 1884, Knatchbull-

Hugessen may have cast himself for a role as the far-seeing prophet who predicted the need for another redistribution bill in twenty years' time. It is also the case that there is no mention in the diary of the negotiations he conducted with Spofforth, the Conservative chief agent, in 1865/6 with a view to himself becoming a Conservative. Nevertheless, a judgement has been made of inherent credibility and material has been taken from it so long as it does not markedly clash with what has been taken from other less suspect contemporary material.

It is, in fact, only with the Halifax *Journal* that any serious problem arises, though even here it is likely that the appearance of the original would reveal that no problem exists. The copy that has been used is a typed copy, prepared perhaps for J. G. Lockhart's life of Halifax's son. The original seems to have been written along with, or immediately after, the events it deals with. It covers the period from June 1866 to mid-1867 and seems designed to justify Halifax's attempts to hold back Russell and Gladstone at their moments of greatest intrepidity. It is unlikely that the diary is an invention, but it has been necessary to bear in mind the desire Halifax undoubtedly felt in writing it to present Gladstone and Russell (and especially Russell) in an unfavourable light, and to clear himself of responsibility for the Liberal collapse in 1867. It has also been felt, without much confidence, that Halifax's account of his activities between June 18 and June 25 may have been less than frank—that he may have been aiming to establish a Liberal/Conservative party under his guidance or leadership rather than anyone else's. The attitude revealed by the *Journal* however, coheres in general with the attitude revealed in the letters Halifax wrote in 1866/7 to Earl Grey and to Brand. Given a fundamental identity of view between these two sources it has on the whole been accepted as a suspect, but useful, source of material about the attitude of a central and well-informed parliamentary Whig and about the opinions he records as prevailing in the Liberal party. When combined with these other diaries, and with innumerable letters written to one another by politicians, it has been thought safe to base upon them the account of the political atmosphere which constitutes the framework of this book.

However, although the parliamentary atmosphere of 1867 is attested by a large body of first-hand material, the amount of direct evidence about the minds and intentions of the major actors is extremely slender. By direct evidence we mean letters in which a politician explains the grounds and objectives of his policies with what we take to be an absence of tactical intent, or with a tactical intention that is readily discernible. This is extremely rare. Bright's letters to his wife, Bright's diary entries and his correspondence with fellow-Radicals, with Gladstone and Russell and with Reform League leaders constitute evidence of this sort. They do not conclusively sustain the impression given here of Bright's attitude to each stage in the parliamentary process. Elcho's letters were collected by Elcho year by year for most of his life. The preservation of both sides of his correspondence provides a massive record of his work. Even if it was collected for our benefit, it reveals so much, both good and bad, intentionally and unintentionally, about Elcho's character that we need no more, except to know, what we shall never know, whether he really thought he could lead a major party. Russell in these years was breaking up physically and mentally. His correspondence could hardly be the work of a man who was deceiving posterity. It has been used as evidence of Russell's condition, though that condition involved such monumental indecisiveness as to make a consistent account difficult to achieve.

In Gladstone's and Disraeli's correspondence, on the other hand, there is little sign of any opening of the mind. To Gladstone correspondence seems to have been a public act with a public purpose: he did not use it at this time as a means of reaching decisions. Like Disraeli, he had few intimates and was under heavy pressure. Once the session began one discovers as much about his frame of mind from reading Acland's letters to him as from reading Gladstone's letters themselves. Nevertheless, at certain points it is possible to establish Gladstone's party and policy orientation with as much certainty as can reasonably be expected.

Before he went abroad for the winter of 1866, Gladstone took pains in writing to Brand to show that he did not intend to identify himself with Bright: he gave this as one reason for going abroad.[1] It is as certain as anything can be that he was thinking in terms of party advantage, calculating that, so long as the Liberal party was not tarred with Bright's brush, it would reap the reward of the failure Disraeli would face in producing a successful bill. There is no reason to doubt that this is what Gladstone thought, even if only in the public sense that this was how he believed a Whig chief whip expected a potential Liberal leader to talk: Chapter III is based on this assumption. Once Gladstone returned from Italy, however, the material for constructing his intentions is oblique. Halifax, Russell, Brand, Acland and others wrote a great deal more to Gladstone than Gladstone wrote to them. He had very little correspondence with Bright, or with so intimate a follower as Granville. The Argyll papers are missing. Few Gladstone letters of importance survive from the four months which follow January 1867. It has been necessary to interpret these letters, his speeches, other people's views of his actions, the letters of Halifax, Acland and others to him and his actual decisions in the light of the context in which he was thinking in 1865 and mid- and late-1866. It cannot be maintained that the account given in chapter v(ii) of his difficulties in these months has anything resembling the certainty or definitiveness of the account given in the preceding chapter of his attitude before his holiday began. If the material is studied with different assumptions, or if a different view is taken of the context on which interpretation rests, the outcome might be different.

It might be different in a particular sense. It might impute to Gladstone a desire, not to destroy Disraeli's government and the Disraeli bill (though that objective is unmistakable until March 22 1867), but, at any rate thereafter, to conduct himself so as to avoid the odium among Whigs of having in office to propose a bill which went farther than they would want a bill to go. It might, that is to say, impute to Gladstone a desire not to return to office until the Reform question was out of the way, thus at the same time both avoiding the need he would face in office to propose a household suffrage bill in order to satisfy his radical wing, and of satisfying them nevertheless by leaving the impression that he wanted Disraeli to go as far as household suffrage pure and simple himself. This view has been rejected because it is far from clear that in March anyone could have expected Disraeli to do what he did in May, and survive in office. Unless we impute to Gladstone (what is highly improbable) a sympathetic prevision of the success Disraeli achieved in the course he took, it is much more reasonable to assume that he expected Disraeli to fall, and wished to hasten the process. The simpler explanation has been preferred, not least because it seems likely that Gladstone disliked the idea of household suffrage pure and simple and wished to impose his preferences on the Liberal party, whatever difficulties its members would face with their constituents as a consequence. This in its turn depends on the assumption that, when Heathcote found Gladstone thoroughly upset by the prospect of household suffrage pure and simple in committee,[1] Gladstone was talking like one earnest churchman to another, and not like a party politician fishing for support. The material is not extensive. It can be read either way, and may well be read in other ways by other historians in the future. In 1866 and 1867 where party calculation was concerned Gladstone moved crabwise. He was certain of his general intention—to shift the Palmerstonian alliance slightly leftward, but he wanted to keep the alliance in existence. To keep it in existence, while satisfying all its elements, necessitated a measure of calculated deception. If, at various times, he deceived his contemporaries, it is possible that he has deceived us.

Nor is construction of Disraeli's intentions made easier by an absence of letters from Disraeli once the session began. As with Gladstone, so with him. There is desire to make the Conservative party the centre of the scene by attaching to it as many floating groups as possible, while seeming to Conservatives to be abandoning as few as possible of the planks in their platform. There is abundant evidence of his desire to detach Whigs and Adullamites from the Palmerstonian coalition[2] and convincing evidence of his desire to avoid fusion in mid-1866,[3] but only the most fragmentary material to support the view that his conduct in 1867 was designed to carry the Cave along while not capitulating to it. There is evidence from the Cave's side of unwillingness to enter a coalition except as part of a major reconstruction of the Conservative party. The only direct evidence of unwillingness on Disraeli's part comes from his talks in the summer of 1866 with Northcote, who in any case would suffer from coalition, from the fact that Disraeli said one thing to Northcote and another to a party meeting, and from a single letter in February 1867.[4] There is no evidence that he wanted to capitulate to public agitation and only two pieces of indirect material from late 1866 to suggest that he had then an intention of out-trumping the Liberal party as he did nine months later.[5] In view of his experience in 1858 and 1859 there was no reason why he should expect Radical support and even less reason to do so in a situation in which Russell and Gladstone had replaced Palmerston. There is a good deal of support for the view (which the Liberal leaders held themselves) that he was meditating a procedural trick,[1] but none to show certainly what he expected the outcome to be except that it would damage Liberal unity. It is clear that he wished to be uncommitted about Reform. There is no reason to doubt that he meant what he said when he objected to including Lowe in any fusion that might occur because that would be too decisively the adoption of an anti-Reforming role.[2]

What Disraeli intended beyond that is a matter of contextual plausibility, but the context imposed a high degree of reticence on him. In order to carry the Conservative party along at all, he had to avoid any sign of pressing too hard or wishing to go too far in reforming directions. Despite anxiety to establish the disenfranchising character of Russell's part in the 1832 Act (in working-class directions at least), there is no sign in late 1866 or early 1867 of extensive sympathy for working-class political rights. This is not to say that Disraeli would not have thought it desirable in 1866 to go as far as he did in May 1867 if he could have been certain that the Conservative party would follow. But since neither the Conservative party nor most parts of the Liberal party would have followed if he had made this clear, there is no reason to suggest that he had anything so clearly formulated as an intention. The intention did not begin to be formulated until it had become clear that he would be fighting the next election on a greatly enlarged register with a working-class majority in all the English, Welsh and Scottish boroughs. The context in which he was operating in 1866 was the outcome of a strategy which had destroyed the Russell government by exposing a democratic streak. He could not suddenly become democratic himself. There is, it must be emphasized, no conclusive evidence of this. We do not find Disraeli saying so on paper, and it is not certain that it would be evidence if we did.

There is nothing to show why he committed the government to sketch the terms of the bill it intended to propose before the resolutions were debated on February 25. Buckle places in January his conversion to immediate action, explaining it by reference to the changed state of public feeling. It is not clear, however, in what way either Disraeli's policy or public feeling had changed in January. Disraeli was committed to resolutions in October: in that respect nothing changed until the decision of February 26 to produce a bill instead of continuing with resolutions. The Grey commission was not to be given powers of recommendation, but, as a commission of enquiry, it remained a possibility. It is true that December and January saw the London Trades Council's decision to give corporate support to the League instead of the individual support its members had been allowed to give before. It is true that a crisis of major proportions had arisen in Ireland. But there is no evidence that these considerations affected Disraeli's, or Derby's, judgement and we have assumed that they did not. We have assumed instead that parliamentary opinion was decisive on Parliament's return and that it was the success achieved by Gladstone in avoiding shipwreck on the resolutions which made it necessary to move forward.

In interpreting Disraeli's actions once this step forward had been taken, the difficulties are no less great. For the critical week after February 25, there are about a dozen letters from Disraeli himself. None of them *says* that he wants to appease the public agitation. The nearest he comes to doing so is the suggestion that the government must think not of Parliament but of the country. 'The country', however, could mean a country which was reacting against Bright, or it could mean a country which would not accept duality from a Tory government. He nowhere says that the government must reorganize on a basis of hostility to Gladstone. All he says is that, since Gladstone's speech of February 26 implied that he would propose a £5 rating franchise to distinguish himself from the government's £6, he had 'weakened and embarrassed his position by his programme' and 'committed himself in a manner which may extricate you [i.e. Derby]'. He can be seen trying to persuade Derby that the Carlton Club meeting of February 28 in favour of household suffrage was more united than it was, but we do not know how far he initiated it.[1] In the three weeks following (except indirectly in a conversation reported in Bright's diary) there is no actual statement from him of a desire to meet Radical wishes. Nor does he provide conclusive evidence that he was thinking more of a general election than of carrying a bill. His speeches of March 18 and March 26 were masterpieces of obfuscation. Unless deductions are made from the atmosphere and the feeling others had that he was reacting to Gladstone, they would be difficult to interpret. There is no evidence to support the claim he made in accepting Hodgkinson's amendment on May 17 that the abolition of compounding 'was contained as part of our original scheme',[1] and much to show that the Cabinet thought the opposite. There is no letter in which Disraeli promises Elcho a fixed-line franchise if Elcho would support him on April 12, though there are a number of reports, including one from Elcho himself, that Elcho had received the impression that he had. It is not clear who first gave party Radicals the idea that Disraeli would concede as much as possible: this feeling existed before March 25. All we have are the widely-attested fears felt by Liberals, a few diary entries from Manners, letters from Barrington, Derby and other ministers to each other (which seldom mention Disraeli) and the disgust Hardy showed in his diary at the speed with which Disraeli tried to abandon duality as soon as it had been accepted.

It is certain that Disraeli tried to accept Hibbert's amendment before the division of April 12 and failed to get the Cabinet to accept it in May, but there is no evidence that the proposals of May 3 and 6 were offered, or intended, by Disraeli as a package-deal, and nothing to show that Radicals who supported him saw them in this way. Apart from a remark (in a note to Corry) that Odger was a 'representative man',[2] there is no direct evidence from Disraeli's side of interest in the *opinions* of the popular movement beyond meetings with a London Working Men's Association delegation and a speech he made to a Reform League delegation in which he described them as 'professors of extreme opinions' and pointed out that the question could be settled only by 'compromise' on all sides.[3] Nor is there anything resembling a *letter* in which he says that he is pursuing a compromise. All there are are speeches in which this is said,[4] letters in which he fishes to discover what his colleagues will accept, direct evidence of negotiation with Radicals and a deduction that this is what he is aiming at. It is possible that all of this could be read differently: no doubt another historian could decide that Disraeli knew from the start that the Conservative party would be destroyed at the next election if he did not force it to go as far as he did in May. All we claim is that, if he did think that (as he may in some respects have done) he was controlled in his day-to-day conduct not by so nebulous a thing as a formulated intention, but by the exigencies of the strategic context he had helped to create in the previous session.

For the period up to the passage of Hodgkinson's amendment material, though inadequate, exists because Disraeli had to negotiate with the Cabinet in order to guard his rear. For this period tactical calculations can be extrapolated from the period of the parliamentary recess. For the period after that, the situation is so different that extrapolation is difficult. Disraeli was in command of the situation: he determined governmental policy and did so without extensive consultation. The material for reconstructing the passage of the redistribution clauses, the second wave of restrictive activity and the handling of the Lords' amendments probably does not exist. One can ask why the seats clauses in the bill of March 18 gave nothing to the large cities and provided no advantage to the Conservative party. One can suggest an answer but one cannot justify it. One can ask what the prolonged evasions about the Boundary Commission was intended to do. One can provide an explanation without believing it absolutely. One can deduce from the refusal to propose complete disfranchisement of any existing borough a desire to avoid the offence Gladstone had caused in 1866 by proposing to do so. This desire was almost certainly operative in other directions also, but one will not find Disraeli confirming the deduction. One can observe the pains he took in speaking to the House to emphasize the needs and rights of counties. One can see other politicians saying that a good redistribution was what the counties needed. One can even see that, in 1868, in the counties that he touched, the Conservative party did extraordinarily well. But one cannot find Disraeli saying in as many words that his object in passing the bill was to establish a firmer Conservative hold upon them, or that he had fixed the redistribution to do so.

One can intuit Disraelian skill in letting the House commit itself against Gaselee's motion and Laing's second one, and in favour of Horsfall's and Laing's first, before presenting his own redistribution schedules on that basis. One can see why, until Horsfall's amendment had been accepted, he probably thought it best to avoid naming the four boroughs whose enfranchisement, having been given, was to be withdrawn. One can see him threatening to withdraw the whole bill and fight an election if his redistribution arrangements were not approved of in principle. One can sense the threat to propose a larger more 'territorial' redistribution if the redistribution he proposed was not accepted. One can sense the need he felt at each point at which he abandoned inessentials, to seem positively reactionary in order to convince Tories that he was not abandoning too much. But one cannot claim to know certainly what he thought essential, or whether he may not have been willing at any particular time to concede almost anything (provided Gladstone had not suggested it) in order to carry the bill through its final stages.

Finally, whatever we may wish to think as a matter of doctrine, there is no conclusive evidence to show what view Disraeli took of the party he had 'educated' or of the classes for whose enfranchisement he was responsible. Working-class power could be made a friend of, and brought within, the party system: it could be ostracized as an enemy so as to rally those who feared it. Until it was certain that a bill would pass, Disraeli's *emphasis* was anti-revolutionary. Yet what he *did* cohered with the first objective, and it is certain that he wanted not to be identified with the second. An answer to the question, in what balance did he keep these attitudes, is central to the interpretation we have offered, but the interpretation is a guess. In relation to the Conservative party and the parliamentary process one intuits irony, ruthlessness and a gambler's contempt— a feeling on Disraeli's part that the precariousness of his situation meant that nothing would be lost by affronts as striking as he gave in May 1867 in demonstrating to others that he had it under control. Because the issues had been personal, the ruthlessness had been great. Because disagreement was synthetic, ruthlessness had been accepted. At the moment of victory there seems to have been a desire to show Whigs in particular that he had cured the party of the defects on which they had relied and a claim that he, like other statesmen of the highest rank but unlike Gladstone, combined vision which perhaps he had not had with parliamentary tact, of which the irony embodied in the quotation at the head of this chapter is an example. The 'brazen oratory' at Edinburgh on October 29[1] when he claimed that he had been educating the Conservative party for seven years implied, after the event, a deliberate foresight which we have found unhelpful as an instrument of explanation and a disregard for 'the donkies [who], conscious of the curriculum thro' which they had passed, were [being] brought to cut capers of delight over the very thing they had always kicked against'.[2] When Clarendon visited Knowsley to see his daughter a couple of days later, Derby would not discuss the subject of 'his

Hebrew chief' which was 'evidently a sore one'.[1] The Queen of Holland was a friend of Clarendon and had the prejudices of an English Whig. One sees what she meant, and what Whigs were being made to understand, when she remarked, on Disraeli's arrival as Prime Minister a few months later, that 'the Jewish race is so full of conceit and vanity [that] they do not want merely the *substance* but the *shine* of power [also]'.[2]

In many of these cases evidence of intention is so fragmentary that the author has little confidence that the narrative structure could not be reversed. In assessing the explanation offered in this book, therefore, the reader must take seriously the warning that what an historian makes of material depends on what he puts into it, that what he puts into it is determined by what he thinks could have happened and that in choice of material and direction of narrative this work depends as much on the prior decision to prefer one sort of explanation as on any conclusion that may be thought to emerge unasked from the material on which it is based.

The explanation offered assumes that political decisions cannot be understood as derivative offshoots of pre-existing social conditions. It assumes that, if connections can be established between the two, they must be established in detail.

In one respect a connection has been established. In 1867 Parliament exhibited a profound dislike of the rule of numbers. If the desire to resist had not been so strong, Disraeli could not have persuaded the House of Commons to go as far as it did. If all Conservatives in both Houses of Parliament had behaved like aristocrats of Radical mythology, he could have done nothing at all. But the desire to resist, when coupled with a belief that pressure could be made innocuous as easily by shifting the basis of representation as by preserving it intact, gave Disraeli a wider measure of flexibility than he would otherwise have had. Neither this belief, which he induced, nor the flexibility he gained as a consequence were the necessary consequence of pressure from numbers. Cranborne, Carnarvon, Lowe and Earl Grey were conscious of the same pressure but wanted resistance to be open. Nothing distinguished them from Disraeli except that their position in the political system indicated one reaction where Disraeli's indicated another. No account of the condition of society at large can explain why Parliament allowed itself to

22-2

be led one way rather than another, why one range of options was adopted instead of another or why, out of all the options open to it in 1867, the Conservative party chose one which could be represented either as a capitulation to popular pressure or as a recognition that the people's heart was sound. Between the closed world in which decisions were taken and the external pressures it reflected, the connections were so devious and diverse that no necessity can be predicated of the one in relation to the other. Between the inner political world and society at large on the one hand and between personal and policy objectives on the other, no general connection can be established except whatever can be discovered in each instance about the proportions in which each reacted on the other. The difficulty in assessing the operative pressures is large and must be larger in any case in which the material is less abundant. In the case we have been considering the material is abundant. If this book has shown nothing else, however, it has shown that, whatever may be said positively, abundance of material need not make a negative conclusion less inescapable.

APPENDIXES

APPENDIX I[1]

(i) *Conservative gains*

A.   Seats *not* scheduled in or affected by Boundary Act of 1868

Clitheroe*, E. Cumberland*, Malmesbury, Nottingham, N. Notts, Portsmouth, Boston, Rye, S. Shropshire, Southampton, Stockport, Wallingford, Norwich, Shrewsbury, Buteshire*, Wigtonshire, Monaghan co., Sligo bor. (disfranchised after petition 1868–70), Portarlington*, Brecknock

B.   Seats scheduled in and counties affected by Act of 1868

Ashton, Bath, Penryn and Falmouth (2), [Taunton (disqu. 1869)], Rutlandshire*, E. Worcestershire, Chester*, Hertford*, Worcester, Bolton, Pembroke dist.   Total 32

(ii) *Liberal gains*

A.   Seats *not* scheduled in or affected by Boundary Act of 1868

Bedford, Canterbury, Carlisle, Christchurch, Colchester, Herefordshire, E. Cornwall, Cricklade, Dover, Grantham (2), Hereford city, Bucks, Devonport (2), Ipswich, Tiverton*, Warrington, Wenlock*, Whitby, Wigan, St Ives, Dumfrieshire, Edinburghshire, Perthshire, Haverfordwest, Bandon, Belfast, Carrickfergus, co. Cork, King's co., New Ross, Londonderry city, Newry, Queen's co., Sligo co., Wexford co., Waterford co.

B.   Seats scheduled in and counties affected by Act of 1868

Cheltenham, Derby, Durham city, Exeter, Hastings, Kidderminster, Macclesfield*, Stoke-on-Trent, Sunderland, Cambridge borough (2), Berkshire, Gloucestershire West, Oxfordshire, Carmarthenshire*, Carnarvonshire, Denbigh dist., Merionethshire, Monmouth dist.   Total 57

* Listed by H. J. Hanham (*Elections and party management: Politics in the time of Gladstone and Disraeli*, 1959, p. 406) as constituency with one seat controlled by patron 1868–85.

APPENDIX II

(Omitting Sussex and Dorset where there were
disfranchisements but no division)

1865		1868
6 C, 1 L	Cheshire and South Lancashire (i.e. Staleybridge new borough, South Lancs and Cheshire redrawn with extra constituencies)	11 C
1 C, 3 L	North Lancs (divided with extra seats, Burnley new borough, Lancaster disfranchised)	4 C, 1 L
2 C	West Kent (divided with extra seats and Gravesend new borough)	4 C, 1 L
4 L	Derbyshire (two constituencies redrawn as three)	3 L, 3 C
5 L, 5 C	Devonshire (redrawn with extra seats and Totnes, Ashburton, etc., disfranchised by 1868 Scottish Act)	1 L, 5 C
1 L, 1 C	South Durham (new boroughs: Darlington L 1868 Hartlepool C 1868 Stockton L 1868)	4 L, 1 C
1 L, 3 C	Essex (redrawn with extra constituency and seats)	2 L, 4 C
2 L, 2 C	Lincolnshire (redrawn with extra constituency and seats)	2 L, 4 C
7 C, 1 L	Norfolk (redrawn with extra constituency and seats, Gt Yarmouth and Thetford disfranchised)	6 C
5 C, 1 L	Somerset (redrawn with extra constituency and seats, Wells disfranchised)	6 C
3 L, 1 C	Staffordshire (redrawn with extra constituency and seats, Wednesbury new borough)	4 L, 3 C

344

1865		1868
3 L	East Surrey (divided with extra seats, Reigate disfranchised)	2 L, 2 C
1 L, 1 C	North Riding (Middlesborough new borough)	2 L, 1 C
4 L	West Riding (redrawn with extra constituency and seats, Dewsbury new borough)	5 L, 2 C
2 L	Middlesex (Chelsea–Kensington new borough)	3 L, 1 C
32 L, 34 C	Total	30 L, 57 C

APPENDIX III

THE ACTORS
(Ages in 1867)

(These notes are designed to be of use in understanding the narrative: they do not normally cover careers after 1867. *Indicates ex-Liberals, Peelites or Palmerstonians who had become Conservatives by 1867, became Disraelian, or post-Disraelian, Conservatives later in the century, or who co-operated closely with the Conservative party.)

ACLAND, Thomas (58). Son of baronet and social reformer, and grandson of Henry Hoare, the banker. Ed. Harrow and Christ Church. Close friend of Gladstone with whom he founded a religious fellowship at Oxford. 1831–9 Fellow of All Souls. 1837 Conservative MP. for West Somerset. 1841–7 Young England sympathizer and follower of Peel on Free Trade. Agricultural and educational improver and Volunteer. 1859 beaten at Birmingham as Conservative by Bright. 1865– Liberal MP. for N. Devon (in company with Sir Stafford Northcote after 1866).

ACTON, Sir John (33). Historian, Liberal, Catholic. 1859–65 MP. for Carlow. Granville's step-son. Not in close touch with Gladstone, but admirer.

ADDERLEY, C. B. (53). Born in Leicestershire, succeeded to large family estates in Warwickshire and Staffordshire. Ed. privately and Christ Church. Responsible for development and planning of Birmingham suburb of Saltley, which was built on his land. 1841 MP. (on Peel's advice). Sat for North Staffs until 1878. Took part in foundation of Canterbury, New Zealand and abolition of transportation. Supporter of independence for colonies. 1852 refused junior office. 1858 Vice-President of Education Committee. 1866 Colonial Under-Secretary. Liberal Conservative, friend of Gladstone, Cobden and Bright. Outspoken, longwinded. Strong evangelical.

AKROYD, Edward (57). Born in Halifax, son of worsted manufacturer, worsted manufacturer himself. Volunteer and Deputy Lieutenant for Yorkshire. 1857–9 MP. for Huddersfield, 1865–

MP. for Halifax. Founder of model town of Akroyden: Halifax Union Building Society. Member of Brooks's as well as the Reform Club.

AMBERLEY, Viscount (25). Son of Russell by second wife. MP. for Nottingham at by-election in 1866. Radical Whig. Lady Amberley was the daughter of Lord Stanley of Alderley and a leader of radical salon.

ANSON, Augustus (32). Son of 1st Earl of Lichfield. 1853– Army (India, wounded before Delhi 1857, V.C. at Lucknow). 1859 MP. for Lichfield. Speaker Denison thought he had a 'fine soldier-like style' of speaking.

ARGYLL, 8th Duke of (44). Progressive Whig admirer of Gladstone. 1853 Lord Privy Seal under Aberdeen. 1855–8 Postmaster General. 1859–66 Lord Privy Seal.

AYRTON, Acton Smee (51). Son of lawyer. Radical on military, electoral and religious questions: anti-centralization. 1857– MP. (Radical) for Tower Hamlets. In trouble with the Reform League in 1867.

BAGEHOT, Walter (41). Editor of *The Economist* since 1860.

*BASS, Michael Arthur (30). Son of M. T. Bass. Ed. Harrow and Trinity College, Cambridge. Partner in Burton brewery. 1865– MP. (Liberal) for Stafford (later MP. for E. Staffs and Burton, and, 1886, Lord Burton. Liberal Unionist and Tariff Reformer under Hartington and Chamberlain).

BASS, Michael Thomas (68). Son of Burton brewer. Ed. Burton-on-Trent Grammar School and Nottingham. Deputy Lieutenant for Staffs. 1848– MP. for Derby. Gladstone visited the brewery in 1865. Experience of strikes.

BATH, 4th Marquess of (36). Not a member of Parliament but enemy of Disraeli. Supporter of Gladstone (on semi-Catholic grounds). Anti-1867 bill. Irish landowner.

BAXTER, R. Dudley (40). Son of parliamentary solicitor, born in Doncaster. Ed. Trinity College, Cambridge. Entered father's firm. Lifelong Conservative: sister a missionary in China. Family closely connected with Shaftesbury. Statistician and party draftsman. Not robust: died in 1875.

BEALES, Edmond (64). Son of a Cambridge merchant. Ed. Bury St Edmund's Grammar School, Eton and Trinity College, Cambridge. Called to Bar. Equity draughtsman and conveyancer.

347

Made a county court judge for Cambridgeshire by Gladstone's Lord Chancellor in 1870.

BEESLY, E. S. (36). Son of evangelical minister. Ed. Wadham College, Oxford. Pupil of Richard Congreve. Positivist. Admirer of Bright as the only parliamentary politican worth attending to. Closely connected with working-class political movement in 1860s.

BERESFORD-HOPE, A. J. (47). Son of author and grandson of Lord Decies, Archbishop of Tuam. Married Cranborne's sister. Ed. Harrow and Trinity College, Cambridge (prizeman). President of Institute of British Architects. Rich man, with a number of houses. Proprietor of *Saturday Review*. 1842–5 and 1857–9 MP. for Maidstone, 1865– MP. for Stoke. Heavy orator.

*BORTHWICK, Algernon (37). Son of editor of *Morning Post*. Ed. Paris and King's College, London. 1852 on father's death became editor of the *Morning Post*. Failed to buy paper, but controlled it. Palmerstonian opponent of free trade. Not yet married. Not yet as powerful as he was to become.

BOUVERIE, E. P. (49). Second son of 3rd Earl of Radnor. Ed. Harrow and Trinity College, Cambridge. 1840 précis writer to Palmerston. 1843 called to the Bar. 1844–74 MP. for Kilmarnock. 1850–2 junior office under Russell. 1853–5 chairman of Committees under Aberdeen. 1855–8 office under Palmerston. 1859–65 2nd Church Estates Commissioner. Whig/Liberal enemy of Gladstone: office seeker.

*BOWYER, Sir George (56). Son of Berkshire squire. Ed. RMC, Woolwich and Middle Temple. Called to Bar. Equity draughtsman and conveyancer. Jurisprudentialist and lawyer. Author of a large number of books. 1850 converted to Catholicism. 1852–68 MP. for Dundalk (1874–80 Home Rule MP. for Wexford). Eighth baronet, Knight of Malta, Knight Commander of the Order of Pius IX and deputy lieutenant for Berkshire. Expelled from the Reform Club in 1876.

BRADLAUGH, Charles (34). Son of solicitor's clerk. Ed. elementary schools, then office boy. Atheist and free-thinker. 1850–3 private in Army. 1853 clerk in solicitor's office. Public speaker in London and provinces in favour of free-thought. 1860, foundation of *National Reformer*, atheist newspaper. Primary interest religion, politics at this time a by-product.

BRAND, Henry (53). Son of 22nd Baron Dacre and grandson of a dean of Limerick. Ed. Eton. 1846 private secretary to Sir George Grey. 1852–68 MP. for Lewes. 1855–8 junior office under Palmerston. 1859 for a short time Keeper of the Privy Seal to the Prince of Wales. 1859–67 Chief Whip.

BRIGHT, John (56). Son of Rochdale cotton manufacturer. Ed. Quaker schools in Rochdale and elsewhere in Yorkshire and Lancashire. Partner in family firm combined with temperance lecturing, etc., in early years. Member of Rochdale Cricket Club. Anti-Corn Law League leader. 1843–7 MP. (Radical) for Durham. 1847–57 MP. for Manchester (defeated in 1857). 1857– MP. for Birmingham.

BROWN, John (41). Queen Victoria's gillie.

CAIRNS, Sir Hugh (48). Ed. Trinity College, Dublin (1st in classics). 1844 English Bar, 1856 QC. 1858–9 Solicitor-General. *Dod* records him (1864) as opposed to 'lowering the borough franchise as low as £5'. Much admired by Newdegate as defender of protestantism. 1866 Attorney-General, but resigned in October to become Lord Justice of Appeals no doubt in view of uncertainty of government's prospects. Disraeli thought that if he had had imagination he could have done anything he wanted to politically. Baron February 1867.

CAMBRIDGE, 2nd Duke of (48). Grandson of George III. Ed. by a canon of Worcester and a guards officer. Married an actress. 1837 onwards served in British Army including (1843) service at Leeds during industrial disturbances. Served in Ireland and Crimea. 1854– General Commanding in Chief of British Army. Unenthusiastic friend of Volunteer movement. In 1867 not notably out of touch with politicians. In charge of troops on July 22 and May 6. There are hints that he was an Adullamite. Elcho claimed he suggested Earl Spencer to succeed Lansdowne as leader of the Cave.

CARNARVON, 4th Earl of (36). Son of 3rd Earl. Ed. Eton and Christ Church. Never sat in the House of Commons. 1858–9 junior office under Derby. 1866–7 Colonial Secretary.

CHELMSFORD, 1st Lord (73). Entered Royal Navy as midshipman but changed to Bar at twenty-four. 1834 QC., 1844 Solicitor-General. 1845 and 1852 Attorney General. MP. 1840–58, 1858–9 and 1866–8 Lord Chancellor.

CLANRICARDE, 1st Marquess of (65). Married Canning's daughter. Irish landowner. Ambassador to Russia. Lord Privy Seal and Postmaster-General in 1850s. No office after 1858.

CLARENDON, 4th Earl of (67). Ed. St John's College Cambridge. Son of landed family of middling fortune; began life as diplomat. 1839–41 Lord Privy Seal, 1840–1 Chancellor of Duchy of Lancaster. 1847–52 Lord Lieutenant of Ireland. 1853–8 Foreign Secretary. 1864–5 Chancellor of Duchy of Lancaster. 1865–6 and 1868–70 Foreign Secretary. Sharp-tongued; in 1867 said to be getting deaf. Enemy of Disraeli. Brother of C. P. Villiers.

CLEVELAND, 4th Duke of (64). Ex MP. (Whig) and, as Lord Harry Vane, a whip.

CLIVE, George (61). MP. for Hereford and Recorder of Wokingham. Relative of General Grey. Liberal. 1859–62, minor office.

COLERIDGE, John Duke (46). Son of a judge. Ed. Eton and Balliol (fellow of Exeter). 1847 Bar, 1861 QC. Recorder of Falmouth. Liberal publicist. MP. 1865. 'Silver-tongued.'

CONGREVE, Richard (49). Ed. Rugby and Wadham. Fellow of Wadham. Leader of positivists. Taught Beesly and Harrison.

COWEN, JOSEPH (67). Manufacturer of fire-bricks and coal-owner in Newcastle. Aldermanic Radical. Creator of reform movement in Newcastle and area. MP. for Newcastle on Tyne 1865– .

CRANBORNE, Lord (37). Younger son of 2nd Marquess of Salisbury (who had a been Conservative minister in 1852 and 1868). Ed. Eton and Christ Church (4th in mathematics, secretary and treasurer of Union). 1853 Fellow of All Souls. 1851–3 in Australia. 1853–68 MP. for Stamford. 1857 married daughter of lawyer against father's disapproval; consequent financial stringency. Extensive journalism from 1859 onwards for *Saturday Review* and *Quarterly Review*. 1865 Viscount Cranborne on death of elder brother. 1866–7 India Secretary. Lord Eustace Cecil was his younger brother.

CRAWFORD, R. W. (54). Partner in East India mercantile firm in London, director of Bank of England. MP. (briefly) 1851 and 1857– (for City of London). A leading Liberal backbencher.

CROSSLEY, Sir Francis (50). Halifax carpet manufacturer. 1849–50 Mayor of Halifax. 1852–9 Liberal MP. for Halifax, 1859–69 for West Riding, 1869–72 for West Riding (N). Philanthropist, baronet (1863). Member of Brooks's Club.

DELANE, J. T. (50). Son of barrister, born in London and brought up in Berkshire. Ed. private schools, King's College, London and Magdalen College, Oxford. Vigorous horseman, not a scholar. Called to the Bar, editor of *The Times* at twenty-four. A Palmerstonian enemy of Russell. Wide contacts in society. Lived at Ascot in house built on the land sold to him by Cobden. Died 1879.

DE GREY AND RIPON, 2nd Earl (40). Christian socialist. Junior office under Palmerston 1859-63. 1863-6 in Cabinet. A Volunteer. MP. (Liberal) 1853-7 and 1857-9. 1859 succeeded father as Earl of Ripon.

DERBY, 14th Earl of (68). Son of 13th earl in Whig family. Ed. Eton and Christ Church. 1822 MP. (Whig). 1830 Chief Secretary for Ireland in Earl Grey's government. 1833-4 Whig Colonial Secretary, resigned over Russell's attack on the Irish Church. 1841 Peel's Colonial Secretary. 1844 called to House of Lords. 1845 declined to form Cabinet on Peel's resignation: formed the nucleus of the Protectionist party in 1846. 1852 and 1858 Conservative Prime Minister.

DILLWYN, Lewis Llewellyn (53). Father a quaker country gentleman. Swansea potter and naturalist. Deputy Lieutenant for Glamorgan, friend of Dissenters, Captain in Glamorgan Rifles. Pro ballot and abolition of church rates. MP. for Swansea (Liberal) since 1855.

DUNKELLIN, Lord (40). Son of Clanricarde. Army in Ireland, Crimea and India 1846-56 (prisoner at Sebastopol). MP. (Liberal) for Galway 1857- . Not a very creditable figure; friend of W. H. Gregory.

EARLE, Ralph Anstruther (32). Son of Liverpool family of Whig opinions. Ed. Harrow. Attaché at Paris Embassy 1854—and Disraeli's informant inside the Embassy from 1857. MP. from 1859, Disraeli's secretary from about the same time. Resigned seat in 1868 and went into business in Ottoman Empire, etc. Died in 1879.

*ELCHO, Lord (49). Son of 9th Earl of Wemyss, married Lichfield's sister. Ed. Christ Church, Oxford. 1841-6 MP. (Conservative) for E. Gloucestershire. 1847- MP. for Haddingtonshire. Palmerstonian.

ELLICE, Edward, jnr. (57). Son of Edward Ellice, MP. 1836- .

Ed. Trinity College, Cambridge. 'Strong Liberal'. Related to Halifax, the Greys, etc. Vendetta with Gladstone.

ENFIELD, Lord (37). Son of Earl of Stafford. Ed. Eton and Christ Church (honorary 4th in classics). Volunteer. Junior office 1865–6. Whig MP. 1852–7 (Tavistock), 1857– (Middlesex).

FAWCETT, Henry (34). Son of Wiltshire squire. Ed. King's College London and Trinity Hall, Cambridge (Wrangler, Fellow 1856). Blinded in shooting accident in early manhood. 1863 Professor of Political Economy at Cambridge. 1865 MP. (Liberal/Radical) for Brighton.

FORSTER, W. E. (49). Son of Quaker missionary and nephew of Sir T. Fowell Buxton. Born in Dorset, ed. Quaker schools in Bristol and Tottenham. Started work in woollens in Norwich and Darlington, and then Bradford on borrowed capital. Successful woollen manufacturer. Renounced Quakerism on marriage to Matthew Arnold's sister in 1850. Defeated at Leeds in 1859 as advanced Liberal. Elected for Bradford in 1861. Competent parliamentarian: earnest and ambitious.

GASELEE, S. (60). Son of judge. Ed. Winchester and Balliol. 1832 Bar. 1840 Sergeant-at-Law. 1865 MP. for Portsmouth.

GIBSON, T. Milner (60). Born in W. Indies. Son of army officer. Minor gentry. Ed. Trinity College, Cambridge. 1846–8 minor office under Russell. 1859 President of Poor Law Board. 1859–65 President of the Board of Trade. Pro ballot in 1853. Radical friend of Bright. MP. intermittently since 1837. Ministerial pension (£2,000 p.a.).

*GOSCHEN, George (36). Grandson of Leipzig publisher, son of banker who arrived in England in 1814 to found firm of Fruhling and Goschen. Ed. Blackheath, Saxe Meiningen, Rugby (head of school) and Oriel (double first in classics). President of Union, and member of 'Essay Club'. 1853–66 in father's firm in England and British Columbia. 1859 director of the Bank of England. 1864 published *Theory of the Foreign Exchanges*. 1863 Liberal MP. for City of London. Pro ballot, anti-Church Rates, etc. Not a follower of Bright. November 1865 Vice-President of the Board of Trade, January 1866 Chancellor of the Duchy of Lancaster.

GRANVILLE, 2nd Earl (52). Son of 1st Earl and grandson of a Duke of Devonshire. Ed. Christ Church, Oxford. MP. (Whig) 1837–46.

1846 junior office. 1851–2 Foreign Secretary, 1852–84, 1855–8 and 1859–66, Cabinet office.

GRAVES, S. R. (49). Born and educated in Ireland. Liverpool ship-owner. 1860 Mayor of Liverpool. Author. MP. (Conservative).

GREGORY, W. H. (50). Son of Irish landowner. Ed. Harrow and Christ Church. Palmerstonian. 1842–7 MP. for Dublin. 1857– MP. for Galway County. Married Yeats's Lady Gregory of Coole.

GREY, General Charles (63). Son of 2nd Earl Grey, born at Howick. Ed. at home, entered army at seventeen. Private secretary to his father during period as Prime Minister from 1830 to 1834, equerry to Queen Victoria from about 1840, private secretary to Prince Albert 1849-61. Queen's secretary. MP. for Chipping Wycombe 1831 and for High Wycombe 1832–7. Gladstone proposed to his wife, Disraeli was beaten by him at elections in 1832.

GREY, Sir George (68). Grandson of 1st Earl Grey; mother a Whitbread and friend of William Wilberforce, father superintendent of naval dockyard at Portsmouth. Ed. at home and at Oriel College, Oxford (first). Lapsed ordinand, married bishop's daughter and called to bar 1826. 1832 MP. for Devonport, 1834–41 junior office, 1846–52 and 1855–8 Home Secretary. 1859-61 Chancellor of Duchy of Lancaster. 1861–6 Home Secretary. Safe, sensible Whig of high moral quality and respectability. From 1846, on uncle's death, owner of Falloden, but recipient of ministerial pension (£2,000 p.a.).

GREY, Henry 3rd Earl (65). Eldest son of Grey of the Reform bill. 1846–52 Colonial Secretary.

GROSVENOR, Earl (42). Son of 2nd Marquess of Westminster by second daughter of 1st Duke of Sutherland. Married to the fifth daughter of the 2nd Duke. Ed. Balliol. 1847–69 Liberal MP. for Chester. Not prominent politically until 1866. Philanthropist, sportsman, Derby winner in 1873 and 1882.

HALIFAX, 1st Viscount (67). Son of 2nd baronet and daughter of Recorder of Leeds. Married fifth daughter of 2nd Earl Grey. Ed. Eton and Oriel (double first 1821). 1826 MP., 1832–65 MP. for Halifax, 1865 MP. for Ripon. 1832 junior office: resigned in 1839. Not an advanced Whig. 1846–52 Chancellor of the Exchequer. 1852–5 President of the Board of Control. 1855–8 First Lord of the Admiralty. 1859–66 India Secretary. 1870–4 Lord Privy Seal. Cr. Viscount Halifax February 25 1866.

HARRISON, Frederic (36). Son of prosperous London merchant. Ed. King's College School, London and Wadham College, Oxford (under Congreve). 1854–6 Fellow of Oriel. 1858 called to the Bar. Journalist and lawyer with close connections with working-class politics in the 1860s.

*HARTINGTON, Marquess of (34). Eldest son of 7th Duke of Devonshire. Ed. Trinity College, Cambridge, 1863–6. Minor office under Palmerston and Russell. 1866 War Secretary. Volunteer. Liberal Whig with no strong enthusiasm for movement.

HARTWELL, Robert (*c.* 50). Secretary of London Working Men's Association. Ex-Chartist. Compositor and journalist. Assistant to Troup, the editor of *The Beehive*.

HAYTER, A. D. (35). Son of Liberal ex-Chief Whip (Sir W. G. Hayter). Ed. Eton and Brasenose (scholar). Army 1860–6. Author 1865– . MP. (Liberal) Wells.

HEATHCOTE, Gilbert (37). Eldest son of Lord Aveland. Ed. Harrow and Trinity College, Cambridge. Voted for Derby's Reform bill in 1859. MP. (Liberal) for Boston 1852–6, for Rutland 1856– . Regular but not very active Adullamite.

HEATHCOTE, Sir William (66). Fellow of All Souls. Keble's squire at Hursley and Carnarvon's guardian. Son of prebendary of Winchester. Ed. Winchester and Oriel College, Oxford where Keble was his tutor. MP. for University of Oxford, 1854– . Disraeli found him 'too churchy'.

HERBERT, Auberon (29). Youngest brother of Carnarvon. Ed. Eton and St John's College, Oxford (Fellow). Fought Isle of Wight as Conservative in 1865. Ended life as Liberal/Radical champion of innumerable progressive causes.

HIBBERT, J. T. (43). Son of founder of Oldham machinist firm. Ed. Shrewsbury and St John's College, Cambridge. 1849 Bar. 1862 MP. for Oldham. Interest in sanitary questions. Junior office under Gladstone in 1870s and 1880s.

HODGKINSON, Grosvenor (49). Newark solicitor. Ed. King Edward's School, Louth. 1859 MP. (Liberal) for Newark.

HORSFALL, T. B. (62). Liverpool merchant and son of Liverpool merchant. 1847–8 Mayor of Liverpool in period of disturbance. 1852–3 MP. (Conservative) for Derby, 1853– for Liverpool.

HORSMAN, Edward (60). Lugubrious Scot, related to the Earls of Stair. Ed. Rugby and Trinity College, Cambridge. Called to the

Scottish bar but did not practise. MP. from 1836. Fought a duel in defence of the Queen in 1840. 1841 junior office. Hostile to bishops. 1855–7 Chief Secretary for Ireland. Died 1876.

HOWELL, George (34). Son of mason who was in financial difficulties. Began work at eight, mortar boy at ten. 1847 began work as Chartist. 1853 bricklayer in Bristol. Early member of Y.M.C.A. 1854– in London, making name in 1859 builders' strike. 1864 ceased to work as bricklayer. Member of Junta. 1861–2 secretary to London Trades Council. 1864–7 secretary of Reform League.

HUBBARD, J. G. (62). Son of Russia merchant. Ed. privately and in Bordeaux. Entered father's firm. 1838 director of Bank of England. 1853–89 chairman of public works loan commission. 1859–68 MP. for Buckingham (defeated in 1868 and became MP. for City of London 1874–7. 1887 1st Lord Addington). High Church enemy of ritualism.

HUTT, Sir William (66). Son of lesser gentry in Isle of Wight. Married well. MP. since 1832; Vice-President of the Board of Trade 1860–65. Not very advanced Liberal.

HUGHES, Thomas (44). Son of clerical lesser gentry family. Ed. Rugby and Oriel College, Oxford. 1848 called to Bar. Author of *Tom Brown's Schooldays*, etc. Radical on electoral and Church issues but strong churchman. 1865 MP. for Lambeth with strong working-class and Reform League support. Volunteer.

JONES, Ernest (48). Son of equerry to Duke of Cumberland. Ed. in Holstein. Man of fashion in London; called to Bar but did not practise. 1846 onward active Chartist. Died 1869.

*KNATCHBULL-HUGESSEN, E. (39). Son of Kent baronet and MP. Born Knatchbull. Ed. Eton and Magdalen College, Oxford. MP. for Sandwich (Liberal) 1857– . Family Conservative.

KNIGHTLEY, Sir Rainald (48). Son of Northamptonshire landowner. MP. for South Northamptonshire since 1852. Friend of Newdegate, enemy of Disraeli.

LAING, Samuel (55). Son of author. Ed. Houghton-le-Spring Grammar School and St John's College, Cambridge (Fellow 1834). Called to Bar. 1834 private secretary to Henry Labouchère. 1844 onwards involved in railway development. 1852 chairman of Crystal Palace Company. 1852–7, 1859–60, 1865–8 MP. for Wick. 1859–60 junior office. 1860–5 Finance Minister in India. In old age wrote *Problems of the Future, The Antiquity of Man*, etc. Disraeli thought him the 'ablest' member of the Cave apart from Lowe.

LAIRD, John (62). Retired Birkenhead shipbuilder. Ex-chairman of Birkenhead Commissioners. Deputy Lieutenant for Cheshire. MP. (Conservative) for Birkenhead from 1861.

LAMBERT, John (52). Son of Wiltshire surgeon. Roman Catholic. Ed. St Gregory's, Downside. 1831–57 Salisbury solicitor (strong free trade and sanitary reformer). 1854 first Roman Catholic mayor of Salisbury. 1857 Poor Law Inspector. 1863 Poor Law Board adviser on poverty (owing to American Civil War). 1866 refused post in Jamaica. Responsible for electoral statistics of 1866–7. Author of works on church music. Advanced Liberal; wrote in newspapers.

LANSDOWNE, 4th Marquess of (died 1866 at the age of 50). Son of 3rd Marquis. 1847–56 MP. (Liberal) for Calne. 1847– junior office under Russell. 1856–8 junior office under Palmerston.

LAWLEY, Francis (42). Son of 1st Lord Wenlock. Ed. Oxford. Fellow of All Souls. 1852–3 MP. for Beverley. Gladstone's secretary until compelled to resign from House of Commons as a result of speculation in funds. Friend of Catherine Gladstone. Racing man.

LICHFIELD, 2nd Earl of (42). Married daughter of 2nd Marquis of Abercorn. Précis writer to Palmerston when young. Whig. Strike experience in Staffordshire. MP. 1847–54.

LOWE, Robert (56). Son of Nottinghamshire rector. Ed. Winchester and University College, Oxford. Private tutor in Oxford. 1835–6 Fellow of Magdalen. Anti-tractarian. 1838 rejected for chair of Greek at Glasgow. 1842 called to Bar and went to Australia to practise. Successful practise and land investments in Sydney. 1850– *Times* leader-writer in England. 1852 MP. for Kidderminster. 1852–5 joint secretary at Board of Control. 1855–8 Paymaster-General. 1859 assaulted and defeated at Kidderminster. MP. for Calne. 1859–64 Vice-President of Education Committee until forced to resign by attack from Cranborne.

LOWRY-CORRY, H. (64). Second son of Earl of Belmore, married Shaftesbury's sister. Ed. Christ Church, Oxford. 1834–5, 1841–5, 1845–6 and 1858–9 junior office. July 1866 office outside Cabinet and Church Estates Commissioner. MP. (Tyrone) since 1826.

LYTTELTON, 4th Lord (50). Worcestershire landowner. He and Gladstone married sisters. Ed. Eton and Trinity College, Cambridge. 1846 junior office under Peel. Anti-Palmerstonian on grounds of tone; religious, not democratic. Committed suicide.

McLaren, Duncan (67). Son of Scottish farmer, apprenticed to draper at twelve: set up as draper on his own. 1832–51 member of Edinburgh town council. 1851 Provost of Edinburgh. 1865-81 MP. for Edinburgh. Three wives, one John Bright's sister.

Malmesbury, 3rd Earl of (60). Hampshire landowner. 1852 and 1858–9 Foreign Secretary. 1866–8 Lord Privy Seal. Regarded as reactionary, unyielding rural Tory. Wrote a book on Game Laws.

Manners, Lord John (47). Ed. Eton, Trinity College, Cambridge. Young Englander. Friend of Disraeli. MP. 1841– . Author of *Plea for National Holidays.*

Marx, Karl (49). Living in London, preparing 'Capital' for publication. Not a member of the Reform League, but, as part of First International, connected with some of those who were. Proud of his influence in League. It is possible that Derby had never heard of him.

May, Sir Erskine (52). Historian. Clerk in House of Commons.

Mayne, Sir Richard (71). Son of an Irish judge. Ed. Trinity College Dublin and Cambridge. 1822 called to Bar. The creator of the London police force. 1850 Chief Commissioner.

Naas, Lord (45), MP. (Kildare) 1847–52, (Coleraine) 1852–7, (Cockermouth) 1857–68. Chief Secretary for Ireland 1852, 1858–9, 1866–8. The Conservative Party's Irish expert. Stabbed to death while Viceroy of India 1872.

Newdegate, C. N. (51). Ed. Eton, King's College, London and Christ Church. MP. for N. Warwickshire since 1843. Enemy of Catholicism and 'the ultramontane organization...the revolutionary element, always discontented, till possessed of supreme power, it renders odious what it possesses.' 'Attached to the principles of the Constitution as established in 1688.'

Northcote, Sir Stafford (49). Grandson of 7th baronet. Ed. Eton and Balliol at both of which places he rowed. Read for Bar and became private secretary to Gladstone. Religious but not a tractarian. 1850 secretary to Great Exhibition. Joint author of Northcote–Trevelyan report (1853). MP. 1855– .

Odger, George (47). Son of a Cornish miner. Shoemaker. Made name in building trades lockout in 1859. 1862–77 secretary of

London Trades Council. Advocate of direct political action by Trades Unions.

O'Donoghue, The (34). Daniel O'Donoghue, nephew of O'Connell. Ed. Stonyhurst. Spent way through inheritance in 'twenties. MP. (Tipperary) 1857–65. MP. for Tralee 1865–. Voted against Derby on Reform in 1859, but against Palmerston on July 8 1864. One of very few who voted against suspending Habeas Corpus in Ireland in 1866.

Osborne, Bernal (59). Born Bernal. Son of MP. and art collector with West Indian fortune and Spanish and Jewish ancestry. Ed. Charterhouse and Trinity College, Cambridge. 1831–41 Army. 1841 MP. for Chipping Wycombe. 1847 onwards MP. for a wide variety of constituencies with some of which he quarrelled. 1852 junior office under Palmerston. Socially accomplished; popular speaker.

Pakington, Sir John (68). Born John Russell. Ed. Eton and Oriel College, Oxford. Assumed name of Pakington and family estates on death of mother's uncle. 1837–74 MP. for Droitwich. Supported Maynooth in 1845 but against repeal of Corn Laws. Anti-penny post as 'truckling to democracy'. 1852 War and Colonial Secretary. 1858–9 and 1866 First Lord of Admiralty. On religio-political questions extremely flexible.

Palmer, Sir Roundell (55). Son of clerical family, married a Waldegrave. Ed. Rugby, Winchester and Trinity College, Oxford. Fellow of Magdalen. 1837 called to Bar. 1849 QC. MP. 1847–52, 1853–7 and 1861– . 1861–3 Solicitor-General. 1863–6 Attorney-General.

Patten, John Wilson (65). Son of minor landed family in Lancashire. 1830–1 MP. for Lancashire, 1832–74 for N. Lancashire. Friend of Derby; daughter wrote to ask Derby to give him office in 1867. June 1867 Chancellor of the Duchy of Lancaster.

Peel, General Jonathan (68). Fifth son of Prime Minister's father. Ed. Rugby. Entered army before Waterloo but not an active soldier. 1826–30 MP. for Norwich. 1831–68 for Huntingdon. 1841–6 junior office under father. 1852 no office. 1858–9 and 1866–7 War Secretary. Horseracing, Derby winner 1844. Popular in Conservative party and a lynch-pin of party Toryism, but an enemy of Disraeli as the enemy of his brother.

*Peel, Sir Robert, jnr. (45). Son of the Prime Minister. Ed. Harrow

and Christ Church. Diplomatic Service in Spain and Switzer-
land. 1850 succeeded father as MP. for Tamworth. 1855–7
junior office under Palmerston. 1861–5 Chief Secretary of Ireland. Improvident, fine presence, gay manner but political failure
(after becoming a Tory, ended life as a Home Ruler).

PLATT, John (50). Mechanical engineering manufacturer in
Oldham. Ed. in Cheshire. Mayor of Oldham. High Sheriff of
Caernarvonshire. Advanced Liberal. MP. (Oldham) 1865– .

POTTER, George (35). Born in Warwickshire, apprenticed to car-
penter in Coventry. 1854 came to London. 1859 made reputation
in builders' lockout. 1864 headed deputation to Garibaldi. 1861
founded *The Beehive*. Founder of London Working Men's
Association.

POTTER, T. B. (50). Ed. Rugby and University College, London.
MP. for Rochdale on Cobden's death in 1865.

*ROEBUCK, J. A. (64). Born in India, son of Civil Servant there and
ed. in Canada. Called to Bar in England. 1843 QC., agent for
House of Assembly of Lower Canada. 1832–7 and 1841–7 MP.
(Radical) for Bath, strongly anti-Whig. 1849–68 and 1874–9 MP.
for Sheffield. Pro-South in American Civil War. Pro-Austria in
Italy. Pro-Turk in 1870s. Made a Privy Councillor by Disraeli.

RUSSELL, 1st Earl (75). Younger son of 6th Duke of Bedford. Ed.
Westminster and Edinburgh. MP. from 1813 onwards. 1820 onwards, centre of movement in House of Commons for parliamentary reform. Introduced Reform bill in 1831 and 1832 as
Paymaster-General.

SALISBURY, Marchioness of (43). Daughter of 2nd Earl de la Warr,
married 2nd Marquess of Salisbury in 1847. Stepmother of Cranborne. Married 15th Earl of Derby (q.v. Stanley) after death
of husband.

SALISBURY, 2nd Marquess of (76). Conservative peer. Lord President of Council 1858–9. No office in 1866–7. Father of Cranborne (q.v.). Second wife Mary, Marchioness of Salisbury (q.v.).

SHAFTESBURY, 7th Earl of (66). Philanthropist, son of chairman of
committees in House of Lords and 6th earl. Ed. Harrow and
Christ Church (first). 1826–46 and 1847–51 MP. (Conservative).
Relative of Palmerston and supporter. Critic of Peel. 1828 junior
office under Wellington. 1834–5, junior office under Peel.

SMITH, J. B. (73). Retired merchant, ex-President of Manchester

Chamber of Commerce; first chairman of Anti-Corn Law League. MP. (Stirling dist.) 1847–52, for Stockport 1852– .

SOMERSET, 12th Duke of (63). Palmerstonian Whig. Never a member of the House of Commons. 1859–66 First Lord of the Admiralty. Enemy of Disraeli.

SPOFFORTH, M. (43). Principal Conservative agent (but see Hanham *op. cit.* p. 357), member of firm of Baxter, Rose, Norton and Company.

*STANHOPE, 5th Earl (62). Historian. Ed. Christ Church. MP. (Conservative) 1830–2 and 1835–52. 1834–5 and 1845–6 junior office under Peel. *History of War of Succession in Spain*, pub. 1832, *History of England, 1713–83*, pub. 1836–63, *Life of Pitt*, 1861, etc. Peelite: one of Peel's literary executors. Only slowly pushed back to Conservative party in 1860s.

STANLEY, Lord (41). Later 15th Earl of Derby, son of 14th Earl (q.v.). Ed. Rugby (expelled from Eton for kleptomania) and Trinity College, Cambridge. An 'Apostle'. 1848 defeated as protectionist at Lancaster, elected at King's Lynn. 1852–3 Foreign Under-Secretary. 1855 refused Palmerston's offer of colonial secretaryship. 1854 supported Bright and Cobden in resistance to entering Crimean War. 1858–9 Cabinet office 1866–8 Foreign Secretary. 1870 married Cranborne's mother after death of Cranborne's father, the 2nd Marquess of Salisbury. Lowe predicted that he would 'die the most irresolute old man in England'. Disraeli thought he would do anything for office.

STANSFELD, James, jnr. (47). Son of solicitor and judge of county court, Halifax. Brewing connections. Ed. University College, London. Bar 1849. 1859– MP. (Radical) for Halifax. 1863–4 junior office until resignation because of Mazzini scandal. 1866– , junior office.

TAYLOR, P. A. (48). Grandson of George Courtauld and member of Courtauld firm. Economic Radical, ally of Cowen. MP. for Leicester 1862– .

TAYLOR, T. E. (55). Conservative Chief Whip. Elder son of younger brother (ordained) of Marquess of Headfort. Married a Tollemache. Army 1829– . 1858–9 Junior Whip. 1859–68 Chief Whip. Irishman. MP. for Dublin Co. since 1841.

TORRENS, W. T. McCullagh (54). Son of family of minor literary Irish gentry. Ed. Trinity College Dublin. Called to English and

Irish Bars. 1834 Irish Special Poor Law Commissioner. Member
of Anti-Corn Law League. MP. 1848–52 (Dundalk), 1857–65
(Yarmouth), 1865– (Finsbury). Close interest in social questions,
author of *Memoirs of Melbourne*.

WALPOLE, Spencer (59). Descendant of Sir Robert Walpole and of
Nelson and nephew of Spencer Perceval. Ed. Eton (Head of
School) and Trinity College, Cambridge. Called to Bar. QC.
1846. 1846 MP. for Midhurst, 1856–82 MP. for Cambridge
University. 1852–3 and 1858–9 Home Secretary. Resigned over
Reform policy in 1859. General agreement, even before July
1866, that he was 'too weak for troublous times'. Awarded
ministerial pension in early 1867 (£2,000 p.a.).

WILSON, George (59). Son of Derbyshire and Manchester corn-
miller, began in corn and shifted to starch and gum manufactur-
ing. 1841 chairman of Anti-Corn Law League. Involved in development of electric telegraph, railway director, etc. A Sande-
manian.

BIBLIOGRAPHY

I. MANUSCRIPT SOURCES

The material from which this book has been made consists primarily of such letters written by politicians to one another as may be found in the following collections (* indicates the most important for the subject; † indicates the most fragmentary).

Where a letter which has been seen in a manuscript collection is also available in published form, I have, nevertheless, quoted almost invariably from the manuscript. I have not often thought it necessary to compare the published with the manuscript version.

My method of working in a manuscript collection is to copy extensively almost everything which might be relevant to the subject even when I am unlikely to understand the significance of the material I have copied until I have seen most of the other collections. This means that I have in my possession a vast body of verbatim notes from manuscript letters. It means, also, that in visiting an archive I need to copy at high speed. In cases where manuscript collections are close at hand and accessible, I have in some cases paid a second visit in order to check the quotations this book contains from them. With other collections it has been either impossible, or impracticable, to do so. In these cases I have relied on my accuracy as a high-speed notetaker of material which, when the notes were taken, may well not always have been intelligible. If it should turn out that my accuracy is not great, I hope it may be agreed that, if inaccuracies have crept in, they have not significantly affected the interpretation put on the letters into which they have been inserted.

Beesly MSS (papers of E. S. Beesly, Library of University College, London).

Belvoir MSS (papers of Lord John Manners, 8th Duke of Rutland, Belvoir Castle, Leicestershire, by permission of the Duke of Rutland).

*Bishopsgate MSS (papers of the Reform League at the Bishopsgate Institute, London).

Braborne MSS (papers of E. Knatchbull-Hugessen, 1st Lord Braborne, in Kent County Record Office).

Brand MSS (papers of Henry Brand, 1st Viscount Hampden, in the Journal Office of the House of Commons, by permission of the late Viscount Hampden).

Bright MSS (papers of John Bright in the British Museum).

*Bright MSS (papers in Library of University College, London).

†Cairns MSS (papers of Sir Hugh Cairns, 1st Earl Cairns in possession of Rear-Admiral the Earl Cairns).

†Carlingford MSS (papers of Chichester Fortescue, 1st Baron Carlingford, in Somerset County Record Office, Taunton, by permission of Lord Strachie).

Carnarvon MSS (papers of the 4th Earl of Carnarvon in Public Record Office).

Clarendon MSS (papers of the 4th Earl of Clarendon in the Bodleian, Oxford, by permission of Rt Hon. the Earl of Clarendon).

†Congreve MSS (papers of Richard Congreve, the positivist, in the Bodleian, Oxford).

Congreve MSS (similar papers in the British Museum).

Cowley MSS (papers of the 1st Earl Cowley in Public Record Office, London).

*Cranbrook MSS (papers of Gathorne Hardy, 1st Earl of Cranbrook, East Suffolk County Record Office, by permission of the Earl of Cranbrook).

*Derby MSS (papers of the 14th Earl, in possession of Mr Robert Blake, by permission of the Earl of Derby).

—— (papers of the 15th Earl, i.e. Stanley, Knowsley Hall, Prescot, by permission of the Earl of Derby).

Ellice MSS (papers of Edward Ellice jnr. in the National Library of Scotland).

*Garrowby MSS (*see* Halifax MSS).

*Gladstone MSS (papers of W. E. Gladstone in the British Museum).

†Halifax MSS (papers of the 1st Viscount Halifax in the British Museum).

—— (papers of the 1st Viscount Halifax at Garrowby, Yorkshire, Garrowby MSS deposited in York Central Library by permission of the Earl of Halifax).

†Harewood MSS (papers of Lord Dunkellin in Leeds Central Library, by permission of the Earl of Harewood).

Harrison MSS (papers of Frederic Harrison in the Library of the London School of Economics).

Howick MSS (papers of 3rd Earl Grey in the Prior's Kitchen, Durham).

*Hughenden MSS (papers of Benjamin Disraeli, 1st Earl of Beaconsfield at Hughenden Manor, by permission of the National Trust).

Iddesleigh MSS (papers of Sir Stafford Northcote, 1st Earl of Iddesleigh, in the British Museum).

Knowsley MSS (see Derby MSS).

Lansdowne MSS (papers of the 4th Marquess of Lansdowne at Bowood, by permission of the Marquess of Lansdowne).

Malmesbury MSS (papers of the 3rd Earl of Malmesbury at Hurn Court, Hampshire, by permission of the Earl of Malmesbury).

Mayo MSS (papers of the 6th Earl of Mayo, i.e. Naas, in the National Library of Ireland, Dublin).

Mill/Taylor MSS (correspondence of John Stuart Mill in the Library of the London School of Economics).

†Richmond MSS (papers of the 6th Duke of Richmond in West Sussex County Record Office, Chichester).

Ripon MSS (papers of the 1st Marquess of Ripon, i.e. de Grey, in the British Museum).

Royal Archives (Windsor Castle).

*Russell MSS (papers of the 1st Earl Russell in the Public Record Office, London).

*Salisbury MSS (papers of the 3rd Marquess of Salisbury, i.e. Cranborne, in the Library of Christ Church, Oxford, by permission of the Marquess of Salisbury).

J. B. Smith MSS (papers of J. B. Smith, MP. for Stockport, in Manchester Central Library).

*Wemyss MSS (papers of the 10th Earl of Wemyss, i.e. Elcho, at Longniddry House, East Lothian, by permission of the Earl of Wemyss).

George Wilson MSS (papers of George Wilson in Manchester Central Library).

The following collections were inspected but found to contain nothing, or nothing of consequence:

Acland MSS (papers of Sir Thomas Dyke Acland in the Bodleian, Oxford).

Bath MSS (papers of the 4th Marquess of Bath at Longleat, by permission of the Marquess of Bath).

Ward Hunt MSS (papers of George Ward Hunt, MP., in Northamptonshire County Record Office).

Monk Bretton MSS (papers of the 1st Lord Monk Bretton in the Bodleian, Oxford).

Cardwell MSS (papers of the 1st Viscount Cardwell in Public Record Office, London).

The Journal of George Hadfield (Manchester Central Library).

The following collections are known to exist, would probably provide material of consequence but, for one reason or another, have not been consulted:

Chatsworth MSS (papers of the 8th Duke of Devonshire).

Chelmsford MSS (papers of the 1st Lord Chelmsford).

Hampton MSS (papers of Sir John Pakington, 1st Lord Hampton).

McLaren MSS (papers of Duncan McLaren).

St Aldwyn MSS (papers of Sir Michael Hicks Beach, 1st Viscount St Aldwyn).

Sherbrooke MSS (papers of Robert Lowe, 1st Viscount Sherbrooke—said to be a small and disappointing collection).

Winmarleigh MSS (papers of John Wilson Patten, 1st Lord Winmarleigh).

The author wishes to acknowledge the gracious permission of H.M. the Queen to make use of material from the Royal Archives. He is grateful to the other owners of collections for permission to make use of them, and to librarians and archivists for making them available. He is grateful to the staff of the National Register of Archives for answering enquiries.

2. PRINTED SOURCES

The following official printed sources have been used:

Hansard, parliamentary debates: 1865–8.

House of Commons division lists not printed in *Hansard* (by courtesy of the Clerk of the House of Commons).

Parliamentary Accounts and Papers:

	vol.	
1860	XII	Report on probable increase in electors in counties and boroughs (Earl Grey's commission).
1861	I	Appropriation of Seats bill (Sudbury and St Albans).
1866	V	Franchise bill (England and Wales) of 1866.
		Redistribution of Seats bill of 1866.
		Franchise bill (Scotland) of 1866.
		Franchise bill (Ireland) of 1866.
1867	IV	Parliamentary Registration bill.
1867	V	Representation of the People bill 1867 (Reform bill of 1867).
		Private Members Reform bill (Ireland).
		Reform bill (Scotland) of 1867.
		Corrupt Practices and Elections (Trial) bill.
		Parliamentary Elections bill.
1867–8	I	Boundary bill (with amendments).
	IV	Reform bill (Scotland) cont.
		Parliamentary Elections bill cont.
		Private Members Reform bill (Ireland) of 1867 cont.
	VIII	Select Committee report on boundaries.
	XX	Boundary Commissioners' report.

RETURNS

| 1866 | LVII | Electoral returns boroughs and counties 1865. |

1866   LVII   Electoral returns boroughs and counties 1865.

1867   LVI   Returns of population and...direct taxes...in... boroughs...in S. Devon, W. Kent, N. Lancashire, Lincolnshire (parts of Lindsey), Middlesex, S. Staffordshire and E. Surrey and areas of counties.

1867   LVII   Returns as to seven parliamentary boroughs to be given third members.

1860   LV

1862   LXIX

1867   LVI ⟩ Various returns of numbers of compounders in England and Wales.

1867   LX

1867–8   LVI

3. PUBLISHED WORKS

The following published works have been used. Works marked with an asterisk contain first-hand material of significance or quantity for the Reform crisis. Most biographies are listed according to the names under which their subjects are known in the text of this book. Thus Trevelyan's *Bright* appears under Bright, not Trevelyan.

Acland, Sir Thomas Dyke, Bt. *Memoirs and Letters of the Right Honourable Sir Thomas Dyke Acland*, ed. A. H. D. Acland, privately printed, 1902.

Acton, Sir J. E. E. D. *Ignaz von Döllinger/Lord Acton Briefwechsel 1850–1869*, ed. Conzemius.

Adderley, Charles Bowyer. *Life of Lord Norton 1814–1905: Statesman and Philanthropist*, by W. S. Childe-Pemberton, 1909.

Althoz, J. L. 'The Political Behaviour of English Catholics 1850–1867', *Journal of British Studies*, IV (1963), pp. 89–104.

*Amberley, Viscount. *Amberley Papers. The Letters and Diaries of Lord and Lady Amberley*, ed. Bertrand and Patricia Russell, 2 vols, 1937.

Archbold, J. F. *The Poor Law*, 10th edn. 1860.

Argyll, 8th Duke of. *George Douglas, 8th Duke of Argyll (1823–1900): Autobiography and Memoirs*, ed. the Dowager Duchess, 2 vols, 1906.

Bagehot, Walter. *The English Constitution*, 2nd edn. ed. R. H. S. Crossman, 1963.

Baxter, R. Dudley. *The New Reform Bill: The Franchise Returns Critically Examined*, 1866.

—— *Re-distribution of Seats and the Counties*, 1866.

—— *Results of the General Election*, 1869.

—— *In Memoriam R. Dudley Baxter, M.A.*, by Mary D. Baxter, 1878.

Borthwick, Algernon. *Lord Glenesk and the 'Morning Post'*, by R. Lucas, 1910.

Bradlaugh, Charles. *Charles Bradlaugh, A Record of his Life and Work*, by H. B. Bonner, 2 vols, 1895.

—— *Reform or Revolution*, 1867.

Brand, C. 'The Conversion of the British Trade Unions to Political Action', *American Historical Review*, xxx (1924–5), pp. 251–70.

Briggs, Asa and Saville, J. (eds.). *Essay in Labour History*, 1960.

Briggs, Asa. *Victorian People: Some Reassessments of People, Institutions, Ideas and Events, 1851–1867*, 1954.

—— *The Age of Improvement 1783–1867*, 1959.

Bright, Sir Charles Tilston. *Life Story of Sir Charles Tilston Bright, Civil Engineer*, by Charles Bright, 1908.

Bright, John. **Life of John Bright*, by G. M. Trevelyan, 1913.

—— **Diaries of John Bright*, ed. R. A. J. Walling, 1930.

—— *Public Addresses of John Bright, MP.*, ed. J. E. Thorold Rogers, 1879.

—— *Public Letters of the Right Hon. John Bright, MP.*, ed. H. J. Leech, 1885.

—— *Speeches...by John Bright, MP.*, ed. J. E. Thorold Rogers, 2 vols, 1869.

—— *John Bright, Victorian Reformer*, by H. Ausubel, 1966.

Broadhurst, Henry. *Henry Broadhurst, MP. The Story of his Life...told by Himself*, 1901.

Bruce, H. A. *Letters of Rt Hon. H. A. Bruce, G.C.B., Lord Aberdare of Duffryn*, 2 vols, privately printed, 1902.

Buchanan, R. A. *Trades Unions and Public Opinion 1850–75* (Cambridge Ph.D. thesis).

*Burghclere, Lady. *A Great Lady's Friendships, Letters to Mary, Marchioness of Salisbury, Countess of Derby, 1862–1890*, 1933.

Burn, W. L. *The Age of Equipoise*, 1964.

Buxton, Charles. *Ideas of the Day on Policy*, 1868.

Carlyle, Thomas. 'Shooting Niagara: and After?', *Macmillan's Magazine*, xvi (1867), 319–36, reprinted in *Miscellaneous Essays* (Library Edition), vol. vii.

*Carnarvon, 4th Earl of. *Life of Henry Edward Molyneux Herbert, Fourth Earl of Carnarvon, 1831–1890*, by Sir Arthur Hardinge, 3 vols, 1925.

Cartwright, Julia. *Journals of Lady Knightley of Fawsley 1856–1884*, 1915.

Childers, Hugh Culling Eardley. *Life and Correspondence of the Right Hon. Hugh C. E. Childers, 1827–1896*, by Spencer Childers, 2 vols, 1901.

Chilston, Viscount. *W. H. Smith*, 1965.

Christie, O. F. *The Transition from Aristocracy, 1832–1867*, 1927.
—— *The Transition to Democracy, 1867–1914*, 1934.
*Clarendon, 4th Earl of. *Life and Letters of George William Frederick, Fourth Earl of Clarendon*, by Sir Herbert Maxwell, 2 vols, 1913.
Clark, G. Kitson. *The Making of Victorian England*, 1963.
Cole, G. D. H. *British Working-Class Politics, 1832–1914*, 1941.
—— *A Short History of the British Working-Class Movement, 1789–1947*, 1948.
*Coleridge, 1st Lord. *Life and Correspondence of John Duke, Lord Coleridge, Lord Chief Justice of England*, by E. H. Coleridge, 2 vols, 1904.
Collins, H. J. and Abramsky, S. *Karl Marx and the British Labour Movement*, 1965.
Cowen, Joseph. *Life and Speeches of Joseph Cowen MP.*, by E. R. Jones, 1886.
Cox, Homersham. *History of the Reform Bills of 1866 and 1867*, 1868.
Cranborne, Lord. *Life of Robert, Marquis of Salisbury*, by Lady Gwendolin Cecil, 4 vols, 1921–32.
—— *Quarterly Review*, 1866, January, 'The Coming Session'; April, 'The Reform bill'; July, 'The Change of Ministry'; 1867, October, 'The Conservative Surrender'.
de Grey. *Life of the First Marquess of Ripon*, by L. Wolf, 2 vols, 1921.
Delane, John Thadeus. *John Thadeus Delane, Editor of 'The Times'*, by A. I. Dasent, 2 vols, 1908.
Denison, John Evelyn. *Notes from my Journal when Speaker of the House of Commons*, by Viscount Ossington, privately printed, 1899.
Derby, 14th Earl of. *Lord Derby and Victorian Conservatism*, by W. D. Jones, Oxford 1956.
Disraeli, Benjamin. *Selected Speeches of the late Earl of Beaconsfield*, ed. by T. E. Kebbel, 1882.
—— **Life of Benjamin Disraeli, 1st Earl of Beaconsfield*, by W. F. Monypenny and G. E. Buckle, 6 vols, 1910–1920 (vol. IV referred to as Buckle, *Disraeli* IV).
—— 'Church and Queen'. *Five Speeches delivered by Rt Hon. B. Disraeli, MP., 1860–1864*, 1865.
—— *Speeches on Parliamentary Reform*, ed. by Montague Corry, 1867.
—— *Mr Gladstone's Finance...reviewed by the Rt Hon. B. Disraeli*, 1862.
—— *Disraeli*, by Robert Blake, 1966.
Duncombe, T. H. *Life and Correspondence of Thomas Slingsby Duncombe*, 2 vols, 1868.
Dunsmore, M. R. *The Working Classes, the Reform League and the Reform Movement in Lancashire and Yorkshire*, Sheffield M.A. Thesis.

Earle, Ralph. G. B. Henderson, *Crimean War Diplomacy*, 1947, pp. 267–90.

Elcho, Lord. *Memories 1818–1912 by the Earl of March and Wemyss*, privately printed, Edinburgh, 1912.

Essays on Reform, 1867.

Fawcett, Henry. *Life of Henry Fawcett*, by Leslie Stephen, 1886.

Forster, W. E. *Life of the Right Honourable William Edward Forster*, by T. Wemyss Reid, 2 vols, 1888.

Gash, Norman. *Politics in the Age of Peel*, 1953.

Gill, Conrad and Briggs, Asa. *History of Birmingham*. 2 vols, 1952.

Gillespie, F. E. *Labor and Politics in England, 1850–1867*, Durham, N.C., 1927.

Gladstone, William Ewart. *Gladstone: A Biography*, by Sir Philip Magnus, 1954.

—— **Life of William Ewart Gladstone*, by John Morley, 3 vols, 1903.

—— *A Chapter of Autobiography*, by W. E. Gladstone, 1868.

—— *Gladstone to his Wife*, ed. A. Tilney Bassett, 1936.

—— *Rise of Gladstone to the Leadership of the Liberal Party 1859 to 1868*, by W. E. Williams, Cambridge, 1934.

Good, W. W. *Political, Agricultural and Commercial Fallacies*, 1866.

Goschen, 1st Viscount. *Life of George Joachim Goschen, First Viscount Goschen, 1831–1907*, by A. R. D. Elliot, 2 vols, 1911.

—— *Lord Goschen and his Friends (The Goschen Letters)*, ed. by Percy Colson, 1946.

Granville, 2nd Earl. *Life of Granville George Leveson-Gower, Second Earl Granville, K.G.*, by Lord Edmond Fitzmaurice, 2 vols, 1905.

Gregory, Sir William. *Autobiography*, ed. by Lady Gregory, 1894.

Grey, Sir George. *Memoir of Sir George Grey, Bart, G.C.B.*, by Mandell Creighton, privately printed, Newcastle, 1884.

Grey, Henry, Earl. *Reform of Parliament*, 1858.

Hanham, H. J. *Elections and Party Management: Politics in the time of Gladstone and Disraeli*, 1959.

**Hardy, Gathorne. *Gathorne Hardy, First Earl of Cranbrook: A Memoir*, by A. E. Gathorne Hardy, 2 vols, 1910.

Hare, Thomas. *Treatise on the Election of Representatives*, 1859.

Harris, William. *History of the Radical Party in Parliament*, 1885.

Harrison, Frederic. *Autobiographic Memoirs*, by Frederick Harrison, 1911.

Harrison, Royden. *Before the Socialists, 1861–1881*, 1965.

Hartington, Marquess of. *Life of Spencer Compton, Eighth Duke of Devonshire*, by Bernard Holland, 2 vols, 1911.

Heathcote, Sir William. *A Country Gentleman of the Nineteenth Century*, by F. Awdry, 1906.

Herbert, Auberon. *Crusader for Liberty, a Life of Auberon Herbert*, by S. H. Harris, 1943.

Herrick, F. H. 'The Reform Bill of 1867 and the British Party System', *Pacific Historical Review*, III (1934), 216–33.

—— 'The Second Reform Movement in Britain 1850–65', *Journal of the History of Ideas*, IX (1948), 174–92,

Hill, R. L. *Toryism and the People, 1832–1846*, 1929.

Holyoake, George Jacob. *Sixty Years of an Agitator's Life*, by G. J. Holyoake, 2 edn, 2 vols, 1893.

—— *Life and Letters of George Jacob Holyoake*, by Joseph McCabe, 2 vols, 1908.

—— *Bygones Worth Remembering*, 2 vols, 1905.

Hughes, Thomas. *Thomas Hughes: The Life of the Author of 'Tom Brown's Schooldays'*, by E. C. Mack and W. H. G. Armytage, 1952.

Hylton, 2nd Lord. *The Jolliffes of Staffordshire*, privately printed, 1892.

Jones, Ernest. *Ernest Jones, Chartist*, by John Saville, 1952.

Kebbel, T. E. *History of Toryism*, 1886.

—— *Lord Beaconsfield and Other Tory Memories*, 1907.

Kennedy, A. L. *'My Dear Duchess', Social and Political Letters to the Duchess of Manchester 1858–69*, 1956.

Kent, C. B. R. *English Radicals*, 1899.

Kimberley, 1st Earl of. *A Journal of Events during the Gladstone Ministry, 1868–1874*, by John, First Earl of Kimberley, ed. Ethel Drus, 1958.

Labouchere, Henry Du Pre. *Life of Henry Labouchere*, by A. L. Thorold, 1913.

Law, H. W. and Irene. *Book of the Beresford Hopes*, 1925.

Layard, Sir Austen Henry. *Sir A. Henry Layard G.C.B., D.C.L.* Autobiography and Letters, ed. W. N. Bruce, 2 vols, 1903.

—— *Layard of Ninevah*, by Gordon Waterfield, 1963.

*Lowe, Robert. *Life and Letters of Rt Hon. Robert Lowe, Viscount Sherbrooke*, by A. P. Martin, 2 vols, 1893.

—— *Speeches and Letters on Reform*, 1867.

Ludlow, J. M. *Life of J. M. Ludlow*, by N. Masterman, 1963.

Lytton, R. B. *Personal and Literary Letters of the Earl of Lytton*, ed. by Lady Betty Balfour, 1906.

McCarthy, Justin. *Reminiscences*, 2 vols, 1899.

—— *A History of Our Own Times*, 3 vols, 1905.

—— *Portraits of the Sixties*, 1903.

Maccoby, S. *English Radicalism 1853–86*, 1938.

MacDowell, R. B. *British Conservatism 1832–1914*, 1959.

McCready, H. W. 'British Labour and the Royal Commission on Trades Unions, 1867–9', *University of Toronto Quarterly*, XXIV (1954–5), 390–409.
—— 'British Labour's Lobby, 1867–75', *Canadian Journal of Economics and Political Science*, XXII (1956), 141–60.
*McLaren, Duncan. *Life and Work of Duncan McLaren*, by J. B. Mackie, 2 vols, Edinburgh, 1888.
*Malmesbury, 3rd Earl of. *Memoirs of an ex-Minister*, by the Earl of Malmesbury, 2 vols, 1884.
*Manners, Lord John. *Lord John Manners and his Friends*, by Charles Whibley, 2 vols, 1925.
Marx, Karl and Engels, Friedrich. *Selected Correspondence*, 1956.
—— *Marx and Engels on Britain*, 1962.
Masheder, R. *Dissent and Democracy*, 1864.
May, Sir Eskine. *Constitutional History of England*, vol. III, 1860–1911, ed. F. Holland, 1912.
Miall, Edward. *Life of Edward Miall*, by Arthur Miall, 1884.
Mill, John Stuart. *Autobiography*, by J. S. Mill, World's Classics edn. Oxford 1923.
—— *J. S. Mill: Letters*, ed. H. S. R. Elliot, 2 vols, 1910.
—— *The Life of John Stuart Mill*, by M. St J. Packe, 1954.
Molesworth, W. N. *History of England, 1830–1874*, vol. III, 1874.
Moore, D. C., 'The Other Face of Reform', *Victorian Studies* V (1961).
—— 'Concession or Cure: The Sociological Premises of the First Reform Act', *Historical Journal* IX, no. 1 (1966).
Morier, Sir Robert. *Memoirs of Sir Robert Morier*, by Mrs Rosslyn Wemyss, 1911, vol. II.
Morley, Samuel. *Life of Samuel Morley*, by Edwin Hodder, 1887.
Mundella, Anthony John. *A. J. Mundella, 1825–1897. The Liberal Background to the Labour Movement*, by W. H. G. Armytage, London, 1951.
Naas, Lord. *Life of the Earl of Mayo*, by W. W. Hunter, 2 vols, 1875.
Norman, E. R. *The Catholic Church and Ireland in the Age of Rebellion, 1859–1873*, 1965.
*Northcote, Sir Stafford. *Life, Letters and Diaries of Sir Stafford Northcote, First Earl of Iddesleigh*, by Andrew Lang, 1899.
—— *The Case of Sir E. Wilmot*, 1847.
—— *Twenty Years of Financial Policy*, 1862.
Oliphant, L. *Memoir of the Life of Lawrence Oliphant and of Alice Oliphant, his wife*, by H. O. W. Oliphant, 2 vols, 1891.
Osborne, Ralph Bernal, *Life of Ralph Bernal Osborne, MP.*, by P. H. Bagenal, privately printed, 1884.

Owen, David, *English Philanthropy 1660–1960*, 1965.

Palmer, Roundell. *Memorials Personal and Political 1865–95*, by the Earl of Selbourne, 2 vols, 1898.

Park, J. H. *The English Reform Bill of 1867*, 1920.

Paul, Herbert. *History of Modern England*, 5 vols, 1904–6.

Pelling, Henry. *A History of British Trade Unionism*, 1963.

Petrie, Sir Charles, *The Carlton Club*, 1955.

Read, Donald. *The English Provinces c. 1760–1960*, 1964.

*Roebuck, John Arthur. *Life and Letters of John Arthur Roebuck*, by R. E. Leader, 1897.

Russell, 1st Earl. *Life of Lord John Russell*, by Sir Spencer Walpole, 2 vols, 1889.

—— *Later Correspondence of Lord John Russell*, ed. G. P. Gooch, 2 vols, 1925.

Salisbury, Marquess of. See Cranborne.

Saville, John (ed.). *Democracy and the Labour Movement*, 1954.

Scrope, Poulett, *No Vote, No Rate*, 1867.

Seymour, Charles. *Electoral Reform in England and Wales*, New Haven and London, 1915.

Shaftesbury, 7th Earl of. *Life and Work of the Seventh Earl of Shaftesbury, K.G.*, by E. Hodder, 3 vols, 1886.

—— *Shaftesbury*, by G. F. A. Best, 1964.

—— *Speeches, 1838–1867*, 1868.

Shaw Lefevre, G. *The Personal Payment of Rates*, 1868.

Smith, F. B. *The Making of the Second Reform Bill*, 1966.

Smith, Paul, *Disraelian Conservatism and Social Reform*, 1967.

Somerset, 12th Duke of. *Letters of 12th Duke of Somerset*, ed. by W. H. Mallock and Lady G. Ramsden, 1893.

Southgate, Donald. *The Passing of the Whigs*, 1962.

Stanley, Lord. *Speeches and Addresses of Edward Henry, XVth Earl of Derby*, ed. Sanderson and Roscoe, 2 vols, 1894.

Stansfeld, James. *James Stansfeld, A Victorian Champion of Sex Equality*, by J. L. and Barbara Hammond, 1932.

Steele, E. D. *Irish Land Reform and English Liberal Politics 1865–70* (Cambridge Ph.D. thesis).

Thomas, J. Alun. *The House of Commons, 1832–1901. A Study of its Economic and Functional Character*, 1939.

Thompson, F. M. L. *English Landed Society in the Nineteenth Century*, 1963.

The Times: History of the Times—The Tradition Established 1841–1884, 1939.

Thring, 1st Lord. *Practical Legislation*, 1902.

Torrens, William McCullagh. *Twenty Years in Parliament*, by W. M. Torrens, 1893.

Trevelyan, G. O. *George Otto Trevelyan, a Memoir*, by G. M. Trevelyan, 1932.

Victoria, Queen. *Letters of Queen Victoria*, second series, ed. G. E. Buckle, 3 vols, 1926–8.

Vincent, J. R. *The Formation of the Liberal Party 1857–68*, 1966.

Waldegrave, Frances, Countess. *Strawberry Fair: A Biography of Frances Countess Waldegrave 1821–79*, by O. W. Hewett, 1956.

*Walpole, Sir Spencer. *The History of Twenty-five Years*, vol. II, 1865–70, 1904.

White, W. *The Inner Life of the House of Commons*, 2 vols, 1897.

Whyte, J. H. *The Independent Irish Party, 1850–9*, 1958.

Wilberforce, Bishop Samuel. *Life of Rt Rev. Samuel Wilberforce*, by A. R. Ashwell and R. G. Wilberforce, 3 vols, 1880.

Winter, James. 'The Cave of Adullam and Parliamentary Reform', *English Historical Review*, vol. LXXXI (January 1966).

5. The following works of reference have been used:

Dod's *Parliamentary Companion*.
Dictionary of National Biography.
Men of The Time.
Burke's Peerage, Baronetage and Knightage.
McCalmont's Parliamentary Poll-Book, 7th edition.
Modern English Biography by Frederic Boase, 1892.
Bateman's *Great Landowners of Great Britain and Ireland*, 1883.

NOTES

Where the location of a letter cannot be in doubt, the reference has been abbreviated, i.e. there are no page references to Lady Burghclere's *A Great Lady's Friendships* (see bibliography) and no catalogue references to the Hughenden MSS except when a letter is undated.

95922 references are to the Bishopsgate MSS; RA to the Royal Archives; PRO to the Public Record Office; PA and P to Parliamentary Accounts and Papers; Add. MSS references are to the British Museum's Additional Manuscripts; UCL to the Bright MSS at University College, London. Hardy, *Diary* refers to the diary of Gathorne Hardy, later 1st Earl of Cranbrook, among the Cranbrook MSS; Knatchbull-Hugessen, *Diary* to the political diary of E. Knatchbull-Hugessen, later 1st Lord Braborne, among the Braborne MSS; Halifax, *Journal* is a typed copy of a diary kept by the 1st Viscount Halifax and now among the Garrowby MSS. Northcote, *Diary* is a typed version of Sir Stafford Northcote's diary for 1866 (Add. MSS 50063 A).

PAGE 2

1 M. Cowling, *Mill and Liberalism*, 1963.
2 *Hansard*, May 20 1867 (781–2). W. Bagehot, *The English Constitution*, pp. 272–3. Lowe to Lady Salisbury, May 14 1867, *A Great Lady's Friendships*.
3 R. H. S. Crossman, Bagehot, p. 45 (see note 2 above).

PAGE 7

1 [J.] Morley, [*The Life of W. E.*] *Gladstone*, 1903, II, p. 464.

PAGE 9

1 Gladstone to General Grey, June 22 1866, RA 32/22.
2 March and Wemyss [i.e. Elcho], *Memories 1818–1912*, I, p. 366.
3 Horsman to Elcho, December 24 1866, Wemyss MSS.

PAGE 10

1 For a list see Derby to Disraeli, June 10 1866, Hughenden MSS.
2 Bright to his wife, June 12 1866, U.C.L.
3 Cf. Rt Hon. R. Lowe, MP., *Speeches and Letters on Reform*, 1867.

PAGE 12

1 S. H. Walpole to Queen [July 23 1866], Windsor RA F 14. Derby to General Grey, February 6 1867, Derby MSS Box 192/1.

PAGE 13

1 *Hansard*, February 25 1867 (946–9). N. Lancashire, N. Lincolnshire, West Kent, East Surrey, Middlesex, South Staffordshire and South

Devon, were to be divided in order to give two seats to each new division, South Lancashire in order to give one seat to each division. The twelve new parliamentary boroughs were to be Hartlepool, Darlington, Burnley, Staleybridge, St Helen's, Dewsbury, Barnsley, Middlesborough, Croydon, Gravesend, Torquay and an unspecified Black Country town.

PAGE 15
1 Reform League notice 95922/4.
2 Bright to Russell, July 13 1867, PRO 30 22/16 D.
3 Speech at Ormskirk, December 19 (*The Times*, December 20 1867).
4 Cf. Knatchbull-Hugessen, *Diary*, April 13 1867.

PAGE 16
1 Speech at Edinburgh, October 29 1867 (*The Times*, October 30 1867).
2 Lord Eustace Cecil to Cranborne (Salisbury) November 28 (n.y. but 1868), Salisbury MSS.
3 Elcho to Grosvenor (n.d. but late 1867), Wemyss MSS.
4 Lowe to Lady Salisbury, September 10 1867, *A Great Lady's Friendships*.
5 J. B. Smith to Duncan McLaren, December 26 1867, J. B. Smith MSS (923. 2. s. 341).
6 McLaren's address to his constituents in [J. B.] Mackie, [*Life and work of Duncan*] *McLaren*, 1888, II, 167–8.
7 C. Seymour, *Electoral Reform in England and Wales*.

PAGE 17
1 [G. M.] Trevelyan, [*The Life of John*] *Bright*, p. 362.
2 Royden Harrison, *Before the Socialists 1861–1881*, pp. 78–137.
3 *Ibid.* p. 111.

PAGE 18
1 *Ibid.* p. 132.

PAGE 19
1 Cf. Beales's letter to potential patrons of the Reform League, March 8 1867, 95922/20.
2 Cf. G. H. Whalley's vote with Disraeli on April 12 after a visit to, and discussion with, the Executive Committee of the League. (Minutes of Executive Committee, April 12 1867, 95922/4.)
3 Beales to George Wilson, April 19 1867, George Wilson MSS.
4 Bright to Congreve, November 24 1866, Congreve MSS (Bodleian Eng. Lett. c. 185).

5 Mill to Fawcett, January 1 1866. Mill-Taylor Correspondence, vol. LVII. F. H. Berkeley MP. to Howell, June 14 1866, 95922/20.

1 Clarendon to Russell, December 20 1865, quoting Stanley, *Later Correspondence of Lord John Russell*, ed. Gooch, pp. 340–1.
2 Trevelyan, *Bright*, p. 373 quoting Gladstone.
3 Bright to his wife, May 12 1867, UCL.
4 Thomas Hughes to de Grey, May 10 1867, Add. MSS 43548. Gladstone to Russell, June 8 1867, PRO 30 22/16 D.
5 See Bright's three letters to J. B. Smith, October 28 and November 15 1865 and January 7 1866 for Bright wrestling with the question whether he should accept office if offered it, and making the historian wonder whether it was vanity, ambition or Quaker modesty which made him wrestle.
6 Bright to his wife, March 3 1867 ff., UCL.
7 Bright to J. B. Smith, October 28 1865, J. B. Smith MSS.
8 Beesly to Howell, January 26 1867, 95922/20.
9 For Carlyle see 'Shooting Niagara' in *Miscellaneous Essays* (Library edition), vol. VII.

1 Cf. Lord John Manners, *Journal*, February 20 and July 6 1867, Belvoir MSS.

1 Lowe, *Speeches and Letters on Reform*. Frederic Harrison to Beesly, February 22 1867. Harrison MSS Section A 1865/7.
2 See Mill to T. B. Potter, March 16 1865 in Gillespie, *Labor and Politics in England 1850–67*, p. 140.
3 *The Amberley Papers* (ed. Bertrand and Patricia Russell, 1937), II, 39. *Hansard*, May 30 1867 (1357 ff.). Mill to Fawcett, January 1 1866, Mill-Taylor Correspondence.
4 Hon. Auberon Herbert who in 1865 was bottom of the poll when he stood as a Conservative for Newport, Isle of Wight and joined the Liberal party in 1866.
5 *Hansard*, May 30 1867 (1361).
6 Galway to Disraeli, March 6 1867, Hughenden MSS.

1 Cf. J. A. Shaw-Stewart to Cranborne, April 15 1867 in Lady G. Cecil, [*Life of Robert, Marquis of*] *Salisbury*, I, 261–2.
2 A. J. Beresford-Hope, *Hansard*, June 27 1867 (630).
3 Beresford-Hope, *Hansard*, June 21 1867 (280).

PAGE 24

1 Beresford-Hope, *Hansard*, June 24 1867 (443).
2 Russell to Brand, October 2 1866, Brand MSS.
3 Lord Nelson to Derby, December 17 1866, Derby MSS Box 113/4.
4 Lord John Manners to Disraeli, October 24 1866, Hughenden MSS.
5 Spofforth to Disraeli, October 18 1867, Hughenden MSS.

PAGE 25

1 Hardy, *Diary*, February 12 and May 7 1867. Cf. General Grey to Derby, May 7 1867, Derby MSS Box 159. Derby to Disraeli, December 3 1866, Hughenden MSS.
2 General Grey to Earl Grey, December 3 1866, Howick MSS.
3 Memo by Chelmsford, the Lord Chancellor, agreeing with Buckingham, August 1866. For Buckingham see Buckingham memo August 1 1866. Both Derby MSS Box 163. For Walpole's note see Derby MSS Box 153/3.
4 Lord John Manners to his brother, July 28 1866, Belvoir MSS.
5 Lord John Manners to his brother, December 4 1866, *ibid.*
6 Bright to Congreve, November 24 1866, Congreve MSS (Bodleian).
7 Shaftesbury to Derby, October 19 1866, Derby MSS Box 114/1.

PAGE 26

1 *Ibid.*
2 Sir George Bowyer in *Hansard*, March 18 1867 (50).
3 Percy Wyndham MP. for W. Cumberland in *Hansard*, March 26 1867 (615).
4 Disraeli in *Hansard*, May 17 1867 (726).

PAGE 27

1 Clarendon to Russell, September 9 1866, PRO 30 22/16 D.
2 *Ibid.* September 2 1866, reporting his brother, C. P. Villiers, after a visit to Wolverhampton.

PAGE 28

1 *Ibid.* September 9 1866.

PAGE 29

1 W. E. Gladstone, *A Chapter of Autobiography*, 1868, pp. 60 and 61. Though this essay was written in preparation for the election of 1868, I have used it as evidence of the direction in which Gladstone's opinions were moving in 1866/7.
2 Gladstone to Lord Lyttleton, March 28 1866, Add. MSS 44536.
3 Argyll to Gladstone, November 3 1865, Add. MSS 44100.
4 Gladstone in *Hansard*, July 2 1867 (877).

PAGE 30

1 Hardy, *Diary*, July 30 1867.
2 Cf. Stanley to Adderley, December 29 1866, Knowsley MSS.
3 Edward Ellice to Halifax, April 17 1867, Garrowby MSS.
4 Gladstone to Lord Lyttleton, April 1865 in Morley, *Gladstone*, ii, 133.
5 F. Foljambe, MP. for East Retford quoted in Halifax, *Journal*, March 30 1867, Garrowby MSS.
6 Knatchbull-Hugessen, *Diary*, October 27 1867, reporting Granville reporting Stanley of Alderley.
7 Halifax in *Journal*, March 30 1867, Garrowby MSS

PAGE 31

1 Gladstone to George Wilson, October 1 1864, George Wilson MSS.
2 Lord John Manners to his brother July 28 1866, Belvoir MSS. J. S. Mill, *Autobiography* (World's Classics edition), pp. 246–7.
3 Cf. Beales to Ernest Jones, June 2 and 22 1866, 95922/20.

PAGE 32

1 Harrison to Beesly, February 22 1866 and three undated letters, Harrison MSS Section A 1865–7. Beesly to Howell, January 14 [1867], 95922/20.
2 Harrison to Howell, September 5 [1866], 95922/20 D. For Walpole and Derby deciding not to remove Harrison's name from the royal commission despite the inflammatory nature of articles in the *Commonwealth* and *Fortnightly Review* see Walpole to Derby, February 11 1867, Derby MSS Box 153/4.
3 Quoted in F. E. Gillespie, *Labor and Politics in England 1850–67*, p. 140.
4 Beesly to Howell, March 15 1866, 95922/20.
5 Beesly to Harrison, March 1 1867, UCL. For Corry, see Corry to Mrs Disraeli, February 25 1867, Hughenden MSS.

PAGE 33

1 Beales to Disraeli, June 11 1866, Hughenden MSS.
2 Beales to Ernest Jones, June 22 1866, 95922/20.
3 Reform League Executive Committee Minutes, January 4 1867, 95922/4.

PAGE 34

1 E. D. Steele, *Irish Land Reform and English Liberal Politics 1865–70* (Cambridge Ph.D. thesis), pp. 54–5.
2 These were also, to some extent, explained away—at least in one case. Cf. *Morning Star*, October 6 1866 for modification of its first report of Bright's Manchester speech of September 26 1866 which contained his first warning and threat.
3 *Hansard*, March 26 1867 (636).
4 *Ibid*. (636–7).

PAGE 35

1 See p. 19, n. 4.
2 *Hansard*, May 3 1867 (1960).
3 Bright to Howell, July 19 and 20 (letters) and telegram 'Do not publish my letter', July 20 1866, 95922/20. The letter of denunciation is printed in Trevelyan, *Bright*, pp. 360–1, though Trevelyan does not mention that Bright tried to stop Howell publishing it.

PAGE 36

1 Fawcett to Howell, January 4 1866. Lusk to Howell, May 19 1866, both 95922/20. Mill, *Autobiography*, pp. 246–7. R. A. Buchanan, *Trades Unions and Public Opinion 1850–75*, p. 89 (unpublished thesis, Cambridge University Library). *Hansard*, May 3 1867 (1968–9 and 1978). Bright to Howell, January 30 1867, 95922/20. R. Culling Hanbury to Howell, September 20 1866, 95922/20.
2 A proponent of the bloomer.
3 Bright to Howell, December 20 1866, 95922/20.

PAGE 37

1 *We'll rally round the League, boys*, see Executive Committee Minutes, January 25 1867, 95922/4.
2 Reform League Executive Council Minutes, May 17 1866, Executive Committee, December 21 1866, 95922/4.
3 *Amberley Papers*, II, 12.
4 H. B. Bonner, *Life of Charles Bradlaugh*, I, 231; *National Reformer*, February 17 1867.
5 Marx to Engels, July 27 1866 in *Marx and Engels on Britain*, p. 541.

PAGE 38

1 See below, chapter V.
2 S. Walpole, *The History of Twenty-Five Years*, II, ch. ix, written by Walpole's son, gives an account of Walpole's view. It is based on Walpole's papers which I have not seen.

PAGE 39

1 For an unsubstantiated suggestion that they ought to have been see J. R. Vincent, *The Formation of the Liberal Party 1857–1868*, Appendix 2. For one area where there seems to have been no connection see Dunsmore, chapter I.
2 *Morning Star*, December 4 1866.
3 Hardy, *Diary*, February 18 1866.

PAGE 40

1 Gladstone in *Hansard*, March 18 1867 (39 and 45) and March 25 (500)
2 Royden Harrison, *Before the Socialists 1861–81*, p. 133.

PAGE 41

1 Royden Harrison, *Before the Socialists 1861–81*, p. 135.
2 *Ibid.*
3 Derby to Disraeli, December 22 1866, Hughenden MSS.
4 Disraeli to Stanley, Easter Sunday 1867, Knowsley MSS.
5 Stanley to Disraeli, April 23 [1867], Hughenden MSS.

PAGE 42

1 Colville to Stanley [May 8 1867], Knowsley MSS.
2 Royden Harrison, *Before the Socialists 1861–81*, p. 107.
3 Hardy, *Diary*, May 9 1867.
4 Walpole to Derby May 7 and Isabella Walpole to Derby May 8 1867, Derby MSS Box 153. See Derby to the Queen, May 11 1867, for his anxiety to 'reliev[e] his colleagues...of any public imputation of having sacrificed him to save themselves from censure with regard to the Park meetings', Derby MSS Box 194/1.
5 Royden Harrison, *Before the Socialists 1861–81*, p. 106.
6 *Ibid.* p. 112.

PAGE 44

1 Lowe to Lady Salisbury, May 19 1867, *A Great Lady's Friendships*.
2 R. D. Baxter to Derby, March 23 1867, Derby MSS Box 52/7.
3 Stanley to Disraeli, April 23 1867, Hughenden MSS.

PAGE 45

1 Parliamentary Accounts and Papers 1867, LVI, pp. 453 ff. and 459 ff. compared with 1867, LX, pp. 33 ff. show about thirty boroughs where the Small Tenements Acts had not been adopted in most parishes and twenty-nine where no Small Tenements or Local Rating Act was in force.
2 The list of these constituencies is in PA and P 1867, LVI, p. 460. See also Lambert, Memo March 13 1867, Hughenden MSS.
3 J. B. Smith in *Hansard*, May 9 1867 (321); Bright in *Hansard*, March 26 1867 (633–4).

PAGE 46

1 There are many ways of presenting the statistics which measure the proposed increases in the electorate. If one presents the increase established in the working-class majority by Hodgkinson's amendment in the form adopted by Baxter in February in presenting the bill of February 23, one gets an increase of 486,000 less $\frac{1}{2}$ (for non-registration) = 243,000, of whom 90,000 less $\frac{1}{2}$ were not necessarily working-class at all. So that the probable increase was slightly less than 200,000.
2 F. H. Herrick, 'The Second Reform Movement in Britain', in *Journal of the History of Ideas*, IX and 'The Reform Bill of 1867 and the British Party System' in *Pacific Historical Review*, III.

PAGE 47

1 Elcho to Marsden, May 21 1867, Wemyss MSS.
2 Grosvenor to Derby, May 14 1867, Derby MSS Box 164.
3 Stanley to Canon Blakesley, August 3 1867, Knowsley MSS.

PAGE 48

1 Russell to Brand, October 18 1866, Brand MSS; Knatchbull-Hugessen, *Diary*, October 27 1866.
The following rough estimate of the social composition of the House of Commons is given for what it is worth (the material was taken from Bateman, *Great Landowners of Great Britain and Ireland* 1883 and Dod's *Parliamentary Companion* 1867).

	Conservative party	Liberal party
(i) Aristocracy and gentry including heirs and landed manufacturers	150	130
(ii) Bateman connections (i.e. younger sons, non-landed and more distant)	40	80
(iii) Merchants, bankers, manufacturers	30*	115§
(iv) Lawyers, authors, civil engineers, tenant-farmer, dons, etc., i.e. professions	20†	80¶
(v) Unidentified, i.e. non-Bateman	c. 45‡	c. 20

* Includes 4 from (i).
† Includes 4 from (ii).
‡ Some of (v) should probably go into (iii).
§ Includes 30 from (i) and (ii).
¶ Includes 20 from (i) and (ii).
2 *Hansard*, March 18 1867 (45).

PAGE 49

1 *Hansard*, April 12 1867 (1694).
2 E. P. Bouverie to Edward Ellice, February 27 1867, Ellice MSS.
3 Argyll to Gladstone, March 12 and April 27 1867, Add. MSS 44100.
4 George Denman to Gladstone, May 1 1867, Add. MSS 44412.
5 T. D. Acland to Gladstone, April 13 1867, Add. MSS 44092.
6 Russell to Bright, July 10 1867, PRO 30 22/16 D.

PAGE 50

1 Stanley to Canon Blakesley, August 3 1867, Knowsley MSS.
2 Sir W. Bagge to Derby in Derby to Disraeli, May 12 1866, Hughenden MSS; R. Bagge to Stanley, March 17 1866, Knowsley MSS.
3 Malmesbury to Derby, June 11 1867, Derby MSS Box 144.

4 *A Journal of Events during the Gladstone Ministry 1868–74 by John, 1st Earl of Kimberley*, ed. by Ethel Drus, Camden Miscellany 1958, entry for July 16 1870, p. 17. *Hansard*, March 25 1867 (529).
5 *Hansard*, March 25 1867 (522).
6 For Holyoake see Gillespie, *Labor and Politics in England, 1850–67*, p. 158. For Ludlow, see J. M. Ludlow to Howell, June 26 1865, 95922/20

PAGE 51

1 Stanley to Canon Blakesley, August 3 1867, Knowsley MSS
2 Disraeli to Derby, February 28 1867, Derby MSS Box 146.
3 *Ibid.*
4 See above note 1.
5 Malmesbury to Derby, June 11 and September 5 1867, Derby MSS Box 144.
6 Elcho to Grosvenor, February 4 and to Marsden, May 21 1867, Wemyss MSS.

PAGE 52

1 Derby to Disraeli, February 1867, Hughenden MSS.
2 See p. 51, n. 6.
3 N. Kendall, MP. for E. Cornwall, *Hansard*, April 11 1867 (1541).
4 *Hansard*, April 27, 1866 (86).

PAGE 53

1 *Ibid.* (86).
2 List compiled from PA and P 1867–8 X.
3 *Hansard*, June 24 1867 (467–8).

PAGE 54

1 Adderley to Disraeli, January 29 [1866] Hughenden MSS.
2 C. Bright, *Life Story of Sir Charles Tilston Bright*, pp. 266–7.
3 *Hansard*, June 20 1867 (215).
4 *Hansard*, April 11 1867 (1555).

PAGE 55

1 *Hansard*, June 25 (514) and May 3 (1963) both 1867. For Neate's advocacy of direct political action by the trades unions see Gillespie, *Labor and Politics in England 1850–67*, p. 206.
2 *Hansard*, May 2 1867 (1883).
3 E. Baines to George Wilson, May 3 1864, George Wilson MSS. *Morning Star*, October 9 1866.
4 Memo (unsigned) from E. W. Watkin transmitted to Disraeli through Sir Philip Rose, Hughenden MSS B/XI/E/12, n.d. but after May 2.

PAGE 56

1 *Hansard*, June 24 1867 (457).
2 *Hansard*, May 13 1867 (473) and May 17 (703–4).

PAGE 57

1 Carnarvon in House of Lords, *Hansard*, March 4 1867 (1290).
2 Clarendon to Russell, September 5 1866, PRO 30 22/16 D. Earl Grey to Halifax, March 17 and April 2 1866, Garrowby MSS.
3 *Hansard*, March 25 1867 (539). Cf. 'the rabble' April 12 1867 (1602).

PAGE 58

1 *Hansard*, May 9 1867 (321).
2 *Hansard*, May 17 1867 (711).

PAGE 62

1 Russell to Brand, October 9 1866, Brand MSS.

PAGE 63

1 Gladstone to Brand, October 30 1866, Brand MSS. Gladstone to Grosvenor, August 18 1866 (copy), Add. MSS 44337.
2 Beesly to Howell, October 18 1865, 95922/20.

PAGE 65

1 Lord Nelson to Derby, December 17 1866, Derby MSS Box 113/4.

PAGE 66

1 S. Walpole, *The History of Twenty-five Years*, pp. 194 ff. For Beresford-Hope and Bagehot see *Hansard*, April 12 (1605–7) and *The Day*, March 25 1867 (quoting *The Economist*).
2 Bright in conversation, Trevelyan, *Bright*, p. 207.
3 Halifax, *Journal*, April 1 1867.
4 Acland to Gladstone [April 14], Add. MSS 44092.
5 *Ibid.*
6 Bright, *Diaries*, March 1 1867, p. 296. Disraeli to his wife, Hughenden MSS A/I/A324.

PAGE 67

1 Hardy, *Diary*, July 18 1866.
2 Lord John Manners, *Journal*, June 7 1866, Belvoir MSS. Northcote to Corry, June 11 1867 B/XX/N/3, Hughenden MSS. Disraeli to Derby, June 14 1867, Derby MSS Box 146.

PAGE 68

1 Newdegate, *Hansard*, May 31 1867 (1406). Cf. Disraeli, same date (1421) and June 17 (1956).
2 E.g. Carnarvon, *Journal* in Hardinge, [*Life of H. E. H. M. Herbert, 4th Earl of*] *Carnarvon*, 1925, I, 348. Exeter to Derby, March 9 1867, Derby MSS Box 111/2. Cranborne to Disraeli (quoting Lord Campbell), February 12 1867, Hughenden MSS. Sir William Heathcote to Gladstone, March 21 1867, Add. MSS 44209. Sir John Trollope's entry in

Dod, *Parliamentary Companion*. Dudley Baxter drafted the outline of a bill for this purpose. Acland suggested that Gladstone should propose separate arrangements for the small boroughs (April 2 1867, Add. MSS 44092). Newdegate's speeches throughout the session are relevant.

3 Laing, *Hansard*, June 17 1867 (1943).

4 Newdegate, *Hansard*, May 31 1867 (1410) says a third of the whole county electorate.

PAGE 70

1 Derby to Adderley, May 10 1866, Derby MSS 190/2.

PAGE 71

1 I.e. about 180 seats were situated in constituencies which altered geographically between 1865 and 1868. About 480 seats did not change geographically, and of these 170 were in constituencies where a change occurred in party representation in 1868.

2 Derby to Disraeli, August 4 1865, Derby MSS Box 190/2 (a copy: I think the original is not at Hughenden). Taylor to Disraeli [June 19 1866], Hughenden MSS. Knatchbull-Hugessen, *Diary*, March 22 1866.

3 Of these ninety, thirty-one were in constituencies whose boundaries were altered by the Boundary Act of 1868 (and in these the Liberal party gained nineteen and the Conservative party twelve).

PAGE 72

1 See below, p. 225.

2 In making these calculations I have omitted Dorset, since it was affected only by the disfranchisement of Lyme Regis, and Sussex, which was affected by the disfranchisement of Arundel in order to provide an extra Scottish seat in the 1868 Scottish Act. The loss of one Liberal seat in East Sussex was predicted by Baxter in 1866 on the assumption that a marked lowering of the county occupation franchise would neutralize the importance of the Brighton freeholders' county votes in relation to Conservative freeholders in the smaller towns. Baxter to Disraeli, May 14 1866, Hughenden MSS.

3 Lord John Manners to Derby, January 14 1867 (Derby MSS Box 161) for the view that the Conservative party would suffer from any large increase in the county electorate unless either borough freeholders' votes were removed from the county register or the larger county divisions were divided. For an attempt to question the belief that there was a Conservative swing in Lancashire in 1868, see J. R. Vincent, 'The Effect of the Second Reform Bill in Lancashire', in *Historical Journal* 1967 or 1968 (forthcoming).

PAGE 73

1 Baxter to Corry, March 16 1867, Hughenden MSS B/XX/J/89.

2 Lord John Manners, *Journal*, June 23 1867, Belvoir MSS. F. B. Smith, *The Making of the Second Reform Bill* quoting White, *The Inner Life of*

the House of Commons, II, 71–2 suggests that Disraeli accepted Horsfall's motion off the cuff. He may have decided to add Leeds at the last moment but it is unlikely that Horsfall's motion was decided in this way. White was doorkeeper to the House of Commons: his book (edited by his son), consists of the parliamentary sketches he wrote for the *Illustrated Times*. It is interesting but is not necessarily a guide to policy. Lord John Manners (*Journal* for June 23) suggests that the Cabinet had made the main decision of principle a week before (Belvoir MSS).

3 That all boroughs with more than 250,000 inhabitants according to the 1861 Census should have three MP.s
4 *Hansard*, July 2 1867 (888 ff.) and July 4 (993).
5 *Hansard*, July 1 1867 (836–8).
6 *Hansard*, July 2 1867 (879–880).
7 *Ibid.* (888).

PAGE 74

1 Glyn to Gladstone, July 3 1867, Add. MSS 44347.
2 Where 'no Conservative is to be found in its limits and it has returned a Whig since it was first registered', Lord Henry Lennox to Disraeli, June 1 1867, Hughenden MSS.
3 Russell to Gladstone, January 15 1868 [1867 written], Add. MSS 44293.

PAGE 75

1 Ayrshire, Clackmannanshire, Renfrewshire, Lanarkshire, Roxburghshire and Selkirk. The bill also provided for the division of Ayrshire, Lanarkshire and Aberdeenshire, the latter of which was to have two MP.s for each of its two divisions.

PAGE 76

1 E.g. Butler-Johnstone, *Hansard*, March 26 1867 (571 ff.), Hon. H. G. Liddell, March 26 (614), Hon. Percy Wyndham, March 26 (615) and Baron Dimsdale, June 3 (1529).
2 *Hansard*, May 31 1867 (1401 ff.).
3 H. A. Bruce to de Grey, May 31 1867, Add. MSS 43534.
4 I.e. six seats in six boroughs—Arundel, Ashburton, Dartmouth, Honiton, Thetford, Wells—which were removed (in order to provide for Scotland) in 1868, plus five seats in five boroughs—Buckingham, Evesham, Helston, Marlborough, Northallerton—which continued to have separate representation after 1868. There were also five Irish constituencies—Downpatrick, Dungarvon, Kinsale, Mallow, Portarlington—with populations (1861 census) smaller than 5,000, which would not have been affected by Gaselee's motion, and which were not affected by the Irish Reform *Act* of 1868, though Portarlington had been scheduled for disfranchisement in the Irish Reform *bill*.

Disraeli's Boundary Commissioners examined 222 boroughs and recommended alterations to the boundaries of seventy-one pre-1867 boroughs, ten Welsh districts, nine new boroughs and two divisions of counties. The Select Committee was instructed to look again at twenty-nine of the seventy-one pre-1867 boroughs and four of the nine new ones. In the case of fifteen of the largest boroughs it recommended that no boundary alteration should be made. It also suggested that two others should be added to the list. The government's bill of March 26, based on the original Commissioners' report, was then amended: when passed it altered seventy-nine constituencies in all.

5 Malmesbury to Derby, June 2 1867, Derby MSS Box 144. Malmesbury's figures imply that nothing was lost in the end. Cf. Dimsdale, in *Hansard*, June 3 (1530) before the government scheme was adopted, saying that the agricultural interest would lose twelve seats.

PAGE 77

1 *Hansard*, May 31 1867 (1399).
2 *Hansard*, June 13 1867 (1969).
3 Lowe to Lady Salisbury, June 3 1867 in *A Great Lady's Friendships*.
4 Lord Henry Lennox to Disraeli, June 2 1867, Hughenden MSS.
5 Lord Hill-Trevor to Derby, March 13 1867, Derby MSS Box 106. R. D. Baxter, memo on seats between 7,000 and 10,000, Derby MSS Box 52/7. A. D. Hayter, *Hansard*, April 8 1867 (1279).

PAGE 78

1 Disraeli to Derby [n.d.], Tuesday [but June 1867], reporting E. P. Bouverie, Derby MSS Box 146/3.
2 H. A. Bruce to de Grey, May 31 1867, Add. MSS 43534. Knatchbull-Hugessen in *Hansard*, June 3 1867 (1542 ff.), but cf. Hardy, *Diary*, June 2 1867 for the view that those Conservatives who thought this 'would be grievously disappointed'.
3 Cf. Acland to Gladstone, April 5 1867, Add. MSS 44092. Also Edward Ellice and Moncreiff (R. D. Baxter to Derby, March 23 1867, Derby MSS Box 52/7) for the view that household suffrage would be conservative in Coventry even without duality.
4 Bright to Russell, July 13 1867, PRO 30 22/16 D.
5 Bright in 1859 quoted in Gillespie, *Labor and Politics in England, 1850–67*, p. 159.

PAGE 79

1 Bright, *Diaries*, March 1 1867, p. 297. Cf. Russell to Gladstone, March 4 1867, Add. MSS 44293.
2 Bright in *Hansard*, April 12 1867 (1670).
3 Bright to his wife, August 8 1867, UCL.
4 Derby to Disraeli, November 18 1866, Derby MSS Box 146.

PAGE 80

1 Derby to Disraeli, August 4 1865, Derby MSS Box 190.
2 Spofforth to Derby, August 2 1865, Derby MSS Box 104.
3 Hardy, *Diary*, September 25 1865.
4 I.e. 'Your' could mean either Derby's *or* Disraeli's. Cf. Northcote, *Diary*, February 3 1866, Add. MSS 50063 A and Lang, *Life, Letters and Diaries of Sir Stafford Northcote*, pp. 138–61. 'Long talk with Dis. this afternoon. He says he communicated with Lord D. after the election, putting before him...the necessity of reconstruction; that he told him that he thought reconstruction could not be carried through without a change of leader in one or the other House, and that he was willing to give up the lead in the Commons in order to facilitate it; that Lord D. rejected that idea, *and did not seem to appreciate the alternative.*'
5 Disraeli to Derby, August 6 1865, Derby MSS Box 146.
6 Derby to Disraeli, August 12 1865, Hughenden MSS.
7 Disraeli to Derby, September 3 1865, Derby MSS Box 146.

PAGE 81

1 Derby to Disraeli, August 12 1865, Hughenden MSS.
2 Clarendon to Granville, October 21 1865, PRO 30 29/29 A.
3 Lord John Manners to Disraeli, December 26 1865, Hughenden MSS.
4 Robert Lowe to his brother, July 26 1865, Patchett Martin, *Life and Letters of Robert Lowe, Viscount Sherbrooke*, II, 241.

PAGE 82

1 Quoted in Masheder, *Dissent and Democracy*, p. 243.
2 Derby to Disraeli, August 4 1865, Derby MSS Box 190.
3 Naas to Derby, October 24 1865, Derby MSS Box 104.

PAGE 83

1 Spofforth to Disraeli, October 30 1865, Hughenden MSS.
2 Earle to Disraeli, November 4 1865, Hughenden MSS.
3 Disraeli to Derby, August 6 1865, Derby MSS Box 146.
4 Spofforth to Disraeli, November 2 1865, Hughenden MSS.
5 Elcho to Disraeli, May 11 1865, Hughenden MSS.
6 Disraeli to Derby, September 3 1865, Derby MSS Box 146.
7 Disraeli to Derby, November 24 1865, Derby MSS Box 146.

PAGE 84

1 Granville to Russell, March 26 1866, PRO 30 29/22 A.
2 Sir George Grey to Brand, November 1 1865, Brand MSS.
3 Who went to the Lords as Lord Halifax in February 1866.
4 Brand to Russell, February 3 1866, PRO 30 22/16.
5 L. Wolf, *Life of First Marquess of Ripon* (i.e. de Grey), I, 212–14.
6 Unsigned memorandum, October 23 1865, PRO 30 22/15. Gladstone to Russell, October 24 1865, PRO 30 22/15.

7 Gladstone to Russell, October 27 1865, Add. MSS 44292.
8 Bouverie to Ellice, October 26 1865, Ellice MSS.
9 Gladstone to Russell, February 1 1866, PRO 30 22/16. Argyll to Gladstone February 2 1866, Add. MSS 44100.

PAGE 85

1 Milner Gibson to Bright, January 11 1866, Add. MSS 43388.
2 Gladstone to Sir George Grey, March 6 1866, Add. MSS 44162.
3 For Goschen's view of Bright and class conflict see Goschen to Cobden, n.d. in *Lord Goschen and His Friends* (*The Goschen Letters*), ed. by Percy Colson, pp. 19–20. For his father's view see Eliot's *Goschen*, I, 80–1. For Sir William Hutt see Hutt to Gladstone, October 20 1865 and January 13 1866, Add. MSS 44409. Cf. Cranborne in *Quarterly Review*, CIX, 252–3. For Knatchbull-Hugessen's opinions see Spofforth to Disraeli, December 9 1865, Hughenden MSS, quoting Knatchbull-Hugessen.
4 Gladstone to Russell, October 24; Russell to Peel, November 16; the Queen to Russell, November 12; unsigned memorandum, n.d. [after November 12], all 1865 and all PRO 30 22/15.
5 Gladstone to Russell, December 6 1865, PRO 30 22/15.

PAGE 86

1 Gladstone to Russell, December 8; and Russell to Granville, December 7 1865, PRO 30 29/18 and 29 A.
2 Stanley to Disraeli, November 16 1865, Hughenden MSS.
3 Gladstone to Russell, October 30 1865, PRO 30 22/15.
4 Cf. the Queen's conversation with Russell, October 29 1866 in Buckle, *Letters of Queen Victoria 1862–78*, I, 281–3.
5 Russell to Gladstone, December 9 1865; Gladstone to Russell, December 11 1865, both Add. MSS 44292.
6 Elcho to Stanley of Alderley, November 1 1865 and to Kinglake, March 1866, Wemyss MSS.
7 Russell to Gladstone, n.d. Add. MSS 44292. Cf. unsigned memorandum, November 25 1865, PRO 30 22/15—one of a series of memoranda recording Russell's conversation at Pembroke Lodge, and written by one of his staff or family. Cf. Northcote, *Diary*, March 8 1866.

PAGE 87

1 Unsigned memorandum, October 23 1865, PRO 30 22/15. For confirmation of this view from Forster himself, see Northcote, *Diary*, March 14 1866, Add. MSS 50063A, Morley, *Gladstone*, II, 123 and T. Wemyss Reid, *Life of W. E. Forster*, I, 362.
2 Bright to Gladstone, February 10 1866, Add. MSS 44112.
3 Cf. Clarendon to Lady Salisbury, Maxwell, *Life and Letters of the Fourth Earl of Clarendon*, II, 309.
4 Somerset to Russell, October 20, 21 and 23 1865, PRO 30 22/15.
5 Wood to Russell, January 30 1866, PRO 30 22/16.

PAGE 88

1 For Russell's memorandum, Gladstone's supporting letter and memoranda from members of the Cabinet (dated March 6–8 1866), see PRO 30 22/16.
2 The Duke of Somerset (memorandum No. 4), *loc. cit.*
3 Sir George Grey to Russell, April 29 1866, PRO 30 22/16.
4 Russell to Brand, April 28 1866, Brand MSS.
5 Sir George Grey to Russell, January 6 1866, PRO 30 22/15.
6 Villiers to Russell, December 23 1865, PRO 30 22/15. Masheder, *Dissent and Democracy*, p. 246. Cf. 'certainly less than one-tenth', Gladstone in *Hansard*, May 11 1864 (316). For the returns themselves see PA and P LVII 1866, pp. 47–51 and 215–521.
7 Russell to Brand, October 27 1865, Brand MSS.

PAGE 89

1 Cf. Gladstone to Russell, December 27 1865, Add. MSS 44292.
2 Cf. Gladstone to Villiers, December 27 1865, Add. MSS 44408.

PAGE 90

1 Halifax to Earl Grey, April 5 1866, Howick MSS; Halifax to Russell, March 23 1866, PRO 30 22/16.
2 Cf. Speaker Denison to Sir George Grey, Morley, *Gladstone*, II, 198–9.
3 Unsigned memorandum, n.d. [but about November 12 1865], PRO 30 22/15.
4 General Grey's memorandum, March 23 1866, RA F 14/7.
5 Cf. Gladstone to Russell, October 23 1865, Morley, *Gladstone*, II, 153; Gladstone to Russell, January 1 1866, PRO 30 22/15.
6 Unsigned memorandum, November 14 1865, PRO 30 22/15.
7 Cf. his remarks (when de Grey was offered the India Office instead of Argyll) on the importance of a regular ladder of promotion (Gladstone to Russell, February 1 1866, PRO 30 22/16).

PAGE 91

1 Cf. Bright to Gladstone, February 10 1866, Add. MSS 44112.
2 Cf. General Grey's memorandum, March 23 1866, RA F 14/16.

PAGE 92

1 Spofforth to Disraeli, January 5 1866, Hughenden MSS.
2 Derby to Pakington, November 10 1865, Derby MSS Box 190.
3 Hardy, *Diary*, March 9 1866.
4 Derby to Carnarvon, November 7 1865, Derby MSS Box 190; Derby to Malmesbury, November 6 1865 in Malmesbury, *Memoirs of an Ex-Minister*, II, 342–3.
5 Cf. Stanley to Disraeli, November 8 1865, Hughenden MSS.

PAGE 93

1 Lang, *Northcote*, p. 135.
2 And whose arrival would, one might add, ruin so many of their political prospects in the Conservative party.
3 Northcote, *Diary*, February 4 1866.
4 Taylor to Disraeli, June 27 1866 (letter I), Hughenden MSS.
5 Malmesbury, *Diary*, March 11 1866 in *Memoirs of an ex-Minister*, II, 349. Cf. Halifax, *Journal*, March 17 1867, for Bath still hoping for a Gladstone/Cranborne coalition in 1867.
6 Hardy to Cairns, December 26 1865, Cairns MSS.
7 Northcote, *Diary*, Add. MSS 50063A, March 3 1866.

PAGE 94

1 Northcote, *Diary*, March 6 1866, Add. MSS 50063 A (omitted from Lang's reprinting of the diary, Lang, p. 151). Cf. *The Times*, February 2 1866 (suggesting Somerset as a possible successor if the government was to remain Liberal).
2 Northcote, *Diary*, March 7 1866 Add. MSS 50063A.
3 Northcote, *Diary*, February 3 1866, *loc. cit.*
4 Derby to Pakington, November 10 1865. Derby MSS Box 190.
5 I have found no evidence to suggest that they were, or that Gladstone approached, or thought of approaching, the Conservative leaders for *any* general political purpose between October 1865 and July 1866. He seems to have asked Northcote to defend the government against attacks on its handling of the Cattle Plague question, but, as Northcote records in his diary (February 6 1866, *loc. cit.*), 'I didn't see why I should'.
6 Cf. Bright to Villiers, n.d. PRO 30 22/15.

PAGE 95

1 *Quarterly Review*, CXIX (1866), 268.
2 Northcote, *Diary*, March 16 1866, Add. MSS 50063A.
3 *Ibid.* February 22 1866.
4 Hardinge, [*Life of H. H. M. Herbert, Fourth Earl of*] *Carnarvon*, I, 277.

PAGE 96

1 Memorandum, Brand to Gladstone, March 22 1866, Add. MSS 44194.
2 Halifax to Earl Grey, April 5 1866, Howick MSS.
3 *Hansard*, March 23 and April 19, 1866 (843–4), (862–3) and (1166).
4 Hardy, *Diary*, April 27 1866. Cf. Lowe to his brother, April 8 1866 in Patchett Martin, *Robert Lowe, Viscount Sherbrooke*, II, 277 and Elcho to Ellice, April 25 1866, Ellice MSS.
5 Cf. the caution (perhaps what Cranborne meant by the 'dreamy sentimentalism') of his speech in Glasgow: Parliament 'will seek...neither to continue, nor to set up, nor in any manner to favour dominion, or the

undue influence of one class compared with another but in a fair adjustment of common rights and common interests to make provision for the happiness and for the strength and prosperity of the country' (*The Times*, November 2 1865).
6 Stanley to Disraeli, January 21 1866, Hughenden MSS.

PAGE 97
1 Granville to Brand, January 16 1867, Brand MSS.
2 Derby to Whiteside, January 19 1866, Derby MSS Box 190.
3 Disraeli to Derby, n.d., Derby MSS Box 146. The Russell resignation rumour is almost certainly the same as the rumour reported in *The Times* on February 28 1866, which may have arisen from something the Prince of Wales said to Delane or from the fact that Russell, having said 'in joke and for chaff' to the Duke of Somerset after a Cabinet meeting '"Oh, I shall have to give up the reins of Government to you"', inspired the Duke to tell the Duchess in the presence of their daughter Lady Gwendoline Ramsden who 'ran off at once to tell her husband, who told his connection Horsman, who ran to Lowe, and Lowe into Delane's arms, and so it was...printed and believed to be true' (B. and P. Russell ed., *Amberley Papers*, I, 476). There is no evidence that Russell offered to resign at any time between October 1865 and June 1866, though it is clear that some Cabinet ministers would have liked him to. For the reliability of the anecdote about Sir Charles Phipps's death, cf. 'Whilst I was dressing got the fatal telegram from Dr Jenner saying that dear Sir Charles had died at half p. 5 this morning' (Queen Victoria's *Diary*, 24 February 1866). I am grateful to Miss Jane Langton, the Assistant Registrar in the Royal Archives, for kindly supplying this reference. The Queen seems not to have seen Russell that day, part of which she spent in London calling on Lady Phipps.
4 Northcote, *Diary*, Add. MSS 50063A, February 28 1866.
5 *Ibid.* February 19 1866.
6 Cf. Elcho to Grosvenor, May 8 1866, Wemyss MSS.
7 *Hansard*, April 12 1866 (1156).
8 Horsman to Elcho, February 25, 1867, Wemyss MSS.

PAGE 98
1 Northcote, *Diary*, Add. MSS 50063A, March 24 1866.
2 Wemyss MSS. Kerrison to Disraeli, Hughenden MSS, B/XXI/K/114.
3 Bouverie to Ellice, October 25 and November 1 1865, Ellice MSS.
4 Bouverie to Ellice, January 24 and March 14 1866, *loc. cit.*
5 Bouverie to Ellice, March 14 1866, *loc. cit.*
6 Spofforth to Disraeli, December 9 1865, January 9 and April 5 1866, Hughenden MSS (for Knatchbull-Hugessen). For election petitions see Taylor to Derby, December 6 1865, Derby MSS Box 104. Election petitions were presented in the case of sixteen or seventeen constituen-

cies in which at least one Liberal MP. had been elected. In seven of these cases involving nine MP.s the petition was successful. Apart from Colonel Crosland none of the MP.s who were petitioned against seems to have been notably reactionary, but the numbers involved are small and I do not know how many more reactionary Liberals who might have been petitioned against were in the end spared.

PAGE 99

1 Cf. Russell to Sir George Grey, December 10 1865, PRO 30 22/15.
2 See Russell's memorandum to Cabinet, February 12 1866, PRO 30 22/16.
3 Russell to Sir George Grey, December 10 1865, PRO 30 22/15. Cf. Brand to Gladstone, January 15 1866, Add. MSS 44194.
4 Sir George Grey to Russell, January 6 1866, PRO 30 22/16.
5 Russell to Sir George Grey, January 7 1866 in Gooch, *Russell*, II, 343.

PAGE 100

1 Brand to Gladstone, January 15 1866, Add. MSS 44193. For the Cabinet division on the question, see Gladstone's Cabinet note of January 29 1866 ' Shall there be any redistribution of seats? Aye, Somerset, Cardwell. Postpone, Wood, Goschen, de Grey, Villiers. No, Chancellor, Grey, Gladstone, Russell, Clarendon, Argyll, Gibson, Stanley [of Alderley] ', Add. MSS 44636.
2 Cf. Gladstone to Russell, March 22 1866; Brand to Russell, March 29 1866, both PRO 30 22/16; Granville to Russell, March 26 1866, PRO 30 29/22 A.
3 Sir George Grey to Russell, April 29 1866, PRO 30 22/16.
4 Accepted by the Cabinet on May 2: Russell to the Queen, May 3 1866, PRO 30 22/16.
5 Brand to Russell, April 1 1866, PRO 30 22/16.

PAGE 101

1 Lord E. Bruce to Gladstone, April 25 1866, Add. MSS 44410; Clarendon to Granville, n.d. [but beginning of April] in Maxwell, *Clarendon*, II, 313.
2 *Speeches of John Bright*, ed. Thorold Rogers, II, 155–6. For the effect of Bright's support see Granville to Russell, March 26 1866, PRO 30 29/29 A; Brand to Clarendon, April 21 1866 in Maxwell, *Clarendon*, II, 314; Lord E. Bruce to Gladstone, April 25 1866, Add. MSS 44410.
3 Cf. General Grey's desire in October 1865 to see Lowe Chancellor of the Duchy as a makeweight to Amberley's influence on Russell (General Grey to Earl Grey, October 20 1865, Howick MSS).
4 Cf. ' I believe that we shall never be safe until some patriotic individual burns down Pembroke Lodge' (de Grey to Wood, January 11 1866 in Maxwell, *Clarendon*, II, 306); and ' I hear Brand don't at all like holding

his conferences with Lady Russell one of the party' Bouverie to Ellice, February 4 1866, Ellice MSS).

5 Northcote, *Diary*, March 3 1866, Add. MSS 50063A.
6 Bouverie to Ellice, January 16 1866, Ellice MSS.
7 Bouverie to Ellice, April 1 1866, *loc. cit.*
8 Elcho to Grosvenor, May 8 1866, Wemyss MSS.
9 Elcho to Grosvenor, n.d. [1866], *loc. cit.*

PAGE 102

1 Elcho to Ellice, April 25 1866, Ellice MSS.
2 Bouverie to Ellice, April 4 1866, *loc. cit.*
3 Cranborne in *Quarterly Review* (1866), cxx, p. 261.
4 Northcote, *Diary*, March 16 1866, Add. MSS. 50063A.
5 Clarendon to Russell, September 9 1866, PRO 30 22/15.
6 Cf. Granville to Gladstone, April 24 and July 4 1866, Add. MSS 44165, reporting the government Chief Whip in the House of Lords.
7 *Amberley Papers*, I, 485.
8 *Loc. cit.* p. 486.
9 Cf. Bouverie to Ellice, April 10 1866, Ellice MSS.

PAGE 103

1 General Grey's memorandum, April 29 1866, RA F 14/44. Cf. General Grey to Earl Grey, April 30 1866, Howick MSS.
2 Halifax to General Grey, June 21 1866, RA C 32/23.
3 Sir George Grey to General Grey, June 21 1866, RA C 32/21.
4 Elcho to Disraeli, June 2 1866, Hughenden MSS recording Delane's account of conversation with Halifax.
5 Clarendon to Russell, June 23 1866, Clarendon MSS dep. c. 104.
6 Brand to Russell, June 23 1866, PRO 30 22/16.
7 General Grey's memorandum, April 24 1866; Granville to General Grey, April 24 1866; the Queen to Russell (draft and letter), RA F 14/33, /35, /37 and RA C 15/51.

PAGE 104

1 RA C 32/11, 14, 15 and 23.
2 Russell to Brand, April 29 1866, Brand MSS.
3 Russell to the Queen, June 1 1866, RA F 14/63.
4 *Ibid.* June 9, 1866, RA F 14/69.
5 General Grey's memorandum, June 10 1866, RA F 14/70.
6 Gladstone to Russell, June 20 1866, PRO 30 22/16.

PAGE 105

1 Speech at Liverpool, April 5 1866 (*The Times*, April 6 1866).
2 Gladstone to Russell, June 20 1866, PRO 30 22/16.
3 *Ibid.*
4 Clarendon to Russell, June 25 1866 in Maxwell, *Clarendon*, II, 317.

5 Bright to Gladstone, June 24 1866, Add. MSS 44112.

6 Gladstone to President and Secretary of London Working Men's Association, July 2 1866 (press cutting), Add. MSS 44755.

PAGE 106

1 Elcho to Disraeli, June 21 1866, Hughenden MSS.

2 Hardy, *Diary*, June 21 1866.

3 The chief source for suspicion of Halifax is an almost illegible note (dated June 29 1867, Add. MSS 44411) from David Robertson (*né* Marjoribanks), MP. for Berwickshire—in which he describes for Gladstone's benefit a meeting of backbenchers conducted by F. Foljambe, R. W. Crawford and Sir John Johnstone at Foljambe's house. The meeting, ostensibly called in order to decide what sort of attitude to take to the possibility of the government staying in office, was prefaced by a declaration from the chair by Johnstone that he was a 'liberal-conservative' and followed by the allegation, aimed at Gladstone, that, though an attempt had been made to draft a resolution to enable the government to stay in office which 'had been prepared by a friend of the government (who...turned out to be...Ch. Wood, now Lord Halifax), it had been unreasonably rejected'. Robertson and other 'liberals' objected to this because it seemed to lay the blame on Gladstone and read out a letter Gladstone had written Robertson that day or the day before. The meeting reached no agreement and is of no importance in itself except as suggesting that there may have been more to Halifax's intervention than is implied in the account given in his *Journal* for this period. But there is not enough evidence to justify more than a suspicion.

PAGE 107

1 Derby to the Queen, June 28 1866, RA C 32/50; Northcote, *Diary*, June 28, Add. MSS 50063A; Hardy, *Diary*, June 29 1866.

2 There is no direct evidence of this: there are only clues. There is his reluctance to accept the Foreign Office in 1865: the fact that he was mentioned by Conservatives as one whom the Adullamites would accept as leader: there are Russell's complaints that 'Lord Clarendon is mixed up in these intrigues...[which] had been going on among Lord Elcho and that party who wished to induce Lord Derby, if the Government should fall, to refuse to form a government in order that the Queen might send for the Horsman and Lowe party' (unsigned memorandum, March 24 1866, PRO 30 22/16). There is Clarendon's attempt to open the Queen's mind to the possibility that, if the Russell Government were defeated, Derby might refuse to form a government (General Grey's memorandum, March 23 1866, RA F 14/16). There is the judgement of Lord Cowley, the ambassador to Paris, in a letter to Lady Salisbury: 'It is a great pity that Lord Derby cannot be persuaded to retire...he will not be able...to form a strong government but I do not see why Lord Stanley should not...Clarendon must bitterly repent having had any-

thing to do with the Russell Cabinet. What a position he would have had at this moment had he kept away from that dangerous source of mischief' (Cowley to Lady Salisbury, 29 June 1866, *A Great Lady's Friendships*).

3 Somerset to Derby, June 29 1866, Derby MSS Box 114; Derby to General Grey, June 29 1866, Derby MSS Box 190.

4 Disraeli to Derby, June 27 1866, Derby MSS Box 146. Hodder, *Shaftesbury*, III, 211.

5 Shaftesbury to Derby, June 29 1866 (two letters) and June 30 1866, Derby MSS Box 114. For Shaftesbury's 'shrinking from office', see Shaftesbury to Robert Baxter (who acted as intermediary for Disraeli and Derby), and Baxter to Disraeli, Hughenden MSS B/XXI/B/183 and 184.

6 Derby to the Queen and to General Grey, July 23 1866, Derby MSS Box 190. Cf. Taylor to Disraeli, July 28 [1866], Hughenden MSS.

7 Disraeli to Derby, Tuesday morning [3 July] 1866, Derby MSS Box 146.

8 Disraeli to Derby, Tuesday morning 6 a.m. [July 1866], Derby MSS Box 146.

PAGE 108

1 Grosvenor to Lansdowne, June 30 1866, Lansdowne MSS.

2 Derby, memorandum in Derby to Disraeli, n.d. [June 30 1866], Hughenden MSS B/XX/S/349.

3 W. H. Gregory to Derby, June 30 1866, Derby MSS Box 111. For Lansdowne's pledge of support for Derby's government 'if, as I hope and believe, it is established upon principles which will admit of the cooperation of moderate and constitutional Whigs', see Lansdowne (who died a week later) to Derby, June 30 1866, Derby MSS Box 112.

4 Derby to Disraeli, n.d. [St James's Square 7.20 p.m. June 22 or June 23], Hughenden MSS.

5 Elcho to Disraeli, June 21 1866, Hughenden MSS.

6 Elcho to Earle, June 26 1866, Wemyss MSS.

PAGE 109

1 Disraeli to Derby, June 23 1866, Derby MSS Box 146.

2 Buckle, *Disraeli*, IV, 439.

3 Elcho to Lansdowne, June 19 1866, Lansdowne MSS.

4 Lord Colville to Derby, Thursday 2 p.m. June 28 1866 (Derby MSS Box 110), reporting a visit from Gilbert Heathcote 'as an ambassador from the Adullamite Camp' to say that 'various Adullamites' on comparing notes 'at the Ball last night' found that 'no overtures had been made to any of them or to Lord Lansdowne' and adding that an overture 'had been, and is expected by them'. Cf. Elcho to Cairns, June 28, for Elcho trying to induce Cairns to advocate coalition (Wemyss MSS) and Sir H. Edwards to Disraeli, June 29 1866, Hughenden MSS B/XXI/E/67.

5 Unsigned memorandum, March 24 1866, PRO 30 22/16.

6 Disraeli to Derby, June 25 1866, Derby MSS Box 146.

NOTES TO PAGES 110-113

PAGE 110

1 Elcho to Horsman, January 15 1866, Wemyss MSS.
2 Elcho to W. H. Gregory, May 19 1866, *loc. cit.*
3 Earle to Disraeli, n.d., Hughenden MSS B/XX/E/379.
4 *Ibid.*
5 Cf. Lowe to Lansdowne, January 16 [?] 1866, Lansdowne MSS.
6 Cf. H. A. Bruce to de Grey, October 22 1865, Add. MSS 43534.
7 Cf. Grosvenor to Lansdowne, June 30 1866, Lansdowne MSS.

PAGE 111

1 Horsman to Elcho, December 17 1865, Wemyss MSS; Horsman to Lansdowne, June 30 1866, Lansdowne MSS.
2 Lytton to John Forster, *Personal and Literary Letters of the Earl of Lytton*, I, 214.
3 Northcote, *Diary*, March 23 1866 Add. MSS 50063A.
4 Unsigned memorandum, March 24 1866 (reporting Queen's conversation with Russell), PRO 30 22/16.
5 Northcote, *Diary*, February 22 and March 23 1866, Add. MSS 50063A.
6 Cf. 'Gladstone's failure as a leader becomes more manifest every day: but they have taken a long time to discover it' (Lowe to his brother, February 20 1866, Patchett Martin, *Robert Lowe, Viscount Sherbrooke*, II, 268). Cf. Lowe to Mrs Billiard of Sydney, *loc. cit.* p. 279. It would be interesting to know what is omitted from Martin's rendering (II, 294) of Lowe's letter of May 24 1866 to Mrs Billiard: 'I have reached a position I never expected in my wildest dreams to attain...[Martin's omission] You know I never was very ambitious and always cared more for the fight than for the prize.'
7 Clarendon to Russell, June 30 [1866], PRO 30 22/16.

PAGE 112

1 It was, for example, Granville who carried the Cabinet's conciliatory message to Lowe in December 1865, though cf. Granville to Russell, March 26 1866 (PRO 30 29/22 A), for Granville's irritation.
2 Northcote, *Diary*, Add. MSS 50063A, February 22 1866.
3 General Grey's memorandum, June 22 1866, RA C 32/16.
4 Which Clarendon thought Disraeli particularly wanted, and Derby particularly wanted him not to have (Clarendon to Russell, June 29 1866, PRO 30 22/16).
5 Northcote, *Diary*, Add. MSS 50063A, March 2 1866.
6 Taylor to Disraeli, June 27 1866, Hughenden MSS.
7 Knightley to Derby, July 3 1866, Derby MSS Box 112.

PAGE 113

1 Cf. W. E. H. Lecky, prefatory memoir to *Speeches and Addresses of Edward Henry, XVth Earl of Derby* (i.e. Stanley), I, ix-xliv.
2 Earle to Disraeli, November 4 1865, Hughenden MSS.

3 Though not at the end of February, cf. Northcote *Diary*, Add. MSS 50063A, February 28, 1866.
4 Northcote, *Diary*, Add. MSS 50063A, June 28 1866.
5 Selborne (i.e. Roundell Palmer), *Memorials Personal and Political, 1865–95*, I, 62.
6 D. Robertson, MP. to Gladstone, June 30 1866, Add. MSS 44411.
7 Malmesbury's *Diary*, June 22 and 27 1866 in *Memoirs of an ex-Minister*, I, 356–7.

PAGE 114

1 Spofforth to Disraeli, November 4 1865, Hughenden MSS.
2 Cf. General Grey's memorandum of conversation with Derby, June 30 1866, RA C 32/65.
3 Derby to Adderley, May 10 1866, Derby MSS Box 190
4 Northcote, *Diary*, Add. MSS 50063A, February 22 1866, reporting Northcote's conversation with Jolliffe.
5 General Grey's memorandum of conversation with Derby, June 29 1866, RA C 32/48.
6 General Grey's memorandum of conversation with Derby, June 30 1866, RA C 32/65.
7 Horsman to Lansdowne, Lansdowne to Horsman, Grosvenor to Lansdowne, all June 30 1866, Lansdowne MSS.
8 Northcote, *Diary*, Add. MSS 50063A, June 28 1866.
9 Taylor to Disraeli [June 27 1866], Hughenden MSS.
10 Northcote, *Diary*, Add. MSS 50063A, June 28 1866.

PAGE 115

1 Disraeli to Derby, June 25 1866 (letter I), Derby MSS Box 146.
2 Northcote, *Diary*, Add. MSS 50063A, June 29 1866.
3 Cf. Milner Gibson to Bright, June 30 1866, Add. MSS 43388 (reporting conversation with Northcote).
4 Disraeli to Derby, June 25 1866 (letter II), Derby MSS Box 146.
5 Derby to General Grey, June 29 [1866], 10 p.m., Derby MSS Box 190. Cf. Derby to Disraeli, n.d. Wednesday, Hughenden MSS B/XX/S/347 (in relation to Shaftesbury).

PAGE 116

1 Disraeli to Derby, June 25 1866, Derby MSS Box 146.
2 Northcote, *Diary*, Add. MSS 50063A, June 28 1866.

PAGE 117

1 Cf. Derby to General Grey, July 2 1866, Derby MSS Box 190 ('must ask you to prepare Her Majesty's mind for my possible failure ultimately to construct a government').
2 Earle to Disraeli, n.d. Hughenden MSS B/XX/E/376.
3 Hardy, *Diary*, June 20 and 21 1866 (including Carnarvon's approval of Lansdowne).

4 Cf. 'They seem to have given up the idea of Lord Derby making way to Lord Granville and concentrate their efforts upon the plan of inducing you to go to the House of Lords. Horsman thinks he can lead the House of Commons!!!' (Earle to Disraeli, n.d. [but during the last week of June], Hughenden MSS B/XX/E/409).

5 E.g. Somerset who, despite his 'cold manner' was less of a 'party man' than Granville and therefore, perhaps, more acceptable to 'moderate Conservatives' (General Grey's memorandum, June 28 1866, RA C 32/49).

6 *Ibid.*

7 Northcote, *Diary*, Add. MSS 50063A, February 5, March 8 and 25 1866.

PAGE 118

1 Malmesbury to Derby, November 8 1865, Derby MSS Box 146. Knatchbull-Hugessen, *Diary*, June 27 1866. Cf. Derby's early brake on the distribution of peerages, etc., in July/August 1866, in face of the flood of applications, e.g. Derby to Sir George Sinclair, August 13 1866 says he had received thirty-two applications for peerages (Box 191/2). For the fears felt by potential Conservative ministers at the effect of fusion on their own prospects, see Northcote, *Diary*, March 25 1866.

2 Disraeli to Derby, July 2 1866, Derby MSS Box 146.

PAGE 120

1 Earl Spencer to Elcho, January 21 1867, Wemyss MSS.

PAGE 121

1 E.g. Russell to Gladstone, July 12 1866, Add. MSS 44293.

2 Russell to Gladstone, July 31 1866, *ibid.*

3 Russell to Gladstone, August 1 1866, *ibid.*

4 Russell to Gladstone, August 31 1866, *ibid.*

5 Russell to Gladstone, September 7 and 27 1866, *ibid.*

6 Halifax, *Journal*, February 4 1867.

7 *Ibid.* February 17 1867.

8 *Ibid.* February 13 1867.

9 Clarendon to Russell, September 9 1866, PRO 30 22/16 D.

10 Brand to Halifax, October 1 1866, Garrowby MSS. Granville had been asked to form a government when Derby resigned in 1859. Brand's expectation was based, presumably, on the assumption that the Whig/Adullamite bid to erode the Conservative party by forming a broad-based coalition, which had been foiled by Derby and Disraeli in July 1866, would be irresistible once Derby's government had turned out to be inadequate.

11 Knatchbull-Hugessen, *Diary*, October 27 1866. Cf. Bouverie to Ellice, December 18 1866 (Ellice MSS) for Bouverie's view that Gladstone could not lead and that Sir George Grey was dissatisfied. Cf. also Halifax, *Journal*, February 4 1867 for Granville and Clarendon as possibili-

ties. Cf. Stansfeld to Halifax for Granville, November 11 1866, Garrow-by MSS.

12 Corry to Disraeli, October 19 1866, Hughenden MSS, reporting at second hand the views of Sir George Grey.

13 Clarendon, PRO 30 22/16 D (August 14 1866) reporting to Russell that his brother-in-law had 'heard from three different persons that Gladstone had bought the whole of the contents of the Kremer's toyshop and ordered them to be sent home and that Mrs Gladstone had gone to the shop and countermanded the order. I have heard of her having had to do this several times within the last few months...a melancholy proof of his tendency and of what Fergusson who knew him well always told me would be his destiny if he lived long enough and gave himself no rest'. Cf. Morley, *Gladstone*, II, 181.

PAGE 122

1 *Hansard*, April 27 1866 (130).
2 Gladstone to Bishop Wilberforce, July 25 1865 in Morley, *Gladstone*, II, 150.
3 Gladstone to Russell, October 18 1865, PRO 30 22/15.
4 Knatchbull-Hugessen, *Diary*, June 30 1866.
5 Russell to Brand, October 2 1866, Brand MSS.
6 Brand to Halifax, October 1 1866, Garrowby MSS; Clarendon to Gladstone, February 13 1867, Add. MSS 44133; Sir George Grey to Brand, October 9 1866, Brand MSS; Russell to Brand, December 10 1866, Brand MSS; Gladstone to Brand, October 30 1866, Brand MSS.

PAGE 123

1 Clarendon to Russell, July 19 and August 10 1866, PRO 30 22/16 D.
2 Russell to Brand, October 1 and December 10 1866, Brand MSS; Brand to Gladstone, November 26 1866, Add. MSS 44193; Gladstone to Brand, October 30 1866, Brand MSS.
3 Clarendon to Russell, September 9 1866, PRO 30 22/16 D.
4 Brand to Gladstone, October 23 1866, Add. MSS 44193.
5 I.e. the Brecknock by-election of October 4 1866 in which Lord Brecknock 'gave us no assistance which was equivalent to turning his back upon his brother-in-law, Churchill', Brand to Gladstone, September 9 1866, Brand MSS.
6 Clarendon to Russell, September 16 1866, PRO 30 22/16 D.
7 Argyll to Gladstone, November 4 1866, Add. MSS 44100.

PAGE 124

1 Speaker Denison to Brand, October 12 1866, quoting Sir Erskine May, Brand MSS.
2 Sir George Grey to Brand, October 9 1866, Brand MSS.
3 Sir George Grey to Brand, October 19 1866, Brand MSS; Argyll to Gladstone, November 4 1866, Add. MSS 44100.

4 Brand to Gladstone, October 23 1866, Add. MSS 44193.
5 Gladstone to Brand, October 30 1866, Brand MSS.
6 Gladstone to Brand, July 21, August 13 and September 6 1866, Brand MSS.
7 Brand to Halifax, October 20 1866, Garrowby MSS; Speaker Denison to Brand, October 12 1866, Brand MSS.

PAGE 125

1 Brand: draft October 3 1866, Brand MSS.
2 Brand to Gladstone, October 7 1866, Add. MSS 44193.
3 Brand to Halifax, October 1 1866, Garrowby MSS.
4 Brand to Halifax, October 1 1866, Garrowby MSS. Stansfeld was too ill to attend this particular banquet on October 8. W. E. Forster, however, spoke after Bright instead, warning the audience of the possibility that 'Disraeli, like Sir Robert Peel might close his career by sacrificing his party and producing a really liberal bill', *Morning Star*, October 8, 1866.
5 Gladstone to Brand, January 7 1867, Brand MSS.
6 Argyll to Gladstone, January 18 1866, Add. MSS 44100.
7 Somerset to de Grey, January 24 1867, Add. MSS 43622. Acland to Gladstone, February 15 1867, Add. MSS 44092.
8 Halifax to Brand, February 13 1867, Brand MSS. Brand to Halifax, January 29 1867, Garrowby MSS.

PAGE 126

1 Brand to Gladstone, January 11 1867, Add. MSS 44194; Argyll to Gladstone, January 18 1867, Add. MSS 44100.
2 Brand to Gladstone, December 17 1866 and January 26 1867, Add. MSS 44193 and 44194.
3 Bouverie to Halifax, January 23 1867, Garrowby MSS; H. A. Bruce to de Grey, February 3 1867, Add. MSS 43534; F. Lawley to Gladstone enclosing Sir Henry Hoare, ex-MP. for Windsor to Lawley, January 10 1867, Add. MSS 44412.
4 Granville to Halifax, January 31 1867, Garrowby MSS.
5 Halifax to Gladstone, February 15 1867, Add. MSS 44184.
6 Clarendon to Halifax, February 19 1867, Garrowby MSS.
7 *Ibid.*
8 Halifax, *Journal*, February 7 1867.
9 Halifax, *Journal*, February 15, 16 and 17 for failure to commit the party to a £6 rating franchise, because Stansfeld thought reformers would want more, and because Clarendon and Halifax wanted to avoid commitment altogether.
10 Russell to Gladstone, January 29 and February 8 1867, Add. MSS 44293. Knatchbull-Hugessen, *Diary*, February 17 1867.
11 Halifax, *Journal*, February 4 and 12 1867.

PAGE 127

1 Halifax to Gladstone, February 15 1867, Add. MSS 44184. Cf. A. W. Kinglake to Gladstone, February 18 and Poulett Scrope to Gladstone, February 1867, Add. MSS 44412.

2 Hardy, *Diary*, July 10 1866 for Lowe's and Horsman's satisfaction at Derby's refusal to give pledges about Reform on taking office in 1866.

3 Add. MSS 44337.

4 Brand to Gladstone, November 26 1866 (Add. MSS 44193) and to Russell, July 22 and August 28 (PRO 30 22/16 D).

PAGE 128

1 Elcho to Grosvenor, January 12 1867, Wemyss MSS.

2 *The Day* was published from March 19 until May 4 1867. For its working, see Elcho to Grosvenor and to Hutton *passim*, Wemyss MSS. Cf. T. E. Kebbell (the leader-writer) in *Lord Beaconsfield and other Tory memories*, p. 39.

PAGE 129

1 Elcho to Horsman, June 30 1866, Wemyss MSS.

2 Elcho to Holyoake, August 1 1866, Wemyss MSS.

3 Elcho to Walpole, September 9 1866 and November/December *passim*, Wemyss MSS.

4 Chelmsford to Derby, November 12 1866, Derby MSS Box 152; Northcote to Derby, September 23 1866, *loc. cit.* Box 162; Carnarvon to Derby, December 27 1866, *loc. cit.* Box 163; Lowe to Lady Salisbury, September 2 1866 in *A Great Lady's Friendships*.

PAGE 130

1 Derby to Lord Stradbroke, August 19 1866, Derby MSS Box 191/1.

PAGE 131

1 Cf. Duncan McLaren to Gladstone, August 14 1866, Add. MSS 44411 referring to Scotland. The lists of diners and speakers in *The Morning Star*, etc., confirm this.

PAGE 132

1 Derby to Disraeli, September 27 1866, Hughenden MSS.

2 Derby to Disraeli, Hughenden MSS B/XX/S/373, 375, 380 and 381, Disraeli to Derby, November 18, December 24 and 29 1866, Derby MSS Box 146.

PAGE 133

1 Derby to the Queen, January 10 1867, Derby MSS Box 192/1.

2 Derby to Pakington, December 4 1866, Derby MSS Box 193/1.

3 Naas to Derby, July 2 1866, Derby MSS Box 155; Carnarvon to Derby, July 2 1866, *loc. cit.* Box 163; Walpole to Derby, July 3 1866, *loc. cit.* Box 153.

4 Pakington to Derby, February 1 and to Disraeli, February 3 1867, both Hughenden MSS; Carnarvon to Disraeli, February 4 1867, Hughenden MSS; Cranborne to Disraeli, January 2 1867 [writes 1866], B/XX/Ce/12 enclosing Elcho to Cranborne, December 30, B/XX/Ce/12c, Hughenden MSS.

5 E.g. Derby to Lichfield, January 25 1867 offering office to Anson, Lichfield's brother, Derby MSS Box 193/1.

PAGE 134

1 Derby to Disraeli, February 2 1867, Hughenden MSS B/XX/S/405.
2 Disraeli (July 29) and Salisbury (July 5) 1866 to Derby, Derby MSS Boxes 146 and 114.
3 See Derby MSS Box 52/5 for draft. Derby to Disraeli, September 16 1866 shows Derby sending Baxter's draft to Disraeli (omitted by Buckle, *Disraeli*, IV, 453).

PAGE 135

1 Derby to Disraeli, October 9 and 19 1866, Hughenden MSS.
2 Derby to Disraeli, December 22 1866, *ibid*.

PAGE 136

1 Northcote to Derby, October 17 1866, Derby MSS Box 162.
2 Cf. e.g. General Grey to Derby, January 29 1867, Derby MSS Box 159.
3 General Grey to the Queen, October 13 1866, RA F 14/94. Cf. Northcote to Derby October 14 1866 reporting General Grey saying that, although Russell would not co-operate, 'Sir George Grey and others might take a different view', Derby MSS Box 162. See also General Grey to Derby, October 28 1866, Box 159, for slightness of his contact with Liberal Whigs. Northcote to Disraeli, October 9 1866, Iddesleigh MSS.
4 Disraeli to Derby, October 21 1866, Derby MSS Box 146.
5 Northcote to Disraeli, October 9 1866, *ibid*. General Grey's memos. October 13 1866, RA F 14/93 and 94. Cf. General Grey to Earl Grey, October 11 1866, Howick MSS; Northcote to Derby, October 14 and 17 1866, Derby MSS Box 162; General Grey to Derby, October 28 1866, Derby MSS Box 159.
6 Derby to the Queen, November 1 1866, Derby MSS Box 192/1.

PAGE 137

1 Derby to Disraeli, October 30 and December 27 1866, Derby MSS Box 146.
2 Cf. General Grey memo. to the Queen, November 16 1866, RA A 35/14 for sharp comments when Reform was not mentioned as a subject which was 'engaging the attention of the Cabinet, though London is full of all sorts of reports on the subject'. Derby to General Grey (January 4) and to the Queen (January 10) 1867, Box 192/1 and 193/1.
3 Derby to the Queen, January 10, February 6 and February 14 1867, Derby MSS Box 192/1.

4 Hardy, *Diary*, November 3 1866.
5 Derby to Disraeli, December 2 1866, Hughenden MSS.

PAGE 138

1 Derby to the Queen, January 10 1867, Derby MSS Box 192/1.
2 Perhaps because it was not desirable that General Grey should know what was going on. I have found no direct evidence that Derby distrusted General Grey, beyond a passing suspicion of Grey's power to influence the Queen to prefer a £6 Rating bill at the beginning of March (Derby to Disraeli, n.d. Hughenden MSS B/XX/S/415). It is, however, not impossible, in a question where secrecy was thought to matter, that Grey's close connections with the Halifax/Grey Whigs made extreme discretion desirable, even though Grey made a point of having to a large extent dropped them when the Russell government went out of office.
3 Derby to General Grey, January 30 1867, Derby MSS Box 193/1.
4 For the published version see *Hansard*, February 11 1867 (Table of Contents, description of page 214). For earlier drafts see Derby MSS Box 191/2, and Box 146 n.d. and Hughenden MSS B/XX/S/374. There is also a draft at the back of Lord John Manners's *Journal*, Belvoir MSS.
5 Derby to General Grey, February 7 1867, Derby MSS Box 192/1.
6 Cf. Derby to Disraeli, n.d. Hughenden MSS B/XX/S/408.

PAGE 139

1 Derby to General Grey, February 6 and 7 1867, Derby MSS Box 192/1.
2 Cf. Cranborne to Disraeli for understanding that the resolution referring to the commission 'shall be purged of every expression which may refer any question of principle to [it]'. Hughenden MSS B/XX/Ce/14 dated February 1 1867.
3 Disraeli to Derby, November 18 1866, Derby MSS Box 146.
4 *Ibid.*

PAGE 140

1 Malmesbury, *Memoirs of an Ex-Minister*, II, 365. Bright, *Diaries*, February 11 1867, p. 205; Ravensworth to Derby, February 20 1867, Derby MSS Box 113/10; Derby to the Queen, February 14 1867, Derby MSS Box 191/2; Hardy, *Diary*, February 12 1867; Knatchbull-Hugessen, *Diary*, February 17 1867; Halifax, *Journal*, February 11 1867.
2 Halifax to Gladstone, February 15 1867, Add. MSS 44184.
3 Resolution 3, 'that, while it is desirable that a more direct representation should be given to the labouring class, it is contrary to the constitution of this Realm to give to any one class, or interest, predominating power over the rest of the community'.
4 Derby to the Queen, February 14 1867, Derby MSS Box 192/1.
5 *Hansard*, February 11 1867 (215 and 226).

PAGE 141

1 Carnarvon, *Journal*, February 16 1867 in Hardinge, *Carnarvon*, I, 344.
2 Adderley to Stanley, and Stanley to Adderley, September 17 and 18 1866, Knowsley MSS.
3 Hardinge, *Carnarvon* (*Journal*), I, 336-7.

PAGE 142

1 Knatchbull-Hugessen, *Diary*, June 27 1866.

PAGE 143

1 Hardinge, *Carnarvon* (*Journal*), I, 336.
2 *Ibid.* I, 341.
3 Disraeli to Derby, February 4 1867, Derby MSS Box 146.

PAGE 144

1 Hardinge, *Carnarvon* (*Journal*), I, 341; Carnarvon to Disraeli, February 2 1867, Hughenden MSS.
2 Northcote to Disraeli memo. January 16 1867, Hughenden MSS; Naas to Derby, January 30 1867, Derby MSS Box 155/2.
3 Nelson to Derby, December 17 1866, Derby MSS Box 113/4.
4 Carnarvon to Disraeli, February 2 1867, Hardinge, *Carnarvon*, I, 342.
5 Peel to Derby, February 7 1867, Derby MSS Box 161.

PAGE 145

1 Disraeli to Derby, February 7 1867 and n.d. Thursday, Derby MSS Box 146. Cf. 'the principle of Plurality of Votes, if adopted by Parliament, would facilitate the settlement of the Borough Franchise on an extensive basis'. (Resolution 5, *Hansard*, February 11 1867, Table of Contents, description of p. 214.)
2 Disraeli to Derby, February 7 and n.d. Thursday 1867, Derby MSS Box 146.
3 Lady G. Cecil, *Salisbury*, I, 230.
4 Lord Henry Lennox to Disraeli, January 3 1867, Hughenden MSS.
5 Hardinge, *Carnarvon* (*Journal*), I, 344.
6 The Queen to General Peel, February 17 1867 in Derby MSS Box 159. Disraeli memo in Buckle, *Letters of Queen Victoria 1862-78*, I, 396 ff.

PAGE 146

1 Memo. February 17, Grosvenor to Derby in Derby MSS Box 52/6.

PAGE 147

1 Lady G. Cecil, *Salisbury*, I, 222 ff. I have quoted from the letter to Elcho which was written the day after Cranborne's letter to Derby rather than from the memorandum, which was written a good deal later. The Elcho

letter is short, but gives a different emphasis, i.e. a party-advantage emphasis, not an emphasis on the general political dangers to be expected from a large working-class enfranchisement in the small boroughs. There can, however, be little doubt that both elements entered into Cranborne's calculations at the time at which he thought of resigning.

PAGE 148

1 Baxter's memorandum on the proposed franchise, February 23 1867, Derby MSS Box 146.
2 Cranborne to Elcho, February 25 1867, Wemyss MSS. Cf. Carnarvon to Derby, February 25 and March 2 1867, Derby MSS Box 163.
3 Carnarvon to Derby, February 25 1867, *loc. cit.*
4 Cf. Northcote, *Diary,* February 5 1866, Add. MSS 50063A, cf. Cranborne to his father, January 9 1867, Salisbury MSS leaving an impression of support for, or at least of lack of hostility to, Disraeli.

PAGE 149

1 Corry to Disraeli, Friday February 22 [1867], Hughenden MSS.
2 720,000 working-class, 90,000 other classes.
3 Cranborne to Elcho, February 25 1867 (two letters) and Elcho to Grosvenor, February 23, Wemyss MSS.

PAGE 150

1 General Grey to Derby, February 26 1867, Derby MSS Box 159.
2 *Quarterly Review* (1866), cxx.
3 Cf. Cranborne to Disraeli, January 2 1867 (written 1866), Hughenden MSS B/XX/Ce/12 and 12 *a.*
4 Carnarvon to Derby, February 25 1867, Derby MSS Box 163. There is a long letter from Sir William Heathcote to Carnarvon (PRO 30/6/145 dated March 2 1867) discussing Carnarvon's position and written as a guardian to his ward, which leaves little doubt that Carnarvon had no part in a general conspiracy and that he and probably Cranborne took so long to make up their minds because 'being young in office they found it very difficult' (Halifax, *Journal,* March 17 quoting Earl Grey reporting Carnarvon.) General Grey's letter (see note 1 above) may indicate a connection between Halifax and Cranborne which has not survived on paper. It is also the case that Elcho thought Halifax was trying to make himself Prime Minister. Halifax himself (in this respect differing from Brand who wanted, if possible, to keep the government in office until the Liberal party was more certainly united) was searching for signs of Cabinet disunity, inaction about Reform and resignation, in the hope, as he told Gladstone, of establishing a new government which would be 'sure of the support of the reasonable Conservatives (*many of whom regret last year*) for any fair measure... [which would be] safeguard[ed by their support] against any ultra [*i.e.* radical] pressure', and which would

be able therefore to 'give the country what it wants...a Reform bill'. (Halifax to Gladstone, February 15 1867, Add. MSS 44184.) Halifax, however, specifically mentions the probability of 'the Liberal party' forming the government. Even if one assumes that he was doing this disingenuously in order to hold out a carrot to encourage Gladstone to act judiciously in the weeks ahead, it is unlikely that he was thinking of an actual coalition and likely, if he was, that Northcote or Stanley rather than Cranborne were the ministers he would think of as its Conservative members. In fact, although Halifax and Cranborne had the same general objective—to attract to their respective parties the great body of central opinion—it is almost certain that, if either was conscious of the other's intentions, they would be competing rather than co-operating in trying to establish a coalition. Although there was close and continuous contact between Earl Grey and General Grey and between Earl Grey and Carnarvon (as well as between Cranborne and Elcho) and although Halifax knew what went on in Cabinet—probably through the knowledge which Clarendon got through Stanley or through his daughter's marriage to Derby's son—the absence of concert between these various conspirators makes it extremely unlikely that there was a *conspiracy* to bring down the government. Cf. Halifax, *Journal*, February 21/23 1867.
5 Cranborne to Elcho, March 21 1867, Wemyss MSS.

PAGE 151

1 Cranborne to Disraeli, February 1 1867, Hughenden MSS.
2 Cranborne to Disraeli, February 22 1867, Hughenden MSS.
3 Hardinge, *Carnarvon (Journal)*, I, 348.

PAGE 152

1 Halifax, *Journal*, February 25 1867.
2 *Hansard*, February 25 (984).
3 Halifax, *Journal*, February 26 1867.
4 *Hansard*, February 25 (982–92) and February 26 (1022 ff.).

PAGE 153

1 *Hansard*, February 25 (990).
2 Disraeli in *Hansard*, March 5 (1343); Disraeli to Derby, February 27 1867 in Buckle, *Disraeli*, IV, 506–7.
3 *Hansard*, February 26 1867 (1021–2).
4 *Hansard*, February 26 (1024).
5 Brand to Halifax, March 2 1867, Garrowby MSS; Gladstone to Halifax, March 1 1867, *loc. cit.*

PAGE 154

1 Disraeli to Derby, February 26 1867, Derby MSS Box 146 quoting Walpole.

PAGE 155

1 *Hansard*, February 26 1867 (1022); Stanley to Disraeli, February 26 1867, Hughenden MSS; Hardy, *Diary*, February 27 1867; Lord J. Manners to Malmesbury, February 26 1867 in Malmesbury, *Memoirs of an ex-Minister*, II, 367.
2 Cranborne to Carnarvon, February 28 1867, Carnarvon MSS, PRO 306/137.
3 Carnarvon to Derby, February 25 1867, Derby MSS Box 163.
4 Disraeli to Derby, n.d. but February 25 1867, Derby MSS Box 146.

PAGE 156

1 Derby to Disraeli, 6.45 [or 8.45] a.m. Hughenden MSS B/XX/S/405.

PAGE 157

1 Derby to the Queen, February 25 1867, Box 192/1; Derby to Disraeli, February 26 1867, Hughenden MSS; General Grey to Disraeli, February 27 and 28 1867, Hughenden MSS; Walpole to Malmesbury, March 2 1867, Malmesbury MSS.
2 'I have little doubt that, by the time we get into committee on our bill, he will be prepared to try 5 against 6, and probably succeed... [so] it would hardly seem that the Queen could interpose with any advantage,' Disraeli to Derby, February 28 1867 in Buckle, *Disraeli*, pp. 506–7. Cf. Halifax, *Journal*, February 15, 16 and 18 (for Russell's and Gladstone's failure to unite the Liberal party on a £6 rating franchise) and February 21 (for advanced Liberals being hostile to a £6 rating suffrage).
3 Disraeli to Derby, February 26 1867, Derby MSS Box 146 and Derby to Disraeli, February 26, 10.00 p.m. Hughenden MSS.
4 Baxter to Disraeli, February 28 1867, Hughenden MSS.

PAGE 158

1 *Ibid.*
2 Disraeli to Derby, February 26 1867, Derby MSS Box 146.

PAGE 159

1 For Disraeli's first mention of Household Suffrage without checks see Disraeli to Derby, February 28 1867, Derby MSS Box 146.
2 Cranborne to Derby, March 1 1867, Derby MSS 52/5. Cf. Carnarvon to Derby, March 2 1867, *loc. cit.* Box 163.

PAGE 160

1 Bright to his wife, March 3 1867, UCL.
2 Derby to the Queen, February 25 1867, Derby MSS Box 192/1.
3 Cf. Derby to Disraeli, February 28 1867, Hughenden MSS B/XX/S/412.
4 Disraeli to Derby, February 26 1867, Derby MSS Box 146.

PAGE 161

1 Cf. J. S. Mill, *Autobiography*, p. 245.
2 Malmesbury to Derby, March 1 1867, Derby MSS Box 144.
3 Northcote to Derby, March 2 1867, Derby MSS Box 162.
4 E. C. Egerton to Derby, March 1 1867, Derby MSS Box 111/2; Richmond to Derby, March 4 1867, Derby MSS Box 113.

PAGE 162

1 Manners to Malmesbury, February 28 1867 in Malmesbury, *Memoirs of an Ex-Minister*, ii, 367–8.

PAGE 163

1 Derby to Disraeli, February 28 1867 reporting the Carlton Club meeting which he did not attend, Hughenden MSS.
2 Disraeli to Derby, February 28 [1867], Derby MSS Box 146 for Disraeli reporting that the Conservative MP. for Cheltenham had 'given motion of a question...the object of which, I am told, is to show that a rating franchise is quite conservative enough *without checks*' (my italics).
3 E.g. Manners to Disraeli, February 28 1867, Hughenden MSS.
4 Laird to Derby, March 2 and 8 1867, Derby MSS Box 112/7.
5 Derby to Disraeli, n.d. Wednesday, but February 27 1867, forwarding draft resolutions from Grosvenor, Hughenden MSS B/XX/S/463.
6 Derby to Disraeli, n.d. 2 p.m. Hughenden MSS B/XX/S/466.
7 Elcho to Grosvenor, March 3 1867, quoting Cranborne, Wemyss MSS.
8 Disraeli to the Queen, February 26 1867, Buckle, *Letters of Queen Victoria, 1862–78*, i, 402.

PAGE 164

1 Lord John Manners, *Journal*, February 24 1867, Belvoir MSS.
2 Derby to General Peel, March 1 1867, Derby MSS Box 193/1.
3 E. C. Egerton to Derby, March 1 1867, Derby MSS Box 111/2.
4 Derby to General Peel, to Carnarvon and to Cranborne, all March 1 1867, Derby MSS Box 193/1.
5 Northcote, note dated March 1 [1867] in Add. MSS 50015. I have assumed that it was Carnarvon. It is unlikely to have been Peel, who was a good deal senior to Northcote. Since whoever it was was 'much distressed', Carnarvon seems to fill the role best.

PAGE 165

1 Derby to Disraeli, n.d. Hughenden MSS B/XX/S/461.

PAGE 166

1 Knatchbull-Hugessen, *Diary*, March 2 1867.
2 Halifax to Gladstone, February 28 1867, Add. MSS 44184.
3 Lord John Manners to Malmesbury, March 12 1867, Malmesbury MSS for Manners 'greatly doubt[ing] this House of Commons passing any Reform bill'.

PAGE 167

1 Derby to Lord Denman, February 28 1867, Derby MSS Box 193/1.
2 Bright, *Diaries*, March 1 1867. Bright to his wife, March 3 1867, UCL. Cf. Sir George Grey to Halifax, March 4 1867, Garrowby MSS, for suggestion that Bright was willing to support a £5 rating bill from the Liberal party.
3 Bright to Disraeli, March 9 1867 in Trevelyan, *Bright*, pp. 381–2. For Stanley, see *Hansard*, March 5 (1364–5).
4 *Hansard*, April 12 1867 (1670).

PAGE 168

1 See p. 167, n. 3 above. Cf. Knatchbull-Hugessen, *Diary*, March 6 1867; cf. Malmesbury to Derby March 3 and 8 1867, Derby MSS Box 144.
2 Duality (i.e. giving second votes to direct taxpayers and to householders of houses rated at more than £10 p.a.) 'compensated' for the increase in the working-class vote by an increase in the votes of property owners, including small ones.
3 Lord John Manners to Malmesbury March 6 and 9 1867, Malmesbury MSS, and to his brother, March 9 1867, Belvoir MSS.
4 Malmesbury to Derby, March 8 1867. See above, note 1.
5 See below, p. .
6 Naas to Derby, March 8 1867, Derby MSS Box 155/3 for Naas advocating the retention of restrictions but, since duality would probably be defeated, suggesting that the Irish principle—for compulsory compounding in respect of houses rated at less than £5 p.a.—be adopted instead.
7 J. W. Henley to Derby, July 1866, Derby MSS Box 190/2.
8 Hardy, *Diary*, March 10 and 26 1867.
9 *Ibid.* April 11, March 24 and April 13 1867.

PAGE 169

1 Derby to Disraeli, n.d., enclosing Earle to Derby, March 18 1867, Hughenden MSS B/XX/S/422 and 422a.
2 Derby to Disraeli, March 14 1867, Hughenden MSS.
3 Cf. S. Walpole, *The History of Twenty-five Years*, II, 186; Disraeli note, Hughenden MSS B/XI/J/7.
4 Disraeli to Derby, February 28 1867, Derby MSS Box 146. For Baxter's memo dated February 28 see Hughenden MSS B/XX/J/74.
5 Dudley Baxter to Disraeli, March 14 1867, Hughenden MSS.
6 Lord John Manners, *Journal*, March 11–16, Belvoir MSS; S. Walpole, see above, note 3; Thring, *Practical Legislation*, p. 7.

PAGE 170

1 Derby to Naas, March 10 1867, Derby MSS Box 192/1. Also Derby to Disraeli, n.d. but March 9 according to Corry, Hughenden MSS B/XX/S/419.

2 H. G. Liddell, *Hansard*, March 26 (610); Cairns to Disraeli, March 6 1867, Hughenden MSS for objections to plurality, though not the reasons.

3 J. Lowther, MP. *Hansard*, March 25 (544–5).

4 Derby to Disraeli, February 2 1867, Hughenden MSS; Lord John Manners, *Journal*, March 23 1867, Belvoir MSS; Barrington to Malmesbury March 19 and 21 1867, Malmesbury MSS.

5 Cairns to Derby, March 22 1867, reporting conversation with Hardy, Derby MSS Box 52/5.

6 Baxter to Disraeli, February 11 1867, Hughenden MSS.

PAGE 171

1 Derby to Naas, March 10 1867 for Derby asserting that, if all compounders had both to claim in order to be registered as voters and to pay the full tenants' rate on doing so, they would do so 'in small numbers judging from the past', Derby MSS Box 192/1.

2 Sir John Walsh to Derby, March 23 1867, Derby MSS Box 114/8.

PAGE 172

1 *Hansard*, March 18 1867 (9).

2 *Ibid.* (12).

3 *Ibid.* (13).

4 *Hansard*, March 26 1867 (642–3).

5 *Ibid.* (645).

PAGE 173

1 E.g. Locke in *Hansard*, March 14 1867 (1810 ff.).

2 Especially about the number of compound householders, *Hansard*, February 25 1867 (982–4) and March 14 (1814).

3 *Hansard*, March 18 1867 (18) and March 25 (470–1).

4 *Hansard*, March 26 1867 (644).

5 R. D. Baxter, *The Times*, April 8 1867.

6 Knatchbull-Hugessen, *Diary*, March 30 1867.

7 Gladstone to Russell, March 27 1867, PRO 30 22/16 D.

8 Gladstone to Russell, *loc. cit.*

9 Knatchbull-Hugessen, *Diary*, March 30 1867.

10 *Hansard*, March 26 1867 (644).

11 *Hansard*, March 25 1867 (509). Cf. Knatchbull-Hugessen contrasting Disraeli 'in concluding yield[ing]...the dual vote' while Hardy 'who had spoken first from the front bench had plainly hinted that they would not yield', *Diary*, March 30 1867.

PAGE 174

1 *Hansard*, March 18 1867 (12).

2 *Hansard*, March 26 1867 (642 ff.).

PAGE 176

1 Grosvenor, memo on Cave meeting, see p. 146. Northcote to Disraeli, February 27 1867, Hughenden MSS.
2 R. D. Baxter: memo on loss of dual vote, n.d. but March 1867, Hughenden MSS B/XI/E/5. Corry to Disraeli, March 23 1867, Hughenden MSS.
3 *Hansard*, April 8 1867 (1302 ff.) for Northcote, March 25 1867 (504 ff.) for Hardy, March 5 (1364 ff.) for Stanley.

PAGE 177

1 Heathcote to Cranborne, March 31 1867, Salisbury MSS.
2 Derby to Disraeli, n.d. Hughenden MSS B/XX/S/351.
3 For a list of Conservatives who moved below the gangway after Cranborne's and the other resignations, see Knatchbull-Hugessen, *Diary*, March 8 1867.
4 Lonsdale to Disraeli, March 2 1867, Hughenden MSS; Baring to Disraeli, March 17 (two letters), *loc. cit.* Disraeli to Derby, n.d. but March 1867, Derby MSS Box 146.
5 Lord Percy to Derby, November 18 1866, Derby MSS Box 113/4; General Grey to the Queen, February 4 1867, RA A 35/38; Halifax, *Journal*, March 18 and 20 1867.
6 Cairns to Derby, March 22 1867 reporting Hardy, Derby MSS Box 52/5.
7 Derby to Marlborough and vice versa, February 20 1867, Derby MSS Box 192/1 and 113.

PAGE 178

1 Ward Hunt to Derby, March 16 1867, Derby MSS Box 112/3; Disraeli to Derby [March 16 1867], Derby MSS Box 146.
2 Carnarvon to Richmond, March 14 1867, Richmond MSS. Carnarvon to Earl Grey, March 20 1867, Howick MSS.
3 Carnarvon in House of Lords, *Hansard*, March 4 1867 (1290).

PAGE 179

1 Exeter to Cranborne, March 9 1867, Salisbury MSS.
2 A. E. Gathorne Hardy, *Gathorne Hardy, First Earl of Cranbrook*, I, 172.
3 Hardy, *Diary*, February 26 1867.
4 E.g. Hardy, *Diary*, March 3 1867.
5 Hardy, *Hardy*, I, 203; Hardy, *Diary*, March 5 and 7 1867. *Hansard*, March 25, 1867 (504 ff.); Lord John Manners, *Journal*, June 7 1867, Belvoir MSS; Buckingham to Derby, n.d. (pencilled July 1867 but obviously March), Derby MSS Box 163.
6 Cairns to Disraeli, April 17, 20 and 29 1867, Hughenden MSS; Hardy, *Diary*, April 22 1867; Cairns to Derby, March 22 1867, Derby MSS Box 52/5; Hardy to Cairns, May 2 1867, Hughenden MSS B/XX/Ha/6.

PAGE 180

1 *Twenty Years of Financial Policy* (1862).
2 *The Case of Sir E. Wilmot* (1847).
3 Northcote to Disraeli, February 28 1867, Iddesleigh MSS.
4 *Hansard*, April 8 (1302).
5 Buckingham to Derby, March 2 1867, Derby MSS Box 163.
6 Derby to Disraeli, n.d. Hughenden MSS, B/XX/S/459. Lord John Manners, *Journal*, March 20 and 23 1867, Belvoir MSS.
7 Hardinge, *Carnarvon (Journal)*, I, 350.
8 W. B. Brett in *Hansard*, May 9 1867 (280).
9 Walpole to Malmesbury, March 2 1867, Malmesbury MSS.

PAGE 181

1 Buckingham to Derby, March 24 1867, Derby MSS.
2 Manners to Lady Derby, February 27 1868, Belvoir MSS.
3 Carnarvon to Earl Grey, March 20 1867, Howick MSS.
4 M. Morris to Naas, March 15 1867, Mayo MSS.
5 Halifax, *Journal*, March 16 1867.
6 Exeter to Cranborne, March 9 and March 25 1867, Salisbury MSS; Exeter to Derby, March 9 1867, Derby MSS Box 111.

PAGE 182

1 *Hansard*, April 1 1867 (907–8).
2 *The Times*, April 8, reporting Disraeli, on receiving a Lancashire Conservative delegation at Downing Street.
3 Cf. Taylor to Disraeli, April 10 1867, Hughenden MSS.

PAGE 183

1 Cf. Lowe to Lady Salisbury, April 17 1868 (*A Great Lady's Friendships*) for the view that Cranborne would be more dangerous to Disraeli as a peer because in the Commons he was 'isolated'.
2 Cf. Lord Henry Lennox to Disraeli (Hughenden MSS B/XX/Lx/250), for the 'evil influence of Mr Pecocke Sandford'.
3 Acland to Gladstone, March 22 1867 reporting Adderley's account of a Cabinet meeting, which, of course, Adderley had not attended, i.e. 'A member of the government (name enclosed)' with 'Adderley' written on separate sheet, Add. MSS 44092.
4 Cf. Exeter to Cranborne, March 25 1867, Salisbury MSS.
5 Halifax, *Journal*, April 2 1867 reporting Lord Sydney reporting a 'discontented' Conservative county MP. who had been sent for by Disraeli to be told this.
6 Beresford-Hope in *Hansard*, May 20 1867 (812).
7 Heathcote to Cranborne, May 4 1867, Salisbury MSS, reporting conversation with Peel.
8 Derby to Disraeli, n.d. Sunday night, Hughenden MSS B/XX/S/459.

PAGE 184

1 *Hansard*, March 7 1867 (1469).
2 Brand to Halifax, January 31 1867, Garrowby MSS; Granville to Halifax, January 31 1867, *ibid.*; Sir George Grey to Brand, January 1 1866 [actually 1867], Brand MSS.
3 Halifax to Brand, February 13 1867, Garrowby MSS.

PAGE 185

1 Clarendon to Halifax, February 19 1867, Garrowby MSS.
2 Lawley to Anson, February 23 1867, Wemyss MSS.
3 *Ibid.*
4 Halifax to Gladstone, February 15 1867, Add. MSS 44184; Spencer to Granville, February 24 1867 in Granville to Gladstone, Add. MSS 44165; Moncreiff to Brand, February 24 1867, Brand MSS, and to Gladstone, January 31 1867, Add. MSS 44412.
5 Elcho to Grosvenor, January 25 1867, Wemyss MSS. Cf. Bouverie to Halifax, January 23 1867, Garrowby MSS.

PAGE 186

1 Bouverie to Ellice, February 25 1867, Ellice MSS.
2 Gregory to Elcho, June 27 1866, Wemyss MSS.
3 Elcho to Grosvenor, February 4 1867, Wemyss MSS; Gregory to Gladstone, March 1 1867, Add. MSS 44412; Derby to Cranborne, September 28 1866, Derby MSS Box 191/2 for unwillingness to make the Galway party too strong by making Gregory Irish Secretary. Also for Gregory's hostility to the Irish Church.
4 Lowe to Lady Salisbury, October 15 1866 (*A Great Lady's Friendships*) reporting his own remarks to Cardwell.
5 Elcho to Sidney Smith, n.d. but mid-February 1867, Wemyss MSS. Moncreiff to Brand, February 24 1867, Add. MSS 44194.
6 Lawley to Catherine Gladstone, February 10 1867, Add. MSS 44412.
7 Elcho to G. J. Holyoake, August 1 1866, Wemyss MSS.
8 Elcho to Sidney Smith, n.d. but mid-February 1867, Wemyss MSS.

PAGE 187

1 Grosvenor to Gladstone [February 22] but possibly earlier, Add. MSS 44337; Grosvenor to Elcho, n.d. Wemyss MSS; Elcho to Grosvenor, February 25 1867, Wemyss MSS; Spencer to Granville, February 24 1867, Add. MSS 44165; Gladstone to Halifax, March 1 1867, Garrowby MSS for satisfactory character of the talk and of the possibility that Grosvenor would abandon plurality if necessary.
2 I have assumed that the reference to 'the Duchess' in Grosvenor's letter (see above, note 1) is to Harriet, Duchess of Sutherland who was both Grosvenor's mother-in-law and a close friend of Gladstone.

3 *The Times*, February 27 1867.
4 The first mention I have discovered of a £5 rating bill as a thing to unite the Liberal party is in Halifax, *Journal*, February 17: it came from Stansfeld.

PAGE 188

1 Bagehot to Earl Grey, March 15 1867, Howick MSS.
2 Brand to Gladstone, March 16 1867, Add. MSS 44194.
3 Argyll to Gladstone, March 12 1867, Add. MSS 444100.
4 Cf. Gladstone to Russell, March 27 1867, PRO 30 22/16 D for the best evidence of unwillingness to agree on the measure.
5 Heathcote to Cranborne, March 16 1867 reporting conversation with Gladstone, Salisbury MSS.

PAGE 189

1 Russell to Gladstone, March 9, 17 and 18 1867, Add. MSS 44293; Halifax, *Journal*, March 19 1867.
2 David Robertson to Gladstone, March 17 1867, Add. MSS 44412.
3 Knatchbull-Hugessen, *Diary*, March 18 1867.
4 Halifax, *Journal*, March 18 1867; Russell to Gladstone, March 27 1867, Add. MSS 44293.

PAGE 190

1 Heathcote to Cranborne, March 16 1867 reporting conversation with Gladstone, Salisbury MSS.
2 *Ibid.*

PAGE 191

1 Clarendon to Gladstone (February 18 1867, Add. MSS 44133); Russell to Gladstone (March 9 1867, Add. MSS 44293) and Bouverie to Ellice (December 18 1866, Ellice MSS) all use this phrase of Tory attempts to deal with Reform.
2 Heathcote to Gladstone, March 21 1867, Add. MSS 44209.
3 Halifax, *Journal*, March 18 1867.
4 Acland to Gladstone, March 22 1867, Add. MSS 44092 quoting Wilson Patten.
5 Halifax, *Journal*, March 16 1867.

PAGE 192

1 T. Hankey to Gladstone, March 28 1867, Add. MSS 44412.
2 For Gladstone's speech see above, p. 153. Cf. Disraeli to Derby, February 27 1867, Derby MSS Box 146.
3 Halifax to Gladstone, February 28 1867, Add. MSS 44184.
4 T. Hankey to Gladstone, March 28 1867, Add. MSS 44412; Sir George Grey to Gladstone, March 22 1867, Add. MSS 44162.

5 Halifax, *Journal*, March 16 1867, for Brand's, Horsman's and Forster's views.
6 F. H. F. Berkeley to Gladstone, March 21 1867, Add. MSS 44412.

PAGE 193

1 For Enfield's approach to Hardy see Hardy, *Diary*, March 26 1867; Halifax, *Journal*, March 25, 26 and 28: also March 21 for Halifax hearing of a 'meeting of considerable numbers (but I did not hear where) in favour of passing the second reading'.
2 Brand to Gladstone, March 16 1867, Add. MSS 44194 enclosing Glyn to Brand same date; Heathcote to Cranborne, March 16 1867, Salisbury MSS.
3 Carnarvon to Cranborne, April 2 1867, Salisbury MSS.
4 See above, note 2.
5 E. B. Lytton to his father, March 19 1867, *Personal and Literary Letters of the Earl of Lytton*, I, 217–18.
6 Halifax, *Journal*, March 18 1867, though cf. Knatchbull-Hugessen, *Diary*, March 23 1867 for slightly different view.
7 Halifax, *Journal*, March 19.
8 *Ibid.*

PAGE 194

1 Halifax to Gladstone [April 4 1867], Add. MSS 44184 (ff. 165–9).
2 Lowe to Gladstone, March 21 1867, Add. MSS 44301. For Bright see Bright to his wife, March 20 1867, UCL.

PAGE 195

1 Cranborne to Gladstone quoted in Clarendon to Gladstone, March 22 1867, Add. MSS 44133; Halifax, *Journal*, March 27 1867; Heathcote to Gladstone, March 21 1867, Add. MSS 44209.
2 Cf. Russell to Gladstone, March 27 1867, Add. MSS 44293.
3 Gladstone to Halifax, March 1 1867, Garrowby MSS.
4 Most of whose houses were rated at less than £5 p.a.
5 Acland to Gladstone, April 5 1867, Add. MSS 44092.
6 Heathcote to Cranborne, April 2 1867, Salisbury MSS reporting Gladstone's desire for secrecy.
7 *The Times*, April 6 1867.
8 Heathcote to Cranborne, April 5 1867, quoting Gladstone, Salisbury MSS.

PAGE 196

1 Elcho to Grosvenor, n.d. Letter 53, Wemyss MSS for Elcho reporting Locke's conversation with an Irish member.
2 E.g. Halifax, Sir George Grey and Cardwell, see Halifax, *Journal*, March 27 1867.

3 For the Tea-Room negotiations see Akroyd to Elcho, April 6 and 7 1867, Wemyss MSS; Halifax, *Journal*, April 7; Clay to Disraeli, n.d. Hughenden MSS B/XX/C/250.

4 Taylor to Disraeli, n.d. [but April 7 in pencil], Hughenden MSS B/XX/T/86.

5 For the Tea-Room meeting itself see J. B. Smith (reported in *Morning Star*, April 19 1867) and *Morning Star*, April 10; cf. Knatchbull-Hugessen, *Diary*, April 13 1867.

PAGE 198

1 Heathcote to Gladstone, April 11 1867, Add. MSS 44209.

2 Elcho to Grosvenor, April 3 1867, quoting Cranborne, Wemyss MSS.

3 Heathcote to Gladstone, April 11 1867, Add. MSS 44209.

4 J. W. Henley, *Hansard*, April 11 1867 (1562).

PAGE 199

1 *The Times*, April 9 1867, for list.

2 Locke at party meeting April 5 1867 (*The Times*, April 6).

3 Elcho to Grosvenor, April 3 1867, Wemyss MSS reporting the opinions of A. J. Otway, MP. for Chatham.

4 *The Times*, April 6 1867.

PAGE 200

1 Halifax, *Journal*, April 18 1867; *The Times*, April 9. *The Times*'s report was mistaken if it was intended to imply that the Tea-Room delegation consisted of advanced Liberals. On the other hand Halifax's analysis seems to leave too little allowance, if the names of the organizers are taken into account, of the fact that it was a predominantly non-Whig movement.

2 Brand (Add. MSS 44755, n.d.) divided the Liberals who did not vote with Gladstone into five categories—'Lord Grosvenor's followers', 'advanced Liberals in favour of household suffrage', 'those desiring to save the bill or the government', 'men voting in fear of dissolution or from worse motives' and those who were absent through dissaffection. He found only four in the second category—Dalglish, Dillwyn, Ewing and Steel, who were all present at the Tea-Room meeting. Dalglish and Ewing, however, sat for Scottish seats, Dillwyn for Swansea. Brand put Hodgkinson into the fourth class and Whalley of Peterborough into the third, though either could as well have gone into the second. Hibbert and Platt of Oldham did not vote: both could have been placed in the second category if one did not have the feeling that their enthusiasm was for a settlement in which they had played a part rather than for household suffrage itself. Brand's list is not quite accurate but on no computation can one find more than half a dozen English Radicals voting with Disraeli.

3 Bowyer, McEvoy, Corbally: possibly Brady, Rearden, Stock and McKenna (see Knatchbull-Hugessen, *Diary*, April 13, 1867 for the last four). *Hansard*, March 21 1867 (363–8) for McEvoy's introduction of his bill and May 30 (1363–6) for evidence of packing. Cf. Barrington to Disraeli, March 19 1867, Hughenden MSS.
4 Argyll to Gladstone, April 23 1867, Add. MSS 44100.
5 A. W. Kinglake to Gladstone, April 10 1867, Add. MSS 44412.

PAGE 201
1 Akroyd to Joshua Appleyard, April 23 1867, J. B. Smith MSS.
2 *Ibid.*
3 See p. 183, n. 5.
4 Acland to Gladstone, April 3 and 5 1867, quoting Bonham-Carter reporting views of unnamed MP.s, Add. MSS 44092.
5 Brand memo. Add. MSS 44755, see p. 200, n. 2.
6 Knatchbull-Hugessen, *Diary*, April 13 1867.
7 Acland to Gladstone, April 5 1867, Add. MSS 44092.

PAGE 202
1 Grosvenor to Elcho, March 3 1867, Wemyss MSS.
2 Elcho to G. Murray, March 1 1867, Wemyss MSS.

PAGE 203
1 See p. 202, n. 1.
2 David Robertson to Gladstone, March 17 1867, Add. MSS 44412.
3 Duke of Cleveland reported in Halifax, *Journal*, February 24 1867.

PAGE 204
1 Elcho to Grosvenor, March 3 1867, Wemyss MSS.
2 Elcho to Horsman and to Grosvenor, February 25 1867, Wemyss MSS.
3 *Hansard*, March 26 1867 (622).

PAGE 205
1 Akroyd to Appleyard, April 23 1867, J. B. Smith MSS.

PAGE 206
1 Trevelyan, *Bright*, pp. 370–1.
2 *Hansard*, March 14 1867 (1815–16).
3 Elcho to Grosvenor, March 19 1867, Wemyss MSS.
4 Moncreiff to Brand, February 24, 1867, Add. MSS 44194.

PAGE 207
1 Though 'I observed that, whatever our faults as a party, this exclusiveness was not one, to which [Lowe] cordially assented.' Hardinge, *Carnarvon (Journal)*, I, 337.
2 Lowe to Lady Salisbury, October 15 1866, *A Great Lady's Friendships*.

PAGE 208

1 Clarendon to Gladstone, February 13 1867, reporting Lowe, Add. MSS 44133.
2 Granville to Gladstone, February 11 1867, reporting Lowe, Add. MSS 44165.
3 Lowe to Elcho, February 20 1867, Wemyss MSS.
4 Grosvenor to Elcho, January 23 1867 and Elcho to Lowe, February 19 1867, Wemyss MSS.
5 Anson, Elcho, Grosvenor, Gilbert Heathcote and Marsh. McKenna also voted with Disraeli, but was not an Adullamite.

PAGE 209

1 Anson to Derby, January 28 1867, Derby MSS Box 110/2.
2 See memorandum of Cave meeting February 17 1867, Derby MSS Box 52/6.
3 Lord Exmouth to Derby, March 2 [1867] reporting conversation with Elcho in the Carlton Club, of which Elcho was still a member, Derby MSS Box 106.

PAGE 211

1 Grosvenor to Gladstone, March 26 1867, Add. MSS 44337.
2 Elcho to Hutton (of *The Day*) March 29 1867, Wemyss MSS.

PAGE 212

1 Grosvenor to Gladstone, March 26 1867, Add. MSS 44337.
2 Hankey said 'all but 50 supported it', Hankey to Gladstone, March 28 1867, Add. MSS 44412. Cf. William Cowper to Gladstone, March 30 1867, *ibid*.
3 Grosvenor to Elcho, n.d. Monday evening [probably February 23] 1867, Wemyss MSS.
4 Elcho to Percy, March 30 1867, *ibid*.
5 Elcho to Grosvenor, March 30 1867 reporting conversation with Lawley, *ibid*.
6 Elcho to Grosvenor, March 30 1867, *ibid*.
7 Grosvenor to Gladstone, April 3 1867, Add. MSS 44337.

PAGE 213

1 Grosvenor to Elcho quoting Gladstone to Grosvenor, Wednesday night April 3 1867, Wemyss MSS.
2 Grosvenor to Gladstone, April 3 1867, Add. MSS 44337.
3 Elcho to Akroyd, April 7 1867, Wemyss MSS.
4 Letter from Grosvenor to the Cave (drafted by Elcho), n.d. [April 1867], Wemyss MSS.
5 Elcho to Grosvenor, n.d. April 1867, Wemyss MSS.

PAGE 214

1 Knatchbull-Hugessen, *Diary*, April 13 1867.
2 Grosvenor to Gladstone, April 3 1867, Add. MSS 44337.
3 Heathcote to Gladstone, March 28 1867, Add. MSS 44209.
4 *The Beehive*, March 30 1867.

PAGE 215

1 Grosvenor to Gladstone, April 3 and 4 1867, Add. MSS 44337.
2 For date of tabling of amendment see Taylor to Disraeli, April 10 1867, Hughenden MSS.
3 Elcho to Grosvenor, April 13 1867, Wemyss MSS.
4 Cf. Akroyd to Elcho, April [13 or 14], Wemyss MSS.
5 '...your only chance of safety is to obtain a formal promise that if in clause 3 line 5, Grosvenor moves to insert..."of the rateable value of £5 or upwards", the government will vote for the motion. A promise to this effect would prevent D[israeli] from urging household suffrage in committee', Cranborne to Elcho, March 24 1867, cf. Cranborne to Elcho, April 7, both Wemyss MSS.
6 Elcho to Grosvenor, April 13 1867, Wemyss MSS.

PAGE 216

1 Elcho to Grosvenor, April [?] 1867, Wemyss MSS.
2 Elcho to Grosvenor, *ibid.*; *Hansard*, April 11 1867 (1505-6) for Grosvenor's attempt to delay discussion until after the recess.

PAGE 217

1 Heathcote to Gladstone, April 10 1867, Add. MSS 44209.
2 *Ibid.*
3 Halifax, *Journal*, April 10 1867.

PAGE 218

1 Heathcote to Gladstone, April 11 1867, Add. MSS 44209.
2 Russell to Gladstone, April 19 1867, Add. MSS 44293.
3 Russell to Gladstone, April 29 1867, *ibid.*
4 Russell to Gladstone, April 30 1867, *ibid.*

PAGE 219

1 Russell to Gladstone, April 23 1867, *ibid.*
2 Halifax, *Journal*, April 13 1867. Cf. Gladstone to Guildford Reform Association (*Morning Star*, April 16).
3 For Gladstone's resignation of the day-to-day lead see Gladstone to R. W. Crawford, MP. for City of London (published letter), April 18 1867, Add. MSS 44412. For Gladstone explaining away the impression he had left that he resigned in 'despondency' see Gladstone to Brand, April 27 1867 (Brand MSS), 'The friendly critics note a tone of "despon-

dency ": that is all owing to Granville and others who cut off a fine peacock's tail that I had appended.'
4 Acland to Gladstone, April 16 1867, Add. MSS 44092.
5 Lambert to Lawley, April 15 1867, Add. MSS 44412.
6 See Chapter III above.
7 Heathcote to Gladstone, April 10 1867, Add. MSS 44209.
8 For *Morning Star* see April 16 1867; for the others see notes to 219–20.
9 Acland to Gladstone, March 30 1867, quoting Neate, Add. MSS 44209.

PAGE 220

1 Lawley to Catherine Gladstone, April 26 1867 and Thomas Hughes to Gladstone, April 13, Add. MSS 44412.
2 Denman to Gladstone, May 1 1867, *ibid.*
3 Acland to Gladstone, March 30 1867, Add. MSS 44209.
4 *Ibid.*
5 Acland to Gladstone, April 16 1867, *ibid.*
6 George Denman to Gladstone, May 1 1867, Add. MSS 44412.
7 The O'Donoghue to Gladstone, March 30 1867, Add. MSS 44412.
8 See note 5 above.
9 Gladstone to Crawford, published letter of April 18 1867, Add. MSS 44412.
10 E.g. Halifax, *Journal*, April 13 1867 dating the end of his intimacy from some time before April 8. Cf. the beginning of Brand's holiday abroad to recover from the strain he had suffered in the previous year.
11 See note 9 above.
12 *Morning Star*, May 6 (letter dated May 4).

PAGE 221

1 Cf. Lawley to Gladstone, April 29 1867, Add. MSS 44412 for Lambert's view that the bill, if modified, might still break up the Cabinet.
2 Knatchbull-Hugessen, *Diary*, April 13 1867.

PAGE 223

1 Brand to Gladstone, April 29 1867, Add. MSS 44194.
2 Acland to Gladstone [April 14 1867], Add. MSS. 44092.
3 Disraeli in *Hansard*, April 12 1867 (1687–8). Derby to Disraeli, n.d. but probably March 26 1867, Hughenden MSS B/XX/S/425. Cf. Knatchbull-Hugessen, *Diary*, July 16 1867 for effect of Gladstone's interventions.

PAGE 224

1 *Hansard*, June 28 1867 (684–702).
2 See below, p. 276–7.
3 See *Hansard*, June 24 1867 (485–6) and below, p. 276–7.
4 *Hansard*, June 25 1867 (521–2).
5 Derby to the Queen, June 26 1867, Derby MSS Box 194/1; Hardy, *Diary*, May 31 1867.

6 Knightley and Gaselee, in *Hansard*, May 27 1867 (1189), and Sandford, May 29 1867 (1243). For Cranborne's complaint about reprinting see *Hansard*, June 3 (1545).

7 *Hansard*, July 1 1867 (794).

PAGE 225

1 Baxter to Disraeli, May 14 1866, Hughenden MSS.

PAGE 226

1 Baxter to Derby, July 25 1866, Derby MSS Box 110/3.

2 Beresford-Hope in *Hansard*, May 28 1867 (1234).

3 *Hansard*, May 28 1867 (1235).

4 *Ibid.* (1242).

5 For division on Fawcett's motion see *Hansard*, June 27 (647), for Berkeley's motion see July 12 (1447).

6 Cumulative voting proposals could take either of two forms. In the most conservative form, when coupled with duality or other sorts of plural voting, it involved specially qualified voters (e.g. property owners or possessors of educational qualifications) being given two or more votes in a constituency and being entitled to cast all of them for one candidate in a three-member constituency. In the less conservative form (as Cairns formulated it in March and as he succeeded, from the House of Lords, in interpolating it into the Act in the summer of 1867) it merely entitled electors to cast all their votes for a number of candidates one fewer than there were seats to be elected to (i.e. they could vote for only two candidates in a three-cornered constituency, etc.). Cairns and the Cave proposed this in March on the assumption that forty or more three-cornered constituencies would be created, though very few new three-cornered constituencies were in fact created by the Act.

PAGE 227

1 For Cairns's calculation in March see Cairns to Disraeli, March 4 1867, Hughenden MSS.

2 *Hansard*, June 24 1867 (457).

3 *Hansard*, June 24 (471 and 476-9) for defeat of Colvile's (copyholder) and Hussey Vivian's (leaseholder) motion by 171 to 151 and 256 to 230. F. B. Smith, *The Making of the Second Reform Bill*, pp. 205-206, makes something of the fact that, owing to a technical oversight, the Act did not specifically forbid owners of borough leases and copyholds valued at between £5 and £10 p.a. to vote in counties. Since, however, they could not vote in two places in respect of the same property, the effect of removing the £10 occupation franchise limit in the boroughs was to enable them to vote there, which many of them could not do before, and thus to ensure that they would not vote on the county electoral roll, unless they took pains to do so.

4 Banks Stanhope, *Hansard*, June 24 1867 (463).

PAGE 228

1 For Adderley, *Hansard*, June 24 1867 (461, 466–9 and 476). For polling-places see *Hansard*, June 27 1867 (618).
2 *Hansard*, May 23 1867 (999).
3 *Ibid.* (999–1000).

PAGE 229

1 *Ibid.* (1002).
2 *Ibid.* (1006).
3 *Hansard*, May 27 1867 (1149).

PAGE 230

1 Labouchère, *Hansard*, June 20 1867 (214).
2 Cranborne, *ibid.* (192).
3 Karslake, *ibid.* (207).
4 *Ibid.* (215).
5 Bright, *ibid.* (225 ff.).
6 Denman, *ibid.* (211 ff.).
7 Synan, *ibid.* (213).
8 See Disraeli's remarks in *Hansard* (220 ff.).
9 Cf. Derby to Disraeli, May 12 1866, Hughenden MSS for importance of borough freeholders in counties and for political impossibility of removing them altogether. No proposal was made by the government in 1867 to do so, though both Dyott and Griffith as private members made proposals to do so partially, see *Hansard*, July 1 (782–91) and July 8 1867 (1227). For Newdegate's view of importance of the freeholder question in the counties see *Hansard*, June 8 1868 (1280). Newdegate opposed Dyott's motion, however.
10 Cf. Gladstone to George Wilson, June 1 1867, George Wilson MSS.

PAGE 231

1 *Hansard*, June 25 1867 (531).
2 *Ibid.* (522 ff.).
3 *Hansard*, June 20 1867 (266 ff.).
4 Derby to Disraeli, June 10 1866, Hughenden MSS.
5 A. Montagu to [?] June 27 1866, Hughenden MSS B/XI/G/4. Darby Griffith in *Hansard*, June 25 (523).

PAGE 232

1 *Hansard*, June 25 1867 (527). Cf. Gillespie, *Labor and Politics in England, 1850–67*, pp. 173–4.
2 For the Boundary Act of 1868 see above, p. 76, n. 4. For Gaselee, see *Hansard*, February 14 1868 (732 ff.) and April 20 (1014).
3 *Hansard*, July 1 1867 (813 ff.).

PAGE 233

1 *Ibid.* (837). Cf. Lowe to Lady Salisbury, May 28 1867 for the view that 'the moment he says a thing is serious, shoals of men go over to him whatever the question', *A Great Lady's Friendships.*
2 *Hansard*, July 2 1867 (868–70).
3 See J. B. Smith in *Hansard*, July 4 1867 (998–9).

PAGE 234

1 See below, ch. VIII. There is something approaching a hint of this in Disraeli's remarks on Laing's motion for the allocation of third seats to a number of English boroughs, *Hansard*, June 17 1867 (1959) which the government resisted by eight votes in a middle-sized division, but cf. Gladstone, *Hansard*, June 17 1867 (1960).

PAGE 235

1 Morley, *Gladstone*, II, 225–6. 'Never have I undergone a stranger emotion of surprise than when, as I was entering the House, our Whip met me and stated that Disraeli was about to support Hodgkinson's motion. But so it was, and the proposition was adopted without disturbance, as if it had been an affair of trivial importance.'
2 43 Eliz. c. 2.
3 59 Geo. 3, c. 12, also *Hansard*, May 9 1867 (334) and Sturges Bourne, etc. see Hibbert in *Hansard*, May 9 1867 (267 ff.).

PAGE 237

1 Taylor to Disraeli, March 25 (misdated May 25), April 25 (dated Tuesday night but obviously April 25) and April 26 1867; also two undated letters, one of them headed 'Thursday night', Hughenden MSS B/XX/T/94, 89, 90, 91 and 93.
2 Barrington to Disraeli, April 7 1867, referring to a speech by Torrens, Hughenden MSS.

PAGE 238

1 Barrington to Disraeli, April 10 1867, Hughenden MSS.
2 Manners, *Journal*, April 14 1867, Belvoir MSS.
3 Manners, *Journal*, April 14 1867, Belvoir MSS; Disraeli to Derby, April 12 1867, Derby MSS Box 146.
4 *Hansard*, April 12 1867 (1589 ff.).
5 There was considerable dispute about the extent to which Derby's name was involved. I have assumed, without much confidence, that it was not.
6 *Hansard*, April 12 1867 (1587 ff.) and (1706 ff.) and May 6 (7 ff.).
7 Osborne had told Brand, the Liberal Chief Whip, that he would raise it, *Hansard*, April 12 (1698) and assumed that Brand would tell Taylor.
8 Hibbert in *Hansard*, May 3 1867 (11).
9 I.e. Gladstone (?).

PAGE 239
1 *Hansard*, April 12 1867 (1593).
2 *Ibid.* (1596–7).
3 Hardy, *Diary*, April 13 1867.
4 Halifax, *Journal*, April 12 1867.

PAGE 240
1 Elcho to Grosvenor, April 13, 28 and 29 1867, Wemyss MSS.
2 Bright in *Hansard*, May 2 1867 (1903).
3 See Baxter's memo. of February 23 1867, Derby MSS Box 52/4.

PAGE 242
1 Reform League Executive Committee Minutes, February 22 1867 95922 [/4]. All references to the Executive Committee or Council are to be found in 95922/4 unless otherwise stated.

PAGE 243
1 For a list of its most respectable members, see *Morning Star*, October 18 1866. This includes fourteen Liberal MP.s (Bazley, Hibbert, Thos. Barnes, P. A. Taylor, R. N. Philips, T. B. Potter, Duncan McLaren, Fawcett, Platt, Onslow, Charles Gilpin, Whitworth, Holden and Sir Francis Crossley as well as T. H. Green, Edward Caird, Thorold Rogers, Handel Cossham and Humphrey Sandwith).
2 See E. R. Jones, *Life and Speeches of Joseph Cowen, MP.*, chapter IV.
3 Bright at Leeds, October 8 1866 (*Morning Star*, October 9).

PAGE 244
1 George Wilson at Reform Union Conference in Manchester, November 19 1866 (*Morning Star*, November 20).

PAGE 245
1 E.g. Bright at Rochdale, January 30 1867 (*Morning Star*, January 31) and Duncan McLaren's letter to the *Morning Star*, April 10.

PAGE 246
1 Reform League Executive Committee, February 22 1867.
2 Baxter Langley to Howell, May 14 1866, 95922/20.
3 To list those who were elected to the Executive Committee in September 1866, when neither Potter, Beesly, Hartwell, Ernest Jones nor Marx's other friend, Eccarius, received enough votes, 95922/4.
4 Quotation from Gladstone's 1865 Chester speech used as a Reform League motto, 95922/4.

PAGE 247
1 Cf. Marx to Engels, May 1 1865 in *Marx and Engels on Britain*, pp. 539–40.

PAGE 248

1 For minutes of joint Reform League Executive/Trades Delegates meeting of January 18 1867, see 95922/4.
2 Quoted in Gillespie, *Labor and Politics in England, 1850–67*, pp. 156–7.

PAGE 249

1 See Reform League Executive Committee, September 22 1865 for attack on Bright for 'verging to Conservatism'.
2 Marx to Engels in *Marx and Engels on Britain*, p. 540; Mill, *Autobiography*, pp. 246–7.
3 Bright at Birmingham, August 27 1866 (*Morning Star*, August 28), and speech of December 3 1867 (*Morning Star*, December 4).
4 Bright at Rochdale, January 30 1867 (*Morning Star*, January 31).
5 Bright at National Reform League Banquet, Manchester, September 25 1866 (*Morning Star*, September 26).

PAGE 250

1 Bright at Birmingham, August 27 1867 (*Morning Star*, August 28).
2 See Reform League Executive Committee minutes, November 10 and December 8 1865 for condemnation of Reform Union but *passim* 1865/6.

PAGE 251

1 See resolution proposed by George Odger and carried at Reform League Executive Committee, March 20 1866.
2 Reform League Executive Council, March 9 1866.
3 Reform League Executive Council, June 22 1866. Cf. minutes of July 6 1866 for desire to work with Reform Union 'and other Reform bodies'.
4 *Morning Star*, June 28 1866.

PAGE 252

1 *Ibid.*
2 *Morning Star* (July 25 and July 24 1867).
3 *Morning Star* (July 4 1867).
4 Bright at Manchester, September 24 1867 (*Morning Star*, September 25).
5 *Morning Star*, July 27 1867. For the meetings of July 24 and 30 see *Morning Star*, July 25 and 31 1867.
6 *Morning Star*, August 1 1866.
7 *Morning Star*, September 4 1866.
8 *Morning Star*, August 6 and September 3 1866.
9 *Morning Star*, September 27 1866.

PAGE 253

1 *Ibid.*
2 *Morning Star*, October 6 1866.

3 See by-election speech on re-election in Buckinghamshire in the *Morning Star*, July 14 1866.

4 *Morning Star*, October 8 1866.

5 *Morning Star*, October 19 1866.

6 *Morning Star*, October 11 1866.

7 *Morning Star*, October 18 1866.

8 *Morning Star*, October 23 1866.

9 In a speech at Islington, November 13 1866 (*Morning Star*, November 14).

PAGE 254

1 *Morning Star*, November 14 1866.

2 Reform League Executive Council, June 8 1866. This phrase was used in an attack on Lord Stanley in 1866; it was applied on June 8 to the Liberal government. It might well have been used in 1867 of the Liberal party.

3 *Morning Star*, September 27 1866 and October 9 (for W. Riding Liberal MP.s refusing to attend the Manhood Suffrage Association meeting in Leeds). Cf. Beales's letter to the *Morning Star* (December 8) for Beales's anxiety about conflict between League and London Working Men's Association.

4 *Morning Star*, November 22 1866.

5 *Morning Star*, December 4 1866.

6 *Morning Star*, November 26 1866.

7 *Morning Star*, December 19 1866.

8 *Morning Star*, January 2 1867.

9 *Ibid.*

PAGE 255

1 *Ibid.*

2 *Morning Star*, January 29 1867.

3 *Morning Star*, January 25 1867.

4 *Morning Star*, February 6 1867.

5 *Morning Star*, February 12 1867.

6 *Morning Star*, February 13 1867.

7 *Morning Star*, February 26 1867.

PAGE 256

1 *Morning Star*, February 16 1867.

2 *Morning Star*, February 17 1867.

3 *Morning Star*, February 26 1867.

4 *Ibid.*

5 E.g. at the Reform League and Trades Delegates meeting on February 28, see *Morning Star*, March 1 1867.

6 *Morning Star*, March 4 1867. Cf. Beales's draft public letter March 8 1867, 95922/20.

7 *Reynolds' News*, March 3 1867.
8 *Morning Star*, March 18 1867.
9 *Morning Star*, March 14 and *Reynolds' News*, March 24 1867.
10 *Reynolds' News*, March 24 1867.
11 *Morning Star*, March 20 1867.
12 *Morning Star*, March 23 and 26 1867. *Reynolds' News*, March 31 1867. Cf. The O'Donoghue to Gladstone, March 30 1867 for Reform League impression that Gladstone 'had receded somewhat from your position of last year'. Add. MSS 44412.

PAGE 257

1 *Morning Star*, March 28 1867.
2 *Morning Star*, April 2 1867.
3 *Morning Star*, April 10 1867.
4 *Morning Star*, April 9 1867.

PAGE 258

1 Cf. Lambert's memo. on the Lodger Franchise, July 19 1867, Hughenden MSS.

PAGE 259

1 *Reynolds' News*, April 14 1867.
2 Reform League Executive Committee Minutes, April 12 1867.
3 *Reynolds' News*, April 14 1867.
4 *Reynolds' News*, April 21 1867.
5 *Morning Star*, April 16 1867.
6 *Reynolds' News*, April 28 1867.

PAGE 260

1 C. Bradlaugh, *Reform or Revolution*, p. 7 (first article in *National Reformer*, reprinted as a pamphlet).
2 Reform League Executive Committee, April 18 1867.
3 P. A. Taylor, MP. at Union/League meeting, *Morning Star*, May 11 1867.
4 For meetings at Birmingham, Leeds and London see *Morning Star*, April 23, 24 and 27 1867.
5 *Morning Star*, May 11 1867.

PAGE 261

1 See below, p. 263, n. 4.
2 Reform League Executive Committee, April 18 1867.
3 H.O. OS 7854/8.
4 Reform League Executive Committee, April 18 ff. 1867.

PAGE 262

1 Chelmsford (Lord Chancellor) to Derby, July 26 1866. Derby MSS Box 153/3.
2 *Morning Star*, July 20, 23, 24 and 27 1867; S. Walpole, *The History of Twenty-Five Years*, II, ch. IX. J. S. Mill, *Autobiography* and H. Broadhurst, *The Story of His Life*, pp. 34–40 provide accounts of July 23.
3 Hardy, *Diary*, July 26 1866. S. Walpole, *The History of Twenty-five Years*, II, 169–75; Mill, *Autobiography*, pp. 246–7.

PAGE 263

1 Reform League Executive Committee, November 23 1866.
2 *Morning Star*, November 29 1866.
3 Bright at Birmingham, August 27 1866 (*Morning Star*, August 28).
4 For the Trades meeting of December 3 see *Morning Star*, November 26; and see also November 27 for Lord John Manners refusing Hartwell (on behalf of Potter) permission to assemble in Green Park. Cf. also *Morning Star*, January 25 1867 for decision not to use the Parks on February 11.
5 Derby to the Queen, November 20 1866, Derby MSS Box 193/1.

PAGE 264

1 Walpole to Derby, April 24 1867, Derby MSS Box 153/3.
2 Derby to the Queen, May 1 1867, Derby MSS Box 192/1.
3 Derby to the Queen, April 27 1867, Derby MSS Box 193/2.

PAGE 265

1 S. Walpole, *The History of Twenty-Five Years*, II, 197[1].
2 Walpole to Derby, April 30 1867, Derby MSS Box 153/4.
3 *Morning Star*, May 2 1867 for copy of the notice.
4 Thomas Hughes to Auberon Herbert, May 5 1867, Derby MSS Box 52/8. Reform League Executive Committee, May 3 and 6 1867.
5 Carnarvon's brother, see above, p. 22, n. 4.

PAGE 266

1 Auberon Herbert to Thomas Hughes, May 5 1867, Derby MSS Box 52/8.

PAGE 267

1 About a dozen Conservative MP.s voted with Ayrton, about half a dozen Adullamites with the government. *Hansard*, May 2 1867 (1908–11).
2 *Hansard*, May 2 1867 (1888).
3 I.e. without Disraeli's connivance if, indeed, there was no connivance on this occasion.

PAGE 268

1 See p. 241.
2 Naas's Tenant Improvement Bill. Cf. Hardy, *Diary*, May 1 1867 for discontent.
3 Hardy, *Diary*, July 19 1866; also see below, p. 304 n. 1.
4 Cairns to Disraeli, April 17, 20 and 29 1867, Hughenden MSS.

PAGE 269

1 *Hansard*, May 2 (1875–6).
2 *Hansard*, May 3 (2024).
3 *Hansard*, May 6 (15 ff.).

PAGE 270

1 Derby to the Queen, May 5 and 7, and to General Grey, May 8, Derby MSS Boxes 192/1 and 194/1. Hardy would have had to resign as an MP. on appointment and fight a by-election. Cf. Hardy, *Diary*, May 6 1867. Cf. Lowe to Lady Salisbury, May 6 1867, *A Great Lady's Friendships*.
2 Derby to the Queen, May 5 1867, Derby MSS Box 192/1.
3 Derby to the Queen, May 7 1867, Derby MSS Box 194/1, and Hardy, *Diary*, May 7 1867.
4 Derby to General Grey, May 8 1867, Derby MSS Box 194/1.

PAGE 271

1 For division list see *Hansard*, May 9 1867 (357–61).
2 Sir Leonard Palk paired because he disapproved of the motion. Palk to Disraeli, May 10 1867, Hughenden MSS.
3 *Hansard*, May 9 1867 (345).
4 *Hansard*, May 3 1867 (2023). Cf. McLaren to Gladstone, August 14 and 30 1866, Add. MSS 44411.

PAGE 272

1 Walter Morrison to H. Brown, May 14 1867, *Western Daily News*, J. B. Smith MSS.
2 Lowe to Lady Salisbury, May 14 1867, *A Great Lady's Friendships*.
3 *Morning Star*, May 13 1867.

PAGE 273

1 Cf. *The Times* for the view that 'not one of the 25,000 who followed Mr Beales...did not pay £10 a year for his rent or his lodgings', May 13 1867.

PAGE 274

1 *Hansard*, May 13 1867 (432–3).
2 Gladstone memo. of meeting of May 17 1867, Add. MSS 44755.
3 Disraeli on introducing Scottish Reform bill, *Hansard*, May 13 1867 (403).
4 Derby to Grosvenor, May 13 1867, Derby MSS Box 194/1.

5 Halifax, *Journal*, March 29 1867.

6 Derby to the Queen, May 11 and 15 1867, RA A/35/67; Derby to Grosvenor, May 13 1867, Derby MSS Box 194/1; Stanhope to Derby, May 14 1867, Derby MSS Box 114/3; the Queen to Derby, May 14, RA A/35/68.

PAGE 275

1 Bright to his wife, May 12 1867, UCL.

2 Derby to the Queen, May 13 1867, Derby MSS Box 194/1.

PAGE 276

1 Grosvenor to Derby, May 14 1867, Derby MSS Box 164.

2 There were two other amendments—one from Denman (*Hansard*, May 13, col. 443) which was accepted in part: one from Disraeli (col. 444) which was covered by the discussion on May 9 and which was accepted with only the briefest discussion on May 13.

PAGE 277

1 Glyn to Gladstone, May 12 1867, Add. MSS 44347.

2 *Hansard*, May 13 1867 (453–4).

3 Gladstone in *Hansard*, May 9 1867 (299).

PAGE 278

1 E.g. Huddersfield.

2 Fawcett in *Hansard*, May 9 1867 (318).

3 For dislike of the Small Tenements Acts see Colonel Bartellot, *Hansard*, April 11 1867 (1549), Sir William Heathcote, April 11 (1542), Beresford-Hope April 12 (1603 ff.). For personal payment of rates being inconvenient and a ground for further agitation see Coleridge, April 11 (1554). For W. E. Forster being against connecting the franchise with the Small Tenements Acts, though not against the Small Tenements Acts themselves, see April 12 (1608). For threats of agitation against the personal payment principle see Cowen, April 12 (1639–40). For Small Tenements Acts as oppression of the poor see J. W. Henley, April 11 (1555–6). For transfer of agitation to vestries, see Cranborne, April 11 (1570). For uncertainty about size of constituencies see Cranborne, April 11 (1571). For corruption see April 11 (1572). Also cf. Hibbert, May 9 (268), J. B. Smith, May 9 (323) and Bright, May 9 (330).

4 Cf. Hardy, *Hansard*, April 12 (1656).

PAGE 279

1 'If the working classes were induced to claim the franchise under this bill, a little wholesome pressure would be put upon the upper classes... among [whom] there was so much apathy and indifference...[and] who...would...find their legitimate influence in no degree diminished ...[since]...intelligence...education and even wealth, when properly expended, would always command respect in this country, among the working classes.' Hon. H. G. Liddell, *Hansard*, April 12 1867 (1632).

2 Manners to Derby, January 14 1867, Derby MSS Box 161 for need to be 'very careful not to make County constituencies impossibilities to country gentlemen of moderate fortunes'. Also see Northcote to Derby, October 17 1866, Derby MSS Box 162 reporting the Queen's dislike of 'the purchasing power of the "noveaux riches"'. Cf. Baxter to Corry, March 16 1867 reporting Banks Stanhope on bribery, Hughenden MSS.

3 *Hansard*, July 2 1867 (892–9) and July 4 (1007 ff.).

4 *Hansard*, July 4 1867 (1019 ff.).

5 Cranborne in *Hansard*, June 20 1867 (192).

6 *Hansard*, March 25 1867 (522–4).

7 *Ibid.* (544).

8 Cf. Lord Hill-Trevor to Derby, March 13 1867, Derby MSS Box 105.

PAGE 280

1 Hardy, *Diary*, May 20 1867. Manners, *Journal*, May 18 1867, Belvoir MSS.

2 Heathcote to Cranborne, May 19 1867, Salisbury MSS.

3 Grosvenor to Derby, May 14 1867, Derby MSS Box 164.

4 *Hansard*, May 9 1867 (324).

PAGE 281

1 W. Foote, agent for Swindon, to Spofforth, November 23 1867, Hughenden MSS.

PAGE 282

1 G. J. Holyoake, *Bygones Worth Remembering*, II, 42–6. Argyll to Gladstone, April 6 1867, Add. MSS 44100. *Hansard*, May 17 1867 (738 ff. and 754–5). Lord John Manners, *Journal*, May 18 1867, Belvoir MSS.

PAGE 283

1 G. Greene in *Hansard*, May 9 1867 (312).

2 For Bright's part, see Bright to his wife, May 12 1867, UCL.

PAGE 284

1 It would be interesting to know whether Hodgkinson's interest in abolishing compounding arose from a fear that the Poor Law overseers in Newark would respond to the large increase in the electorate, which the bill would have established, by adopting the Small Tenements Acts (i.e. by *introducing* compounding in order to *restrict* the franchise).

2 Bright to his wife, May 11 1867, UCL.

3 *Ibid.*

PAGE 285

1 I.e. Gladstone preferred Childers's.

2 *Hansard*, May 13 1867 (472–3).

3 *Hansard*, May 17 1867 (725).

4 *Hansard*, May 17 1867 (735–6), May 30 (1363).

5 Cf. J. B. Smith to [?] May 28 1867 for Disraeli 'pushing the bill as hard as he can', J. B. Smith MSS. Cf. also James Clay in *Hansard*, May 17 (1743) and Disraeli to Hardy, May 18 1867 in Buckle, *Disraeli*, IV, 541.

6 E. Levy to A. Montagu, May 28 1867, Hughenden MSS B/XX/M/413*a*.

7 The House sat thereafter at 12 instead of at 2. Knatchbull-Hugessen, *Diary*, May 29 1867.

8 See *Hansard*, June 18 (17). Cf. Chichester Fortescue on June 28 (703 ff.) for allegation that Disraeli had made a bargain with Irish MP.s to leave Irish representation alone in order to keep support on the English bill. In this Chichester Fortescue was probably right, but the abandonment of an Irish bill, which had been promised on a number of occasions throughout the session, may also be seen as a recognition that Disraeli's object had shifted from keeping a series of policy options open in case of a general election to pressing the passage of the English bill as soon as possible. It was obviously impossible to introduce, and pass, an Irish bill if the English bill was to pass that session. There was also the security consideration in the Irish case.

9 Disraeli in *Hansard*, May 24 1867 (1023).

10 For the short debate on this see *Hansard*, May 28 1867 (1206–32).

11 Grosvenor to Gladstone, March 26 1867, Add. MSS 44337; Hankey to Gladstone, *c.* March 28 1867, Add. MSS 44412; Argyll to Gladstone, May 15 1867, Add. MSS 44100; Elcho to Grosvenor, March 25 1867, Wemyss MSS and Halifax, *Journal*, February 24 1867.

PAGE 289

1 Northcote, *Diary*, Add. MSS 50063A, March 8 1866.

PAGE 290

1 Knatchbull-Hugessen, *Diary*, April 13 1867.

2 Grosvenor to Elcho, March 3 1867, Wemyss MSS.

3 See H. W. McCready, 'British Labour and the Royal Commission on Trades Unions 1867–9', *University of Toronto Quarterly*, XXIV (1954–5), p. 314 and Lord John Manners to Disraeli, October 24 1866, Hughenden MSS.

PAGE 291

1 Dunkellin to W. H. Gregory, Christmas Day 1865, Harewood MSS.

2 See above chapters I and II.

PAGE 292

1 On March 5 1867, see above, p. 176 n. 3.

2 I.e. the line-up with the Reform Union adopted by Gladstone after May 11.

PAGE 295
1 See above, p. 81.
2 See above, chapter II.

PAGE 296
1 Stanley to Disraeli, February 15 1867, Hughenden MSS. Cf. Sir Henry
Edwards's speech to Wakefield Working Men's Association for a Conservative MP.s view that 'of all...humbugs on the face of the earth, the
Liberal Whig is the greatest', press cutting enclosed in Edwards to Disraeli, April 26 [1867], Hughenden MSS.
2 Russell to Gladstone, March 17 1867, Add. MSS 44293.
3 Bright to Gladstone, July 31 1867, Add. MSS 44112.

PAGE 297
1 Cf. Sir Philip Magnus, *Gladstone*, pp. 105 ff. Acton to Döllinger,
November 1865 in ed. Conzemius, *Ignaz von Döllinger/Lord Acton,
Briefwechsel 1850–1869*, I, 415–16.
2 Cf. *Observations on Mr Gladstone's denunciations...of millowners...
in a speech...[of] 7 October 1862 by a merchant*, 1862.

PAGE 298
1 For patronage see Acland to Gladstone, March 30 1867, Add. MSS
44092. For mystification see Cf. N. Kendall, MP. in *Hansard*, May 9
1867 (317).

PAGE 299
1 See above, p. 96

PAGE 300
1 See Gillespie, *Labor and Politics in England, 1850–67*, p. 245.

PAGE 301
1 See Sir Robert Phillimore's diary in Morley, *Gladstone*, II, 234 and
Halifax, *Journal* entry, April 20 1867, but written later.

PAGE 302
1 For Bright see Trevelyan, *Bright*, pp. 206–7. For the Irish see J. H.
Whyte, *The Independent Irish Party 1850–9*, pp. 55–7 and 151–3.
2 For Palmerston see Buckle, *Disraeli*, IV, 235–7; for Gladstone see
Buckle, *Disraeli*, IV, 156–61.
3 *Hansard*, July 8 1864 (1300–6).
4 Disraeli to Derby, December 24 1866, Derby MSS Box 146.

PAGE 303

1 See above, pp. 130–4.
2 For the Malt Tax movement see Northcote, *Diary*, February 20 1866, Sir Fitzroy Kelly to Disraeli, February 19 1866, Hughenden MSS. Cf. W. W. Good, *Political, Agricultural and Commercial Fallacies*, pp. 43 ff.
3 Lord Henry Lennox to Disraeli, various dates, in Hughenden MSS B/XX/Lx/240, 244, 247, 256 and 257. For impossibility of increasing naval expenditure while in a minority in the existing House, see Derby to Pakington, January 16 1867, Derby MSS.

PAGE 304

1 For the Conscience Clause see Derby to Beauchamp, July 1 1866 and January 16 1867, Derby MSS Box 110 and 192. Lord R. Montagu to Disraeli, two letters in Hughenden MSS B/XXI/M. J. G. Hubbard to Disraeli in Hughenden MSS B/XX/H. Cranborne to Disraeli, June 29 1866, Pakington to Disraeli July 1 1866, Lord J. Manners to Disraeli, October 24 1866, all Hughenden MSS. For Catholics see Earle to Disraeli, n.d. [July 1866], Hughenden MSS B/XX/E/386 and 408 and Bowyer to Disraeli, July 5 1866, Hughenden MSS. Hardy, *Diary*, July 21 1866. Disraeli to Corry, October 17 1866, Hugenden MSS, and to Derby, July 23 1866, Derby MSS Box 146. For Irish Catholics see below, p. 306 and Althoz and Norman in bibliography.
2 *Hansard*, May 31 1867 (1421).
3 See above, p. 113.
4 Disraeli to Stanley, November 6 1865, Knowsley MSS.
5 Disraeli to Derby, July 12 1866, Derby MSS Box 146.

PAGE 305

1 Disraeli to Derby, September 24 1866, Derby MSS Box 146.
2 Somerset Beaumont to Disraeli, July 4 1866, Hughenden MSS. For the *Owl* circle of which Knatchbull-Hugessen was a member, see Knatchbull-Hugessen, *Diary*, July 30 1867 and *passim*.
3 See *W. H. Smith* by Viscount Chilston (1965), pp. 47–61. For Sir Hugh Rose see Derby to General Grey, July 16 1866 and July 20, Derby MSS. For Bath see Bath to Derby, June 24 and 25 1867, Derby MSS Box 164.
4 Cf. Paul Smith, *Disraelian Conservatism and Social Reform*, p. 86.
5 *Ibid*. p. 71.
6 *Ibid*. pp. 66–7.
7 For Lord Arthur Clinton's interest in Irish policy, for his attempts to obtain office from Gladstone and Derby and for the pretence that he supported both parties, see his letters to Gladstone (n.d. Tuesday 1866 in Add. MSS 44410), and to Disraeli (Hughenden MSS B/XXI/C), asking for governorships abroad in January 1867 and for the governorship of New South Wales on March 13 1867.

NOTES TO PAGES 305-314

8 Shaftesbury to Disraeli, October 19 1866 ('Beware of being thought a High Church government'), Derby MSS Box 114. Cf. Shaftesbury, *Diary*, March 9 1867 quoted in Hodder, *Shaftesbury*, III, 217.

9 Paul Smith, *Disraelian Conservatism and Social Reform*, p. 50.

PAGE 306

1 For Stanley's persuasion of Whiteside see his letter to Whiteside dated July 7 1866, Knowsley MSS. See also Knatchbull-Hugessen, *Diary*, July 4 1866. For the vote of April 12 see memo. by Barrington, n.d. in Derby MSS 52/4.

2 For Clanricarde see *The Greville Memoirs 1814–60*, March 2 1858, p. 347.

3 See Derby to Lord Stradbroke, August 1, to the Queen, July 12, and to Cairns, July 12, all 1866, all Derby MSS.

4 For the buttering of Clanricarde see, e.g. Disraeli to Derby, July 12 1866, Derby MSS and Malmesbury to Naas, April 1 1867, Mayo MSS. Dr F. B. Smith, *The Making of the Second Reform Bill*, p. 83, suggests that Gregory and Clanricarde were alienated from Gladstone because of the threat Gladstone presented to Irish landowners. The truth, however, seems to be that Gregory was a more extreme tenant-righter than either Gladstone or Disraeli and that Clanricarde was willing to go as far as Disraeli or Derby (see Sir William Gregory's *Autobiography*, pp. 242–4, for Gladstone finding Gregory's Land bill objectionable. Cf. Derby to Cranborne, September 28 1866, Derby MSS, Box 191/2 for the same reaction).

PAGE 307

1 For Stanley as the idol of the intelligentsia see Sir Robert Morier to Mrs Rosslyn Wemyss in Rosslyn Wemyss, *Memoirs of Sir Robert Morier*, II, 85. Cf. Hammond (Under-Secretary at the Foreign Office) to Cowley in FO 519/192 *passim*. For Stanley as friend of the working classes see the critical resolution passed at the Reform League Executive Council, June 8 1866. See also Disraeli to Stanley, November 2, 6 and 7, Knowsley MSS, for Disraeli's wooing of him.

PAGE 310

1 Lord Henry Lennox to Disraeli, October 25 1866, Hughenden MSS.

PAGE 313

1 C. Seymour, *Electoral Reform in England and Wales*.

2 See bibliography.

PAGE 314

1 *Before the Socialists 1861–1881*, chapter III.

2 See bibliography.

3 In the form in which it was presented as a Ph.D. thesis at Cambridge (Cambridge University Library).

4 See bibliography.

PAGE 315

1 See bibliography.

PAGE 318

1 See above, p. 277.
2 Kimberley, *Journal*, p. 17.
3 *Hansard*, March 26 (610). Barrington to Malmesbury, March 19 and 21 1867, Malmesbury MSS.
4 Paul Smith, *Disraelian Conservatism and Social Reform*, p. 53.

PAGE 319

1 Beauchamp to Derby, January 18 1867, Derby MSS Box 110.
2 *Hansard*, June 21 1867 (271–4 and 277–8).
3 In the votes on Gaselee's and on Laing's second motion.

PAGE 320

1 For the debate see *Hansard*, July 8 1867 (1228–50).

PAGE 321

1 Roebuck to Disraeli, July 4 1867, Hughenden MSS. Cf. August 20 1867, 'seldom happens to me to acknowledge kindness'.

PAGE 322

1 *Hansard*, June 24 (451 and 454–5).
2 See above, p. 305.
3 See Hanham, *Elections and Party Management*, p. 383, quoting Sir Alfred Pease.
4 See below, p. 329–30.

PAGE 323

1 See above, p. 98.
2 See above, p. 111 n. 6.
3 See above, p. 215–16.
4 See above, p. 109.
5 See above, p. 106 n. 3. For hinting at resignation see Wood to Russell, October 18 1865, PRO 30 22/15.

PAGE 324

1 For Hutt, Bouverie, Hugessen and Peel see above, pp. 85–98.
2 See Richmond to Derby, September 27 1866, Derby MSS Box 113/10 and Lord John Manners to his brother, October 24 1866, Belvoir MSS.

PAGE 325

1 Sir Henry Bulwer to Lady Salisbury, October 5 1866 in *A Great Lady's Friendships*. Lytton to John Foster in *Personal and Literary Letters of the Earl of Lytton*, March 6 1866.

2 Cf. *Hansard*, June 20 1867 (192) 'the greatest wealth is with a very different class...[from] the landed interest to which I have the honour to belong'.

3 See above, p. 277.

4 Derby to Disraeli letters written between July and December 1866 and preserved at Hughenden.

5 Disraeli letters to Derby all in Derby MSS Box 146.

PAGE 326

1 For Derby's illnesses see Malmesbury, *Diary*, July 9 1866, *c.* January 22 1867 and April 13 1867 in Malmesbury, *Memoirs of an ex-Minister*, I, pp. 361, 365 and 369; Hardy, *Diary*, April 1 and June 30 1867 and Derby to General Grey, May 8 1867, Derby MSS Box 194/1, and to Disraeli, June 28 [1867], Hughenden MSS.

2 Disraeli to Cranborne, December 26 1866, Salisbury MSS.

3 See above, chapter II.

PAGE 327

1 For Peel, Bouverie and Hutt see above, pp. 85–98. For Clinton see p. 305 n. 7. For Baillie-Cochrane's desire for 'the opportunity of work' and his 'disappointment at finding [him]self separated from all his old friends' after '20 years at a loss of more than £20,000 for my party' since he became an MP., see his letters to Carnarvon of August 21 [1866], PRO 30 6/137, and enclosure in Malmesbury to Derby of May 10 1867, Derby MSS. Cochrane wrote a number of books including an autobiography, *In the Days of the Dandies* which, however, has little political interest. Disraeli made him a peer in 1880.

For Earl Percy, whose religious eccentricity did him no good, who had no claim to office on grounds of ability and whose manner 'certainly' was 'not fascinating', see his letters to Derby of November 18 1866 and February 12 1867. He refused to be called to the House of Lords and declined the Treasurership on the ground that if, in July 1866, Derby had found it 'necessary to strengthen your position...that one of the oldest and staunchest Conservative families...should have a voice', etc., he would have helped but that it was now a 'matter of entire indifference to me personally'.

PAGE 328

1 The letters to Malmesbury are in the Malmesbury MSS. The Derby letter to Naas has been used in the copied form which Derby retained. Brand's letters to Gladstone are in Add. MSS 44194, and to Halifax in the Garrowby MSS. Their letters to him are in the Brand MSS. Copies of Elcho's letters to Grosvenor and Grosvenor's replies are all in the Wemyss MSS.

PAGE 331

1 See above, p. 124.

PAGE 333

1 See above, p. 188.
2 See above, chapter II.
3 *Ibid.*
4 See above, chapter II. For the letter see Disraeli to Derby, February 27 1867 (2nd letter), Derby MSS Box 146.
5 i.e. a conversation between Cranborne and his mother in which his mother, having met Disraeli at Carnarvon's house in the winter of 1866 and finding him unwilling to talk to her about politics, decided that he meant 'to translate into statute law the sentiments of his novels—the Crown and the People—as against the aristocracy and the middle class' (*A Great Lady's Friendships*, p. 101). But cf. also Derby's alarm and irritation at Disraeli's suggestion of enfranchisement for every borough with population above 100,000—because that would involve finding forty-one seats, Derby to Disraeli, December 27 1866, Hughenden MSS.

PAGE 334

1 See Hardinge, *Carnarvon*, p. 335 for Disraeli, while staying at Highclere, 'suggesting as a detail to omit all mention of Reform in the Queen's speech—to lead the opposition to believe that they could move an amendment on the Address and then just before the Address to let the secretary to the Treasury announce that on a certain day [the] question of Reform would be considered'.
2 See above, p. 115.

PAGE 335

1 Disraeli to Derby, February 27 1867 (2nd letter). For the Carlton Club meeting see Disraeli to Derby, February 28 and Derby to Disraeli, February 28 1867 (Derby MSS Box 146 and Hughenden MSS). Cf. Buckle, IV, *Disraeli*, 487–8.

PAGE 336

1 *Hansard*, May 17 1867 (723).
2 Disraeli to Corry, Good Friday 1867, Hughenden MSS B/XX/J/20.
3 See *Morning Star*, April 3 1867.
4 E.g. *Hansard*, July 8 1867 (1243).

PAGE 338

1 Speech at Edinburgh, October 29 1867 (*The Times*, October 30).
2 Clarendon to Gladstone, November 4 1867, Add. MSS 44133.

PAGE 339

1 *Ibid.*
2 The Queen of Holland to Lady Salisbury, February 22 1867, *A Great Lady's Friendships*.

1 This is a very rough list. It includes only gains among MP.s who can fairly certainly be said to have voted regularly for one party or the other. Some Liberal losses, especially in Ireland (e.g. Louth and Dungarvan) cannot be counted as Conservative gains. What looks in McCalmont like a Liberal gain in Mayo (1865 Bingham LC; Browne L—1868 Moore L; Bingham C) was in effect a Conservative gain, since Bingham was a regular Conservative voter throughout except on the Irish Church in 1868 and Moore, a Catholic and anti-landlord candidate, sat on the Conservative side of the House (see White: *Inner Life of the House of Commons*, II, 157–8). Dod's and McCalmont's Liberal/Conservative classifications are unreliable: their designations of Irish MP.s need thorough examination.

INDEX

[Note: Bright, Derby, Disraeli, Gladstone and Russell are mentioned too frequently for an index of references to be practicable. They have therefore not been included.]

Clarendon, 4th Earl of, fears increased working-class electorate, 46; views on Liberal party, 81, 122; criticizes Gladstone, 101, 102, 298; opposes dissolution, 103; possibility of leadership, 106, 107, 108, 109, 111, 134; and possible coalition, 114, 115, 117, 150, 201, 394; sees danger of Bright, 123; and commission, 136; supports fixed-line franchise, 274; and also, 57, 87, 88, 97, 100, 296, 323, 338, 339, 396, 400

Clay, James, 194, 195, 196, 199, 239, 302

Clay, Sir William, 45, 97, 299

Clay's Act of 1851, 174, 175, 237, 269

Cleveland, 4th Duke of, 106

Clinton, Lord Arthur, 327, 424

Clive, George, 97

Cobden, Richard, 22, 82, 179, 246, 248

Colchester, Baroness, 93

Cole, G. D. H., 315

Colebrooke, Sir Edward, amendment of, 228, 229

Coleridge, John D., 54, 296

Coleridge's Instruction, 14, 166, 194–7, 199, 213, 215, 216, 217, 257, 285, 292

Colvile, C. R., 227

Commission of enquiry, suggestion for, 135–9

Congrieve, Richard, 20, 31, 34

Conscience Clause, the, 303, 321

Corbally, M., 417

Corn Laws, repeal of, 252–3

Corry, Montague, 32, 169, 255, 305, 336

counties, enfranchisement, 50, 74, 53, 173, 275; 1832 franchise qualification of fifty pounds, 8; proposed reductions from fifty pounds to twenty, 13; to fourteen, 134, 225; to ten, 50; qualification lowered from fifteen pounds to twelve pounds, 14, 72, 223, 233; landed interest in, 225, 231, 232; urban element in, 225, 255; registers, 70; representation, 73, 76, 78, 171, 228; divisions, 72–3; proposed seat redistribution, 9, 17, 68, 69

Coventry, 386

Cowen, J., 243, 244, 245, 246, 249, 260

Cox, Homersham, 313

Cranborne, Lord, threatens resignation, 13, 150, 151, 155, 209; resignation, 173, 177, 179, 180, 181, 241, 256, 291, 297, 300, 302; conservative Anglican in politics, 21, 22, 23; and Park closing, 38; wants to limit working-class enfranchisement, 46, 59, 96, 148, 149, 157, 159, 160, 163, 164, 165, 173; dislikes Disraeli, 66; helps to divide Liberals, 101; and possible coalition, 112, 116, 117, 133; and Adullamites, 129, 132; supports five pound rating, 147, 198; wants moderate Reform policy, 150, 156; limitations, 182–3; and Coleridge's Instruction, 194, 215, 216; does not want rated residential suffrage, 208, 211; opposes Conscience Clause, 303, 321; and also, 5, 6, 20, 85, 95, 102, 134, 141, 145, 158, 166, 168, 187, 208, 228, 229, 240, 253, 325, 339, 421

Crawford, R. W., 226, 394

Creasey, Sir Edward, 37

Cricklade, 53

Crosland, T. P., 10, 392

Crossley, Sir Francis, 231

Cullen, Cardinal, 3, 8

Culture and Anarchy, 4

cumulative voting, 62, 146, 162, 203, 226, 421

Daily Telegraph, the, 4, 8, 285

Dalglish, Robert, 200, 273, 416

Dalkeith, Earl of, 177

The Day, 401

De Grey, 3rd Earl, 83, 94, 97, 389

de Lolme, J. L., 37

Delane, J. T., 103, 317, 391, 393

Denman, George, 219, 320; amendment of, 224, 276, 277

Dent, John, 196

Dering, Sir Edward C., 299

Devonshire, 7th Duke of, 106, 177

Devonshire, 73, 179

Dewsbury, 69

Dickson, Colonel L. S., 36, 245, 246

Dillwyn, Lewis L., 238, 239, 299, 416

Dimsdale, Baron, 176

INDEX

Dod, *Parliamentary Companion*, 319
Doulton, Henry, 10, 200, 299
Droitwich, 92, 177, 187
duality, abandonment of, 14, 168, 173,
  180, 182, 189; doubts on abandonment of, 177, 179; criticism of, 183,
  191, 206, 210, 212, 256; support
  for, 143, 146, 157, 162, 165, 167,
  211, 226; impossibility of, 176; and
  also, 79, 166, 169, 170, 174, 203, 240
Dublin, 39
Duckworth, Sir John, 231
Dunkellin, Lord, 9, 97, 98, 99, 106,
  107, 186, 204, 271, 299, 306; amendment of, 134, 172
Dunstable, 319–20
Dyott, R., 230, 422

Earle, Ralph A., 83, 110, 113, 117,
  168, 169, 177, 182, 185, 304
Ecclesiastical Titles Act, 200
Edinburgh, 16, 311, 338; demonstrations in, 12
Edwards, Sir Henry, 320, 433
Egerton, Algernon F., 320
Elcho, Lord, as leader of Cave, 9, 10,
  11, 134; tries to increase its influence 290–1; belief in political
  education of the masses, 23; responsibility for extensive nature of
  1867 Bill, 46, 47; view of democracy, 51; criticism of Gladstone,
  82, 214, 299; suggests commission,
  86, 128, 135; asks for statistics, 88;
  initiates and supports Grosvenor's
  amendment, 96, 97, 100; and
  possible coalition, 108, 109, 110,
  150, 394, 395; suggests Trade
  Union commission, 129, 305; committed to duality, 183, 208, 209, 210;
  supports Gladstone's six pound
  rating, 186, 187; supports rated
  residential suffrage with retrictions,
  208, 209, 210, 211; supports compounding below five pounds, 211,
  212; does not want election, 213,
  215, 216; loses trust of Cave, 295;
  letters, 328, 331, 336; and also, 6,
  12, 16, 28, 51, 63, 95, 98, 101, 102,
  120, 147, 148, 149, 151, 153, 200,
  240, 292, 300, 301, 309, 323
electorate, change in size of, 14, 16,

24, 44, 46, 47, 48, 60, 174, 175, 176,
  206, 248
Ellice, Edward, Jnr., 100, 184, 185,
  298; amendment of, 228
Essex, 73, 169
Eversley, 1st Viscount, 231, 299
Ewing, H. E. C., 200, 299, 416
Exeter, 3rd Marquess of, 181

Factory Acts Extension, 305
faggot votes, 228, 229, 318
Falkirk, 75
fancy franchises, 13–14, 141, 145, 146,
  165, 171, 180, 226, 255, 256
Farrer, T. H., 329
Fawcett, Henry, 2, 36, 58, 199, 226,
  246, 279
Finsbury, 196
Fitzwilliam, C. W. W., 200, 298
fixed-line franchise, 14, 163, 194,
  195, 201, 205, 209, 210, 215, 259,
  281, 293; policy rejected, 218, 289;
  see also Coleridge's Instruction,
  and rating-franchise
Foljambe, F., 378, 394
Foreign Office, the, 112
Forster, W. E., 28, 85, 87, 105, 218,
  219, 231, 253, 275, 285, 289, 292, 296,
  310, 321, 400
Fort, Richard, 271
Fortescue, Chichester S., 85, 432
Foster, W. O., 271

Galashiels, 75
Galway, 6th Viscount, 22
Galway, 107
Garibaldi, 246
Gaselee, Stephen, 22, 76, 230, 232,
  272, 337, 385
Gash, Norman, 314
Gibson, T. Milner, 84
Gillespie, F. E., 315
Gilpin, R. T., 319–20
Gladstone, Mrs, 187, 399
Glasgow, 75; demonstrations in, 12
Glyn, G. C., 193, 296
Goldney, Gabriel, 44, 150, 162, 277,
  318
Goldsmid, Sir Francis, 56
Goschen, George, 28, 85, 87, 97,
  98, 100, 277, 296
Governor Eyre controversy, 92

Horsman, Edward, 9, 12, 56, 82, 84, 89, 93, 95, 97, 100, 108, 110, 111, 114, 186, 204, 208, 209, 251, 282, 292, 299, 323, 391
Hotham, 3rd Baron, 176
Houghton, 1st Baron, 254
household suffrage, bill for, 12–13, 14, 45, 149, 157; advocates of, 15, 16, 260; counterpoises to, 19, 43, 47, 60, 143–5, 146, 148, 151, 158, 159, 163, 165, 167, 170, 175, 178, 183, 188, 190, 194, 195, 203, 204, 210, 222, 237, 253, 289, 293–4, 300; rural, 53; 'cow house suffrage', 55–6; opposition to, 121, 155, 159, 177, 186, 205, 208, 218–19; 'pure and simple', 175, 181, 189, 190, 191, 192, 194, 199, 201, 203, 204, 211, 214, 221, 259, 273, 276, 277, 281, 283, 284, 294, 300, 332, 333; and also, 11, 41, 46, 51, 52, 54, 55, 79, 187, 193, 200, 201, 233, 256, 257, 271, 335
House of Commons, social composition of, 381
Howell, George, 35, 38, 61, 246, 247, 379
Hubbard, J. G., 177, 182, 183, 321
Hughes, Thomas, 2, 32, 33, 36, 58, 246, 265
Hull, 196
Hunt, G. Ward, 177, 218
Huntingdon, 69
Hutt, Sir William, 85, 324, 327
Hyde Park, meetings in, July 1866, 33, 35, 36, 129, 249, 261, 295; Good Friday 1867, 8, 12, 261; May 6 1867, 18, 42, 43, 44, 241, 261, 263, 264, 266, 272–3, 275; closing of, 38, 131, 247, 251, 262, 264, 266

Ireland, dissension over, 130; land-owners of, 10, 34, 130, 200; Fenian outrages in, 39, 266, 322; proposed redistribution of seats, 70, 71, 385; promise of Reform bill for, 285; delaying of Reform bill for, 432; Reform Act of 1868, 15, 385; University bill, 200; Lord Lieutenant of, 177, 304; Lord Chancellor of, 304, 306; Solicitor General of, 107;

Land bill for, 186, 268, 306; and also, 170, 328
Irish Church, disestablishment of, 71, 75; Catholics, 304, 306; and also, 28, 93, 114, 252, 260, 297, 301, 303–4
Islington, 36

James, Edward, 321
Jervis, H. Jervis-White-, 160, 162
Johnstone, Sir John, 395
Jolliffe, W. G. H., 1st Baron Hylton, 95, 112
Jones, Ernest, 31, 32, 33

Karslake, Sir J. B., 229
Keighley, 73, 319, 320
Kent, 73; County Record Office, 329
Kerrison, Sir Edward, 98
Kilmarnock, 74
Kimberley, 1st Earl of, 296, 318
Kinglake, A. W., 272
King's Lynn, 50
Kitson Clark, G., 314
Knaresborough, 321
Knatchbull-Hugessen, Edward H., 71, 85, 98, 121, 213, 217, 299; diary of, 323, 324, 328, 329–30
Knightley, Sir Rainald, 34, 112, 116, 166, 176, 183

Labouchere, Henry, 54, 229, 230
Laing, Samuel, 10, 23, 24, 65, 204, 209, 211, 232, 233, 271, 299, 319, 323, 337; amendment of, 73, 76–7, 89, 223–4, 423
Laird, John, 160, 162
Lambert, John, 88, 96, 99
Lambeth, 36
Lancashire South, 69, 317; merchants and manufacturers of, 242, 243; and also, 72, 254
Lancaster, Duchy of, 98, 107, 112
landed interest, 19–20, 27, 48, 49, 50, 51, 52–3, 54, 56, 60, 68, 70, 75, 76, 81, 131, 134, 185, 192, 225, 227, 229, 231, 232, 304
Langley, Baxter, 245, 246
Lansdowne, 4th Marquess of, 9, 10, 106, 107, 108, 114, 115, 128, 256
Layard, Austen Henry, 53, 97
Leeds, 9, 70, 73, 232; demonstrations

447

Morning Star, the, 8, 30, 82, 219, 220, 242, 317, 378
Morris, Michael, 107, 306
Morrison, Walter, 196, 271–2

Naas, Lord, 67, 170, 306, 328, 409
Neate, Charles, 55, 219
Newark, 284
Newcastle-on-Tyne, 50, 305; demonstrations in, 12, 244, 245, 246
Newcastle, 6th Duke of, 304, 305
Newdegate, Charles N., 50, 320, 384, 422
Newman, Cardinal, 28, 29
Northamptonshire, 181
Northcote, Sir Stafford, in Derby's cabinet, 67; views on Church matters, 93; possible place in coalition, 111, 112, 115, 333, 390; contact with Cave, 129; and Commission of enquiry, 135, 136; supports household suffrage with counterpoises, 144, 176; against lowering borough franchise, 179–80, follows moderate policy, 307; diary of, 328, 329; and also, 94, 95, 164, 238, 333
Northumberland House, 177
Northumberland North, 305
Nottingham, 238

O'Connell, D., 246, 253
Odger, George, 24, 95, 246, 247, 336
Odham, 200, 284, 319
O'Donoghue, The, 39, 219, 246
Oliphant, L., 299
Osborne, Bernal, 2, 238, 246
Owen, David, 314
Oxford Anglicanism, 28, 29, 297

Pakington, Sir John, 92, 119, 129, 133, 141, 177, 187, 208, 267, 303, 321
Palmer, Sir Roundell, 112, 113, 226, 296
Palmerston, 3rd Viscount, death of, 8, 28, 32, 64, 80–1, 96, 113, 119, 122, 299, 310, 314; and also, 2, 8, 9, 20, 27, 61, 65, 82, 83, 85, 87, 92, 93, 98, 101, 121, 161, 250, 298, 301, 302, 303, 323
Park, J. H., 6, 319
Paul, Herbert, 1, 313

Peebles and Selkirk, 74, 75
Peel, Arthur, 320
Peel, General Jonathan, threatens resignation, 13, 141, 144, 147, 150, 162, 165, 209; wishes to limit working-class enfranchisement, 59, 149; and possible coalition, 112; against household suffrage, 145, 155, 156, 159, 160, 164; resignation of, 177, 184, 256, 297, 300; high reputation of, 178–9; does not get Conservative support, 182–3; and also, 42, 66, 94, 113, 148, 157, 325
Peel, Sir Robert (elder), 5, 20, 62, 82, 116, 253, 308, 310
Peel, Sir Robert (younger), 85, 98, 107, 115, 271, 274, 299, 304, 320, 324, 327
Pennant, E. G. Douglas- (1st Baron Penrhyn), 231
Percy, Earl, 327, 437
Peto, Sir Samuel M., 304
Phillimore, Sir Robert, 93
Phipps, Sir Charles, 97
Pim, J., 10, 321
Platt, John, 16, 200, 299, 416
plurality, *see* duality
Plymouth, 272
polling places, increase of, 228
Poor Law Board, 99, 169
Poor Law machinery, 88
Poor rate, payment of, 13, 236; 1563 Act, 235
Potter, Edmund, 196
Potter, George, 24, 26, 30, 33, 39, 61, 202, 247, 248, 249, 254, 260, 263, 288; Trades' March of, 254, 263
Potter, T. B., 33, 105, 246, 254
Primrose Hill, demonstration on, 36, 37, 246, 268
Public agitation; demonstrations, 12, 17–18, 24–6, 31, 132; limited political effect of, 3, 26–7, 42–3, 285, 335, 336; possible political effect of, 17–18, 35, 60, 61, 125, 131, 161, 241, 242–66, 272–3; and also, 3, 55, 274, 285, 286, 288, 291, 301, 333
public opinion, 3, 4, 5, 39, 47, 60, 81, 91, 131, 161, 241, 280, 297, 234–5

Quarterly Review, 95

INDEX

seats, redistribution of, 16, 17, 46, 52, 67, 68, 69, 70, 71–9, 99, 100, 123, 171, 225, 232, 233, 256, 258, 275, 296, 337, 384, 385; agricultural, 60
Seats bill 1865, 8–9, 10, 11
Seats bill 1866, 68, 69, 70, 100, 102, 204
Seymour, C., 6, 16, 17
Shaftesbury, 7th Earl of, 25, 28, 33, 107, 113, 115, 119, 177, 261, 299, 304, 305, 324, 328
Sheffield, 57, 232, 284, 321; Trade Unions, 36; violence in, 39
Shoreham, 53
Sinclair, Sir George, 398
Small Tenements Act, 142, 158, 235, 240, 278, 280, 380
Smith, F. B., 6, 57, 314, 421
Smith, J. B., 16, 196, 271, 273, 275, 276, 284
Smith, Paul, 314
Smith, W. H., 305
Social Science Association, 36
Somerset, 12th Duke of, 83, 84, 87, 88, 97, 99, 101, 106, 107, 112, 136, 298, 303, 391
Spencer, Earl, 98, 120, 187
Spofforth, M., 77, 80, 83, 323, 330
Staffordshire, 72; iron workers' strike, 39, 290
Stalybridge, 69
Stansfeld, James, 28, 36, 125, 218, 219, 260, 275, 292, 296, 400
Stanhope, 5th Earl, 274
Stanley of Alderley, 2nd Baron, 86, 89
Stanley, Lord, relations with League, 30; sounded out by Disraeli, 41–2; possibility of Cabinet place, 86, 91; Russell's attempts to win over, 64, 91, 92, 310; relations with Cave, 97, 104; as possible premier of coalition, 110, 112–14, 207; and possible coalition, 111, 127, 134, 394; supports household suffrage with restrictions, 167, 168, 176, 183; and Hibbert's amendment, 238, 239; and also, 93, 96, 106, 187, 253, 291, 292, 304, 305, 306–7, 323, 426
Stanley, W. O., 199
Star, Morning, 4, 265
Steel, John, 299
Stockport, 16, 57

Stuart, Colonel W., 320
Sudbury, 82
Suffolk, East, 98
Sunday Trading bill 1855, 264
Surrey, 72
Sutherland, Harriet, Duchess of, 187, 256, 413
Swansea, 238

Tamworth, 316
Taylor, P. A., 33, 36, 58, 246, 260
Taylor, Colonel T. E., 80, 213, 238, 240, 241, 267, 268, 305
Tea-Room revolt, 14, 16, 166, 196, 198, 199, 200, 215, 216, 217, 218, 220, 240, 257, 271
Teynham, 16th Baron, 245, 254
Thetford, 50, 74
Thompson, F. M. L., 314
Thring, Henry, 169
Tilston-Bright, Sir Charles, 54
Times, The, 83, 93, 103, 125, 170, 231, 240, 265, 311, 317
Tiverton, 320
Tomline, George, 299
Torrens, W. T. McC., 239, 246, 285, 299, 305, 322; amendment of, 14, 20, 196, 276–7
Tower Hamlets, 13, 55, 69
Trade, Board of, 85, 179–80, 329
Trades' March, 25, 254, 263
Trades Unions, 27–8, 51, 58, 83, 290, 297; Royal Commission on, 32, 305
Trafalgar Square, political rally in, 12, 26, 37, 255, 263
Trevelyan, G. M., 1, 6, 17, 313, 379
Trollope, Sir J., 228, 229

urban freeholders, county votes of, 72

Victoria, Queen, 9, 12, 21, 32, 35, 94, 97, 103, 104, 106, 107, 111, 113, 114, 117, 124, 126, 134, 136, 137, 138, 139, 140, 145, 149, 157, 274, 304, 328
Vincent, J. R., 314, 379, 384
Vivian, H. H., 227
Volunteers, the, 9, 11
voting papers, 171, 229, 255, 279; abolished, 229–30, 233

Walling, R. A. J., 329

450